Name
Pg. No#
Date
Makeup
Test - Quiz

Using Algebra

Using Algebra

KENNETH J. TRAVERS
Professor of Mathematics Education
University of Illinois
Urbana, Illinois

LEROY C. DALTON
Chairman, Mathematics Department
Wauwatosa Secondary Schools
Wauwatosa, Wisconsin

VINCENT F. BRUNNER
Mathematics Department
Nicolet High School
Milwaukee, Wisconsin

LAIDLAW BROTHERS · PUBLISHERS
A Division of Doubleday & Company, Inc.
RIVER FOREST, ILLINOIS

Palo Alto, California   Dallas, Texas   Atlanta, Georgia   Toronto, Canada

About the cover: The cover design was made from a photograph of a highly magnified view of elon crystals, a substance used as a photographic developer.

EDITORIAL STAFF

Project Director: Eugene M. Malecki

Staff Editors: Gene S. Kuechmann, Max V. Lyles, Jeffrey Wells

Production Editor: Roberta S. Randorf

Art Director: Gloria Muczynski

ILLUSTRATORS

Cover and Title Pages: Donald Meighan

Text: John D. Firestone & Associates, Paul Hazelrigg

ISBN 0–8445–**1945**–6

Copyright © 1974 by Laidlaw Brothers, Publishers

A Division of Doubleday & Company, Inc.

Printed in the United States of America

67890   2109876

Contents

Optional

Optional

Special Topics

Algebra: What and Why?

In a sense, algebra is an extension of arithmetic, so you are already familiar with many ideas of algebra. The main purpose of this chapter is to agree on the terms and symbols we will use when referring to these ideas. We will also begin to answer the questions

What is algebra?   and   **Why study algebra?**

Three methods for describing a **set** are shown below. Notice that the set is named by a capital letter.

Complete listing	$S = \{0, 1, 2, 3, 4, 5, 6, 7, 8, 9, 10\}$
Partial listing	$S = \{0, 1, 2, 3, \cdots, 10\}$
Set-builder notation	or $S = \{x \mid x$ is a whole number less than $11\}$ $S = \{x \mid x < 11\}$ ←if we have agreed that x stands for a whole number

The *braces* { } mean "the set whose members (or elements) are." In the partial listing method, the dots mean *the pattern continues*. Set-builder notation is read as shown below.

$$\{x \mid x \text{ is a whole number less than } 11\}$$

The set of all x such that x is a whole number less than 11.

We can say: 4 is a member of S.   11 is not a member of S.

$$4 \in S \qquad\qquad 11 \notin S$$

Finite sets	Infinite sets
$T = \{0, 1, 2, 3, \cdots, 10\}$	$W = \{0, 1, 2, 3, 4, \cdots\}$
$V = \{x \mid x$ is a student in your class$\}$	$E = \{0, 2, 4, 6, \cdots\}$
$\varnothing = \{\ \}$	$O = \{n \mid n$ is an odd number$\}$
A count of the members will end.	A count of the members may be continued without end.

The **empty (or null)** set is named $\varnothing$ or { }. It contains no members and is finite.

The exercises in this book are of three kinds. (Answers to selected exercises are given at the back of the book.)

Exercises in the set labeled	Will help you to
Ⓐ	Review the basic ideas you have just studied.
Ⓑ	Practice using the basic ideas.
Ⓒ	Extend the basic ideas or consider interesting sidelights or preview later work.

EXERCISES 1.1

Ⓐ Which symbol, $\in$ or $\notin$, should replace each ▓ ?

$$W = \{x \mid x \text{ is a whole number}\} \qquad E = \{0, 2, 4, 6, 8, \cdots\}$$
$$L = \{a, b, c, d, e, f, g\} \qquad D = \{1, 3, 5, 7, 9, \cdots\}$$

1. a ▓ L
2. x ▓ L
3. 0 ▓ E
4. 10 ▓ D
5. a ▓ W
6. 0 ▓ D
7. 11 ▓ E
8. $1,000,000$ ▓ W
9. 10 ▓ E

Is the set *clearly defined*? If *not*, explain why.

10. the set of all good men *doesn't explain about the set of all good men*

11. the set of all senators in the United States Senate *doesn't finish what about the set of senators*

Is the set *finite* or *infinite*?

12. the set of all books belonging to your school library *infinite*

13. the set of all books belonging to the Library of Congress *infinite*

14. the set of all books in the world *infinite*

15. $\{0, 3, 6, 9, 12, \cdots\}$ *finite*

16. $\{0, 3, 6, 9, \cdots, 21\}$ *finite*

Ⓑ Describe each set by a complete listing or by a partial listing, whichever is better.

17. whole numbers less than 6
18. whole numbers less than 12
19. even whole numbers
20. odd whole numbers
21. whole numbers greater than 7
22. whole numbers greater than 0
23. whole numbers greater than 15 but less than 27
24. whole numbers greater than 5 but less than 6

Describe each set; let x stand for a whole number; use these symbols.

Symbol	=	<	>
Meaning	is equal to	is less than	is greater than

Example: $\{1, 2, 3, \cdots, 12\} = \{x \mid x > 0 \text{ and } x < 13\}$.

25. $\{2, 3, 4, 5, 6, \cdots\}$
26. $\{8, 9, 10, 11, 12, \cdots\}$ 7 < 8
27. $\{0, 1, 2, 3, \cdots, 103\}$
28. $\{0, 1, 2, 3, \cdots, 621\}$
29. $\{2, 3, 4, 5, 6, \cdots, 103\}$
30. $\{8, 9, 10, 11, \cdots, 621\}$
31. $\{8, 10, 12, 14, 16, \cdots\}$
32. $\{13, 15, 17, 19, 21, \cdots\}$
33. $\{1, 3, 5, 7, \cdots, 35\}$
34. $\{0, 2, 4, 6, \cdots, 98\}$
35. $\{18, 20, 22, 24, \cdots, 102\}$
36. $\{91, 93, 95, 97, \cdots, 291\}$
37. $\{7\}$
38. $\{0\}$
Ⓒ 39. $\{\ \}$
40. $\varnothing$
41. $\{0, 3, 6, 9, 12, \cdots\}$
42. $\{0, 4, 8, 12, 16, \cdots\}$
43. $\{0, 5, 10, 15, \cdots, 105\}$
44. $\{10, 20, 30, 40, \cdots, 1000\}$
45. $\{2, 3, 5, 7, 11, 13, 17, \cdots\}$
46. $\{2, 3, 5, 7, 11, \cdots, 101\}$

List the members that $\cdots$ stands for in each case.

47. $\{2, 4, 8, 16, 32, \cdots, 2048\}$
48. $\{3, 9, 27, 81, \cdots, 59049\}$
49. $\{4, 9, 16, 25, 36, \cdots, 144\}$
50. $\{0, 1, 8, 27, 64, \cdots, 1000\}$
51. $\{\frac{1}{2}, \frac{1}{3}, \frac{1}{4}, \frac{1}{5}, \frac{1}{6}, \cdots, \frac{1}{13}\}$
52. $\{0, \frac{1}{3}, \frac{2}{3}, 1, 1\frac{1}{3}, 1\frac{2}{3}, \cdots, 4\}$
53. $\{\frac{1}{4}, \frac{1}{2}, \frac{3}{4}, 1, \frac{5}{4}, \frac{3}{2}, \cdots, 4\}$
54. $\{\frac{1}{2}, \frac{1}{3}, \frac{1}{5}, \frac{1}{7}, \frac{1}{11}, \cdots, \frac{1}{37}\}$

In the picture, the set of guitars is a *subset* of the set of musical instruments shown. We define *subset* as follows.

> If every member of set S is also a member of set T, then S is a **subset** of T. "$S \subseteq T$" is read "S is a subset of T."

A *set diagram* can be used to show that $S \subseteq T$.

$S = \{1, 3, 5, 7, 9\}$

$T = \{0, 1, 2, 3, 4, 5, 6, 7, 8, 9\}$

By the definition above, a set is a subset of itself. Also, we consider the empty set, $\varnothing$, to be a subset of every set.

Equal sets	$\{1, 2, 3\} = \{2, 3, 1\}$	contain the same members
Equivalent sets	$\{1, 2, 3\}$ $\{a, b, \$\}$	members can be matched one-to-one

Sets S and T are *equal* when they are subsets of each other. If sets X and Y are *equivalent*, we say there is a one-to-one correspondence between their members.

EXERCISES 1.2

Ⓐ Exercises 1–8 refer to the sets below.

$C = \{0, 1, 2, 3\}$ $D = \{2, 0\}$ $E = \{1, 3, 2, 0\}$ $F = \{1, 2, 3, 4\}$

1. Is D a subset of C?

2. Is D a subset of E?

3. Is D a subset of F?

4. Is E a subset of F?

5. Are C and E equal?

6. Are C and F equal?

7. Are C and E equivalent?

8. Are C and F equivalent?

9. Are equal sets always equivalent?

10. Are equivalent sets always equal?

Ⓑ Choose the best one of (a) $S = T$; (b) S and T are equivalent but not equal; (c) S and T are not equivalent.

11. $S = \{x \mid x$ is a whole number$\}$
$T = \{0, 1, 2, 3, 4, \cdots\}$

12. $S = \{n \mid n$ is an even whole number$\}$
$T = \{0, 2, 4, 6, 8, \cdots\}$

13. $S = \{0, 1, 2, 3, 4, 5, 6, 7\}$
$T = \{0, 1, 2, 3, \cdots, 7\}$

14. $S = \{0, 2, 4, 6, \cdots, 20\}$
$T = \{0, 2, 4, \cdots, 20\}$

15. $S = \{1, 3, 5, 7, 9\}$
$T = \{0, 2, 4, 6, 8\}$

16. $S = \{a, b, c, d, e\}$
$T = \{b, c, d, e, f\}$

17. $S = \{1, 3, 5, 7, 9\}$
$T = \{1, 3, 5, 7\}$

18. $S = \{a, b, c\}$
$T = \{a, b, c, d, e\}$

19. $S = \{x \mid x \text{ is a whole number}\}$
$T = \{y \mid y \text{ is a whole number}\}$

20. $S = \{e \mid e \text{ is an even number}\}$
$T = \{n \mid n \text{ is an even number}\}$

21. $S = \{0, 2, 4, 6, 8, \cdots, 20\}$
$T = \{1, 3, 5, 7, 9, \cdots, 21\}$

22. $S = \{0, 2, 4, 6, 8, \cdots, 16\}$
$T = \{1, 3, 5, 7, 9, \cdots, 17\}$

23. $S = \{0, 2, 4, 6, 8, 10, \cdots\}$
$T = \{1, 3, 5, 7, \cdots\}$

24. $S = \{e \mid e \text{ is an even number}\}$
$T = \{o \mid o \text{ is an odd number}\}$

Choose the best one of **(a)** $C \subseteq D$; **(b)** $D \subseteq C$; **(c)** both $C \subseteq D$ and $D \subseteq C$; **(d)** neither $C \subseteq D$ nor $D \subseteq C$.

25. $C = \{a, b, c\}$
$D = \{a, b, c, d\}$

26. $C = \{\alpha, \beta, \gamma, \delta\}$
$D = \{\beta, \gamma, \delta\}$

27. $C = \{1, 2, 3, 4\}$
$D = \{3, 1, 4, 2\}$

28. $C = \{0, 1, 2, 3, \cdots, 101\}$
$D = \{x \mid x \text{ is a whole number less than 102}\}$

29. $C = \{0, 2, 4, 6, 8\}$
$D = \{1, 3, 5, 7, 9\}$

30. $C = \{0, 2, 4, 6, 8, \cdots\}$
$D = \{1, 3, 5, 7, 9, 11, \cdots\}$

© Find *all* the subsets of $S = \{3, 6, 9, 12\}$ that contain

31. exactly one member.

32. exactly two members.

33. exactly three members.

34. exactly four members.

35. no members.

36. only numbers less than 3.

37. only odd numbers.

38. only even numbers.

39. only numbers greater than 8.

40. only numbers less than 8.

How many distinct subsets does each set have?

Example: *Given set:* $\{a\}$
Subsets: $\varnothing$ and $\{a\}$
Number of subsets: 2

41. $\{a, b\}$ **42.** $\{a, b, c\}$ **43.** $\{a, b, c, d\}$

44. any set S if S contains 5 members

45. any set S if S contains n members

Choose any point on a line. Label it A and assign it the number 0. Then 0 is called the **coordinate** of A. Choose a point to the right of A on the line. Label this point B and assign it the coordinate 1. Line segment AB (also written $\overline{AB}$) is a *unit segment*. Now assign whole numbers to other points on the line according to the number of units each point is to the right of the 0-point.

whole-number line

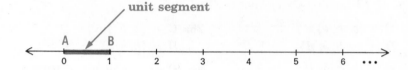

The set of **natural numbers**, often called the **positive integers**, is an important subset of the whole numbers.

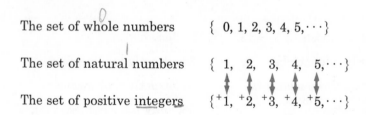

The set of whole numbers $\{\ 0, 1, 2, 3, 4, 5, \cdots\}$

The set of natural numbers $\{\ 1,\ \ 2,\ \ 3,\ \ 4,\ \ 5, \cdots\}$

The set of positive integers $\{{}^+1,\ {}^+2,\ {}^+3,\ {}^+4,\ {}^+5, \cdots\}$

Just as positive integers are matched with points to the right of the 0-point, **negative integers** may be matched with points to the left of the 0-point. The two numbers matched with points the *same distance* but in *opposite directions* from the 0-point are called **opposites**. 0 is said to be its own opposite.

integer line

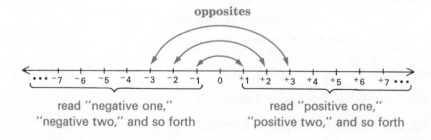

opposites

read "negative one," "negative two," and so forth

read "positive one," "positive two," and so forth

We usually denote the set of integers in one of these four ways.

I $\{\cdots, {}^-4, {}^-3, {}^-2, {}^-1, 0, {}^+1, {}^+2, {}^+3, {}^+4, \cdots\}$

{integers} $\{\cdots, {}^-4, {}^-3, {}^-2, {}^-1, 0, 1, 2, 3, 4, \cdots\}$

Some subsets of I and the names we will use for them are shown below.

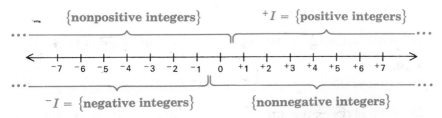

Sets of numbers are **graphed** on a number line by drawing points with the proper coordinates.

Example 1: Graph $\{{}^-4, 0, {}^+2, {}^+3, {}^+5, {}^+6\}$.

SOLUTION:

Example 2: Graph $\{{}^-2, 0, {}^+2, {}^+4, {}^+6, {}^+8, {}^+10, \cdots\}$.

SOLUTION:

meaning the pattern
of points continues

EXERCISES 1.3

Ⓐ What is the coordinate of each point?

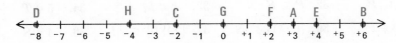

1. A	2. B	3. C	4. D
5. E	6. F	7. G	8. H

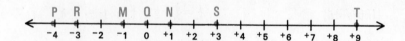

9. What is the coordinate of the next integer point to the right of T? $^+10$

10. What is the coordinate of the integer point 5 units to the right $^+14$ of T?

11. What is the coordinate of the next integer point to the left of P? $^-3$

12. What is the coordinate of the integer point 4 units to the left of P? $^-8$

13. Points R and ____ have coordinates which are opposites.

14. Points N and ____ have coordinates which are opposites.

15. The coordinate of ____ is neither positive nor negative.

16. The coordinate of ____ is its own opposite.

17. Which points shown have coordinates in ^+I?

18. Which points shown have coordinates in ^-I?

Exercises 19–48 refer to the sets below. True or False?

$$P = \{^-1, \, ^-2, \, ^-3, \, ^-4, \cdots\} \qquad M = \{0, \, ^+1, \, ^+2, \, ^+3, \cdots\}$$
$$S = \{0, \, ^-1, \, ^-2, \, ^-3, \cdots\} \qquad T = \{^+1, \, ^+2, \, ^+3, \, ^+4, \cdots\}$$

19. $M = \, ^+I$ 20. $P = \, ^-I$ 21. $T \subseteq M$ 22. $M \subseteq T$

23. $0 \in P$ 24. $0 \notin T$ 25. $0 \in S$ 26. $0 \notin M$

27. $S = \, ^-I$ 28. $T = \, ^+I$ 29. $P = M$ 30. $P = T$

31. $S \subseteq P$ 32. $P \subseteq S$ 33. $^+5 \in M$ 34. $^+5 \in T$

35. $^-4 \notin P$ 36. $\{0, \, ^+1\} \subseteq S$ 37. $\{^-1, 0\} \subseteq M$ 38. $^-4 \notin S$

Ⓑ 39. $P \subseteq I$ 40. $M \subseteq I$ 41. $S \subseteq I$ 42. $T \subseteq I$

43. $\{0\} \subseteq I$ 44. $\{0\} \subseteq M$ 45. $\{0\} \subseteq T$ 46. $\{0\} \subseteq P$

47. P and T are equivalent.   48. S and M are equivalent.

Exercises 49–73. Draw a separate number line to graph each set.

49. {2, 8, 9}   **50.** {3, 5, 6}   **51.** {0, 5, 10}   **52.** {0, 8, 16}

53. {0, 1, 2, 3}   **54.** {0, 2, 4, 8}   **55.** {$^-1$, 0, $^+1$}   **56.** {$^-2$, $^-1$, $^+5$}

57. ^+I **58.** ^-I **59.** {0}   **60.** I

61. {$^-3$, $^-2$, $^-1$, 0, $^+1$, $^+2$, $^+3$}   **62.** {$^-6$, $^-4$, $^-2$, 0, $^+2$, $^+4$, $^+6$}

63. {3, 6, 9, 12, 15, $\cdots$}   **64.** {0, 4, 8, 12, 16, $\cdots$}

65. {$\cdots$, $^-6$, $^-5$, $^-4$, $^-3$}   **66.** {$^-4$, $^-2$, 0, $^+2$, $^+4$, $^+6$, $^+8$, $\cdots$}

67. {nonnegative integers}   **68.** {nonpositive integers}

69. {odd positive integers}   **70.** {even nonnegative integers}

71. {even negative integers}   **72.** {0, $\frac{1}{2}$, 1, 1$\frac{1}{2}$, 2, 2$\frac{1}{2}$, 3, 3$\frac{1}{2}$, $\cdots$}

73. {$\cdots$, $^-(\frac{6}{4})$, $^-(\frac{5}{4})$, $^-(\frac{4}{4})$, $^-(\frac{3}{4})$, $^-(\frac{2}{4})$, $^-(\frac{1}{4})$, 0, $\frac{1}{4}$, $\frac{2}{4}$, $\frac{3}{4}$, $\frac{4}{4}$, $\frac{5}{4}$, $\frac{6}{4}$, $\cdots$}

74. Are ^+I and {nonnegative integers} equivalent? Why?

Exercises 75–77. The drawing shows an undersea research base on the edge of an underwater cliff. A weighted line from the supply ship above helps the divers record their findings and regulate the rate at which they go up and down.

75. A diver starts at the base level (0 fathoms) and goes down 8 fathoms and then up 3 fathoms. At what level is he?

76. From the $^-8$-fathom level, a diver goes up 3 fathoms and then down 5 fathoms. At what level is he?

77. From the $^-5$-fathom level, how many fathoms would a diver have to go up to get to the $^+5$-fathom level?

Exercises 78–81. What is the opposite of each of the following ?

78. 200 feet below sea level   **79.** A profit of 2 dollars

80. 7° above zero (temperature)   **81.** A loss of 3 yards (football)

82. In Exercises **78-81**, which integer would best express
  a. each item given ?   **b.** the opposite of each item?

Can You Do This?

The highway from Ayville to Efton is seventeen miles long and perfectly straight. Beetown, Seaburg, Deeville, and Eaton also lie along this stretch of highway, and the distance between any two of the six towns, in miles, is an integer (not 0).

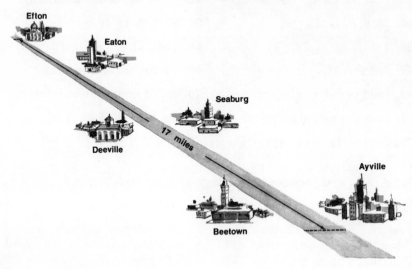

Can you complete the mileage chart?

	Ayville	Beetown	Seaburg	Deeville	Eaton
Beetown	5				
Seaburg		2			
Deeville					
Eaton	16		3		
Efton	17				

When one integer is divided by another integer (not zero), the result is a *rational number*.

$$8 \div 2 = \tfrac{8}{2} = 4 \qquad 3 \div 6 = \tfrac{3}{6} = \tfrac{1}{2}$$

A **rational number** is any number which can be named by a fraction that has integers for its numerator and denominator, but the denominator cannot be 0.

Q is often used to name the set of rational numbers, since every member of Q is a Quotient of two integers. To graph rational numbers, draw a number line as you do to graph integers. Now, however, points may be located *between* integer points. The unit segments may be subdivided into halves, thirds, fourths, or any convenient fractional part.

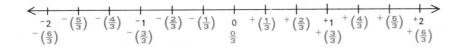

rational
number
lines

Example 1: What are the coordinates of points A, B, and C shown on the second rational number line above?

SOLUTION:
Each unit segment has been subdivided into tenths. (Labeling the 0-point as $\tfrac{0}{10}$ tells the subdivision at a glance.)

$A \leftrightarrow {}^{+}(\tfrac{5}{10})$ or ${}^{+}(\tfrac{1}{2})$ $\qquad$ $B \leftrightarrow {}^{+}(\tfrac{16}{10})$ or ${}^{+}(\tfrac{8}{5})$ $\qquad$ $C \leftrightarrow {}^{-}(\tfrac{13}{10})$

Example 2: Graph $\{{}^{-}1, {}^{-}(\tfrac{1}{2}), 0, {}^{+}(\tfrac{1}{2}), {}^{+}1, {}^{+}(\tfrac{3}{2}), {}^{+}2, \cdots\}$

SOLUTION:

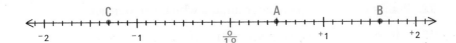 $\cdots$

On a number line, the number graphed farther to the left is the lesser. The number graphed farther to the right is the greater.

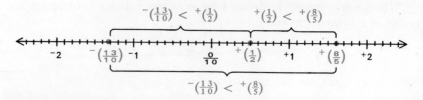

EXERCISES 1.4

Ⓐ Exercises 1–14 refer to the number line below.

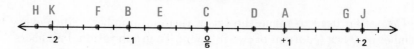

1. Each unit segment has been subdivided into ____.

What is the coordinate of each point?

2. A	**3.** B	**4.** C	**5.** D

6. E   **7.** F   **8.** a point $\frac{1}{5}$ unit to the right of J

9. G   **10.** H   **11.** a point $\frac{3}{5}$ unit to the left of H

12. Points E and ____ have coordinates which are opposites.

13. Which points have coordinates in ^-I?

14. Which points have coordinates in Q but not in I?

15. Define *rational number*.   16. Is I a subset of Q? Why?

Exercises 17–34. Refer to a number line if necessary to decide which symbol, =, <, or >, should replace each ●.

17. 8 ● 9   **18.** 1501 ● $^-$1500

19. $\frac{1}{2}$ ● $\frac{2}{4}$ **20.** $^+\left(\frac{5}{4}\right)$ ● $^+1$

21. $^-\left(\frac{1}{2}\right)$ ● $^-\left(\frac{2}{4}\right)$ **22.** $^-\left(\frac{4}{3}\right)$ ● $^-1$

23. $^+\left(\frac{2}{6}\right)$ ● $^+\left(\frac{3}{6}\right)$ **24.** $^-\left(\frac{1}{2}\right)$ ● $^-\left(\frac{3}{5}\right)$

25. $^-\left(\frac{5}{7}\right)$ ● 0   **26.** $\frac{0}{5}$ ● $\frac{0}{9}$

Ⓑ 27. $^+\!\left(\frac{3}{4}\right)$ ⬤ $^+\!\left(\frac{2}{3}\right)$ 28. $^+\!\left(\frac{4}{7}\right)$ ⬤ $^+\!\left(\frac{3}{5}\right)$

29. $^-\!\left(\frac{3}{4}\right)$ ⬤ $^-\!\left(\frac{2}{3}\right)$ 30. $^-\!\left(\frac{4}{7}\right)$ ⬤ $^-\!\left(\frac{3}{5}\right)$

31. $^+\!\left(\frac{5}{8}\right)$ ⬤ $^+\!\left(\frac{3}{5}\right)$ 32. $^+\!\left(\frac{3}{5}\right)$ ⬤ $^+\!\left(\frac{5}{8}\right)$

33. $^-\!\left(\frac{5}{8}\right)$ ⬤ $^-\!\left(\frac{3}{5}\right)$.   34. $^-\!\left(\frac{3}{5}\right)$ ⬤ $^-\!\left(\frac{5}{8}\right)$

35. Is every positive rational number greater than 0? Why?

36. Is every negative rational number less than 0? Why?

Exercises 37–48. Draw a separate number line to graph each set. Subdivide the unit segments appropriately in each case.

37. $\left\{^-\!\left(\frac{3}{2}\right),\ ^-1,\ ^-\!\left(\frac{1}{2}\right),\ 0,\ ^+\!\left(\frac{1}{2}\right),\ ^+1,\ ^+\!\left(\frac{3}{2}\right)\right\}$

38. $\left\{^-2,\ ^-\!\left(\frac{4}{3}\right),\ ^-\!\left(\frac{2}{3}\right),\ 0,\ ^+\!\left(\frac{2}{3}\right),\ ^+\!\left(\frac{4}{3}\right),\ ^+2\right\}$

39. $\left\{^-\!\left(\frac{9}{2}\right),\cdots,\ ^-\!\left(\frac{3}{2}\right),\ ^-1,\ ^-\!\left(\frac{1}{2}\right),\ 0,\ ^+\!\left(\frac{1}{2}\right),\ ^+1,\ ^+\!\left(\frac{3}{2}\right),\cdots,\ ^+\!\left(\frac{9}{2}\right)\right\}$

40. $\left\{^-4,\cdots,\ ^-2,\ ^-\!\left(\frac{4}{3}\right),\ ^-\!\left(\frac{2}{3}\right),\ 0,\ ^+\!\left(\frac{2}{3}\right),\ ^+\!\left(\frac{4}{3}\right),\ ^+2,\cdots,\ ^+4\right\}$

41. $\left\{\cdots,\ ^-\!\left(\frac{3}{2}\right),\ ^-1,\ ^-\!\left(\frac{1}{2}\right),\ 0,\ ^+\!\left(\frac{1}{2}\right),\ ^+1,\ ^+\!\left(\frac{3}{2}\right),\cdots\right\}$

42. $\left\{\cdots,\ ^-2,\ ^-\!\left(\frac{4}{3}\right),\ ^-\!\left(\frac{2}{3}\right),\ 0,\ ^+\!\left(\frac{2}{3}\right),\ ^+\!\left(\frac{4}{3}\right),\ ^+2,\cdots\right\}$

43. $\left\{\cdots,\ ^-\!\left(\frac{3}{4}\right),\ ^-\!\left(\frac{2}{4}\right),\ ^-\!\left(\frac{1}{4}\right),\ \frac{0}{4},\ ^+\!\left(\frac{1}{4}\right),\ ^+\!\left(\frac{2}{4}\right),\ ^+\!\left(\frac{3}{4}\right),\cdots\right\}$

44. $\left\{\cdots,\ ^-\!\left(\frac{6}{5}\right),\ ^-\!\left(\frac{4}{5}\right),\ ^-\!\left(\frac{2}{5}\right),\ \frac{0}{5},\ ^+\!\left(\frac{2}{5}\right),\ ^+\!\left(\frac{4}{5}\right),\ ^+\!\left(\frac{6}{5}\right),\cdots\right\}$

45. $\left\{\cdots,\ ^-\!\left(\frac{6}{6}\right),\ ^-\!\left(\frac{4}{6}\right),\ ^-\!\left(\frac{2}{6}\right),\ \frac{0}{6},\ ^+\!\left(\frac{2}{6}\right),\ ^+\!\left(\frac{4}{6}\right),\ ^+\!\left(\frac{6}{6}\right),\cdots\right\}$

46. $\left\{\cdots,\ ^-\!\left(\frac{3}{7}\right),\ ^-\!\left(\frac{2}{7}\right),\ ^-\!\left(\frac{1}{7}\right),\ \frac{0}{7},\ ^+\!\left(\frac{1}{7}\right),\ ^+\!\left(\frac{2}{7}\right),\ ^+\!\left(\frac{3}{7}\right),\cdots\right\}$

Ⓒ **47.** all rational numbers between $^+\!\left(\frac{3}{4}\right)$ and $^-\!\left(\frac{1}{2}\right)$, including $^+\!\left(\frac{3}{4}\right)$ and $^-\!\left(\frac{1}{2}\right)$

48. all rational numbers greater than or equal to $^-\!\left(\frac{5}{3}\right)$

49. Given any two different rational numbers, how can you find a third rational number between them?

50. If Q is the set of rational numbers, what might each of the following be?

　　　　　　a. ^+Q　　　　　　　　b. ^-Q

p9 q

We can subdivide the units on a rational number line into *subunits* as small as we please. Can we, by doing this, finally assign a rational number to every point on the line?

It sounds amazing, but *there are more points on a number line than there are rational numbers*! Numbers like $\sqrt{2}$ and π can be matched to points on a number line, but they are not rational numbers. (They cannot be expressed as quotients of integers.) Numbers like $\sqrt{2}$ and π are **irrational numbers**.

The set of rational numbers and the set of irrational numbers are subsets of the set of **real numbers**. There is a one-to-one correspondence between the set of real numbers and the set of all points on a line. That is, for each real number there is a point on the line, and for each point there is a real number.

> A **real number** is any number for which a decimal expansion can be found.

	Real number	Its decimal expansion	
rational numbers	$^+3$ 0 $^-(\frac{1}{11})$ $^+(\frac{2}{3})$	$^+3.000\cdots = {}^+3.\overline{0}$ $0.000\cdots = 0.\overline{0}$ $^-0.0909\cdots = {}^-0.\overline{09}$ $^+0.666\cdots = {}^+0.\overline{6}$	a set of digits repeats
irrational numbers	$^+\pi$ $^-\sqrt{2}$	$^+3.141592653\cdots$ $^-1.414213562\cdots$	digits do not repeat in a pattern

Example: Graph **a.** the set of all real numbers less than $^-2$;

                  b. the set of all real numbers greater than or equal to $^+(\frac{1}{5})$ but less than $^+3$.

SOLUTIONS:

    a.   **b.**

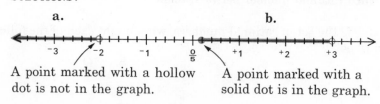

A point marked with a hollow dot is not in the graph.   A point marked with a solid dot is in the graph.

Zero is a real number, and all other real numbers are either positive (greater than 0) or negative (less than 0). It is sometimes useful to consider distance from the 0-point without regard to direction.

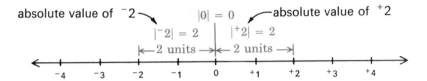

The **absolute value** of a positive number or 0 is the number.
The **absolute value** of a negative number is its opposite.

EXERCISES 1.5

Ⓐ 1. Any rational number can be named as the ____ of two integers.

2. Name two numbers which are not rational numbers.

3. Why are the numbers you named in Exercise **2** not rational numbers? Are they real numbers?

4. The set of rational numbers and the set of irrational numbers are subsets of ____ .

5. Is there a one-to-one correspondence between the set of all points on a line and the set of rational numbers?

6. Can $\sqrt{2}$ and π be graphed on a number line?

7. The opposite of $^+\sqrt{2}$ is ____ .   8. The opposite of $^-\pi$ is ____ .

9. There is a one-to-one correspondence between the set of all points on a line and the set of ____ numbers.

10. Name a real number which is neither positive nor negative.

11. In graphing, a hollow dot shows that the coordinate of that point (is, is not) in the set being graphed.

12. In graphing, a solid dot shows that the coordinate of that point (is, is not) in the set being graphed.

Give the absolute value of each real number.

13. $^+9$ **14.** $^-9$ **15.** 4 **16.** $^+(0.5000\cdots)$

17. $^-(\frac{1}{2})$ **18.** $^+(\frac{1}{2})$ **19.** 0 **20.** $^-(0.3333\cdots)$

21. $^-\sqrt{3}$ **22.** $^+\pi$ **23.** $^-\sqrt{2}$ **24.** $^-(1.4142\cdots)$

25. Can the absolute value of a real number be negative?

26. Do a number and its opposite have the same absolute value?

Ⓑ Copy and complete.

27. $|^+15| = $ ____   **28.** $|^+(\frac{4}{5})| = $ ____

29. $|^-37| = $ ____   **30.** $|^-(\frac{8}{9})| = $ ____

31. $|0| = $ ____   **32.** $|$___$| = 0$

33. $|^+\sqrt{2}| = $ ____   **34.** $|^-\sqrt{2}| = $ ____

For each of Exercises 35–50 draw a separate number line. Then graph the set of real numbers which are

35. greater than $^+3$.

36. greater than $^-2$.

37. less than $^+3$.

38. less than $^-2$.

39. greater than $^-(\frac{2}{3})$.

40. greater than $^+(\frac{3}{4})$.

41. less than $^-(\frac{2}{3})$.

42. less than $^+(\frac{3}{4})$.

43. greater than or equal to $^+(\frac{1}{2})$.

44. greater than or equal to $^-(\frac{5}{4})$.

45. less than or equal to $^-(\frac{1}{2})$.

46. less than or equal to $^+(\frac{5}{4})$.

47. greater than $^-(\frac{2}{3})$ but less than $^+(\frac{2}{3})$.

48. greater than $^-2$ but less than $^-(\frac{3}{4})$.

49. greater than or equal to $^-(\frac{1}{4})$ but less than $^+(\frac{3}{4})$.

50. greater than $^-(\frac{3}{4})$ but less than or equal to 0.

Ⓒ For each of Exercises 51–53 draw a separate number line. Then graph the set of real numbers whose absolute values are

51. less than $\frac{3}{2}$ **52.** greater than $\frac{3}{2}$ **53.** equal to 4

Exercises 1–12 refer to the sets described below. True or false ?

$P = \{5, 10, 15, 20\}$ $S = \{1, 3, 5, 7, \cdots, 51\}$

$T = \{y \mid y$ is an even whole number$\}$ $V = \{1, 3, 5, 7, 9, \cdots\}$

$W = \{x \mid x$ is a whole number$\}$ $X = \{0, 2, 4, 6, 8, \cdots\}$

1. $25 \in P$ **2.** $25 \notin S$ **3.** $18 \notin S$ **4.** $18 \in W$

5. $P \subseteq S$ **6.** $T \subseteq W$ **7.** $V = X$ **8.** $T = V$

9. T and V are equivalent.   **10.** X and V are equivalent.

11. V is a finite set.   **12.** S is an infinite set.

Name every point graphed whose coordinate fits the description.

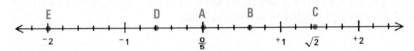

13. $^-(\frac{3}{5})$ **14.** in ^-I

15. in I but not in ^-I **16.** in Q but not in I

17. the opposite of the coordinate of **B**

18. in the set of real numbers but not in Q

Which symbol, $>$, $<$, or $=$, should replace each ◍ ?

19. $^-2$ ◍ $^-1$ **20.** $^-(\frac{7}{6})$ ◍ 0 **21.** $^+(\frac{5}{16})$ ◍ 0 **22.** 0 ◍ $\frac{0}{7}$

Give the absolute value.

23. $^-16$ **24.** $^+36$ **25.** $^-(\frac{2}{3})$ **26.** 0

Draw a separate number line to graph each set.

27. $\{^-2, ^-1, 0, ^+1, ^+2\}$

28. $\{\cdots, ^-(\frac{3}{3}), ^-(\frac{2}{3}), ^-(\frac{1}{3}), 0, ^+(\frac{1}{3}), ^+(\frac{2}{3}), ^+(\frac{3}{3}), \cdots\}$

29. all real numbers greater than $^-(\frac{3}{2})$ but less than or equal to $^+2$

1.6 VARIABLES AND EXPRESSIONS

Numbers are important in your study of algebra. Operations on numbers, such as addition, subtraction, multiplication, and division, are also important. One or more of these operations are usually involved in expressions (phrases) we write about numbers.

closed expressions $\left\{\begin{array}{l} 375 \\ (15 - 3) \div 2 \\ 37 \cdot 5 \end{array}\right.$ open expressions $\left\{\begin{array}{l} x \\ 2 \cdot y \text{ or } 2y \\ 5x - 4 \end{array}\right.$

A **closed expression** names a number that is the *value* of the expression. (Since the expressions $37 \cdot 5$, 37×5, and $37(5)$ all name the product of 37 and 5, they all have a value of 185.)

Grouping symbols, such as *parentheses* ( ) and *brackets* [ ], can be used as in Example **1** below to give the order in which operations are to be done to evaluate an expression.

Examples:

1. $[(2 \cdot 5) + 8] \div (4 - 1)$
    $= [10 + 8] \div 3$
    $= 18 \div 3$
    $= 6$

2. $2 \cdot 5 + 8 \div 4 - 1$
    $= 10 + 2 - 1$
    $= 12 - 1$
    $= 11$

If no grouping symbols are used, as in Example **2** above, the agreed-upon order is

order of operations

1. Multiplication and division in order from left to right;

2. Addition and subtraction in order from left to right.

An **open expression** contains at least one **variable**, usually a letter, sometimes another symbol. The variable represents any number in a given **replacement set**, and the expression can be evaluated for each member of the replacement set. It may help to think of the expression in terms of a "pattern frame," as shown on the next page.

Replacement set:	{1, 2, 3}		
Open expression:	$5x - 4$		
Closed expressions:	$5 \cdot 1 - 4$	$5 \cdot 2 - 4$	$5 \cdot 3 - 4$
Values:	1	6	11

EXERCISES 1.6

(A) Multiple Choice: Choose *all* correct answers.

1. "15 times 3" may be written as ___ .

    a. 153   **b.** 15×3 **c.** $15 \cdot 3$ **d.** $15(3)$ **e.** $15x$

2. "4 times some number" may be written as ___ .

    a. $4x$ **b.** $4y$ **c.** $4 \cdot x$ **d.** $4 \cdot 3$ **e.** 43

3. "Some number divided by 7" may be written as ___ .

    a. $n \div 7$ **b.** $7 \div n$ **c.** $\frac{n}{7}$ **d.** $\frac{7}{n}$ **e.** $7n$

For each case, what is the open expression? What closed expressions can be formed?

4. 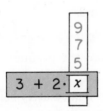   **5.** 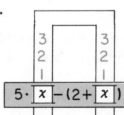   **6.**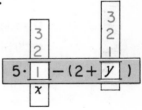

How is each statement below illustrated by Exercise 5 or 6?

7. If the same variable occurs more than once in an expression, each use of the variable must be replaced by the same numeral in forming a closed expression.

8. If an expression has more than one variable, they need not be replaced by the same numeral in forming a closed expression.

What is the first step in evaluating each expression?

9. $(16 - 4) \div 2$

10. $3(2 + 7)$

11. $16 - 4 \div 2$

12. $3 \cdot 2 + 7$

13. $16 - [4 \div (2 - 1)]$

14. $3[9 - (6 - 2)]$

15. $(16 - 4) \div 2 - 1$

16. $16 - 4 \div 2 - 1$

For the given expression and replacement set, what closed expressions can be formed?

17. $\frac{9}{y}$ $\{1, 2, 3\}$

18. $\frac{x}{2} + 1$ $\{0, 1, 2, 3, \cdots\}$

19. $r + 5$ $\{^-1, 0, 1\}$

20. $2n - 1$ $\{1, 2, 3, 4, \cdots\}$

Ⓑ **21–28.** Evaluate each closed expression in Exercises **9–16.**

Write an open expression for each of the following.

29. the sum of a number n and 3

30. the sum of 7 and a number m

31. six more than x

32. five increased by b

33. 12 less than y

34. 8 decreased by t

35. the product of 4 and r

36. the product of m and 9

37. b divided by c

38. n divided by m

39. 15 decreased by $4t$

40. 49 less than $2r$

41. a less 7

42. 49 less $2r$

43. 9 increased by the product of 3 and y

44. 6 more than the product of 5 and t

45. the next integer after some given integer p

46. the integer immediately before some given integer q

47. the number which is half some given number n

48. the number which is twice some given number m

49. the number of feet in k yards

50. the number of inches in r feet

51. the number of cents in q quarters

52. the number of cents in x dollars

53. the number of nickels in c cents

54. the number of dimes in c cents

Evaluate the given open expression for each member of the given replacement set. Describe the set of values by a complete or partial listing, whichever is better.

55. $r + 7$ $\{0, 1, 2\}$

56. $12 - x$ $\{2, 4, 6, 8\}$

57. $2n$ $\{0, 1, 2, 3, \cdots\}$

58. $\frac{n}{2}$ $\{0, 1, 2, 3, \cdots\}$

59. $2n + 1$ $\{0, 1, 2, 3, \cdots\}$

60. $2n + 2$ $\{0, 1, 2, 3, \cdots\}$

61. $2x - 1$ $\{0, 1, 2, 3, \cdots\}$

62. $2(x - 1)$ $\{0, 1, 2, 3, \cdots\}$

63. $4x - 2x$ $\{0, \frac{1}{2}, \frac{3}{4}, 2\}$

64. $3x + x$ $\{1, 2, 3, 4\}$

© **65.** $|x|$ $\{\cdots, {}^-3, {}^-2, {}^-1, 0, {}^+1, {}^+2, {}^+3, \cdots\}$

66. $2 \cdot |x|$ $\{\cdots, {}^-3, {}^-2, {}^-1, 0, {}^+1, {}^+2, {}^+3, \cdots\}$

67–74. Using set-builder notation, describe each set of values you found in Exercises **57–64.**

75. If the length of a rectangular frame is x centimeters and its width is y centimeters, write an open expression for **(a)** its perimeter; **(b)** its area.

76. If the time is $t - 2$ hours, what time will it be in $1\frac{1}{2}$ hours? In 45 minutes? What time was it $1\frac{1}{2}$ hours ago?

77. Maria is three times as old as Carlos was four years ago. If Carlos is d years old, what will Maria's age be six years from now?

1.7 EXPRESSIONS AND SENTENCES

Some mathematical symbols may be compared with parts of speech in English. Numerals are used in mathematical expressions as nouns are used in English phrases, variables are used like pronouns, and operation symbols are used like conjunctions. Grouping symbols are the punctuation marks. To write mathematical sentences, we must include **relation symbols** to serve as "mathematical verbs."

Relation symbol	=	<	>
Meaning	*is equal to*	*is less than*	*is greater than*

Connecting expressions by the symbol = forms a sentence called an **equation**. Connecting expressions by < or > forms a sentence called an **inequality**. Sentences may be *closed* or *open*.

closed sentences
$$\begin{cases} 4 + 3 = 5 \\ 12 - 7 < 6 \\ 3 > 2(4 - 1) \end{cases}$$

open sentences
$$\begin{cases} x + 3 = 5 \\ 12 - y < 6 \\ 3 > 2(d - 1) \end{cases}$$

A closed sentence is either true or false. (Which closed sentences above are true?) An open sentence is neither true nor false.

For the open sentence and replacement set below, four closed sentences can be formed, two true and two false.

$$5 \cdot 0 + 7 < 17 \rightarrow 7 < 17 \quad \text{true}$$

$$5 \cdot 1 + 7 < 17 \rightarrow 12 < 17 \quad \text{true}$$

$$5 \cdot 2 + 7 < 17 \rightarrow 17 < 17 \quad \text{false}$$

$$5 \cdot 3 + 7 < 17 \rightarrow 22 < 17 \quad \text{false}$$

$$5 \cdot \boxed{x} + 7 < 17$$

The *solution set* (or *truth set*) in this case is {0, 1}. Each member of the solution set is called a *solution*. To *solve an open sentence* means to find its solutions.

What is algebra? The rest of this book will be spent answering this question. For now, we can say that algebra is the study of a set and the operations we can perform on its members. In this course, the set is the set of real numbers. The operations are, for the most part, the familiar operations of arithmetic. We want to learn what properties the real numbers have under these operations.

Why study algebra? Most people study algebra to learn how to solve problems in everyday life. Therefore, a large part of this book will be devoted to using algebra in problem solving.

EXERCISES 1.7

Ⓐ For each diagram, what is (a) the open sentence? (b) the replacement set? (c) the solution set?

1.

$$12 - \boxed{y} > 3$$

with scale 10, 9, 8, 7

2.

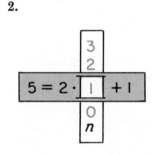

$$5 = 2 \cdot \boxed{} + 1$$

with scale 3, 2, 1, 0, n

3.

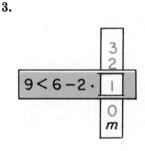

$$9 < 6 - 2 \cdot \boxed{}$$

with scale 3, 2, 1, 0, m

4. The solution set of an open sentence is a subset of the ____ of the variable.

5. For each solution of an open sentence, a (true, false) closed sentence is formed.

6. If a (true, false) closed sentence is formed for each member of the replacement set, the solution set is the empty set.

7. If a (true, false) closed sentence is formed for each member of the replacement set, the solution set is the replacement set.

Which symbol, =, <, or >, should replace each ▦ ?

8. $4 + 3$ ▦ 5

9. $3 + 6$ ▦ $6 + 3$

10. $2(7 - 1)$ ▦ 12

11. $2 \cdot 7 - 1$ ▦ 12

12. 8 ▦ $5 \div \frac{1}{2}$

13. $3 \cdot 4 - 2 \cdot 6$ ▦ 1

14. $5 \cdot 8 - 4$ ▦ $3(12)$

15. $4(7 \div 2)$ ▦ 16

16. $3 \cdot 5 - 2 \cdot 7$ ▦ 1

Ⓑ Solve each open sentence using the given replacement set.

17. $3r + 5 = 11$; $\{0, 1, 2, 3, 4\}$ 18. $3r + 5 = 11$; $\{0, 2, 4, 6, 8\}$

19. $3r + 5 < 11$; $\{0, 1, 2, 3, 4\}$ 20. $3r + 5 < 11$; $\{0, 2, 4, 6, 8\}$

21. $3r + 5 > 11$; $\{0, 1, 2, 3, 4\}$ 22. $3r + 5 > 11$; $\{0, 2, 4, 6, 8\}$

23. $2(x + 1) = 3$; $\{0, \frac{1}{2}, 1, \frac{3}{2}\}$ 24. $3y + y = 12$; $\{1, 3, 5, 7\}$

25. $n + 1 = 4$; $\{0, 1, 2, 3, \cdots\}$ 26. $m - 1 = 4$; $\{0, 1, 2, 3, \cdots\}$

27. $2x = 10$; $\{0, 1, 2, 3, \cdots\}$ 28. $s \div 2 = 7$; $\{0, 1, 2, 3, \cdots\}$

29. $|x| = 4$; $\{^-4, 0, ^+2, ^+3, ^+5, ^+6\}$ 30. $|x| > 0$; $\{^-1, 0, 1\}$

31. $|x| = 0$; $\{^-2, ^-1, 0, ^+1, ^+2\}$ 32. $|x| < 0$; $\{^-1, ^-(\frac{1}{2}), 0, ^+(\frac{1}{2})\}$

33. $n + n = 2n$; ^+I 34. $3c + 2c = 5c$; ^+I

35. $n + n < 2n$; ^+I 36. $3c + 2c > 5c$; ^+I

Write an open sentence for each of the following. In each case use only one variable, but you may use it more than once.

37. Lanetta traded 255 pennies for nickels and dimes, getting 6 more nickels than dimes.

Ex. 37

38. Scott has $3.00 in nickels and dimes. He has 3 fewer dimes than nickels.

Ⓒ 39. Elroy has 7 fewer dimes than nickels but his dimes are worth more than his nickels.

40. Sue is 3 years younger than Rosharon, and the sum of their ages is less than their father's age of 39.

41. The sum of two consecutive integers is 43.

$$\xleftarrow{\hspace{1em}} \overset{\displaystyle n-1}{+} \quad \overset{\displaystyle n}{+} \quad \overset{\displaystyle n+1}{+} \quad \overset{\displaystyle n+2}{+} \quad \overset{\displaystyle n+3}{+} \xrightarrow{\hspace{1em}}$$

42. In a socket-wrench set, two sockets differ by $\frac{1}{8}''$, and the socket which is midway between them is the $\frac{7}{16}''$ size.

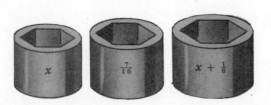

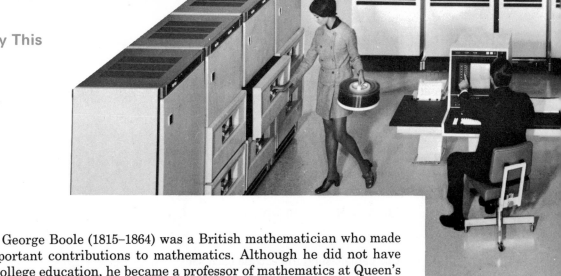

George Boole (1815–1864) was a British mathematician who made important contributions to mathematics. Although he did not have a college education, he became a professor of mathematics at Queen's College in Dublin. Modern computers like the one shown use a mathematics related to the *Boolean algebra* which he developed.

An "addition" table and a "multiplication" table for Boolean algebra are shown below. Are $\oplus$ and $\otimes$ like the usual operations of addition and multiplication?

$\oplus$	1	0
1	1	1
0	1	0

$\otimes$	1	0
1	1	0
0	0	0

Evaluate each "Boolean expression."

1. $1 \oplus 0$

2. $0 \oplus 1$

3. $1 \otimes 0$

4. $0 \otimes 1$

5. $1 \oplus 1$

6. $1 \otimes 1$

7. $0 \oplus 0$

8. $0 \otimes 0$

9. $(1 \oplus 0) \oplus 1$

10. $(1 \oplus 0) \otimes 1$

11. $(1 \otimes 0) \oplus 1$

12. $(1 \otimes 1) \oplus 0$

Which of the following statements are always true in Boolean algebra? The replacement set for a and b is $\{0, 1\}$.

13. $a \oplus 0 = 0 \oplus a$

14. $1 \oplus (a \otimes b) = (1 \oplus a) \otimes (1 \oplus b)$

15. $a \oplus 1 = 1 \oplus a$

16. $0 \oplus (a \otimes b) = (0 \oplus a) \otimes (0 \oplus b)$

17. $a \otimes 0 = 0 \otimes a$

18. $1 \otimes (a \oplus b) = (1 \otimes a) \oplus (1 \otimes b)$

19. $a \otimes 1 = 1 \otimes a$

20. $0 \otimes (a \oplus b) = (0 \otimes a) \oplus (0 \otimes b)$

CHAPTER REVIEW

1.1 **1.** Describe the set S of whole numbers less than 20 but greater than 12 using **(a)** set-builder notation, **(b)** complete listing, and **(c)** partial listing. Is S finite or infinite?

1.2 In Exercises 2–5, which statements about the given sets are true?

$$A = \{0, 2, 4, 6\} \qquad B = \{2, 4, 6, 8\} \qquad C = \{2, 4, 6, 0\}$$

2. $A = B$ **3.** $\varnothing \subseteq C$ **4.** $C = A$ **5.** $B \subseteq B$

1.3 Use partial listing to describe each set.

6. {negative integers}   **7.** {nonpositive integers}

Graph each set.

8. $\{^-5, \, ^-1, 0, 2, 4\}$ **9.** {odd positive integers}

1.4 **10.** Find the coordinates of points M, N, P, and T.

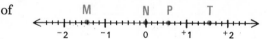

1.5 Describe each subset of the real numbers graphed.

11.    **12.**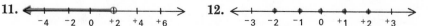

1.6 Identify each expression as open or closed. Then evaluate each expression, using $\{0, 1, 3\}$ as the replacement set for each variable.

13. $7 - (x \div 1)$ **14.** $(4 + 2) \cdot 3$ **15.** $24 \div 2 - 2 \cdot x$

16. Write an expression for the number of quarts in g gallons.

1.7 Identify each sentence as open or closed. Solve each open sentence, using $\{0, 1, 3\}$ as the replacement set.

17. $5 + (x \cdot 3) = 14$ **18.** $4x + 2x > 6$ **19.** $(7 \cdot 1 + 9 \cdot 3) \div 2 = 17$

Which term or symbol best completes each sentence?

a. equivalent   **b.** closed expression   **c.** finite   **d.** $\subseteq$

e. replacement set   **f.** closed sentence   **g.** infinite   **h.** equal

i. solution set   **j.** open expression   **k.** member   **l.** $<$

1. $\{1, 2, 3\}$ is ____ to $\{\sqrt{2}, \frac{1}{2}, 7\}$.

2. $^-6$ is a(n) ____ of I.

3. $\{0, 2, 4, \cdots\}$ is a(n) ____ set.

4. $9 + 6 \cdot 3$ is a(n) ____.

5. Each ____ contains a variable.

6. ^-I ____ I

7. $\{^-1, 1, \frac{1}{2}\}$ is ____ to $\{\frac{1}{2}, ^-1, 1\}$.

8. $^-4$ ____ $^+4$

9. Three closed sentences can be formed from $3x + 2 = 14$ if $\{2, 4, 6\}$ is the ____ for x.

10. The ____ of an open sentence contains those members in the replacement set for which true sentences can be formed.

In Exercises 11–14, graph each set.

11. $\{^-4, ^-3, ^-2, ^-1, 0, ^+1, ^+2, ^+3, \cdots\}$

12. all real numbers greater than $^-4$

13. all real numbers less than or equal to $^-4$

14. $\{^-\left(\frac{16}{4}\right), ^-\left(\frac{15}{4}\right), ^-\left(\frac{14}{4}\right), ^-\left(\frac{13}{4}\right), ^-\left(\frac{12}{4}\right), \cdots\}$

15. Evaluate $2(t - 3) + 7$ for each member of the replacement set $\{3, 4, 5, 6\}$.

16. Write an open expression for "9 less than the number of centimeters in m meters."

17. Write an open sentence for "A certain number of nickels along with twice as many dimes is worth $2.00."

Solve. The replacement set is $\{0, 1, 2, 3, 4, 5\}$.

18. $2x + 3 = 7$ **19.** $3 > 8 - y$ **20.** $2n + n < 12$

21. Find: **a.** $|^+7|$ **b.** $|^-13|$ **c.** $|0|$

Chapter 2

The Operations and Their Properties

To most people, a building may seem like a jumble of steel, brick, and other materials. But each part has a purpose and is related to the other parts in a meaningful way. The way the parts are made and put together is the *structure* of the building.

Algebra has a structure too. The better you understand its structure, the better you can "put it all together," and the more sense it makes.

The foundation of a building, also called its *substructure*, underlies and supports the rest of it. This chapter will "pour the concrete" for the foundation of algebra.

Each **directed line segment** drawn below indicates a part of the real number line and a direction. Each represents the real number labeling it.

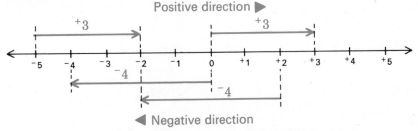

Directed line segments may be used to find sums.

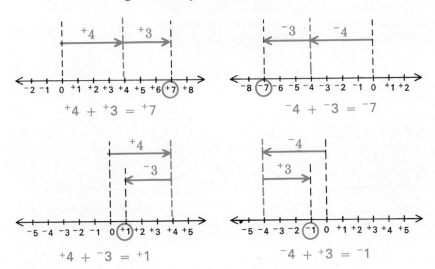

To add more than two numbers, you first add two of them and then to that sum you add a third number, and so on. For example, you can find $^-4 + {}^+8 + {}^-3 + {}^-2$ as follows.

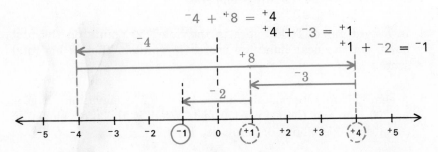

If *a, b, c, d,* ⋯ are real numbers, then

$$a + b + c = (a + b) + c,$$

$$a + b + c + d = [a + b + c] + d = [(a + b) + c] + d,$$

and so on, for sums of more than four addends.

EXERCISES 2.1

(A) What addition sentence is illustrated in each case?

1.
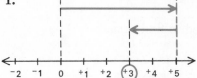

2.
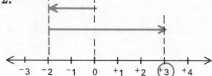

3.
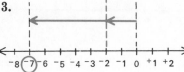

4.
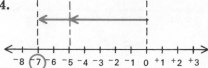

5.
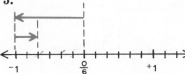

6.

Use real numbers to answer these questions.

7. The temperature is 0°, and then there is a 4° rise followed by a 5° drop. What is the resulting temperature?

8. In a card game, Todd "goes in the hole" 50 points on the first hand. On the next hand, he scores 75 points. What is his total score then?

9. A chair lift for skiers starts at sea level (0 feet elevation). It goes up 700 feet and then down 50 feet. What is the final elevation (number of feet above or below sea level)?

10. On a trip through a cave, you start at sea level and go down 325 feet. Then you go up 75 feet to a lunchroom. What is the elevation of the lunchroom?

11. A football team gains $5\frac{1}{2}$ yards on one play and loses $7\frac{1}{2}$ yards on the next play. What was the total yardage on the two plays?

Find each sum by referring to the number line below and thinking of the directed line segments you could draw.

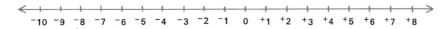

12. $^+7 + {}^-4$

13. $^-5 + {}^+2$

14. $^-2 + {}^-4$

15. $^-5 + {}^-3$

16. $^-4 + {}^+7$

17. $^+2 + {}^-5$

18. $^-4 + {}^-2$

19. $^-3 + {}^-5$

20. $^+4 + 0$

21. $0 + {}^+4$

22. $0 + {}^-10$

23. $^-10 + 0$

24. $^+5 + {}^-5$

25. $^+3 + {}^-3$

26. $^-8 + {}^+8$

Ⓑ Find each sum. (Use a number line if necessary.)

27. $(^+2 + {}^-5) + {}^+4$

28. $(^+5 + {}^-3) + {}^+4$

29. $^+2 + ({}^-5 + {}^+4)$

30. $^+5 + ({}^-3 + {}^+4)$

31. $(^-3 + {}^+4) + {}^-5$

32. $(^-7 + {}^+6) + {}^-2$

33. $^-3 + ({}^+4 + {}^-5)$

34. $^-7 + ({}^+6 + {}^-2)$

35. $^-3 + {}^+7 + {}^-2 + {}^-8$

36. $^-4 + {}^-3 + {}^-5 + {}^-2$

37. $^+10 + {}^-5 + {}^-2 + {}^+2$

38. $^-13 + {}^+7 + {}^-6 + {}^+13$

39. $^-9 + {}^+9 + {}^-16 + {}^+15$

40. $^+12 + {}^-12 + {}^+20 + {}^-22$

41. $^+(\frac{2}{5}) + {}^-(\frac{2}{5})$

42. $^-(\frac{3}{7}) + {}^+(\frac{3}{7})$

43. $^+(\frac{4}{5}) + {}^-(\frac{1}{5})$

44. $^-1 + {}^+(\frac{1}{2})$

45. $^-(\frac{1}{3}) + {}^+1$

46. $^-(\frac{1}{2}) + {}^-(\frac{1}{4})$

Ⓒ **47.** $^+(\frac{1}{2}) + {}^-(\frac{1}{3})$

48. $^+0.25 + {}^-0.75$

49. $^-5.5 + {}^-2.45$

50. Addition is called a **binary** operation because it assigns to every *two* real numbers a third real number. (*Bi* means "two.") Name another binary operation.

2.2 PROPERTIES OF ADDITION

Consider set E and set S below. Add any two members of E. Is the sum in E?

$$E = \{0, {}^+2, {}^+4, {}^+6, {}^+8, \cdots\}$$

$$S = \{\cdots, {}^-5, {}^-3, {}^-1, 0, {}^+2, {}^+4, {}^+6, \cdots\}$$

Since the sum of *any* two members of E is also in E, we say that set E is *closed under addition,* or addition of the members of set E has the *closure property.* Set S is not closed under addition. Why?

Addition of real numbers has several such properties. These properties are so basic that we take them for granted. That is, even though it is impossible to check all cases, we assume that addition of real numbers has these properties.

properties
of
addition

Let a, b, and c be any real numbers.

1. $(a + b)$ is a real number.   Closure prop. of $+$

2. $a + b = b + a$ Commutative prop. of $+$

3. $(a + b) + c = a + (b + c)$ Associative prop. of $+$

4. There is exactly one real number 0, called the **additive identity**:
   $a + 0 = 0 + a = a.$ Identity prop. of $+$

5. For each a there is exactly one real number $-a$, called the **additive inverse** of a:
   $a + (-a) = -a + a = 0.$ Inverse prop. of $+$

When the replacement set for a is the set of real numbers, as above, a represents negative as well as nonnegative numbers. Notice that, in stating the inverse property of addition, we have used the symbol $-a$ to represent the **additive inverse** (or **opposite**) of a. The following examples illustrate that $-a$, like a, represents both nonnegative and negative numbers.

Examples: If   then

$$a = {}^+3 \qquad -a = -({}^+3) = {}^-3$$

$$a = {}^-3 \qquad -a = -({}^-3) = {}^+3$$

$$a = 0 \qquad -a = -(0) = 0.$$

EXERCISES 2.2

Ⓐ Find $-a$ in each case.

1. $a = {}^+8$ **2.** $a = {}^+12$ **3.** $a = {}^-5$ **4.** $a = {}^-9$

5. $a = {}^+(\frac{2}{5})$ **6.** $a = {}^+(\frac{7}{8})$ **7.** $a = {}^-(\frac{4}{7})$ **8.** $a = {}^-(\frac{3}{4})$

Exercises 9–38. Which property is illustrated by each sentence? Each letter represents any real number.

9. The same sum results if two real numbers are added in either order.

10. The sum of any real number and 0 is identical to the given real number.

11. The sum of two real numbers is also a real number.

12. The sum of any real number and its opposite is 0.

13. The same sum results if three real numbers are added by grouping the first two or the last two.

14. $a + (b + c) = (a + b) + c$ **15.** ${}^+6 + [-({}^+6)] = 0$

16. $-({}^-11) + {}^-11 = 0$ **17.** $r + s = s + r$

18. $({}^+4 + {}^+3)$ is a real number.   **19.** $x + 0 = x$

20. $(a + b) + c = c + (a + b)$ **21.** ${}^+3 + ({}^+3 + {}^-3) = {}^+3 + 0$

22. $r + (s + t) = (s + t) + r$

Ⓑ **23.** $y + (-y) = 0$ **24.** $-m + m = 0$

25. $(x + y) + 0 = x + y$ **26.** $0 + (r + s) = r + s$

27. $b + [b + (-b)] = b + 0$ **28.** $(-k + k) + (-n) = 0 + (-n)$

29. $(w + z)$ is a real number.   **30.** $(-m + n)$ is a real number.

31. $({}^-5 + {}^+6) + {}^+8 = {}^+8 + ({}^-5 + {}^+6)$

32. $^-(\tfrac{1}{2}) + (^-11 + {}^+9) = (^-11 + {}^+9) + {}^-(\tfrac{1}{2})$

33. $^-6 + [-(^-6) + {}^-6] = {}^-6 + 0$

34. $[-({}^+5) + {}^+5] + [-(^-7)] = 0 + [-(^-7)]$

35. $(a + b) + (c + d) = (c + d) + (a + b)$

36. $(a + b) + (c + d) = (b + a) + (c + d)$

37. $[a + (b + c)] + d = a + [(b + c) + d]$

38. $(w + x) + (y + z) = w + [x + (y + z)]$

Show how each sum may be found by using the properties of addition.

Example:

$$
\begin{aligned}
({}^+7 + {}^+8) + {}^-7 &= ({}^+8 + {}^+7) + {}^-7 & \text{Comm. prop. of } + \\
&= {}^+8 + ({}^+7 + {}^-7) & \text{Assoc. prop. of } + \\
&= {}^+8 + 0 & \text{Inv. prop. of } + \\
&= {}^+8 & \text{Ident. prop. of } +
\end{aligned}
$$

39. $^-6 + ({}^+5 + {}^-5)$ **40.** $(^-4 + {}^+4) + {}^+8$

41. $({}^+9 + {}^+11) + {}^-11$ **42.** $^-17 + ({}^+17 + {}^-25)$

43. $(^-15 + {}^-13) + {}^+15$ **44.** $^+43 + (^-27 + {}^-43)$

45. $({}^+32 + {}^-19) + [-({}^+32)]$ **46.** $-(^-23) + ({}^+10 + {}^-23)$

© Each letter represents any real number. Show how the properties of addition may be used to simplify each expression.

47. $a + [b + (-b)]$ **48.** $-t + (t + t)$

49. $(c + d) + (-d)$ **50.** $-a + (b + a)$

A Fun Thing

Let $\{ \cdots, U4, U3, U2, U1, N0, J1, J2, J3, J4, \cdots \}$ be a set of "things."

Unthings   Nonthing   Just things

Let $\oplus$ stand for an operation that "puts things together." Let $\rightarrow$ stand for "this is what you get." See the examples below.

A. $J1 \oplus J2 \rightarrow J3$ **B.** $U1 \oplus U2 \rightarrow U3$

$\quad\quad J3 \oplus J5 \rightarrow J8$ $\quad\quad U3 \oplus U5 \rightarrow U8$

C. $J3 \oplus N0 \rightarrow J3$ **D.** $J4 \oplus U4 \rightarrow N0$

$\quad\quad U5 \oplus N0 \rightarrow U5$ $\quad\quad J7 \oplus U2 \rightarrow J5$

$\quad\quad N0 \oplus N0 \rightarrow N0$ $\quad\quad J3 \oplus U9 \rightarrow U6$

The number given in the name of each thing is its *strength*. If you put two "just things" together, you get a "just thing" whose strength is the combined strength of the two. (See the examples in **A**.) Also, if you put two "unthings" together, you get an "unthing" whose strength is the combined strength of the two. (See **B**.) If you put the "nonthing" together with any "thing," you get that "thing." (See **C**.)

The cartoon and the examples in **D** illustrate what happens when you put together a "just thing" and an "unthing." Find out what you get for each of the following.

1. $J6 \oplus J8$ **2.** $U5 \oplus U9$ **3.** $U10 \oplus J3$ **4.** $U8 \oplus J12$

5. $J8 \oplus J6$ **6.** $U9 \oplus U5$ **7.** $J3 \oplus U10$ **8.** $J12 \oplus U8$

9. $J7 \oplus N0$ **10.** $N0 \oplus J2$ **11.** $U11 \oplus N0$ **12.** $N0 \oplus U17$

13. $J8 \oplus U8$ **14.** $J13 \oplus U13$ **15.** $J21 \oplus U21$ **16.** $J18 \oplus U31$

2.3 ADDITION MADE EASY

If two real numbers are both positive or both negative, they are said to have the *same sign*. If one real number is positive and the other is negative, they are said to have *opposite signs*.

●   *a* is positive; *b* is positive   *a* is negative; *b* is negative

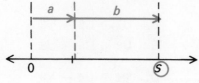 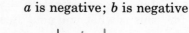

       Sum is positive.   Sum is negative.

●   *a* is positive; *b* is negative;   *a* is negative; *b* is positive;
            $|a| > |b|$ $|a| > |b|$

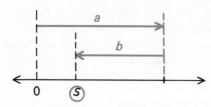 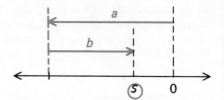

       Sum is positive.   Sum is negative.

Finding sums on the number line suggests the following rules.

addition of real numbers

●   To add two real numbers with the same sign:

1. Add their absolute values.

2. Let the sum have the same sign as the two addends.

●   To add two real numbers with opposite signs and different absolute values:

1. Subtract the lesser absolute value from the greater absolute value.

2. Let the result have the same sign as the addend with the greater absolute value.

Examples:

1. $^+19 + {}^+21 = {}^+(|{}^+19| + |{}^+21|)$
$= {}^+(19 + 21)$
$= {}^+40$

2. $^-16 + {}^-35 = {}^-(|{}^-16| + |{}^-35|)$
$= {}^-(16 + 35)$
$= {}^-51$

3. $^+12 + {}^-7 = {}^+(|{}^+12| - |{}^-7|)$
$= {}^+(12 - 7)$
$= {}^+5$

4. $^+15 + {}^-23 = {}^-(|{}^-23| - |{}^+15|)$
$= {}^-(23 - 15)$
$= {}^-8$

To add two real numbers with opposite signs and different absolute values:

another way to
add numbers with
opposite signs

1. Express the addend with the greater absolute value as some number plus the additive inverse of the other addend.

2. Use the properties of addition to find the sum.

Examples:

How much of this will offset this?

Express $^+12$ as $^+5$ plus the opposite of $^-7$.

5. $^+12 + {}^-7$

$= ({}^+5 + {}^+7) + {}^-7$
$= {}^+5 + ({}^+7 + {}^-7)$
$= {}^+5 + 0$
$= {}^+5$

Use the properties of addition.

How much of this will offset this?

Express $^-23$ as the opposite of $^+15$ plus $^-8$.

6. $^+15 + {}^-23$

$= {}^+15 + ({}^-15 + {}^-8)$
$= ({}^+15 + {}^-15) + {}^-8$
$= 0 + {}^-8$
$= {}^-8$

Use the properties of addition.

EXERCISES 2.3

Ⓐ Find each sum.

1. $^+7 + {}^+9$ 2. $^+8 + {}^+5$ 3. $^+9 + {}^+8$ 4. $^+7 + {}^+6$

5. $^-7 + {}^-9$ 6. $^-8 + {}^-5$ 7. $^-9 + {}^-8$ 8. $^-7 + {}^-6$

9. $^+10 + {}^+3$ 10. $^+5 + {}^+10$ 11. $^+5 + {}^+20$ 12. $^+20 + {}^+7$

13. $^-10 + {}^-3$ 14. $^-5 + {}^-10$ 15. $^-5 + {}^-20$ 16. $^-20 + {}^-7$

17. $^-1 + {}^+6$ 18. $^-2 + {}^+6$ 19. $^-3 + {}^+6$ 20. $^-4 + {}^+6$

21. $^+1 + {}^-6$ 22. $^+2 + {}^-6$ 23. $^+3 + {}^-6$ 24. $^+4 + {}^-6$

25. $^+9 + {}^-8$ 26. $^+5 + {}^-10$ 27. $^+7 + {}^-8$ 28. $^-7 + {}^+8$

29. $^+10 + {}^-3$ 30. $^-10 + {}^+3$ 31. $^-9 + {}^+8$ 32. $^-5 + {}^+10$

Ⓑ 33. $^-17 + {}^+11$ 34. $^+13 + {}^-8$ 35. $^-15 + {}^+9$ 36. $^-19 + {}^+13$

37. $^-11 + {}^+7$ 38. $^-12 + {}^+16$ 39. $^+18 + {}^-9$ 40. $^-14 + {}^+19$

41. $^+20 + {}^-5$ 42. $^+30 + {}^-10$ 43. $^+84 + {}^+90$ 44. $^-72 + {}^-32$

45. $^-18 + {}^+22$ 46. $^+27 + {}^-33$ 47. $^-23 + {}^+14$ 48. $^-82 + {}^+70$

49. $^-90 + {}^-64$ 50. $^-22 + {}^-34$ 51. $^+87 + {}^+48$ 52. $^+98 + {}^+87$

53. $^-237 + {}^+4$ 54. $^+464 + {}^-3$ 55. $^-791 + {}^-4$ 56. $^-829 + {}^-4$

Example: $^-12 + {}^-5 + {}^+9 = (^-12 + {}^-5) + {}^+9$
$$= {}^-17 + {}^+9$$
$$= {}^-8$$

57. $^-64 + {}^+4 + {}^-104$ 58. $^-64 + {}^+4 + {}^+104$

59. $^+52 + {}^-11 + {}^+164$ 60. $^+52 + {}^-11 + {}^-164$

61. $^-64 + {}^-4 + {}^-104$ 62. $^-52 + {}^-11 + {}^-164$

63. $^-18 + {}^+23 + {}^+148$ 64. $^-13 + {}^+23 + {}^+148$

65. $^+35 + {}^-15 + {}^-173$ 66. $^+47 + {}^-61 + {}^-197$

67. $^+(\frac{2}{7}) + {}^+(\frac{3}{7})$ 68. $^-(\frac{2}{7}) + {}^-(\frac{3}{7})$ 69. $^-(\frac{2}{7}) + {}^+(\frac{3}{7})$

70. $^+0.5 + {}^+0.3$ 71. $^-0.9 + {}^-0.6$ 72. $^-0.12 + {}^+0.23$

Ⓒ 73. $^+(\frac{3}{4}) + {}^-(\frac{1}{2})$ 74. $^-(\frac{3}{8}) + {}^+(\frac{1}{2})$ 75. $^-(\frac{1}{2}) + {}^+(\frac{1}{6})$

76. $^-(\frac{2}{3}) + {}^-(\frac{3}{4})$ 77. $^-(\frac{2}{3}) + {}^+(\frac{3}{4})$ 78. $^+(\frac{2}{3}) + {}^-(\frac{3}{4})$

79. $^+11.7 + {}^-3.4$ 80. $^-3.1 + {}^-5.3$ 81. $^-8.3 + {}^+2.4$

Example: Find $^-38 + {}^-724 + {}^+1245 + {}^+347$.

SOLUTION:

$$
\begin{array}{ccc}
{}^-38 & {}^+1245 & |{}^+1592| \longrightarrow 1592 \\
{}^-724 & {}^+347 & -|{}^-762| \longrightarrow -762 \\
\hline
{}^-762 & {}^+1592 & {}^+830 \\
\end{array}
$$

82. $^+349 + {}^-726 + {}^-42 + {}^-1009$

83. $^-648 + {}^+88 + {}^-8 + {}^+352$

84. $^-3.8 + {}^-1.5 + {}^+8.9 + {}^+8.2$

85. $^+8.2 + {}^-0.7 + {}^-0.1 + {}^-1.1$

86. Bill's savings account has $231.33 in it on the first of the month. Then Bill withdraws $10 on the fifth of the month. He withdraws $17.50 on the tenth; deposits $18.25 on the fifteenth; deposits $8.75 on the twentieth; and withdraws $9.50 on the last day of the month. Without figuring any interest earned, how much is now in his account?

87. Tanya's uncle gave her a share of stock. For the next five days the price (in dollars) of the share on the stock exchange changed as follows: rose $\frac{1}{4}$; fell $\frac{1}{8}$; fell $\frac{3}{8}$; rose $\frac{1}{4}$; rose $\frac{5}{8}$. What was the net change over the five days?

Copy and complete the table.

	Subset of Real Numbers	Property of Addition				
		Closure	Commutative	Associative	Identity	Inverse
88.	Positive Integers	Yes			No	
89.	Negative Integers					
90.	Nonnegative Integers			Yes		
91.	Nonpositive Integers					No
92.	Integers					
93.	Rational Numbers				Yes	

2.4 SUBTRACTION

If something in mathematics can be shown to be "just like" another thing, then we can get along without one of them. This section might be called "How to Get Along Without Subtraction."

You know that addition and subtraction are **inverse operations**. Each operation "undoes" the other. So, if you add 3 to a given number and then subtract 3, you get the given number.

$$5 + 3 - 3 = 5$$

$$18 + 3 - 3 = 18$$

$$n + 3 - 3 = n$$

Let's extend this pattern to addition and subtraction of any real numbers as follows.

Addition and subtraction are inverse operations.	$n + {}^+5 - {}^+5 = n$	(I)
	$n + {}^-5 - {}^-5 = n$	(II)

But you also know that the same "undoing" effect occurs with addition of a number and its additive inverse.

Addition of a number and its additive inverse	$n + {}^+5 + {}^-5 = n$	(III)
	$n + {}^-5 + {}^+5 = n$	(IV)

Notice that the black parts of sentences I and III are exactly alike. Notice also that the red parts indicate we are subtracting ${}^+5$ in case I and adding ${}^-5$ in case III.

Similarly, for sentences II and IV the black parts are exactly alike. But in case II we are subtracting ${}^-5$, and in case IV we are adding ${}^+5$.

Thus, it appears that subtracting a number is the same as adding its additive inverse.

To subtract any real number b from any real number a, add the additive inverse of b to a. In symbols,

$$a - b = a + (-b).$$

Examples:

$$1. \quad {}^+7 - {}^+9 = {}^+7 + {}^-9 \qquad 2. \quad {}^-23 - {}^+8 = {}^-23 + {}^-8$$
$$= {}^-2 \qquad\qquad\qquad\qquad = {}^-31$$

EXERCISES 2.4

(A) How should each sentence be completed?

1. ${}^+7 - {}^+2 = {}^+7 +$ _____
2. ${}^+7 - {}^-2 = {}^+7 +$ _____
3. ${}^-7 - {}^+2 = {}^-7 +$ _____
4. ${}^-7 - {}^-2 = {}^-7 +$ _____
5. ${}^-2 - {}^+7 = {}^-2 +$ _____
6. $0 - {}^+3 = 0 +$ _____
7. $0 - {}^-3 = 0 +$ _____
8. ${}^+5 -$ _____ $= {}^+5 + {}^-9$
9. ${}^+5 -$ _____ $= {}^+5 + {}^+9$
10. ${}^+5 - 0 = {}^+5 +$ _____

Use the subtraction property to express each difference as a sum.

11. $0 - {}^+9$
12. $0 - {}^+11$
13. ${}^-8 - {}^+13$
14. ${}^+34 - {}^-20$
15. ${}^+48 - {}^-30$
16. ${}^-29 - {}^-17$

(B) Find each difference.

17. ${}^+21 - {}^+35$
18. ${}^+76 - {}^+109$
19. ${}^+21 - {}^-35$
20. ${}^+76 - {}^-109$
21. ${}^-21 - {}^+35$
22. ${}^-76 - {}^+109$
23. ${}^-21 - {}^-35$
24. ${}^-76 - {}^-109$
25. ${}^+35 - {}^+21$
26. ${}^+109 - {}^+76$
27. ${}^+35 - {}^-21$
28. ${}^+109 - {}^-76$
29. ${}^-35 - {}^+21$
30. ${}^-109 - {}^+76$
31. ${}^-35 - {}^-21$
32. ${}^-109 - {}^-76$
33. ${}^+511 - {}^+511$
34. ${}^-2478 - {}^-2478$

35. $(^+9 - {}^+5) - {}^+6$

36. $(^-7 - {}^-5) - {}^-3$

37. $^+9 - (^+5 - {}^+6)$

38. $^-7 - (^-5 - {}^-3)$

39. $(^-16 - {}^+5) - {}^-18$

40. $(^+21 - {}^-4) - {}^+6$

41. $^-16 - (^+5 - {}^-18)$

42. $^+21 - (^-4 - {}^+6)$

43. $^+(\frac{5}{7}) - {}^+(\frac{2}{7})$ **44.** $^+(\frac{3}{7}) - {}^+(\frac{5}{7})$ **45.** $^+(\frac{3}{7}) - {}^-(\frac{2}{7})$

46. $^+(\frac{1}{7}) - {}^-(\frac{2}{7})$ **47.** $^+(\frac{1}{2}) - {}^+(\frac{1}{3})$ **48.** $^+(\frac{1}{3}) - {}^+(\frac{1}{2})$

49. $^-(\frac{1}{3}) - {}^-(\frac{1}{2})$ **50.** $^+(\frac{1}{2}) - {}^-(\frac{1}{3})$ **51.** $^-(\frac{1}{2}) - {}^-(\frac{1}{3})$

52. $^+0.9 - {}^-0.5$ **53.** $^-1.7 - {}^-0.6$ **54.** $^+0.29 - {}^+0.23$

Exercises 55–60. Which sets are closed under subtraction?

55. Positive integers

56. Negative integers

57. Integers

58. Rational numbers

59. Positive real numbers

60. Real numbers

61. Is subtraction of real numbers commutative?

62. Is subtraction of real numbers associative?

63. In a certain game, Ann has a score of $^+25$ points. Then she draws a penalty card which tells her to subtract 50 points from her score. What is her new score?

64. Cole has borrowed against future allowances, and his allowance account is now $^-8$ dollars. If he washes the family car, he can deduct 2 dollars of this debt. What will his allowance account be then?

© **65.** Subtraction of real numbers does not have the identity property. But it is often said to have the right identity property. What does this mean?

66. Subtraction of real numbers can be said to have the inverse property. What would be the *subtractive inverse* of any real number a?

Find each sum.

1. $^+7 + {}^-2$ 2. $^+7 + {}^+2$ 3. $^-7 + {}^-2$

4. $^-7 + {}^+2$ 5. $^-16 + {}^+5$ 6. $^-16 + {}^-5$

7. $^+16 + {}^-5$ 8. $^+16 + {}^+5$ 9. $^+20 + {}^-21$

10. $(^+3 + {}^-7) + {}^-6$ 11. $^+3 + (^-7 + {}^-6)$

12. $(^-8 + {}^-5) + {}^+2$ 13. $^-8 + (^-5 + {}^+2)$

Which property of addition is illustrated by each sentence?

14. $^-6 + {}^+9 = {}^+9 + {}^-6$ 15. $-(^+7) + (^+7) = 0$

16. $^-9 + 0 = {}^-9$ 17. $(^+6 + {}^-2)$ is a real number.

18. $^+7 + {}^-7 = 0$ 19. $(^-5 + {}^+2) + {}^-1 = {}^-5 + (^+2 + {}^-1)$

Find each difference.

20. $^+15 - {}^+4$ 21. $^+15 - {}^-4$ 22. $^-15 - {}^-4$

23. $^-15 - {}^+4$ 24. $^-20 - {}^-10$ 25. $^+20 - {}^-10$

26. $^+20 - {}^+10$ 27. $^-20 - {}^+10$ 28. $^-32 - {}^+12$

2.5 MULTIPLICATION

In multiplying real numbers, there are four cases to consider.

I. *Positive number times positive number:*

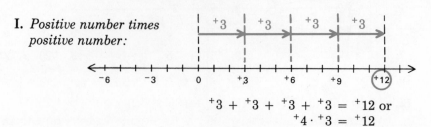

$$^+3 + {}^+3 + {}^+3 + {}^+3 = {}^+12 \text{ or}$$
$$^+4 \cdot {}^+3 = {}^+12$$

II. *Positive number times negative number:*

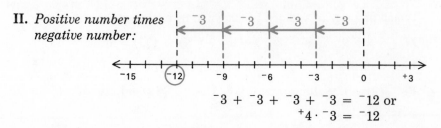

$$^-3 + {}^-3 + {}^-3 + {}^-3 = {}^-12 \text{ or}$$
$$^+4 \cdot {}^-3 = {}^-12$$

III. *Negative number times positive number:* Consider $^-4 \cdot {}^+3$. You know that $4 \cdot 3 = 3 \cdot 4$. Let us assume that $^-4 \cdot {}^+3 = {}^+3 \cdot {}^-4$. Since $^+3 \cdot {}^-4 = {}^-4 \cdot {}^+3$, it follows that $^-4 \cdot {}^+3 = {}^-12$.

Consider $^+4 \cdot 0$. Does $^+4 \cdot 0 = 0 + 0 + 0 + 0$? Thus, $^+4 \cdot 0 = 0$. Let us assume the following.

multiplication property of 0

Let a be any real number: $a \cdot 0 = 0$.

IV. *Negative number times negative number:* To determine $^-4 \cdot {}^-3$, look for a pattern in the sentences below.

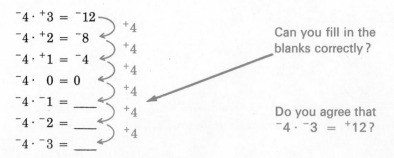

Can you fill in the blanks correctly?

Do you agree that $^-4 \cdot {}^-3 = {}^+12$?

Here is another way to think about these different products.

water running in at
3 gallons per minute

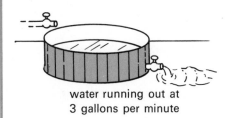

water running out at
3 gallons per minute

1. 4 minutes from now there will be 12 gallons more in the tank.

$$^+4 \cdot {}^+3 = {}^+12$$

2. 4 minutes ago, there were 12 fewer gallons in the tank.

$$^-4 \cdot {}^+3 = {}^-12$$

1. 4 minutes from now there will be 12 fewer gallons in the tank.

$$^+4 \cdot {}^-3 = {}^-12$$

2. 4 minutes ago, there were 12 gallons more in the tank.

$$^-4 \cdot {}^-3 = {}^+12$$

Just as in addition of real numbers, the concept of absolute value may be used to simplify the multiplication process.

- To multiply two real numbers with the same sign, find the product of their absolute values. Let the product be positive.

- To multiply two real numbers with different signs, find the product of their absolute values. Let the product be negative.

Examples:

1. $^-8 \cdot {}^-4 = {}^+(|{}^-8| \cdot |{}^-4|)$

$= {}^+(8 \cdot 4)$

$= {}^+32$

2. $^-7 \cdot {}^+6 = {}^-(|{}^-7| \cdot |{}^+6|)$

$= {}^-(7 \cdot 6)$

$= {}^-42$

To multiply more than two numbers, you first multiply two of them, and then you multiply that product by the third number, and so on.

If $a, b, c, d, \cdots$ are real numbers, then

$$a \cdot b \cdot c = (a \cdot b) \cdot c,$$

$$a \cdot b \cdot c \cdot d = [a \cdot b \cdot c] \cdot d = [(a \cdot b) \cdot c] \cdot d,$$

and so on, for products of more than four factors.

Example 3: $\quad {}^-4 \cdot {}^+5 \cdot {}^-7 = ({}^-4 \cdot {}^+5) \cdot {}^-7$

$$= {}^-(|{}^-4| \cdot |{}^+5|) \cdot {}^-7$$

$$= {}^-(4 \cdot 5) \cdot {}^-7$$

$$= {}^-20 \cdot {}^-7$$

$$= {}^+(|{}^-20| \cdot |{}^-7|)$$

$$= {}^+(20 \cdot 7)$$

$$= {}^+140$$

EXERCISES 2.5

Ⓐ Find each product.

1. ${}^+5 \cdot {}^+3$ **2.** ${}^+4 \cdot {}^+6$ **3.** ${}^+4 \cdot {}^-5$ **4.** ${}^+3 \cdot {}^-8$

5. ${}^-4 \cdot {}^+6$ **6.** ${}^-5 \cdot {}^+7$ **7.** ${}^-8 \cdot {}^-9$ **8.** ${}^-5 \cdot {}^-13$

9. ${}^+12 \cdot {}^+1$ **10.** ${}^+1 \cdot {}^+12$ **11.** ${}^+1 \cdot {}^-17$ **12.** ${}^-17 \cdot {}^+1$

13. ${}^-1 \cdot {}^-1$ **14.** ${}^-1 \cdot {}^-1 \cdot {}^-1$

15. ${}^-1 \cdot {}^-1 \cdot {}^-1 \cdot {}^-1$ **16.** ${}^-2 \cdot {}^-1 \cdot {}^+3 \cdot {}^-1$

17. ${}^+2 \cdot {}^+1 \cdot {}^+3 \cdot {}^-2 \cdot {}^+1$ **18.** ${}^-1 \cdot {}^-2 \cdot {}^+3 \cdot {}^-1 \cdot {}^-1 \cdot {}^-1$

19. What is the sign of the product of an odd number of negative numbers, if none of the factors is zero?

20. What is the sign of the product of an even number of negative numbers, if none of the factors is zero?

21. On a diet, Bill lost 4 pounds and Ben lost three times as many pounds. What real number expresses Ben's weight loss?

22. If John lost \$2 per day for five days, what real number represents his loss?

Express each sum as a product.

23. $^+7 + {}^+7 + {}^+7 + {}^+7$ **24.** $^-8 + {}^-8 + {}^-8 + {}^-8 + {}^-8$

25. $^-5 + {}^-5 + {}^-5$ **26.** $^+12 + {}^+12 + {}^+12 + {}^+12$

Ⓑ Find each product.

27. $^+2 \cdot {}^+(\frac{1}{2})$ **28.** $^-4 \cdot {}^-(\frac{1}{4})$ **29.** $^+(\frac{1}{9}) \cdot {}^+9$ **30.** $^-(\frac{1}{17}) \cdot {}^-17$

31. $^+18 \cdot {}^-7$ **32.** $^-27 \cdot {}^+8$ **33.** $^-12 \cdot {}^-16$ **34.** $^-36 \cdot {}^-12$

35. $(^+4 \cdot {}^-3) \cdot {}^-5$ **36.** $(^+6 \cdot {}^-2) \cdot {}^-4$

37. $^+4 \cdot ({}^-3 \cdot {}^-5)$ **38.** $^+6 \cdot ({}^-2 \cdot {}^-4)$

39. $(^-8 \cdot {}^-4) \cdot {}^-6$ **40.** $(^-7 \cdot {}^-5) \cdot {}^-3$

41. $^-8 \cdot ({}^-4 \cdot {}^-6)$ **42.** $^-7 \cdot ({}^-5 \cdot {}^-3)$

43. $^-8 \cdot {}^+11 \cdot 0 \cdot {}^-74$ **44.** $^-7 \cdot {}^+12 \cdot 0 \cdot {}^-47$

45. $^-1 \cdot {}^+14 \cdot {}^-2 \cdot {}^-4$ **46.** $^+15 \cdot {}^-2 \cdot {}^-1 \cdot {}^-6$

47. $^-5 \cdot {}^-4 \cdot {}^-7 \cdot {}^-3 \cdot {}^-11$ **48.** $^-13 \cdot {}^-3 \cdot {}^-2 \cdot {}^-9 \cdot {}^-4$

49. $^-24 \cdot {}^+12$ **50.** $^-13 \cdot {}^+34$ **51.** $^+25 \cdot {}^-14$

52. $^+36 \cdot {}^-8$ **53.** $^-124 \cdot {}^-74$ **54.** $^-236 \cdot {}^-58$

55. $^-345 \cdot {}^+89$ **56.** $^-747 \cdot {}^+29$ **57.** $^+(\frac{3}{5}) \cdot {}^-(\frac{2}{7})$

58. $^+(\frac{3}{5}) \cdot {}^-(\frac{4}{11})$ **59.** $^-(\frac{2}{7}) \cdot {}^+(\frac{4}{7})$ **60.** $^-(\frac{4}{9}) \cdot {}^+(\frac{5}{9})$

61. $^+0.7 \cdot {}^-0.8$ **62.** $^-0.4 \cdot {}^+0.9$ **63.** $^-0.6 \cdot {}^-0.7$

64. $^+0.3 \cdot {}^+0.9$ **65.** $^+3 \cdot {}^+(\frac{8}{9})$ **66.** $^-5 \cdot {}^+(\frac{7}{8})$

Ⓒ **67.** $^-(\frac{5}{4}) \cdot {}^+(\frac{9}{10})$ **68.** $^-(\frac{6}{7}) \cdot {}^-(2\frac{1}{4})$ **69.** $^+(\frac{9}{5}) \cdot {}^-(2\frac{5}{6})$

70. $^+0.4 \cdot {}^-0.12$ **71.** $^-0.16 \cdot {}^-0.16$ **72.** $^-1.5 \cdot {}^+1.25$

73. Suppose a girl walks *forward* at a rate of 3 steps per second. We take a movie of the girl, and show it at 2 times the normal *reverse* (*backward*) speed. The screen will show the girl walking *backward* at $2 \cdot 3$ or 6 steps per second. This is an example for $^-2 \cdot 3 = {}^-6$. How can you use this method to give examples for $2 \cdot 3 = 6$, $2 \cdot {}^-3 = {}^-6$, and $^-2 \cdot {}^-3 = 6$?

2.6 DIVISION

You can check the result of a division problem by multiplying the quotient by the divisor. The product obtained should equal the dividend. For example,

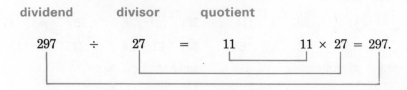

This idea can be used to discover rules for division of real numbers. In each case below, n must have the same value in both open sentences.

$$\text{I.} \quad {}^+12 \div {}^+3 = n \longleftrightarrow n \times {}^+3 = {}^+12$$
$$\text{II.} \quad {}^+12 \div {}^-3 = n \longleftrightarrow n \times {}^-3 = {}^+12$$
$$\text{III.} \quad {}^-12 \div {}^+3 = n \longleftrightarrow n \times {}^+3 = {}^-12$$
$$\text{IV.} \quad {}^-12 \div {}^-3 = n \longleftrightarrow n \times {}^-3 = {}^-12$$

Your knowledge of multiplication can be used to determine the value of n in each case.

In case I, since ${}^+4 \times {}^+3 = {}^+12$, it follows that ${}^+12 \div {}^+3 = {}^+4$.

In case II, since ${}^-4 \times {}^-3 = {}^+12$, it follows that ${}^+12 \div {}^-3 = {}^-4$.

In case III, since ${}^-4 \times {}^+3 = {}^-12$, it follows that ${}^-12 \div {}^+3 = {}^-4$.

In case IV, since ${}^+4 \times {}^-3 = {}^-12$, it follows that ${}^-12 \div {}^-3 = {}^+4$.

Notice that in cases I and IV the dividend and divisor have the same sign. In cases II and III, they have opposite signs. Thus, these examples suggest the following rules.

division of real numbers

- To divide two real numbers with the same sign, find the quotient of their absolute values. Let the quotient be positive.

- To divide two real numbers with opposite signs, find the quotient of their absolute values. Let the quotient be negative.

Examples:

1. $^+75 \div {}^+3 = {}^+(75 \div 3)$
$$= {}^+25$$

2. $^-42 \div {}^-7 = {}^+(42 \div 7)$
$$= {}^+6$$

3. $^+100 \div {}^-10 = {}^-(100 \div 10)$
$$= {}^-10$$

4. $^-30 \div {}^+6 = {}^-(30 \div 6)$
$$= {}^-5$$

In finding the quotient $a \div b$, the divisor b cannot equal 0. Consider what happens in the following two cases when we try to divide by 0.

A. $^+4 \div 0 = n \quad \longleftrightarrow \quad n \times 0 = {}^+4$

B. $0 \div 0 = n \quad \longleftrightarrow \quad n \times 0 = 0$

In case **A**, no matter what replacement we make for n, $n \times 0 \neq {}^+4$ (rather $n \times 0 = 0$). There is no number n such that $n \times 0 = {}^+4$. In case **B**, any number n will make $n \times 0 = 0$ true. Since there is either no value of n or the values of n are unlimited, we say *division by 0 is not defined.*

However, the dividend can be 0, as long as the divisor is not 0.

$$0 \div {}^+4 = n \quad \longleftrightarrow \quad n \times {}^+4 = 0$$

Since $0 \times {}^+4 = 0$, it follows that $0 \div {}^+4 = 0$.

EXERCISES 2.6

Ⓐ What number does n represent in each case?

1. $^-32 \div {}^+8 = n$ because $n \times {}^+8 = {}^-32$.

2. $^-48 \div {}^-6 = n$ because $n \times {}^-6 = {}^-48$.

3. $^+72 \div {}^+8 = n$ because $n \times {}^+8 = {}^+72$.

4. $^+16 \div {}^-2 = n$ because $n \times {}^-2 = {}^+16$.

5. $0 \div {}^+5 = n$ because $n \times {}^+5 = 0$.

6. $0 \div {}^-2 = n$ because $n \times {}^-2 = 0$.

Find each quotient.

7. $^+9 \div {}^-1$ 8. $^-9 \div {}^+1$ 9. $^-9 \div {}^-1$ 10. $^+9 \div {}^+1$

11. $^-4 \div {}^+2$ 12. $^-4 \div {}^-2$ 13. $^+4 \div {}^-2$ 14. $^+4 \div {}^+2$

15. $^-6 \div {}^+3$ 16. $^+6 \div {}^-3$ 17. $^-6 \div {}^-3$ 18. $^+6 \div {}^+3$

19. $^+8 \div {}^+2$ 20. $^-8 \div {}^-2$ 21. $^-8 \div {}^+2$ 22. $^+8 \div {}^-2$

23. $^-9 \div {}^-3$ 24. $^-9 \div {}^+3$ 25. $0 \div {}^-3$ 26. $0 \div {}^+3$

Ⓑ 27. $^-18 \div {}^+3$ 28. $^-18 \div {}^-3$ 29. $^+18 \div {}^+3$ 30. $^+18 \div {}^-3$

31. $^-30 \div {}^-5$ 32. $^+30 \div {}^+5$ 33. $^+30 \div {}^-5$ 34. $^-30 \div {}^+5$

35. $^+45 \div {}^+5$ 36. $^-45 \div {}^-5$ 37. $^-45 \div {}^+5$ 38. $^+45 \div {}^-5$

Example: $^-1.21 \div {}^-0.11 = 1.21 \div 0.11 \rightarrow 0.11)\overline{1.21}^{\,11}$

39. $2.5 \div {}^-0.5$ 40. $^-0.32 \div 0.8$ 41. $^-0.45 \div {}^-0.05$

42. $14.4 \div 1.2$ 43. $^-1.19 \div 0.17$ 44. $^-17.5 \div {}^-0.35$

45. $22.8 \div 0.57$ 46. $4.50 \div {}^-2.5$ 47. $^-2.79 \div 3.1$

48. $2.99 \div {}^-2.3$ 49. $^-75 \div 0.25$ 50. $^-92 \div {}^-0.23$

51. For one week the following daily low temperatures in degrees Fahrenheit were recorded at a weather bureau. Find the average daily low temperature.

Day	Sun.	Mon.	Tues.	Wed.	Thurs.	Fri.	Sat.
Temperature	$^+10°$	$^+4°$	$0°$	$^-8°$	$^-12°$	$^-2°$	$^+1°$

52. Mr. Collins reported the following gains and losses (in dollars) on his investments for 5 months: $^+320$, $^-80$, $^+100$, $^-120$, $^-20$. What was his monthly average?

Ⓒ Evaluate each expression. Before doing these exercises, review the "order of operations" in Section 1.6.

53. $^-8[^+2 - {}^+18 \div {}^-9]$ 54. $^+5 + {}^-9 \div {}^+3 - {}^-2 \cdot {}^+6$

55. $^+13 + {}^-8 \cdot {}^+4 \div {}^-16$ 56. $^-55 \div {}^-11 \cdot {}^-7 \div {}^+5$

57. $^-4[(^+18 - {}^+10) \div ({}^+6 + {}^+2)]$ 58. $^+34 \div {}^-17 + {}^-10 \div {}^-2$

Until now, we have denoted a negative number by using a raised minus sign. The regular minus sign has been used to denote "the opposite of" or "the additive inverse of." So ⁻3 means "negative 3" while −3 means "the additive inverse of 3." However, since the additive inverse of 3 is ⁻3, it follows that −3 = ⁻3.

Therefore, from now on, we will use the regular minus sign to denote negative numbers. The raised plus will no longer be used to denote positive numbers. The raised ⁺ and ⁻ are helpful when first learning about positive and negative numbers, but using the regular − and omitting the plus is more common. Also, parentheses will not be used unless necessary.

Old notation	⁻10	⁻($\frac{1}{2}$)	⁺2	⁺($\frac{2}{3}$)
New notation	−10	−$\frac{1}{2}$	2	$\frac{2}{3}$

In Section 2.6, you learned the rules for division of real numbers. We sometimes express a quotient by a fraction. Remember that $a \div b = \frac{a}{b}$.

Consider $-2 \div 3$ and $2 \div (-3)$. Expressing each quotient as a fraction, we have

$$-2 \div 3 = \frac{-2}{3} \quad \text{and} \quad 2 \div (-3) = \frac{2}{-3}.$$

According to the rules for division, each quotient is negative. Therefore,

$$\boxed{\frac{-2}{3} = \frac{2}{-3} = -\frac{2}{3}.}$$

This illustrates that a fraction which names a negative number can be written in three ways. For example, $-\frac{1}{2}$ can also be expressed as $\frac{-1}{2}$ or $\frac{1}{-2}$.

Now consider $-2 \div (-3)$. By the rules for division, the quotient is positive. Therefore,

$$-2 \div (-3) = \frac{-2}{-3} = \frac{2}{3}.$$

You have performed operations with positive numbers named by fractions before. The same procedures apply when negative numbers are involved.

Examples:

1. $-\dfrac{2}{3} \cdot \dfrac{1}{5} = -\left(\dfrac{2 \cdot 1}{3 \cdot 5}\right) = -\dfrac{2}{15}$

2. $-\dfrac{5}{7} \cdot \left(-\dfrac{3}{8}\right) = \dfrac{5 \cdot 3}{7 \cdot 8} = \dfrac{15}{56}$

3. $\dfrac{5}{9} \div \left(-\dfrac{1}{4}\right) = \dfrac{5}{9} \cdot \left(-\dfrac{4}{1}\right) = -\left(\dfrac{5 \cdot 4}{9 \cdot 1}\right) = -\dfrac{20}{9}$

4. $-\dfrac{3}{4} \div \left(-\dfrac{5}{7}\right) = -\dfrac{3}{4} \cdot \left(-\dfrac{7}{5}\right) = \dfrac{3 \cdot 7}{4 \cdot 5} = \dfrac{21}{20}$

Notice that the negative answers above are stated in the form $-\frac{2}{15}$ (not $\frac{-2}{15}$ or $\frac{2}{-15}$). Also, the positive answers are stated in the form $\frac{21}{20}$ (not $\frac{-21}{-20}$). We will agree that, in this book, this is **standard form** for such answers. Your teacher may want you to give all your answers in standard form.

EXERCISES 2.7

Ⓐ Express each of the following by a fraction.

1. $7 \div 3$ **2.** $3 \div (-7)$ **3.** $-7 \div (-8)$ **4.** $-3 \div 7$

Express each of the following fractions in two other ways. For example, $-\frac{1}{2} = \frac{-1}{2} = \frac{1}{-2}$.

5. $-\dfrac{1}{5}$ **6.** $\dfrac{3}{-7}$ **7.** $\dfrac{-2}{9}$ **8.** $\dfrac{3}{-10}$

How should each sentence be completed?

9. $\dfrac{1}{3} \div \dfrac{2}{5} = \dfrac{1}{3} \cdot \underline{\hspace{1cm}}$ **10.** $\dfrac{2}{5} \div \left(-\dfrac{1}{4}\right) = \dfrac{2}{5} \cdot \underline{\hspace{1cm}}$

11. $\dfrac{3}{8} \div \left(-\dfrac{4}{7}\right) = \dfrac{3}{8} \cdot \underline{\hspace{1cm}}$ **12.** $-\dfrac{2}{7} \div \dfrac{3}{10} = -\dfrac{2}{7} \cdot \underline{\hspace{1cm}}$

Find each product.

13. $\frac{7}{8} \cdot \frac{1}{5}$

14. $\frac{3}{7} \cdot \frac{1}{4}$

15. $\frac{1}{6} \cdot (-\frac{1}{3})$

16. $\frac{1}{8} \cdot (-\frac{7}{9})$

17. $-\frac{2}{7} \cdot (-\frac{4}{3})$

18. $-\frac{9}{16} \cdot (-\frac{3}{4})$

19. $-\frac{7}{10} \cdot \frac{7}{10}$

20. $-\frac{5}{14} \cdot \frac{1}{3}$

21. $\frac{8}{21} \cdot \frac{4}{3}$

22. $\frac{1}{20} \cdot \frac{3}{10}$

23. $\frac{-2}{15} \cdot \frac{4}{5}$

24. $\frac{-3}{11} \cdot \frac{2}{7}$

25. $\frac{9}{13} \cdot \frac{-2}{11}$

26. $\frac{3}{5} \cdot \frac{-2}{5}$

27. $\frac{7}{-25} \cdot \frac{-9}{8}$

28. $\frac{-3}{4} \cdot \frac{9}{-5}$

29. $-\frac{7}{20} \cdot \frac{7}{15}$

30. $-\frac{6}{13} \cdot \frac{4}{11}$

Find each quotient.

31. $\frac{2}{5} \div \frac{5}{3}$

32. $\frac{3}{5} \div \frac{2}{3}$

33. $\frac{6}{25} \div (-\frac{5}{4})$

34. $\frac{7}{10} \div (-\frac{3}{7})$

35. $-\frac{4}{7} \div (-\frac{7}{2})$

36. $-\frac{7}{8} \div (-\frac{3}{5})$

37. $\frac{-4}{9} \div \frac{1}{2}$

38. $\frac{-7}{11} \div \frac{11}{5}$

39. $\frac{4}{13} \div \frac{9}{10}$

40. $\frac{10}{3} \div \frac{3}{7}$

41. $\frac{3}{-2} \div \frac{4}{11}$

42. $\frac{9}{-5} \div \frac{4}{13}$

43. $\frac{9}{8} \div \frac{4}{-9}$

44. $\frac{5}{4} \div \frac{6}{-17}$

45. $\frac{14}{-3} \div \frac{-1}{5}$

Ⓒ Study the following example.

Example:

$$-\frac{2}{3} \div \frac{5}{7} = \frac{-\frac{2}{3}}{\frac{5}{7}} = \frac{-\frac{2}{3} \cdot \frac{7}{5}}{\frac{5}{7} \cdot \frac{7}{5}} = \frac{-\frac{2}{3} \cdot \frac{7}{5}}{1} = -\frac{2}{3} \cdot \frac{7}{5}$$

46. Show that $\dfrac{7}{6} \div \left(-\dfrac{2}{5}\right) = \dfrac{7}{6} \cdot \left(-\dfrac{5}{2}\right).$

47. Show that $\dfrac{a}{b} \div \dfrac{c}{d} = \dfrac{a}{b} \cdot \dfrac{d}{c}.$

2.8 PROPERTIES OF MULTIPLICATION

Multiplication of real numbers has five properties that are similar to the five properties of addition of real numbers discussed in Section 2.2. Again, these properties are so basic that we take them for granted.

properties
of
multiplication

Let a, b, and c be any real numbers.

1. $(a \cdot b)$ is a real number.   Closure prop. of $\cdot$

2. $a \cdot b = b \cdot a$ Commutative prop. of $\cdot$

3. $(a \cdot b) \cdot c = a \cdot (b \cdot c)$ Associative prop. of $\cdot$

4. There is exactly one real number 1, called the **multiplicative identity**: $a \cdot 1 = 1 \cdot a = a$.   Identity prop. of $\cdot$

5. For each nonzero a, there is exactly one real number $\frac{1}{a}$, called the **multiplicative inverse** of a: $a \cdot \frac{1}{a} = \frac{1}{a} \cdot a = 1$.   Inverse prop. of $\cdot$

In the statement of the inverse property, note that a cannot be zero. That is, 0 does not have a multiplicative inverse because $\frac{1}{0}$ is not defined.

Note that every nonzero real number a has exactly one multiplicative inverse $\frac{1}{a}$. However, this multiplicative inverse can be denoted by more than one symbol. For example, the multiplicative inverse of $\frac{3}{4}$ is

$$\frac{1}{\frac{3}{4}}. \quad \text{But} \quad \frac{1}{\frac{3}{4}} = 1 \div \frac{3}{4} = 1 \cdot \frac{4}{3} = \frac{4}{3}.$$

So, $\frac{4}{3}$ is the standard form for the multiplicative inverse of $\frac{3}{4}$.

The multiplicative inverse of a number is sometimes called the **reciprocal** of the number. The product of any number and its reciprocal is 1.

Since $\quad 4 \cdot \frac{1}{4} = 1, \quad \frac{1}{4}$ is the multiplicative inverse of 4.

Since $\quad -3 \cdot (-\frac{1}{3}) = 1, \quad -\frac{1}{3}$ is the multiplicative inverse of -3.

Since $\quad \frac{3}{5} \cdot \frac{5}{3} = 1, \quad \frac{5}{3}$ is the multiplicative inverse of $\frac{3}{5}$.

Since $\quad -\frac{8}{5} \cdot (-\frac{5}{8}) = 1, \quad -\frac{5}{8}$ is the multiplicative inverse of $-\frac{8}{5}$.

The following examples suggest another multiplication property.

If	then	and
$a = 3$	$-a = -3$	$-1 \cdot a = -3$
$a = -2$	$-a = -(-2) = 2$	$-1 \cdot a = 2$
$a = 0$	$-a = 0$	$-1 \cdot a = 0.$

multiplication property of -1

Let a be any real number.

$$-a = -1 \cdot a$$

Using the properties already given in this section, we can show why the following properties must be true.

multiplication properties of opposites

Let a and b be any real numbers.

$$(-a)b = -ab \qquad a(-b) = -ab \qquad (-a)(-b) = ab$$

For example,

$$(-a)b = (-1 \cdot a)b \qquad \text{Mult. prop. of } -1$$
$$= -1(ab) \qquad \text{Assoc. prop. of } \cdot$$
$$= -ab. \qquad \text{Mult. prop. of } -1$$

So, $(-a)b = -ab$.

In a similar way, it can be shown that

$$a(-b) = -ab \quad \text{and} \quad (-a)(-b) = ab.$$

EXERCISES 2.8

Ⓐ What is the multiplicative inverse (if any) of each number?

1. 5   **2.** -7 **3.** $\frac{3}{7}$ **4.** 1

5. $-\frac{1}{6}$ **6.** -1 **7.** 0   **8.** $-\frac{3}{2}$

Name the property illustrated by each sentence. Each letter represents any real number.

9. The product of any real number and 1 is identical to the given number.

10. The same product results if any two real numbers are multiplied in either order.

11. The product of any nonzero real number and its reciprocal is 1.

12. The product of any two real numbers is also a real number.

13. The same product results if any three real numbers are multiplied by grouping the first two or the last two.

14. The product of any real number and -1 is the opposite of the given real number.

15. The product of any two real numbers is equal to the product of their opposites.

16. The opposite of the product of any two real numbers is equal to the product of either one of the real numbers and the opposite of the other.

17. $-7 \cdot (-\frac{1}{7}) = 1$ **18.** $-12 \cdot (-8) = -8 \cdot (-12)$

19. $[-3 \cdot (-5)] \cdot 8 = -3 \cdot (-5 \cdot 8)$ **20.** $(-5 \cdot 8)$ is a real number.

21. $24 \cdot 1 = 24$ **22.** $-24 = -1 \cdot 24$

23. $7(-6) = -(7 \cdot 6)$ **24.** $(-8)(-4) = 8 \cdot 4$

Ⓑ **25.** $\frac{4}{5} \cdot (-\frac{8}{9}) = -\frac{8}{9} \cdot \frac{4}{5}$ **26.** $-\frac{5}{6} \cdot (-\frac{7}{11}) = -\frac{7}{11} \cdot (-\frac{5}{6})$

27. $-\frac{1}{2} \cdot (\frac{2}{3} \cdot 5) = (-\frac{1}{2} \cdot \frac{2}{3}) \cdot 5$ **28.** $6 \cdot (-\frac{3}{4} \cdot 4) = [6 \cdot (-\frac{3}{4})] \cdot 4$

29. $-\frac{2}{3} \cdot 1 = -\frac{2}{3}$ **30.** $-\frac{5}{6} \cdot 1 = -\frac{5}{6}$

31. $\frac{7}{8} \cdot \frac{1}{\frac{7}{8}} = 1$

32. $-\frac{4}{13} \cdot \frac{1}{-\frac{4}{13}} = 1$

33. $-\frac{3}{4} = -1 \cdot \frac{3}{4}$

34. $-1 \cdot \frac{2}{3} = -\frac{2}{3}$

35. $[w \cdot (-c)]$ is a real number.

36. $(-a \cdot b)$ is a real number.

37. $(2 \cdot \frac{1}{2}) \cdot s = 1 \cdot s$

38. $[-6 \cdot (-\frac{1}{6})] \cdot w = 1 \cdot w$

39. $(-c + d) \cdot 1 = -c + d$

40. $(-m + n) \cdot 1 = -m + n$

41. $x(-y) = -xy$

42. $(-x)(-y) = xy$

Show how each product may be found by using the properties of multiplication to evaluate the given expression.

Example: Evaluate $(-8 \cdot 9) \cdot (-\frac{1}{8})$.

$$\text{SOLUTION:} \quad (-8 \cdot 9) \cdot (-\tfrac{1}{8}) = [9 \cdot (-8)] \cdot (-\tfrac{1}{8}) \quad \text{Comm. prop. of } \cdot$$
$$= 9 \cdot [-8 \cdot (-\tfrac{1}{8})] \quad \text{Assoc. prop. of } \cdot$$
$$= 9 \cdot 1 \quad \text{Inv. prop. of } \cdot$$
$$= 9 \quad \text{Ident. prop. of } \cdot$$

43. $-5 \cdot (4 \cdot \frac{1}{4})$

44. $(5 \cdot \frac{1}{5}) \cdot (-6)$

45. $[7 \cdot (-\frac{1}{12})] \cdot (-12)$

46. $-13 \cdot (-\frac{1}{13} \cdot 9)$

47. $[-34 \cdot (-15)] \cdot (-\frac{1}{34})$

48. $-\frac{1}{42} \cdot [-18 \cdot (-42)]$

© Copy and complete the table.

	Subset of Real Numbers	Property of Multiplication				
		Closure	Commutative	Associative	Identity	Inverse
49.	Positive Integers	Yes				
50.	Negative Integers	No		Yes		
51.	Nonnegative Integers					
52.	Nonpositive Integers					
53.	Integers					
54.	Rational Numbers					

SELF-QUIZ: 2.5 to 2.8

Find each product.

1. $-2 \cdot 5$
2. $-2 \cdot (-5)$
3. $2 \cdot 5$
4. $2 \cdot (-5)$
5. $6 \cdot (-8)$
6. $6 \cdot 8$
7. $-6 \cdot (-8)$
8. $-6 \cdot 8$
9. $3 \cdot (-16)$
10. $-7 \cdot (-10)$
11. $35 \cdot (-5)$
12. $-25 \cdot 15$

Which property of multiplication is illustrated by each sentence?

13. $[5 \cdot (-6)]$ is a real number.
14. $0 \cdot 7 = 0$
15. $-7 \cdot 3 = 3 \cdot (-7)$
16. $-16 \cdot 1 = -16$
17. $-6 \cdot (-\frac{1}{6}) = 1$
18. $-5 \cdot (3 \cdot 4) = (-5 \cdot 3) \cdot 4$

Find each quotient.

19. $-20 \div 5$
20. $20 \div 5$
21. $20 \div (-5)$
22. $-20 \div (-5)$
23. $32 \div (-8)$
24. $-32 \div (-8)$
25. $32 \div 8$
26. $-32 \div 8$
27. $-50 \div 2$
28. $76 \div (-4)$
29. $-90 \div (-5)$
30. $150 \div (-3)$

Find each product or quotient.

31. $\frac{3}{7} \cdot (-\frac{4}{5})$
32. $(-\frac{1}{9}) \div \frac{1}{4}$
33. $-\frac{6}{11} \cdot (-\frac{3}{7})$
34. $\frac{2}{9} \cdot (-\frac{1}{5})$
35. $-\frac{7}{16} \cdot \frac{1}{3}$
36. $-\frac{3}{7} \div (-\frac{5}{9})$
37. $\frac{5}{14} \cdot (-\frac{3}{8})$
38. $\frac{6}{5} \div \frac{13}{9}$
39. $-\frac{4}{15} \cdot \frac{4}{15}$

Earlier we agreed on standard form for indicating if a fraction names a positive or a negative number. We will now extend our agreement on **standard form for fractions** to include *reducing to lowest terms.* As you probably recall, a fraction is in lowest terms if no factor greater than 1 is common to its numerator and denominator.

Examples: Express each of the following in standard form.

1. $\dfrac{8}{12}$ 2. $\dfrac{-5}{10}$

SOLUTIONS:

1. $\dfrac{8}{12} = \dfrac{2 \cdot 4}{3 \cdot 4}$

$\quad = \dfrac{2}{3} \cdot \dfrac{4}{4}$

$\quad = \dfrac{2}{3} \cdot 1$

$\quad = \dfrac{2}{3}$

2. $\dfrac{-5}{10} = -\dfrac{5}{10}$

$\quad = -\left(\dfrac{1 \cdot 5}{2 \cdot 5}\right)$

$\quad = -\dfrac{1}{2} \cdot \dfrac{5}{5}$

$\quad = -\dfrac{1}{2} \cdot 1 = -\dfrac{1}{2}$

In Example 1, notice that $\frac{8}{12}$ could first be renamed as $\frac{4 \cdot 2}{6 \cdot 2}$, which reduces to $\frac{4}{6}$. But then $\frac{4}{6}$ can be renamed as $\frac{2 \cdot 2}{3 \cdot 2}$, which reduces to $\frac{2}{3}$.

A **mixed numeral** represents a sum. For example,

$$5\tfrac{1}{3} = 5 + \tfrac{1}{3} \qquad -3\tfrac{1}{2} = -3 + (-\tfrac{1}{2}).$$

EXERCISES 2.9

(A) Express each fraction in standard form.

1. $\frac{6}{15}$ 2. $-\frac{4}{8}$ 3. $\frac{-12}{16}$ 4. $\frac{4}{12}$

5. $-\frac{4}{20}$ 6. $\frac{-6}{18}$ 7. $-\frac{14}{21}$ 8. $\frac{10}{16}$

9. $-\frac{20}{25}$ 10. $\frac{12}{36}$ 11. $-\frac{16}{40}$ 12. $\frac{-20}{30}$

Ⓑ Find each product.

Example: $\dfrac{2}{3} \cdot \dfrac{-6}{7} = -\left(\dfrac{2}{\overset{}{\underset{1}{3}}} \cdot \dfrac{\overset{2}{6}}{7}\right)$

$$= -\dfrac{2 \cdot 2}{1 \cdot 7}$$

$$= -\dfrac{4}{7}$$

13. $\dfrac{2}{3} \cdot \dfrac{3}{5}$ **14.** $-\dfrac{1}{2} \cdot \dfrac{2}{7}$ **15.** $\dfrac{6}{7} \cdot \dfrac{7}{8}$ **16.** $\dfrac{-3}{5} \cdot \dfrac{-10}{9}$

17. $-\dfrac{9}{16} \cdot \dfrac{8}{21}$ **18.** $\dfrac{7}{18} \cdot \dfrac{9}{28}$ **19.** $-\dfrac{3}{14} \cdot \dfrac{7}{15}$ **20.** $\dfrac{11}{20} \cdot \dfrac{5}{22}$

21. $\dfrac{2}{13} \cdot \dfrac{-13}{40}$ **22.** $-\dfrac{6}{25} \cdot \dfrac{8}{15}$ **23.** $\dfrac{9}{16} \cdot \dfrac{24}{25}$ **24.** $-\dfrac{8}{3} \cdot \dfrac{-33}{40}$

25. $\dfrac{9}{40} \cdot \dfrac{20}{3}$ **26.** $-\dfrac{6}{11} \cdot \dfrac{44}{3}$ **27.** $-\dfrac{18}{23} \cdot \dfrac{23}{27}$ **28.** $\dfrac{9}{10} \cdot \left(-\dfrac{9}{10}\right)$

Find each quotient.

Example: $-\dfrac{9}{16} \div \left(-\dfrac{3}{4}\right) = \dfrac{9}{16} \div \dfrac{3}{4}$

$$= \dfrac{\overset{3}{9}}{\underset{4}{16}} \cdot \dfrac{\overset{1}{4}}{\underset{1}{3}}$$

$$= \dfrac{3 \cdot 1}{4 \cdot 1}$$

$$= \dfrac{3}{4}$$

29. $-\dfrac{7}{16} \div \dfrac{1}{2}$ **30.** $-\dfrac{6}{7} \div \dfrac{3}{4}$ **31.** $-\dfrac{7}{30} \div \dfrac{7}{10}$ **32.** $\dfrac{11}{24} \div \dfrac{11}{12}$

33. $\dfrac{13}{40} \div \dfrac{26}{5}$ **34.** $\dfrac{5}{18} \div \dfrac{-5}{3}$ **35.** $\dfrac{-11}{30} \div \dfrac{33}{10}$ **36.** $-\dfrac{8}{13} \div \dfrac{4}{39}$

37. $-\dfrac{4}{35} \div \dfrac{-12}{7}$ **38.** $\dfrac{7}{34} \div \dfrac{21}{-8}$ **39.** $\dfrac{2}{25} \div \dfrac{-6}{35}$ **40.** $-\dfrac{9}{40} \div \left(-\dfrac{25}{1}\right)$

41. $\dfrac{20}{21} \div \left(-\dfrac{5}{7}\right)$ **42.** $\dfrac{9}{25} \div \dfrac{3}{5}$ **43.** $-\dfrac{10}{11} \div \dfrac{-2}{3}$ **44.** $\dfrac{18}{5} \div \dfrac{3}{10}$

Find each sum.

Example: $-\dfrac{7}{11} + \dfrac{3}{11} = \dfrac{-7 + 3}{11}$

$$= \dfrac{-4}{11} = -\dfrac{4}{11}$$

45. $\dfrac{1}{5} + \left(-\dfrac{3}{5}\right)$ **46.** $\dfrac{2}{7} + \left(-\dfrac{1}{7}\right)$ **47.** $-\dfrac{1}{8} + \dfrac{5}{8}$ **48.** $-\dfrac{9}{16} + \dfrac{3}{16}$

49. $-\dfrac{11}{12} + \dfrac{1}{12}$ **50.** $\dfrac{3}{10} + \dfrac{3}{10}$ **51.** $-\dfrac{5}{18} + \dfrac{5}{18}$ **52.** $\dfrac{3}{20} + \dfrac{11}{20}$

53. $-\frac{4}{3} + \left(-\frac{8}{3}\right)$ **54.** $\frac{7}{25} + \frac{9}{25}$ **55.** $-\frac{5}{21} + \frac{1}{21}$ **56.** $\frac{3}{17} + \left(-\frac{2}{17}\right)$

57. $-\frac{6}{5} + \left(-\frac{13}{5}\right)$ **58.** $-\frac{11}{30} + \frac{1}{30}$ **59.** $\frac{3}{14} + \frac{9}{14}$ **60.** $\frac{13}{50} + \frac{19}{50}$

Find each sum. **Example:** $-\frac{3}{8} + \left(-\frac{1}{3}\right) = -\frac{9}{24} + \left(-\frac{8}{24}\right)$

$$= \frac{-9 + (-8)}{24}$$

$$= \frac{-17}{24} = -\frac{17}{24}$$

61. $\frac{1}{4} + \left(-\frac{1}{8}\right)$ **62.** $-\frac{5}{6} + \left(-\frac{1}{3}\right)$ **63.** $\frac{9}{10} + \frac{2}{5}$ **64.** $\frac{1}{6} + \frac{5}{12}$

65. $-\frac{3}{5} + \frac{2}{3}$ **66.** $\frac{3}{2} + \frac{1}{7}$ **67.** $\frac{5}{9} + \left(-\frac{1}{2}\right)$ **68.** $\frac{4}{15} + \left(-\frac{3}{5}\right)$

69. $\frac{9}{20} + \left(-\frac{1}{4}\right)$ **70.** $-\frac{3}{8} + \frac{1}{5}$ **71.** $\frac{2}{9} + \frac{1}{6}$ **72.** $-\frac{2}{3} + \left(-\frac{1}{7}\right)$

73. $\frac{6}{13} + \frac{1}{2}$ **74.** $-\frac{1}{6} + \left(-\frac{1}{4}\right)$ **75.** $\frac{5}{18} + \left(-\frac{1}{2}\right)$ **76.** $\frac{3}{16} + \left(-\frac{5}{4}\right)$

Find each difference. **Example:** $\frac{6}{15} - \left(-\frac{1}{3}\right) = \frac{6}{15} + \frac{1}{3}$

$$= \frac{6}{15} + \frac{5}{15}$$

$$= \frac{6 + 5}{15}$$

$$= \frac{11}{15}$$

77. $\frac{3}{16} - \left(-\frac{1}{16}\right)$ **78.** $\frac{9}{10} - \left(-\frac{1}{10}\right)$ **79.** $\frac{5}{8} - \frac{4}{8}$ **80.** $-\frac{5}{6} - \frac{1}{6}$

81. $\frac{9}{20} - \frac{1}{10}$ **82.** $\frac{5}{6} - \left(-\frac{1}{3}\right)$ **83.** $-\frac{11}{12} - \frac{1}{6}$ **84.** $-\frac{1}{3} - \left(-\frac{1}{9}\right)$

85. $\frac{3}{2} - \frac{1}{3}$ **86.** $-\frac{3}{4} - \frac{1}{5}$ **87.** $\frac{4}{3} - \left(-\frac{1}{4}\right)$ **88.** $-\frac{5}{6} - \frac{1}{4}$

89. $\frac{7}{9} - \left(-\frac{3}{2}\right)$ **90.** $-\frac{4}{15} - \frac{2}{3}$ **91.** $\frac{6}{5} - \frac{1}{4}$ **92.** $-\frac{2}{9} - \left(-\frac{1}{3}\right)$

© Evaluate each expression.

93. $1\frac{1}{2} \cdot \left(-2\frac{3}{4}\right)$ **94.** $-2\frac{1}{3} \cdot \left(-3\frac{1}{2}\right)$ **95.** $-4\frac{1}{2} \div 1\frac{1}{2}$ **96.** $6\frac{1}{3} \div 1\frac{1}{6}$

97. $2\frac{1}{2} + 2\frac{1}{2}$ **98.** $-6\frac{1}{3} + 5\frac{2}{3}$ **99.** $-1\frac{3}{4} + 1\frac{1}{2}$ **100.** $2\frac{2}{3} + \left(-3\frac{1}{6}\right)$

101. $5\frac{1}{4} - 2\frac{3}{4}$ **102.** $6\frac{1}{9} - \left(-5\frac{4}{9}\right)$ **103.** $-3\frac{1}{5} - 4\frac{1}{3}$ **104.** $6\frac{1}{8} - 5\frac{1}{3}$

105. $4\frac{1}{5} \cdot 5\frac{5}{9}$ **106.** $-2\frac{1}{7} \div 1\frac{3}{7}$ **107.** $-7\frac{1}{5} + 6\frac{2}{3}$ **108.** $-8\frac{1}{4} - 3\frac{5}{6}$

2.10 THE DISTRIBUTIVE PROPERTY

$2 \cdot (100 + 50)$ $2 \cdot 100$ $2 \cdot 50$

For a promotional stunt, a bicycle shop hired teen-agers and their younger brothers and sisters to ride two bicycles-built-for-two, two unicycles, and two tricycles. Each teen-ager was given 100 circulars to deliver, and each younger student was given 50 circulars to deliver. As you can see, the students on the bicycles-built-for-two would deliver the same number of circulars as those on the unicycles and tricycles since $2 \cdot (100 + 50) = 2 \cdot 100 + 2 \cdot 50$.

This example illustrates an important property of addition and multiplication of real numbers. It is called the *distributive property of multiplication over addition* or just the *distributive property*.

distributive property

Let *a*, *b*, and *c* be any real numbers.

$a \cdot (b + c) = a \cdot b + a \cdot c$, and

$(b + c) \cdot a = b \cdot a + c \cdot a$.

Which property of multiplication tells you that $(b + c) \cdot a = b \cdot a + c \cdot a$ if you know that $a \cdot (b + c) = a \cdot b + a \cdot c$?

As you know, the equals sign means that two expressions name the same number. Thus, when we write $x = y$, we mean that x can be substituted for y (and y for x) in an expression which involves x or y. It follows that if $x = y$, then $y = x$.

Therefore, the distributive property can be written in different ways.

If $a \cdot (b + c) = a \cdot b + a \cdot c$, then $a \cdot b + a \cdot c = a \cdot (b + c)$.

If $(b + c) \cdot a = b \cdot a + c \cdot a$, then $b \cdot a + c \cdot a = (b + c) \cdot a$.

The following examples illustrate how the distributive property can be used.

Examples:

1. $-27(\frac{1}{3} + \frac{1}{9})$

   $= -27 \cdot \frac{1}{3} + (-27) \cdot \frac{1}{9}$

   $= -9 + (-3)$

   $= -12$

2. $\frac{16}{5} + \frac{9}{5} = 16 \cdot \frac{1}{5} + 9 \cdot \frac{1}{5}$

   $= (16 + 9) \cdot \frac{1}{5}$

   $= 25 \cdot \frac{1}{5}$

   $= 5$

3. $87 \cdot 4 + 87 \cdot (-6)$

   $= 87 \cdot [4 + (-6)]$

   $= 87 \cdot (-2)$

   $= -174$

4. $4\frac{5}{7} \cdot (-7) = (4 + \frac{5}{7}) \cdot (-7)$

   $= 4 \cdot (-7) + \frac{5}{7} \cdot (-7)$

   $= -28 + (-5)$

   $= -33$

EXERCISES 2.10

Ⓐ Use the distributive property to complete each sentence.

1. $-3 \cdot (-6 + 8) =$ _____ + _____

2. $5 \cdot (-7 + 6) =$ _____ + _____

3. $4 \cdot 11 + (-2) \cdot 11 = [$_____ + _____$] \cdot$ _____

4. $(-5)8 + (-5)4 =$ _____ $\cdot ($_____ + _____$)$

5. $0 \cdot [13 + (-9)] =$ _____ + _____

6. $(\frac{1}{3} + \frac{1}{4}) \cdot 12 = $ _____ + _____

7. $\frac{6}{11} + \frac{8}{11} = ($ _____ + _____ $) \cdot \frac{1}{11}$

8. $\frac{7}{2} + \frac{9}{2} = \frac{1}{2} \cdot ($ _____ + _____ $)$

Ⓑ Evaluate each expression by using the distributive property.

9. $-3[4 + (-2)]$ **10.** $-3[5 + (-3)]$

11. $-4(7) + (-4)3$ **12.** $-5(8) + (-5) \cdot 2$

13. $-8[-5 + (-6)]$ **14.** $-9[-4 + (-7)]$

15. $7[-10 + (-9)]$ **16.** $11[(-9) + (-8)]$

17. $-12 \cdot 5 + (-18) \cdot 5$ **18.** $13(-4) + 17(-4)$

19. $-10(1 + \frac{1}{2})$ **20.** $12[-1 + (-\frac{1}{4})]$

21. $24 \cdot (\frac{1}{3} + \frac{1}{4})$ **22.** $-36(\frac{1}{6} + \frac{1}{4})$

23. $-\frac{12}{7} + (-\frac{2}{7})$ **24.** $-\frac{19}{5} + \frac{4}{5}$

25. $\frac{1}{3}[9 + (-24)]$ **26.** $\frac{1}{5}(-20 + 15)$

27. $47 \cdot 8 + (-7) \cdot 8$ **28.** $-11 \cdot 12 + 71 \cdot 12$

Use the distributive property to complete each sentence.

29. $4x + 5x = (4 + 5)$ _____   **30.** $9y + 3y = (9 + 3)$ _____

31. $r(s + t) = rs + $ _____   **32.** $(x + y)z = xz + $ _____

33. $(3 + 4)x = 3x + $ _____   **34.** $(6 + 2)z = 6z + $ _____

35. $mt + nt = ($ _____ + _____ $)t$ **36.** $($ _____ + _____ $)g = ag + bg$

37. _____ $+ 6z = (1 + 6)z$ **38.** $3m + $ _____ $= (3 + 1)m$

39. $[5 + (-3)]x = 5x + $ _____   **40.** $[7 + (-2)]y = 7y + $ _____

Ⓒ **41.** $(5 - 3)x^2 = 5x^2 - $ _____   **42.** $(7 - 2)y^2 = 7y^2 - $ _____

43. $x + 5x = ($ _____ $+ 5)x$ **44.** $6y + y = (6 + $ _____ $)y$

45. $4mn + 4ms = 4m($ _____ $+ s)$ **46.** $3a(x + y) = 3ax + $ _____

47. $6rs + 6rt = $ _____ $(s + t)$

48. $-2wz + (-2wy) = -2w(z + $ _____ $)$

Try These Puzzles

1. If it takes 3 minutes to boil an egg, how many minutes does it take to boil 3 eggs?

2. If it takes 1 minute to make each cut, how long will it take to cut a 10-foot pole into 10 pieces of equal length?

3. If 3 cats can catch 3 mice in 3 minutes, how long will it take 100 cats to catch 100 mice?

4. There is a long-established custom among the justices of the United States Supreme Court. Before each session of the Court, each justice shakes the hand of every other justice. This custom has led to a problem with which the justices like to puzzle their friends. Since there are nine justices, how many handshakes take place when the custom of shaking hands is followed? (Neither 81 nor 72 is the correct answer.)

5. The census taker, counting the residents of a small village, was questioning the owner of a small shack. He pointed to another gentleman who lay fast asleep on the porch. "Who is he?" he asked. The man replied, "Brothers and sisters have I none, but that man's father is my father's son." Who was the sleeping man?

CHAPTER REVIEW

2.1 What addition sentence is illustrated by each drawing?

1.
2.

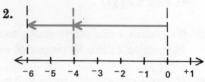

3.
4.

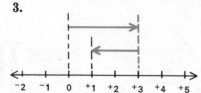

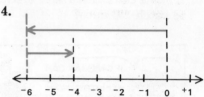

2.2 What property of addition is illustrated by each sentence?

5. $-3 + 4 = 4 + (-3)$ **6.** $-7 + 0 = -7$

7. $[6 + (-3)] + 5 = 6 + (-3 + 5)$ **8.** $6 + (-6) = 0$

9. $[7 + (-3)]$ is a real number.

2.3 Find each sum.

10. $3 + (-4)$ **11.** $4 + (-3)$ **12.** $-4 + (-3)$ **13.** $4 + 3$

14. $7 + (-6)$ **15.** $-7 + (-6)$ **16.** $-11 + 2$ **17.** $-6 + (-5)$

18. $14 + (-4)$ **19.** $-2 + (-8)$ **20.** $9 + 3$ **21.** $-9 + 3$

2.4 Find each difference.

22. $7 - (-5)$ **23.** $-7 - 5$ **24.** $-7 - (-5)$ **25.** $7 - 5$

26. $-9 - 6$ **27.** $-12 - (-6)$ **28.** $3 - 11$ **29.** $-6 - 16$

30. $30 - (-15)$ **31.** $-49 - 12$ **32.** $-38 - (-6)$ **33.** $50 - 28$

2.5 Find each product.

34. $6 \cdot (-2)$ **35.** $-6 \cdot (-2)$ **36.** $6 \cdot 2$ **37.** $-6 \cdot 2$

38. $9 \cdot (-1)$ **39.** $-12 \cdot (-4)$ **40.** $7 \cdot (-6)$ **41.** $-9 \cdot (-7)$

42. $25 \cdot (-4)$ **43.** $-50 \cdot 5$ **44.** $-9 \cdot 10$ **45.** $12 \cdot 15$

Find each quotient.

46. $-8 \div 1$ **47.** $-8 \div (-1)$ **48.** $8 \div (-1)$

49. $24 \div 3$ **50.** $-72 \div 9$ **51.** $-40 \div (-8)$

52. $21 \div 7$ **53.** $63 \div (-9)$ **54.** $-42 \div (-6)$

55. $-7.2 \div (-0.8)$ **56.** $0.48 \div 0.6$ **57.** $-3.2 \div 0.4$

Express each fraction in standard form.   2.7

58. $\frac{-2}{5}$ **59.** $\frac{3}{-7}$ **60.** $\frac{-2}{-3}$ **61.** $\frac{-2}{3}$

Find each product or quotient.

62. $\frac{4}{7} \cdot \frac{3}{5}$ **63.** $-\frac{5}{9} \cdot \frac{2}{7}$ **64.** $\frac{1}{6} \div (-\frac{5}{7})$ **65.** $-\frac{4}{3} \div \frac{5}{11}$

66. $-\frac{4}{15} \cdot (-\frac{1}{3})$ **67.** $-\frac{3}{14} \div \frac{5}{9}$ **68.** $\frac{9}{25} \div \frac{4}{3}$ **69.** $\frac{9}{16} \cdot (-\frac{5}{4})$

Which property of multiplication is illustrated by each sentence?   2.8

70. $-5 \cdot (-\frac{1}{5}) = 1$ **71.** $\frac{2}{5} \cdot 1 = \frac{2}{5}$

72. $16 \cdot (-5) = -5 \cdot 16$ **73.** $[-8 \cdot (-2)] \cdot 5 = -8 \cdot [(-2) \cdot 5]$

74. $[-3 \cdot (-7)]$ is a real number.

Evaluate each expression.   2.9

75. $-\frac{6}{10}$ **76.** $\frac{70}{120}$ **77.** $-\frac{3}{7} \cdot \frac{7}{9}$ **78.** $-\frac{3}{5} \div (-\frac{6}{5})$

79. $\frac{3}{10} + (-\frac{7}{10})$ **80.** $-\frac{5}{9} + \frac{-4}{3}$ **81.** $-\frac{3}{11} + \frac{-4}{11}$ **82.** $-\frac{9}{16} - (-\frac{1}{8})$

Use the distributive property to evaluate each expression.   2.10

83. $-3[8 + (-4)]$ **84.** $5 \cdot (-6) + 7 \cdot (-6)$

85. $20(\frac{1}{2} + \frac{1}{4})$ **86.** $\frac{1}{3} \cdot 11 + \frac{1}{3} \cdot 7$

CHAPTER SELF-TEST ◆

For each numbered equation or sentence, match the letter of the property that is illustrated. Assume that the replacement set for each variable is the set of real numbers.

1. $-5 + 9 = 9 + (-5)$
2. $3(-2 + 7) = 3 \cdot (-2) + 3 \cdot 7$
3. $\frac{3}{4} \cdot 0 = 0$
4. $-14 \cdot (-\frac{1}{14}) = 1$
5. $(1 + 2) + (-5) = 1 + [2 + (-5)]$
6. $18 - 7 = 18 + (-7)$
7. $-w = -1 \cdot w$
8. $k(mn) = (km)n$
9. $20 + 0 = 20$
10. $-\frac{3}{4} + \frac{7}{8}$ is a real number.
11. $-\frac{1}{4} \cdot 1 = -\frac{1}{4}$
12. $\frac{2}{3} \cdot (-\frac{1}{2})$ is a real number.
13. $6 \cdot (-7) = -7 \cdot 6$
14. $\frac{2}{3} + (-\frac{2}{3}) = 0$

a. Multiplication prop. of -1
b. Associative prop. of $+$
c. Multiplication prop. of 0
d. Inverse prop. of $+$
e. Commutative prop. of $+$
f. Subtraction prop.
g. Inverse prop. of $\cdot$
h. Commutative prop. of $\cdot$
i. Closure prop. of $+$
j. Associative prop. of $\cdot$
k. Identity prop. of $+$
l. Distributive prop.
m. Closure prop. of $\cdot$
n. Identity prop. of $\cdot$

Evaluate each expression.

15. $-16 + 28$
16. $-24 + 34$
17. $49 - 14$
18. $37 \cdot (-3)$
19. $-72 \div (-9)$
20. $-12 \cdot (-8)$
21. $35 + 77$
22. $84 + (-37)$
23. $-96 \div 16$
24. $344 + (-125)$
25. $112 \div (-28)$
26. $-68 + (-82)$
27. $-4(-11 + 9)$
28. $-(-15) + (-5)$
29. $17 - (-6 + 21)$
30. $3 \cdot (-4) \cdot (-2) \cdot (-5)$
31. $-(-18 + 29)$
32. $-7 \cdot 5 + (-7)6$
33. $\frac{2}{3} \cdot (-\frac{1}{3})$
34. $-\frac{3}{5} \div (-\frac{1}{4})$
35. $-\frac{7}{8} \cdot \frac{16}{21}$
36. $\frac{9}{35} \cdot (-\frac{3}{7})$
37. $-\frac{15}{8} \div (-\frac{5}{4})$
38. $-\frac{3}{5} + \frac{7}{5}$
39. $\frac{1}{4} + (-\frac{1}{3})$
40. $\frac{9}{10} + (+\frac{3}{10})$
41. $-\frac{11}{18} + \frac{1}{6}$

Chapter 3

Working with Expressions and Equations

The foundation of a building not only supports the rest of the building, but also determines what type of structure it can have.

In Chapters 1 and 2, we have put into place a very large and important part of the foundation of algebra. Now we will begin to find out what kind of structure we can build on that foundation.

71

3.1 EXPONENTS

An *exponent* is used to indicate multiplication.

Expression	Meaning	Exponent	Base
4^2	$4 \cdot 4$	2	4
$(-5)^3$	$(-5)(-5)(-5)$	3	-5
x^5	$x \cdot x \cdot x \cdot x \cdot x$	5	x
$3x^2$	$3 \cdot x \cdot x$	2	x
$(3x)^2$	$3x \cdot 3x$	2	$3x$
$x + 4^2$	$x + 4 \cdot 4$	2	4
$(x + 4)^2$	$(x + 4)(x + 4)$	2	$x + 4$

Notice the difference in meaning between $3x^2$ and $(3x)^2$ and between $x + 4^2$ and $(x + 4)^2$.

In general, the expression x^n, where x is any real number and n is any positive integer, means n factors of x. Since $x^1 = x$, we do not usually write 1 as an exponent.

$$\text{exponent} \searrow \qquad \overbrace{}^{n \text{ factors}}$$
$$\text{base} \longrightarrow x^n = x \cdot x \cdot x \cdots x$$

We call x^n "the nth **power** of x" or "x to the nth **power**."

4^2 **may be read** four squared

5^3 **may be read** five cubed

6^4 **may be read** six to the fourth (or fourth power)

The meaning of the exponents can often be used to simplify or evaluate an expression.

Example 1: Find the value. **a.** 4^3 **b.** $(-4)^3$ **c.** -4^3

SOLUTIONS:

a. $4^3 = 4 \cdot 4 \cdot 4$
$\quad = 16 \cdot 4$
$\quad = 64$

b. $(-4)^3 = (-4) \cdot (-4) \cdot (-4)$
$\quad = 16 \cdot (-4)$
$\quad = -64$

c. $-4^3 = -1 \cdot 4^3$
$\quad = -1 \cdot 64$
$\quad = -64$

Example 2: Express $25 \cdot x \cdot x$ as a power of $5x$.

$$\begin{aligned} \text{SOLUTION:} \qquad 25 \cdot x \cdot x &= 5 \cdot 5 \cdot x \cdot x \\ &= 5 \cdot x \cdot 5 \cdot x \\ &= (5x) \cdot (5x) \\ &= (5x)^2 \end{aligned}$$

Example 3: Express $s^3 \cdot s^2$ as a power of s.

$$\begin{aligned} \text{SOLUTION:} \qquad s^3 \cdot s^2 &= (s \cdot s \cdot s)(s \cdot s) \\ &= s \cdot s \cdot s \cdot s \cdot s \\ &= s^5 \end{aligned}$$

Example 4: Evaluate $2x^2 + y^3$ for $x = 3$ and $y = 2$.

$$\begin{aligned} \text{SOLUTION:} \qquad 2x^2 + y^3 &= (2 \cdot 3^2) + 2^3 \\ &= (2 \cdot 3 \cdot 3) + (2 \cdot 2 \cdot 2) \\ &= (2 \cdot 9) + 8 \\ &= 26 \end{aligned}$$

EXERCISES 3.1

Ⓐ What information should fill each blank?

	a. Expression	b. Meaning	c. Exponent	d. Base	e. Value
1.	5^3	$5 \cdot 5 \cdot 5$	___	___	125
2.	2^5	$2 \cdot 2 \cdot 2 \cdot 2 \cdot 2$	___	___	___
3.	n^4	___	___	___	
4.	$(-6)^2$	___	___	___	
5.	___	___	8	-1	___
6.	$(-2)^5$	___	___	___	___
7.	$\left(\frac{1}{3}\right)^3$	___	___	___	___
8.	___	___	7	t	
9.	___	___	___	-3	-27
10.	___	___	4	___	0.0016

Ⓑ Find the value.

11. $(-2)^7$ **12.** $(-3)^5$ **13.** 7^3 **14.** 8^3

15. 3^6 **16.** 4^5 **17.** -5^4 **18.** -4^4

19. $(-5)^4$ **20.** $(-4)^4$ **21.** $(0.2)^5$ **22.** $(0.3)^6$

23. $(\frac{1}{4})^3$ **24.** $(\frac{1}{2})^4$ **25.** $(-\frac{1}{5})^4$ **26.** $(-\frac{1}{6})^3$

27. $(-0.4)^3$ **28.** $(-0.3)^3$ **29.** $(0.02)^5$ **30.** $(0.03)^4$

31. $(2 \cdot 3)^2$ **32.** $(4 \cdot 2)^2$ **33.** $2^2 \cdot 5^3$ **34.** $3^2 \cdot 4^3$

Evaluate each expression for $m = 2$ and $n = 5$.

35. $m^3 - n$ **36.** $n^2 - m$ **37.** $(m + n)^2$ **38.** $(n + 2m)^2$

39. $2m + n^2$ **40.** $m^2 + 3n$ **41.** m^n **42.** n^m

Express as a power of the given base.

43. $a \cdot a \cdot a \cdot a$; base a **44.** $b \cdot b \cdot b \cdot b \cdot b$; base b

45. 625; base 25 **46.** 729; base 9

47. 625; base 5 **48.** 729; base 3

49. $xy \cdot xy \cdot xy$; base xy **50.** $yz \cdot yz \cdot yz \cdot yz$; base yz

51. $8 \cdot x \cdot x \cdot x$; base $2x$ **52.** $9 \cdot y \cdot y$; base $3y$

53. $t^5 \cdot t \cdot t \cdot t$; base t **54.** $n^4 \cdot n \cdot n$; base n

55. $m^3 \cdot m^4$; base m **56.** $p^5 \cdot p^2$; base p

Ⓒ **57.** $(-x)(-x)(-x)$; base x **58.** $(-2) \cdot (-2) \cdot (-2)$; base 2

59. $(-3)(-3)(-3)$; base -3 **60.** $(-x) \cdot (-x) \cdot (-x)$; base $-x$

61. $(-7) \cdot 7 \cdot 7 \cdot y \cdot y \cdot y$; base $-7y$ **62.** $(-5) \cdot 5 \cdot 5 \cdot x \cdot x \cdot x$; base $-5x$

Try This

Simplify $2^5 \cdot 9^2$ and observe the unusual result.

Equivalent Expressions

Expressions that have the same value	Expressions that have the same value for the same replacements of the variables	
$2 \cdot 4$	$-4(3x)$	$(8x^2y)(-2xy)$
$4 \cdot 2$	$-2^2(3x)$	$-16(x^2y)(xy)$
2^3	$3(-4x)$	$-2^4x^3y^2$
8	$-12x$	$-16x^3y^2$

The last expression is considered the simplest in each case.

Since each expression names a product, we can derive the simplest expression in a column from any of the others by using properties of multiplication. We say we are "finding the product" or "simplifying the expression."

Example 1: Find: **a.** $-4(3x)$ **b.** $(\frac{1}{3}t)(-12)$

SHORT SOLUTIONS:

a. $-4(3x) = -12x$ **b.** $(\frac{1}{3}t)(-12) = -4t$

Markings like the arrows above are included in *short solutions* only to show you how the answer is found.

DETAILED SOLUTIONS:

a. $-4(3x) = (-4 \cdot 3)x$ Assoc. prop. of $\cdot$

           $= -12x$ Multiplication

b. $(\frac{1}{3}t)(-12) = (-12)(\frac{1}{3}t)$ Comm. prop. of $\cdot$

            $= (-12 \cdot \frac{1}{3})t$ Assoc. prop. of $\cdot$

            $= -4t$ Multiplication

As shown above, reasons can be given for the steps of *detailed solutions.*

Consider the product $r^2 \cdot r^3$.

$$r^2 \cdot r^3 = (r \cdot r)(r \cdot r \cdot r) \longleftarrow \begin{array}{l} \text{2 factors} \\ \text{3 factors} \end{array}$$
$$= r \cdot r \cdot r \cdot r \cdot r \longleftarrow \text{2 + 3 factors}$$
$$= r^{2+3} \text{ or } r^5$$

This suggests a shortcut for multiplying expressions containing exponents.

multiplication of powers

Let x be any real number and let m and n be any positive integers. Then

$$x^m \cdot x^n = x^{m+n}$$

Example 2: Simplify $(8x^2y)(-2x^3y^3)$.

SHORT SOLUTION: $(8x^2y^1)(-2x^3y^3) = -16x^5y^4$

DETAILED SOLUTION:

$(8x^2y)(-2x^3y^3) = 8(-2)x^2 \cdot x^3 \cdot y \cdot y^3$	Comm., assoc. props. of $\cdot$
$= 8(-2)x^{2+3}y^{1+3}$	Mult. of powers
$= 8(-2)x^5y^4$	Addition
$= -16x^5y^4$	Multiplication

EXERCISES 3.2

Ⓐ Which expressions below are equivalent to $-24m^5n^6$?

1. $-24n^6m^5$ **2.** $(12m^3n)(-2m^2n^5)$ **3.** $(-4mn)(-6m^4n^5)$

4. $(-n)^6 \cdot 24m^5$ **5.** $-n^6 \cdot 24m^5$ **6.** $(-\frac{1}{2}m^3n)(48m^2n^5)$

Simplify each product.

7. $9(7x)$ **8.** $(18st)(-2)$ **9.** $(-32)(-\frac{1}{4}t)$

10. $(3a)(-4b)$ **11.** $(8r^2)(9r)$ **12.** $2m^2(3m^3)$

Ⓑ 13. $(-7)(3n)$ 14. $(-8)(4r)$ 15. $(12ab)(\frac{1}{3})$

16. $(18de)(\frac{1}{3})$ 17. $(-5c)(-3d)$ 18. $(-9m)(-2n)$

19. $(12m)(3m)$ 20. $(13n)(2n)$ 21. $(7t^3)(3t)$

22. $(8w^4)(3w)$ 23. $(7a^2)(4a^4)$ 24. $(9d^3)(3d^5)$

25. $(7s^4t)(11s^2t^4)$ 26. $(11a^3b)(3a^2b^3)$ 27. $(14m^4)(-2m^3)$

28. $(13s^3)(-2s^5)$ 29. $(-4n^5)(-3s^3)$ 30. $(-9m^2)(-2t^4)$

31. $(5rs)(-3s^2r)$ 32. $(3ad)(-7d^2a)$ 33. $(15def)(2d^2e^2)$

34. $(12mnr)(3n^2r^2)$ 35. $(-3cd)(d^4)$ 36. $(-2st)(t^3)$

Ⓒ Determine the missing factors.

37. $9 \cdot \underline{\hspace{1cm}} = 18n^2$ 38. $3y \cdot \underline{\hspace{1cm}} = 15y^3$

39. $2rs \cdot \underline{\hspace{1cm}} = 14r^3s^4$ 40. $\underline{\hspace{1cm}} \cdot 20tv^2 = 10t^3v^2$

41. $\frac{1}{4}mn \cdot \underline{\hspace{1cm}} = 4m^2n^2$ 42. $(-2)^2 \cdot \underline{\hspace{1cm}} = 4r^3t^2$

Expressions in BASIC

To use a computer, you must "talk" to it in a language it understands. The following expressions are written in a computer language called BASIC.

Expression	A ↑ 2	3 * X	M/2 + (−5)	2 * Y ↑ 3 − (2 * X) ↑ 2
Meaning	a^2	$3x$	$m \div 2 + (-5)$	$2y^3 - (2x)^2$

In BASIC, all letters are capitals. The symbols for operations are similar to those we usually use. Note, however, the different symbols for multiplying, dividing, and for powers. The order of operations in BASIC is the same as we usually use.

Write each of the following expressions in BASIC.

1. $5m^4$ 2. $7r$ 3. $16 \div 2$

4. $(9s)^5$ 5. $(a + b)^2$ 6. $-x + (-3)^2$

7. $\frac{x^2}{y^3}$ 8. $(x + 2)^3 \div (7y)^2$ 9. $2n^3 - 5n^2 + 4x - 3$

3.3 SIMPLIFYING EXPRESSIONS

Addends in an expression are called **terms**.

unlike terms	unlike terms	like terms
↓ ↓	↓ ↓	↓ ↓
$5x + 5y$	$3x^2 + 2x$	$-3xy^2 + 4xy^2$
different variables	same variables, different powers	same variables, same powers

The distributive property can be used to combine like terms to simplify an expression.

Example 1: Simplify.   **a.** $3n - 7n$ **b.** $8x^2y + (4xy + 5x^2y)$

SOLUTIONS:

a. $\begin{aligned} 3n - 7n &= 3n + (-7n) \\ &= [3 + (-7)]n \\ &= -4n \end{aligned}$

b. $\begin{aligned} 8x^2y + (4xy + 5x^2y) &\\ = 8x^2y + (5x^2y + 4xy) &\\ = (8x^2y + 5x^2y) + 4xy &\\ = (8 + 5)x^2y + 4xy &\\ = 13x^2y + 4xy & \end{aligned}$

If an expression has more than two like terms, the following extension of the distributive property is useful to save steps.

extended
distributive
property

If $a, b, c, d, \cdots$ are real numbers, then
$$ab + ac + ad = a(b + c + d),$$
$$ab + ac + ad + ae = a(b + c + d + e),$$
and so on.

Example 2: Simplify $8x^2 + 3x + x + 4x$.

SOLUTION: $\begin{aligned} 8x^2 + 3x + x + 4x &= 8x^2 + (3x + 1x + 4x) \\ &= 8x^2 + (3 + 1 + 4)x \\ &= 8x^2 + 8x \end{aligned}$

EXERCISES 3.3

(A) Complete each sentence.

1. The expression $8x^2 + 3x + 5$ has (some, no) like terms.

2. (Some, No) terms of $8x^2 + 3x + 5$ can be combined.

3. The expression $8x^2 + 3x + 5x^2$ has (some, no) like terms.

4. The simpler expression _____ is equivalent to $8x^2 + 3x + 5x^2$.

5. The expression $2x^2y + 3x^2y^2 + xy^2$ (can, cannot) be simplified.

Simplify (if possible).

6. $-13x + 20x$
7. $19y + 30y$
8. $-24y^2 + 19y^2$
9. $4s^2 + (-5s^2)$
10. $37st + st$
11. $12a^2b + 5a^2b^2$
12. $-28t^3 - 18t^3$
13. $14ab - ab$
14. $-14e - 8e^2$
15. $15j + (-10j)$
16. $7a - 2a + 3a$

(B) 17. $7x + (-3x + 8)$
18. $10x + (5 - 7x)$
19. $20s - 12s + t$
20. $30a - 8a + b$
21. $35rs + 18rs^2$
22. $17pq^2 + 5pq$
23. $-12xy^2 + 3xy^2$
24. $-15a^2b + 2a^2b$
25. $(5x)(2y) + (5x)y$
26. $(3s)(2t) + s(5t)$

From the tubs, choose all expressions equivalent to the given expression.

27. $8x - x + (-3y)$
28. $-9w + 6t + 8w$
29. $x + (-2x) - 5x$
30. $4r^2 - (2r^2 - r)$

Ex. 27, 28

Ex. 29, 30

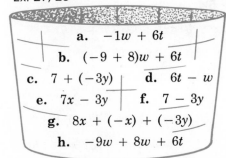

Ex. 27, 28
a. $-1w + 6t$
b. $(-9 + 8)w + 6t$
c. $7 + (-3y)$
d. $6t - w$
e. $7x - 3y$
f. $7 - 3y$
g. $8x + (-x) + (-3y)$
h. $-9w + 8w + 6t$

Ex. 29, 30
a. $4r^2 - 2r^2 - r$
b. $2r^2 + r$
c. $1x - 7x$
d. $(4 - 2)r^2 + r$
e. $-6x$
f. $4r^2 - 2r^2 + r$
g. $3r^3$
h. $1x + (-2x) + (-5x)$
i. $1 + (-2) + (-5)x$

First, apply the distributive property and then simplify the resulting expression by combining like terms.

Example: $3(x + 2) + 5(2x + 1) = 3x + 6 + 10x + 5$
$$= 13x + 11$$

31. $5(6x - 5) + 2(6x - 5)$ **32.** $7(9y - 7) + 3(9y - 7)$

33. $3t + 7(2t - 9)$ **34.** $5r + 3(7r - 2)$

35. $8(2x - 6y) - 8(2x - 6y)$ **36.** $9(2t - 9r) - 9(2t - 9r)$

37. $6x(5x + 4y) - x(2x - 3y)$ **38.** $7y(4x - 2y) - y(5x + y)$

39. $12(5x + 4y) - 7(5x + 4y)$ **40.** $14(2x + 3y) - 3(2x + 3y)$

Simplify.

41. $(21x - 8) - (9x + 5)$ **42.** $(28y - 9) - (2y + 1)$

43. $7x^2 + (-3x^2) - 5x^2$ **44.** $9y^2 - 2y^2 + (-4y^2)$

45. $2a - 3b - 15a$ **46.** $-4c + 3d - 17c$

47. $3(r + 2t) + 5t$ **48.** $7(n + 3s) + 2s$

49. $6x + 8x - (-9x)$ **50.** $7y - 12y - (-4y)$

51. $6(x - 3y) + 2(x + 7y)$ **52.** $9(a + 2b) + 3(a - 4b)$

53. $4xy - 12xy^2 + 7xy$ **54.** $9ab - 6ab^2 + 11ab$

© Use the distributive property to simplify each expression.

Example: $(3x + 5)(4x + 7) = (3x + 5)4x + (3x + 5)7$
$$= (3x \cdot 4x + 5 \cdot 4x) + (3x \cdot 7 + 5 \cdot 7)$$
$$= 12x^2 + 20x + 21x + 35$$
$$= 12x^2 + 41x + 35$$

55. $(6x + 2)(5x + 3)$ **56.** $(5x + 3)(7x + 6)$

57. $(3x - 5y)(-7x + 9y)$ **58.** $(14a + 7b)(6a - 5b)$

Find the value.

1. $(-3)^5$ **2.** $2^3 \cdot (-3)^2$ **3.** $(5 \cdot 3)^2$ **4.** $(0.4)^2$

Evaluate each expression for $x = 2$ and $y = 3$.

5. $x^3 + y$ **6.** y^x **7.** $(3x + y)^2$ **8.** $7y + (2x)^2$

Express as a power of the given base.

9. 225; base 15   **10.** $a \cdot a \cdot a \cdot b^2 \cdot b$; base ab

Find each product.

11. $8(-2r)$ **12.** $(-2a)(-3a)$ **13.** $(3pq) \cdot 5$

14. $(-18)(\frac{1}{3}s)$ **15.** $(7n^2)(-3mn)$ **16.** $5(2x)(3y^2)$

Simplify.

17. $9d - 2c + 4d$

18. $-3p^2q - (-7p^2q)$

19. $4x^2y + 2xy - 3x^2y$

20. $5a + (-2a) + 3a$

21. $12(\frac{1}{2}x + \frac{1}{3})$

22. $5(3m - 2n) + 2(m + n)$

23. $4p(2m) - (-3pm)$

24. $12(2m + 2n)$

25. $7(a - 2p) + 3(a - 2p)$

3.4 EQUATIONS: $x + b = c$

In Chapter 1, we solved open sentences by substituting the members of the replacement set, one at a time, and noting which of the resulting closed sentences were true. Unless the replacement set has only a few members, however, this can be difficult or even impossible.

We can use the following property to help solve certain types of equations.

addition property of equality

Let a, b, and c be any real numbers.

If $a = b$, then $a + c = b + c$.

We will now use this property to simplify $x - 3 = 5$.

$x - 3 = 5$	Given
$x + (-3) = 5$	Subtr. prop.
$[x + (-3)] + 3 = 5 + 3$	Add. prop. of $=$
$[x + (-3)] + 3 = 8$	Addition
$x + [(-3) + 3] = 8$	Assoc. prop. of $+$
$x + 0 = 8$	Inv. prop. of $+$
$x = 8$	Ident. prop. of $+$

So, if $x - 3 = 5$, then $x = 8$. The solution of $x = 8$ is obviously 8. But 8 is also the solution of *each* equation in the chain of equations above! (How can you check this?)

Open sentences that have the same solution set are said to be **equivalent**. Thus, to solve an equation, we can use the properties of equality and real numbers to write a chain of equivalent equations until we find one whose solution set is obvious.

You should always *check* your work. Substitute the solution of the last equation of the chain for the variable in the first (given) equation. If a true closed sentence is formed, the solution is correct.

Example: Solve $x + 7 = 2$ if the replacement is {integers}.

SHORT SOLUTION:

$$x + \quad 7 = \quad 2$$
$$\underline{+ (-7) \quad +(-7)}$$
$$x \qquad = \quad -5$$

The solution set of this equation is obviously $\{-5\}$.

DETAILED SOLUTION:

$$x + 7 = 2$$
$$(x + 7) + (-7) = 2 + (-7)$$
$$(x + 7) + (-7) = -5$$
$$x + [7 + (-7)] = -5$$
$$x + 0 = -5$$
$$x = -5$$

Check: $-5 + 7 = 2$ ◀ Is this true?
$2 = 2$ ◀ Yes (it simplifies to this true sentence).

The answer may be written $\{-5\}$, $x = -5$, or just -5. Can you give a reason for each step of the detailed solution?

EXERCISES 3.4

Ⓐ Which number would you add to both sides to solve each equation?

1. $x + 4 = 5$

2. $x + 12 = 10$

3. $x + 15 = 15$

4. $x - 12 = 4$

5. $18 + x = 20$

6. $x - 8 = 15$

7. $8 = x - 7$

8. $13 + x = 10$

9. $24 = 8 + x$

10. $x + 1 = 6$

11. $x + 23 = 23$

12. $11 = x - 8$

13. $x + (-7) = 4$

14. $x + (-9) = 5$

15. $x + 9 - 13 = 12$

16–30. Solve each equation in Exercises **1–15** if the replacement set for x in each case is {integers}.

Ⓑ From the crates, choose all equations equivalent to the given equation.

31. $x - 5 = 7$

32. $x + 5 = -7$

33. $-6 = x + 4$

34. $4 = x - 6$

Ex. 31, 32

a. $x = 12$ **b.** $[x + (-5)] + 5 = 12$
c. $x = -12$ **d.** $x + 2 - 5 = 9$
e. $(x + 5) + (-5) = -2$ **f.** $x = 2$
g. $x = -2$ **h.** $x + (-5) = 7$

Ex. 33, 34

a. $x = -10$ **b.** $0 = x - 10$ **c.** $x = 10$
d. $4 + 6 = [x + (-6)] + 6$
e. $0 = x + 10$ **f.** $4 = x + (-6)$
g. $(-6) + (-4) = (x + 4) + (-4)$

Solve each equation. The replacement set is {rational numbers}.

35. $x + 34 = 14$

36. $x + 41 = 21$

37. $x - 17 = 9$

38. $x - 14 = 15$

39. $9 + x = 21$

40. $12 + x = 38$

41. $12 - x = 33$

42. $5 - x = 23$

43. $24 - 18 + x = 5$

44. $17 - 11 + x = 12$

45. $w + (-44) = 56$

46. $z + (-52) = 24$

47. $m + \frac{1}{2} = \frac{3}{2}$

48. $n + \frac{1}{4} = \frac{5}{4}$

49. $s - \frac{1}{5} = \frac{3}{5}$

50. $t - \frac{1}{7} = \frac{2}{7}$

51. $-14 = x - 16$

52. $-17 = x - 8$

53. $c - \frac{5}{8} = -\frac{3}{8}$

54. $d - \frac{5}{9} = -\frac{1}{9}$

Ⓒ Supply the reason for each step.

55.
$$x + 8 = -17$$
$$[x + 8] + (-8) = -17 + (-8)$$
$$[x + 8] + (-8) = -25$$
$$x + [8 + (-8)] = -25$$
$$x + 0 = -25$$
$$x = -25$$

56.
$$x - 9 = 12$$
$$x + (-9) = 12$$
$$[x + (-9)] + 9 = 12 + 9$$
$$[x + (-9)] + 9 = 21$$
$$x + [(-9) + 9] = 21$$
$$x + 0 = 21$$
$$x = 21$$

Write a detailed solution for each equation, giving the reason for each step. The replacement set is {integers}.

57. $x + (-5) = 17$

58. $x - 20 = 7$

59. $11 = x - 19$

60. $-8 = x - 15$

Solve for x. Assume a, b, c, and d are rational numbers and the replacement set for x is {rational numbers}.

61. $x + b = a$

62. $x - c = d$

63. $-d = x - c$

64. $a = x + b$

65. $a - b + x = d$

66. $c + d + x = a$

67. Solve $t + 2 = 9$ for each replacement set (U) listed.

    a. $U = $ {integers}   **b.** $U = $ {negative integers}   **c.** $U = \{7\}$

To solve an equation like $4x = -24$, we can use the following property of equality.

Let a, b, and c be any real numbers.

If $a = b$, then $ca = cb$.

Example 1: Let {integers} be the replacement set. Solve.

$$\textbf{a.} \quad -4x = -24 \qquad \textbf{b.} \quad \tfrac{1}{2}x = 3$$

SHORT SOLUTIONS:

a. $-4x = -24$
$\quad \times(-\tfrac{1}{4}) \quad \times(-\tfrac{1}{4})$
$\qquad\qquad x = 6$

b. $\tfrac{1}{2}x = 3$
$\quad \times 2 \quad \times 2$
$\qquad x = 6$

DETAILED SOLUTIONS:

a. $\quad -4x = -24$	Given	**b.** $\tfrac{1}{2}x = 3$
$-\tfrac{1}{4}(-4x) = -\tfrac{1}{4}(-24)$	Mult. prop. of $=$	$2(\tfrac{1}{2}x) = 2 \cdot 3$
$-\tfrac{1}{4}(-4x) = 6$	Multiplication	$2(\tfrac{1}{2}x) = 6$
$[(-\tfrac{1}{4})(-4)]x = 6$	Assoc. prop. of $\cdot$	$(2 \cdot \tfrac{1}{2})x = 6$
$1x = 6$	Inv. prop. of $\cdot$	$1x = 6$
$x = 6$	Ident. prop. of $\cdot$	$x = 6$

Check: $-4(6) = -24$
$\qquad\quad -24 = -24 \quad \textsf{T}$

Check: $\tfrac{1}{2}(6) = 3$
$\qquad\qquad 3 = 3 \quad \textsf{T}$

The distributive property can be used to derive an equation of the type $ax = c$ from an equation of the type $ax + dx = c$.

Example 2: Simplify $15x + (-7)x = 16$.

SOLUTION: $15x + (-7)x = 16$
$\qquad\quad [15 + (-7)]x = 16$
$\qquad\qquad\qquad 8x = 16 \quad \longleftarrow$ How would you solve this equation?

EXERCISES 3.5

Ⓐ By what number would you multiply both sides to solve each equation?

1. $2x = 18$

2. $-3x = -9$

3. $13 = 13x$

4. $\frac{1}{2}a = 21$

5. $-\frac{1}{3}w = 5$

6. $-7s = 28$

7. $-9t = -45$

8. $-12b = 60$

9. $-8 = \frac{1}{4}r$

Simplify each equation by using the distributive property as in Example 2.

10. $2x + 3x = 30$

11. $-7r + (-2r) = -36$

12. $6x - 2x = 12$

13. $9x + (-4x) = 55$

14. $-3x + 12x = -18$

15. $2x + x = -24$

16–30. Solve each equation in Exercises **1–15** if the replacement set for each variable is {integers}.

Ⓑ Fish out of the lake the equations equivalent to the given equations.

31. $-5x = 35$

32. $7x = -35$

33. $3x - x = 18$

34. $x + 2x = -21$

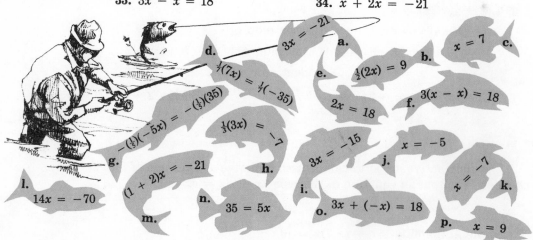

Solve each equation. Let the replacement set be {rational numbers}.

35. $3m = -42$

36. $-6w = 48$

37. $x + 3x = 20$

38. $4x + x = 30$

39. $-\frac{1}{2}w = 7$

40. $-\frac{1}{3}z = 9$

41. $x + (-8) = 2$

42. $x - 6 = 9$

43. $9x - 5x = 40$

44. $7x - 3x = 44$

45. $-5t = -55$

46. $-7t = -49$

47. $m + m = -16$

48. $-c + (-c) = 14$

49. $-x + 13x = -60$

50. $-x + 9x = -64$

51. $\frac{1}{2}w + \frac{3}{2}w = 8$

52. $\frac{1}{3}s + \frac{5}{3}s = 12$

© Supply the reason for each step in the solutions.

53.
$$-9w = -4$$
$$(-\tfrac{1}{9})(-9w) = (-\tfrac{1}{9})(-4)$$
$$(-\tfrac{1}{9})(-9w) = \tfrac{4}{9}$$
$$[(-\tfrac{1}{9})(-9)]w = \tfrac{4}{9}$$
$$1w = \tfrac{4}{9}$$
$$w = \tfrac{4}{9}$$

54.
$$8t + (-5t) = -1$$
$$[8 + (-5)]t = -1$$
$$3t = -1$$
$$\tfrac{1}{3}(3t) = \tfrac{1}{3}(-1)$$
$$\tfrac{1}{3}(3t) = -\tfrac{1}{3}$$
$$(\tfrac{1}{3} \cdot 3)t = -\tfrac{1}{3}$$
$$1t = -\tfrac{1}{3}$$
$$t = -\tfrac{1}{3}$$

For Exercises 55–58, write a detailed solution for each equation, giving the reason for each step. The replacement set is {rational numbers}.

55. $12w = -5$

56. $-5t = 3$

57. $6x + (-11x) = 20$

58. $-7y + 11y = -24$

Solve each equation. The replacement set is {rational numbers}.

59. $\frac{4}{3}x = 4$

60. $\frac{8}{5}y = 5$

61. $4x - 3 = 9$

62. $5y - 6 = 14$

63. $-3w \div 4 = 13$

64. $-5z + 2 = 17$

Solve for x. Assume a, b, c, and d are nonzero rational numbers and the replacement set for x is {rational numbers}.

65. $ax = b$

66. $cx = d$

67. $ax - cx = d$

68. $bx + dx = c$

3.6 SOLVING PROBLEMS

In this section we will use equations of the types studied in the preceding two sections to solve practical problems.

Example 1: Nancy borrowed $1.25 to help pay for a $7.75 album. How much money of her own did Nancy use to pay for the album?

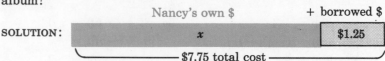

SOLUTION:

Let x = number of Nancy's own dollars spent on the album.

$$x + 1.25 = 7.75$$
$$x = 6.50$$

▶ Be sure you can complete the missing steps.

Check: $6.50 + 1.25 = 7.75$
$$7.75 = 7.75$$

So Nancy used $6.50 of her own to help pay for the album.

The main steps used to solve this problem, and similar problems, can be shown in a *flow chart*.

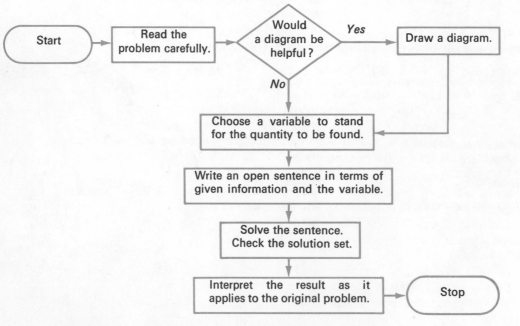

Example 2: Mike has saved the same amount each month for 4 months. He saved a total of $5.20. How much did he save each month?

SOLUTION: Let n = the amount Mike saved each month.

number of months $\quad 4n = 5.20 \longleftarrow$ total saved

amount each month $\quad n = 1.30$

Check: $4(1.30) = 5.20$

$5.20 = 5.20 \quad$ T

Mike saved $1.30 each month.

EXERCISES 3.6

Ⓐ For each problem, tell **(a)** which quantity you would represent by a variable and **(b)** the equation you would use to solve the problem.

1. In 12 years, Ivan will be 27 years old. How old is he now?

2. Seven years ago, Lila was nine years old. How old is she now?

3. Eight times a certain number is 48. What is the number?

4. If Nina had $100 more, she would have enough to pay for her $550 motorcycle. How much money does Nina have now?

5. Mark has 7 quarters. How many dollars is this?

6. The radius of the sun is 696,000 kilometers, which is about 109 times the radius of the earth. What is the radius of the earth?

7. After climbing Mount Baldy, Art descended to a point 320 feet lower than the peak. There he found a marker that indicated that he was still 5,460 feet above sea level. How many feet above sea level is the peak of Mount Baldy?

8. Objects on the moon weigh about $\frac{1}{6}$ as much as they weigh on earth. What does Stan weigh here if he weighs 28 pounds on the moon?

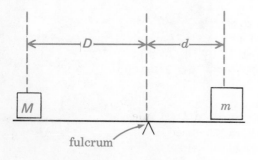

9. The speed of a falling object increases 9.8 meters per second each second it falls. If a rock that was pushed off an overhanging cliff is falling 39.2 meters per second, how many seconds has it been falling?

10. Rachel drove 720 miles in 16 hours. What was her average speed?

11. If the Panama Express travels 660 miles at an average speed of 55 miles per hour, how long does the trip take?

12. The area of a triangle is found by multiplying one-half the length of the base by the height. The area of a triangle is 56 square inches. If the base measures 14 inches, find the height.

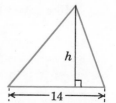

Ⓑ 13–24. Solve each problem in Exercises 1–12.

25. When Cindy and Kathy took part in the Walk-for-Development last fall, they walked a combined distance of 45 miles. If Cindy walked twice as far as Kathy, how far did they each walk?

26. Monty's sponsors in the Walk-for-Development paid 50¢ a mile, and their contribution on Monty's behalf was $11.50. How far did Monty walk?

27. Jack put some money in a savings account a year ago. He now has $564.30 in the account, which pays $4\frac{1}{2}\%$ annual interest. How much did Jack deposit originally?

A simple lever is in balance when $MD = md$, where M and m are the masses of the objects on the lever, while D and d are their distances from the fulcrum.

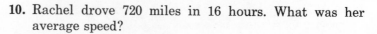

28. Gina weighs 104 pounds and sits on a seesaw 8 feet from the fulcrum. If Juan weighs 130, how far from the fulcrum should he sit to balance the seesaw?

29. If an object with mass 164 grams is 20 centimeters from the fulcrum of a lever, what is the mass of an object 80 centimeters from the fulcrum that will balance the lever?

30. Colleen borrowed $500 from the Money-to-Spend Loan Company to buy a new car. When she repaid the money a year later, she had to pay $532.50. What rate of interest did the company charge?

31. Birds of one endangered species laid only 22 eggs last year, half of which hatched. If this doubled their number, how many of this species were there before the eggs hatched?

32. A flock of 12 rare cranes has only 2 birds more than half as many as it had last year. How big was the flock last year?

© **33.** A new subdivision of Oldburgh occupies 240 hectares and will be zoned for single-family housing (R), multiple-family housing (M), commerce (C), and industry (I). Areas zoned R, I, and C are to be respectively two, three, and six times larger than the area zoned M. How many hectares will there be in each category?

34. At 8 A.M., a Boeing 707 and a Douglas DC-8 leave terminals located 3,000 miles apart and travel toward each other. If the average speed of the 707 is 560 miles per hour and the average speed of the DC-8 is 640 miles per hour, at what time will the two planes pass each other?

35. At 6 P.M., two supersonic jets leave terminals located 2,600 miles apart and travel toward one another. The average speed of one jet is one and one-half times the average speed of the other. If they pass each other at 7 P.M., what is the average speed of each plane?

SELF-QUIZ: 3.4 to 3.6

Tell whether the equations in each pair are equivalent.

1. $x - 7 = 5$
   $x + (-7) = 5$

2. $5x = -40$
   $-5x = 40$

3. $n + 10 = 3$
   $n + 3 = 10$

4. $15y = -20$
   $3y = -4$

5. $-8 + s = -6 + 2$
   $s = -12$

6. $7t - 5t = 10$
   $[7 + (-5)]t = 10$

Solve each equation. The replacement set is {rational numbers}.

7. $-9 = x + 6$

8. $-6w = 18$

9. $r - 9 + 17 = 0$

10. $\frac{1}{5}s = 8$

11. $7 - x = -3$

12. $-5t + 11t = 1$

Solve each problem by the use of an equation.

13. Eighteen years from now, Liz will be 32. How old is she now?

14. Wayne receives four times as much weekly allowance as his kid brother Ron, and together they receive $3.75. How much does each receive?

15. The Rag Rug Carpet Company sells its carpet in rolls containing 126 square yards of carpet 3 yards wide. How long is each piece of carpet?

To solve some equations, we can combine methods used earlier. The replacement set in these examples is {integers}.

Example 1: Solve $3x + 8 = 20$.

SHORT SOLUTION:

$$
\begin{array}{rcl}
3x + & 8 & = & 20 \\
& + (-8) & & + (-8) \\
\hline
3x & & = & 12 \\
\times \frac{1}{3} & & & \times \frac{1}{3} \\
\hline
x & & = & 4
\end{array}
$$

DETAILED SOLUTION:

$$3x + 8 = 20$$
$$[3x + 8] + (-8) = 20 + (-8)$$
$$[3x + 8] + (-8) = 12$$
$$3x + [8 + (-8)] = 12$$
$$3x = 12$$
$$\tfrac{1}{3}(3x) = \tfrac{1}{3} \cdot 12$$
$$\tfrac{1}{3}(3x) = 4$$
$$(\tfrac{1}{3} \cdot 3)x = 4$$
$$x = 4$$

Check: $3 \cdot 4 + 8 = 20$
$20 = 20$ T

Notice that, in solving the equation above, we first "isolate" the variable. That is, we find an equivalent equation of the form $ax = c$.

Example 2: Solve $4x + 7 = -2x + 31$.

SOLUTION:

$$
\begin{array}{rcl}
4x + & 7 & = & -2x + & 31 \\
+ 2x & & & + 2x \\
\hline
6x + & 7 & = & & 31 \\
& + (-7) & & & + (-7) \\
\hline
6x & & = & & 24 \\
\times \frac{1}{6} & & & & \times \frac{1}{6} \\
\hline
x & & = & & 4
\end{array}
$$

First find an equivalent equation of the form $ax + b = c$.

Check: $4 \cdot 4 + 7 = -2 \cdot 4 + 31$
$23 = 23$ T

EXERCISES 3.7

Ⓐ Tell **(a)** which real number must be added to both sides of the first equation to obtain the second equation, and **(b)** which real number each side of the second equation must be multiplied by to obtain the third equation.

1. $2x + 1 = 5$	$2x = 4$	$x = 2$
2. $3x - 4 = 8$	$3x = 12$	$x = 4$
3. $-7x + 7 = 0$	$-7x = -7$	$x = 1$
4. $-5y - 9 = 1$	$-5y = 10$	$y = -2$
5. $11 = 8 - 3x$	$3 = -3x$	$x = -1$
6. $-13 = 6x - 10$	$-3 = 6x$	$x = -\frac{1}{2}$
7. $-\frac{1}{2}x + 5 = -1$	$-\frac{1}{2}x = -6$	$x = 12$
8. $\frac{3}{4}x - 8 = -7$	$\frac{3}{4}x = 1$	$x = \frac{4}{3}$
9. $11x + 13 = -9$	$11x = -22$	$x = -2$
10. $12 = \frac{1}{6}t + 7$	$5 = \frac{1}{6}t$	$t = 30$

Tell how each equation was derived from the equation to its left.

11. $5x + 2 = 3x - 8$	$2x + 2 = -8$	$2x = -10$	$x = -5$
12. $x - 16 = 7x + 2$	$-16 = 6x + 2$	$-18 = 6x$	$x = -3$
13. $-3x + 4 = 2x - 6$	$4 = 5x - 6$	$10 = 5x$	$x = 2$
14. $9x - 2 = 8 + 6x$	$3x - 2 = 8$	$3x = 10$	$x = \frac{10}{3}$
15. $7r - 5 = -4r + 6$	$11r - 5 = 6$	$11r = 11$	$r = 1$
16. $10 - s = s + 16$	$10 = 2s + 16$	$-6 = 2s$	$s = -3$

Ⓑ Tell whether the equations in each pair are equivalent.

17. $4x - 9 = 3; 4x = 12$

18. $7x - 4 = 10; 7x = 14$

19. $2x + 5 = 17; x = 6$

20. $3x + 4 = 13; x = 3$

21. $4x + 11 = -3x; 7x = 11$

22. $5x + 9 = -3x; 8x = 9$

23. $8 - 4x = 8x - 4; x = 1$

24. $7 - 5x = 7x - 5; x = 1$

Solve each equation. The replacement set is {rational numbers}.

25. $2x + 1 = 13$ **26.** $3x + 2 = 14$

27. $5x - 2 = 3$ **28.** $4x - 3 = 5$

29. $-6x + 4 = 16$ **30.** $-5x + 7 = 17$

31. $3 - 4x = 0$ **32.** $5 - 6x = 0$

33. $12s - 10 = 14$ **34.** $10t - 9 = 11$

35. $\frac{1}{3}s - 2 = 4$ **36.** $\frac{1}{5}t - 1 = 5$

37. $-15 = 3t - 9$ **38.** $-12 = 2s - 20$

39. $3s + 8 = s$ **40.** $5w + 9 = 2w$

41. $\frac{1}{5}w + \frac{2}{5} = -\frac{3}{5}$ **42.** $\frac{1}{4}r + \frac{3}{4} = -\frac{1}{4}$

43. $5m = 11 - 2m$ **44.** $6n = 26 - 3n$

45. $4y - 7 = -3y$ **46.** $3x - 9 = -6x$

47. $2x + 7 = -x + 9$ **48.** $2x + 5 = -2x + 8$

49. $\frac{2}{3}x - 2 = 4$ **50.** $\frac{3}{4}x - 4 = 8$

51. $4x - 6 = 3x - 4$ **52.** $3x - 4 = 2x - 6$

53. $\frac{5}{2}x + 12 = 2$ **54.** $\frac{7}{2}x - 4 = 10$

55. $-5w + 4 = 3w - 12$ **56.** $-4w + 8 = 5w - 10$

57. $-17r - 13 = -12r - 11$ **58.** $-19s - 14 = -12s - 11$

© **59.** $\frac{1}{3}x - \frac{5}{3} = -\frac{2}{3}x + \frac{1}{3}$ **60.** $\frac{2}{5}x - 2 = \frac{1}{5}x + 4$

61. $-\frac{5}{6}y - \frac{1}{6} = -\frac{2}{6}y + \frac{11}{6}$ **62.** $\frac{3}{7}w + 8 = w + 4$

63. $\frac{4}{3}s - \frac{2}{3}s + 5 = s - 3$ **64.** $\frac{2}{7}t - \frac{5}{7}t = \frac{3}{7}t + 1$

65. $-4(2x - 5) = -4x + 10$ **66.** $9x - 13 = 6x - (5x - 7)$

Write detailed solutions, giving the reason for each step.

67. $3x + 19 = -5$ **68.** $4x + 17 = -3$

Show that each of the following equations is equivalent to an equation of the form $mx + n = 0$. Then solve each equation for x.

69. $ax = c$ **70.** $x + b = c$

71. $ax + b = c$ **72.** $ax + b = cx + d$

3.8 PRACTICE WITH EQUATIONS

Each equation you have considered so far has had a single rational number in its solution set. Can an equation of any of the types you have studied have more than one solution? Can such an equation have an empty solution set?

Example 1: Solve $2(3x + 4) = 6x + 8$, where the replacement set is {rational numbers}.

SOLUTION:

$$
\begin{aligned}
2(3x + 4) &= 6x + 8 \\
6x + 8 &= 6x + 8 \\
+(-6x) \quad\quad &+ (-6x) \\
\hline
8 &= 8
\end{aligned}
$$

→ We have used the given equation to derive the true closed sentence $8 = 8$, so the given equation is true for every rational replacement for x. Thus, its solution set is the replacement set or {rational numbers}. An equation whose solution set is the replacement set is called an **identity**.

Example 2: Solve. The replacement set is {integers}.

a. $2(x - 2) = 2(x + 1)$ **b.** $3(x + 2) = x + 7$

SOLUTIONS:

a.
$$
\begin{aligned}
2(x - 2) &= 2(x + 1) \\
2x - 4 &= 2x + 2 \\
-2x \quad\quad &-2x \\
\hline
-4 &= 2
\end{aligned}
$$

b.
$$
\begin{aligned}
3(x + 2) &= x + 7 \\
3x + 6 &= x + 7 \\
+(-x - 6) \quad\quad &+(-x - 6) \\
\hline
2x &= 1 \\
x &= \tfrac{1}{2}
\end{aligned}
$$

→ In **a**, we have used the given equation to derive a false closed sentence, so the given equation is false for every replacement for x. Thus, its solution set is $\varnothing$.

→ In **b**, the given equation is equivalent to an equation that obviously does not have a solution in {integers}, so its solution set is also $\varnothing$ for the given replacement set.

EXERCISES 3.8

Ⓐ Match each equation with its solution set. The replacement set is {rational numbers}.

a. {rational numbers}   **b.** ∅   **c.** {0}

1. $3x = x$
2. $x + 3 = x + 3$
3. $x + 4 = 4$
4. $3x - 4 - x = 2x - 4$
5. $2x + 3 = 2x - 5$
6. $3(x - 1) = 3x$
7. $2(3x - 4) = 3(2x + 4)$
8. $3x + 7 = x + 7$
9. $5(2x + 1) = 10x + 5$
10. $-7x = -10x + 3x$

Ⓑ Solve each equation. The replacement set is {rational numbers}.

11. $2m + 8 = m + 3$
12. $3n + 5 = 2n + 1$
13. $3(2x + 1) = 6x + 3$
14. $2(x + 2) = 2x + 4$
15. $-2(3x - 4) = -4x$
16. $-3(2x - 5) = -3x$
17. $4(-2t + 3) = -5t + 3$
18. $5(-3r + 4) = -10r + 5$
19. $3(2x - 5) = 6x + 8$
20. $4(2x - 3) = 8x + 6$
21. $8 - (7x + 5) = -x$
22. $7 - (5x + 5) = -x$
23. $3x = 9x - (3x - 18)$
24. $2x = 12x - (7x - 15)$
25. $-(18x - 21) = 7x - 29$
26. $-(17x - 43) = 6x - 26$
27. $3(x - 3) - 2(x + 1) = 5$
28. $2(x - 4) - 3(x - 1) = 4$
29. $2(5s - 2) = 3(3s + 4)$
30. $5(4t - 2) = 2(2t - 1)$
31. $3r + 5 = 2(r - 1)$
32. $5f + 1 = 4(f - 2)$
33. $-7(1 + j) + 7j - 4 = 3$
34. $8k - 2 - 8(1 + k) = 6$
35. $14(x - 2) = 5(2x - 7)$
36. $13(2x + 3) = 6(3x + 9)$
37. $3v + 7 = 3(v + 2) + 1$
38. $9c - 5 = 3(3c - 1) - 2$

Ⓒ 39. Describe the replacement sets for which $x - 3 = 2x - 4$ would have each of the following solution sets.

a. ∅   **b.** the replacement set

c. neither ∅ nor the replacement set

3.9 MORE ABOUT SOLVING PROBLEMS

Some problems call for more complicated equations than we used earlier, while others call for more than one answer.

Example 1: For a football game, West High priced student tickets at 75¢ and adult tickets at $1.25. The gate receipts were the same as if each ticket were sold for 95¢. If 400 adult tickets were sold, how many student tickets were sold?

SOLUTION:

	Rate $\times$ number of tickets $=$ receipts		
Student rate	$75 \times$	x	$= 75x$
Adult rate	$125 \times$	400	$= 125(400)$
Single rate	$95 \times$	$x + 400$	$= 95(x + 400)$

$$95(x + 400) = 75x + 125(400)$$
$$95x + 95(400) = 75x + 125(400)$$
$$95x - 75x = 125(400) - 95(400)$$
$$20x = 30(400)$$
$$x = 600$$

> Be sure you can complete the missing steps.

Check: $95(600 + 400) = 75(600) + 125(400)$
$95000 = 95000$ T

They sold 600 student tickets.

Example 2: The sum of three consecutive even integers is four times the smallest of the three integers. What are the integers?

SOLUTION: Let x, $x + 2$, and $x + 4$ be the integers.

$$x + (x + 2) + (x + 4) = 4x$$
$$3x + 6 = 4x$$
$$x = 6$$
$$x + 2 = 8$$
$$x + 4 = 10$$

> Be sure you can complete the missing steps.

Check: $6 + 8 + 10 = 4 \cdot 6$
$24 = 24$ T

The integers are 6, 8, and 10.

The replacement set for the variable is usually obvious from the problem. For instance, in Example 1, the variable represents a certain number of tickets. Would the replacement set include all rational numbers? Negative integers? Why would {nonnegative integers} be the best choice for the replacement set?

Example 3: Ann and Chris rode their bikes toward each other from points on a straight road 24 miles apart. If Chris rode 3 miles per hour faster than Ann and they met in 2 hours, how fast did each ride?

SOLUTION: Let r = Ann's rate in miles per hour;
$r + 3$ = Chris's rate in miles per hour.

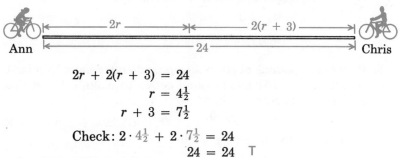

$$2r + 2(r + 3) = 24$$
$$r = 4\tfrac{1}{2}$$
$$r + 3 = 7\tfrac{1}{2}$$

Check: $2 \cdot 4\tfrac{1}{2} + 2 \cdot 7\tfrac{1}{2} = 24$
$$24 = 24 \quad \text{T}$$

Ann rode $4\tfrac{1}{2}$ miles per hour; Chris rode $7\tfrac{1}{2}$ miles per hour.

EXERCISES 3.9

Ⓐ Study each problem and the three equations which follow it. Then choose the equation that fits the problem.

1. One integer is 6 more than 5 times another, and their sum is 36. Find the integers.
   a. $x + (5x - 6) = 36$ **b.** $x + (5x + 6) = 36$
   c. $x + 5(x + 6) = 36$

2. Sophie wants to buy a $93 pair of skis. They cost $12 less than 3 times the amount of money she has saved. How much has she saved?
   a. $3(x - 12) = 93$ **b.** $3x - 12 = 93$
   c. $3x = 93 - 12$

3. A rectangular playground is 80 meters longer than it is wide. If 960 meters of fencing enclose it, find its length.

    a. $w + (w + 80) = 960$ **b.** $2w + 2w + 80 = 960$

    c. $2w + 2(w + 80) = 960$

4. Four years ago, Mal's age was two years more than three times Rico's present age. If the sum of their present ages is fifty, how old are they?

    a. $x - 4 = 3(50 - x) - 2$ **b.** $x - 4 = 3(50 - x) + 2$

    c. $x - 4 = 3(50 - x - 4) + 2$

5. Twelve years from now, Mona's age will be four years less than twice her present age. How old is she now?

    a. $x + 12 = 2x - 4$ **b.** $x - 12 = 2x - 4$

    c. $x + 12 = 2(x + 12) - 4$

6. How many pounds of 80-cents-a-pound coffee must be mixed with 16 pounds of 110-cents-a-pound coffee to make a blend that can be sold at 92 cents a pound?

    a. $80x + 110(16) = 92$ **b.** $80x + 110(16) = 92x$

    c. $80x + 110(16) = 92(x + 16)$

Ⓑ **7–12.** Solve each of the problems in Exercises **1–6**.

Solve each problem.

13. Find three consecutive integers whose sum is 54. (HINT: Let x, $x + 1$, and $x + 2$ represent the integers.)

14. Find three consecutive integers whose sum is 45.

15. Find three consecutive even integers whose sum is 48.

16. Find three consecutive odd integers whose sum is 99. (HINT: Let x, $x + 2$, and $x + 4$ represent the integers.)

17. In a two-digit number, the tens digit is 4 more than the units digit. The sum of the digits is 10. Find the number.

18. The tens digit of a two-digit number is 3 less than the ones digit. The sum of the digits is 11. Find the number.

19. A football field is 40 feet longer than twice its width. Its perimeter is 1,040 feet. Find its dimensions.

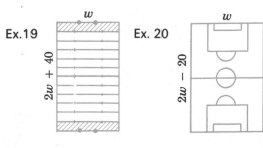

Ex.19   Ex. 20

20. A soccer field is 20 yards shorter than twice its width. Its perimeter is 350 yards. Find its dimensions.

21. How many pounds of 80-cents-a-pound candy must Judy mix with 10 pounds of 96-cents-a-pound candy to give her a mixture that she can sell for 90 cents a pound?

22. How many pounds of 95-cents-a-pound candy must Fred mix with 10 pounds of 80-cents-a-pound candy to give him a mixture he can sell for 90 cents a pound?

23. Max bought a used bicycle for which he paid $5 more than one-half of its price when new. If the bike cost him $40, what was its original price?

24. On her paper route, Sonya now has 3 more than twice as many customers as she had when she started. If Sonya has 95 customers, with how many did she start?

25. Pat was given 29 nickels and dimes in exchange for $2 in bills. How many nickels and how many dimes did she get?

26. Paula bought 45 six-cent and eight-cent postage stamps for $3. How many of each kind did she buy?

27. Of three consecutive integers, twice the sum of the first two is 18 more than 3 times the third. Find the integers.

28. Of three consecutive integers, 3 times the sum of the first and third is 74 more than 4 times the second. Find the integers.

29. Tom and Elsa rode their motorbikes toward each other from points 168 miles apart. If Elsa rode 4 miles per hour slower than Tom and they met in 3 hours, how fast did Elsa ride?

Ex. 30

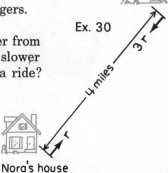

30. Sherm started walking toward Nora's house, 4 miles away, at the same time that Nora started walking toward Sherm's house. If they met 30 minutes later, and Sherm walked 3 times as fast as Nora, how fast did Sherm walk?

© **31.** The highest mountain peak (Mount Everest) is 19,810 meters above the deepest point in the oceans (southwest of Guam in the Pacific). The depth of the deepest point in the oceans is 6,710 meters less than twice the height of Mount Everest. Find the height of Mount Everest and the depth of the deepest point in the oceans.

32. Tony scored 92 points on a test, receiving 8 points for each correct answer and losing 4 points for each incorrect answer. If the number he had correct was 7 more than twice the number he had incorrect, how many did he have correct?

33. Jeanne can paddle her canoe 5.5 miles an hour in still water. If it took her 5 hours to paddle up the Blue River and 3 hours to return, what was the rate of flow of the river?

I've almost got the answer, but for the life of me I can't remember what the problem was!

The dictionary defines a formula as "a general fact, rule, or principle expressed in symbols."

$I = prt$ > interest = principal × annual rate × time
               dollars   dollars   hundredths   years

$E = IR$ > voltage = current × resistance
            volts   amperes   ohms

$F = \frac{9}{5}C + 32$ > Fahrenheit temp. = $\frac{9}{5}$ × Centigrade temp. + 32
            degrees   (or Celsius) degrees

Example 1: Use the formula for engine power shown below to write a formula for the number of pistons needed for a given horsepower and piston size. That is, solve the given formula for n.

$$H = 0.4d^2n, \text{ or}$$

horsepower = 0.4 × (diameter of pistons)^2 × number of cylinders
                      inches

SOLUTION:

$$H = 0.4d^2n$$
$$\times \frac{1}{0.4d^2} \quad \times \frac{1}{0.4d^2}$$

◀ since we know that d stands for a nonzero real number

$$\frac{H}{0.4d^2} = n \quad \text{or} \quad n = \frac{H}{0.4d^2}$$

Example 2: Find the horsepower of an 8-cylinder engine with pistons 3 inches in diameter.

SOLUTION: $H = 0.4d^2n$
$= 0.4(3)^2 \cdot 8$
$= 29.8$ So the engine has 29.8 horsepower.

Example 3: Convert 86° Fahrenheit to degrees Celsius.

SOLUTION:
$$F = \tfrac{9}{5}C + 32$$
$$86 = \tfrac{9}{5}C + 32$$
$$+(-32) \qquad +(-32)$$
$$54 = \tfrac{9}{5}C$$
$$\times \tfrac{5}{9} \qquad \times \tfrac{5}{9}$$
$$30 = C \qquad\qquad \text{The temperature is } 30°C.$$

EXERCISES 3.10

Ⓐ In Exercises 1–14, use the information given and the geometric formulas below to find the required quantity. Use 3.14 for π.

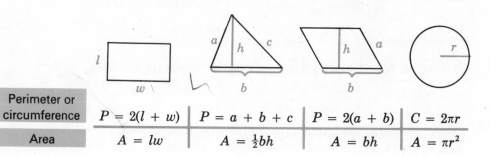

Perimeter or circumference	$P = 2(l + w)$	$P = a + b + c$	$P = 2(a + b)$	$C = 2\pi r$
Area	$A = lw$	$A = \frac{1}{2}bh$	$A = bh$	$A = \pi r^2$

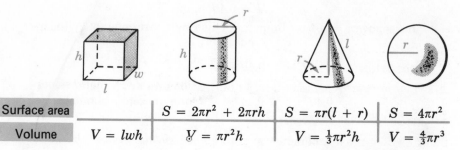

Surface area		$S = 2\pi r^2 + 2\pi rh$	$S = \pi r(l + r)$	$S = 4\pi r^2$
Volume	$V = lwh$	$V = \pi r^2 h$	$V = \frac{1}{3}\pi r^2 h$	$V = \frac{4}{3}\pi r^3$

1. perimeter of a rectangle
   $l = 5$ meters, $w = 3$ meters

2. area of a rectangle
   $l = 9$ meters, $w = 6$ meters

3. area of a triangle
   $b = 12$ inches, $h = 5$ inches

4. area of a parallelogram
   $b = 9$ inches, $h = 7$ inches

5. volume of rectangular solid; $l = 5$ feet, $w = 4$ feet, $h = 6$ feet

6. perimeter of a parallelogram; $a = 3$ feet, $b = 4$ feet

Ⓑ 7. surface area of a cylinder
   $r = 25$ meters, $h = 75$ meters

8. surface area of a cone
   $r = 11$ meters, $l = 9$ meters

9. volume of a cylinder
   $r = 7$ inches, $h = 10$ inches

10. volume of a cone
    $r = 10$ feet, $h = 6$ feet

11. volume of a sphere
    $r = 30$ inches

12. surface area of a sphere
    $r = 10$ centimeters

13. area of a circle
    $r = 8$ inches

14. circumference of a circle
    $r = 8$ centimeters

Use the formulas given in this section to find the following.

15. the voltage in a circuit if $I = 7$ amperes and $R = 8$ ohms

16. the interest on $2,700 at 7.5% yearly interest for 2 years

17. the Fahrenheit temperature if the Celsius temperature is 45°

18. the horsepower of an 8-cylinder engine whose pistons measure 3.5 inches in diameter

19. the interest on $2,300 at 6.2% yearly interest for 3 years

20. the voltage in a circuit if $R = 6$ ohms and $I = 9$ amperes

21. the horsepower of a 6-cylinder engine whose pistons measure 3.5 inches in diameter

22. the Fahrenheit temperature if the Celsius temperature is 35°

For Exercises 23–28, use the formula $d = rt$, where d is the distance traveled, r is the rate of travel, and t is the time traveled.

23. How far can a person go in 7 hours at 80 kilometers per hour?

24. How far can a person go in 6 hours at 55 miles an hour?

25. How fast must a person travel to go 344 miles in 8 hours?

26. How fast must a person travel to go 686 kilometers in 7 hours?

27. How long does it take to travel 434 miles at 62 miles per hour?

28. How long does it take to travel 290 miles at 58 miles per hour?

Solve the formula for the variable called for.

29. $d = rt$ for t

30. $E = IR$ for I

31. $E = mc^2$ for m

32. $W = \frac{1}{2}mv^2$ for m

33. $P = 2(l + w)$ for l

34. $P = 2(a + b)$ for b

© **35.** $A = \frac{1}{2}h(a + b)$ for h

36. $A = p + prt$ for p

37. $T^2 = 4\pi^2 \dfrac{L}{g}$ for g

38. $v^2 = \dfrac{2GM}{r}$ for r

CHAPTER REVIEW ◆

Give the information that should fill each blank.

a. Expression	b. Meaning	c. Exponent	d. Base	e. Value
1. 3^4	_____	_____	_____	_____
2. _____	_____	3	4	_____
3. $(-2)^4$	_____	_____	_____	_____

3.2 Simplify each product.

4. $-6(8s)$ **5.** $(-9t)(-7t)$ **6.** $(12ab)(-\frac{1}{2}a^2)$

3.3 Determine whether the expressions in each pair are equivalent.

7. $-5x + 10x - 2y$ **8.** $4x^2 - 2z - x^2$
$-5(x + 2) - 2y$ $3x^2 + (-2z)$

Simplify each expression.

9. $17y^2 - 34y^2$ **10.** $8t - (-7t + 3)$

11. $-9c + 4d - 3c$ **12.** $-4(5x - 3) + (5x - 3)$

13. $(5w)3z + (5w)6z$ **14.** $8(2x - 11y) - 2(x - 2y)$

3.4 Determine whether the equations in each pair are equivalent.

15. $x - 12 = 8$ **16.** $22 - y = 16$
$x + (-12) = 8$ $y = -6$

Solve. Let the replacement set be {integers}.

17. $x - 9 = -3$ **18.** $13 - t = 5$

19. $16 - 7 + x = 4$ **20.** $y - \frac{3}{7} = \frac{4}{7}$

3.5 Solve. Let the replacement set be {rational numbers}.

21. $-7x = 21$ **22.** $\frac{1}{3}w = 8$ **23.** $8x - 5x = 9$

Solve each problem by writing and solving a suitable equation.   3.6

24. Nine years ago, Dave was eight years old. How old is he now?

25. In a bicycle marathon, Antonia rode 3 times as far as Andy did.
    If together they rode 44 miles, how far did each ride?

Solve. The replacement set is {rational numbers}.   3.7

26. $-5x + 8 = -12$ 27. $7t = -36 - 2t$

28. $-6s + 9 = 5s - 13$ 29. $12w - 21 = 21 + 5w$

30. $-5(2x + 4) = -10x - 20$ 31. $4(3x - 1) = 3(4x + 2)$ 3.8

32. $-3(6x - 7) = -12x - 9$

33. $-11(-2x - 3) + 7(-4x + 3) = 0$

Solve each problem by the use of an equation.   3.9

34. White Cloud is 6 years older than Eagle Feather. Eight years
    ago White Cloud was 4 times as old as Eagle Feather. How old are
    White Cloud and Eagle Feather now?

35. Hilda has 4 more dimes than quarters. If the total value of her
    dimes and quarters is $2.15, how many does she have of each?

36. The formula for the volume of a square pyramid is $V = \frac{1}{3}s^2h$.   3.10
    Find V if $s = 20$ meters and $h = 15$ meters.

37. Solve the formula $A = p + prt$ for r.

38. Find the surface area and volume of
    water in a circular pool that is 8
    meters across and 2 meters deep.

CHAPTER SELF-TEST

Which term best completes each sentence?

a. exponent	**b.** base	**c.** unlike terms
d. like terms	**e.** equivalent	**f.** empty set
g. distributive property		**h.** replacement set
i. addition property of =		**j.** associative property of +
	k. multiplication property of =	

1. The property used to simplify $-4x + 7x$ is the ____.

2. The 3 in the expression $(-2)^3$ is a(n) ____.

3. The expressions $5xy$ and $-9xy$ are called ____.

4. The property used to solve $x - 6 = 5$ is the ____.

5. The solution set for $3(5x - 8) = 15x - 24$ is the ____.

6. ____ equations have the same solution set.

7. The ____ is the solution set of $2x + 7 = 5x - 3x$.

Simplify each expression.

8. $5x - 4y - 6x$ **9.** $(3s)2t + (3s)t$ **10.** $9r - (4r - 8)$

Solve. The replacement set is {rational numbers}.

11. $x - 12 = -3$ **12.** $-6t + 8 = 7 - 4t$

13. $-17x + 6x = 22$ **14.** $4s - 9 = 2(2s - 3) - 3$

15. Dick is 3 times as old as Dee and the sum of their ages is 48. How old is each? (Write and solve a suitable equation.)

16. Find V if $V = \pi r^2 h$, $r = 6$ inches and $h = 10$ inches. (Use 3.14 for π.)

17. Solve $A = \frac{1}{2}bh$ for h.

Chapter 4

Inequalities and Compound Sentences

In algebra, as in everyday life, it is sometimes necessary to deal with quantities that are *not* equal. We use *inequalities* to describe how unequal quantities are related.

You will find that, like equations, inequalities can be used to solve problems.

4.1 ORDER AND GRAPHING

A sentence containing < or > is an **inequality** which tells about the *order* of numbers on a number line.

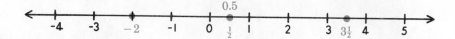

Sentence	How to read	Tells us that
$-2 < \frac{1}{2}$	-2 *is less than* $\frac{1}{2}$.	-2 is graphed to the *left* of $\frac{1}{2}$.
$3\frac{1}{2} > \frac{1}{2}$	$3\frac{1}{2}$ *is greater than* $\frac{1}{2}$.	$3\frac{1}{2}$ is graphed to the *right* of $\frac{1}{2}$.
$0.5 = \frac{1}{2}$	0.5 *is equal to* $\frac{1}{2}$.	0.5 and $\frac{1}{2}$ correspond to the *same* point.

For any pair of real numbers, if a is one of the numbers and b is the other, then either $a < b$, $a = b$, or $a > b$. This is called the *comparison property* of real numbers.

The solution sets of some open sentences are graphed as follows. In each case the replacement set is the set of real numbers.

Sentence	How to read	Graph
$x < 3$	*x is less than 3*	
$y > -2$	*y is greater than* -2	
$r \le -\frac{1}{2}$	*r is less than or equal to* $-\frac{1}{2}$	
$m \ge 1.5$	*m is greater than or equal to 1.5*	
$s \ne -1$	*s is not equal to* -1	

Notice how a solid dot ● or a hollow dot ○ is used to show whether a certain point is in the graph.

EXERCISES 4.1

Ⓐ Which symbol, $<$, $=$, or $>$, should replace each ▦?

1. 2 ▦ 3   **2.** 7 ▦ -5 **3.** 0 ▦ -4

4. 0.7 ▦ 0.8   **5.** -0.7 ▦ -0.8 **6.** -8 ▦ 8

7. $\frac{1}{2}$ ▦ $\frac{1}{4}$ **8.** $\frac{3}{2}$ ▦ 1.5   **9.** $\frac{3}{11}$ ▦ $\frac{1}{11}$

Match each inequality with the graph of its solution set.

10. $y \neq 2.5$ **a.** [number line: ray shaded left from about -2, solid dot at -2; marks -3 -2 -1 0 1 2 3 4]

11. $r \geq 2$ **b.** [number line: shaded ray left from 3 with open circle at 3; marks -3 -2 -1 0 1 2 3 4]

12. $r \leq -2$ **c.** [number line: shaded ray right from 1, solid dot at 1; marks -3 -2 -1 0 1 2 3 4]

13. $y < 3$ **d.** [number line: shaded both directions with open circle at 2; marks -3 -2 -1 0 1 2 3 4]

14. $n > 4 - 7$ **e.** [number line: shaded ray right from -3 with open circle at -3; marks -3 -2 -1 0 1 2 3 4]

Ⓑ Graph each sentence. In each case the replacement set is the set of real numbers.

15. $x < 2$ **16.** $y < -1$ **17.** $m > -3$

18. $n > 3$ **19.** $s \geq -5$ **20.** $s \geq -1$

21. $y \leq \frac{1}{4}$ **22.** $x \leq -3.5$ **23.** $m \neq 1.5$

Ⓒ Use set-builder notation to describe each set graphed below.

24.

25.

26.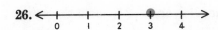

27.

4.2 COMPARING NUMBERS

Notice that if we add 6 to -2 we get 4.

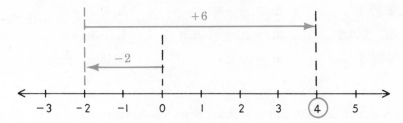

The sentences

$$-2 + 6 = 4 \quad \text{and} \quad -2 < 4$$

seem to say much the same thing about -2 and 4. That is, saying we can add the positive number 6 to -2 and get 4 is much like saying -2 is less than 4. (Or, -2 is graphed to the left of 4.)

Other Examples

$-4 + 7 = 3$ tells us that $-4 < 3$

$3 + 4 = 7$ tells us that $3 < 7$ (also $4 < 7$)

$0 + 2.3 = 2.3$ tells us that $0 < 2.3$

$-\frac{4}{2} + \frac{1}{2} = -\frac{3}{2}$ tells us that $-\frac{4}{2} < -\frac{3}{2}$

> If some positive number can be added to any real number a to obtain another real number b, then a is less than b.

Example 1: Use $<$ or $=$ to compare the numbers in each pair below.

    a. $3, 8$ **b.** $5, -6$ **c.** $-\frac{5}{2}, -2.5$

SOLUTION: **a.** $3 < 8$, since $3 + 5 = 8$.

    b. $-6 < 5$, since $-6 + 11 = 5$.

    c. $-\frac{5}{2} = -2.5$, since $-\frac{5}{2}$ and -2.5 name the same number.

Example 2: Compare the rational numbers in each pair below.

a. $\dfrac{5}{7}, \dfrac{9}{11}$

b. $\dfrac{-3}{8}, \dfrac{5}{-12}$

SOLUTION: In each case, first express the two numbers with the same denominator. Then it is easy to compare them.

a. $\left.\begin{array}{l} \dfrac{5}{7} = \dfrac{55}{77} \\[2ex] \dfrac{9}{11} = \dfrac{63}{77} \end{array}\right\}$ and $\dfrac{55}{77} < \dfrac{63}{77}$. So, $\dfrac{5}{7} < \dfrac{9}{11}$.

b. $\left.\begin{array}{l} \dfrac{-3}{8} = -\dfrac{9}{24} \\[2ex] \dfrac{5}{-12} = -\dfrac{10}{24} \end{array}\right\}$ and $-\dfrac{10}{24} < -\dfrac{9}{24}$. So, $\dfrac{5}{-12} < \dfrac{-3}{8}$.

A shortcut for comparing two rational numbers is to multiply the numerator of each rational number by the denominator of the other and compare the products.

$$\dfrac{5}{7} < \dfrac{9}{11} \quad \text{because} \quad 5 \cdot 11 < 9 \cdot 7$$

IMPORTANT: This shortcut can be used with any two rational numbers. But, you must be careful to first express each rational number so that the denominator is positive.

$\dfrac{5}{-12} \;\fbox{?}\; \dfrac{-3}{8}$

Right: $\dfrac{-5}{12} < \dfrac{-3}{8}$ because $\begin{array}{l} -5 \cdot 8 < 12(-3) \\ -40 < -36 \end{array}$ or

Wrong: $\dfrac{5}{-12} > \dfrac{-3}{8}$ because $\begin{array}{l} 5 \cdot 8 > -12(-3) \\ 40 > 36 \end{array}$ or

Let $\dfrac{a}{b}$ and $\dfrac{c}{d}$ be any rational numbers with positive denominators. Then, whichever symbol, $<$, $=$, or $>$, makes one of the following two sentences true also makes the other true.

$$\dfrac{a}{b} \;\fbox{}\; \dfrac{c}{d} \quad \longleftarrow \; \begin{array}{c} \text{means the} \\ \text{same as} \end{array} \; \longrightarrow \quad ad \;\fbox{}\; bc$$

EXERCISES 4.2

Ⓐ Which number in each pair is the lesser? Tell what positive number can be added to the lesser number to obtain the greater number.

1. 2, 8   2. 5, 1   3. 0, 3   4. 4, -2

5. $-1, -3$ 6. $-7, 5$ 7. $-2, 0$ 8. $-\frac{1}{2}, \frac{1}{2}$

9. 2, 10   10. 1.6, 1.9   11. $-2.1, 1.0$ 12. $\frac{1}{4}, \frac{3}{4}$

Ⓑ Which symbol, $<$, $=$, or $>$, should replace each ●?

13. 3 ● 4   14. 9 ● 3   15. 4 ● -4

16. -2 ● 5   17. -2 ● -1 18. -5 ● -8

19. 0.3 ● 0.1   20. 1.5 ● 2.1   21. -0.5 ● $-\frac{1}{2}$

22. -0.4 ● $\frac{-4}{10}$ 23. 0.3 ● 0.2   24. -0.3 ● -0.2

Compare the rational numbers in each pair by first expressing them with the same denominator.

25. $\frac{1}{2}, \frac{1}{4}$ 26. $\frac{1}{3}, \frac{1}{5}$ 27. $\frac{2}{3}, \frac{3}{5}$ 28. $\frac{3}{8}, \frac{2}{6}$

29. $\frac{-1}{4}, \frac{1}{-2}$ 30. $\frac{4}{-5}, \frac{-2}{3}$ 31. $\frac{4}{7}, \frac{6}{11}$ 32. $\frac{4}{11}, \frac{3}{10}$

33. $\frac{1}{-3}, \frac{2}{-5}$ 34. $\frac{3}{-7}, \frac{2}{-5}$ 35. $\frac{-2}{7}, \frac{-4}{9}$ 36. $-\frac{9}{13}, -\frac{11}{15}$

37–48. Use the shortcut to compare the numbers in Exercises **25–36**.

Ⓒ Equalities and inequalities are related as follows:

Let a, b, and k be real numbers and k be positive:

1. $a < b$ means there is a k so that $a + k = b$.
2. $a + k = b$ means $a < b$.

Use this definition to translate each inequality into an equality and vice versa.

49. $3 < 4$ 50. $-2 < -1$ 51. $7 < 9$

52. $-4 < 4$ 53. $-3 < 5$ 54. $-7.9 < 4.2$

55. $-3 + 4 = 1$ 56. $-6 + 3 = -3$ 57. $-5 + 11 = 6$

There are three properties of equality which you probably use often, perhaps without realizing it.

Let *a*, *b*, and *c* be any real numbers.

1. $a = a$ Reflexive prop. of $=$

2. If $a = b$, then $b = a$.   Symmetric prop. of $=$

3. If $a = b$ and $b = c$, then $a = c$.   Transitive prop. of $=$

Do the inequalities $<$ and $>$ also have similar properties? Look at the following examples for $<$. (You can easily find the same types of examples for $>$.)

$5 < 5$	◀ **False**
If $4 < 5$, then $5 < 4$.	◀ **False**
If $4 < 5$ and $5 < 6$, then $4 < 6$.	◀ **True**

From the first two examples, you can see that the inequality $<$ is neither reflexive nor symmetric. But, from the third example, it looks like $<$ may be transitive. Let's use a number line to look at more examples like the third one.

Statement	Graph of Numbers
If $-3 < 2$ and $2 < 4$, then $-3 < 4$.	
If $-6 < -2$ and $-2 < 3$, then $-6 < 3$.	
If $-8 < -5$ and $-5 < -2$, then $-8 < -2$.	

These examples suggest that the transitive property is true for $<$. (It is also true for $>$.)

Let *a*, *b*, and *c* be any real numbers.

1. If *a* < *b* and *b* < *c*, then *a* < *c*.

2. If *a* > *b* and *b* > *c*, then *a* > *c*.

Examples: Use the transitive properties to derive a new sentence from each of the following.

    1. $-2 < 5$ and $5 < 9$

    2. $3x + 2 > 4s - 1$ and $4s - 1 > 29$

SOLUTIONS:

1. $-2 < 5$ and $5 < 9$. Since the bold numerals are the same, we can conclude that

$$-2 < 9.$$

We are not amazed by the fact that $-2 < 9$, but it is important that new properties do not give results which conflict with known facts.

2. $3x + 2 > 4s - 1$ and $4s - 1 > 29$. Since the two bold expressions represent the same number (regardless of the replacement for *s*), we can conclude that

$$3x + 2 > 29.$$

Notice that $5 > 4$ and $4 < 5$ say the same thing about the order of 4 and 5. We can generalize as follows.

If *a* > *b* is true, then *b* < *a* is true.

If *b* < *a* is true, then *a* > *b* is true.

EXERCISES 4.3

all od problems

Ⓐ Tell what property each statement illustrates.

  1. $-5 = -5$ **2.** If $4 = 3 + 1$, then $3 + 1 = 4$.

  3. If $6 = 2 \cdot 3$, then $2 \cdot 3 = 6$.   **4.** If $x = 7$ and $7 = y$, then $x = y$.

  5. If $6 < a + 1$ and $a + 1 < x$, then $6 < x$.

Translate each $<$ inequality into a $>$ inequality, and vice versa.

6. $x < 2$ **7.** $y < 4$ **8.** $m > 7$

9. $a > 0$ **10.** $2x > 6$ **11.** $x - 1 < 17$

12. $-1 < 0$ **13.** $8 > 2y + 2$ **14.** $2y + 1 < 2y - 1$

Ⓑ Use the transitive properties to derive a new sentence.

15. $6 < 9$ and $9 < 21$ **16.** $-3 < 0$ and $0 < 5$

17. $5x < 12$ and $12 < 7x$ **18.** $2x < 4$ and $4 < y$

19. $14 = 7t$ and $7t = 7 + 7$ **20.** $12 = 4n$ and $4n = 8 + 4$

21. $5 - 7a > a$ and $a > 36$ **22.** $7 - 5b > b$ and $b > 16$

23. $-3x > -2d$ and $-2d > r$ **24.** $-17q > -2m$ and $-2m > q$

25. In swimming competition, Jodi's time was less than Connie's, and Connie's time was less than Vicki's. Vicki's time was 12 seconds. What can you conclude about Jodi's time?

26. Becky is shorter than her mother who is shorter than Bill. How do Becky and Bill compare in height?

27. Last summer Joel earned more money than Howard. Howard earned more than $150. How much did Joel earn?

28. Jim's baseball team has won more games than Ted's team, and Ted's team has won more than 8 games. What can you conclude about the number of games won by Jim's team?

Ⓒ What can we conclude from each statement? Explain your answer.

29. $x < y$ and $y < z$ and $z < w$.

30. $a > b$ and $b > c$ and $c > d$ and $d > e$.

4.4 SOLVING INEQUALITIES

An important property of inequalities is that we can add the same number to both sides of a true inequality and the resulting inequality will also be true.

Examples

$3 < 6$	$-3 < 5$	$-3 < -1$
$3 + 2 < 6 + 2$	$-3 + 7 < 5 + 7$	$-3 + (-6) < -1 + (-6)$
$5 < 8$	$4 < 12$	$-9 < -7$

Similar examples can be given for $>$.

addition properties of $<$ and $>$

Let a, b, and c be any real numbers.

1. If $a < b$, then $a + c < b + c$.

2. If $a > b$, then $a + c > b + c$.

We can use these properties to help solve inequalities.

Example 1: Solve $y + 2 < 5$. The replacement set is $\{-1, 0, 2, 4\}$.

SHORT SOLUTION:
$$y + 2 < \quad 5$$
$$\underline{+(-2) \quad +(-2)}$$
$$y < 3$$

DETAILED SOLUTION:

$y + 2 < 5$	Given
$[y + 2] + (-2) < 5 + (-2)$	Add. prop. of $<$
$[y + 2] + (-2) < 3$	Addition
$y + [2 + (-2)] < 3$	Assoc. prop. of $+$
$y + 0 < 3$	Inv. prop. of $+$
Solution set $\longrightarrow y < 3$	Ident. prop. of $+$
is $\{-1, 0, 2\}$.	

You should check the solutions in the given inequality.

Check:
$-1 + 2 < 5$	$0 + 2 < 5$	$2 + 2 < 5$
$1 < 5$	$2 < 5$	$4 < 5$

In the detailed solution we derived a sequence of equivalent open sentences, ending with a sentence whose solution set is obvious. The solution set is graphed below.

Example 2: Solve $3x + 7 > 4x$ with the set of real numbers as the replacement set.

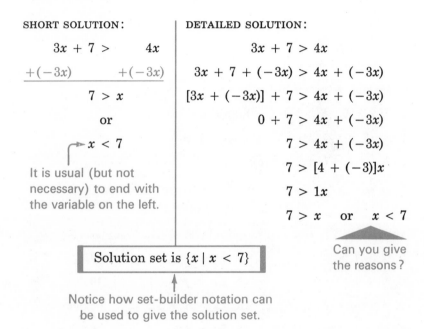

SHORT SOLUTION:

$$3x + 7 > 4x$$
$$\underline{+(-3x) +(-3x)}$$
$$7 > x$$

or

$$x < 7$$

It is usual (but not necessary) to end with the variable on the left.

DETAILED SOLUTION:

$$3x + 7 > 4x$$
$$3x + 7 + (-3x) > 4x + (-3x)$$
$$[3x + (-3x)] + 7 > 4x + (-3x)$$
$$0 + 7 > 4x + (-3x)$$
$$7 > 4x + (-3x)$$
$$7 > [4 + (-3)]x$$
$$7 > 1x$$
$$7 > x \quad \text{or} \quad x < 7$$

Can you give the reasons?

Solution set is $\{x \mid x < 7\}$

Notice how set-builder notation can be used to give the solution set.

Since the solution set is an infinite set, you cannot check every solution. Try a few values. The graph can help you choose appropriate values to check.

From now on, we will assume that the replacement set for each variable is the set of real numbers. Any exceptions will be called to your attention if not obvious.

replacement set agreement

Example 3: Solve $5t + 7 < 13 + 4t$.

SOLUTION:

$$5t + 7 < 13 + 4t$$
$$\underline{+(-4t) \qquad\qquad +(-4t)}$$
$$t + 7 < \qquad 13$$
$$\underline{+(-7) \quad +(-7)}$$
$$t < \qquad 6$$

The solution set is $\{t \mid t < 6\}$. (You should also check.)

EXERCISES 4.4

Ⓐ Which symbol, $<$ or $>$, should replace each ▓?

1. If $2 < 9$, then $2 + (-3)$ ▓ $9 + (-3)$.

2. If $13 > -1$, then $13 + 6$ ▓ $-1 + 6$.

3. If $-8.1 < -3.2$, then $6 + (-8.1)$ ▓ $6 + (-3.2)$.

4. If $\frac{3}{4} > \frac{1}{3}$, then $\frac{3}{4} + 18$ ▓ $\frac{1}{3} + 18$.

What would you add to both sides to solve each inequality below?

5. $x + 7 > 12$	**6.** $y + 2 > 14$	**7.** $x - 3 < -4$
8. $y - 7 < -9$	**9.** $2m < m - 4$	**10.** $4n < 3n - 8$
11. $4 > m + 4$	**12.** $11 > n + 11$	**13.** $6m > 7m + 9$
14. $11m > 10m - 4$	**15.** $3q > 2q - 20$	**16.** $5t > 6t - 8$

Ⓑ **17–20.** Solve and graph each inequality in Exercises 5–8. The replacement set is $\{-2, 0, 2, 4, 6\}$.

21–28. Solve and graph each inequality in Exercises 9–16. (Recall the replacement set agreement stated on page 119.)

Solve each inequality. (Remember to check your solutions!)

29. $-4x < -5x - 8$	**30.** $-3y < -4y + 7$
31. $-8a < -9a + 2$	**32.** $-5c < -6c - 9$
33. $8t - 6 > 9t + 4$	**34.** $9s + 5 > 10s - 7$

35. $6r + 9 < 5r - 3$

36. $12m - 8 < 11m + 6$

37. $\frac{5}{6}x + 7 < 1 - \frac{1}{6}x$

38. $\frac{3}{8}x + 2 < 3 - \frac{5}{8}x$

39. $-3.5x < -4.5x + 2.8$

40. $2.5x < 1.5x - 7.6$

© **41.** $3(2x - 8) < 5x$

42. $2(3y + 7) < 5y$

43. $7x > 8(x - 3)$

44. $9x > 2(5x - 3)$

45. $4(2t - 3) > 12t + 2$

46. $-3(6n + 2) > -11n - 1$

Supply the missing reasons for the following steps in verifying the addition property of $<$.

$a < b$	Given
$a + k = b$ (k is positive)	**47.** _____
$c + a + k = c + b$	**48.** _____
$c + a < c + b$	**49.** _____
$a + c < b + c$	**50.** _____

Both sides of a true inequality can be multiplied by the same number to obtain another true inequality. But, we must be careful!

Examples with a Positive Multiplier

$1 < 5$	$7 > 3$	$-8 < -\frac{1}{2}$
$2 \cdot 1 < 2 \cdot 5$	$5 \cdot 7 > 5 \cdot 3$	$3(-8) < 3(-\frac{1}{2})$
$2 < 10$	$35 > 15$	$-24 < -\frac{3}{2}$

When both sides of an inequality are multiplied by a *positive* number, the result is another inequality of the same type. But, if both sides of an inequality are multiplied by a *negative* number, the *order changes*.

Examples with a Negative Multiplier

$2 < 7$	$7 > -2$	$-10 < -\frac{1}{4}$
$-1 \cdot 2 > -1 \cdot 7$	$-3 \cdot 7 < -3(-2)$	$-8(-10) > -8(-\frac{1}{4})$
$-2 > -7$	$-21 < 6$	$80 > 2$

multiplication properties of $<$ and $>$

Let a, b, and c be any real numbers.

1. For c *positive:*
- If $a < b$, then $ca < cb$.
- If $a > b$, then $ca > cb$.

2. For c *negative:*
- If $a < b$, then $ca > cb$.
- If $a > b$, then $ca < cb$.

These properties can be used to solve inequalities.

Example 1: Solve $3x < 7$.

SHORT SOLUTION:

$$3x < 7$$
$$\underline{\times \tfrac{1}{3} \qquad \times \tfrac{1}{3}}$$
$$x < \tfrac{7}{3}$$

DETAILED SOLUTION:

$3x < 7$	Given
$\tfrac{1}{3}(3x) < \tfrac{1}{3}(7)$	Mult. prop. of $<$
$\tfrac{1}{3}(3x) < \tfrac{7}{3}$	Multiplication
$(\tfrac{1}{3} \cdot 3)x < \tfrac{7}{3}$	Assoc. prop. of $\cdot$
$1 \cdot x < \tfrac{7}{3}$	Inv. prop. of $\cdot$
$x < \tfrac{7}{3}$	Ident. prop. of $\cdot$

The solution set is $\{x \mid x < \tfrac{7}{3}\}$. (You should also check.)

Example 2: Solve $14 - 5y > 11$.

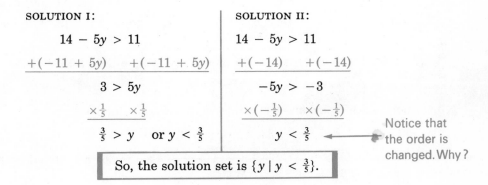

SOLUTION I:

$$14 - 5y > 11$$
$$\underline{+(-11 + 5y) \qquad +(-11 + 5y)}$$
$$3 > 5y$$
$$\underline{\times \tfrac{1}{5} \qquad \times \tfrac{1}{5}}$$
$$\tfrac{3}{5} > y \quad \text{or } y < \tfrac{3}{5}$$

SOLUTION II:

$$14 - 5y > 11$$
$$\underline{+(-14) \qquad +(-14)}$$
$$-5y > -3$$
$$\underline{\times (-\tfrac{1}{5}) \qquad \times (-\tfrac{1}{5})}$$
$$y < \tfrac{3}{5}$$

Notice that the order is changed. Why?

So, the solution set is $\{y \mid y < \tfrac{3}{5}\}$.

Example 3: Solve $-5x + 4 < 3x - 8$.

SOLUTION:
$$-5x + 4 < 3x - 8$$
$$-5x + 4 + [-3x + (-4)] < 3x - 8 + [-3x + (-4)]$$
$$-8x < -12$$
$$\text{or} \begin{cases} (-\tfrac{1}{8})(-12) < (-\tfrac{1}{8})(-8x) \\ (-\tfrac{1}{8})(-8x) > (-\tfrac{1}{8})(-12) \end{cases}$$

Either of these is correct for the fourth step. But be careful! Be sure the *order* or *sense* is correct.

$$x > \tfrac{12}{8}$$
$$x > \tfrac{3}{2}$$

So, the solution set is $\{x \mid x > \tfrac{3}{2}\}$.

EXERCISES 4.5

Ⓐ Which symbol, $<$ or $>$, should replace each ▒ ?

1. If $5 < 7$, then $5 \cdot 2$ ▒ $7 \cdot 2$.

2. If $-4 < 5$, then $(-4)(-2)$ ▒ $5(-2)$.

3. If $-8 < -2$, then $3(-8)$ ▒ $3(-2)$.

4. If $-3 < 12$, then $(-3)(-3)$ ▒ $(-3)12$.

5. If $\frac{1}{4} < \frac{1}{2}$, then $\frac{1}{4}(-3)$ ▒ $\frac{1}{2}(-3)$.

6. If $4.5 < 7.8$, then $3(4.5)$ ▒ $3(7.8)$.

What would you multiply both sides by to solve each inequality?

7. $3x < 15$	**8.** $4y < 12$	**9.** $4m > 7$	**10.** $6 > 5q$
11. $-6n > 12$	**12.** $7 > -2t$	**13.** $6q < 21$	**14.** $11n < 21$
15. $\frac{1}{3}r > 9$	**16.** $0.6 < 0.8s$	**17.** $-\frac{3}{4}m > 9$	**18.** $\frac{1}{5} > \frac{3}{5}y$

Ⓑ **19–30.** Solve and graph each inequality in Exercises 7–18.

Solve each inequality. (Remember to check your solution!)

31. $3 - 2t < 7$	**32.** $5 - 6g < 21$	**33.** $3r - 12 > 9$
34. $2s - 15 > 6$	**35.** $m - 1 > 9 - 4m$	**36.** $n - 3 > 7 - 4n$
37. $-7 < 5y - 8$	**38.** $-11 < 3x - 7$	**39.** $0 < 5m - 2$
40. $0 < 6n - 11$	**41.** $\frac{1}{3}x > \frac{4}{3}x$	**42.** $\frac{1}{4}y > \frac{5}{4}y$
43. $-6x + 8 > 0$		**44.** $0 < 5 - 9t$
45. $0.5x > 1.5x + 6.8$		**46.** $0.4y > 2.4y + 5.8$
47. $6m - 3 + 5m < 0$		**48.** $7n - 5 + 2n < 0$
Ⓒ **49.** $\frac{1}{2}(x + 2) < \frac{3}{2}x$		**50.** $\frac{1}{4}(y - 4) < \frac{5}{4}y$
51. $-3(a + 5) < 5(a - 3)$		**52.** $-7(c + 2) < 4(c - 3)$
53. $9(5 - 3x) > -4(3x + 3)$		**54.** $7(7 - 4t) > -5(2t + 5)$

Many problems in algebra and in everyday life involve inequalities.

Example 1: A summer camp needs a boat and motor. The Community Chest will donate the money on the condition that the camp spends less than $1500 for both. The camp decides to buy a boat for $1065. How much can be spent on the motor?

SOLUTION:

- Read the problem carefully.

- Choose a variable.

  Let x = cost of the motor. (in dollars)

  Then $x + 1065$ = cost of motor and boat. (in dollars)

- Determine how the cost of the motor, the cost of the boat, and the total money are related.

  (cost of the motor) + (cost of the boat) < total money

- Translate this relationship into an open sentence.

  $$x + 1065 < 1500$$

- Solve the open sentence and check your results.

  $x + 1065 < 1500$

  $x < 435$ So, solution set = $\{x \mid x < 435\}$.

  Since the solution set is an infinite set, you cannot check every solution. Try a few values.

- Interpret the solution.

  Since the solution set is $\{x \mid x < 435\}$, we conclude that the camp can spend some amount less than $435 for the motor.

Example 2: The sum of three consecutive *odd* integers is greater than 219. What is the smallest of the three integers?

SOLUTION:

- Read the problem carefully.

- Choose a variable.

  Let x = the smallest of the three integers.

  $x + 2$ = the second odd integer.

  $x + 4$ = the third odd integer.

- Make a sketch from the given information.

- Translate the problem into an open sentence.

  $$x + (x + 2) + (x + 4) > 219$$

IMPORTANT: The replacement set for x is limited to the set of odd integers. Why? By our replacement set agreement, the replacement set is usually the real numbers. But, in solving problems you must be alert to how the nature of the problem can limit the results.

- Solve the open sentence and interpret the solution.

  $$x + (x + 2) + (x + 4) > 219$$
  $$3x + 6 > 219$$
  $$3x > 213$$

  You should check a ⟶ $x > 71$
  few values to make
  sure that any number greater than 71
  will make the original sentence true.

  Since x must be an odd integer, the smallest of the three odd integers can be any member of $\{73, 75, 77, \cdots\}$.

EXERCISES 4.6

Ⓐ Translate each word sentence into an inequality.

1. 5 is greater than x.

2. 7 is less than y.

3. $y - 2$ is less than 3.

4. $2m$ is greater than 6.

Choose a variable and then translate each word sentence into an inequality.

5. A number is less than 10.

6. A number is greater than -6.

7. Three times a number is greater than 12.

8. Twice a number is less than -20.

9. Three times a number is less than the number increased by 12.

10. One-half a number is greater than the number plus 17.

11. Seven less than twice a number is greater than the number increased by 3.

12. Nineteen more than the product of 3 and a number is less than the number increased by 2.

Ⓑ Solve each problem.

13. The sum of a number and 12 is more than 3 times the number. What is the number?

14. The sum of 5 times a number and 5 is less than the number decreased by 9. What is the number?

15. Martha has more than 20 nickels and dimes. There are 7 more nickels than dimes. What is the smallest number of nickels that Martha might have?

16. The sum of two consecutive integers is less than 23. What is the smaller integer?

17. The sum of two consecutive odd integers is greater than 37. What is the smaller integer?

18. The supermarket will pay you $1.50 an hour for working after school and on weekends. What is the fewest number of hours you can work and earn more than $25.00 a week?

19. Hamburgers cost 25¢ and a Coke is 15¢. If you want to buy one Coke, what is the most hamburgers you could also buy and spend less than $1.00?

20. At a certain parking lot, you pay 75¢ for the first hour and 50¢ for each additional hour (or part of an hour). What is the greatest number of hours you could leave a car in the lot and still spend less than $3.00?

ⓒ **21.** To make a profit, a factory must produce 3 times as many radios as TV's. The number of radios must exceed the number of TV's by more than 5200. How many TV's should be produced?

22. Do Exercise **18** again, but this time assume the supermarket deducts a 15% income tax from your pay and you still want your take-home pay to be more than $25.00.

23. Do Exercise **19** again, but this time assume you must pay a 5% sales tax.

24. A man has $12,000 to invest. He decides to invest part of the money at 6% and the rest at 7%. How much of the $12,000 must he invest at 7% to get more than $750 in interest each year?

25. A salt solution that a food processor uses to preserve pickles must be more than 8% salt. By mistake, an employee adds too much water and ends up with 100 gallons of 6% salt solution. How much water must be evaporated from the solution to make it usable in preserving pickles?

Which symbol, $<$, $=$, or $>$, should replace each ◍ ?

1. 13 ◍ 8

2. 0 ◍ -11

3. -7 ◍ -6

4. 8 ◍ -1

5. $-\frac{1}{2}$ ◍ -0.5

6. -1.8 ◍ -8.1

7. $\frac{7}{12}$ ◍ $\frac{4}{5}$

8. $\frac{-4}{11}$ ◍ $\frac{1}{-4}$

9. $\frac{3}{-5}$ ◍ $\frac{4}{-7}$

Which property is illustrated by each of the following?

10. Either $2 < 1$, $2 = 1$, or $2 > 1$.

11. If $x + 2 > 5$, then $(x + 2) + (-2) > 5 + (-2)$.

12. If $6 > 3$ and $3 > -6$, then $6 > -6$.

Graph the solution set of each sentence.

13. $x < 5$

14. $x \neq -\frac{1}{2}$

15. $x \geq 4$

16. If $m < n$ and $n < p$, what can you conclude about m and p?

Solve and graph each sentence.

17. $x + 7 < 12$

18. $3x - 9 > 2x + 17$

19. $3x > 15$

20. $6x - 11 < 2x + 7$

21. $21 < 27x$

22. $9 - 3x > 4(2x - 1)$

23. Kim does baby-sitting on Friday nights and Saturdays for 75¢ an hour. Find the fewest number of hours she can baby-sit and earn more than $5.00 a week.

4.7 INTERSECTION AND UNION OF SETS

Two operations on sets are finding the *union* and the *intersection*. The union or intersection of two sets is a single set, just as a single number is the sum or product of two numbers.

▶ The **intersection** of two sets A and B, written $A \cap B$, is the set of members which are in *both A and B*.

▶ The **union** of two sets A and B, written $A \cup B$, is the set of members which are either in A **or** in B, **or** in both.

$A = \{1, 2, 3, 4\}$

$B = \{2, 4, 6, 8\}$

Sets A and B have some members in common. But, neither of these sets is a subset of the other.

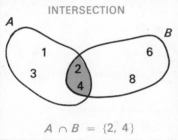

INTERSECTION

$A \cap B = \{2, 4\}$

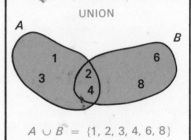

UNION

$A \cup B = \{1, 2, 3, 4, 6, 8\}$

$A = \{1, 3, 5\}$

$B = \{2, 4, 6\}$

Sets A and B have no common members. That is, A and B are *disjoint sets*.

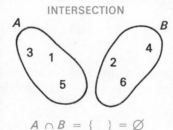

INTERSECTION

$A \cap B = \{ \ \} = \varnothing$

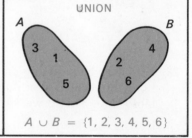

UNION

$A \cup B = \{1, 2, 3, 4, 5, 6\}$

$A = \{1, 3, 5\}$

$B = \{1, 2, 3, 4, 5\}$

Here, set A is a subset of set B. Note that $A \cap B = A$ and $A \cup B = B$.

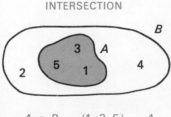

INTERSECTION

$A \cap B = \{1, 3, 5\} = A$

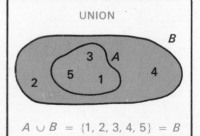

UNION

$A \cup B = \{1, 2, 3, 4, 5\} = B$

Example 1: $A = \{1, 3, 5, 7\}$ $B = \{2, 4, 6, 8\}$ $C = \{3, 4, 5, 6\}$

Find: **a.** $A \cap B$ **b.** $B \cap A$ **c.** $A \cap C$

d. $C \cap A$ **e.** $B \cap C$ **f.** $C \cap B$

SOLUTIONS: Using the definition of intersection, we get:

a. $A \cap B = \varnothing$ **b.** $B \cap A = \varnothing$

c. $A \cap C = \{3, 5\}$ **d.** $C \cap A = \{3, 5\}$

e. $B \cap C = \{4, 6\}$ **f.** $C \cap B = \{4, 6\}$

Example 2: $M = \{0, 1, 2, 3\}$ $N = \{0, 1, 2, 3, 4\}$ $P = \{0, 1, 2, 3, 4, 5\}$

Find: **a.** $M \cap N, M \cap P,$ and $N \cap P$

b. $M \cup N, M \cup P,$ and $N \cup P$

SOLUTIONS: Note that $M \subseteq N, M \subseteq P,$ and $N \subseteq P$. We find that:

a. $M \cap N = M, M \cap P = M,$ and $N \cap P = N$

b. $M \cup N = N, M \cup P = P,$ and $N \cup P = P$

> In general, if $A \subseteq B$, then
>
> $A \cap B = A$ and $A \cup B = B$.

EXERCISES 4.7

Ⓐ Find the intersection of the sets.

1. $\{1, 2\} \cap \{2, 3\}$ **2.** $\{2, 3\} \cap \{1, 2\}$

3. $\{2, 3\} \cap \{1, 2, 3, 4\}$ **4.** $\{1, 2, 3, 4\} \cap \{2, 3\}$

5. $\{3, 6, 9, 12\} \cap \{4, 8, 12, 16\}$ **6.** $\{4, 8, 12, 16\} \cap \{3, 6, 9, 12\}$

7. $\{-4, -2, 0\} \cap \{-2, 0, 2\}$ **8.** $\{-2, -1, 0, 1, 2\} \cap \{-1, 0, 1\}$

9. $\{1, 2, 3, \cdots\} \cap \{2, 4, 6, \cdots\}$ **10.** $\{3, 6, 9, \cdots\} \cap \{1, 2, 3, \cdots\}$

Find the union of the sets.

11. $\{1, 3\} \cup \{2, 4\}$ **12.** $\{2, 4\} \cup \{1, 3\}$

13. $\{2, 4\} \cup \{1, 2, 3, 4\}$ **14.** $\{1, 2, 3, 4\} \cup \{2, 4\}$

15. {4, 8, 12, 16} ∪ {2, 4, 6}　　**16.** {2, 4, 6} ∪ {4, 8, 12, 16}

17. {1, 2, 3, 4} ∪ {1, 3}　　**18.** {5, 10, 15, 20} ∪ {8, 10, 12}

19. {1, 3, 5,···} ∪ {2, 4, 6,···}　　**20.** {−2, −1, 0,···} ∪ {1, 2, 3,···}

Ⓑ Use the given sets to find each union or intersection.

$A = \{-8, -6, -4\}$　$B = \{-8, 6, -4\}$　$C = \{8, 6, 4\}$　$D = \{8, -6, 4\}$

21. $A \cap B$	**22.** $B \cap C$	**23.** $C \cap B$	**24.** $B \cap A$
25. $A \cap A$	**26.** $C \cap C$	**27.** $B \cup B$	**28.** $D \cup D$
29. $D \cup C$	**30.** $B \cup A$	**31.** $A \cup B$	**32.** $C \cup D$

Use the given sets to find each union or intersection.

$E = \{-3\}$　　$G = \{-9, -7, -5, -3\}$　　$I = \{integers\}$

$F = \varnothing$　　$H = \{-7, -5, 5, 7, 9, 11\}$

33. $E \cap F$	**34.** $F \cap H$	**35.** $E \cup G$	**36.** $E \cup I$
37. $G \cap H$	**38.** $H \cap G$	**39.** $F \cup G$	**40.** $F \cup H$
41. $I \cup G$	**42.** $H \cup I$	**43.** $F \cap I$	**44.** $G \cap I$

Ⓒ Grouping symbols are sometimes used when performing operations on sets. For example, $(A \cup B) \cap C$ means that we find the union of A and B first and then find the intersection of this set with C. Use the given sets to find the following.

$A = \{2, 4\}$　　$B = \{3, 5\}$　　$C = \{2, 3, 4, 5\}$　　$N = \{1, 2, 3,···\}$

45. $(A \cap B) \cap C$　　　　**46.** $A \cap (B \cap C)$

47. $(A \cup B) \cup C$　　　　**48.** $A \cup (B \cup C)$

49. $(A \cup N) \cup B$　　　　**50.** $A \cup (N \cup B)$

51. $(B \cap C) \cap N$　　　　**52.** $B \cap (C \cap N)$

53. $(A \cap B) \cup (A \cap C)$　　**54.** $(B \cap C) \cup (B \cap N)$

55. $(A \cup B) \cap (C \cap N)$　　**56.** $(A \cap B) \cup (C \cup N)$

Some Properties of Set Operations

$$A = \{1, 2, 4, 5\} \qquad B = \{2, 3, 4, 6\} \qquad C = \{1, 4, 6, 7\}$$

These sets and the ways they are related can be pictured as shown in the diagram. Are the following statements true?

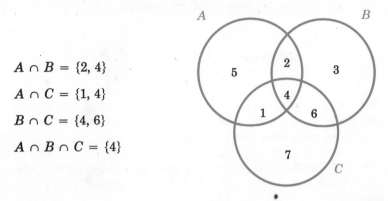

$A \cap B = \{2, 4\}$

$A \cap C = \{1, 4\}$

$B \cap C = \{4, 6\}$

$A \cap B \cap C = \{4\}$

Represent each of the following by shading a portion of a diagram like the one above.

1. $A \cup B$ 2. $B \cup A$

3. $A \cap B$ 4. $B \cap A$

5. $A \cap (B \cup C)$ 6. $(A \cap B) \cup (A \cap C)$

7. $A \cup (B \cap C)$ 8. $(A \cup B) \cap (A \cup C)$

The shaded area should be the same for **1** and **2**, **3** and **4**, **5** and **6**, and **7** and **8**. You might now predict that:

$A \cup B = B \cup A$ ←————— $\cup$ is commutative.

$A \cap B = B \cap A$ ←————— $\cap$ is commutative.

$A \cap (B \cup C) = (A \cap B) \cup (A \cap C)$ ←——— $\cap$ distributes over $\cup$.

$A \cup (B \cap C) = (A \cup B) \cap (A \cup C)$ ←——— $\cup$ distributes over $\cap$.

Each of these properties can be shown to be true in general.

4.8 SOLVING COMPOUND SENTENCES

In algebra, as in English, we can connect two simple sentences to form a compound sentence.

Compound Sentences	
"And" sentence	$5 < x$ and $x < 7$
"Or" sentence	$y < -3$ or $y > 4$

As you can see, an "and" sentence is formed by joining two sentences with the word *and*. For such a sentence to be true, *both* of the joined sentences must be true.

An "or" sentence is formed by joining two sentences with the word *or*. Such a sentence is true if *at least one* of the joined sentences is true.

Simple Sentences		"And" Sentence	"Or" Sentence
p	q	p and q	p or q
True	True	True	True
True	False	False	True
False	True	False	True
False	False	False	False

Consider the sentence

$$x > 5 \quad \text{and} \quad x < 7.$$

The graph for each of the two simple sentences is sketched alongside the number line below.

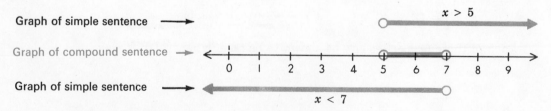

Graph of simple sentence $\longrightarrow$ $x > 5$

Graph of compound sentence $\rightarrow$

Graph of simple sentence $\longrightarrow$ $x < 7$

The points which are common to the graphs of the two simple sentences are shown in red. Notice that

$$\{x \mid x > 5 \text{ and } x < 7\} = \{x \mid x > 5\} \cap \{x \mid x < 7\}.$$

solving an "and" sentence

1. Find the solution sets of the two simple sentences.
2. Then, find the *intersection* of those sets.

Example 1: Solve and graph $2y > y - 3$ and $2y + 5 < 1$.

SOLUTION: $2y > y - 3$ and $2y + 5 < 1$

$y > -3$ and $2y < -4$

$y > -3$ and $y < -2$

So, the solution set is $\{y \mid y > -3\} \cap \{y \mid y < -2\}$.

Graph: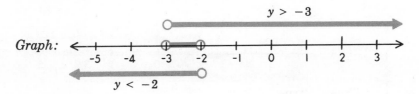

The sentence "$y > -3$ and $y < -2$" means the same as "$-3 < y$ and $y < -2$," which is often written in a shorter way as

$$-3 < y < -2.$$

So, the solution set found above can be described as

$$\{y \mid -3 < y < -2\}.$$

Now consider the sentence

$$x < -3 \quad \text{or} \quad x > 1.$$

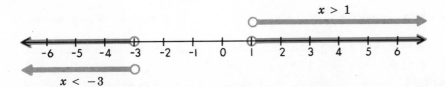

The points which are in the graphs of one or both of the simple sentences are shown in red. Notice that

$$\{x \mid x < -3 \text{ or } x > 1\} = \{x \mid x < -3\} \cup \{x \mid x > 1\}.$$

solving an "or" sentence

1. Find the solution sets of the two simple sentences.
2. Then, find the *union* of those sets.

Example 2: Solve and graph $3x + 5 > -1$ or $2x < x + 3$.

SOLUTION: $3x + 5 > -1$ or $2x < x + 3$

$$3x > -6 \text{ or } x < 3$$

$$x > -2 \text{ or } x < 3$$

So, the solution set is $\{x \mid x > -2\} \cup \{x \mid x < 3\}$. Notice that this is the set of all real numbers.

Graph:

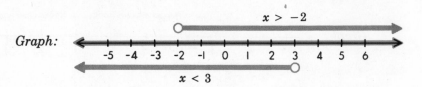

Each of the symbols $\leq$ and $\geq$ is actually a shortcut for writing an "or" sentence in which one of the simple sentences is an equality and the other is an inequality. For example:

$$y \leq -3 \quad \text{means} \quad y < -3 \quad \text{or} \quad y = 3.$$

$$x \geq 7 \quad \text{means} \quad x > 7 \quad \text{or} \quad x = 7.$$

EXERCISES 4.8

(A) Tell whether each compound sentence is true or false.

1. $2 < 4$ and $2 > 0$

2. $4 > 1$ and $3 < 2$

3. $6 > 4$ or $4 < 6$

4. $-5 < -2$ or $2 < 3$

5. $-2 < -8$ or $-2 > -1$

6. $2x + 1 > 2x$ or $x < x$

7. $6 < 4$ and $4 < 6$

8. $m > m$ and $2m < m + m$

Ⓑ Rewrite each compound sentence using "and" or "or." Indicate the solution set as a union or an intersection of sets. Then graph it.

Example: $x \geq 5$

    a. $x > 5$ or $x = 5$

    b. $\{x \mid x > 5\} \cup \{x \mid x = 5\}$

    c.

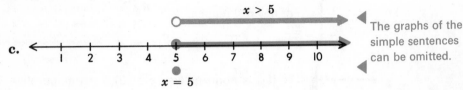

The graphs of the simple sentences can be omitted.

9. $x \leq -3$ **10.** $x \leq 7$ **11.** $x \geq 6$

12. $x \geq -5$ **13.** $-3 < x < 5$ **14.** $-4 < x < 12$

15. $7 > x > 3$ **16.** $-3 > x > -8$ **17.** $x \neq -5$

18. Express $\{x \mid 4 < x < a + 2\}$ as the intersection of two sets.

Find the solution set and graph each sentence.

19. $x < 5$ and $x > 3$ **20.** $y < 2$ and $y > -2$

21. $x < 5$ or $x > 3$ **22.** $y < 2$ or $y > -2$

23. $x = 3$ or $x = 7$ **24.** $y = -3$ or $y = -5$

25. $m = 3$ and $m = 12$ **26.** $n = 13$ and $n = -1$

27. $x > 5$ or $x > 7$ **28.** $p > -3$ or $p > 6$

29. $x < -3$ or $x > 3$ **30.** $s < 4$ or $s > 7$

31. $7x \leq x + 2$ **32.** $5y \leq 2y - 6$

33. $3x - 7 \geq 2$ **34.** $5y - 12 \geq 3$

35. $3x - 2 < 7$ or $x > 3x - 1$

36. $2x - 4 < 5$ or $x > 2x - 4$

37. $x - 7 < 12$ and $x + 2 = 3$

38. $7x - 3 < -3$ and $5x - 1 = 11$

Ⓒ **39.** $-2x + 7 = -5$ and $2x < x + 2$

40. $5(x - 3) + 2 < 7$ and $5x > 4(2x - 3)$

41. $2 - 5(2x - 3) > 2$ or $3x < 2(x - 8)$

The following definition will help you review the idea of *absolute value*.

> For any real number x:
> $$\text{If } x \geq 0, \text{ then } |x| = x.$$
> $$\text{If } x < 0, \text{ then } |x| = -x.$$

IMPORTANT IDEAS:

1. If x is nonnegative ($x \geq 0$), then its absolute value is x itself.

2. If x is negative ($x < 0$), then its absolute value is $-x$, its additive inverse (or opposite). In this case $-x$ *is positive*.

For example, $|7| = 7$ since $7 \geq 0$.

$|-3| = -(-3) = 3$ since $-3 < 0$.

$|0| = 0$ since $0 \geq 0$.

We can now translate open sentences involving absolute value into more familiar types of sentences.

Open Sentence	Translation	Graph
$|x| = 3$	$x = 3$ or $x = -3$	
$|x| < 3$	$-3 < x < 3$	
$|x| > 3$	$x > 3$ or $x < -3$	
$|x| \leq 3$	$x \leq 3$ and $x \geq -3$	
$|x| \geq 3$	$x \geq 3$ or $x \leq -3$	

Example 1: Solve and graph $|x + 7| = 4$.

    SOLUTION: $|x + 7| = 4$ means $x + 7 = 4$ or $x + 7 = -4$

$$x = -3 \text{ or } x = -11$$

Solution set: $\{-3, -11\}$

    Graph:

Example 2: Solve and graph $|x + 3| < 4$.

    SOLUTION: $|x + 3| < 4$ means $-4 < x + 3 < 4$

$$-4 < x + 3 \text{ and } x + 3 < 4$$

$$-7 < x \text{ and } x < 1$$

$$-7 < x < 1$$

Solution set: $\{x \mid -7 < x < 1\}$

    Graph:

Example 3: Solve and graph $|x - 7| \geq 4$.

    SOLUTION: $|x - 7| \geq 4$

$$x - 7 \geq 4 \text{ or } x - 7 \leq -4$$

$$x \geq 11 \text{ or } x \leq 3$$

Solution set: $\{x \mid x \geq 11 \text{ or } x \leq 3\}$

    Graph:

EXERCISES 4.9

Ⓐ Translate each sentence into an equivalent sentence without the absolute value symbol.

1. $|x| = 7$ **2.** $|y| = 6$ **3.** $|x| = \frac{1}{4}$ **4.** $|y| = \frac{1}{2}$

5. $|x| = 3.7$ **6.** $|y| = 8.3$ **7.** $|x| < 5$ **8.** $|t| < 8$

9. $|p| < \frac{3}{2}$ 10. $|q| < \frac{7}{8}$ 11. $|x| > 7$ 12. $|y| \le 9$

13. $|m| > \frac{1}{2}$ 14. $|n| \ge \frac{1}{4}$ 15. $|s| > 4.3$ 16. $|t| > 3.7$

Ⓑ 17–32. Solve and graph each sentence in Exercises 1–16.

Solve each open sentence.

33. $|x - 3| = 12$ 34. $|p - 2| = 7$ 35. $|m + 7| = 3$

36. $|n - 8| = 9$ 37. $|2m| = 6.8$ 38. $|2n| = 3.4$

39. $|x - 5| < 2$ 40. $|y - 7| < 4$ 41. $|m + 7| < 3.5$

42. $|n - 2| < 7.6$ 43. $|3t - \frac{1}{2}| < \frac{7}{2}$ 44. $|2s - \frac{3}{2}| < \frac{9}{2}$

45. $|4r - 2| < 8$ 46. $|3p - 6| < 7$ 47. $|c + 3| > 5$

48. $|d - 5| > 2$ 49. $|6 - c| \ge 2$ 50. $|4 - d| \le 7$

Ⓒ Examine each sentence very carefully. Then solve the sentence. (HINT: Can the absolute value of a real number ever be negative; that is, can it be less than 0 ?)

51. $|x| = 0$ 52. $|x| > 0$

53. $|x| < 0$ 54. $|x| = -2$

55. $|x| > -2$ 56. $|x| < -2$

The problems in this section involve the terms *at least*, *at most*, and *between*. These terms can be represented by symbols.

Example	Open Sentence	Equivalent Open Sentence
x is at least 2.	$x \geq 2$	$x > 2$ or $x = 2$
x is at most 7.	$x \leq 7$	$x < 7$ or $x = 7$
x is between -2 and 9.	$-2 < x < 9$	$-2 < x$ and $x < 9$

Example 1: A washing machine is 32 pounds heavier than the matching dryer. Together the two machines weigh at least 410 pounds. How much does the dryer weigh?

SOLUTION:

- Read the problem carefully.

- Choose a variable.

  Let $x =$ the weight of the dryer. (in pounds)

  Then $x + 32 =$ the weight of the washer. (in pounds)

- Now decide how these weights are related and translate the relationship into an open sentence.

  (weight of dryer) + (weight of washer) is at least 410

  $$x + (x + 32) \geq 410$$

- Solve the open sentence and check your results.

  $$x + (x + 32) \geq 410$$
  $$2x + 32 \geq 410$$
  $$2x + 32 > 410 \quad \text{or} \quad 2x + 32 = 410$$
  $$2x > 378 \quad \text{or} \quad 2x = 378$$
  $$x > 189 \quad \text{or} \quad x = 189$$
  $$x \geq 189$$

Is $189 + (189 + 32) \geq 410$? If x is greater than 189 is the sentence still true?

- Interpret the solution: The solution set is $\{x \mid x \geq 189\}$. Thus, we conclude that the dryer weighs 189 pounds or more.

Example 2: Sheila decides to buy a dress and shoes and spend at most $23. As she shops she buys a dress for $12.75. How much can she then spend for shoes?

SOLUTION:

Let x = dollars Sheila can spend for shoes. Then $12.75 + x$ = dollars Sheila spends. This must be at most $23. Thus we get the open sentence,

$$12.75 + x \leq 23.00.$$
$$12.75 + x < 23.00 \text{ or } 12.75 + x = 23.00$$
$$x < 10.25 \text{ or } x = 10.25$$

So, solution set = $\{x \mid x \leq 10.25\}$. We conclude that Sheila can pay $10.25 or less for shoes.

Example 3: What numbers satisfy the condition: If 6 times a number is increased by 7, the result is between 3 and 8?

SOLUTION: Let x be the number. Then $6x + 7$ denotes 6 times the number, increased by 7. This must represent a number between 3 and 8. So we get,

$$3 < 6x + 7 < 8.$$
$$3 < 6x + 7 \text{ and } 6x + 7 < 8$$
$$-4 < 6x \text{ and } 6x < 1$$
$$\tfrac{-4}{6} < x \text{ and } x < \tfrac{1}{6}$$
$$-\tfrac{2}{3} < x \text{ and } x < \tfrac{1}{6}$$

That is, $\qquad -\tfrac{2}{3} < x < \tfrac{1}{6}.$

Thus, the solution set is $\{x \mid -\tfrac{2}{3} < x < \tfrac{1}{6}\}$, and so the number must be between $-\tfrac{2}{3}$ and $\tfrac{1}{6}$.

EXERCISES 4.10

Ⓐ Translate each statement into an open sentence.

1. A number is at most 7.
2. A number is at most -3.
3. A number is at least -6.
4. A number is at least 5.
5. A number is between 0.25 and 0.75.
6. A number is between $\frac{1}{4}$ and $\frac{1}{2}$.
7. Four times a number is at most $\frac{2}{3}$.
8. Eight times a number is at most $-\frac{2}{3}$.
9. Two times a number is at least 6.
10. $\frac{3}{4}$ of a number is at least -3.
11. If 9 times a number is decreased by 2, the result is between -4 and 3.
12. If 4 times a number is increased by 4, the result is between $\frac{1}{2}$ and $\frac{1}{4}$.

Ⓑ 13–24. Solve and graph your open sentences for Exercises 1–12.

25. If a number is multiplied by 6 and then 8 is added to the result, the total is at least 50. Find the number.

26. The sum of two consecutive positive integers is at most 12. What are the integers?

27. Six times a number is between 12 and 24. Find the number.

For each graph, write the compound open sentence whose solution set is shown.

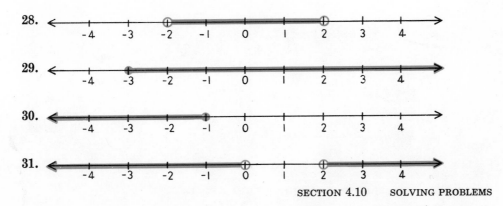

28.
29.
30.
31.

32. The drugstore will pay you $1.75 an hour for working part time on Saturdays and Sundays. How many hours must you work to earn at least $15.00 a week?

33. José and Leon plan to share the cost of buying a racing bike. Leon agreed to pay $17.00 more than José. The models they are interested in cost between $99.00 and $189.00. How much will José have to pay?

34. The length of a rectangle is twice its width. If the perimeter is between 10 meters and 22 meters, what are the possible values of the width?

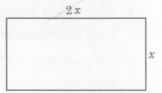

35. Separate 138 into two parts so that one part is greater than or equal to 2 more than $\frac{1}{2}$ the other part.

36. If 6 is added to a number the result is at least 13, and if 5 is subtracted from the same number the result is at most 9. Find the number.

37. A salesman is paid $5000 a year plus 5% of the amount of sales he makes. What must his sales amount to if his annual income is to be between $12,000 and $18,000?

38. If 6 times a number is added to 13 the result is between 5 and 25. Find the number.

39. Smiths had 4 gallons of paint on hand, and they bought more paint on 3 occasions, buying the same amount each time. Altogether they used between 22 and 28 gallons of paint and they had none left over. How much paint did they buy in each of the 3 purchases?

Graph the solution set of each sentence.

1. $m \neq 2$ **2.** $x > -1$ **3.** $s \leq 1.5$ **4.** $t \geq 0$

Which symbol, $<$, $=$, or $>$, should replace each ▦?

5. 6 ▦ 3 **6.** 1 ▦ -1 **7.** -0.8 ▦ -0.7

8. -4 ▦ 0 **9.** 0.5 ▦ $\frac{1}{2}$ **10.** -1.5 ▦ $\frac{3}{2}$

11. $\frac{1}{2}$ ▦ $\frac{1}{3}$ **12.** $-\frac{1}{4}$ ▦ $-\frac{1}{3}$ **13.** $\frac{4}{9}$ ▦ $\frac{5}{7}$

Translate each $<$ inequality into $>$ inequality, and vice versa.

14. $7 < m$ **15.** $x + 5 < 13$

16. $-2 > -8$ **17.** $2x - 1 > x + 3$

Use the transitive properties to derive a new sentence.

18. $3 < 4$ and $4 < 9$ **19.** $-5 > -8$ and $-8 > -11$

20. $2x = 14$ and $14 = 3m$ **21.** $12q < -2m$ and $-2m < 8$

Solve and graph.

22. $x + 3 < 7$ **23.** $y - 3 > 1$

24. $4x + 5 < 17$ **25.** $8 - 2x < 7x + 9$

26. $5x > 10$ **27.** $14 > 7m$

28. $3y < 21$ **29.** $3 - 4t < 11$

30. $\frac{1}{5}x > \frac{3}{5}x$ **31.** $0.3m < 2.7m + 1.2$

32. Pamela has 72 coins whose total value is less than $2.12. If each
of the coins is either a penny or a nickel, how many nickels might
there be?

33. If you are paid $1.25 an hour, how many hours must you work
to make more than $12.00?

34. If 7 times a number is decreased by 8, the result is less than 27.
Find the number.

4.7   If $M = \{-1, 1, 3, 5\}$, $N = \{-2, 0, 2, 4\}$, and $G = \{-2, 3\}$, find:

35. $M \cap G$ 36. $M \cap N$ 37. $N \cap G$

38. $M \cup G$ 39. $N \cup G$ 40. $M \cup N$

4.8   Solve and graph.

41. $x < 4$ and $x > 2$ 42. $y > 1$ or $y < -1$

43. $x \leq -2$ 44. $1 < m < 3$

4.9   45. $|y| = 4$ 46. $|x + 1| = 3$

47. $|x + 2| < 9$ 48. $|t - 2| \leq 4$

4.10   49. If 3 times a number is decreased by 5, the result is between 25 and 31. Find the number.

50. A salesman wants to spend at most $85.00 to buy gifts for two good customers. If he spends $38.50 for one gift, how much can he then spend for the other?

Which term best completes each sentence?

a. at most   **b.** between   **c.** intersection

d. union   **e.** inequality   **f.** absolute value

g. comparison property   **h.** transitive property of >

1. $7x + 1 < 6$ is a(n) _E_ .

2. "If $x > 6m$ and $6m > 9$, then $x > 9$" is an example of the _H_ .

3. $\{-2, -1, 0, 1, 2\}$ is the _D_ of $\{-1, 1\}$ and $\{-2, 0, 2\}$.

4. If x is negative, then $-x$ is the _f_ of x.

5. The sentence, $-2 < x < 3$, is read "x is _B_ -2 and 3."

Which symbol, < or >, should replace each ▦ ?

6. 2 ▦ 5   **7.** -1.2 ▦ -2.1 **8.** $\frac{-2}{3}$ ▦ $\frac{1}{4}$

9. If $x < 5$ and $5 < w$, then x ▦ w.

Solve and graph.

10. $x < -2$ **11.** $y \neq 3.5$ **12.** $x + 3 \leq 13$

13. $3n > 6$ **14.** $4m - 22 < 7m$ **15.** $|t| \geq 5$

If $A = \{-1, 0, 1\}$, $B = \{-3, -1, 1, 3\}$, and $C = \{-2, 0, 2\}$, find:

16. $A \cap B$ **17.** $A \cup C$ **18.** $B \cap \{0, 1, 2\}$

19. Five times a number is at least $\frac{2}{3}$. Find the number.

20. At a hamburger stand, you are told that by working 8 hours a week you can expect to earn between $12.00 and $15.00 in tips and wages. How much would you be earning an hour?

Suppose you wanted an electronic computer to find the solutions to the following inequality.

Inequality: $4x + 3 < 11$ **Replacement set:** $\{-2, 0, 2, 4, 6\}$

One of your first steps would be to outline a plan of how the computer might solve the inequality. You would probably make a **flow chart** like the one below.

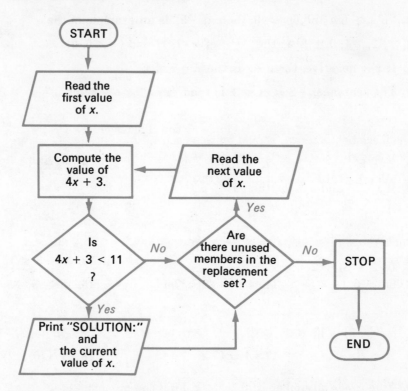

When this plan is properly translated into a language the computer understands, the computer would solve the inequality and produce the following "PRINT OUT."

SOLUTION: -2

SOLUTION: 0

Make a flow chart to show a plan for solving:

1. $x - 3 < 7$ **2.** $y + 5 \neq -1$ **3.** $2x - 7 \leq 11$

Exercises 1–8 refer to the following sets of integers.   Ch. 1

$M = \{-5, -6, -7, \cdots\}$ $N = \{3, 4, 5\}$ $S = \{x \mid x > -4\}$

$P = \{-3, -2, -1, 0, \cdots\}$ $T = \{-8, -9, -10\}$ $V = \{-3, -2, -1, 0\}$

Name *one* of the given sets to complete each statement correctly.

1. $S =$ _____   2. $T \subseteq$ _____

3. _____ $\subseteq$ {negative integers}   4. _____ is a finite set.

5. Sets N and _____ are equivalent.

6. The graph shows set _____.   Ex. 6

7. Set _____ is described in set-builder notation.

8. If S is the replacement set, _____ is the solution set of $x < 1$.

9. Evaluate $3x + 7$ using V above as the replacement set for x.

10. Graph $\{t \mid t > \frac{-1}{2}\}$, where t is a real number.

11. Which of the following does {rational numbers} contain?

    a. $|-5|$ **b.** $-\frac{7}{2}$ **c.** $-\frac{\pi}{2}$ **d.** $3\sqrt{2}$

Which property is illustrated by each sentence?   Ch. 2

12. $(-2 + 5) + 1 = -2 + (5 + 1)$ 13. $9 = 0 + 9$

14. $\frac{1}{7} \cdot 7 = 1$ 15. $-3 + 3 = 3 + (-3)$

16. $4(3 + 2) = 4 \cdot 3 + 4 \cdot 2$ 17. $(3 \cdot 2) \cdot 4 = 3 \cdot (2 \cdot 4)$

18. $-\frac{3}{5} + \frac{3}{5} = 0$ 19. $1 \cdot (-16) = -16$

Evaluate. (If the value is a fraction, express it in standard form.)

20. $-\frac{5}{8} + \frac{-3}{8}$ 21. $-7 - (-3)$ 22. $7 \cdot 5$

23. $7 \div 3.5$ 24. $-4 \cdot 6$ 25. $(-\frac{5}{9})(-\frac{1}{2})$

26. $-4 - 15$ 27. $24(\frac{1}{3} + \frac{1}{2})$ 28. $16 - (-\frac{9}{3})$

29. $\frac{7}{11} - \frac{4}{11}$ 30. $21 \div (-3)$ 31. $-\frac{3}{2} \div (-\frac{4}{9})$

32. $(-\frac{1}{2} + \frac{1}{2}) + 6$ 33. $-24 \div 3$ 34. $\frac{5}{3} + (-\frac{2}{3})$

35. $7 \cdot 79 + 3 \cdot 79$ 36. $(4.1 + 3.2) \cdot 0$ 37. $0 \div (4 - 7)$

38. Identify the exponent and the base in each expression.

  a. x^2 **b.** -3^5 **c.** $2(mn)^2$ **d.** $4xy^3$ **e.** $(-2)^4$

Simplify each expression.

39. $-12b^2d + 3b^2d$ **40.** $(9t^2)(-2t)$ **41.** $4 \cdot 3sm \cdot 2s^2$

42. $4r - 2t - 3r$ **43.** $3(2m + n) - 2(2m + n)$

Solve. Let {rational numbers} be the replacement set.

44. $4x + 3 = 6$ **45.** $x + 7 = -3$

46. $x - \pi = 0$ **47.** $5x - 3 = 7x + 5$

48. $9(x + 12) = 3(36 + 3x)$ **49.** $6(x + 1) = 3(2x + 4)$

50. Write a formula for the number of feet (f) an object has fallen if this is 16 times the square of the time (t) the object has fallen (in seconds).

51. Find three consecutive integers whose sum is 54.

Assume n is positive. Using the properties of $<$, determine in each case whether $m < n$ or $n < m$.

52. $m - 5 < n - 5$ **53.** $3m < 3n$ **54.** $m + n < 2n$

55. $mn < n^2$ **56.** $-m < -n$ **57.** $m < 0$

Solve each sentence and graph the solution set.

58. $-3s < 14$ **59.** $7t + 2 < 3t + 14$ **60.** $y = 3$ or $2y = 10$

61. $2x \neq 8$ **62.** $8r + 5 \geq 9r + 7$ **63.** $5m = 20$ and $m > 4$

64. $13n \leq 39$ **65.** $4 < 2t < 8$ **66.** $3|x| > 9$

67. The Green Thumb Glove Company has enough yarn to make one pair more of red gloves than of blue gloves. There is enough yarn altogether to make more than 32 gloves, but fewer than 36. How many gloves of each color can they make?

Ex. 68

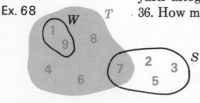

68. From the illustration, determine:

  a. $S \cup T$ **b.** $S \cap T$ **c.** $S \cup W$

  d. $S \cap W$ **e.** $T \cup W$ **f.** $T \cap W$

A Closer Look
at Real Numbers

The student shown above is taking a rather long look at a certain
real number.

You are studying the algebra of real numbers. And now is a good
time to consider these numbers in more detail.

5.1 POWER OF A PRODUCT

In Chapter 3, you saw that when multiplying powers with the same base, you can add exponents. For example,

$$3^2 \cdot 3^5 = 3^{2+5} = 3^7.$$

In general,

multiplication of powers

Let a be any real number, and let m and n be any positive integers. Then,

$$a^m \cdot a^n = a^{m+n}.$$

Another useful property of powers can be developed for working with powers of products.

$$
\begin{aligned}
(2 \cdot 5)^3 &= (2 \cdot 5)(2 \cdot 5)(2 \cdot 5) &\quad \text{Def. of exponent} \\
&= (2 \cdot 2 \cdot 2)(5 \cdot 5 \cdot 5) &\quad \text{Comm. and assoc. props. of } \cdot \\
&= 2^3 \cdot 5^3 &\quad \text{Def. of exponent}
\end{aligned}
$$

In general,

power of a product

Let a and b be any real numbers, and let m be any positive integer. Then,

$$(a \cdot b)^m = a^m \cdot b^m.$$

Notice that in the first property above all bases must be the same number, but the exponents need not. In the second property all exponents must be the same number, but the bases need not.

Examples: Simplify each expression. (Each base is a real number.)

1. $b^2 \cdot b^3$ 2. $(4t)^3$ 3. $(-2y)^3(-2y)^5$ 4. $(xy)^3 y^2$

SOLUTIONS:

1. $\begin{aligned} b^2 \cdot b^3 &= b^{2+3} &\quad \text{Multiplication of powers} \\ &= b^5 \end{aligned}$

2. $(4t)^3 = 4^3 \cdot t^3$ Power of a product

       or $64t^3$

3. $(-2y)^3(-2y)^5 = (-2y)^8$ Multiplication of powers

                   $= (-2)^8 y^8$ Power of a product

                 or $256y^8$

4. $(xy)^3 y^2 = (x^3 \cdot y^3)y^2$ Power of a product

              $= x^3(y^3 \cdot y^2)$ Associative property of $\cdot$

              $= x^3 \cdot y^{3+2}$ Multiplication of powers

              $= x^3 \cdot y^5$

EXERCISES 5.1

Ⓐ Give the name of the property of powers illustrated by each equation. (Each base is a real number.)

1. $5^4 \cdot 5^3 = 5^{4+3}$ **2.** $2 \cdot 2^3 = 2^{1+3}$

3. $(2 \cdot 5)^5 = 2^5 \cdot 5^5$ **4.** $(rs)^8 = r^8 \cdot s^8$

5. $3^4 \cdot y^4 = (3y)^4$ **6.** $(5r)^2(5r)^5 = (5r)^7$

7. $w^8 = w^6 \cdot w^2$ **8.** $a^2 \cdot a^2 = a^{2+2}$

9. $a^2 \cdot a^2 = (a \cdot a)^2$ **10.** $(-4z)^3 = (-4)^3 z^3$

Simplify each expression. (Each base is a real number.)

11. $y^8 \cdot y^3$ **12.** $m^5 \cdot m$ **13.** $(4b)^2$

14. $(3q)^3$ **15.** $4 \cdot 4^2$ **16.** $3 \cdot 3^2$

Ⓑ **17.** $(-3)^2(-3)^3$ **18.** $(-2)^2(-2)^3$ **19.** $(-1)^3(-1)^5$

20. $(-1)^7(-1)^3$ **21.** $(2x)^3$ **22.** $(3x)^2$

23. $(-2s)^3$ **24.** $(-3r)^2$ **25.** $(-2m)^2$

26. $(-3k)^3$ **27.** $(-2s)^5$ **28.** $(-3r)^4$

29. $x^{18} \cdot x^4$ **30.** $y^7 \cdot y^{11}$ **31.** $(9y)(9y)$

32. $(6x)(6x)$ **33.** $(-7m)(-7m)$ **34.** $(-5q)(-5q)$

HINT: For Exercises 35–42, recall that

$$-3^2 = -1 \cdot 3^2 = -9 \quad \text{but} \quad (-3)^2 = (-3)(-3) = 9.$$

35. $-3^2 \cdot 3^3$ **36.** $-2^4 \cdot 2^3$ **37.** $-3^2 \cdot 3^4$

38. $-2^4 \cdot 2^2$ **39.** $(-3)^2(-3)^4$ **40.** $(-2)^4(-2)^2$

41. $(-6)^2(-6)$ **42.** $(-4)^3(-4)$ **43.** $x^4(xy)^2$

44. $(rs)^3 s^4$ **45.** $(km)^5 k^3$ **46.** $c^4(dc)$

47. $(x^2y^3)(x^3y^2)$ **48.** $(s^4t^3)(s^2t^3)$ **49.** $(x^3y^5)(y^2x^6)$

50. $(t^5s^4)(s^5t^3)$ **51.** $(m^2n^3)(m^3n^5)$ **52.** $(x^5y^2)(x^2y^3)$

53. $(m^2n)(mn^2)$ **54.** $(xy^3)(x^3y)$ **55.** $(rs)^2(rs)^4$

56. $(mn)^4(mn)^2$ **57.** $(3z)^3(3z)^2$ **58.** $(2x)^4(2x)^3$

59. $(5m)^3(2m)^4$ **60.** $(4r)^2(3r)^3$ **61.** $(4s^5)(7s^4)$

62. $(6r^8)(5r^4)$ **63.** $(-2x^3)(7x^5)$ **64.** $(-5m^6)(-3m^3)$

65. $(2s^3t^4)(3s^2t^3)$ **66.** $(5x^5y^3)(4y^2x^3)$ **67.** $(-2m^3n^2)(-7m^2n^4)$

68. $(6x^5y^3)(-3x^3y^2)$ **69.** $(-3r)^2(-3r)^3$ **70.** $(-2s)^4(-2s)^3$

© **71.** $s^7 \cdot s^2 \cdot s^3$ **72.** $x^3 \cdot x^6 \cdot x$ **73.** $y^7 \cdot (-y^6) \cdot y$

74. $-t^4 \cdot t^5 \cdot t^2$ **75.** $(xyz)^2(xyz)^3$ **76.** $(rst)^6(rst)^2$

77. $(-s)(-4s)^3(2s)^2$ **78.** $(-2r)^4(3r)^3(-1)$

79. $(-4x^2y)(-x^2y^3)(-5y^4)$ **80.** $(-2a^3cd^2)(-acd)^3(8a^2b)$

81. $(-3rs^2)(-r^3s^2)(-8r^5)$ **82.** $(4x^2)(2x)^2(-3x^4)$

Simplify each expression. (Each base is a real number, and each exponent is a positive integer.)

83. $3^x \cdot 3^{2x+4}$ **84.** $4^y \cdot 4^{y-3}$

85. $a^2(a^{x+1} + a^y)$ **86.** $b^3(b^q + b^{n+2})$

We say that we have *factored* 12 when we express 12 as the product of two or more integers (for example, $12 = 3 \cdot 4$). We call 3 and 4 **factors** (or **divisors**) of 12. Notice that 12 can be factored as the product of different pairs of *positive* integers.

$$12 = 1 \cdot 12 \qquad 12 = 2 \cdot 6 \qquad 12 = 3 \cdot 4$$

However, 7 can be factored as the product of only a single pair of *positive* integers.

$$7 = 1 \cdot 7$$

Any integer, greater than 1, whose only positive integer factors are itself and 1 is a **prime** number.

Thus, 7 is prime, but 12 is not. The first ten primes are:

$$2 \quad 3 \quad 5 \quad 7 \quad 11 \quad 13 \quad 17 \quad 19 \quad 23 \quad 29$$

An integer that is not prime can be factored as a product of primes.

Example 1: Factor 90 as a product of primes.

SOLUTION: Starting with any pair of factors, such as "9 and 10" or "3 and 30," you can proceed as below.

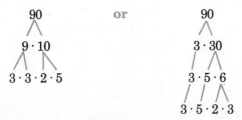

Notice that, except for the order in which they are listed, the same prime factors have been found in both cases above. This illustrates the following important property of positive integers.

Any positive integer that is not prime can be factored as a product of primes in only one way, except for the order of the factors.

Example 2: Completely factor -140.

SOLUTION: First, you can factor -140 as $-1 \cdot 140$. Then you can factor 140 by the method in Example **1**. Another way to do the factoring follows.

$$
\begin{aligned}
-140 &= -1 \cdot 140 \\
&= -1 \cdot 2 \cdot 70 \\
&= -1 \cdot 2 \cdot 2 \cdot 35 \\
&= -1 \cdot 2 \cdot 2 \cdot 5 \cdot 7 \\
&= -1 \cdot 2^2 \cdot 5 \cdot 7
\end{aligned}
$$

Notice that the primes are "factored out" in order, proceeding until the last factor is prime. Then exponent form is used to state the result.

EXERCISES 5.2

Ⓐ Tell whether or not each integer is prime.

1. 5	**2.** 6	**3.** 8	**4.** 11	**5.** 9
6. 13	**7.** 15	**8.** 17	**9.** 19	**10.** 33

Express each of the following in exponent form.

11. $2 \cdot 2 \cdot 3$ **12.** $-1 \cdot 2 \cdot 3 \cdot 3$ **13.** $-1 \cdot 2 \cdot 2 \cdot 3 \cdot 3$

14. $2 \cdot 2 \cdot 2 \cdot 3 \cdot 3$ **15.** $-1 \cdot 2 \cdot 2 \cdot 2 \cdot 3 \cdot 3 \cdot 5$ **16.** $3 \cdot 3 \cdot 5 \cdot 5 \cdot 5 \cdot 7 \cdot 7$

Completely factor each integer, expressing each result in exponent form.

17. 6	**18.** -9	**19.** 8	**20.** -10
21. -25	**22.** -49	**23.** 12	**24.** 18
Ⓑ **25.** -24	**26.** -36	**27.** 81	**28.** 32
29. 100	**30.** 150	**31.** -125	**32.** -75

33. 135	34. 245	35. 48	36. 42
37. −64	38. −72	39. 128	40. 144
41. 200	42. 300	43. −250	44. −350
45. −216	46. −192	47. 600	48. 750
49. 224	50. 168	51. −121	52. −169
53. −363	54. −338	55. 625	56. 343
© 57. 221	58. 187	59. −399	60. −391

A method for finding all primes less than a certain number is considered below. First, list the numbers 2, 3, 4, 5, · · ·, 29.

61. The first prime you have listed is _____.

62. Every second number after the first prime contains _____ as a factor. Thus, each of these numbers (is, is not) prime, and you should cross them off the list:

②, 3, 4̸, 5, 6̸, 7, 8̸, 9, 1̸0̸, 11, 1̸2̸, · · ·, 29.

63. The next prime is _____.

64. Every third number after the second prime contains _____ as a factor. Cross these numbers off the list:

②, ③, 4̸, 5, 6̸, 7, 8̸, 9̸, 1̸0̸, 11, 1̸2̸, · · ·, 29.

65. Some numbers, like 6 and 12, would be crossed off twice. Why?

66. The next prime is _____.

67. Which numbers would you cross off now?

68. The next prime is _____.

69. All numbers that contain any combination of 2, 3, and 5 as factors would already have been eliminated. So the next number that is not prime would have to be 7 · _____ or _____.

70. But your list goes up to only 29. So the remaining numbers must be _____.

71. Using the preceding method, find all primes less than 100.

72. Using reference books, find out who *Eratosthenes* was, and what the method used above for finding primes is called.

An Unsolved Problem

Consider the expression $n^2 - n + 11$, where the replacement set for n is $\{1, 2, 3, 4, 5, \cdots\}$.

If $n =$	$n^2 - n + 11 =$
1	$1^2 - 1 + 11$ or 11
2	$2^2 - 2 + 11$ or 13
3	$3^2 - 3 + 11$ or 17

Notice that each value found for $n^2 - n + 11$ above is prime. Do you think that this expression produces a prime number for every member of the replacement set?

Mathematicians have tried to find an expression which would result in a prime when it is evaluated for *any* positive integer. As yet, no one has succeeded.

The expression above fails to produce a prime for $n = 11$ because

$$11^2 - 11 + 11 = 121 \qquad \text{and} \qquad 121 = 11 \cdot 11.$$

A similar expression,

$$n^2 - n + 41,$$

yields primes for $n = 1$ through $n = 40$ but fails for $n = 41$. Still another expression is

$$n^2 - 79n + 1601.$$

If you are curious as to the smallest positive integer for which this expression fails, you will have to find out on your own.

You might guess that the answer is 1601. But it is really much less than that. Even so, to find the answer by computing would involve a lot of work, and you would need a list of primes. A much easier way is to read the following reference.

Eves, Howard, *An Introduction to the History of Mathematics*, 3rd ed., New York: Holt, Rinehart and Winston, 1969, pages 148–149.

When reducing a fraction to lowest terms, you find the *greatest common factor* of the numerator and denominator. Prime factors can be very useful for this purpose.

Example 1: Express $\frac{84}{-180}$ in standard form.

SOLUTION:

$$\frac{84}{-180} = -\frac{84}{180}$$

First, take care of the sign.

$$= -\frac{2^2 \cdot 3 \cdot 7}{2^2 \cdot 3^2 \cdot 5}$$

Completely factor both numerator and denominator.

$$= -\frac{(2^2 \cdot 3) \cdot 7}{(2^2 \cdot 3) \cdot 3 \cdot 5}$$

Find the greatest common factor by grouping the common prime factors.

$$= -\frac{(2^2 \cdot 3)}{(2^2 \cdot 3)} \cdot \frac{7}{3 \cdot 5}$$

$$= -1 \cdot \frac{7}{15} = -\frac{7}{15}$$

In a similar way, prime factors are also useful when multiplying or dividing with fractions.

Example 2: Find the product $\left(-\frac{8}{15}\right)\left(-\frac{21}{32}\right)$.

SHORT SOLUTION:

$$\left(-\frac{8}{15}\right)\left(-\frac{21}{32}\right) = \frac{\overset{1}{\cancel{8}} \cdot \overset{7}{\cancel{21}}}{\underset{5}{\cancel{15}} \cdot \underset{4}{\cancel{32}}}$$

$$= \frac{1 \cdot 7}{5 \cdot 4}$$

$$= \frac{7}{20}$$

Notice that no prime factors are common to the numerator and denominator.

DETAILED SOLUTION:

$$\left(-\frac{8}{15}\right)\left(-\frac{21}{32}\right) = \frac{8 \cdot 21}{15 \cdot 32}$$

$$= \frac{2^3 \cdot 3 \cdot 7}{3 \cdot 5 \cdot 2^5}$$

$$= \frac{(2^3 \cdot 3) \cdot 7}{(2^3 \cdot 3) \cdot 2^2 \cdot 5}$$

$$= \frac{(2^3 \cdot 3)}{(2^3 \cdot 3)} \cdot \frac{7}{2^2 \cdot 5}$$

$$= 1 \cdot \frac{7}{20} = \frac{7}{20}$$

Example 3: Find the quotient $\frac{25}{12} \div (-\frac{15}{16})$.

SHORT SOLUTION: | DETAILED SOLUTION:

$$\frac{25}{12} \div \left(-\frac{15}{16}\right) = -\left(\frac{25}{12} \cdot \frac{16}{15}\right)$$

$$= -\frac{\overset{5}{\cancel{25}} \cdot \overset{4}{\cancel{16}}}{\underset{3}{\cancel{12}} \cdot \underset{3}{\cancel{15}}}$$

$$= -\frac{5 \cdot 4}{3 \cdot 3}$$

$$= -\frac{20}{9}$$

Notice that no prime factors are common to the numerator and denominator.

$$\frac{25}{12} \div \left(-\frac{15}{16}\right) = -\left(\frac{25}{12} \cdot \frac{16}{15}\right)$$

$$= -\frac{5^2 \cdot 2^4}{2^2 \cdot 3 \cdot 3 \cdot 5}$$

$$= -\frac{(2^2 \cdot 5) \cdot 2^2 \cdot 5}{(2^2 \cdot 5) \cdot 3^2}$$

$$= -\frac{(2^2 \cdot 5)}{(2^2 \cdot 5)} \cdot \frac{2^2 \cdot 5}{3^2}$$

$$= -1 \cdot \frac{2^2 \cdot 5}{3^2}$$

$$= -\frac{20}{9} \quad (\text{or } -2\frac{2}{9})$$

EXERCISES 5.3

Ⓐ In each case, find the greatest common factor of the numerator and denominator, giving your answer in exponent form. Then change the fraction to standard form.

1. $\dfrac{2 \cdot 3}{3 \cdot 5}$

2. $\dfrac{2 \cdot 3^2}{3^2 \cdot 5}$

3. $\dfrac{2 \cdot 3}{3^2 \cdot 5}$

4. $\dfrac{2 \cdot 3 \cdot 5}{2 \cdot 5 \cdot 7}$

5. $\dfrac{2^3 \cdot 3^2}{2^2 \cdot 3^3}$

6. $\dfrac{3^3 \cdot 5^2}{3^2 \cdot 5^3}$

7. $\dfrac{2^4 \cdot 3^2}{2^2 \cdot 3^2 \cdot 5}$

8. $\dfrac{3^3 \cdot 5^2 \cdot 7}{3^4 \cdot 5^3}$

9. $\dfrac{5^2 \cdot 7^2}{5^3 \cdot 7}$

10. $\dfrac{2^2 \cdot 3^4 \cdot 7}{2^3 \cdot 3^5}$

11. $\dfrac{5^2 \cdot 7^3 \cdot 11}{5 \cdot 7^5}$

12. $\dfrac{2^3 \cdot 3^5 \cdot 17}{2^4 \cdot 3^5 \cdot 11}$

Change each fraction to standard form.

13. $\frac{2}{4}$

14. $\frac{-3}{9}$

15. $\frac{4}{-12}$

16. $\frac{30}{40}$

17. $\frac{9}{6}$

18. $\frac{-6}{12}$

19. $\frac{16}{24}$

20. $\frac{27}{-6}$

Ⓑ 21. $\frac{12}{18}$

22. $\frac{18}{24}$

23. $\frac{-18}{36}$

24. $\frac{-24}{42}$

25. $\frac{12}{27}$ 26. $\frac{18}{27}$ 27. $\frac{27}{-21}$ 28. $\frac{42}{-27}$

29. $\frac{65}{70}$ 30. $\frac{72}{75}$ 31. $\frac{-96}{63}$ 32. $\frac{-72}{63}$

33. $\frac{48}{72}$ 34. $\frac{24}{84}$ 35. $\frac{75}{-90}$ 36. $\frac{56}{-70}$

Find each product and express it in standard form.

37. $\frac{3}{22} \cdot \frac{11}{9}$ 38. $\frac{13}{25} \cdot \frac{5}{39}$ 39. $\frac{-4}{15} \cdot \frac{5}{6}$

40. $\frac{7}{16} \cdot \frac{-8}{9}$ 41. $\left(-\frac{7}{12}\right)\left(-\frac{15}{28}\right)$ 42. $\left(-\frac{15}{28}\right)\left(-\frac{7}{25}\right)$

43. $\frac{15}{4} \cdot \frac{12}{5}$ 44. $\frac{14}{9} \cdot \frac{6}{7}$ 45. $\left(-\frac{18}{49}\right)\left(\frac{14}{27}\right)$

46. $\left(\frac{16}{33}\right)\left(-\frac{11}{32}\right)$ 47. $\frac{36}{65} \cdot \frac{13}{27}$ 48. $\frac{20}{33} \cdot \frac{44}{25}$

49. $\frac{-18}{35} \cdot \frac{35}{18}$ 50. $\frac{42}{12} \cdot \frac{-12}{42}$ 51. $\frac{65}{72} \cdot \frac{56}{39}$

52. $\frac{64}{81} \cdot \frac{27}{56}$ 53. $\frac{63}{-64} \cdot \frac{-40}{91}$ 54. $\frac{-34}{35} \cdot \frac{21}{-85}$

Find each quotient and express it in standard form.

55. $\frac{7}{12} \div \frac{7}{9}$ 56. $\frac{5}{12} \div \frac{5}{8}$ 57. $\frac{-13}{18} \div \frac{26}{9}$

58. $\frac{-11}{16} \div \frac{33}{8}$ 59. $\frac{1}{8} \div \frac{-7}{24}$ 60. $\frac{1}{7} \div \frac{-9}{28}$

61. $\frac{34}{45} \div \left(-\frac{51}{20}\right)$ 62. $\left(-\frac{48}{49}\right) \div \frac{36}{35}$ 63. $\frac{55}{52} \div \frac{88}{39}$

64. $\frac{35}{96} \div \frac{65}{84}$ 65. $\left(-\frac{13}{19}\right) \div \left(-\frac{26}{38}\right)$ 66. $\left(-\frac{17}{23}\right) \div \left(-\frac{51}{46}\right)$

67. $\frac{38}{75} \div \frac{57}{50}$ 68. $\frac{23}{55} \div \frac{69}{44}$ 69. $\frac{-21}{-62} \div \frac{63}{58}$

70. $\frac{28}{29} \div \frac{-42}{-58}$ 71. $\frac{13}{48} \div \frac{65}{72}$ 72. $\frac{70}{27} \div \frac{80}{81}$

© Change each fraction to standard form. (Each letter represents a prime number.)

73. $\dfrac{2^3 b^2}{2^2 b^3}$ 74. $\dfrac{3^2 x^3}{3^3 x^4}$ 75. $\dfrac{2^3 3^3 a^2}{2^3 3^2 a^3}$

76. $\dfrac{5^2 c^3 d^2}{5c^2 d^3}$ 77. $\dfrac{-7rs^3}{7^2 r^2 s}$ 78. $\dfrac{11x^3 y^5}{-11^2 xy^3}$

79. $\dfrac{a^3 b^2 c^5}{a^4 b^2 c^3}$ 80. $\dfrac{rs^5 t^3}{r^4 s^3 t^4}$ 81. $\dfrac{x^3 y^3 z^2}{x^4 y^4 z^3}$

82. $\dfrac{m^5 n^3 v}{m^2 n^4}$ 83. $-\dfrac{k^7 m^6}{m^5 v^3}$ 84. $-\dfrac{u^2 v^3 w^2}{uvw}$

When adding or subtracting with fractions, you often find the *least common denominator* (**LCD**). Recall that the LCD is the least positive integer which contains each given denominator as a factor. Prime factors can be used to find the LCD.

Example 1: Find the sum $\frac{11}{24} + \frac{7}{20}$.

SOLUTION:

$$\frac{11}{24} + \frac{7}{20} = \frac{11}{2^3 \cdot 3} + \frac{7}{2^2 \cdot 5}$$

> Completely factor each denominator. Then choose the *greatest* power of each prime factor.

→ LCD is $2^3 \cdot 3 \cdot 5$.

$$= \frac{11 \cdot 5}{2^3 \cdot 3 \cdot 5} + \frac{7 \cdot 2 \cdot 3}{2^2 \cdot 5 \cdot 2 \cdot 3}$$

> Multiply the numerator and the denominator of each fraction by those prime factors that are in the LCD but not in the given denominator.

$$= \frac{55}{2^3 \cdot 3 \cdot 5} + \frac{42}{2^3 \cdot 3 \cdot 5}$$

$$= \frac{55 + 42}{2^3 \cdot 3 \cdot 5}$$

$$= \frac{97}{2^3 \cdot 3 \cdot 5} = \frac{97}{120}$$

> Since neither 2, 3, nor 5 is a factor of 97, the result is in standard form.

Example 2: Find the sum $-\frac{11}{12} + \frac{7}{15}$.

SOLUTION:

$$-\frac{11}{12} + \frac{7}{15} = \frac{-11}{2^2 \cdot 3} + \frac{7}{3 \cdot 5}$$

→ LCD is $2^2 \cdot 3 \cdot 5$.

$$= \frac{-11 \cdot 5}{2^2 \cdot 3 \cdot 5} + \frac{2^2 \cdot 7}{2^2 \cdot 3 \cdot 5}$$

$$= \frac{-55 + 28}{2^2 \cdot 3 \cdot 5}$$

$$= \frac{-27}{2^2 \cdot 3 \cdot 5} = \frac{-9}{2^2 \cdot 5} = -\frac{9}{20}$$

Example 3: Find the difference $-\frac{5}{18} - \frac{3}{10}$.

SOLUTION:

$$-\frac{5}{18} - \frac{3}{10} = \frac{-5}{18} + \frac{-3}{10}$$

$$= \frac{-5}{2 \cdot 3^2} + \frac{-3}{2 \cdot 5} \longrightarrow \text{LCD is } 2 \cdot 3^2 \cdot 5.$$

$$= \frac{-5 \cdot 5}{2 \cdot 3^2 \cdot 5} + \frac{-3 \cdot 3^2}{2 \cdot 5 \cdot 3^2}$$

$$= \frac{-25 + (-27)}{2 \cdot 3^2 \cdot 5}$$

$$= \frac{-52}{2 \cdot 3^2 \cdot 5} = \frac{-26}{3^2 \cdot 5} = -\frac{26}{45}$$

EXERCISES 5.4

Ⓐ State each LCD in completely factored form. Then tell by which prime factors you would multiply the numerator and denominator of each fraction in order to add.

1. $\dfrac{5}{2 \cdot 3} + \dfrac{7}{3 \cdot 5}$ 2. $\dfrac{9}{2^2 \cdot 5} + \dfrac{11}{3 \cdot 5}$ 3. $\dfrac{11}{2^2 \cdot 3 \cdot 7} + \dfrac{25}{2 \cdot 3 \cdot 7}$

4. $\dfrac{5}{2 \cdot 3^2} + \dfrac{1}{2^3}$ 5. $\dfrac{5}{3^2 \cdot 7} + \dfrac{-4}{3 \cdot 5}$ 6. $\dfrac{13}{2 \cdot 3^2 \cdot 5} + \dfrac{17}{2^2 \cdot 3 \cdot 7}$

7. $\dfrac{9}{2^2 \cdot 5} + \dfrac{8}{3 \cdot 5^2}$ 8. $\dfrac{12}{5^3 \cdot 7^2} + \dfrac{18}{5^2 \cdot 7^3}$ 9. $\dfrac{-19}{2^3 \cdot 3^4 \cdot 5^2} + \dfrac{-7}{2^2 \cdot 3 \cdot 5^3}$

10. $\dfrac{15}{2^3 \cdot 7} + \dfrac{21}{2^4 \cdot 5}$ 11. $\dfrac{15}{7^2 \cdot 11} + \dfrac{25}{7 \cdot 13}$ 12. $\dfrac{-3}{5 \cdot 7^3 \cdot 11^2} + \dfrac{15}{7 \cdot 11 \cdot 13}$

Ⓑ Find each sum and express it in standard form.

13. $\frac{2}{5} + \frac{7}{15}$ 14. $\frac{5}{8} + \frac{1}{4}$ 15. $\frac{5}{6} + \frac{1}{8}$

16. $\frac{5}{9} + \frac{1}{6}$ 17. $\frac{4}{15} + \frac{5}{12}$ 18. $\frac{2}{9} + \frac{7}{24}$

19. $\frac{5}{12} + \frac{-3}{32}$ 20. $\frac{-5}{16} + \frac{11}{24}$ 21. $\frac{-13}{30} + \frac{-11}{35}$

22. $\frac{-9}{35} + \frac{-6}{25}$ 23. $\frac{-7}{48} + \frac{5}{42}$ 24. $\frac{7}{72} + \frac{-13}{60}$

Find each difference and express it in standard form.

25. $\frac{5}{12} - \frac{7}{18}$ **26.** $\frac{4}{15} - \frac{8}{25}$ **27.** $\frac{5}{24} - \frac{7}{36}$

28. $\frac{11}{30} - \frac{9}{25}$ **29.** $\frac{23}{96} - \frac{17}{72}$ **30.** $\frac{19}{72} - \frac{5}{84}$

31. $-\frac{7}{48} - \frac{5}{36}$ **32.** $-\frac{7}{36} - \frac{5}{42}$ **33.** $\frac{31}{39} - \left(-\frac{15}{26}\right)$

34. $\frac{5}{33} - \left(-\frac{7}{44}\right)$ **35.** $-\frac{5}{54} - \left(-\frac{7}{60}\right)$ **36.** $-\frac{7}{54} - \left(-\frac{7}{42}\right)$

37. A carpenter is going to use wood dowels (pegs) to join the shelves of a bookcase to the sides. The dowels are to be inserted in holes that are $\frac{1}{2}$ inch deep in the shelves and $\frac{3}{8}$ inch deep in the sides. How long should each dowel be?

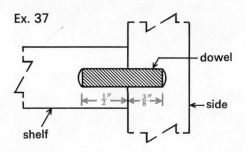

Ex. 37

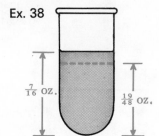

Ex. 38

38. A druggist has a vial containing $\frac{7}{16}$ ounce of medicine. He wants to pour off enough medicine so that $\frac{19}{48}$ ounce is left. How much should he remove?

39. A milling-machine operator must shape a piece of metal stock to $\frac{5}{6}$ its width. The width is now $\frac{9}{10}$ inch. The cutters on the machine must be set at the width after shaping. What should this setting be?

40. A recipe calls for $2\frac{1}{2}$ tablespoons of maple syrup. But the baker has only a teaspoon with which to measure. A teaspoon is $\frac{1}{3}$ tablespoon. How many teaspoons of syrup should be used?

Using the methods of this section, find each sum in standard form.

41. $\frac{1}{4} + \frac{2}{9} + \frac{5}{16}$ **42.** $\frac{1}{4} + \frac{4}{25} + \frac{3}{10}$

43. $\frac{3}{14} + \frac{4}{21} + \frac{5}{28}$ **44.** $\frac{5}{18} + \frac{2}{27} + \frac{4}{9}$

45. $\frac{1}{6} + \frac{-2}{3} + \frac{4}{15}$ **46.** $\frac{-3}{8} + \frac{3}{10} + \frac{6}{25}$

© **47.** $\frac{-5}{12} + \frac{-7}{18} + \frac{11}{30}$ **48.** $\frac{7}{24} + \frac{-5}{36} + \frac{11}{54}$

49. $\frac{-5}{18} + \frac{-2}{21} + \frac{-2}{15}$ **50.** $\frac{11}{30} + \frac{3}{20} + \frac{4}{45}$

51. $\frac{6}{35} + \frac{3}{10} + \frac{4}{21}$ **52.** $\frac{7}{30} + \frac{-8}{45} + \frac{3}{20}$

53. A bonding-machine operator has to set the machine at the total thickness of a three-layer panel. The layers are $\frac{7}{24}$ inch of plastic, $\frac{5}{16}$ inch of asbestos, and $\frac{3}{10}$ inch of steel. What setting should be used?

54. A sheet of copper of the proper width and $\frac{1}{8}$ inch thick is to be rolled into a length of copper tubing with a $1\frac{3}{16}$-inch outside diameter. How large a roller (inside diameter of the tubing) should be used?

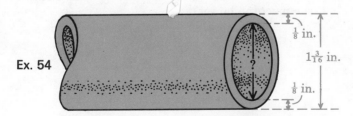

Ex. 54

55. An elite typewriter types one character per $\frac{1}{12}$ inch. A pica typewriter types one character per $\frac{1}{10}$ inch. A secretary wants to use a pica typewriter to retype lines measuring $7\frac{1}{2}$ inches in elite type. Will the retyped lines fit across a sheet $8\frac{1}{2}$ inches wide?

SELF-QUIZ: 5.1 to 5.4

Simplify each expression. (Each base is a real number.)

1. $(2a)^3$
2. $r^4 \cdot r^2$
3. $(xy)^3 x^2$
4. $(c^3 d^4)(c^2 d)$
5. $(2n)^2(-3n^3)$
6. $(-2x)^2(-2x)^3$
7. $(rs)^3(rs)^4$
8. $(3s^2 t^4)(5s^3 t)$
9. $(-7x^4 y^5)(6xy^3)$

Completely factor each integer, expressing each result in exponent form.

10. 50
11. -56
12. -180
13. 288

Change each fraction to standard form.

14. $\frac{-3}{12}$
15. $\frac{18}{32}$
16. $\frac{-63}{-36}$
17. $\frac{72}{96}$

Compute as indicated. Give your results in standard form.

18. $\frac{11}{12} \cdot \frac{9}{11}$
19. $\frac{35}{36} \cdot \frac{-42}{25}$
20. $\left(-\frac{18}{49}\right) \div \frac{27}{14}$
21. $\left(-\frac{33}{40}\right) \div \left(-\frac{66}{35}\right)$
22. $\frac{5}{12} + \frac{7}{18}$
23. $\frac{-11}{36} + \frac{17}{48}$
24. $\frac{5}{24} - \frac{9}{20}$
25. $\left(-\frac{9}{56}\right) - \left(-\frac{4}{63}\right)$

26. A machine makes wire brads (small, thin nails) by chopping pieces of wire to a preset length and flattening one end to form a head. Each piece of wire is shortened $\frac{1}{24}$ inch when the head is formed. To make $\frac{9}{16}$-inch brads, at what chopping length should the machine be set?

Since any rational number is the quotient $\frac{a}{b}$ of two integers, where $b \neq 0$, it can be renamed as a decimal by dividing a by b.

Examples:

1.
$$
\begin{array}{r}
0.3125000\cdots \\
16\overline{)5.0000\cdots} \\
\underline{4\,8} \\
20 \\
\underline{16} \\
40 \\
\underline{32} \\
80 \\
\underline{80} \\
0
\end{array}
$$

$$\tfrac{5}{16} = 0.3125\overline{0}$$

2.
$$
\begin{array}{r}
2.833\cdots \\
6\overline{)17.000\cdots} \\
\underline{12} \\
5\,0 \\
\underline{4\,8} \\
20 \\
\underline{18} \\
20 \\
\underline{18} \\
2
\end{array}
$$

$$\tfrac{17}{6} = 2.8\overline{3}$$

3.
$$
\begin{array}{r}
0.259259\cdots \\
27\overline{)7.000000\cdots} \\
\underline{5\,4} \\
1\,60 \\
\underline{1\,35} \\
250 \\
\underline{243} \\
70 \\
\underline{54} \\
160 \\
\underline{135} \\
250 \\
\underline{243} \\
7
\end{array}
$$

$$\tfrac{7}{27} = 0.\overline{259}$$

The results above are written as **repeating decimals**, using bars to show which digits repeat. If the only repeating digit is 0, as in Example **1**, the decimal is also called a **terminating decimal** because we can (and usually do) write it without the $\overline{0}$. That is,

$$0.3125\overline{0} = 0.3125.$$

The remainder after each division step is shown in red above. If a zero remainder occurs, as in Example **1**, the division can be ended, and a repeating decimal which is also terminating results.

If nonzero remainders start repeating according to a pattern, as in Examples **2** and **3**, the division can be continued "without end," and a repeating decimal which is not terminating results.

Is it possible that, in the division process, the remainders do not start repeating? In other words, are there some rational numbers that cannot be renamed as repeating decimals?

The answer is No. To understand why, recall that any remainder in the division process *must* be less than the divisor. If the divisor is 7, the only possible remainders are

$$0, 1, 2, 3, 4, 5, 6.$$

Since the set of remainders is limited by the size of the divisor, eventually they have to start repeating. Thus, we conclude:

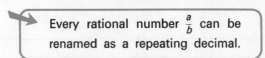

Every rational number $\frac{a}{b}$ can be renamed as a repeating decimal.

The next two examples show why we can also turn this last statement around and say:

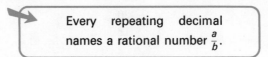

Every repeating decimal names a rational number $\frac{a}{b}$.

Example 4: Rename $0.3\overline{15}$ as a fraction.

SOLUTION:

$$\text{Let} \quad x = 0.31515\cdots.$$

$$\text{I} \quad 1000x = 315.15\cdots \quad \text{II}$$

$$\underline{10x = 3.15\cdots}$$

$$\text{III} \quad 990x = 312.00\cdots$$

$$\text{IV} \quad x = \frac{312}{990} = \frac{2^3 \cdot 3 \cdot 13}{2 \cdot 3^2 \cdot 5 \cdot 11} = \frac{2^2 \cdot 13}{3 \cdot 5 \cdot 11} = \frac{52}{165}$$

I. Multiply both sides of the equation by 10, 100, 1000, 10000, $\cdots$ to "move" the decimal point immediately *in back of* the first complete sequence of repeating digits.

II. Multiply both sides of the *original* equation by 1, 10, 100, 1000, 10000, $\cdots$ to "move" the decimal point immediately *in front of* the first complete sequence of repeating digits.

III. Subtract the members of the equation resulting in II from the members of the equation resulting in I.

IV. Solve the equation resulting in III. (You should also check your result by dividing.)

Example 5: Rename $0.\overline{27}$ as a fraction.

SOLUTION:

Let $\quad x = 0.2727\cdots$.

I

$100x = 27.27\cdots$ II

$1x = 0.27\cdots$

III $\quad 99x = 27.00\cdots$

IV $\quad x = \frac{27}{99} = \frac{3}{11}$

EXERCISES 5.5

Ⓐ **1.** Using a bar, how would you rewrite $25.67373\cdots$?

2. A decimal like $5.36\overline{0}$ is a _____ or a _____ decimal.

3. Every rational number can be renamed as a _____ decimal, and every _____ decimal names a rational number.

In each case, by which number would you multiply both sides of the equation as in steps I and II of Example 4?

4. $x = 2.\overline{7}$ 　　　　　　**5.** $x = 5.6\overline{2}$

6. $x = 0.\overline{273}$ 　　　　　**7.** $x = 3.51\overline{6}$

8. The method of Example 4 can be used to rename a terminating decimal, say $3.25\overline{0}$, as a fraction. But, what is an easier way?

Rename each rational number as a repeating decimal, using a bar to indicate the sequence of repeating digits.

9. $\frac{1}{3}$ 　　　　**10.** $\frac{2}{3}$ 　　　　**11.** $\frac{3}{10}$ 　　　　**12.** $\frac{25}{100}$

13. $2\frac{1}{3}$ 　　　**14.** $3\frac{2}{3}$ 　　　**15.** $\frac{1}{2}$ 　　　　**16.** $\frac{1}{4}$

17. $-7\frac{2}{3}$ 　　**18.** $-5\frac{1}{3}$ 　　**19.** $-\frac{2}{5}$ 　　　**20.** $-\frac{3}{4}$

Ⓑ **21.** $\frac{1}{9}$ 　　　**22.** $\frac{2}{9}$ 　　　**23.** $\frac{5}{8}$ 　　　　**24.** $\frac{7}{25}$

25. $\frac{19}{3}$ 　　　**26.** $\frac{25}{3}$ 　　　**27.** $\frac{31}{9}$ 　　　**28.** $\frac{17}{9}$

29. $\frac{1}{11}$ 　　　**30.** $\frac{2}{11}$ 　　　**31.** $\frac{3}{11}$ 　　　**32.** $\frac{4}{11}$

33. $-\frac{5}{11}$	34. $-\frac{7}{11}$	35. $-\frac{162}{11}$	36. $-\frac{123}{11}$
37. $\frac{5}{32}$	38. $\frac{7}{64}$	39. $\frac{31}{27}$	40. $\frac{50}{37}$
41. $\frac{17}{33}$	42. $\frac{28}{33}$	43. $-\frac{82}{75}$	44. $-\frac{43}{30}$
45. $\frac{1}{7}$	46. $\frac{2}{7}$	47. $\frac{3}{7}$	48. $\frac{4}{7}$

Rename each decimal as a fraction in standard form.

49. $0.\overline{5}$	50. $0.\overline{7}$	51. $2.\overline{1}$
52. $3.\overline{2}$	53. $0.\overline{54}$	54. $0.\overline{72}$
55. $1.1\overline{6}$	56. $1.2\overline{6}$	57. $0.\overline{468}$
58. $0.\overline{612}$	59. $7.25\overline{0}$	60. $9.5\overline{0}$
61. $5.\overline{63}$	62. $4.\overline{81}$	63. $-1.\overline{83}$
64. $-5.1\overline{3}$	65. $-0.1\overline{27}$	66. $-0.2\overline{54}$
67. $0.13\overline{8}$	68. $-0.21\overline{6}$	69. $0.34\overline{09}$

The examples show how any fraction in standard form can be changed to a terminating decimal if its denominator contains prime factors of only 2 or 5 (or both). Using this method, change each fraction in Exercises 70–74 to a decimal.

Examples:

A. $\dfrac{3}{4} = \dfrac{3}{2 \cdot 2} = \dfrac{3 \cdot 5 \cdot 5}{2 \cdot 2 \cdot 5 \cdot 5} = \dfrac{75}{100} = 0.75\overline{0}$

B. $\dfrac{7}{250} = \dfrac{7}{2 \cdot 5 \cdot 5 \cdot 5} = \dfrac{2 \cdot 2 \cdot 7}{2 \cdot 2 \cdot 2 \cdot 5 \cdot 5 \cdot 5} = \dfrac{28}{1000} = 0.028\overline{0}$

70. $\frac{1}{4}$ 71. $\frac{3}{25}$ 72. $\frac{7}{40}$ 73. $\frac{13}{50}$ 74. $\frac{72}{125}$

75. Will a method similar to that of Exercises **70–74** work for a fraction in standard form whose denominator contains at least one prime factor other than 2 and 5 (for example $\frac{1}{3}$, $\frac{1}{6}$, or $\frac{1}{30}$)? Why? Can such fractions be changed to terminating decimals?

76. Find out why $0.\overline{9} = 1.\overline{0}$ by reading: Niven, Ivan, *Numbers: Rational and Irrational*, New York: Random House, Inc., 1961, pages 34–36. Then find a terminating decimal equal to $2.4\overline{9}$.

$$5^2 = 25$$
$$(-5)^2 = 25$$

From the above, you see that

5 is one of two equal factors of 25.

Also,

−5 is one of two equal factors of 25.

We say that 5 and −5 are the **square roots** (or **second roots**) of 25. In symbols we write

$$\sqrt{25} = 5 \qquad \text{and} \qquad -\sqrt{25} = -5.$$

The positive (or principal) square root of 25 equals 5.

The negative square root of 25 equals −5.

Since	We write
$1^2 = 1$	$\sqrt{1} = 1$
$(-1)^2 = 1$	$-\sqrt{1} = -1$
$2^2 = 4$	$\sqrt{4} = 2$
$(-2)^2 = 4$	$-\sqrt{4} = -2$
$3^2 = 9$	$\sqrt{9} = 3$
$(-3)^2 = 9$	$-\sqrt{9} = -3$
$\left(\frac{2}{3}\right)^2 = \frac{4}{9}$	$\sqrt{\frac{4}{9}} = \frac{2}{3}$
$\left(-\frac{2}{3}\right)^2 = \frac{4}{9}$	$-\sqrt{\frac{4}{9}} = -\frac{2}{3}$

As this list suggests, every *positive* real number has two real-number square roots—one positive, the other negative.

However, 0 has only one square root: $\sqrt{0} = 0$. (Since zero is its own opposite, $-\sqrt{0} = -0 = 0$.)

How about *negative* real numbers? Do they have real-number square roots? For example, is there a real number which when multiplied by itself results in −4?

Well, the square root of -4 cannot be a positive real number because a positive times a positive gives a *positive* product. Nor can the square root of -4 be a negative real number since a negative times a negative also gives a *positive* product. And the square root of -4 is certainly not 0 because 0^2 equals 0, not -4.

Thus, we conclude that *negative* real numbers do not have real-number square roots. (In a later course, it is shown that negative numbers do have square roots, but they are not real numbers.)

EXERCISES 5.6

Ⓐ 1. Since $7^2 = 49$, the positive _____ of 49 is 7.

2. Since $(-7)^2 = 49$, the _____ of 49 is -7.

3. $-\sqrt{49}$ is read _____.

4. Every _____ real number has two real-number square roots.

5. The real number _____ has only one square root.

6. _____ real numbers do not have real-number square roots.

Find each square root.

7. $\sqrt{4}$	8. $-\sqrt{25}$	9. $\sqrt{0}$	10. $\sqrt{9}$
11. $\sqrt{1}$	12. $-\sqrt{1}$	13. $\sqrt{\frac{4}{9}}$	14. $-\sqrt{\frac{4}{9}}$
Ⓑ 15. $\sqrt{16}$	16. $\sqrt{36}$	17. $\sqrt{64}$	18. $\sqrt{81}$
19. $-\sqrt{81}$	20. $-\sqrt{64}$	21. $\sqrt{100}$	22. $\sqrt{121}$
23. $-\sqrt{121}$	24. $-\sqrt{100}$	25. $\sqrt{144}$	26. $\sqrt{196}$
27. $\sqrt{169}$	28. $\sqrt{225}$	29. $\sqrt{\frac{9}{16}}$	30. $\sqrt{\frac{1}{16}}$
31. $\sqrt{\frac{1}{25}}$	32. $\sqrt{\frac{16}{25}}$	33. $\sqrt{\frac{25}{4}}$	34. $\sqrt{\frac{25}{9}}$
35. $-\sqrt{\frac{36}{49}}$	36. $-\sqrt{\frac{49}{36}}$	37. $-\sqrt{\frac{64}{49}}$	38. $-\sqrt{\frac{49}{64}}$
Ⓒ 39. $\sqrt{\frac{100}{121}}$	40. $\sqrt{\frac{144}{169}}$	41. $\sqrt{\frac{196}{25}}$	42. $\sqrt{\frac{225}{64}}$
43. $\sqrt{\frac{9}{100}}$	44. $\sqrt{0.09}$	45. $\sqrt{\frac{81}{100}}$	46. $\sqrt{0.81}$
47. $\sqrt{0.25}$	48. $-\sqrt{0.64}$	49. $-\sqrt{1.21}$	50. $\sqrt{2.25}$

Copy and complete the table.

Since	We write	
$2^3 = 8$	$\sqrt[3]{8} = 2$	
$3^3 = 27$	$\sqrt[3]{27} = 3$	
$(-2)^3 = -8$	$\sqrt[3]{-8} = -2$	Third (or cube) roots
51. $(-3)^3 = -27$		
52. $1^3 = 1$		
53. $(-1)^3 = -1$		
54. $4^3 = 64$		
55. $\left(\frac{2}{3}\right)^3 = \frac{8}{27}$		
$2^4 = 16$	$\sqrt[4]{16} = 2$	
$3^4 = 81$	$\sqrt[4]{81} = 3$	Fourth roots
$(-2)^4 = 16$	$-\sqrt[4]{16} = -2$	
56. $(-3)^4 = 81$		
57. $\left(\frac{2}{3}\right)^4 = \frac{16}{81}$		
$2^5 = 32$	$\sqrt[5]{32} = 2$	
58. $3^5 = 243$		Fifth roots
59. $(-2)^5 = -32$		
60. $(-3)^5 = -243$		
$2^6 = 64$	$\sqrt[6]{64} = 2$	Sixth roots
61. $(-2)^6 = 64$		

62. Does a positive real number have more than one real-number "odd" root (cube root, fifth root, and so on)?

63. Does a positive real number have more than one real-number "even" root (square root, fourth root, and so on)?

64. Does a negative real number have any real-number "odd" roots? "Even" roots?

5.7 NONREPEATING DECIMALS

The sign $\sqrt{}$, used to indicate square roots, is called a *radical sign*, and the number expressed under the radical sign is called the *radicand*.

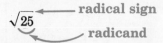

All the radicands considered in the previous section are **perfect squares** because each is the square of a rational number. The square root of a perfect square is therefore a rational number and can be expressed by a repeating decimal.

However, all real numbers are not perfect squares. For example, the following numbers are not perfect squares.

$$2 \quad 3 \quad 5 \quad 6 \quad 7 \quad 8 \quad 10 \quad 11 \quad 12 \quad 13 \quad 14 \quad 15 \quad \tfrac{1}{2} \quad \tfrac{2}{3}$$

The square roots of such numbers cannot be expressed by either fractions or repeating decimals. But we can approximate the square roots by decimals.

Example 1: Find $\sqrt{2}$ correct to the hundredths place.

SOLUTION:

The first three steps are done to find a reasonable first approximation.

$1 < \quad 2 \quad < 4$ Locate the radicand between two con-secutive perfect-square integers.

$\sqrt{1} < \sqrt{2} < \sqrt{4}$
or
$1 < \sqrt{2} < 2$ Locate the given square root between the square roots of the perfect squares.

$\dfrac{1 + 2}{2} = 1.5$ Find the average of the square roots of the perfect squares.

The remaining steps are repetitions of a *dividing step* and an *averaging step* as follows.

<table>
<tr>
<td>

Divide the radicand by the average found in the preceding step. Determine the quotient to one more decimal place than the divisor.

</td>
<td>

Find the **average** of the quotient and divisor from the preceding step. Determine the average to the same number of decimal places as the quotient.

</td>
</tr>
</table>

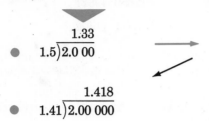

$$\begin{array}{r} 1.33 \\ 1.5\overline{)2.0\ 00} \end{array}$$

$$\frac{1.33 + 1.5}{2} \approx 1.41$$

$$\begin{array}{r} 1.418 \\ 1.41\overline{)2.00\ 000} \end{array}$$

Continue the divide-and-average steps until the divisor and quotient are the same for the decimal places required.

The symbol $\approx$ means "is approximately equal to." We have found that, correct to the hundredths place,

$$\boxed{\sqrt{2} \approx 1.41.}$$

Compute $(1.41)^2$. Is it close to 2?

Example 2: Find $\sqrt{17}$ correct to the thousandths place.

SOLUTION:

▶ $16 < 17 < 25$

▶ $\sqrt{16} < \sqrt{17} < \sqrt{25}$ or $4 < \sqrt{17} < 5$

▶ $\dfrac{4 + 5}{2} = 4.5$

Divide	Average

$$\begin{array}{r} 3.77 \\ 4.5\overline{)17.0\ 00} \end{array}$$

$$\frac{3.77 + 4.5}{2} \approx 4.13$$

$$\begin{array}{r} 4.116 \\ 4.13\overline{)17.00\ 000} \end{array}$$

$$\frac{4.116 + 4.13}{2} = 4.123$$

$$\begin{array}{r} 4.1232 \\ 4.123\overline{)17.000\ 0000} \end{array}$$

$$\boxed{\text{Thus, } \sqrt{17} \approx 4.123}$$

Compute $(4.123)^2$. Is it close to 17?

The divide-and-average method is very similar to a method used by computers. Some computer approximations follow.

$$\sqrt{2} \approx 1.4142135623730950^{48803}$$
$$\sqrt{17} \approx 4.123105625617660549821$$
$$\sqrt{119} \approx 10.908712114635714411502$$

Since the radicands are not perfect squares, there is no limit to the number of digits that can be found in the decimal expansions of $\sqrt{2}$, $\sqrt{17}$, and $\sqrt{119}$. But no repeating sequence of digits will ever occur. That is, such square roots have nonterminating, **nonrepeating** decimal expansions.

EXERCISES 5.7

ⓐ Which of the following are perfect squares?

1. 4	**2.** 9	**3.** 2	**4.** 3	**5.** 16
6. 18	**7.** 36	**8.** 49	**9.** 50	**10.** 121
11. $\frac{4}{9}$	**12.** $\frac{16}{25}$	**13.** $\frac{2}{3}$	**14.** $\frac{3}{5}$	**15.** $\frac{3}{4}$

Which of the following can be expressed by repeating decimals?

16. $\sqrt{4}$	**17.** $\sqrt{2}$	**18.** $\sqrt{17}$	**19.** $\sqrt{31}$
20. $\sqrt{\frac{4}{9}}$	**21.** $\sqrt{\frac{16}{25}}$	**22.** $\sqrt{\frac{2}{3}}$	**23.** $\sqrt{\frac{3}{4}}$

Locate each radicand between two consecutive perfect-square integers. Then locate the square root between the square roots of the perfect squares.

24. $\sqrt{3}$	**25.** $\sqrt{5}$	**26.** $\sqrt{12}$	**27.** $\sqrt{31}$
28. $\sqrt{65}$	**29.** $\sqrt{93}$	**30.** $\sqrt{115}$	**31.** $\sqrt{135}$

32. $\sqrt{\frac{7}{3}}$ (HINT: $\frac{7}{3} = 2.\overline{3}$)

ⓑ Using the divide-and-average method, find each square root correct to the hundredths place.

33. $\sqrt{10}$	**34.** $\sqrt{12}$	**35.** $\sqrt{14}$	**36.** $\sqrt{15}$
37. $\sqrt{20}$	**38.** $\sqrt{21}$	**39.** $\sqrt{28}$	**40.** $\sqrt{33}$

41. $\sqrt{37}$	**42.** $\sqrt{41}$	**43.** $\sqrt{50}$	**44.** $\sqrt{53}$
45. $\sqrt{75}$	**46.** $\sqrt{88}$	**47.** $\sqrt{109}$	**48.** $\sqrt{116}$
49. $\sqrt{130}$	**50.** $\sqrt{136}$	**51.** $\sqrt{417}$	**52.** $\sqrt{431}$

© If a desk calculator which performs division is available, use the divide-and-average method to find each square root correct to the thousandths place.

53. $\sqrt{147}$	**54.** $\sqrt{151}$	**55.** $\sqrt{177}$	**56.** $\sqrt{186}$
57. $\sqrt{198}$	**58.** $\sqrt{234}$	**59.** $\sqrt{335}$	**60.** $\sqrt{942}$
61. $\sqrt{1.25}$	**62.** $\sqrt{\frac{3}{4}}$	**63.** $\sqrt{0.3333}$	**64.** $\sqrt{\frac{1}{3}}$

Using the divide-and-average method, find the following correct to the hundredths place. This time, however, divide the radicand by 2 to find the first approximation.

65. $\sqrt{17}$	**66.** $\sqrt{18}$	**67.** $\sqrt{16}$	**68.** $\sqrt{25}$

69. Can the divide-and-average method as employed in Exercises 65–68 be used to find square roots of perfect squares?

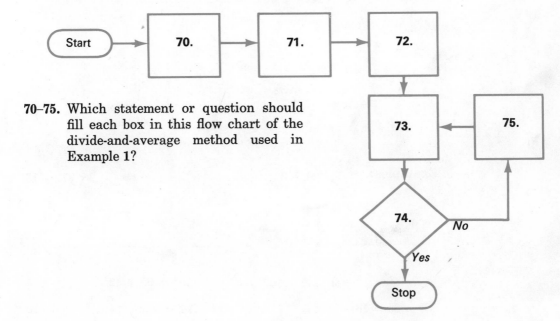

70–75. Which statement or question should fill each box in this flow chart of the divide-and-average method used in Example 1?

We have already seen that every *rational* number has a *repeating* decimal expansion.

> An **irrational number** is a number that has a *nonrepeating* decimal expansion.

Irrational numbers occur as the square roots of certain numbers. They also result from many other mathematical processes. For example, the ratio of the circumference of any circle to its diameter is the irrational number π.

Using a decimal approximation for an irrational number, we can graph it on a real number line. But the *Pythagorean property* (or *Pythagorean theorem*) can also be used to show that irrational numbers "belong" on the real number line.

Pythagorean property

In a right triangle, the square of the hypotenuse is equal to the sum of the squares of the legs.

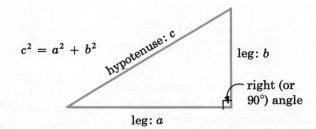

$$c^2 = a^2 + b^2$$

hypotenuse: c

leg: b

right (or 90°) angle

leg: a

Examples:

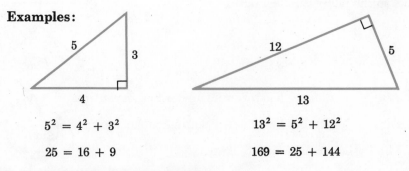

5   3   4

$$5^2 = 4^2 + 3^2$$

$$25 = 16 + 9$$

12   5   13

$$13^2 = 5^2 + 12^2$$

$$169 = 25 + 144$$

We can construct right triangles whose sides have irrational measures. And then use the lengths of these sides to graph irrational numbers on the real number line.

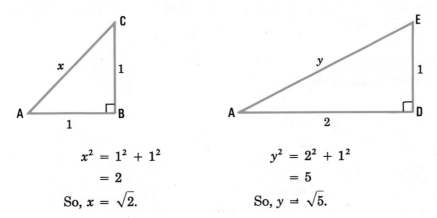

$$x^2 = 1^2 + 1^2$$
$$= 2$$
So, $x = \sqrt{2}$.

$$y^2 = 2^2 + 1^2$$
$$= 5$$
So, $y = \sqrt{5}$.

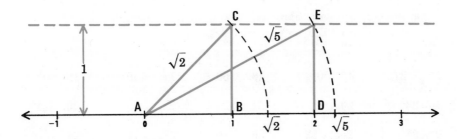

The rational and irrational numbers make up the complete set of real numbers. And they enable us to assign a coordinate to every point on a line.

Since square roots will be used from time to time in this book, it will be convenient to have the table of squares and square roots that is included on page 555. This table gives the irrational square roots to the nearest thousandth.

EXERCISES 5.8

Ⓐ 1. A(n) _____ number has a repeating decimal expansion.

2. A(n) _____ number has a nonrepeating decimal expansion.

3. The Pythagorean property states: _____.

4. The rational and irrational numbers make up the complete set of _____ numbers.

5. The _____ numbers enable us to assign a coordinate to every point on a line.

6. Explain why the length of segment AC is $\sqrt{2}$.

7. What is the length of segment AD?

8. How could you graph $\sqrt{3}$ on a real number line?

Ex. 6–7

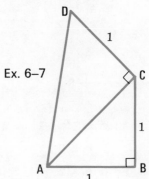

Using the table on page 555, find each of the following.

9. 2^2	**10.** $\sqrt{2}$	**11.** 3^2	**12.** $\sqrt{3}$	**13.** 27^2
14. $\sqrt{27}$	**15.** 50^2	**16.** $\sqrt{50}$	**17.** $\sqrt{59}$	**18.** 59^2
Ⓑ **19.** 23^2	**20.** 28^2	**21.** $\sqrt{23}$	**22.** $\sqrt{28}$	**23.** 82^2
24. 96^2	**25.** $\sqrt{82}$	**26.** $\sqrt{96}$	**27.** $\sqrt{143}$	**28.** $\sqrt{149}$

Find x to the nearest thousandth in each of the following.

29.
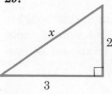

30.
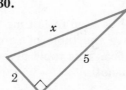

31.
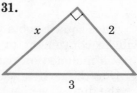

32.
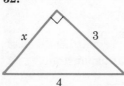

33.
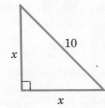

34.
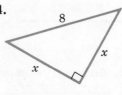

35. To the nearest tenth of a foot, how long is one roof rafter for the garage roof shown below?

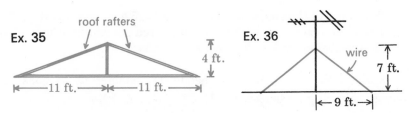

36. To the nearest tenth of a foot, how long is one of the wires needed to brace a TV antenna as shown above? (Allow $\frac{1}{2}$ foot extra at each end for tying.)

37. To the nearest tenth of a kilometer, how long is the pipeline across the square field shown below?

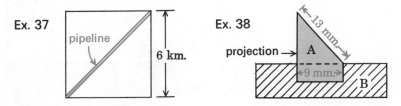

38. Machine part A fits into part B as shown above. To the nearest thousandth of a millimeter, how much should part A project?

© First, construct the necessary right triangles. Then use the measure of each hypotenuse to graph the given set.

39. $\{\sqrt{2}, \sqrt{5}, -\sqrt{2}, -\sqrt{5}\}$ **40.** $\{\sqrt{10}, \sqrt{17}, -\sqrt{10}, -\sqrt{17}\}$

41. $\{\sqrt{3}, \sqrt{6}, -\sqrt{3}, -\sqrt{6}\}$ **42.** $\{\sqrt{7}, \sqrt{8}, -\sqrt{7}, -\sqrt{8}\}$

43. Does $2.\overline{65}$ name a rational or an irrational number? Using $2.\overline{65}$ and the digit 3, we can write

$$2.653653365333653333 \cdots .$$

Is this a repeating decimal? If so, write it using a bar. Does this decimal name a rational or an irrational number?

44. Modern computers have approximated π to over 100,000 decimal places. What is the most accurate approximation of π that you can find by doing some library research?

The Wheel of Theodorus

Theodorus of Cyrene, who lived around 425 B.C., was a philosopher of ancient Greece. It is said that he discovered the construction below, which is therefore called "the wheel of Theodorus."

Notice how "the wheel of Theodorus" enables us to construct segments having measures of $\sqrt{1}$, $\sqrt{2}$, $\sqrt{3}$, $\sqrt{4}$, $\sqrt{5}, \cdots$.

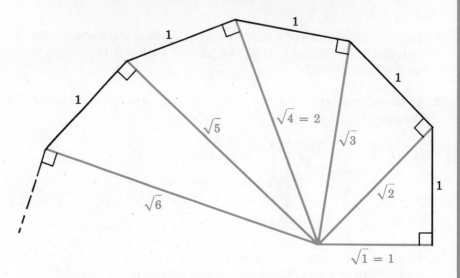

Construct a "wheel" of your own and continue it further. Construct the segments labeled 1 so that each is $\frac{10}{8}$ or $1\frac{1}{4}$ inches long. Then $\frac{1}{8}$ inch will be $\frac{1}{10}$ of your unit segment. Measure the segments having irrational measures to approximate these numbers to the nearest tenth.

What is the measure of the last segment that can be constructed before the "wheel" overlaps?

Can the "wheel" be continued even after it overlaps?

Rename each rational number as a repeating decimal, using a bar to indicate the sequence of repeating digits.

1. $\frac{1}{5}$ **2.** $\frac{5}{6}$ **3.** $\frac{41}{22}$ **4.** $-\frac{8}{37}$

Rename each decimal as a fraction in standard form.

5. $0.4\overline{0}$ **6.** $0.\overline{40}$ **7.** $-1.4\overline{6}$

Find each square root.

8. $\sqrt{49}$ **9.** $\sqrt{81}$ **10.** $-\sqrt{121}$ **11.** $\sqrt{\frac{25}{64}}$

Using the divide-and-average method, find each square root correct to the hundredths place.

12. $\sqrt{65}$ **13.** $\sqrt{83}$

Using the table on page 555, find each of the following.

14. 46^2 **15.** $\sqrt{46}$ **16.** 126^2 **17.** $\sqrt{117}$

Find x to the nearest thousandth.

18.
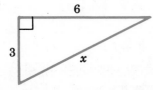

19.
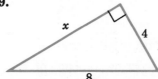

20. For safety, a ladder should be placed $\frac{1}{4}$ of its length away from the wall as shown at the right. How high up a wall will a 12-foot ladder safely reach (to the nearest tenth of a foot)?

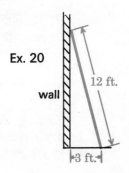

Ex. 20

wall

12 ft.

3 ft.

Considering some examples with specific numbers often *suggests* a general property about an entire set of numbers. Consider the examples using 1, 2, 3, and 4 below.

$$1^2 - 1 + 11 = 11 \qquad 3^2 - 3 + 11 = 17$$
$$2^2 - 2 + 11 = 13 \qquad 4^2 - 4 + 11 = 23$$

The examples *suggest* that for any positive integer n,

$$n^2 - n + 11 \text{ equals a prime.}$$

But we cannot be absolutely certain that this holds true for *all* positive integers. In fact, if we try $n = 11$, then $n^2 - n + 11 = 11^2 - 11 + 11 = 121$, which is *not* prime.

Reasoning that specific examples *suggest* a general conclusion is called **inductive reasoning**. In algebra, inductive reasoning is used very frequently. But we also *prove* conclusions.

We do so by *assuming* that a rather small number of general statements are true. These statements, called **axioms**, are then used to show *why* our conclusions, called **theorems**, must be true.

In algebra, there are eleven axioms that are used very frequently and from which most of our conclusions (theorems) can be proved. You have already considered these axioms in Chapter 2.

axioms

Closure property of $+$	Closure property of $\cdot$
Associative property of $+$	Associative property of $\cdot$
Identity property of $+$	Identity property of $\cdot$
Inverse property of $+$	Inverse property of $\cdot$
Commutative property of $+$	Commutative property of $\cdot$

Distributive property of $\cdot$ over $+$

Earlier, we accepted the multiplication properties of 0 and -1 because examples suggested that they were true. But we can prove these properties by using the axioms.

Example 1: Prove that for every real number a, $\quad 0 \cdot a = 0$.

SOLUTION: Let a be *any* real number.

$0 \cdot a = 0 \cdot a + 0$	Identity prop. of $+$
$\quad = 0 \cdot a + [a + (-a)]$	Inverse prop. of $+$
$\quad = [0 \cdot a + a] + (-a)$	Associative prop. of $+$
$\quad = [0 \cdot a + 1 \cdot a] + (-a)$	Identity prop. of $\cdot$
$\quad = [0 + 1]a + (-a)$	Distributive prop.
$\quad = 1 \cdot a + (-a)$	Identity prop. of $+$
$\quad = a + (-a)$	Identity prop. of $\cdot$
$\quad = 0$	Inverse prop. of $+$

$\boxed{\therefore 0 \cdot a = 0}$ $\qquad$ (The symbol $\therefore$ is read "therefore.")

The **proof** above was written as a chain of *equivalent expressions*. The reason *why* each expression is equivalent to the one preceding it is given to the right, and each reason is an axiom.

After a theorem has been proved, it can be used as a reason in any later proof. Notice how the multiplication property of 0, which we just proved, is used in the next proof.

Example 2: Prove that for every real number a, $\quad -1 \cdot a = -a$.

SOLUTION: Let a be *any* real number.

$-1 \cdot a = -1 \cdot a + 0$	Ident. prop. of $+$
$\quad = -1 \cdot a + [a + (-a)]$	Inv. prop. of $+$
$\quad = [-1 \cdot a + a] + (-a)$	Assoc. prop. of $+$
$\quad = [-1 \cdot a + 1 \cdot a] + (-a)$	Ident. prop. of $\cdot$
$\quad = [-1 + 1]a + (-a)$	Why?
$\quad = 0 \cdot a + (-a)$	Why?
$\quad = 0 + (-a)$	Mult. prop. of 0
$\quad = -a$	Why?

$\boxed{\therefore -1 \cdot a = -a}$

Example 3: Prove that for all real numbers a and b,

$$(-a) + (-b) = -(a + b).$$

SOLUTION: Let a and b be *any* real numbers.

$$(-a) + (-b) = (-1a) + (-1b) \qquad \text{Mult. prop. of } -1$$
$$= -1(a + b) \qquad\qquad \text{Why?}$$
$$= -(a + b) \qquad\qquad\ \text{Why?}$$

$$\boxed{\therefore (-a) + (-b) = -(a + b)}$$

Thus, we have *proved* three theorems.

theorems

Let a and b be any real numbers.

$0 \cdot a = 0$	Multiplication prop. of 0
$-1 \cdot a = -a$	Multiplication prop. of -1
$(-a) + (-b) = -(a + b)$	Addition prop. of opposites

EXERCISES 5.9

(A) 1. Reasoning that specific examples *suggest* a general conclusion is called _____.

2. General statements assumed to be true are called _____.

3. Conclusions proved to be true are called _____.

4. Name the eleven axioms assumed in this section.

5. Name the three theorems proved in this section.

6. True or false? After it has been proved, a theorem can be used as a reason in any later proof.

7. What are the missing reasons in Example 2? In Example 3?

8. *Addition property of opposites:* The sum of the _____ of any two real numbers is equal to the opposite of their _____.

Which axiom or theorem is illustrated? Letters stand for any real numbers.

9. $x(y + z) = xy + xz$

10. $rt + st = (r + s)t$

11. $a(bc) = (ab)c$

12. $m(n + 0) = (n + 0)m$

13. $a(bc) = (bc)a$

14. $m(n + 1) = m(1 + n)$

15. $a + b = 1(a + b)$

16. $m(n + 0) = mn$

17. $m + (n + 1) = (m + n) + 1$

18. $x + 0 = x + (-y + y)$

19. $k \cdot 1 = k\left(a \cdot \frac{1}{a}\right)$, if $a \neq 0$

20. $0(m + n) = 0$

21. $-(r + s) = -1(r + s)$

22. $-(r + s) = (-r) + (-s)$

23. $x + 0 = x + 0(y + z)$

24. $-(a + b) + (a + b) = 0$

Copy and complete each proof. Let *a* and *b* be any real numbers.

25. *Prove:* $(-a)b = -ab$

$\quad$ *Proof:* $(-a)b = (-1a)b$

$\qquad\qquad\quad = -1(ab)$

$\qquad\qquad\quad = -ab$

$\quad \therefore (-a)b = -ab$

26. *Prove:* $a(-b) = -ab$

$\quad$ *Proof:* $a(-b) = (-b)a$

$\qquad\qquad\quad = -ba$

$\qquad\qquad\quad = -ab$

$\quad \therefore a(-b) = -ab$

Ⓒ **27.** *Prove:* $(-1)(-1) = 1$

$\quad$ *Proof:*

$\quad (-1)(-1) = (-1)(-1) + 0$

$\qquad\qquad\quad = (-1)(-1) + [(-1) + 1]$

$\qquad\qquad\quad = (-1)(-1) + [(-1)1 + 1]$

$\qquad\qquad\quad = [(-1)(-1) + (-1)1] + 1$

$\qquad\qquad\quad = -1 \cdot [(-1) + 1] + 1$

$\qquad\qquad\quad = -1 \cdot 0 + 1$

$\qquad\qquad\quad = 0 + 1$

$\qquad\qquad\quad = 1$

$\quad \therefore \underline{\qquad\qquad ? \qquad\qquad}$

28. *Prove:* $-(-a) = a$

$\quad$ *Proof:*

$\quad -(-a) = -1(-a)$

$\qquad\quad = -1(-1a)$

$\qquad\quad = [(-1)(-1)]a$

$\qquad\quad = 1 \cdot a$

$\qquad\quad = a$

29. *Prove:* $(-a)(-b) = ab$

$\quad$ *Proof:*

$\quad (-a)(-b) = (-a)(-1b)$

$\qquad\qquad\quad = [(-a)(-1)]b$

$\qquad\qquad\quad = [(-1)(-a)]b$

$\qquad\qquad\quad = [-(-a)]b$

$\qquad\qquad\quad = ab$

30. Do some library research to find: **(a)** the mathematical definition of the word **field**; **(b)** the names of the field properties.

5.10 BUILDING A PROOF

In the preceding proofs each reason was an axiom or a previously proved theorem. A definition can also be used as a reason.

definitions

Subtraction is the inverse operation of addition. **Division** is the inverse operation of multiplication. That is, for any real numbers m and n,

$$(m - n) + n = m$$

and, if $n \neq 0$,

$$(m \div n) \cdot n = m.$$

Examples: Prove that for any real numbers m and n,

1. $m - n = m + (-n)$.

2. If $n \neq 0$, $m \div n = m \cdot \dfrac{1}{n}$.

SOLUTIONS:

1. Let m and n be any real numbers.

$$
\begin{aligned}
m - n &= (m - n) + 0 & &\text{Ident. prop. of } + \\
&= (m - n) + [n + (-n)] & &\text{Inv. prop. of } + \\
&= [(m - n) + n] + (-n) & &\text{Assoc. prop. of } + \\
&= m + (-n) & &\text{Def. of subtraction}
\end{aligned}
$$

$$\boxed{\therefore\ m - n = m + (-n)}$$

2. Let m and n be any real numbers where $n \neq 0$.

$$
\begin{aligned}
m \div n &= (m \div n) \cdot 1 & &\text{Ident. prop. of } \cdot \\
&= (m \div n)\left[n \cdot \frac{1}{n} \right] & &\text{Why?} \\
&= [(m \div n) \cdot n] \cdot \frac{1}{n} & &\text{Why?} \\
&= m \cdot \frac{1}{n} & &\text{Why?}
\end{aligned}
$$

$$\boxed{\therefore\ \text{if } n \neq 0,\ m \div n = m \cdot \frac{1}{n}}$$

The preceding proofs were written as chains of equivalent expressions. Sometimes a proof is written as a chain of *equivalent sentences*. In such proofs, you may use the properties of equality and inequality as reasons (for example, see the second step below).

Example 3: Prove that for any real numbers a, b, c, and x, where $a \neq 0$,

$$\text{if } ax + b = c, \text{ then } x = \frac{c + (-b)}{a}.$$

SOLUTION: Let a, b, c, and x be any real numbers where $a \neq 0$.

$ax + b = c$	Given
$[ax + b] + (-b) = c + (-b)$	Add. prop. of $=$
$ax + [b + (-b)] = c + (-b)$	Assoc. prop. of $+$
$ax + 0 = c + (-b)$	Inv. prop. of $+$
$ax = c + (-b)$	Ident. prop. of $+$
$(ax) \cdot \dfrac{1}{a} = [c + (-b)] \cdot \dfrac{1}{a}$	Mult. prop. of $=$
$\left(\dfrac{1}{a} \cdot a \right) x = [c + (-b)] \cdot \dfrac{1}{a}$	Comm. and assoc. props. of $\cdot$
$1x = [c + (-b)] \cdot \dfrac{1}{a}$	Inv. prop. of $\cdot$
$x = [c + (-b)] \cdot \dfrac{1}{a}$	Ident. prop. of $\cdot$
$x = [c + (-b)] \div a$	Proved in Example 2
$x = \dfrac{c + (-b)}{a}$	Def. of fraction

$$\therefore \text{ if } ax + b = c, \text{ then } x = \frac{c + (-b)}{a}$$

The following definition is needed as a reason in the exercises.

Multiplication of real numbers named by fractions is defined as follows (where neither b nor d equals 0). **definition**

$$\frac{a}{b} \cdot \frac{c}{d} = \frac{ac}{bd}$$

EXERCISES 5.10

Ⓐ 1. Besides axioms and previously proved theorems, _____ can be used as reasons in a proof.

2. What property stated earlier in this book was proved in Example **1**?

3. What are the missing reasons in Example **2**?

4. What is the first reason in Example **3**? Could we prove that $x = \dfrac{c + (-b)}{a}$ without first being *given* that $ax + b = c$?

5. In what part of the proof in Example **3** were two steps combined? Did we state two reasons? Were both reasons needed?

6. How is $\dfrac{a}{b} \cdot \dfrac{c}{d}$ defined? By this definition, does $\dfrac{ac}{bd} = \dfrac{a}{b} \cdot \dfrac{c}{d}$?

Give a reason for each step in the proof below. Let the variables stand for any real numbers.

Prove: If $x + b < c$, then $x < c + (-b)$.

7.	*Proof:* $\quad x + b < c$	?
8.	$[x + b] + (-b) < c + (-b)$	?
9.	$x + [b + (-b)] < c + (-b)$	?
10.	$x + 0 < c + (-b)$	?
11.	$x < c + (-b)$	?

12. To complete the proof above, we should include:

$\therefore$ _____ ?

Ⓑ Copy and complete each proof. Let *a, b, c,* and *d* be any real numbers.

13. *Prove:*

$a + (b - c) = (a + b) - c$

Proof:

$$a + (b - c) = a + [b + (-c)]$$
$$= [a + b] + (-c)$$
$$= (a + b) - c$$

14. *Prove:*

$(a - b) + c = (a + c) - b$

Proof:

$$(a - b) + c = [a + (-b)] + c$$
$$= [a + c] + (-b)$$
$$= (a + c) - b$$

15. *Prove:* if $a \neq 0$,

$$\frac{a}{a} = 1$$

Proof: $\dfrac{a}{a} = a \div a$

$$= a \cdot \frac{1}{a}$$

$$= 1$$

16. *Prove:* if $a \neq 0$ and $c \neq 0$,

$$\frac{ab}{ac} = \frac{b}{c}$$

Proof: $\dfrac{ab}{ac} = \dfrac{a}{a} \cdot \dfrac{b}{c}$

$$= 1 \cdot \frac{b}{c}$$

$$= \frac{b}{c}$$

17. *Prove:*

$$a(b - c) = ab - ac$$

Proof:

$$a(b - c) = a[b + (-c)]$$

$$= ab + a(-c)$$

$$= ab + (-ac)$$

$$= ab - ac$$

18. *Prove:*

$$a - (b + c) = (a - b) - c$$

Proof:

$$a - (b + c) = a + [-(b + c)]$$

$$= a + [(-b) + (-c)]$$

$$= [a + (-b)] + (-c)$$

$$= (a - b) - c$$

© **19.** *Prove:*

$$a - (b - c) = (a - b) + c$$

Proof:

$$a - (b - c) = a - [b + (-c)]$$

$$= [a - b] - (-c)$$

$$= (a - b) + [-(-c)]$$

$$= (a - b) + c$$

20. *Prove:* $\dfrac{1}{1} = 1$

Proof: $\dfrac{1}{1} = 1 \div 1$

$$= (1 \div 1) \cdot 1$$

$$= 1$$

21. *Prove:* $\dfrac{a}{1} = a$

Proof: $\dfrac{a}{1} = a \div 1$

$$= a \cdot \frac{1}{1}$$

$$= a \cdot 1$$

$$= a$$

22. *Prove:*

if $b \neq 0$, $c \neq 0$, and $d \neq 0$,

$$\frac{a}{b} \div \frac{c}{d} = \frac{a}{b} \cdot \frac{d}{c}$$

Proof: ?

Another Unsolved Problem

Christian Goldbach (1690–1764), a Russian mathematician, used inductive reasoning to predict that

 Every even number greater than 2 can be expressed as the sum of two primes. ▶

For example,

$$4 = 2 + 2 \qquad\qquad 10 = 7 + 3 \text{ or } 5 + 5$$

$$6 = 3 + 3 \qquad\qquad 12 = 7 + 5$$

$$8 = 5 + 3 \qquad\qquad 14 = 11 + 3 \text{ or } 7 + 7$$

Express each of the following as the sum of two primes.

1. 16 **2.** 18 **3.** 20 **4.** 22

5. 24 **6.** 26 **7.** 40 **8.** 50

Nobody has ever been able to find an even number greater than 2 that could not be expressed as the sum of two primes. But neither has anybody been able to prove that Goldbach's statement (called *Goldbach's conjecture*) must be true.

Simplify each expression. (Each base is a real number.)   5.1

1. $x^7 \cdot x^2$ **2.** $(4m)^2$ **3.** $(ab)^2 a^3$

4. $(-3r)^3(2r^3)$ **5.** $(-2n)^4(2n^3)$ **6.** $(st)^4(7s^2t)$

Completely factor each integer. Express results in exponent form.   5.2

7. 28 **8.** -54 **9.** -140 **10.** 128

Change each fraction to standard form.   5.3

11. $\frac{-6}{18}$ **12.** $\frac{20}{48}$ **13.** $\frac{80}{-36}$ **14.** $\frac{63}{105}$

Compute as indicated. Give your results in standard form.

15. $\frac{-7}{18} \cdot \frac{12}{7}$ **16.** $\frac{39}{35} \cdot \frac{25}{26}$

17. $\frac{20}{63} \div \left(-\frac{50}{42}\right)$ **18.** $\left(-\frac{22}{45}\right) \div \left(-\frac{44}{75}\right)$

19. $\frac{-5}{18} + \frac{7}{30}$ **20.** $\frac{11}{12} + \frac{-9}{20}$ 5.4

21. $\frac{8}{25} - \left(-\frac{7}{30}\right)$ **22.** $-\frac{5}{48} - \frac{5}{42}$

23. A drill-press operator needs a drill that is $\frac{3}{32}$ inch wider than a $\frac{5}{24}$-inch metal pin. What size drill does he need?

Rename each rational number as a repeating decimal, using a bar to   5.5
indicate the sequence of repeating digits.

24. $\frac{5}{4}$ **25.** $-\frac{8}{9}$ **26.** $\frac{13}{27}$ **27.** $\frac{12}{7}$

Rename each decimal as a fraction in standard form.

28. $1.2\overline{0}$ **29.** $0.\overline{02}$ **30.** $1.3\overline{8}$

Find each square root.   5.6

31. $\sqrt{64}$ **32.** $-\sqrt{196}$ **33.** $\sqrt{\frac{16}{49}}$ **34.** $-\sqrt{\frac{81}{121}}$

Using the divide-and-average method, find each square root correct to   5.7
the hundredths place.

35. $\sqrt{22}$ **36.** $\sqrt{62}$

Using the table on page 555, find x to the nearest thousandth.

37.

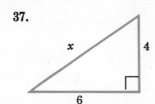

38.

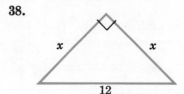

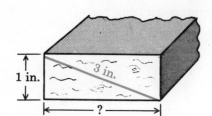

39. A cabinetmaker needs a piece of wood, 1 inch thick, that will give him a surface 3 inches wide when planed on the diagonal as shown at the left. To the nearest tenth of an inch, how wide should the wood be?

5.9 Identify the axiom or theorem illustrated. Let the variables stand for any real numbers.

40. $(-x) + (-y) = -(x + y)$

41. $-1(m + n) = -(m + n)$

42. $-1(a + b) = (-1a) + (-1b)$

43. $r + 0(s + t) = r + 0$

44. $xy = x(y + 0)$

45. $c + d = 1(c + d)$

5.10 Copy and complete each proof. Let the variables stand for any real numbers, where $b \neq 0$.

46. Prove: $\dfrac{a}{b} = a \cdot \dfrac{1}{b}$

Proof: $\dfrac{a}{b} = a \div b$

$= a \cdot \dfrac{1}{b}$

48. Prove: $\dfrac{a}{b} + \dfrac{c}{b} = \dfrac{a + c}{b}$

Proof: $\dfrac{a}{b} + \dfrac{c}{b} = a \cdot \dfrac{1}{b} + c \cdot \dfrac{1}{b}$

$= (a + c)\dfrac{1}{b}$

$= \dfrac{a + c}{b}$

47. Prove: $\dfrac{-a}{b} = -\dfrac{a}{b}$

Proof: $\dfrac{-a}{b} = (-a) \cdot \dfrac{1}{b}$

$= (-1a) \cdot \dfrac{1}{b}$

$= -1\left(a \cdot \dfrac{1}{b}\right)$

$= -1\left(\dfrac{a}{b}\right)$

$= -\dfrac{a}{b}$

Which lettered choice *best* matches each numbered term?

1. Power of a product

2. Unique factoring property

3. Rational numbers

4. Square root

5. Irrational numbers

6. Addition property
of opposites

a. $360 = 2^3 \cdot 3^2 \cdot 5$

b. $\sqrt{\frac{4}{9}}$

c. $a^m \cdot a^n = a^{m+n}$

d. Repeating decimals

e. Nonrepeating decimals

f. $(a \cdot b)^m = a^m \cdot b^m$

g. $(-a) + (-b) = -(a + b)$

Simplify or compute as indicated. (Express fractional results in standard form. Let the variables stand for any real numbers.)

7. $r^2 \cdot r^4$

8. $(2y)^2(2y)^3$

9. $(-2a)^3(-2a)$

10. $(-3m^2n)(-2mn)^2$

11. $\frac{-7}{24} \cdot \frac{27}{14}$

12. $(-\frac{21}{50}) \div (-\frac{36}{35})$

13. $\frac{7}{18} + (-\frac{11}{12})$

14. $-\frac{5}{42} - \frac{11}{54}$

15. Completely factor: -450.

16. Express as a repeating decimal: $\frac{16}{11}$.

17. Express by a fraction in standard form: $0.\overline{21}$.

18. Find: $-\sqrt{169}$.

19. Find: $\sqrt{\frac{121}{49}}$.

20. Find correct to the hundredths place: $\sqrt{28}$.

21. *Solve:* To the nearest tenth of a foot, how long a ramp is needed to reach across an 8-foot ditch if one side of the ditch is 3 feet higher than the other?

Ex. 21

22. Copy and complete the proof.
Let a be any real number.

   Prove: $a - a = 0$

   Proof: $a - a = a + (-a)$
   $= 0$

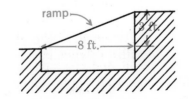

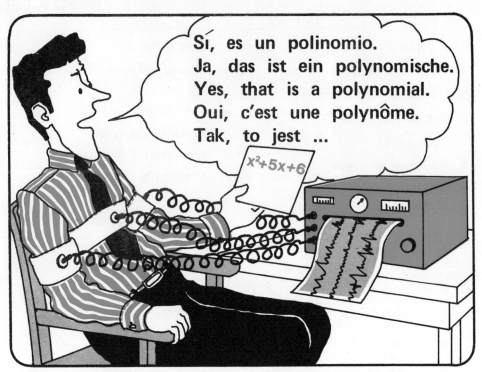

The **poly**linguist is taking a **poly**graph test on **poly**nomials.

Chapter

6

Polynomials

What does the prefix *poly-* mean? A special set of expressions, called polynomials, is very important in algebra. In this chapter, you will find out what a polynomial is and how to add, subtract, and multiply polynomials.

The prefix *mono-* means "one."

Constants (Each names a specific real number.)	Variables (Each stands for any number in a set of real numbers.)	Products (of constants and variables.)
$\frac{1}{2}$	x	$\frac{1}{2}m$
5	r	$-63r$
-63	y	xy
π	m	$3x^2$
$\sqrt{2}$	a	$-5ax^2y^3$

A **monomial** is a constant, a variable, or a product of a constant and one or more variables.

Expressions like the following are not monomials.

$$3x^2 + 7x \qquad 5a - 7 \qquad \frac{5y}{r^2x} \qquad \frac{1}{x} \qquad -5\sqrt{x}$$

The first is the sum of two monomials. The second is the difference of two monomials. The next two include a variable as a divisor. And the last one includes a variable under a radical sign.

The following table shows what we mean by the *numerical coefficient* (or simply *coefficient*) and by the *degree* of a monomial.

Monomial	Coefficient	Degree
$-8x^4y^3$	-8	7
$\sqrt{2}\,a^3b^3$	$\sqrt{2}$	6
$\frac{-9}{4}mn^2$	$-\frac{9}{4}$	3
$-x$ or $-1x^1$	-1	1
x or $1x^1$	1	1
3	3	0
-5	-5	0

Notice that the degree is the sum of the exponents of the variables in a monomial. The degree of a nonzero constant is 0.

A monomial is often called a *term*. The table below reviews what *like terms* are.

Monomials	Like terms?	Why?
$3x$, $6y$	No	Different variables
$2m$, $5m$	Yes	Same variable factors
$6x^3y$, $6x^2y$	No	Different powers of x
$-3ab^2c$, $8ab^2c$	Yes	Same variable factors

EXERCISES 6.1

Ⓐ Which of the expressions are monomials? If the expression is not a monomial, tell why it is not.

1. 4

2. $6m$

3. $\frac{2}{3}$

4. $-11m$

5. $\sqrt{x}$

6. $-\frac{1}{4}q$

7. $\frac{-3}{2}xy$

8. $\frac{5}{4}t$

9. $\frac{5xy}{z}$

10. $-3a\sqrt{m}$

11. $\frac{3}{x}$

12. $\frac{-4}{y^3}$

13. $\sqrt{7}y$

14. $5y^2 - 2$

15. $x + 3x^2$

16. $-3p - 7$

What is the coefficient and the degree of each monomial?

17. $3x$

18. -2

19. 7

20. $-6t^2$

21. $-2r^2s$

22. $8p^2q$

23. $6abc$

24. $-7xyz$

25. $\frac{1}{2}x^4$

26. $-\frac{1}{4}s^2$

27. $\sqrt{11}p^2q^2$

28. $-\sqrt{3}rs^3$

29. a^2

30. $-y^2$

31. $\frac{12}{5}x^2y$

32. $\frac{9}{7}m^2np$

Ⓑ Which pairs of monomials are *like terms*?

33. $3m^2n$, $-7m^2n$

34. $-16st^2$, $5st^2$

35. $8mn^2$, $-12m^2n$

36. $12st^2$, $-24s^2t$

37. -9, 16

38. -2, 32

39. $18x$, $14y$

40. $7r$, $-13s$

41. $3xyz$, $-8xyz$

42. $-4abc$, $-11abc$

43. x^4, $\sqrt{5}x^4$

44. $-\sqrt{3}y^3$, y^3

45. $-7x^2, \ 3x^4$ **46.** $-10y^4, \ 8y^2$ **47.** $9rs^2t^2, \ 12rs^2t^2$

48. $-5mn^2p^2, \ \frac{1}{2}mn^2p^2$ **49.** $3xy, \ -4yx$ **50.** $-5bca, \ 6abc$

© **51–60.** Study the following example. Then find the product of each pair of monomials in Exercises **33–42.**

$$\textbf{Example:} \ (-3x^2y)(4x^2y) = (-3 \cdot 4)(x^2 \cdot x^2)(y \cdot y)$$
$$= -12x^4y^2$$

61–70. Find the sum of each pair of monomials in Exercises **33–42,** and simplify your results if possible.

How Important Are Monomials?

Are monomials of any use? You might be surprised by the great number of formulas whose right members are nothing more than monomials. Here are some of them.

Circumference: $C = 2\pi r$

Area: $A = \pi r^2$

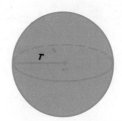

Volume: $V = \frac{4}{3}\pi r^3$

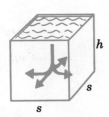

Pressure: $P = \frac{1}{2}sh^2$

Distance traveled: $d = \frac{1}{2}gt^2$

Heat: $Q = \frac{1}{2}RI^2$

The first three should be rather familiar. The last three may not be familiar, but the pictures suggest what these formulas are used for. Can you find other examples of how monomials are used?

6.2 POLYNOMIALS DEFINED

A **polynomial** is a monomial or the sum (or difference) of two or more monomials.

Each monomial in a polynomial is called a *term of the polynomial*. Polynomials are often named according to how many terms they have.

examples of polynomials

Monomials (one term)	Binomials (two terms)	Trinomials (three terms)	Polynomials (of more than three terms)
$\sqrt{5}x$	$x - 5$	$-x^2 - 6x + 5$	$x - 3x^2 - x^4 - 9$
$\frac{1}{2}$	$2y + 15$	$y - 2y^2 + 7y^3$	$z^5 + z^3 + z^2 - z + 2$
$-9y^3$	$3m^2 - m$	$7z + 6yz^2 - 1$	$xy + 2xy^2 + 3x^2y + 4$
$-16m^2n$	$5x^4 - xy$	$m^4 - 13n^2 - 2$	$x - y + 2z - m + s$

The **degree of a polynomial** is the degree of the highest degree monomial that is a term of the polynomial. If a polynomial contains only one variable, it is often convenient to write the polynomial in *descending powers of the variable*.

Polynomial	Degree	In descending powers
$\sqrt{13}m^4$	4	$\sqrt{13}m^4$
$7 - x$	1	$-x + 7$
$3y - 5 + y^2$	2	$y^2 + 3y - 5$
$m^5 - 2m + 7m^2 - 3$	5	$m^5 + 7m^2 - 2m - 3$
$9x - 3x^2 - 5x^3 - 7x^4$	4	$-7x^4 - 5x^3 - 3x^2 + 9x$

EXERCISES 6.2

Ⓐ Tell whether each expression is a polynomial.

1. 37 **2.** -29 **3.** $\sqrt{7}$ **4.** π

5. $3p + 2$ **6.** $5 - 11x$ **7.** $\frac{1}{2}y + 7$ **8.** $6m - \frac{1}{4}$

9. $\dfrac{3x - 7x^2}{1 + x}$ **10.** $\dfrac{3 + 2n}{5n}$ **11.** x^2 **12.** $q^4 - 1$

13. $x - 3x^2 + x^3$ **14.** $-y^4 + 6y - 9$

15. $11t^2 + \dfrac{5}{t} - 11$ **16.** $\dfrac{15}{n^2} - 3n + 11$

17. $\frac{1}{2}s^2 - 6s - \frac{1}{4} + s^2$ **18.** $3m - \frac{1}{2}m^2 + \frac{1}{4}m^3 - m^4$

Ⓑ Tell whether each polynomial is a monomial, binomial, trinomial, or polynomial with more than three terms.

19. $2x$ **20.** $13m^2x^3y$

21. $-5 - 2x$ **22.** $-3 - 5y$

23. $x^4 + 2 - 3x$ **24.** $y^4 + 5y - 3$

25. $\frac{1}{2}m - \frac{1}{4}m^2$ **26.** $-\frac{1}{4}n + \frac{1}{2}n^2$

27. $5 - 2p + 6p^2$ **28.** $4 - 12q^2 + 3q$

29. $\sqrt{2}x + \sqrt{11}x^2$ **30.** $-y + \sqrt{7}y^2$

31. $2 - \frac{1}{2}t - \sqrt{2}t^2$ **32.** $4 - \frac{1}{4}s - s^2$

33. $x - 7x^3 + x^4 - 3x^2$ **34.** $x^2 - 3x - 7 + 12x^3$

35. $m^2 - 11 - m$ **36.** $n^2 - 23 - n$

37. $6y + 7y^2 - 2 - 5y^3$ **38.** $2m - 4m^2 + 17 - 10m^3$

39–58. Find the degree of each polynomial in Exercises **19–38.**

59–68. Refer to Exercises **29–38.** Rewrite each of the polynomials in descending powers of the variable.

Ⓒ Write a polynomial for the perimeter of each figure.

69.

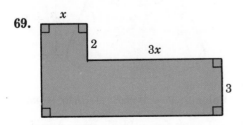

70.

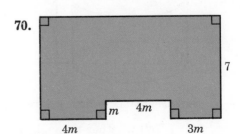

Numbers can be expressed in polynomial form, using powers of 10.

Place-value form	Expanded form	Polynomial form
27	20 + 7 or $2 \cdot 10 + 7$	$2 \cdot 10^1 + 7$
392	300 + 90 + 2 or $3 \cdot 100 + 9 \cdot 10 + 2$	$3 \cdot 10^2 + 9 \cdot 10^1 + 2$
705	700 + 0 + 5 or $7 \cdot 100 + 0 \cdot 10 + 5$	$7 \cdot 10^2 + 0 \cdot 10^1 + 5$

Express each number in polynomial form.

71. 32   **72.** 67   **73.** 126   **74.** 1001   **75.** 86205

76. What would it mean to write a polynomial containing one variable in *ascending powers* of the variable? Give three examples.

77–82. Refer to Exercises **33–38.** Rewrite each of the polynomials in *ascending powers* of the variable.

Using Polynomials

Like monomials, polynomials often occur as members of useful formulas. Two examples are given below.

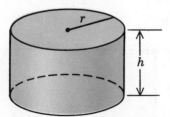

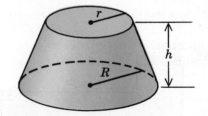

Surface area: $S = 2\pi r^2 + 2\pi rh$ Volume: $V = \frac{1}{3}(\pi hR^2 + \pi hRr + \pi hr^2)$

Tell whether the right member of each formula above is a monomial, binomial, trinomial, or a polynomial of more than three terms.

If each variable in a polynomial is replaced by a constant, the polynomial then names a specific number. Then we can *evaluate the polynomial.*

Let $x = 2$, $y = 3$, and $z = -4$.	
Polynomial	**How to evaluate**
$4xy^3 + 3x^2y^2 - 2x^3y$	$4(2)(3^3) + 3(2^2)(3^2) - 2(2^3)(3)$
	$= 4 \cdot 2 \cdot 27 + 3 \cdot 4 \cdot 9 - 2 \cdot 8 \cdot 3$
	$= 8 \cdot 27 + 12 \cdot 9 - 16 \cdot 3$
	$= 216 + 108 - 48$
	$= 324 - 48$
	$= 276$
$x^4 - 8y^2 + 3z^2$	$2^4 - 8(3^2) + 3(-4)^2$
	$= 16 - 8 \cdot 9 + 3 \cdot 16$
	$= 16 - 72 + 48$
	$= -56 + 48$
	$= -8$

A polynomial is sometimes named according to its degree.

Degree 0	**Degree 1**	**Degree 2**	**Degree 3**
⬇	⬇	⬇	⬇
Constant polynomial	**Linear polynomial**	**Quadratic polynomial**	**Cubic polynomial**
⬇	⬇	⬇	⬇
3	x	x^2	x^3
$\sqrt{2}$	$2q - 7$	$4xy$	$5st^2$
$\frac{1}{2} - 7$	$3 + 5m$	$2y^2 - 1$	$q^3 - 2q + 2$
$-\frac{1}{4}$	$7q - 4y$	$m^2 + 2n^2$	$y^3 - x^2$

The replacements for the variable that make a polynomial equal to 0 are called the *zeros of that polynomial*.

Examples: Find the zeros of the following polynomials. The replacement set is $\{-4, -2, 0, 2, 4\}$ in each case.

1. $2x + 4$	**2.** $5y - 20$
3. $2t^2 - 8$	**4.** $m^2 - 2m - 8$

SOLUTIONS: In Examples **1** and **2**, we can set each polynomial equal to zero and solve the equations.

1. $2x + 4 = 0$	**2.** $5y - 20 = 0$
$2x = -4$	$5y = 20$
$x = -2$	$y = 4$
The zero is -2.	The zero is 4.

For Examples **3** and **4**, we can find the zeros by evaluating the polynomials for each replacement.

3.

t	$2t^2 - 8 = ?$
-4	$2(-4)^2 - 8 = 24$
-2	$2(-2)^2 - 8 = 0$
0	$2(0)^2 - 8 = -8$
2	$2(2)^2 - 8 = 0$
4	$2(4)^2 - 8 = 24$

The zeros are -2 and 2.

4.

m	$m^2 - 2m - 8 = ?$
-4	$(-4)^2 - 2(-4) - 8 = 16$
-2	$(-2)^2 - 2(-2) - 8 = 0$
0	$(0)^2 - 2(0) - 8 = -8$
2	$(2)^2 - 2(2) - 8 = -8$
4	$(4)^2 - 2(4) - 8 = 0$

The zeros are -2 and 4.

EXERCISES 6.3

Ⓐ Tell whether each polynomial is linear, quadratic, or cubic.

1. $4x$	**2.** $15y$	**3.** $11p^2$	**4.** $x^3 - 6x$
5. $-3q^2$	**6.** $4t^3 - 17t$	**7.** $5x + 7$	**8.** $12 + 3n$
9. $p^2 - 4p + 6$		**10.** $17r + r^2 - 4$	
11. $n^3 - 6n^2 + 4n - 2$		**12.** $6x^3 + 3x^2 - 7$	

13. Which polynomials in Exercises 1–12 are constant polynomials?

14. What is the zero of a polynomial like $8z$? 0

Let $x = -3$, $y = 5$, $z = -2$, $s = 4$, and $t = 6$. Then evaluate each polynomial.

15. $3x$ **16.** $5s$ **17.** $7z$ **18.** $-3y$

19. $4z^2$ **20.** $-3y^2$ **21.** $-2t^2$ **22.** $6x^2$

23. $x^2 - 2$ **24.** $t^2 + 3$ **25.** $4z^2 + 6$ **26.** $-3y^2 - 10$

Ⓑ **27.** $s^2 - t^2$ **28.** $x^2 + y^2$ **29.** $xz - z^2$ **30.** $st + 2t^2$

31. $x^2 - 6x + 7$ **32.** $x^2 - 4x + 12$

33. $y^2 + 16y - 2$ **34.** $y^2 + 7y - 13$

35. $s^2t + st^2$ **36.** $4s^2t + 2st^2$

37. $x^4 + 4x^2 - 7$ **38.** $y^4 + 4y - 11$

39. $12x^2y^2 - t^2$ **40.** $7s^2t^2 - x^2$

41. $\frac{1}{2}xy + stz$ **42.** $\frac{1}{4}st + xyz$

43. $0.5x^2 - xt$ **44.** $0.7y^2 - ys$

45. $xy + ys - st$ **46.** $st - ys + xy$

47. $\frac{1}{2}x^2 + z^2 - \frac{1}{4}t^2$ **48.** $\frac{1}{4}z^2 + \frac{1}{2}s^2 - x^2$

49. $t^3 + 4t^2 + 6t - 7$ **50.** $3s^3 + 5s^2 + 8s - 17$

Let the replacement set for each variable be $\{-4, -3, -1, 1, 3, 4\}$. Then find the zeros of each polynomial if there are any.

51. $3x - 12$ **52.** $5y - 20$ **53.** $x^2 - 1$ **54.** $x^2 - 9$

55. $x^2 + 4x$ **56.** $x^2 + 3x$ **57.** $2x^2 - 54$ **58.** $3p^3 - 81$

59. $5x^2 - 17x + 6$ **60.** $7y^2 - 22y + 3$

61. $m^2 - 7m - 30$ **62.** $n^2 - 3n - 4$

Ⓒ Let the replacement set for each variable be the real numbers. Then see if you can find a zero for each polynomial.

63. $20 - \frac{1}{2}y + 6$ **64.** $2(x - 2) + 4$

65. $x^3 - 2x^2$ **66.** $y^3 - 27$

67. $x^2 - 6x + 8$ **68.** $x^2 - 13x + 12$

1. Copy and complete the chart.

Monomial	Coefficient	Degree
5		
$\sqrt{3}p$		
$-\frac{1}{2}x^2y$		
$-11mn^3$		

2. Separate the set $\{4, -6x^2, 3mn, \sqrt{2}x^2, \sqrt{5}, \frac{1}{2}x^2, -15mn\}$ into subsets of like terms.

Answer Exercises 3–9 for the polynomials listed at the right.

3. Which are monomials?

4. Which are binomials?

5. Which are trinomials?

6. Which are constant polynomials?

7. Which are linear polynomials?

8. Which are quadratic polynomials?

9. Which are cubic polynomials?

a. $4xy$

b. $x + 7$

c. $\sqrt{2}x^3 - 2$

d. $m^2 - 2m + 3$

e. $a^3 - 2a$

f. $\frac{1}{2}x^2 + \frac{1}{4}$

g. $m^2 - \sqrt{5}m + 2$

h. 17

i. $\sqrt{7}a^3$

10. Write $3x - 7x^3 - 5 + 4x^2$ in descending powers of the variable.

Let $x = -4$, $y = 6$, and $m = -2$. Then evaluate each polynomial.

11. $4x + 6$

12. $m^2 + y - 2x$

13. $-x^2 + 2x + y^2$

Find the zeros of each polynomial. The replacement set for each variable is $\{-4, -2, 0, 2, 4\}$.

14. $2x - 8$

15. $y^2 - 4$

16. $m^2 - 6m + 8$

Finding Zeros by Computer

Electronic computers affect each of us more each day. They are used by schools for scheduling; by cities for traffic control; by farmers to study costs and production; by professional football teams to analyze competing teams; by stores to keep track of inventories and charge accounts; by airlines for reservations—the list of uses is almost endless.

A computer could help us solve certain algebra problems. For example, we could use a computer to help find the zeros of a polynomial like

$$x^2 + 0.6x - 0.16.$$

"This computer is almost human. It makes a lot of mistakes!"

We might first outline a plan in a flow chart. Then, we would need to write a program telling the computer exactly what we want it to do. Suppose the following was obtained as part of the "PRINT-OUT" from the computer.

X	X↑2 + 0.6*X − 0.16	VALUE
−1.400	(−1.40)↑2 + 0.6∗(−1.40) − 0.16 =	0.960
−1.200	(−1.20)↑2 + 0.6∗(−1.20) − 0.16 =	0.560
−1.000	(−1.00)↑2 + 0.6∗(−1.00) − 0.16 =	0.240
−0.800	(−0.80)↑2 + 0.6∗(−0.80) − 0.16 =	−0.000
−0.600	(−0.60)↑2 + 0.6∗(−0.60) − 0.16 =	−0.160
−0.400	(−0.40)↑2 + 0.6∗(−0.40) − 0.16 =	−0.240
−0.200	(−0.20)↑2 + 0.6∗(−0.20) − 0.16 =	−0.240
−0.000	(−0.00)↑2 + 0.6∗(−0.00) − 0.16 =	−0.160
0.200	(0.20)↑2 + 0.6∗(0.20) − 0.16 =	0.000
0.400	(0.40)↑2 + 0.6∗(0.40) − 0.16 =	0.240
0.600	(0.60)↑2 + 0.6∗(0.60) − 0.16 =	0.560
0.800	(0.80)↑2 + 0.6∗(0.80) − 0.16 =	0.960

Explain what you think the computer was instructed to do. (Refer to page 77 for the meanings of ↑ and ∗.) What do you guess to be the zeros of the polynomial?

6.4 ADDITION

To add two polynomials we simply place a plus sign between them and then find the simplest name for the result. To find the *simplest name for a polynomial* we combine all like terms and then arrange the terms in descending powers of a variable.

Example 1: Add $3z + 7$ and $9z + 2$.

SHORT SOLUTION:

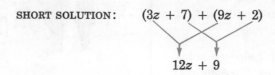

$$12z + 9$$

DETAILED SOLUTION:

$(3z + 7) + (9z + 2)$	Given
$= (3z + 9z) + (7 + 2)$	Assoc. and comm. props. of $+$
$= (3 + 9)z + (7 + 2)$	Dist. prop.
$= 12z + 9$	Addition

Since we know that the distributive property can always be used to combine like terms, we sometimes arrange the polynomials in vertical columns of like terms and then add.

Example 2: Add $3x^2 + 2$ and $7x^2 - 6x + 3$.

SHORT SOLUTION:

$$(3x^2 + 2) + (7x^2 - 6x + 3)$$

$$10x^2 - 6x + 5$$

VERTICAL METHOD:

$$
\begin{array}{r}
3x^2 + 2 \\
(+)\ 7x^2 - 6x + 3 \\
\hline
10x^2 - 6x + 5
\end{array}
$$

The *horizontal method* shown in the *short solutions* is probably the more convenient. (Of course, the colored arrows can be left out.) This method allows us to find the sum in simplest form without rewriting the problem as is required by the *vertical method*.

Example 3: Add $3s^2 + 5st - 7t^2$ and $6s^2 - 7st + 6t^2$.

SHORT SOLUTION:

VERTICAL METHOD:

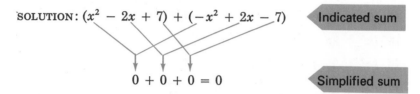

$$(3s^2 + 5st - 7t^2) + (6s^2 - 7st + 6t^2)$$

$$9s^2 - 2st - t^2$$

$$3s^2 + 5st - 7t^2$$

$$(+)\ 6s^2 - 7st + 6t^2$$

$$9s^2 - 2st - t^2$$

A special case follows.

Example 4: Add $x^2 - 2x + 7$ and $-x^2 + 2x - 7$.

SOLUTION: $(x^2 - 2x + 7) + (-x^2 + 2x - 7)$ ◄ Indicated sum

$$0 + 0 + 0 = 0$$ ◄ Simplified sum

What polynomial can we add to $3x - 6$ to get a sum of zero as in Example 4 above? We simply choose the polynomial with each term the opposite of the corresponding term in the given polynomial.

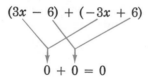

$$(3x - 6) + (-3x + 6)$$

$$0 + 0 = 0$$

To find the **opposite (additive inverse) of a polynomial,** change each term of the polynomial to its opposite.

opposite of
a polynomial

Polynomial	Opposite
$5a$	$-(5a)$ or $-5a$
$-x^2 + 8x$	$-(-x^2 + 8x)$ or $x^2 - 8x$
$y^3 - y + 2$	$-(y^3 - y + 2)$ or $-y^3 + y - 2$

EXERCISES 6.4

Ⓐ Find the opposite of each polynomial.

1. $5x^2$

2. $-6y^2$

3. $x - 7$

4. $y + 2$

5. $0.3m^2 - 2m$

6. $0.6n^2 - 4n$

7. $\frac{1}{2}x^2 - 4x + \frac{1}{2}$

8. $\frac{1}{4}y^2 - 7y + \frac{1}{4}$

9. $2a + 3b - 2c$

10. $7a + 2b - 3c$

Add the polynomials.

11. $(3x + 2) + (4x - 7)$

12. $(6k - 3) + (5k + 2)$

13. $(5y + 9) + (6y - 11)$

14. $(11s + 7) + (4s + 4)$

15. $(x^2 - 2x + 3) + (x^2 - 7x + 7)$

16. $(y^2 - 3y + 9) + (y^2 - 12y + 2)$

17. $(2x - 2y + 3z) + (5x - 6y - 12z)$

18. $(4a - 6b + 2c) + (3a + 2b - 4c)$

Ⓑ Use the vertical method to add the polynomials.

19. $(7y - 3) + (5y + 5)$

20. $(10m + 7) + (-3m + 2)$

21. $(6a - 7ab) + (6ab + 10b)$

22. $(7s - 8st) + (2st + 3t)$

23. $(\frac{1}{4}x - 9) + (\frac{1}{4}x - 9)$

24. $(\frac{1}{2}y - 12) + (\frac{1}{2}y + 12)$

Use the horizontal method to add the polynomials.

25. $3p + (4p + 7)$

26. $8m + (9m - 2)$

27. $(11t - 4) + 5t$

28. $(13n - 5) + (-8n)$

29. $(3x^2 - 2) + (9x^2 + 6)$

30. $(4y^2 + 2) + (-5y^2 - 3)$

31. $(12p^2 - 3) + (12p^2 + 3)$

32. $(-3n^2 + n) + (6n^2 - 2n)$

33. $(3t^2 - 6t) + (2t^2 - 7)$

34. $(6s^2 - 4s) + (3s + 6)$

35. $(5m - 4) + (6m^2 - 11)$

36. $(10t^2 - 5t) + (10t - 5)$

37. $(6q + 4) + (-6q - 4)$

38. $(3 + 6z) + (-3 - 6z)$

39. $(7x^2 - 3y^2) + (7x^2 + 3y^2)$

40. $(3m^2 - 9n^2) + (-3m^2 - 9n^2)$

210   CHAPTER 6   POLYNOMIALS

41. $(x^2 + 7) + (-x^2 - 7)$ **42.** $(-y^2 + 12) + (y^2 - 12)$

43. $(3xy + 4xy^2 + 7xy^3) + (-3xy + 4xy^2 - 7xy^3)$

44. $(9mn - 2mn^2 - 5mn^3) + (-9mn + 4mn^2 + 5mn^3)$

45. $(0.1r + s - t) + (r - 0.2s - t)$

46. $(0.4m - n + p) + (m + n + 0.6p)$

Write a polynomial for the perimeter of each figure.

47.

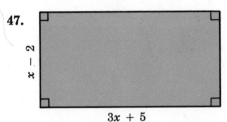

$3x + 5$

$8x + 6$

48.

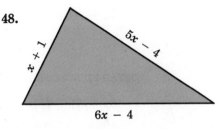

$6x - 4$

$12x - 7$

Add the polynomials.

49. $8xy - 7x^2y + 2x^3y, \quad 2xy - 5x^2y + 9x^3y$

50. $3xy + 12xy^2 - 7xy^3, \quad 2xy + 4xy^2 - 7xy^3$

51. $2mnp^2 - 7m^2n^2, \quad 5m^2n^2 - 12p^2$

52. $2abc^2 - 9a^2b^2, \quad 11a^2b^2 + 7b^2$

53. $3a - 6b + 5c - d, \quad 2a - 6b - 5c + d$

54. $4m - 9n - 6p + 5q, \quad 7m + 9n - 6p - 5q$

© Add the polynomials. Give detailed solutions with reasons for each step. You may combine steps when convenient.

55. $3x - 7, \quad 7x + 4$ **56.** $5x + 7, \quad 11x - 9$

57. $2x - 3, \quad 13x + 11$ **58.** $4x + 6, \quad 7x - 12$

59. $2m^2 + 4m + 12, \quad 8m - 6$ **60.** $3a^2 - 14a + 17, \quad 11a + 2$

61. $2x^2 + 7x - 2, \quad x^2 - 3x + 11$

62. $9y^2 - 2y + 7, \quad 3y^2 + 6y - 13$

6.5 SUBTRACTION

The subtraction property, $a - b = a + (-b)$, can be used to subtract one polynomial from another.

Example 1: From $5x - 7$, subtract $11x + 4$.

SHORT SOLUTION:

$$(5x - 7) - (11x + 4)$$
$$(5x - 7) + [-11x + (-4)]$$

$$-6x - 11$$

DETAILED SOLUTION:

$(5x - 7) - (11x + 4)$	Given
$= [5x + (-7)] + [-(11x + 4)]$	Subtr. prop.
$= [5x + (-7)] + [-11x + (-4)]$	Opposite of a poly.
$= [5x + (-11x)] + [-7 + (-4)]$	Assoc. and comm. props. of $+$
$= [5 + (-11)]x + [-7 + (-4)]$	Dist. prop.
$= -6x + (-11)$	Addition
$= -6x - 11$	Subtr. prop.

Carefully study the first two steps above. Notice how the subtraction problem was changed into an addition problem involving the opposite of a polynomial.

> In general, subtracting a polynomial is equivalent to adding its opposite.

Example 2: From $2z - 8$, subtract $5z + 2$.

SOLUTION:

$$(2z - 8) - (5z + 2)$$
$$= (2z - 8) + (-5z - 2)$$
$$= (2z - 5z) + (-8 - 2)$$
$$= -3z - 10$$

Example 3: Simplify $(8x^2 - 6x + 7) - (4x^2 + 3x - 12)$.

SOLUTION: $(8x^2 - 6x + 7) - (4x^2 + 3x - 12)$

$$= (8x^2 - 6x + 7) + (-4x^2 - 3x + 12)$$
$$= (8x^2 - 4x^2) + (-6x - 3x) + (7 + 12)$$
$$= 4x^2 - 9x + 19$$

EXERCISES 6.5

Ⓐ Find the opposite of each polynomial.

1. $3x$ **2.** $-7y$ **3.** $2x^2 + 6$ **4.** $-9y^2 + 5$

5. $\frac{1}{2}a^2 - 0.3a + \frac{1}{3}$ **6.** $2m^3 - 6m^2 + m - 3$

Simplify each difference of polynomials.

7. $(3p - 11) - (7p + 2)$ **8.** $(6k + 9) - (-2k - 3)$

9. $(-2m - 2) - (6m + 4)$ **10.** $(17x + 2) - (12x - 9)$

11. $(-8n - 8) - (2n - 3)$ **12.** $(-6y + 7) - (6y + 3)$

13. $(9s - 12) - (-9s - 12)$ **14.** $(4t - 2) - (4t - 2)$

15. $(11x + 13) - (11x - 13)$ **16.** $(13y - 2) - (13y + 2)$

17. $(a - 16) - (7a - 16)$ **18.** $(9t + \frac{1}{2}) - (-3t - \frac{1}{4})$

Ⓑ **19.** $(x - 2y) - (3x - 7y)$ **20.** $(y - 3z) - (2y - 12z)$

21. $(9x^2 + 5x) - (6x^2 - 7x)$ **22.** $(12y^2 + 4y) - (9y^2 - 8y)$

23. $(x^2 - 5x + 7) - (x^2 + 5x - 7)$

24. $(y^2 - 7y + 11) - (y^2 + 7y - 11)$

25. $(x^2 - 11x + 4) - (x^2 - 2x + 11)$

26. $(y^2 + 10y - 13) - (y^2 - 7y - 2)$

27. $(4x^2 - 14x + 2) - (8x^2 + 2x - 7)$

28. $(6p^2 - 12p - 6) - (9p^2 - 3p + 7)$

29. $(5st - 7s) - (12st - 2s)$ **30.** $(3pq - 2p) - (12pq - 6p)$

31. $(x^2 - y^2) - (x^2 + y^2)$ **32.** $(s^2 - t^2) - (s^2 + t^2)$

33. $(\frac{1}{4}x^2 - \frac{1}{4}x) - (\frac{1}{4}x^2 + \frac{1}{2}x)$ **34.** $(\frac{1}{4}y^2 - \frac{1}{2}y) - (\frac{1}{2}y^2 + \frac{1}{4}y)$

Use the vertical method to find each difference.

Example:
$$\begin{array}{r} 3x^2 - 6x + 7 \\ (-)\ \ x^2 + 7x + 2 \\ \hline \end{array} \quad \leftarrow \text{means} \rightarrow \quad \begin{array}{r} 3x^2 - 6x + 7 \\ (+) -x^2 - 7x - 2 \\ \hline 2x^2 - 13x + 5 \end{array}$$

35.
$$\begin{array}{r} 7y^2 \qquad\ + 4 \\ (-)\ 3y^2 - 2y - 6 \\ \hline \end{array}$$

36.
$$\begin{array}{r} 4x - 11 \\ (-)\ 3x^2 + 4x - 11 \\ \hline \end{array}$$

37.
$$\begin{array}{r} 2m^2n^2 - 6mn - 13 \\ (-)\ 6m^2n^2 - 3mn - \ \ 7 \\ \hline \end{array}$$

38.
$$\begin{array}{r} 5x^2t^2 - 6xt + 17 \\ (-)\ 11x^2t^2 + 4xt - \ \ 6 \\ \hline \end{array}$$

39. $(5x^2 + 7) - (15x + 2)$

40. $(11p^2 - 11) - (-2p + 7)$

Simplify each difference of polynomials.

41. $(5x^2y^2 + 6xy - 1) - (x^2y^2 - 5xy - 1)$

42. $(0.2t^2 - 0.7t) - (0.4t^2 + 0.8t)$

43. $(8x^2 - 4x + 3) - (7x - 11)$

44. $(12y^2 + 9y - 13) - (11y - 21)$

45. $(13p - 13) - (-18p^2 + 13p - 7)$

46. $(12m - 10) - (2m^2 + 12m - 12)$

© Simplify each expression.

47. $(x - 2) + (x + 3) + (x - 7)$

48. $(x^2 - 2x) - (x - 7) + (x^2 + 2x - 2)$

49. $(m^2 - 8m) + (6m - 2) - (m^2 - 2m + 2)$

50. $(s^2 - 6s - 12) - (3s^2 + 2s - 6) + (-6s^2 - 2s + 5)$

Simplify. Give detailed solutions with reasons for each step. You may combine steps when convenient.

51. $(x - 7) - (3x + 4)$

52. $(3x^2 - 7x + 5) - (2x^2 + 2x - 8)$

We can use the distributive property of multiplication over addition to multiply one polynomial by another.

Example 1: Multiply $3m$ and $4m - 7$.

SHORT SOLUTION:	DETAILED SOLUTION:	
$3m[4m - 7]$	$3m[4m - 7]$	Given
$= 3m \cdot 4m - 3m \cdot 7$	$= 3m[4m + (-7)]$	Subtr. prop.
$= 12m^2 - 21m$	$= 3m \cdot 4m + 3m(-7)$	Dist. prop.
	$= (3 \cdot 4)(m \cdot m) + 3(-7)m$	Assoc. and comm. props. of $\cdot$
	$= 12m^2 + (-21)m$	Multiplication
	$= 12m^2 - 21m$	Subtr. prop.

To find a product like $(-4x)(5x^2 + 6x - 2)$, we use the extended distributive property.

$$(-4x)(5x^2 + 6x - 2) = (-4x)(5x^2) + (-4x)(6x) - (-4x)(2)$$
$$= -20x^3 - 24x^2 + 8x$$

In the following example, note how useful the distributive property can be when we multiply two binomials.

Example 2: Multiply $3x - 5y$ and $2x + 6y$.

SOLUTION:

$$(3x - 5y)(2x + 6y) = (3x - 5y)(2x) + (3x - 5y)(6y)$$
$$= (3x \cdot 2x - 5y \cdot 2x) + (3x \cdot 6y - 5y \cdot 6y)$$
$$= 6x^2 - 10xy + 18xy - 30y^2$$
$$= 6x^2 + (-10 + 18)xy - 30y^2$$
$$= 6x^2 + 8xy - 30y^2$$

Note use of distributive property.

In the second step above, notice that each term of the first binomial is multiplied by each term of the second binomial. This suggests that we can arrange the polynomials vertically and find the product as shown on the next page.

$$3x - 5y$$
$$(\times)\ \ 2x + 6y \qquad\qquad (3x - 5y)2x$$
$$\overline{\quad\ 6x^2 - 10xy} \qquad\quad (3x - 5y)6y$$
$$(+)\qquad\quad 18xy - 30y^2 \qquad -10xy + 18xy$$
$$\overline{6x^2 + 8xy - 30y^2}$$

Example 3: Find the product $(x + 2)(x^2 + 4x + 6)$.

SOLUTION I: (Horizontal method)

$$\begin{aligned}
(x + 2)(x^2 + 4x + 6) &= (x + 2)x^2 + (x + 2)4x + (x + 2)6 \\
&= x^3 + 2x^2 + 4x^2 + 8x + 6x + 12 \\
&= x^3 + (2 + 4)x^2 + (8 + 6)x + 12 \\
&= x^3 + 6x^2 + 14x + 12
\end{aligned}$$

SOLUTION II: (Vertical method)

$$x^2 + 4x + 6$$
$$(\times)\qquad\quad x + 2 \qquad\qquad (x^2 + 4x + 6)x$$
$$\overline{x^3 + 4x^2 + 6x} \qquad\qquad (x^2 + 4x + 6)2$$
$$(+)\qquad\quad 2x^2 + 8x + 12$$
$$\overline{x^3 + 6x^2 + 14x + 12}$$

EXERCISES 6.6

Ⓐ Find each product.

1. $7(p + 1)$

2. $(q - 5)4$

3. $5a(3a - 6b)$

4. $(2x + 5y)7x$

5. $(2m + 3n)2n$

6. $3s(6r - 4s)$

7. $(5x - 4)(-5x)$

8. $(-7y)(11y + 3)$

9. $-7xy(2xy - 8)$

10. $(7xy + 9)(-5xy)$

11. $4mn(6m^2n^2 + 5mn)$

12. $3ab(7a^2b^2 - 9ab)$

13. $6x(2x^2 - 3x + 2)$

14. $(4y^2 + 5y - 7)4y$

Ⓑ **15.** $2ab(3a^2 + 7ab - 6b^2)$

16. $(6m^3 - 2m^2 + 3m)5mn$

17. $-3p^2(11p^2 + 6pq + 12q^2)$

18. $(13s^2 + 2st + t^2)(-4t^2)$

19. $x^3(x^3 - x^2 + x - 2)$

20. $(3y^3 + 2y^2 + y - 1)y^3$

Find each product. Use the horizontal method.

21. $(x + 2)(x + 3)$

22. $(y - 5)(y - 1)$

23. $(m - 5)(m + 5)$

24. $(s + 6)(s - 6)$

25. $(r - 10)(r - 11)$

26. $(t + 12)(t + 12)$

27. $(7 - y)(7 + y)$

28. $(5 - x)(5 + x)$

29. $(2s - 7)(2s + 7)$

30. $(5t - 7)(5t + 7)$

31. $(\frac{1}{2}x + \frac{1}{2})(\frac{1}{2}x - \frac{1}{2})$

32. $(\frac{1}{4}p - \frac{1}{2})(\frac{1}{4}p + \frac{1}{2})$

33. $(3t + 2s)(2t + 4s)$

34. $(5m + 4n)(3m + 2n)$

35. $(5 - 7x)(7 - 5x)$

36. $(3 - 10x)(5 - 2x)$

37. $(3xy + 4)(4xy - 5)$

38. $(2xy - 3)(5xy + 6)$

39. $(x + 2)(x^2 - x + 1)$

40. $(m + 3)(m^2 - m + 2)$

41. $(y - 1)(y^2 - 2y + 1)$

42. $(x - 2)(x^2 - x + 3)$

Find each product. Use the vertical method.

43. $(x - 8)(x - 7)$

44. $(y - 5)(y - 8)$

45. $(x - 5y)(x + 11y)$

46. $(5t - 3)(8t + 9)$

47. $(a + b)(a + ab + b)$

48. $(m + n)(m + 2mn + n)$

49. $(x + y)(x^2 - xy + y^2)$

50. $(r + s)(r^2 - rs + s^2)$

51. $(2a - 2b)(5a^2 + 3ab - b^2)$

52. $(5x - y)(2x^2 + 3xy - 4y^2)$

Write a polynomial for the area of each figure. Simplify the polynomial if possible.

53.

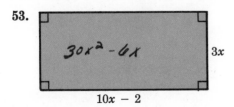

$30x^2 - 6x$

$3x$

$10x - 2$

54.

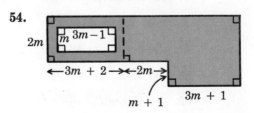

$2m$ m $3m - 1$

$\leftarrow 3m + 2 \rightarrow \leftarrow 2m \rightarrow$

$m + 1$ $3m + 1$

Find each product. HINT: $(a - b)^2$ means $(a - b)(a - b)$.

55. $(6k - 3)^2$ **56.** $(5a - 2)^2$ **57.** $(7 + 8b)^2$

58. $(9 + 6c)^2$ **59.** $(a - b)^2$ **60.** $(a + b)^2$

© Find each product.

61. $(x + y + z)(x + y + z)$ **62.** $(m - n - p)(m - n - p)$

63. $(a + b + c)(2a - 3b + c)$ **64.** $(3x + 2y - z)(x - y + z)$

65. A rectangle is 5 meters longer than it is wide. Find a polynomial that represents the area of the rectangle.

66. A rectangle is 3 times as long as it is wide. Represent the area of a rectangle which is 2 feet longer and 8 feet wider.

A sheet-metal worker cuts 2-inch-square corners out of an x-by-x-inch sheet of metal. The flaps are then folded to form a pan. (See figures.)

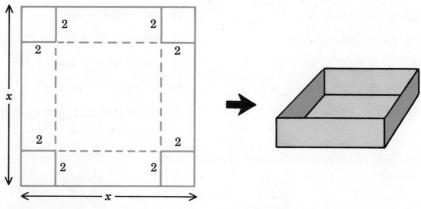

Find:

67. the perimeter of the pan.

68. the area of the bottom of the pan.

69. the volume of the pan.

6.7 ANOTHER LOOK AT MULTIPLICATION

To simplify the product

$$(a + b)(c + d),$$

we could use the distributive property as follows.

$$(a + b)(c + d) = a(c + d) + b(c + d)$$
$$= ac + ad + bc + bd$$

Notice that a shortcut for finding the product of two binomials is simply to add up the products of four pairs of terms.

1. *First terms* of the binomials.

2. *Outside terms* of the binomials.

3. *Inside terms* of the binomials.

4. *Last terms* of the binomials.

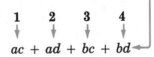

We call this shortcut the **FOIL method** for multiplying two binomials.

The product of two binomials can be illustrated with areas of rectangles.

$$\text{Total area} = \begin{cases} \text{length} \times \text{width} = (a + b)(c + d) \\ \text{sum of small areas} = ac + ad + bc + bd \end{cases}$$

Thus, we again conclude that

$$(a + b)(c + d) = ac + ad + bc + bd.$$

Example 1: Find the product $(x + 2)(x + 4)$ by using

    a.   the distributive property.

    b.   the FOIL method.

    c.   the areas of rectangles.

SOLUTIONS:

a.
$$(x + 2)(x + 4) = x(x + 4) + 2(x + 4)$$
$$= x^2 + 4x + 2x + 2 \cdot 4$$
$$= x^2 + (4 + 2)x + 2 \cdot 4$$
$$= x^2 + 6x + 8$$

Notice how 2 and 4 reoccur in the product as indicated by the small colored arrows above.

b.
$$(x + 2)(x + 4) = x^2 + 4x + 2x + 8$$
$$= x^2 + 6x + 8$$

c.

Total area $= \begin{cases} (x + 2)(x + 4) \\ x^2 + 4x + 2x + 8 \\ \boxed{x^2} + \boxed{6x} + \boxed{8} \end{cases}$

More examples of the FOIL method.
I. $(3x + 4y)(5x + 3y) = 15x^2 + 9xy + 20xy + 12y^2$ $= 15x^2 + 29xy + 12y^2$
II. $(y + 7z)(y - 2z) = y^2 - 2yz + 7yz - 14z^2$ $= y^2 + 5yz - 14z^2$
III. $(4a - 3)(6a - 7) = 24a^2 - 28a - 18a + 21$ $= 24a^2 - 46a + 21$

By the meaning of an exponent, $(a + b)^2 = (a + b)(a + b)$. Thus, the FOIL method can be used to show the following.

$(a + b)^2 = a^2 + 2ab + b^2$	Square of a sum
$(a - b)^2 = a^2 - 2ab + b^2$	Square of a difference
$(a + b)(a - b) = a^2 - b^2$	Product of the sum and difference of two numbers

Example 2: Find the following special products.

     a. $(2x + 4y)^2$ **b.** $(3m - k)^2$ **c.** $(4x + 7y)(4x - 7y)$

SOLUTIONS:

     a. $(2x + 4y)^2 = (2x)^2 + 2 \cdot 2x \cdot 4y + (4y)^2 = 4x^2 + 16xy + 16y^2$

     b. $(3m - k)^2 = (3m)^2 - 2 \cdot 3m \cdot k + (k)^2 = 9m^2 - 6mk + k^2$

     c. $(4x + 7y)(4x - 7y) = (4x)^2 - (7y)^2 = 16x^2 - 49y^2$

EXERCISES 6.7

Ⓐ Find the products. (Look for patterns that repeat.)

  1. $(x + 5)(x + 7)$ **2.** $(b - 3)(b - 7)$ **3.** $(a + 5)(a + 4)$

  4. $(m + 1)(m + 1)$ **5.** $(2 + k)(3 + k)$ **6.** $(a + 4)(a - 5)$

  7. $(y + 2)^2$ **8.** $(y - 1)^2$ **9.** $(m + 5)^2$

10. $(x + 3)(x - 2)$ **11.** $(y + 7)(y - 3)$ **12.** $(x + 3)(2 - y)$

13. $(m + 1)^2$ **14.** $(m + 1)(m - 1)$ **15.** $(m - 1)^2$

16. $(e + f)(e - f)$ **17.** $(mn + 3)(mn - 3)$ **18.** $(s^2 - 9)(s^2 + 9)$

Ⓑ Find each product using shortcuts such as in the example.

Example: $27 \cdot 33 = (30 - 3)(30 + 3) = 900 - 9 = 891$

19. $19 \cdot 21$ **20.** $69 \cdot 71$ **21.** $28 \cdot 32$ **22.** $14 \cdot 16$

23. $63 \cdot 57$ **24.** $48 \cdot 52$ **25.** $24 \cdot 26$ **26.** $36 \cdot 44$

Find the products.

27. $(3x + 5)(5x - 3)$

28. $(7y + 4)(4y - 7)$

29. $(8 - x)(7 + x)$

30. $(11 - p)(7 + p)$

31. $(5m - 3n)(4m - 2n)$

32. $(7p - 8q)(3p - 5q)$

33. $(0.1x + 0.2)(0.2x - 0.3)$

34. $(0.3y - 0.4)(0.2y + 0.6)$

35. $(\frac{1}{2}xy - 2)(\frac{1}{2}xy + 2)$

36. $(\frac{1}{4}mn + 4)(\frac{1}{4}mn - 4)$

37. $(c - 7)(c + 8)$

38. $(d - 6)(d - 8)$

39. $(e + f)(e - f)$

40. $(c - d)(c + d)$

41. $(mn + 3)(mn - 3)$

42. $(xy + 2)(xy - 2)$

43. $(t + 3)^2$

44. $(m + n)^2$

45. $(p - 6)^2$

46. $(r - s)^2$

47. $(3p + 4)^2$

48. $(4q - 8)^2$

Simplify each expression by first finding the binomial products.

49. $(x - 3)(x + 4) + (x + 2)(x + 3)$

50. $(m + 5)(m - 7) + (m - 1)(m + 3)$

51. $(p + q)(p + 2q) - (p - 3q)(p - q)$

52. $(2s - t)(s + 4t) - (s + 2t)(2s + 5t)$

53. $x(x + 4) + (x + 2)(x - 7)$

54. $y(y - 7) + (y - 4)(y - 6)$

55. $p^2 + (7p - 2)(6p + 3)$

56. $q^2 + (8q - 1)(2q - 3)$

57. $5(x + 2)(x + 3)$

58. $6(y + 3)(y + 4)$

59. $x(x + 11)^2$

60. $c(c + d)^2$

61. $y(x + y)(x - y)$

62. $x(x - y)(x + y)$

© **63.** $(a + b)(a - b)^2$

64. $(a - b)(a + b)^2$

65. $(x + 4)(x - 3)^2$

66. $(y + 2)(y - 4)^2$

67. $(x + 2)^3$

68. $(a - b)^3$

Use the FOIL method to show each of the following.

69. $(a + b)^2 = a^2 + 2ab + b^2$

70. $(a - b)^2 = a^2 - 2ab + b^2$

71. $(a + b)(a - b) = a^2 - b^2$

For each expression, tell whether it is a monomial. If it is a monomial, tell   **6.1**
its coefficient and its degree.

1. 3 **2.** $4m$ **3.** $6x + 2$ **4.** $17xy^2$

5. $\dfrac{5t^2}{s}$ **6.** $4 + 3z$ **7.** $\sqrt{2}x^2y$ **8.** $\frac{1}{4}m^2n^2$

Which of the pairs of monomials are like terms?

9. $3c^2,\ 7c^2$ **10.** $2ab,\ 5ac$

11. $5xy^2,\ -3x^2y$ **12.** $7m^2n,\ -9m^2n$

Write each polynomial in descending powers of the variable and tell whether   **6.2**
it is a monomial, binomial, trinomial, or none of these.

13. $5p$ **14.** $-4 + m^4$ **15.** $3 + x^2 - 2x$

16. $3m^2n$ **17.** $6x^2 - 5x^3$ **18.** $x^4 - 3x + 7x^2 + 2x^3$

19. Evaluate each polynomial in Exercises **13–18** for $x = 2$, $m = -4$,   **6.3**
$n = 3$, and $p = 7$.

20. Tell whether each polynomial in Exercises **13–18** is constant, linear, quadratic, cubic, or none of these.

Find each sum, difference, or product.   **6.4**

21. $(3x - 2) + (5x + 7)$ **22.** $(4x) + (x^2 - 2x + 11)$

23. $(4m^2 + 2) + (5m - 7)$ **24.** $(3x^2 - 5x + 9) + (x^2 - 7x)$

25. $(n - 3) - (n + 2)$ **26.** $(4y + 7) - (y - 2)$ **6.5**

27. $(x^2 + 2) - (x + 2)$ **28.** $(9x^2 - 8x + 3) - (5x^2 + 9x)$

29. $(4t)(t - 3)$ **30.** $(6mn)(-3m^2n)$ **6.6**

31. $(6x + 2)(6x - 2)$ **32.** $(p + 1)(p^2 - 2p + 2)$

33. $(2m + 3n)^2$ **34.** $(8p - 7q)(5p + 2q)$ **6.7**

35. $(\frac{1}{2}x + \frac{1}{4})(\frac{1}{2}x - \frac{1}{4})$ **36.** $(3a - 7b)^2$

CHAPTER SELF-TEST

Give an example of each of the following.

1. monomial   **2.** binomial   **3.** trinomial

4. polynomial   **5.** coefficient   **6.** like terms

7. constant polynomial   **8.** linear polynomial

9. quadratic polynomial   **10.** cubic polynomial

11. term of a polynomial   **12.** zero of a polynomial

13. opposite of a polynomial

Simplify each expression. Write each result in descending powers of a variable.

14. $3(x + 6)$

15. $(x^2 + 3) + (x^2 + 4x - 3)$

16. $4x(3x - 7)$

17. $(x^2 - 6x + 2) - (3x^2 + x - 7)$

18.
$$\begin{array}{r} 6x^2 + 2 \\ (+)\ 3x^2 - 12x + 9 \\ \hline \end{array}$$

19.
$$\begin{array}{r} 4x^2 - 7x + 3 \\ (-)\ 2x^2 + 5x - 11 \\ \hline \end{array}$$

20. $5(x^2 + 8x + 2)$

21. $-3x(2x^2 - 5x + 12)$

22. $(x + 2)(x - 7)$

23. $(3x - 3)(6x + 5)$

24. $(3ab - 5)(3ab - 5)$

25. $(x + 3y)(x^2 + 11xy - 12y^2)$

26. $(5m - 3)^2$

27. $3mn(m^2n^2 - 4mn + 11)$

28. $(x + 4y)^2$

29. $(4m - 3n)(m^2 + 7mn + 6n^2)$

Find the zeros of each polynomial. The replacement set is $\{-3, -2, -1, 0, 1, 2\}$ in each case.

30. $4x + 8$ **31.** $2(y - 1)$ **32.** $z^2 - 9$

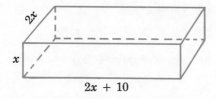

Refer to the box shown at the left. Write a polynomial for its

33. surface area.

34. volume.

Chapter 7   *Factoring Polynomials*

So far you have factored integers. For example:

$$24 = 2^3 \cdot 3$$

$$-30 = -1 \cdot 2 \cdot 3 \cdot 5$$

Now you will factor such algebraic expressions as $5x + 15$ and $4x^2 - 9$.

The student in the picture above is using scissors and paper to show factoring. You may want to try this method after you study the next section.

225

7.1 MONOMIAL FACTORS

When we use the distributive property in the form $ax + bx = x(a + b)$ or $(a + b)x$, we are *factoring* the expression $ax + bx$.

Examples:

1. $5y + 15 = 5 \cdot y + 5 \cdot 3$
$= 5(y + 3)$

monomial factor
polynomial factor

2. $12x^3 - 8x^2 = 4x^2 \cdot 3x - 4x^2 \cdot 2$
$= 4x^2(3x - 2)$

monomial factor
polynomial factor

3. $-6m^2 + 3 = 3 \cdot (-2m^2) + 3 \cdot 1$ or $-3(2m^2) + (-3) \cdot (-1)$
$= 3(-2m^2 + 1)$ or $-3(2m^2 - 1)$

monomial factor
polynomial factor

monomial factor
polynomial factor

The *extended* distributive property is used in the next example.

4. $6x^2 - 12x - 18 = 6 \cdot x^2 - 6 \cdot 2x - 6 \cdot 3$
$= 6(x^2 - 2x - 3)$

monomial factor
polynomial factor

This type of factoring is called **removing a monomial factor.** Integer factors, like the 4 in Example **2,** and the 6 in Example **4,** are not factored into their prime factors. When all coefficients are integers, as in these examples, we say we have "factored the polynomial over the integers."

Some expressions may be factored over the integers in many ways.

$8n^2 + 4n$
$2(4n^2 + 2n)$
$4(2n^2 + n)$
$n(8n + 4)$
$4n(2n + 1)$

$12a^2 - 6ab$	
$2(6a^2 - 3ab)$	$3a(4a - 2b)$
$2a(6a - 3b)$	$a(12a - 6b)$
$3(4a^2 - 2ab)$	$6(2a^2 - ab)$
◀ completely factored form ▶	$6a(2a - b)$

In the completely factored form, no more variable factors can be removed from the polynomial factor. Also, no more integer factors, other than 1 and -1, can be removed.

In this book, we use "factor (the polynomial) completely" to mean "completely factor the polynomial *over the integers.*"

EXERCISES 7.1

Ⓐ Which of the following can be factored over the integers? Why?

1. $3x^2 + \frac{1}{3}$ **2.** $2m + 4$ **3.** $m - n$ **4.** $x - 4x$

5. $9 + 3x$ **6.** $\frac{1}{2}x + \frac{1}{4}y$ **7.** $4y + 2y$ **8.** $3m + 4n$

Name the monomial factor of the completely factored form.

9. $7x + 56$ **10.** $3a - 12$ **11.** $-5n^2 + 20$

12. $-6v - 12$ **13.** $4y^2 - 4$ **14.** $3d^2 + 6d - 9$

15. $4m^2 + 16m$ **16.** $12x - 18y$ **17.** $-2r^2 - 4r - 8$

18. $15a + 3$ **19.** $21b - 7$ **20.** $24n^2 - 12n + 4$

Ⓑ Factor completely by removing a monomial factor. Check by multiplying.

21. $18y - 9$ **22.** $24x - 8$

23. $3x + 6$ **24.** $5y + 10$

25. $4n - 8$ **26.** $2m - 4$

27. $-3r - 15t$ **28.** $-5w - 15s$

29. $3x^2 + 2x$ **30.** $2y^2 + 5y$

31. $3m - 15n$ **32.** $2r - 14s$

33. $ab^2 + b^2$ **34.** $mn^2 + 2n^2$

35. $x^2y + x$ **36.** $xy^2 + y$

37. $7y^3 - 5y^2$ **38.** $3x^3 - 5x^2$

39. $24x^4 - 18x^3 + 12x^2$ **40.** $3y^5 - 6y^4 + 9y^3$

41. $3b^3 + 6b^2 - 12b$ **42.** $5c^3 - 10c^2 + 15c$

43. $28a^3b - 21a^2b + 7ab$ **44.** $32m^3n - 16m^2n + 8mn$

A polynomial factor can sometimes be removed as if it were a monomial factor. Factor the following.

Example: $y(y + 2) + 3(y + 2) = (y + 3)(y + 2)$

45. $(a + b)c + (a + b)d$

46. $(m + n)p + (m + n)q$

47. $x(r + s) - y(r + s)$

48. $t(a + b) - a(a + b)$

49. $(x + 4)y + (x + 4)z$

50. $(m + 3)t - (m + 3)p$

© **51.** $5x(r^2 - 2) + (r^2 - 2)$

52. $6y(s^2 - 3) + (s^2 - 3)$

Example: $2x + 2y + ax + ay = 2(x + y) + a(x + y)$
$$= (2 + a)(x + y)$$

53. $x(m + n) + ym + yn$

54. $wx + wy + x(x + y)$

55. $bx + by + px + py$

56. $ax + ay + 8x + 8y$

57. $x^2y + y + x^2z + z$

58. $m^2 + 4m - 8m - 32$

59. $ab - ac + db - dc$

60. $5x - 10 + px - 2p$

a.

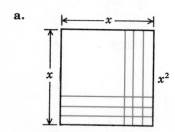

b.

Factoring with Scissors and Paper

Take a large *square* sheet of paper. Call its side x inches long. Thus its area (in square inches) is x^2.

Rule three 1-inch strips on the bottom and also on the right as in **a**.

Cut out and set aside the block of 9 square inches as in **b**. The area of the remaining piece is $(x^2 - 9)$ square inches.

Cut off the bottom three strips and place them as in **c**. The width of the rectangle formed is $(x - 3)$ inches and its length is $(x + 3)$ inches. Thus its area is $(x + 3)(x - 3)$ square inches.

This shows that $x^2 - 9 = (x + 3)(x - 3)$.

Use paper and scissors to factor the following.

c.

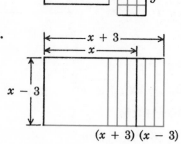

$(x + 3)(x - 3)$

1. $x^2 - 4$ **2.** $x^2 - 16$ **3.** $x^2 - 49$

Notice the pattern that occurs when we find products like $(a + b)(a - b)$ by the FOIL method, explained in Chapter 6.

$$(a + b)(a - b) = a^2 \underbrace{- ab + ab} - b^2$$
$$= a^2 + \quad 0 \quad - b^2$$
$$= a^2 - b^2$$

$$(2x + 3)(2x - 3) = 4x^2 \underbrace{- 6x + 6x} - 9$$
$$= 4x^2 + \quad 0 \quad - 9$$
$$= 4x^2 - 9$$

difference
of two
squares

Now, suppose we reverse these steps.

$$s^2 - t^2 = s^2 + \quad 0 \quad - t^2$$
$$= s^2 \overbrace{- st + st} - t^2$$
$$= (s^2 - st) + (st - t^2)$$
$$= s(s - t) + t(s - t)$$
$$= (s + t)(s - t)$$

Thus, the difference of the squares of two numbers can be factored as the sum of those numbers times their difference.

Example 1: Factor.   **a.** $(4x)^2 - (5y)^2$ **b.** $64x^2 - 9$

SOLUTIONS: **a.** $(4x)^2 - (5y)^2 = (4x + 5y)(4x - 5y)$

         b. $64x^2 - 9 = 8^2x^2 - 3^2$
$$= (8x)^2 - 3^2$$
$$= (8x + 3)(8x - 3)$$

Example 2: Find the difference of the squares of 75 and 25.

SOLUTION: $75^2 - 25^2 = (75 + 25)(75 - 25)$
$$= 100 \cdot 50$$
$$= 5000$$

Removing a monomial factor from a polynomial may leave a difference of two squares.

Example 3: Factor.   **a.** $5a^2 - 5b^2$ **b.** $50p^2 - 32q^2$

SOLUTIONS:

monomial factor

difference of two squares

a. $5a^2 - 5b^2 = 5(a^2 - b^2)$
$$= 5(a + b)(a - b)$$

b. $50p^2 - 32q^2 = 2(25p^2 - 16q^2)$
$$= 2[(5p)^2 - (4q)^2]$$
$$= 2(5p + 4q)(5p - 4q)$$

Sometimes it is useful to multiply a given expression by a factor that will give us a difference of two perfect squares as a product.

Example 4: In each case, by what can you multiply the given binomial so that the product is the difference of two squares?

a. $7 - x$ **b.** $4p + 9q$ **c.** $12m - 5n^2$

SOLUTIONS:

	Given	·	Multiplier	=	Product
a.	$(7 - x)$	·	$(7 + x)$	=	$49 - x^2$
b.	$(4p + 9q)$	·	$(4p - 9q)$	=	$16p^2 - 81q^2$
c.	$(12m - 5n^2)$	·	$(12m + 5n^2)$	=	$144m^2 - 25n^4$

EXERCISES 7.2

(A) Factor completely.

1. $c^2 - d^2$ **2.** $u^2 - w^2$ **3.** $16 - a^2$

4. $25 - b^2$ **5.** $x^2 - 25$ **6.** $y^2 - 81$

7. $64m^2 - 25$ **8.** $9n^2 - 16$ **9.** $4p^2 - 9q^2$

10. $16s^2 - 25t^2$ **11.** $9x^2y^2 - 64$ **12.** $16p^2q^2 - 49$

13. $(x^2)^2 - 25$ **14.** $9x^2 - (6y^2)^2$

By what can you multiply the given binomial so that the product is the difference of two squares? What is the product?

15. $s + t$ **16.** $m - n$ **17.** $p + q$ **18.** $x - y$

19. $4 - m$ **20.** $5 + n$ **21.** $2x - 7$ **22.** $3m + n$

23. $5x + 3y$ **24.** $7r - 5s$ **25.** $6x^2 + 11$ **26.** $7y^2 - 13$

Ⓑ Factor completely. Check by multiplying.

27. $64 - y^2$ **28.** $81 - x^2$ **29.** $x^2 - 25y^2$

30. $p^2 - 16q^2$ **31.** $a^2 - b^2$ **32.** $s^2 - t^2$

33. $144 - 25p^2$ **34.** $121 - 16q^2$ **35.** $49m^2 - 9n^2$

36. $81a^2 - 4b^2$ **37.** $2 - 2y^2$ **38.** $5 - 5x^2$

39. $4p^2 - 36$ **40.** $5q^2 - 45$ **41.** $3t^2 - 27s^2$

42. $5m^2 - 125n^2$ **43.** $7m^2n^2 - 7$ **44.** $11x^2y^2 - 44$

45. $8 - 32s^2t^2$ **46.** $4 - 16m^2n^2$ **47.** $8u^2 - 18v^2$

48. $2w^2 - 32z^2$ **49.** $x^2 - x^2y^2$ **50.** $m^2 - m^2n^2$

51. $13s^2t^2 - 52w^2$ **52.** $11x^2y^2 - 99z^2$ **53.** $6x^2y^2 - 24x^2z^2$

54. $7m^2n^2 - 28m^2p^2$ **55.** $2r^2 - 8n^2$ **56.** $63 - 7t^2$

Use factoring to find the following.

57. $15^2 - 5^2$ **58.** $16^2 - 6^2$ **59.** $121^2 - 21^2$ **60.** $70^2 - 30^2$

61. $19^2 - 1$ **62.** $21^2 - 1$ **63.** $42^2 - 4$ **64.** $53^2 - 9$

65. $81 - 36$ **66.** $64 - 25$ **67.** $12^2 - 13^2$ **68.** $14^2 - 15^2$

Ⓒ Factor each of the following.

Example: $(x + y)^2 - (m + n)^2$
$$= [(x + y) + (m + n)][(x + y) - (m + n)]$$
$$= (x + y + m + n)(x + y - m - n)$$

69. $(x - y)^2 - (m + n)^2$ **70.** $(s - t)^2 - (r - u)^2$

71. $(2x + z)^2 - (2m - 3)^2$ **72.** $(a - 4b)^2 - (c - 6d)^2$

73. $(m^2 + 1)^2 - (n^2 + 3)^2$ **74.** $(x^2 - 2)^2 - (y^2 + 4)^2$

75. $(a^2 + b^2)^2 - (c^2 + d^2)^2$ **76.** $(3xy - 4)^2 - (7xy + 2)^2$

Factor each of the following.

Example: $x^4 - 9 = x^2 \cdot x^2 - 3^2$ or $(x^2)^2 - 3^2$
$$= (x^2 + 3)(x^2 - 3)$$

77. $a^4 - 25$ **78.** $m^6 - 64$ **79.** $n^8 - 36$

Using the pattern of the difference of two squares, factor the following over the real numbers.

Example: $x^2 - 2 = x^2 - (\sqrt{2})^2$
$$= (x + \sqrt{2})(x - \sqrt{2})$$

80. $y^2 - 5$ **81.** $4m^2 - 3$ **82.** $3s^2 - 16$

Timken Roller Bearing Company manufactures stainless steel tubing in many shapes, including those shown here in cross section.

I

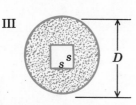

83. What is the wall thickness of type I tubing if $D = 5\frac{3}{4}$ inches and $d = 4\frac{1}{4}$ inches?

84. The cross-sectional area (shaded) of type I tubing is $\frac{1}{4}\pi(D^2 - d^2)$. Find this area for the tubing in Exercise **83**. (Use 3.14 for π.)

II

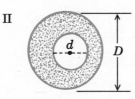

85. Write a formula for the volume of steel per running foot of type I tubing if D and d are measured in inches. Find the volume per running foot for the tubing in Exercise **83**.

86. Write a formula (using a difference of squares) for the cross-sectional area of type II tubing. Find the area if $D = 3\frac{1}{4}$ centimeters and $d = 1\frac{3}{4}$ centimeters.

III

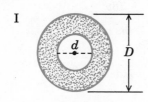

87. Which of these formulas expresses the cross-sectional area of type III tubing?

     a. $\frac{1}{4}\pi(D^2 - s^2)$ **b.** $\frac{1}{4}\pi D^2 - s^2$ **c.** $(\frac{1}{2}\pi D)^2 - s^2$

IV

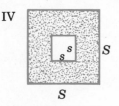

88. Write a formula for the cross-sectional area of type IV tubing. Find this area if $S = 6\frac{3}{4}$ centimeters and $s = 3\frac{1}{4}$ centimeters. Find the volume of steel per running meter of this tubing.

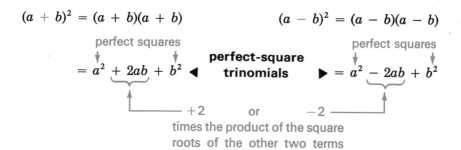

$$(a + b)^2 = (a + b)(a + b) \qquad\qquad (a - b)^2 = (a - b)(a - b)$$

$$= a^2 + 2ab + b^2 \blacktriangleleft \quad \begin{array}{c}\textbf{perfect-square}\\ \textbf{trinomials}\end{array} \quad \blacktriangleright = a^2 - 2ab + b^2$$

perfect squares $\qquad\qquad\qquad$ perfect squares

$+2$ $\qquad$ or $\qquad$ -2

times the product of the square
roots of the other two terms

Reversing the pattern of squaring a binomial shown above, we can now factor perfect-square trinomials.

Examples:

1. $x^2 - 12x + 36 \quad = x^2 - 2 \cdot x \cdot 6 + 6^2 \qquad = (x - 6)^2$

2. $9m^2 - 12mn + 4n^2 = (3m)^2 - 2 \cdot 3m \cdot 2n + (2n)^2 = (3m - 2n)^2$

3. $16r^2 + 40rs + 25s^2 = (4r)^2 + 2 \cdot 4r \cdot 5s + (5s)^2 \quad = (4r + 5s)^2$

It can be useful to add a term to a given expression to "compl   the square," that is, to form a perfect-square trinomial.

Example 4: What term must be added to comple   are?

$\quad$ **a.** $x^2 - 14x \qquad$ **b.** $25s^2 + 90st \qquad\qquad$ **c.** $64m^2 + n^2$

SOLUTIONS:

Given	Perfect-square trinomial	Term added

a. $x^2 - 14x \qquad x^2 - 2 \cdot x \cdot 7 + \,?^2$

$\qquad\qquad\qquad x^2 - 2 \cdot x \cdot 7 + 7^2 \qquad\qquad 7^2$ or 49

b. $25s^2 + 90st \qquad (5s)^2 + 2 \cdot 5s \cdot 9t + \,?^2$

$\qquad\qquad\qquad (5s)^2 + 2 \cdot 5s \cdot 9t + (9t)^2 \qquad (9t)^2$ or $81t^2$

c. $64m^2 + n^2 \qquad (8m)^2 + 2 \cdot ? \cdot ? + n^2$

$\qquad\qquad\qquad (8m)^2 + 2 \cdot 8m \cdot n + n^2 \qquad 2 \cdot 8m \cdot n$ or $16mn$

EXERCISES 7.3

Ⓐ 1. Simplify each perfect-square trinomial in Example 4.

2. Factor each perfect-square trinomial in Example 4.

In Exercises 3–18, identify and factor the perfect-square trinomials. Check your results by multiplying.

3. $x^2 + 2x + 1$

4. $y^2 + 4y + 4$

5. $x^2 + 9x + 9$

6. $y^2 + 8y + 16$

7. $x^2 - 6x + 9$

8. $m^2 - 10m + 25$

9. $n^2 - 8n + 64$

10. $s^2 - 4s + 16$

11. $x^2 + 4xy + 4y^2$

12. $a^2 + 8ab + 16b^2$

Ⓑ 13. $4x^2 + 4xs + s^2$

14. $36y^2 + 12yz + z^2$

15. $5m^2 + 10mn + 12n^2$

16. $7n^2 + 14np + 14p^2$

17. $16x^2 - 24xy + 9y^2$

18. $25x^2 - 30xy + 9y^2$

Complete the square; then factor. Check by multiplying.

19. $x^2 + 10x + \underline{\quad}$

20. $y^2 - 12y + \underline{\quad}$

21. $m^2 - 8m + \underline{\quad}$

22. $n^2 - 6n + \underline{\quad}$

23. $p^2 + \underline{\quad} + q^2$

24. $s^2 + \underline{\quad} + t^2$

25. $4e^2 + \underline{\quad} + f^2$

26. $16x^2 + \underline{\quad} + y^2$

27. $9a^2 - 24ab + \underline{\quad}$

28. $25b^2 - 40ab + \underline{\quad}$

29. $4c^2 + \underline{\quad} + 9d^2$

30. $25u^2 + \underline{\quad} + 4v^2$

31. $16a^2 - \underline{\quad} + 25b^2$

32. $64x^2 - \underline{\quad} + 9y^2$

33. $64x^2 - 80x + \underline{\quad}$

34. $81x^2 - 72x + \underline{\quad}$

Factor.

35. $16s^2 - 8st + t^2$

36. $25m^2 - 10mn + n^2$

37. $x^2 + 20x + 100$

38. $y^2 + 18y + 81$

39. $p^2 - 2pq + q^2$

40. $w^2 - 2wv + v^2$

41. $m^2n^2 - 4mn + 4$

42. $p^2q^2 + 16pq + 64$

43. $81 - 18t + t^2$

44. $49 - 14s + s^2$

45. $25 - 20x + 4x^2$

46. $16 - 24y + 9y^2$

47. $49m^2 + 1 + 14m$

48. $36n^2 + 1 + 12n$

49. $1 - 14p + 49p^2$

50. $1 - 12q + 36q^2$

51. $16x^2 - 40xy + 25y^2$

52. $9p^2 - 24pq + 16q^2$

53. $16x^2y^2 + 1 + 8xy$

54. $25m^2n^2 + 1 + 10mn$

Factor completely. Look for monomial factors, differences of two squares, and perfect-square trinomials.

55. $x^2 - 4$

56. $y^2 - 16$

57. $2x^2 + 4x + 12$

58. $2y^2 + 16x + 4$

59. $4x^2 + 12x + 9$

60. $9y^2 + 12y + 4$

61. $3m^2 + 6m + 15$

62. $5p^2 + 5p + 15$

63. $16x^2 - 25$

64. $25y^2 - 16$

© Factor. Use the patterns of perfect-square trinomials and differences of two squares.

65. $(x^2)^2 + 16x^2 + 64$

66. $y^4 + 12y^2 + 36$

67. $a^4 - 4a^2b^2 + 4b^4$

68. $m^6 - 10m^3 + 25$

69. $(a + b)^2 + 2(a + b) + 1$

70. $(a^2 - 2ab + b^2) - 16$

71. $(m - n)^2 - 2(m - n) + 1$

72. $(c^2 + 2cd + d^2) - 25$

73. $(x + 2)^2 - (y^2 + 4y + 4)$

74. $\frac{1}{4}y^2 + \frac{1}{3}y + \frac{1}{9}$

75. $(x^2 - 8x + 16) - (x^2 - 16x + 64)$

76. $x^2 + x + \frac{1}{4}$

77. If the area of a square is $16s^2 - 8s + 1$, how long is each side?

78. Use factoring to find the following.

    a. $7^2 + 2 \cdot 7 \cdot 3 + 3^2$ **b.** $16 + 2 \cdot 4 \cdot 3 + 9$

79. The Seven-Bar Ranch consists of 55 square miles of land, divided by fences as shown in the diagram. The rancher wants to buy just enough additional land to make his ranch perfectly square. What is the area of the land he needs?

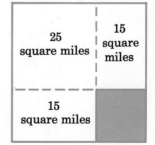

Numbers ending in 5 can be squared by a simple process.

$$(15)^2 = 100(1 \cdot 2) + 25 = 2 \cdot 100 + 25 = 225$$

$$(35)^2 = 100(3 \cdot 4) + 25 = 12 \cdot 100 + 25 = 1225$$

$$(85)^2 = 100(8 \cdot 9) + 25 = 72 \cdot 100 + 25 = 7225$$

In this method, if d is the tens digit of the number you are squaring, find 100 times d times $d + 1$ and add 25.

This works because any number ending in 5 may be expressed as $10d + 5$, where d is an integer. Squaring this binomial, we get:

$$(10d + 5)^2 = (10d + 5)(10d + 5)$$
$$= (10d)^2 + 2 \cdot 10d \cdot 5 + 5^2$$
$$= 100d^2 + 100d + 25$$

$$\text{But } 100d^2 + 100d + 25 = (100d^2 + 100d) + 25$$
$$= 100d(d + 1) + 25$$

Consider, for example, 65^2. Here $d = 6$ and $d + 1 = 7$.

$$d(d + 1) = 42$$
$$100d(d + 1) = 100 \cdot 42 = 4200$$
$$100d(d + 1) + 25 = 4200 + 25 = 4225$$

Use this method to square each of the following numbers.

1. 55 **2.** 75 **3.** 95 **4.** 105 **5.** 355

In preceding sections, we found the products $(a - b)(a + b)$, $(a + b)^2$, and $(a - b)^2$ to decide how to factor certain expressions. Now let us look at another product.

$$(x + r)(x + s) = x^2 + rx + sx + rs$$
$$= x^2 + (\underline{r + s})x + \underline{rs}$$

product of r and s

sum of r and s

Thus, if a trinomial of the form $x^2 + bx + c$ is not a perfect square, we examine it to see if we can find two numbers with product c and sum b.

The two numbers may both be positive, both negative, or one may be positive and the other negative. Carefully examine the examples that follow to learn how to recognize each case.

Example 1: Factor $x^2 + 15x + 54$.

SOLUTION:

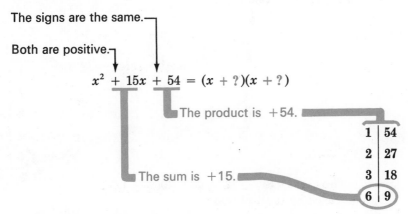

The signs are the same.

Both are positive.

$$x^2 + 15x + 54 = (x + ?)(x + ?)$$

The product is $+54$.

The sum is $+15$.

1	54
2	27
3	18
6	9

Thus, $x^2 + 15x + 54 = (x + 6)(x + 9)$.

Check: $(x + 6)(x + 9) = x^2 + 9x + 6x + 6 \cdot 9$
$$= x^2 + 15x + 54$$

Example 2: Factor $x^2 - 14x + 40$.

SOLUTION:

The signs are the same.

Both are negative.

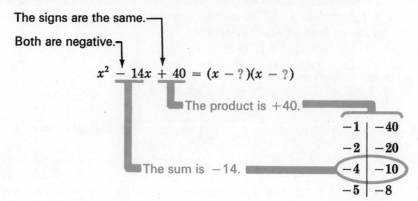

$$x^2 - 14x + 40 = (x - \, ?\,)(x - \, ?\,)$$

The product is $+40$.

The sum is -14.

-1	-40
-2	-20
-4	-10
-5	-8

Thus, $x^2 - 14x + 40 = (x - 4)(x - 10)$.
Check by multiplying.

Example 3: Factor. **a.** $x^2 - 6x - 72$ **b.** $x^2 + 6x - 72$

SOLUTIONS:

The signs are opposite.

The negative number has greater absolute value.

a.

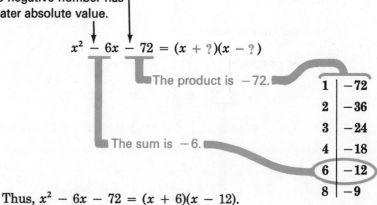

$$x^2 - 6x - 72 = (x + \, ?\,)(x - \, ?\,)$$

The product is -72.

The sum is -6.

1	-72
2	-36
3	-24
4	-18
6	-12
8	-9

Thus, $x^2 - 6x - 72 = (x + 6)(x - 12)$.
Check by multiplying.

b. The solution is the same as for **a** except that the positive number has the greater absolute value.

Thus, $x^2 + 6x - 72 = (x + 12)(x - 6)$. Check.

The factoring we have done so far can be summarized in a flow chart.

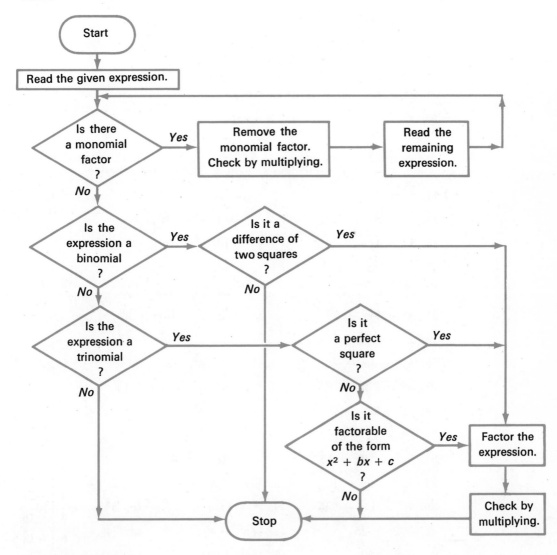

EXERCISES 7.4

Ⓐ Complete the factoring.

1. $x^2 + 7x + 12 = (x + 4)(\quad)$

2. $s^2 - 10s - 24 = (\quad + \quad)(\quad - 12)$

3. $r^2 + 5r - 6 = (\quad)(r - 1)$

4. $k^2 - 12k + 35 = (\quad - 5)(\quad - \quad)$

5. $a^2 + 5a - 24 = (\quad\quad)(a + 8)$

6. $m^2 - 9m + 18 = (m - 3)(m - 6)$

7. $p^2 + 5p + 6 = (p + 2)(p + 3)$

8. $t^2 + 16t - 36 = (t + 18)(t - 2)$

9. $s^2 + 4s - 21 = (s + 7)(s - 3)$

10. $s^2 - 4s - 21 = (s + 7)(s - 3)$

Ⓑ Factor completely, removing a monomial factor first if possible.

11. $x^2 + 4x + 3$

12. $p^2 + 7p + 6$

13. $x^2 - 8x + 7$

14. $y^2 - 6y + 5$

15. $x^2 - 11x + 18$

16. $y^2 - 9y + 14$

17. $m^2 - m - 6$

18. $n^2 - 2n - 8$

19. $r^2 + 9r + 20$

20. $s^2 + 12s + 20$

21. $x^2 - 11x + 28$

22. $y^2 - 13y + 22$

23. $x^2 - 14x - 15$

24. $y^2 - 16y - 17$

25. $m^2 - 4m - 32$

26. $n^2 - n - 30$

27. $p^2 - 17p + 16$

28. $q^2 - 13q + 12$

29. $m^2 + 6m - 27$

30. $n^2 + n - 42$

31. $x^2 - 4x - 12$

32. $s^2 + 16s - 36$

33. $5x^2 + 20x + 15$

34. $3y^2 + 15y + 12$

35. $9x^2 - 6x + 1$

36. $16y^2 - 8y + 1$

37. $5s^2 + 10s - 240$

38. $7t^2 + 14t - 245$

39. $t^2 - 9t + 8$

40. $u^2 + 7u + 10$

41. $36x^2 - 25y^2$

42. $16p^2 - 49q^2$

43. $7y^2 - 28$

44. $5x^2 - 20$

45. $12t^2 - 24t$

46. $18s^2 - 36s$

Ⓒ 47. $m^4 - 49n^2$

48. $g^4 - 9$

49. $n^4 - 81p^2$

50. $x^4 - 11x^2 + 18$

51. $(a + b)^2 + 3(a + b) + 2$

52. $y^4 - 13y^2 + 30$

53. $(m - n)^2 + 7(m - n) + 10$

54. $(x + y)^2 - 6(x + y) - 16$

55. $(4m - n)^2 - 7(4m - n) - 8$

More Factoring with Scissors and Paper

The rectangular region in the picture on page 225 is made up of pieces of paper, each labeled with its area as in figure I below.

a. Find the sum of the areas of the individual pieces of paper; express it as a trinomial.

b. Find the area of the rectangle in terms of the lengths of its sides.

c. Why are your expressions for **a** and **b** equal?

d. Using pieces of paper, illustrate the factoring in Exercises **11**, **12**, and **19** on page 240.

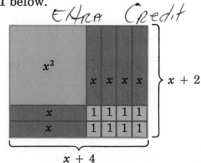

Extra Credit

We can also show the factors of trinomials like $x^2 - 6x + 8$, if we first accept two rules.

1. If two pieces overlap, the areas cancel each other.

2. No area can be canceled more than once.

Start with a square of paper whose sides are x inches long; its area is x^2 square inches.

Lay two strips, each x inches long and 1 inch wide, on the square as shown in figure II. Each strip has an area of x square inches. Then lay four more x-by-1-inch strips on the square as shown in figure III.

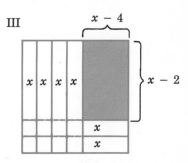

Part of the original square is still uncovered. What is its area in terms of the lengths of its sides?

This area can also be found as follows.

Area of the original square. $\longrightarrow$ x^2

Six strips overlapping the square cancel 6x sq. in. of area. $\longrightarrow$ $-6x$

The equivalent of eight 1-by-1-inch squares is overlapped twice. By rule *2*, we must undo one of these cancellations. $\longrightarrow$ $+8$

Thus, $x^2 - 6x + 8 = (x - 4)(x - 2)$.

e. Using pieces of paper as above, illustrate the factoring of the trinomials in Exercises **13**, **16**, and **26** on page 240.

TRINOMIALS: $ax^2 + bx + c$

If a trinomial of the form $ax^2 + bx + c$ is not a perfect square, to factor it we must find four numbers (m, n, p, and t) related to the coefficients of $ax^2 + bx + c$ as shown below.

$$(mx + n)(px + t) = mpx^2 + mtx + npx + nt$$

$$= mpx^2 + (mt + np)x + nt$$

$$ax^2 + bx + c$$

Example 1: Factor $2x^2 + 7x + 6$.

SOLUTION:

$$2x^2 + 7x + 6 = (?x + ?)(?x + ?)$$

This product is $+6$.

$$= (?x + ?)(?x + ?)$$

This product is $+2$.

Since the only factors of 2 are 2 and 1, only four cases need to be considered.

Possible factors	Middle term
$(2x + 1)(1x + 6)$	$13x$
$(2x + 6)(1x + 1)$	$8x$
$(2x + 2)(1x + 3)$	$8x$
$(2x + 3)(1x + 2)$	$7x$

This is the required middle term.

Thus, $2x^2 + 7x + 6 = (2x + 3)(x + 2)$. Check by multiplying.

Example 2: Factor $8y^2 - 35y + 12$.

SOLUTION:

$$8y^2 - 35y + 12 = (?y - ?)(?y - ?)$$

This product is $+12$.

$$= (?y - ?)(?y - ?)$$

This product is $+8$.

There are 12 cases to consider, all of which are listed here. However, with experience, the factors can often be found without actually considering all the cases.

Possible factors	Middle term	Possible factors	Middle term
$(1y - 1)(8y - 12)$	$-20y$	$(2y - 1)(4y - 12)$	$-28y$
$(1y - 12)(8y - 1)$	$-97y$	$(2y - 12)(4y - 1)$	$-50y$
$(1y - 2)(8y - 6)$	$-22y$	$(2y - 2)(4y - 6)$	$-20y$
$(1y - 6)(8y - 2)$	$-50y$	$(2y - 6)(4y - 2)$	$-28y$
$(1y - 3)(8y - 4)$	$-28y$	$(2y - 3)(4y - 4)$	$-20y$
$(1y - 4)(8y - 3)$	$-35y$	$(2y - 4)(4y - 3)$	$-22y$

This is the required middle term.

Thus, $8y^2 - 35y + 12 = (y - 4)(8y - 3)$. Check.

When the constant term of the trinomial being factored is positive, both factors are sums (as in Example 1) or both are differences (as in Example 2). The constant term is negative only when one factor is a sum and the other a difference. Consider the product of two such factors.

The product of two numbers with opposite signs is negative.

$$(2x + 1)(3x - 2) = 6x^2 - 1x - 2$$

$3x$

$-4x$

The sign of this sum of products depends on which product has the greater absolute value.

Example 3: Factor $3r^2 - 7r - 6$.

SOLUTION: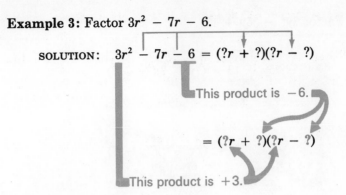

$$3r^2 - 7r - 6 = (?r + ?)(?r - ?)$$

This product is -6.

$$= (?r + ?)(?r - ?)$$

This product is $+3$.

Possible factors	Middle term	Possible factors	Middle term
$(1r + 1)(3r - 6)$	$-3r$	$(3r + 1)(1r - 6)$	$-17r$
$(1r + 6)(3r - 1)$	$17r$	$(3r + 6)(1r - 1)$	$3r$
$(1r + 3)(3r - 2)$	$7r$	$(3r + 3)(1r - 2)$	$-3r$
$(1r + 2)(3r - 3)$	$3r$	$(3r + 2)(1r - 3)$	$-7r$

This is the required middle term.

Thus, $3r^2 - 7r - 6 = (3r + 2)(r - 3)$. Check.

EXERCISES 7.5

Ⓐ 1. At what point in the flow chart on page 239 would you introduce this decision box? Where would you connect the *Yes* and *No* arrows?

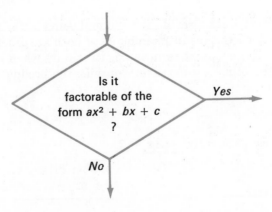

Is it factorable of the form $ax^2 + bx + c$?

Yes

No

Each of the following has $2n + 5$ as a factor; find the other binomial factor in each case.

2. $6n^2 + 23n + 20$ **3.** $6n^2 + 7n - 20$ **4.** $14n^2 + 39n + 10$

5. $4n^2 + 24n + 35$ **6.** $4n^2 - 4n - 35$ **7.** $4n^2 + 20n + 25$

Factor completely.

8. $2x^2 + 5x + 3$ **9.** $2y^2 + 7y + 5$ **10.** $2x^2 + 9x + 10$

Ⓑ **11.** $2y^2 + 11y + 14$ **12.** $2m^2 - 5m + 3$ **13.** $2n^2 - 7n + 5$

14. $3a^2 - 10a + 7$ **15.** $3c^2 - 8c + 5$ **16.** $4x^2 - 8x + 3$

17. $4y^2 - 12y + 5$ **18.** $2m^2 - 7m + 6$ **19.** $2n^2 - 9n + 10$

20. $4a^2 - 19a - 5$ **21.** $6b^2 - 29b - 5$ **22.** $9x^2 - 6x - 8$

23. $9y^2 + 6y - 8$ **24.** $8m^2 + 10m - 3$

25. $10m^2 + 23m - 5$ **26.** $7x^2 + 10x - 8$

27. $5y^2 + 13y - 6$ **28.** $6y^2 - 13y + 6$

29. $8b^2 + 19b - 15$ **30.** $8x^2 - 37x - 15$

31. $8y^2 - 13y - 6$ **32.** $5m^2 + 37m + 14$

33. $8n^2 + 23n + 15$ **34.** $15x^2 - 13x + 2$

35. $15y^2 - 7y - 2$ **36.** $6p^2 - 17p + 12$

37. $8q^2 - 18q + 9$ **38.** $6y^2 + 11y - 10$

39. $16y^2 + 30y + 9$ **40.** $25p^2 - 65p + 36$

Ⓒ **41.** $12s^2 - 16st - 11t^2$ **42.** $16t^2 - 6tx - 7x^2$

Factor completely. More than one type of factoring may be needed.

43. $x^4 - 4x^2$ **44.** $4a^2 + 16a + 16$ **45.** $5b^2 - 30b + 45$

46. $4a^2 - 19a - 5$ **47.** $5(m - n)^2 - 7(m - n) + 2$

48. $12x^2 + 21x + 9$ **49.** $3(x - y)^2 - 7(x - y) + 4$

50. $9c^2 - 24c + 15$ **51.** $20n^2 + 46n - 10$

For what values of t are the trinomials factorable?

52. $3x^2 + tx + 2$ **53.** $3x^2 + tx - 2$

What is the monomial factor of each of the following?

1. $4m + 6n$ **2.** $7p^2 + 14p$

3. $3xy + 9x + 12xz$ **4.** $x^3 - 5x^2$

Factor completely.

5. $9x + 18$ **6.** $11y^2 - 6y$

7. $5mn + 10mn^2 + 5mn^3$ **8.** $12z^2 + 16z$

9. $w^2 - u^2$ **10.** $x^2 - 25y^2$

11. $49m^2 - 16n^2$ **12.** $9m^2n^2 - 64p^2$

13. $u^2 - 10u + 25$ **14.** $t^2 + 14t + 49$

15. $9s^2 - 24st + 16t^2$ **16.** $4x^2 + 36xy + 81y^2$

17. $a^2 + 10a + 16$ **18.** $c^2 - 13c + 12$

19. $x^2 - 4x - 12$ **20.** $y^2 + 15y - 16$

21. $3x^2 - x - 4$ **22.** $5p^2 + 13p + 6$

23. $6y^2 + 3y - 9$ **24.** $4z^2 - 9z - 9$

Sometimes a polynomial that does not look like any of those you have studied so far can be changed to a type you can recognize. This may involve grouping terms, rearranging terms, or removing a monomial factor.

Example 1: **a.** $y^3 - y^2 + y - 1 = (y^3 - y^2) + (y - 1)$ grouping terms

$$= y^2(y - 1) + 1(y - 1)$$

$$= (y^2 + 1)(y - 1)$$

b. $11m - 12 + m^2 = m^2 + 11m - 12$ rearranging terms

$$= (m + 12)(m - 1)$$

c. $-x^2 + 13x - 12 = (-1)(x^2 - 13x + 12)$ removing a monomial factor

$$= (-1)(x - 12)(x - 1)$$

$$\text{or } (12 - x)(x - 1)$$

$$\text{or } (x - 12)(1 - x)$$

d. $-6p^2 - 16p - 10 = (-2)(3p^2 + 8p + 5)$ removing a monomial factor

$$= (-2)(3p + 5)(p + 1)$$

If all coefficients are not integers, removing a monomial factor may leave a polynomial that is factorable over the integers.

Example 2: **a.** $m^2 - \frac{1}{4} = \frac{1}{4}(4m^2 - 1)$

$$= \frac{1}{4}[(2m)^2 - 1^2]$$

$$= \frac{1}{4}(2m + 1)(2m - 1)$$

b. $p^2 - \frac{1}{2}p + \frac{1}{16} = \frac{1}{16}(16p^2 - 8p + 1)$

$$= \frac{1}{16}[(4p)^2 - 2 \cdot 4p \cdot 1 + 1]$$

$$= \frac{1}{16}(4p - 1)^2$$

c. $y^2 + \frac{5}{4}y + \frac{1}{4} = \frac{1}{4}(4y^2 + 5y + 1)$

$$= \frac{1}{4}(4y + 1)(y + 1)$$

You know that removing a monomial factor may leave a factorable polynomial. Similarly, in other types of factoring, one of the factors may itself be factorable.

Example 3: **a.** $x^4 - y^4 = (x^2 \cdot x^2 - y^2 \cdot y^2)$

$$= [(x^2)^2 - (y^2)^2]$$
$$= (x^2 + y^2)(x^2 - y^2)$$
$$= (x^2 + y^2)(x + y)(x - y)$$

b. $a^3 + 3a^2 - a - 3 = (a^3 + 3a^2) - (a + 3)$
$$= a^2(a + 3) - 1(a + 3)$$
$$= (a^2 - 1)(a + 3)$$
$$= (a + 1)(a - 1)(a + 3)$$

EXERCISES 7.6

Ⓐ To factor each expression, which of the following would you do first?

    a. remove a monomial factor   **b.** rearrange the terms

    c. factor as a difference of squares   **d.** group the terms

1. $5x^2 - 45$ **2.** $4n + n^2 + 3$ **3.** $-x^2 - 6x - 9$

4. $a^4 - 16$ **5.** $6x^3 - 24x$ **6.** $m^3 + m^2 - m - 1$

7. $-2x^2 + 8$ **8.** $-2y + 1 + y^2$ **9.** $ax^2 - ay^2 + bx^2 - by^2$

10. $ax^2 - a$ **11.** $-y^2 - 10y - 25$ **12.** $\frac{1}{2}x^2 - \frac{1}{2}a^2$

Ⓑ **13–24.** Factor each expression in Exercises 1–12 completely.

Factor completely.

25. $3x^2 + 15x + 18$ **26.** $2y^2 + 10y + 8$

27. $-t^2 - 12t - 11$ **28.** $-s^2 - 14s - 13$

29. $p^4 - q^4$ **30.** $m^4 - n^4$

31. $x^4 - 10x^2 + 9$ **32.** $y^4 - 17y^2 + 16$

33. $6x^3 + 3x^2 - 3x$

34. $8y^3 + 2y^2 - 6y$

35. $18mn^2 - 50mp^2$

36. $27st^2 - 48sr^2$

37. $25a^2 - 100b^2c^2$

38. $16x^2 - 144y^2z^2$

39. $p^4 + 6p^2 - 7$

40. $q^4 + 8q^2 - 9$

41. $(x - 7)^2 - 4$

42. $(y - 2)^2 - 9$

43. $16 - (m + 4)^2$

44. $25 - (n + 5)^2$

45. $4p^4 - 32p^2 + 64$

46. $3q^4 - 24q^2 + 48$

47. $9x^2y^2 - 36x^2z^2$

48. $16p^2q^2 - 25p^2r^2$

Remove a monomial factor as in Example 2, and then, if possible, factor the polynomial factor completely.

49. $\frac{1}{2}x + 5$

50. $\frac{1}{4}x + 3$

51. $\frac{1}{9}p^2 - 1$

52. $\frac{1}{4}m^2 - 1$

53. $t^2 - \frac{1}{16}$

54. $s^2 - \frac{1}{25}$

55. $\frac{1}{4}x^2 - \frac{1}{9}y^2$

56. $\frac{1}{49}u^2 - \frac{1}{4}v^2$

57. $\frac{1}{4}a^2 + a + 1$

58. $\frac{1}{2}b^2 - 2b + 2$

59. $m^2 - \frac{2}{3}m + \frac{1}{9}$

60. $n^2 + \frac{2}{5}n + \frac{1}{25}$

61. $\frac{1}{2}x^2 + \frac{5}{2}x + 2$

62. $\frac{1}{4}y^2 + 2y + \frac{7}{4}$

63. $\frac{1}{3}p^2 + 4p - 15$

Factor each polynomial completely by grouping terms.

64. $8a^3 + 4a^2 - 2a - 1$

65. $(x - y)^2 - 4 + x - y + 2$

66. $m^2 - 2mn + n^2 - 9$

67. $16 - p^2 + 4pq - 4q^2$

7.7 APPLICATIONS OF FACTORING

Suppose the product of two numbers is 0. What do you know about the numbers?

Let $mn = 0$. If $m \neq 0$, then m has a multiplicative inverse and we may write

$$\frac{1}{m} \cdot mn = \frac{1}{m} \cdot 0.$$

$$\text{Then} \quad \left(\frac{1}{m} \cdot m\right) n = \frac{1}{m} \cdot 0$$

$$\text{and} \quad n = 0.$$

Similarly, if n is not 0, then m is 0. It is possible, of course, that both numbers are 0, since $0 \cdot 0 = 0$. We can now state the property that is the key to solving equations by factoring.

zero product property

Let m and n be real numbers.
If $mn = 0$, then $m = 0$ or $n = 0$, or both.

Example 1: Solve $x^2 - 4 = 0$.

SOLUTION: $x^2 - 4 = 0$ Given

$(x + 2)(x - 2) = 0$ Factoring

$x + 2 = 0$ or $x - 2 = 0$ Zero product property

$x = -2 \qquad x = 2$ Why?

Check: $(-2)^2 - 4 = 0 \qquad 2^2 - 4 = 0$

$0 = 0$ T $\qquad\qquad 0 = 0$ T

Thus, the solution set of $x^2 - 4 = 0$ is $\{-2, 2\}$.

Example 2: Solve $x^2 + 7x = 0$.

SOLUTION: $x^2 + 7x = 0$

$x(x + 7) = 0$

$x = 0$ or $x + 7 = 0$

$x = 0 \qquad x = -7$ Check as in Example 1.

Example 3: Solve $x^2 - 6x = -9$.

SOLUTION:

$$x^2 - 6x = -9$$

$$x^2 - 6x + 9 = 0$$ ◀ First, derive an equation in which one side is 0.

$$(x - 3)(x - 3) = 0$$

$$x - 3 = 0 \text{ or } x - 3 = 0$$

$$x = 3 \qquad x = 3$$ ◀ Two equal solutions, so the solution set is $\{3\}$.

Check: $3^2 - 6 \cdot 3 = -9$
$$-9 = -9 \quad \text{T}$$

Many practical problems involve equations that can be solved by factoring. The steps for solving such problems are the same as those shown in the flow chart on page 88.

Example 4: The length of a rectangular factory building is 8 meters less than four times its width. If the floor area is 252 square meters, what are the length and width of the building?

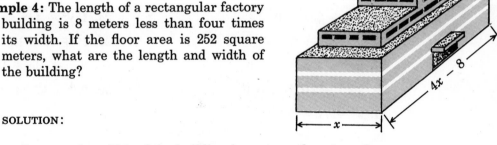

SOLUTION:

Let $x =$ the width of the building in meters; then $4x - 8 =$ the length of the building in meters.

$$x(4x - 8) = 252$$

$$4x^2 - 8x = 252$$

$$x^2 - 2x = 63$$

$$x^2 - 2x - 63 = 0$$

$$(x + 7)(x - 9) = 0$$

$$x = -7 \text{ or } x = 9$$

But a building cannot be -7 meters wide. Thus, the building is 9 meters wide and $4x - 8$, or 28, meters long.

Check this result.

EXERCISES 7.7

Ⓐ Solve; check your solutions.

1. $x(x + 3) = 0$

2. $y(y - 6) = 0$

3. $(x - 2)(x + 3) = 0$

4. $(y + 5)(y + 2) = 0$

5. $(m + 2)(m - 6) = 0$

6. $(s + 7)(s - 8) = 0$

7. $(p - 11)(p + 3) = 0$

8. $(2s + 1)(s - 5) = 0$

9. $4a(a - 12) = 0$

10. $(c - 2)4c = 0$

11. $(t - 3)(t - 3) = 0$

12. $(x + 5)(x - 5) = 0$

13. $a^2 + 4a + 4 = 0$

14. $y^2 - 2y + 1 = 0$

Ⓑ 15. $x^2 - 9 = 0$

16. $y^2 - 16 = 0$

17. $a^2 + 4a + 3 = 0$

18. $b^2 + 5b + 4 = 0$

19. $m^2 - 6m + 9 = 0$

20. $n^2 - 8n + 16 = 0$

21. $x^2 - 8x = 0$

22. $y^2 + 12y = 0$

23. $7x^2 - 28x = 0$

24. $11y^2 + 44y = 0$

25. $s^2 - 5s + 6 = 0$

26. $t^2 + 7t + 12 = 0$

27. $5p^2 + 12p + 7 = 0$

28. $3q^2 - 14q + 11 = 0$

29. $10c^2 - 11c + 3 = 0$

30. $2d^2 - 17d + 21 = 0$

31. $s^2 + 7s = -12$

32. $p^2 - 7p = -10$

33. $z^2 = 3 - 2z$

34. $r^2 - 8 = 2r$

35. $x^2 + 16 = 8x$

36. $y^2 + 25 = 10y$

37. $p^2 + 4p = 21$

38. $z^2 - 8z = -12$

39. $c^2 = 14 - 5c$

40. $m^2 - 6m = 16$

41. $x^2 = 25$

42. $y^2 = 36$

43. $m^2 - 12m = -36$

44. $n^2 - 14n = -49$

45. $s^2 - 2s = 15$

46. $t^2 - 3t = 28$

47. $6p = p^2$

48. $8q = q^2$

49. $14x + 72 = x^2$

50. $18y - 72 = y^2$

51. $5p^2 = 3p + 2$

52. $q^2 = q + 12$

53. $6m^2 + 11m = -4$

54. $6n^2 + n = 15$

55. A rectangle whose area is 160 square meters is 12 meters longer than it is wide. What are its length and width?

56. A rectangle 20 meters longer than it is wide has an area of 125 square meters. What are its length and width?

© **57.** One leg of a right triangle is 2 inches longer than the other. If the hypotenuse is 10 inches, how long are the legs?

58. The length of a rectangle is twice its width. If the length is increased by 2 feet and the width by 3 feet, the area is 30 square feet. Find the original length.

59. A rectangular pool is 8 feet wide and 12 feet long. A walk of uniform width surrounds the pool. If the total area of walk and pool is 320 square feet, how wide is the walk?

Find the zeros of these polynomials.

60. $x(x + 2)(x - 3)$

61. $y(y - 6)(y + 3)$

62. $x^3 - 6x^2 + 5x$

63. $z^3 - 7z^2 + 6z$

The formula for the height (in feet from the starting point) reached after t seconds by an object thrown upward at r feet per second is $h = rt - 16t^2$. So for an object thrown upward at 160 feet per second, $h = 160t - 16t^2$.

64. After how many seconds will the object first be 336 feet above its starting point? When will it be this height again?

65. How high will the object be after 4 seconds?

66. What is the maximum height the object will reach, and how long will it take to reach this height? (HINT: Find the value of h for which $16t^2 - 160t + h$ is a perfect square.)

CHAPTER REVIEW

7.1   Factor completely by removing a monomial factor.

    1. $5m - 5n$ **2.** $6n^2 - n$

    3. $12pq + 6qr$ **4.** $4x - 8x^2 + 12x^3$

7.2   By what can you multiply the given binomial so that the product is the difference of two squares?

    5. $x + 3$ **6.** $3p - 4q$

Factor completely.

    7. $m^2 - n^2$ **8.** $9z^2 - 49$

7.3   **9.** $x^2 - 14x + 49$ **10.** $y^2 + 6yz + 9z^2$

    11. $4t^2 - 20t + 25$ **12.** $16m^2 + 40mn + 25n^2$

7.4   **13.** $r^2 - 14r + 13$ **14.** $a^2 + 5a + 6$

    15. $x^2 + 4x - 32$ **16.** $y^2 - 6y - 16$

7.5   **17.** $2c^2 - 3c - 2$ **18.** $5p^2 + 3p - 2$

    19. $3y^2 - 8y + 4$ **20.** $2m^2 + m - 15$

    21. $t^2 + t - 30$ **22.** $5w^2 + 13w + 6$

7.6   **23.** $6s^2 - 12s + 6$ **24.** $a^2b - 3ab - 4b$

    25. $p^3 - 8p^2 - p$ **26.** $6z^2 - 24$

    27. $x^4 - y^4$ **28.** $2t^2 - 8t + 8$

Remove a monomial factor so that the remaining polynomial has integer coefficients. Then, if possible, factor the polynomial completely.

    29. $\frac{1}{4}m^2 - 9$ **30.** $\frac{1}{2}a^2 - a + \frac{1}{2}$ **31.** $\frac{1}{3}x^2 - 4x + 9$

7.7   Solve.

    32. $x^2 - 6x = 0$ **33.** $x^2 + 12x + 36 = 0$

    34. $m^2 - 49 = 0$ **35.** $2x^2 - 10x = 12$

Which lettered choice *best* matches each numbered item?

1. removing a monomial factor

2. difference of two squares

3. perfect-square trinomial

4. completely factored form

a. $x^2 - 4x + 4$

b. $x^2 - 3x + 2$

c. $3x(x - 2)(x - 1)$

d. $x^2 - 4$

e. $3x(x^2 - 3x + 2)$

Factor completely.

5. $5xy - 20xz$

7. $9s^2 - 36t^2$

9. $4p^2 + 12pq + 9q^2$

11. $y^2 - y - 12$

13. $5x^2 - 28x - 12$

15. $5am^2 - 20a$

17. $r^4 - 3r^2 + 2$

6. $25a^2 - 10a + 1$

8. $x^2 - 7x + 6$

10. $c^2 + 8c + 15$

12. $2x^2 + 17x + 21$

14. $3x^2 - 13x + 14$

16. $2x^2 - 8x + 8$

18. $16x^2y^2 - 81$

Remove a monomial factor so that the remaining polynomial has integer coefficients. Then, if possible, factor the polynomial completely.

19. $\frac{1}{4}h^2k^2 - \frac{1}{4}m^2$

20. $\frac{1}{5}x^2 - 2x + 5$

21. What binomial may be multiplied by $3x + 7y$ so that the product will be the difference of two squares?

Solve.

22. $4t^2 - 16t = 0$

24. $8x^2 + 2x - 15 = 0$

26. $r(2r - 1)(3r + 2) = 0$

23. $s^2 - 11s + 18 = 0$

25. $4m^2 = 16$

27. $9a^2 - 30a = -25$

28. If the length of a rectangle is 4 centimeters more than three times its width and its area is 64 square centimeters, find the length and width of the rectangle.

Ch. 1   Exercises 1–14 refer to the following sets.

I = {integers} W = {whole numbers}

^+I = {positive integers} ^-I = {negative integers}

M = {nonpositive integers} N = {nonnegative integers}

Q = {rational numbers} R = {real numbers}

1. π (is, is not) in Q.   2. $\sqrt{2}$ (is, is not) in R.

3. 0 (is, is not) in ^+I.   4. 0 (is, is not) in N.

5. $\frac{3}{2}$ (is, is not) in R.   6. ^+I (is, is not) a subset of N.

7. $\{0, -1, -2, -3, \cdots\}$ = _____   8. W = _____

9. $|-7|$ (is, is not) in ^-I.

10. The graph shows set _____. $\bullet\ \bullet\ \bullet$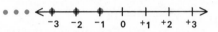

11. Graph set N.

12. $\{x \mid x < 0 \text{ and } x \text{ is an integer}\}$ describes set _____.

13. If ^+I is the replacement set, describe the solution set for $x < 3$.

14. The sets listed (are, are not) all infinite sets.

Ch. 2   Evaluate. (If the result is a fraction, express it in standard form.)

15. $-\frac{3}{7} + \frac{2}{7}$ 16. $\frac{7}{8} \cdot \left(-\frac{1}{3}\right)$ 17. $-3\left(\frac{4}{5} \cdot \frac{1}{3}\right)$

18. $54 \div (-3)$ 19. $-2(-7)$ 20. $21\left(\frac{1}{7} + \frac{1}{3}\right)$

21. $-\frac{3}{7} - \frac{2}{7}$ 22. $\frac{1}{2} \cdot \frac{5}{3}$ 23. $\frac{2}{9} \cdot 33 + \frac{2}{9} \cdot 66$

24. $-\frac{3}{5} \div \left(-\frac{2}{3}\right)$ 25. $\frac{3}{5} - \left(-\frac{1}{5}\right)$ 26. $\left(\frac{7}{9} \cdot \frac{3}{2}\right) \cdot 0$

27. $-\frac{7}{9} - \left(-\frac{2}{9}\right)$ 28. $-7 \div \frac{1}{7}$ 29. $0 \div \left(\frac{2}{7} + \frac{3}{7}\right)$

Which property is illustrated by each sentence?

30. $(7 - 19) \cdot 1 = 7 - 19$ 31. $2 + (3 - 2) = (3 - 2) + 2$

32. $-12 + 12 = 0$ 33. $(4 + n)3 = 12 + 3n$

34. $(9 + 2) + 14 = 9 + (2 + 14)$ 35. $9 \cdot \frac{1}{9} = 1$

36. $3(7x) = (3 \cdot 7)x$ 37. $6 \cdot 3y = 6y \cdot 3$

Simplify.

38. $-4a^2d + 7a^2d$ **39.** $(-7)^2$ **40.** $(-m)^2 + m^2$

41. $-3s + 5s^2 - 4s$ **42.** -7^2 **43.** $(x + y) - 2(x + y)$

Solve. Let {rational numbers} be the replacement set.

44. $6x - 20 = 10x + 4$ **45.** $-\frac{1}{2}n + 3 = 5$

46. $2(15m + 9) = 6(5m + 3)$ **47.** $7y + 3 = -11$

48. $3(6x + 5) = 2(3 + 9x)$ **49.** $9s + s = 4 + 3^2s$

50. A total of 522 people attended three hearings on pollution in Mudville, and at each hearing there were 3 people more than at the hearing before. How many people attended each hearing?

51. Using the formula $C = \frac{5}{9}(F - 32)$, find the Celsius temperature equivalent to 4° Fahrenheit.

52. Solve the formula $S = 2\pi r^2 + 2\pi rh$ for h.

From which of the following can you determine that $m < n$?

53. $m + 3 < n + 7$ **54.** $-2n < -2m$ **55.** $2m < mn$

56. $2m < m + n$ **57.** $\frac{1}{2}m < \frac{1}{3}n$ **58.** $m < a$ and $a > n$

Refer to the graphs of sets S, V, and T. True or False?

59. $S \cup T = \{$real numbers$\}$

60. 3 is in $S \cap T$.

61. $V \cup T = \{$real numbers$\}$

62. 9 is in $S \cup V$.

63. 5 is in $S \cap T$ **64.** $V \cup T = T$ **65.** 5 is in $S \cup T$

66. $S \cap V = \varnothing$ **67.** $V \cap T = \{9\}$ **68.** 9 is in $S \cap V$

Solve each sentence and graph the solution set.

69. $3n \neq -24$ **70.** $7 + 4y > y - 8$

71. $x + 2 > 0$ and $3x < 6$ **72.** $54 \leq 9s$

73. $3 < 9t < 18$ **74.** $\frac{1}{2}m = 3$ or $m + 2 = 7$

Express each of the following as a fraction in standard form.

75. $\frac{12}{54}$ **76.** $\frac{20}{45} \div 2$ **77.** $0.\overline{2}$ **78.** $\frac{12}{72} - \left(-\frac{1}{18}\right)$

79. $0.\overline{20}$ **80.** $\frac{3}{2} \cdot \frac{4}{27}$ **81.** $-\frac{10}{18} + \frac{21}{27}$ **82.** $0.2\overline{0}$

83. $\sqrt{\frac{4}{81}}$ **84.** $\dfrac{2^2 \cdot 3}{2 \cdot 3^3}$ **85.** $\dfrac{28}{9\sqrt{196}}$ **86.** $-\sqrt{\frac{4}{81}}$

87. Simplify. **a.** $n^6 \cdot 3n^2$ **b.** $(2y)^3$ **c.** $(-tr)^3 (3r^2)$

88. Factor completely. **a.** 315   **b.** 92   **c.** -156

89. Express as a repeating decimal. **a.** $\frac{5}{7}$ **b.** $-\frac{5}{9}$ **c.** $\frac{3}{5}$

90. Find $\sqrt{78}$ correct to the hundredths place.

91. If a 17-foot ladder reaches 15 feet up a vertical wall, how far from the wall is the foot of the ladder?

What axiom or theorem is illustrated by each sentence? Each variable stands for any real number.

92. $3 + 0(x + 1) = 3 + 0$ **93.** $r - 12 = [r + (-12)]$

94. $3t = 3(t + 0)$ **95.** $-2 + (-x) = -(2 + x)$

96. $-1 \cdot (n + 3) = -(n + 3)$

97. $-1 \cdot (n + 3) = -1n + (-1 \cdot 3)$

Exercises 98–101 refer to the polynomials listed below.

a. $m + 7$ **b.** $3x - 2y + 1$ **c.** $2n^2$

d. $3 - y$ **e.** $\frac{1}{3}n^2$ **f.** $n^2 - 3$

g. 7   **h.** $x^3 + x + 2$ **i.** $y^3 + 5$

j. $13n$ **k.** $4 - y^3 + 2y$ **l.** $3m^2 - 1 + m^4$

98. Identify each polynomial as a monomial, binomial, or trinomial.

99. Which monomials are like terms?

100. Identify each linear, quadratic, and cubic polynomial.

101. Evaluate each polynomial for $x = 2$, $y = -2$, $m = 3$, and $n = -3$.

Simplify each expression. Write each result in descending powers of a variable.

102. $(7x - 5) + (3x + 4)$

103. $(3m^2 + 2) - (2m^2 + 7)$

104. $4t(7 - t)$

105. $(x + 3)(x^2 - 2x + 1)$

106. $(4y^2 - 2y + 1) + (y^2 + 3)$

107. $(5n^2 + 9n - 1) - (n - 4)$

Simplify each expression.

108. $(4n - 1)(4n + 1)$

109. $(3ab)(-9a^2b)$

110. $(2y - 5x)^2$

111. $(\frac{1}{4}r + \frac{1}{3}s)(\frac{1}{4}r - \frac{1}{3}s)$

Find the zeros of each polynomial if $\{-3, -2, -1, 0, 1, 2\}$ is the replacement set in each case.

112. $n^2 - 4$

113. $3x + 9$

114. $4(y + 2)$

Factor completely.

115. $3x^3 - 9x^2$

116. $a^2 - 4b^2$

117. $4n^2 + 5n - 6$

118. $y^2 + y - 12$

119. $t^2 + 12t + 36$

120. $6x^2 - 17x + 12$

121. $2x^2 - 18x + 28$

122. $m^2 - 18m + 81$

123. $4r^2 + 4r + 1$

124. $14y^2 + 7y - 21$

Remove a monomial factor so that the remaining polynomial has integer coefficients. Then, if possible, factor the polynomial completely.

125. $\frac{1}{6}x^2 + \frac{1}{6}x - 1$

126. $y^2 + \frac{8}{3}y - 1$

Solve.

127. $n^2 + 3n = 0$

128. $4x^2 - 25 = 0$

129. $2m^2 - 11m = 21$

130. $4t^2 + 12t + 9 = 0$

131. Use factoring to find how much greater $(120)^2$ is than $(20)^2$.

132. How much less is the area of a square with sides 32 inches long than the area of a square with sides 92 inches long?

Chapter 8

Linear Sentences in Two Variables

In Chapter 1, pattern frames similar to the one above were used to illustrate open sentences in one variable.

The frame above can be used to illustrate an open sentence with **two** variables, x and y. Such open sentences are the main topic of this chapter.

The *order* in which we list a pair of numbers can be important. For example,

1/2	is *not* the same date as	2/1
▼		▼
Jan. 2		Feb. 1

11:10	is *not* the same time as	10:11
▼		▼
10 minutes after 11		11 minutes after 10

We also use ordered pairs in algebra. For example, let's agree that the replacement for x is listed first and the replacement for y is listed second. Then,

The ordered pair	The ordered pair
(1, 3)	(3, 1)
is a solution for	**is not** a solution for
$2x + y = 5$	$2x + y = 5$
because	because
$2 \cdot 1 + 3 = 5$	$2 \cdot 3 + 1 = 5$
is a true sentence.	is a false sentence.

In algebra, we generally represent *any* ordered pair with the variables x and y, listing x first and y second as

$$(x, y).$$

Example 1: List all the ordered pairs (x, y) that can be formed if the replacement sets are {1, 2} for x and {0, 1, 2} for y.

SOLUTION:

Each replacement for x must be paired with *every* replacement for y as shown at the right.

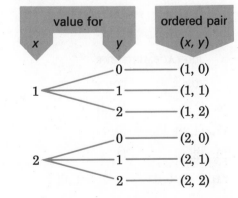

Example 2: Which ordered pairs listed in Example **1** are solutions for $2x + y = 4$?

SOLUTION:

Let (x, y) be	Then $2x + y = 4$ becomes	
(1, 0)	$2 \cdot 1 + 0 = 4$	False
(1, 1)	$2 \cdot 1 + 1 = 4$	False
(1, 2)	$2 \cdot 1 + 2 = 4$	True
(2, 0)	$2 \cdot 2 + 0 = 4$	True
(2, 1)	$2 \cdot 2 + 1 = 4$	False
(2, 2)	$2 \cdot 2 + 2 = 4$	False

Thus, only (1, 2) and (2, 0) from Example **1** are solutions for $2x + y = 4$.

EXERCISES 8.1

Ⓐ **1.** Does $(2, 4) = (4, 2)$? That is, are (2, 4) and (4, 2) the same ordered pair of numbers? Why?

2. Does $(\frac{1}{2}, \frac{2}{6}) = (0.5, \frac{1}{3})$? Why?

Is the given ordered pair a solution for

$$3x + y = 5 \text{ ?}$$

3. (1, 2)   **4.** (2, 1)   **5.** (−1, 2)   **6.** (2, −1)

7. (0, 5)   **8.** (5, 0)   **9.** (2, 0)   **10.** (0, 2)

11. $(\frac{1}{3}, 4)$ **12.** $(4, \frac{1}{3})$ **13.** $(\frac{2}{3}, 3)$ **14.** $(-\frac{1}{3}, 6)$

Ⓑ In each exercise, list all the ordered pairs (x, y) that can be formed.

REPLACEMENT SET		REPLACEMENT SET	
FOR x	FOR y	FOR x	FOR y
15. {1}	{1, 2}	**16.** {2}	{0, 1}
17. {1, 2}	{0, 1}	**18.** {0, 1}	{1, 2}
19. {2, 3}	{1, 2, 3}	**20.** {3, 4}	{2, 3, 4}
21. {−1, 0, 1}	{−2, −1, 0, 1}	**22.** {−2, −1, 0}	{−1, 0, 1, 2}

In each exercise, write the open sentence. Then write all the closed sentences that can be formed and indicate which are true and which are false.

23.

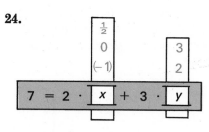

$x - 2 \cdot y = 0$

(values: 2, 0 for x; 2, 1, 0 for y)

24.

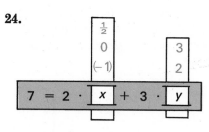

$7 = 2 \cdot x + 3 \cdot y$

(values: $\tfrac{1}{2}$, 0, (−1) for x; 3, 2 for y)

25.

$3 \cdot (-2) + 1 < (-1)$

(values: 0, (−1) for x; 1, 0 for y)

26.

$2 \cdot 2 > 3 \cdot 2 - 4$

(values: 4, 3 for y; 4, 3 for x)

© In each exercise, find 3 ordered pairs (x, y) that are solutions for the open sentence and have the given values for x.

27.

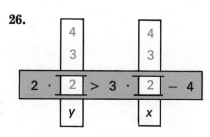

$y = -2 \cdot (-1) + 5$

(values: 1, 0, (−1) for x)

28.

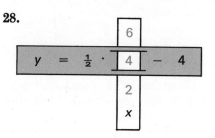

$y = \tfrac{1}{2} \cdot 4 - 4$

(values: 6, 4, 2 for x)

Copy and complete each table.

29.

$y = 2x - 1$	
Let $x =$	Then $y =$
2	?
1	?
0	?
−1	?
−2	?

30.

$3x - 4y = 2$	
Let $x =$	Then $y =$
0	?
?	0
−2	?
?	1
10	?

8.2 THE COORDINATE PLANE

As was shown in Chapter 5, any real number can be graphed on a number line. By using two real number lines together, we can graph any *ordered pair* of real numbers.

coordinate plane

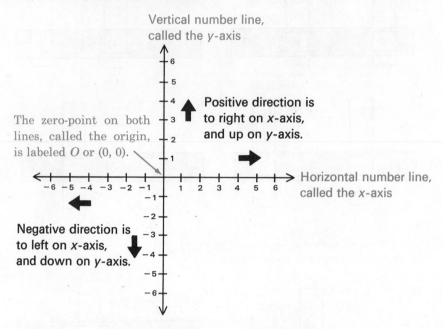

Together, the *x*-axis and *y*-axis are called the **axes**. The axes determine a plane, called the **coordinate plane**.

Example 1: Graph $(2, 5)$ and $(5, 2)$.

SOLUTION:

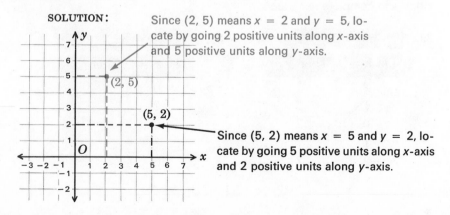

Since (2, 5) means $x = 2$ and $y = 5$, locate by going 2 positive units along x-axis and 5 positive units along y-axis.

Since (5, 2) means $x = 5$ and $y = 2$, locate by going 5 positive units along x-axis and 2 positive units along y-axis.

The **graph** of each ordered pair (x, y) is a *point* in the coordinate plane. The numbers in an ordered pair are called the **coordinates** of the point they locate.

Example 2: What are the coordinates of each point shown in the graph?

SOLUTION:

point	coordinates
A	$(4, 3)$
B	$(-4, 3)$
C	$(-4, -3)$
D	$(4, -3)$
E	$(4, 0)$
F	$(-4, 0)$
G	$(0, 3)$
H	$(0, -3)$
J	$(2\frac{1}{2}, -1\frac{1}{2})$
O	$(0, 0)$

The first number is the **x-coordinate** (or **abscissa**).

The second number is the **y-coordinate** (or **ordinate**).

The axes separate the plane into four **quadrants**, numbered as shown. (Points on the axes are in none of the quadrants.)

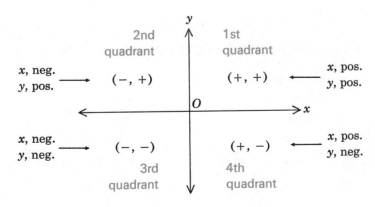

SECTION 8.2   THE COORDINATE PLANE   265

EXERCISES 8.2

Ⓐ Which point shown is the graph of the given ordered pair?

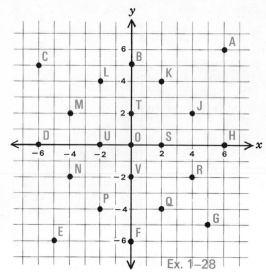

Ex. 1–28

1. (2, 4) **2.** (4, 2)

3. (−2, 4) **4.** (4, −2)

5. (−2, −4) **6.** (−4, −2)

7. (2, −4) **8.** (−4, 2)

9. (2, 0) **10.** (0, 2)

11. (0, −2) **12.** (−2, 0)

What are the coordinates of each point?

13. A **14.** B **15.** C

16. D **17.** E **18.** F

19. G **20.** H **21.** O

Which points graphed above are:

22. in the first quadrant? **23.** in the second quadrant?

24. in the third quadrant? **25.** in the fourth quadrant?

26. on the *x*-axis? **27.** on the *y*-axis?

28. on both axes?

29. The point on both axes is called the _____.

30. The axes determine the _____ plane.

31. The first coordinate of a point is called the _____ (or _____).

32. The second coordinate of a point is called the _____ (or _____).

Ⓑ Graph the ordered pairs, using a separate coordinate plane for each exercise.

33. (0, 2) (0, 1) (0, 0) (0, −1) (0, −2) (0, −3)

34. (3, 0) (2, 0) (1, 0) (0, 0) (−1, 0) (−2, 0)

35. $(1, 2)$ $(1, 1)$ $(1, 0)$ $(1, -1)$ $(1, -2)$ $(1, -3)$

36. $(3, 2)$ $(2, 2)$ $(1, 2)$ $(0, 2)$ $(-1, 2)$ $(-2, 2)$

37. $(3, -5)$ $(2, -5)$ $(1, -5)$ $(0, -5)$ $(-1, -5)$ $(-2, -5)$

38. $(-3, 2)$ $(-3, 1)$ $(-3, 0)$ $(-3, -1)$ $(-3, -2)$ $(-3, -3)$

39. $(2, \frac{1}{2})$ $(1, \frac{1}{2})$ $(0, \frac{1}{2})$ $(-1, \frac{1}{2})$ $(-2, \frac{1}{2})$ $(-3, \frac{1}{2})$

40. $(-1\frac{1}{2}, 2)$ $(-1\frac{1}{2}, 1)$ $(-1\frac{1}{2}, 0)$ $(-1\frac{1}{2}, -1)$ $(-1\frac{1}{2}, -2)$ $(-1\frac{1}{2}, -3)$

41. $(3, 3)$ $(2, 2)$ $(1, 1)$ $(0, 0)$ $(-1, -1)$ $(-2\frac{1}{2}, -2\frac{1}{2})$

42. $(3, -3)$ $(2, -2)$ $(1, -1)$ $(0, 0)$ $(-1, 1)$ $(-2\frac{1}{2}, 2\frac{1}{2})$

Refer to your graphs for Exercises 33–42 to answer Exercises 43–48.

43. If a point is on the y-axis, what is its x-coordinate?

44. If a point is on the x-axis, what is its y-coordinate?

45. All points with an x-coordinate of 1 are on the same [horizontal, vertical] line.

46. All points with a y-coordinate of 2 are on the same [horizontal, vertical] line.

47. All points for which $y = x$ are on a line which slants upward to the [right, left].

48. All points for which $y = -x$ are on a line which slants upward to the [right, left].

In which quadrant or on which axis will (x, y) be graphed if:

49. $x > 0$ and $y > 0$?   **50.** $x < 0$ and $y < 0$?

51. $x > 0$ and $y < 0$?   **52.** $x < 0$ and $y > 0$?

53. $x = 0$?   **54.** $y = 0$?

© On a graph, show five points whose coordinates are solutions for the given equation. Use a separate graph for each exercise.

55. $y = 2x + 1$ **56.** $y = 3x - 2$

57. $y = -2x + 3$ **58.** $y = -\frac{1}{2}x + 4$

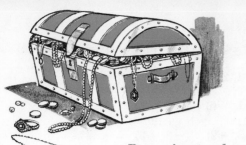

Treasure Hunt—A Graphing Game

Number of players: Two.

Equipment needed: Graph paper and pencils.

Preparing to play: Each player makes two grids—a "treasure" grid and a "map" grid. The players agree on the size of the grids (perhaps from −10 to 10 on both axes) and draw the proper axes.

Treasure grid: The player "buries treasure chests" on this grid by circling intersections as follows.

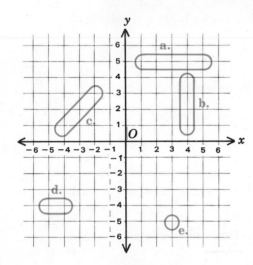

Kind of trea-sure chest	Number of intersections
a. diamonds	5
b. emeralds	4
c. rubies	3
d. gold coins	2
e. silver coins	1

The players agree on whether to "bury" 1 or 2 of each kind of treasure chest. In any chest, all the intersections must be consecutive and lie on a line that is horizontal, vertical, or diagonal.

Map grid: Only the axes are needed on this grid at the start of the game.

Playing the game: The players hide their treasure grids from each other. (You can place your hand or a book in front of your grid.)

Either player can start. The players take turns naming one intersection by calling out its coordinates. The opponent must answer "in" or "out," depending on whether the intersection is inside or outside a treasure chest. If the intersection is the last one inside a chest, then its owner must say "in and found."

To help plan your search, mark both your "ins" and "outs" on your *map* grid. (Use • for an "in" and ○ for an "out.") On your *treasure* grid, mark only your opponent's "ins." The first player to find *all* of the opponent's buried treasure wins the game.

If an open sentence contains two variables, each solution is an ordered pair. And ordered pairs can be graphed. We will now use both of these ideas to graph equations containing two variables, that is, to graph their solution sets.

Example 1: Graph $3x - y = 5$.

SOLUTION: By the replacement-set agreement on page 119, the replacement set for each variable is the set of real numbers. Thus, to find an ordered pair which is a solution of $3x - y = 5$, we can let x equal any real number and solve the resulting equation for y.

A convenient way to find these solutions is to solve the given equation for y *before* making replacements for x:

$$3x - y = 5$$
$$-y = 5 - 3x$$
$$y = -5 + 3x$$
$$y = 3x - 5$$

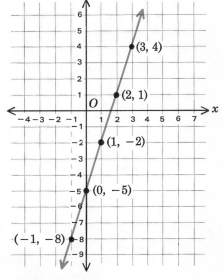

Then make a table as follows.

$y = 3x - 5$		
Let $x =$	Then $y =$	
2	$3 \cdot 2 - 5 = 1$	$\rightarrow (2, 1)$
0	$3 \cdot 0 - 5 = -5$	$\rightarrow (0, -5)$
−1	$3(-1) - 5 = -8$	$\rightarrow (-1, -8)$
3	$3 \cdot 3 - 5 = 4$	$\rightarrow (3, 4)$
1	$3 \cdot 1 - 5 = -2$	$\rightarrow (1, -2)$

Graphing the ordered pairs listed in the table, suggests that the points all lie on a line. In fact, it can be proved that all the points of this line make up the graph of the entire solution set of $3x - y = 5$.

A **linear equation in two variables** is an equation whose graph in the coordinate plane is a line.

standard form of a linear equation

Any linear equation in two variables can be written in the form

$$ax + by = c,$$

where a and b are any real-number coefficients (not both 0), x and y are any variables, and c is any real-number constant.

Notice that in a linear equation each term is a first-degree monomial or a constant.

Example 2: Graph $2x = x - 2y$.

SOLUTION: First, notice that the equation can be put in standard form, where $a = 1$, $b = 2$, and $c = 0$.

$$2x = x - 2y$$
$$x = -2y$$
$$1x + 2y = 0$$

Therefore, this is a linear equation, and you now know its graph is a line.

Two points determine a line, so you need to graph only two solutions of the given equation. As a check, graph at least three solutions. (If the points you locate are not on a line, you have made an error.)

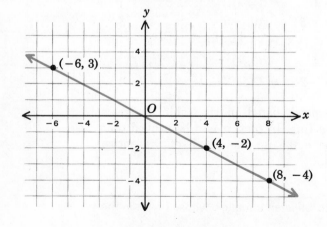

Solve the given equation for y and make a table.

$$2x = x - 2y$$
$$x = -2y$$
$$-\tfrac{1}{2}x = y$$

$y = -\tfrac{1}{2}x$	
Let $x =$	Then $y =$
4	$-\tfrac{1}{2} \cdot 4 = -2$
8	$-\tfrac{1}{2} \cdot 8 = -4$
-6	$-\tfrac{1}{2}(-6) = 3$

Ⓐ 1. An equation whose graph in the coordinate plane is a line is called ____.

2. If an open sentence contains two variables, then each solution is [a single number, an ordered pair].

3. The graph of an ordered pair is [a point, a line].

4. To graph a linear equation in two variables, it is enough to graph ____ solutions. But, we graph at least ____ as a check.

5. In a linear equation, each term is a ____ or a ____.

Tell whether each equation is a linear equation in two variables, and if it is, whether it is in standard form.

6. $3x + 2y = 6$

7. $3x^2 + 2y = 6$

8. $\frac{3}{x} + 2y = 6$

9. $2y = 6 - 3x$

10. $\frac{1}{2}x + (-1)y = 0$

11. $3xy = 1$

12. $1x + 1y = 0$

13. $y = -x$

14. $y = x$

15. $0x + 1y = 3$

16. $y = 3$

17. $y = 3^2$

18. $-1x + 0y = 2$

19. $x = -2$

20. $y = x^3$

21. $2m + 3n = 5$

22. $r = s^3$

How should each table be completed?

23.

$y = x + 2$	
Let $x =$	Then $y =$
a.	0	
b.	-2	
c.	4	

24.

$y = 3x$	
Let $x =$	Then $y =$
a.	0	
b.	2	
c.	-2	

Ⓑ 25.

$y = -2x + \frac{1}{2}$	
Let $x =$	Then $y =$
a.	0	
b.	$\frac{1}{4}$	
c.	3	

26.

$y = -\frac{1}{3}x + 1$	
Let $x =$	Then $y =$
a.	0	
b.	3	
c.	-3	

27–30. Graph the equations in Exercises **23–26**, using a separate pair of axes for each.

Graph the equations, using a separate pair of axes for each.

31. $y = x + 3$ **32.** $y = x + 5$

33. $y = x - 3$ **34.** $y = x - 5$

35. $y = 2x$ **36.** $y = 4x$

37. $y = \frac{1}{2}x$ **38.** $y = \frac{1}{4}x$

39. $y = -2x$ **40.** $y = -4x$

41. $y = -\frac{1}{2}x$ **42.** $y = -\frac{1}{4}x$

43. $y = 2x + 3$ **44.** $y = 4x + 5$

45. $y = -2x + 3$ **46.** $y = -4x + 5$

47. $x - 2y = 6$ **48.** $x - 4y = 20$

49. $x + 2y = 6$ **50.** $x + 4y = 20$

51. $2x + 3y = 12$ **52.** $2x - 3y = -12$

© **53.** Graph the equations, using the *same* pair of axes.

    a. $y = x + 1$ **b.** $y = 2x + 1$ **c.** $y = \frac{1}{2}x + 1$

    d. $y = 0x + 1$ **e.** $y = -2x + 1$ **f.** $y = -\frac{1}{2}x + 1$

    g. What do the lines have in common?

    h. What do the right sides of the equations have in common?

54. Graph the equations, using the *same* pair of axes.

    a. $y = 2x + 1$ **b.** $y = 2x - 1$ **c.** $y = 2x + 2$

    d. $y = 2x + 3$ **e.** $y = 2x + 0$ **f.** $y = 2x - \frac{1}{2}$

    g. Do the lines appear to intersect?

    h. What do the right sides of the equations have in common?

For each equation, make a table of at least 7 solutions. Graph these solutions, using a separate pair of axes for each exercise.

55. $y = x^2$ **56.** $y = x^3 - 12$ **57.** $y = \frac{12}{x}$

58. $xy = 18$ **59.** $n = 2m + 1$ **60.** $n = m^2$

True or false?

1. $(1, -\frac{1}{2}) = (-\frac{1}{2}, 1)$ 2. $(\frac{2}{4}, 0.\bar{3}) = (\frac{1}{2}, \frac{1}{3})$

3. One solution for $4x - 3y = 2$ is $(0, 0)$.

4. One solution for $4x - 3y = 2$ is $(2, 2)$.

5. One solution for $4x - 3y = 2$ is $(\frac{1}{2}, 0)$.

6. List all the ordered pairs (x, y) that can be formed if the replacement set for x is $\{0, 1\}$ and for y it is $\{-\frac{1}{2}, 0, 1\}$.

7. Graph these ordered pairs on the same coordinate plane.

    $(0, 0)$ $(2, 0)$ $(0, 2)$ $(-3, 0)$ $(0, -3)$

    $(2, 4)$ $(-2, -4)$ $(2, -4)$ $(-2, 4)$ $(\frac{1}{2}, -1\frac{1}{2})$

8. If a point is on the x-axis, what is its y-coordinate?

9. In which quadrant are all the points that have both coordinates negative?

Is the equation a linear equation in two variables? If so, is it in standard form?

10. $5x + (-\frac{1}{2})y = 3$ 11. $y = x^2$ 12. $y = 2x - 1$

Graph the equations, using a separate pair of axes for each.

13. $y = 2x - 5$ 14. $y = -\frac{1}{2}x + 4$

15. $2x + 3y = 24$

8.4 SLOPE OF A LINE

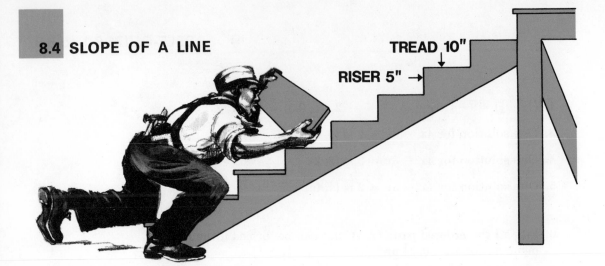

TREAD 10"

RISER 5" →

When a carpenter builds a stairway, he considers the ratio of "riser" to "tread." This tells him the steepness or "slope" of the stairway.

The riser may be thought of as the *vertical change* (or *rise*) of each step. The tread may be considered the *horizontal change* (or *run*) of each step. Thus, for the stairway the carpenter is building above,

$$\text{SLOPE} = \frac{\text{VERTICAL RISE}}{\text{HORIZONTAL RUN}} = \frac{5}{10} = \frac{1}{2}.$$

In algebra, we use similar ideas to define the *slope of a line*. For example, consider the line graphed below.

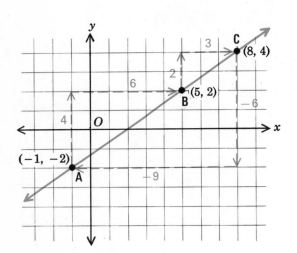

• From point A to point B.

$$\frac{\text{VERTICAL CHANGE}}{\text{HORIZONTAL CHANGE}} = \frac{4 \text{ UNITS UP}}{6 \text{ UNITS RIGHT}} = \frac{+4}{+6} = \frac{2}{3}$$

• From point B to point C.

$$\frac{\text{VERTICAL CHANGE}}{\text{HORIZONTAL CHANGE}} = \frac{2 \text{ UNITS UP}}{3 \text{ UNITS RIGHT}} = \frac{+2}{+3} = \frac{2}{3}$$

• From point C to point A.

$$\frac{\text{VERTICAL CHANGE}}{\text{HORIZONTAL CHANGE}} = \frac{6 \text{ UNITS DOWN}}{9 \text{ UNITS LEFT}} = \frac{-6}{-9} = \frac{2}{3}$$

This example suggests that the slope is the same no matter which two points of the line we use. We will now define *slope of a line* so that it can be found from the coordinates of two points on a line.

> The **slope of a line** that contains points at (x_1, y_1) and (x_2, y_2) is
>
> $$\frac{\text{VERTICAL CHANGE}}{\text{HORIZONTAL CHANGE}} = \frac{y_2 - y_1}{x_2 - x_1},$$
>
> providing that $x_2 - x_1 \neq 0$.

NOTE: The small numerals, $_1$ and $_2$, used above are called *subscripts*. They indicate that x_1 and x_2 (or y_1 and y_2) can have different values.

Example: Find the slope of the line that contains points at

$$(3, -4) \quad \text{and} \quad (-2, 6).$$

SOLUTION: Either ordered pair may be considered (x_2, y_2). Then the other ordered pair is (x_1, y_1). So, the slope can be found in two ways.

Let $(x_2, y_2) = (3, -4)$

and $(x_1, y_1) = (-2, 6)$.

$$\text{SLOPE} = \frac{y_2 - y_1}{x_2 - x_1} = \frac{-4 - 6}{3 - (-2)}$$

$$= \frac{-10}{5}$$

$$= -2$$

Or,

Let $(x_2, y_2) = (-2, 6)$

and $(x_1, y_1) = (3, -4)$.

$$\text{SLOPE} = \frac{y_2 - y_1}{x_2 - x_1} = \frac{6 - (-4)}{-2 - 3}$$

$$= \frac{10}{-5}$$

$$= -2$$

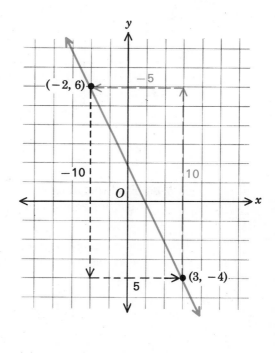

Ⓐ 1. The slope of a line is the ratio of ____ change to ____ change, providing that the ____ change is not 0.

2. What are the $_1$ and $_2$ in y_1 and y_2 called? What do they indicate?

Find the slope of each line by considering the vertical and horizontal changes from point A to point B.

3.

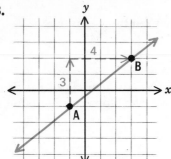

4.

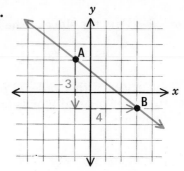

5.

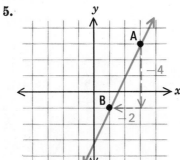

6.

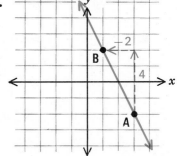

7–10. Find the slope of each line above by considering the vertical and horizontal changes from point B to point A.

For a line containing points at (2, 4) and (3, 6), four students computed the slope as follows. Which were right and which were wrong? Why were they wrong?

11. $\dfrac{6-4}{3-2} = \dfrac{2}{1} = 2$

12. $\dfrac{3-2}{6-4} = \dfrac{1}{2}$

13. $\dfrac{4-6}{2-3} = \dfrac{-2}{-1} = 2$

14. $\dfrac{6-4}{2-3} = \dfrac{2}{-1} = -2$

Ⓑ Find the slope of the line by using the two points given.

15. (2, 3) and (5, 6)   **16.** (3, 2) and (6, 5)

17. (6, 2) and (3, 5)   **18.** (2, 6) and (5, 3)

19. (−6, 2) and (−4, 6)   **20.** (−4, 3) and (−2, 9)

21. (−1, 3) and (−7, 5)   **22.** (−2, 1) and (−6, 2)

23. (−2, −7) and (2, −1)   **24.** (−3, −10) and (3, −2)

25. (−1, −9) and (−5, −1)   **26.** (−3, −8) and (−5, −2)

27. $(\frac{3}{2}, 0)$ and $(\frac{9}{2}, 4)$ **28.** $(\frac{1}{3}, -3)$ and $(\frac{7}{3}, 0)$

29. $(\frac{1}{2}, -\frac{3}{2})$ and $(0, -\frac{7}{2})$ **30.** $(0, -\frac{10}{3})$ and $(\frac{2}{3}, -\frac{8}{3})$

Given three points A, B, and C on a line, find the slope by using

    a. A and B;   **b.** B and C;   **c.** A and C.

	A	B	C		A	B	C
31.	(1, 3)	(3, 5)	(5, 7)	**32.**	(2, 6)	(4, 9)	(6, 12)
33.	(−2, 1)	(0, 4)	(2, 7)	**34.**	(−1, 5)	(2, 7)	(5, 9)
35.	(0, −5)	(2, −6)	(−10, 0)	**36.**	(−6, 0)	(0, −4)	(3, −6)

Ⓒ Find the slope of the line by using the two points given.

37. (2.1, 1.3) and (−1.4, 0.5)   **38.** $(\frac{7}{4}, \frac{2}{3})$ and $(\frac{13}{4}, \frac{1}{2})$

39. (1000000, 4000000) and (1000001, 4000003)

40. A line with points at (1, 1) and (3, y) has slope 5. Find y.

41. A line with points at (x, 0) and (3, −2) has slope $-\frac{1}{2}$. Find x.

42. Which is steeper, a stairway with a riser of 5 inches and a tread of 10 inches or one with a riser of 6 inches and a tread of 8 inches?

43. Which line is steeper: line l with a slope of $\frac{1}{2}$ or line k with a slope of $\frac{3}{4}$?

Using a pair of axes, draw the lines for odd-numbered Exercises 15–29. Then use the lines and their slopes to answer these exercises.

44. A line slanting upward to the [left, right] has positive slope.

45. A line slanting upward to the [left, right] has negative slope.

8.5 WHAT DOES THE SLOPE TELL YOU?

The slope of a line tells about the line's steepness. There are also other facts about lines revealed by their slopes.

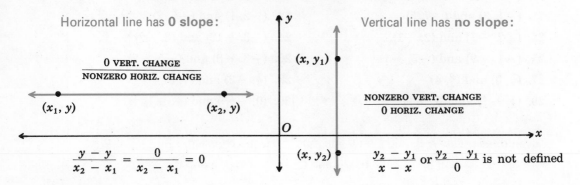

Horizontal line has **0 slope:**

$$\frac{0 \text{ VERT. CHANGE}}{\text{NONZERO HORIZ. CHANGE}}$$

(x_1, y) (x_2, y)

$$\frac{y - y}{x_2 - x_1} = \frac{0}{x_2 - x_1} = 0$$

Vertical line has **no slope:**

(x, y_1)

$$\frac{\text{NONZERO VERT. CHANGE}}{0 \text{ HORIZ. CHANGE}}$$

(x, y_2) $\frac{y_2 - y_1}{x - x}$ or $\frac{y_2 - y_1}{0}$ is not defined

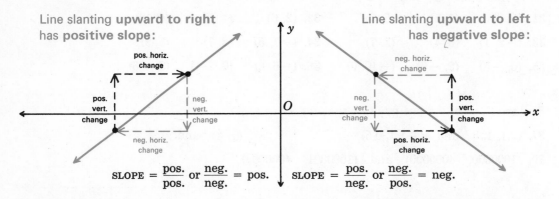

Line slanting **upward to right** has **positive slope:**

pos. horiz. change

pos. vert. change   neg. vert. change

neg. horiz. change

$$\text{SLOPE} = \frac{\text{pos.}}{\text{pos.}} \text{ or } \frac{\text{neg.}}{\text{neg.}} = \text{pos.}$$

Line slanting **upward to left** has **negative slope:**

neg. horiz. change

neg. vert. change   pos. vert. change

pos. horiz. change

$$\text{SLOPE} = \frac{\text{pos.}}{\text{neg.}} \text{ or } \frac{\text{neg.}}{\text{pos.}} = \text{neg.}$$

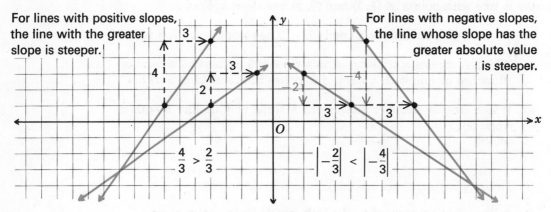

For lines with positive slopes, the line with the greater slope is steeper.

$$\frac{4}{3} > \frac{2}{3}$$

For lines with negative slopes, the line whose slope has the greater absolute value is steeper.

$$\left|-\frac{2}{3}\right| < \left|-\frac{4}{3}\right|$$

In general, for *any* two nonvertical lines, the line whose slope has the greater absolute value is steeper.

Now consider two lines with the same slope. Let the slope be $\frac{3}{2}$, as in the drawing below. Then for every vertical change of 3 and each horizontal change of 2 on one line, there are corresponding changes on the other line.

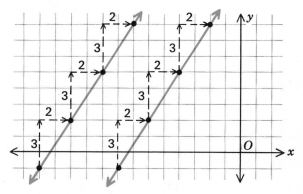

Thus, the lines never approach each other. That is, they are always the same distance apart. In general, for any two distinct lines:

Lines with the same slope are parallel.
Lines with different slopes intersect.

If you know the slope of a line and the coordinates of one point, you can draw the line in the coordinate plane.

Examples: Given the slope and one point of a line, draw the line:

1. slope: $\frac{3}{4}$; point: $(-3, -2)$.   **2.** slope: -3; point: $(5, -4)$.

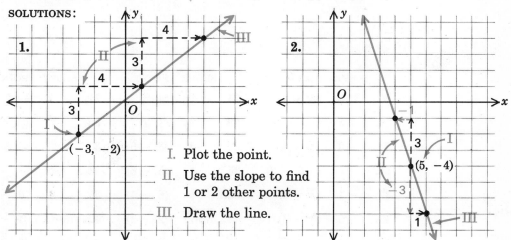

SOLUTIONS:

I. Plot the point.
II. Use the slope to find 1 or 2 other points.
III. Draw the line.

EXERCISES 8.5

Ⓐ **1.** The slope of any _____ line is 0.

2. Any _____ line has no slope.

3. What is the slope of the x-axis? The y-axis?

4. For any line that slants upward to the right, the vertical change and horizontal change always have [the same sign, opposite signs], so the slope is always _____.

5. For any line that slants upward to the left, the vertical change and horizontal change always have [the same sign, opposite signs], so the slope is always _____.

6. Two lines with the same slope [are parallel, intersect].

Given the slopes, tell which line is steeper.

	LINE l	LINE k		LINE l	LINE k		LINE l	LINE k
7.	2	3	8.	-2	-3	9.	2	-3
10.	$\frac{4}{5}$	$\frac{3}{5}$	11.	$-\frac{6}{7}$	$-\frac{3}{7}$	12.	$-\frac{5}{9}$	$\frac{4}{9}$
Ⓑ 13.	$-\frac{1}{2}$	$-\frac{1}{3}$	14.	$-\frac{1}{3}$	$-\frac{1}{4}$	15.	$\frac{3}{5}$	$\frac{4}{7}$
16.	$\frac{7}{8}$	$\frac{6}{7}$	17.	$-\frac{5}{6}$	$-\frac{7}{9}$	18.	$-\frac{9}{8}$	$-\frac{4}{3}$
19.	$-1\frac{1}{5}$	$\frac{9}{4}$	20.	$\frac{8}{13}$	$-\frac{7}{11}$	21.	$-2\frac{2}{3}$	$-2\frac{3}{4}$
22.	$-4\frac{5}{6}$	$-4\frac{4}{5}$	23.	$-\sqrt{2}$	1.1	24.	1.8	$-\sqrt{3}$

Given the slope and one point of a line, draw the line. Use a separate pair of axes for each exercise.

	SLOPE	POINT		SLOPE	POINT		SLOPE	POINT
25.	$\frac{1}{2}$	$(2, 3)$	26.	$\frac{1}{3}$	$(4, 2)$	27.	2	$(-2, 3)$
28.	5	$(-6, 5)$	29.	$-\frac{3}{4}$	$(1, 7)$	30.	$-\frac{2}{5}$	$(7, 3)$
31.	-3	$(5, -4)$	32.	-4	$(8, -6)$	33.	$\frac{4}{3}$	$(-3, -7)$
34.	$\frac{5}{2}$	$(-5, -3)$	35.	$-\frac{4}{3}$	$(5, -6)$	36.	$-\frac{5}{2}$	$(8, -4)$
37.	$-\frac{4}{3}$	$(3, -6)$	38.	$-\frac{5}{2}$	$(6, -4)$	39.	0	$(0, -6)$
40.	0	$(0, -7)$	41.	none	$(2, -8)$	42.	none	$(4, -9)$
Ⓒ 43.	$-2\frac{3}{5}$	$(-2, 3)$	44.	0.25	$(0, 7)$	45.	50%	$(0, 8)$

Graph each equation. Find the slope of the line. Then tell what part of the equation gives the slope.

46. $y = \frac{2}{3}x - 4$

47. $y = -\frac{2}{3}x + 4$

48. $y = 4x$

49. $y = -2x + 5$

50. $y = \frac{3}{4}x - 2$

51. $y = -\frac{5}{2}x$

Experimenting with Perpendicular Lines

Equipment: A sheet of transparent material (such as that used with overhead projectors);

A sheet of graph paper with large squares (at least $\frac{1}{4}$ inch by $\frac{1}{4}$ inch);

An object with a sharp point (such as a compass);

An object for making right angles (such as a T square)

Purpose: To find how slopes of perpendicular lines are related.

Procedure:

1. Carefully scratch a pair of perpendicular lines on the transparent sheet, using the sharp object and the right-angled device.

2. Draw a pair of axes on the graph paper.

3. Place the perpendicular lines on the graph paper so that their intersection is at the intersection of a pair of grid lines, and so that you can easily determine the slope of one of the perpendicular lines. (See diagram.)

4. Determine the corresponding slope of the other line.

5. Record the slopes found in steps **3** and **4**.

6. Repeat steps **3–5** with the perpendicular lines held in various positions on the graph paper.

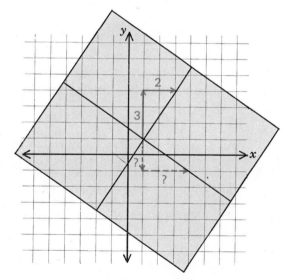

Conclusion: State your conclusion. (Be careful about lines with 0 slope or no slope.) Check your conclusion by referring to a high-school geometry book.

Any nonvertical line will intersect the y-axis at some point. The x-coordinate of this point is 0 (since it is on the y-axis).

Let's say that some line intersects the y-axis at $(0, b)$. Then let any other point on this line be (x, y). We can find the slope of this line as follows.

$$\frac{y - b}{x - 0} \quad \text{or} \quad \frac{y - b}{x}$$

Now, set the slope equal to m and solve the resulting equation for y.

$$\bullet \quad \frac{y - b}{x} = m$$

$$\bullet \quad y - b = mx$$

$$\bullet \quad y = mx + b$$

This result is the equation of the line. Recall where m and b came from:

m from letting it equal the slope;

b from $(0, b)$, where the line intersects the y-axis.

So, when an equation is in the form

$$y = mx + b,$$

its graph is the line having slope m and intersecting the y-axis at $(0, b)$.

Example 1: Given the equation below, find the slope of its graph and the point at which the graph intersects the y-axis.

$$2x + 4y = 12$$

SOLUTION: Solve for y.

$$2x + 3y = 12$$

$$3y = -2x + 12$$

$$y = -\tfrac{2}{3}x + 4$$

Slope $= -\tfrac{2}{3}$ ⸺⸺⸺↑   ↑⸺Graph intersects
                                        y-axis at $(0, 4)$

Any linear equation in two variables for which the coefficient of y is not 0 can be written in the form

$$y = mx + b,$$

where m is the slope of the graph and b (called the **y-intercept**) is the y-coordinate of the point at which the graph intersects the y-axis.

slope-intercept form of a linear equation

Example 2: Given the equation below, find the slope and y-intercept of its graph.

$$3y - 6x + 5 = 0$$

SOLUTION: Solve for y.

$$3y - 6x + 5 = 0$$
$$3y = 6x - 5$$
$$y = 2x + (-\tfrac{5}{3})$$

Note that this sign must be +

Slope ⎯⎯⎯⎯⎯⎯ y-intercept

EXERCISES 8.6

Ⓐ 1. The coordinates of the point at which a nonvertical line intersects the _____ are (0, b).

2. The y-intercept of a line is the _____ of the point at which the line intersects the _____.

3. An equation in the form $y = mx + b$ is in _____ form.

4. For an equation in the form $y = mx + b$, the graph is a line whose _____ is m and whose _____ is b.

5. To put a linear equation in slope-intercept form, solve the equation for _____.

What is the slope and y-intercept of the graph of each equation?

6. $y = \tfrac{1}{2}x + 3$ 7. $y = 3x + \tfrac{1}{2}$ 8. $y = -2x + 7$

9. $y = -\tfrac{3}{4}x + 0$ 10. $y = -\tfrac{3}{4}x$ 11. $y = 6x + (-5)$

12. $y = 6x - 5$ **13.** $y = -\frac{3}{5}x + (-2)$ **14.** $y = -\frac{3}{5}x - 2$

15. $y = 0x - 7$ **16.** $y = -7$ **17.** $y = 0x + 0$

18. $y = 0$ **19.** $y = \frac{x}{2} + 5$ **20.** $y = \frac{3x}{-5} - 9$

Ⓑ Change each equation to slope-intercept form and state the slope and y-intercept of the graph.

21. $y - \frac{2}{3}x = 5$ **22.** $y - \frac{3}{5}x = 7$

23. $3y - 2x = 15$ **24.** $5y - 3x = 35$

25. $-2x + 3y = 15$ **26.** $-3x + 5y = 35$

27. $2x - 3y = -15$ **28.** $3x - 5y = -35$

29. $2x - 3y + 15 = 0$ **30.** $3x - 5y + 35 = 0$

31. $4x - 6y + 30 = 0$ **32.** $6x - 10y + 70 = 0$

33. $3x + 2y = -6$ **34.** $4x + 3y = -6$

35. $2x - 2y + 3 = 0$ **36.** $4x - 4y + 5 = 0$

37. $x - y = 0$ **38.** $x + y = 0$

39. $y - 2 = 0$ **40.** $y + 4 = 0$

41. Graph the equations in odd-numbered Exercises **21–31**, using the same pair of axes. (HINT: Use the y-intercept to locate one point. Then use the slope to locate one or two other points.)

42. Graph the equations in even-numbered Exercises **22–32**, using the same pair of axes. (See HINT in Exercise **41**.)

43–50. Graph each equation in Exercises **33–40**, using a separate pair of axes for each. (See HINT in Exercise **41**.)

Ⓒ **51.** How might the x-intercept of a line be defined?

52. Solve several of the equations in Exercises **21–38** for x. Then, by looking at the graphs, try to find out what the coefficient of y and the constant term represent.

53. What might be a good name for $x = \frac{1}{m}y + a$?

8.7 FINDING EQUATIONS OF LINES

If we are given the slope and y-intercept of a line, it is easy to find the equation of that line.

Example 1: The slope of a line is $\frac{2}{3}$, and its y-intercept is -4. Find the equation of the line.

SOLUTION:
$$Given:\ m = \tfrac{2}{3},$$
$$b = -4.$$

$$Substitute\ in:\ y = mx + b$$
$$y = \tfrac{2}{3}x + (-4)$$

The required equation has been found. If we want to, we can change the equation to standard form as follows.

$$y = \tfrac{2}{3}x + (-4)$$
$$3y = 2x - 12$$
$$-2x + 3y = -12 \quad \text{or} \quad 2x - 3y = 12$$

Example 2: The slope of a line is 2, and the coordinates of a point on this line are $(4, -1)$. Find the equation of the line.

SOLUTION: This time we do not know the y-intercept. But we can use the given facts to find it.

$$y = mx + b$$
$$-1 = 2 \cdot 4 + b$$
$$b = -9$$

Now, using the slope and the y-intercept, we can proceed as in Example 1.

$$y = mx + b$$
$$y = 2x + (-9)$$
$$y = 2x - 9$$

Again, if we want to, we can change to standard form.

Example 3: The coordinates of two points on a line are (1, 2) and (3, −5). Find the equation of the line.

SOLUTION: This time we do not know either the slope or the y-intercept. But we can use the given facts to find them.

First, find the slope.

$$m = \frac{y_2 - y_1}{x_2 - x_1} = \frac{-5 - 2}{3 - 1} = \frac{-7}{2} = -\frac{7}{2}$$

Now, using the slope and the coordinates of *one* of the points, find the y-intercept as in Example **2**.

$$y = mx + b$$
$$2 = -\tfrac{7}{2} \cdot 1 + b$$
$$b = \tfrac{7}{2} + \tfrac{4}{2} = \tfrac{11}{2}$$

Last, find the equation as in Example **1**.

$$y = mx + b$$
$$y = -\tfrac{7}{2}x + \tfrac{11}{2}$$

EXERCISES 8.7

Ⓐ True or False? You can find the equation of any line if you know:

1. its slope.   **2.** the coordinates of a point on the line.

3. its y-intercept.   **4.** its slope and y-intercept.

5. its slope and the coordinates of a point on the line.

6. the coordinates of two points on the line.

Given the slope and y-intercept of a line, find the slope-intercept form of its equation.

	SLOPE	y-INTERCEPT		SLOPE	y-INTERCEPT
7.	2	3	**8.**	3	2
9.	$\tfrac{1}{3}$	−2	**10.**	$-\tfrac{5}{2}$	1
11.	7	0	**12.**	0	3

Ⓑ **13–18.** Change your answers for Exercises **7–12** to standard form.

Given the slope of a line and the coordinates of a point on this line, find the slope-intercept form of the equation of the line. Then change the equation to standard form.

	SLOPE	POINT			SLOPE	POINT
19.	$\frac{2}{3}$	(3, 3)		20.	$\frac{1}{2}$	(1, 3)
21.	2	(3, −2)		22.	3	(1, −3)
23.	$-\frac{2}{3}$	(3, 0)		24.	$-\frac{3}{4}$	(2, 0)
25.	1	(−4, −2)		26.	1	(−5, −4)
27.	−1	(5, 6)		28.	−1	(6, 5)
29.	0	(3, 2)		30.	0	(2, 3)
31.	0	(−5, 0)		32.	0	(−9, 0)
33.	$2\frac{1}{2}$	(2, 1)		34.	$3\frac{1}{3}$	(1, 2)

Given the coordinates of two points on a line, find the slope-intercept form of its equation.

	POINT ONE	POINT TWO			POINT ONE	POINT TWO
35.	(2, 3)	(5, 6)		36.	(3, 2)	(6, 5)
37.	(−6, 2)	(−4, 6)		38.	(−4, 3)	(−2, 9)
39.	(−1, 3)	(−7, 5)		40.	(−2, 1)	(−6, 2)
41.	(−1, −9)	(−5, −1)		42.	(−3, −8)	(−5, −2)
43.	(5, 3)	(1, 3)		44.	(8, −5)	(2, −5)

45. If a line has no slope and it intersects the x-axis at (−2, 0), what is its equation?

46. If a line has no slope and it intersects the x-axis at (a, 0), what is its equation?

© 47–54. If a line has slope m and a point at (x_1, y_1), you can let (x, y) stand for any other point and write

$$\frac{y - y_1}{x - x_1} = m. \quad \text{Then} \quad y - y_1 = m(x - x_1)$$

The last result is the **point-slope form** of a linear equation. Use this form to find the slope-intercept form of each equation in Exercises 19–26.

Find the slope (if any) of the line with points at:

1. (2, 1) and (5, 4)

2. (−1, −3) and (−3, 1)

3. (−4, −5) and (6, −5)

4. (7, 2) and (7, −8)

Given the slopes, tell which line is steeper.

	LINE l	LINE k			LINE l	LINE k
5.	3	4		**6.**	−3	−4
7.	$-\frac{8}{13}$	$\frac{7}{12}$		**8.**	$\frac{5}{2}$	$2\frac{1}{2}$

Given the slope and one point of a line, draw the line. Use a separate pair of axes for each exercise.

	SLOPE	POINT			SLOPE	POINT
9.	$\frac{3}{4}$	(1, 2)		**10.**	$-\frac{3}{4}$	(1, 2)
11.	$-\frac{4}{3}$	(−4, −2)		**12.**	0	(0, −4)
13.	−5	(6, −4)		**14.**	none	(2, 3)

Change each equation to slope-intercept form and state the slope and y-intercept of the graph. Then draw the graph.

15. $y - \frac{3}{2}x = 5$

16. $x + 3y + 12 = 0$

Each exercise gives two facts about a line. Find the slope-intercept form of the equation of the line.

17. slope: 4; y-intercept: −2.

18. slope: $-\frac{2}{5}$; point: (1, 2).

19. point one: (2, −3); point two: (5, 1).

20. Change the answer for Exercise **19** to standard form.

Many formulas are linear equations in two variables. Usually, however, the variables are letters other than x and y. One example is the formula for changing temperatures from Celsius (centigrade) to Fahrenheit.

$$F = \tfrac{9}{5}C + 32$$
$$y = mx + b$$

This formula is in slope-intercept form, where F replaces y, C replaces x, the slope is $\tfrac{9}{5}$, and the y-intercept is 32.

When a linear formula is written in slope-intercept form, we call the variable that replaces x the **independent variable** and the variable that replaces y the **dependent variable**.

Example 1: Show how the formula $F = \tfrac{9}{5}C + 32$ may be found.

SOLUTION: Most people know what the freezing and boiling temperatures of water are on both the Fahrenheit and Celsius scales. Let's write these temperatures as ordered pairs. Since we want F to be the *dependent* variable (replacing y), we list the Fahrenheit temperatures second.

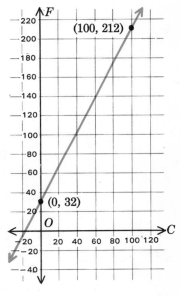

independent variable   dependent variable

$$(x, \quad y)$$
$$(C, \quad F)$$
freezing temperature of water $\rightarrow$ $(0, \quad 32)$
boiling temperature of water $\rightarrow$ $(100, 212)$

The ordered pair $(0, 32)$ gives the y-intercept. But now, we call it the F-intercept or the dependent-variable-intercept. We can also find the slope:

$$\frac{y_2 - y_1}{x_2 - x_1} = \frac{F_2 - F_1}{C_2 - C_1} = \frac{212 - 32}{100 - 0}$$
$$= \tfrac{180}{100} = \tfrac{9}{5}.$$

Since $m = \tfrac{9}{5}$ and $b = 32$, we can write the formula.

$$y = mx + b$$
$$F = \tfrac{9}{5}C + 32$$

A formula related to the preceding one is the formula for changing temperatures the other way, that is, from Fahrenheit to Celsius:

$$C = \tfrac{5}{9}(F - 32).$$

In slope-intercept form this equation becomes

$$C = \tfrac{5}{9}F + (-\tfrac{160}{9}).$$

We could find this formula by using $(32, 0)$ and $(212, 100)$ as the coordinates of two points in its graph. Notice that since we have switched the independent and dependent variables (now C replaces y and F replaces x), we would reverse the order in the two ordered pairs that we used in Example 1.

Of course, a much easier way to find the formula above is to solve for C in the formula from Example 1.

Example 2: Find a formula for converting from nickels to cents.

SOLUTION: This is a simple formula that you can easily find. But it will illustrate some things about many linear formulas.

> Let n = the number of nickels
> and c = the number of cents.

Since we want to change from nickels to cents, n is the *independent* variable and c is the *dependent* variable. So, we are working with ordered pairs like

$$(n, c).$$

We know that two such ordered pairs are

$$(0, 0) \qquad \text{and} \qquad (1, 5).$$

The ordered pair $(0, 0)$ tells us the c-intercept is 0. And the slope is very easy to find.

$$\frac{c_2 - c_1}{n_2 - n_1} = \frac{5 - 0}{1 - 0} = \frac{5}{1} = 5.$$

Since $m = 5$ and $b = 0$, we can write the formula.

$$y = mx + b$$
$$c = 5n + 0$$
$$c = 5n$$

Example **2** illustrates the following. When $(0, 0)$ is a solution for a linear formula, the formula contains a zero constant term. And the coefficient of the independent variable can be found from a single ordered pair. In Example **2**, it can be found from $(1, 5)$.

Notice that in most practical uses it would make no sense to use -3, $\frac{1}{2}$, or $\sqrt{2}$ as replacements for n, the number of nickels, in Example **2**. Therefore, the replacement set for a variable in a linear formula may not be the entire set of real numbers.

EXERCISES 8.8

Ⓐ In the formula $F = \frac{9}{5}C + 32$ from Example 1:

1. The independent variable is _____.

2. Each value found for _____ depends on the value chosen for C.

3. The variable F is called the _____ variable.

4. The slope of the graph is _____.

5. The F-intercept of the graph is _____.

When $(0, 0)$ is a solution for a linear formula:

6. The y-intercept of the graph is _____.

7. The formula contains a zero _____.

8. The _____ of the independent variable can be found from a single ordered pair.

In the formula $c = 5n$ from Example 2:

9. What is the independent variable? The dependent variable?

10. Would the replacement set for n be the entire set of real numbers? Why?

Ⓑ Using the variables given, write a formula for finding:

11. the number (c) of cents in d dimes.

12. the number (c) of cents in d dollars.

13. the number (d) of dimes in c cents.

14. the number (d) of dollars in c cents.

15. the number (i) of inches in f feet.

16. the number (y) of yards in f feet.

17. the perimeter (p) of a square with side s.

18. the circumference (C) of a circle with diameter d.

19. the cost (c) of g gallons at 38.9¢ per gallon.

20. the tax (t) on d dollars at 5¢ per dollar.

21–30. For each formula found in Exercises **11–20**, what would be a good replacement set for the independent variable?

31–36. Solve each formula found in Exercises **15–20** for the independent variable. Then identify the new dependent variable.

In each exercise, a formula is described and two ordered pairs of the proper form are given. Find the formula.

37. A telephone fee (f) equals a charge for each call (c) plus a minimum service charge. (c, f): (10, 3.50) and (0, 2.00).

38. A welfare payment (p) equals an allowance for each child (c) plus a constant amount. (c, p): (3, 225) and (0, 100).

39. The cooking time (t), in hours, for turkey equals so much per pound (p) plus a minimum time. (p, t): (10, 5) and (18, 7).

40. A taxi fee (f), in cents, equals a charge per mile (m) plus a minimum charge. (m, f): (2, 45) and (6, 85).

© 41. The weight (w), in pounds, of an "average" person over five feet tall equals an amount determined by the person's height (h), in inches, plus a constant amount. (h, w): (62, 121) and (72, 176).

42. A salesman's weekly salary (s), in dollars, equals a commission on his sales volume (v), in dollars, plus a minimum amount. (v, s): (6000, 340) and (4000, 260).

43. Describe two more linear formulas like those in Exercises **37–42** which might be used in situations from everyday life.

In some practical applications, slope is expressed as a per cent. For example, an engineer might talk about the *grade* (slope) of a road as being 9%. Since *per cent* means "hundredths,"

$$9\% = \frac{9}{100}.$$

So, the engineer would be saying that the road rises 9 feet vertically for every 100 feet it runs horizontally.

SLOPE = 9%

9 feet

100 feet

Example 1: During takeoff, a certain airplane rises 4.7 yards vertically for every 10 yards it runs horizontally. What is its rate of climb (the slope of its path as a per cent)?

SOLUTION:

SLOPE = 47%

47 yards

100 yards

$$\text{SLOPE} = \frac{\text{VERT. CHANGE}}{\text{HORIZ. CHANGE}} = \frac{4.7}{10}$$

$$= \frac{4.7}{10} \cdot \frac{10}{10}$$

$$= \frac{47}{100} = 47\%$$

In such uses of slope, horizontal change is almost always considered to be positive. Vertical change, however, can be positive (as above) or negative (as follows).

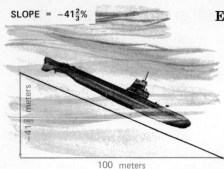

SLOPE = $-41\frac{2}{3}\%$

$-41\frac{2}{3}$ meters

100 meters

Example 2: During its dive, a certain submarine descends 5 meters for every 12 meters it runs horizontally. What is its rate of dive (the slope of its diving path)?

SOLUTION:

$$\text{SLOPE} = \frac{\text{VERT. CHANGE}}{\text{HORIZ. CHANGE}} = \frac{-5}{12}$$

$$= -0.41\frac{2}{3} \quad (\text{or } -0.41\overline{6})$$

$$= -41\frac{2}{3}\% \quad (\text{or } -41.\overline{6}\%)$$

In this case, we have considered the vertical change to be negative. Since the horizontal change is positive, the slope turns out to be negative. But, as long as we know we are talking about the rate of dive of a submarine, it would also be meaningful to state the result as simply $41\frac{2}{3}\%$.

Example 3: The slope of a road is 6%. Write a formula that gives the vertical distance y for any horizontal distance x.

SOLUTION: $\quad y = (6\%)x \quad$ or $\quad y = 0.06x \quad$ or $\quad y = \frac{6}{100}x$

EXERCISES 8.9

(A) **1.** 19% means _____ hundredths.

2. When we express slope as a per cent, we are giving the vertical change for every _____ units of horizontal change.

Express each slope as a per cent.

3. $\frac{21}{100}$ **4.** $\frac{120}{100}$ **5.** $\frac{1}{2}$ **6.** $\frac{1}{4}$

7. 1   **8.** 2   **9.** $\frac{1}{3}$ **10.** $\frac{2}{3}$

Express each per cent by a fraction in standard form.

11. 3%   **12.** 30%   **13.** 10%   **14.** 20%

(B) **15.** 75%   **16.** 82%   **17.** 105%   **18.** 250%

19. $12\frac{1}{2}\%$ **20.** $16\frac{2}{3}\%$ **21.** $14\frac{2}{7}\%$ **22.** $11\frac{1}{9}\%$

The slope is 6%. Find the vertical distance for each horizontal distance below. (HINT: Use the formula in Example 3.)

23. 100 feet   **24.** 50 meters   **25.** 200 yards   **26.** 37 feet

The slope is 6%. Find the horizontal distance for each vertical distance below.

27. 6 feet   **28.** 3 meters   **29.** 12 yards   **30.** 20 feet

Find the slope as a per cent.

31. A railroad track rises 1.5 feet for every 30 feet it runs horizontally.

32. A ski lift rises 8.25 meters for every 11 meters it runs horizontally.

33. Each step of a stairway has a riser of $5\frac{1}{2}$ inches and a tread of 11 inches.

34. A road rises $1\frac{1}{4}$ yards for every 25 yards of horizontal run.

35. A helicopter rises 3 feet for every 2 feet of horizontal run.

36. A ladder reaches $19\frac{1}{4}$ feet up a vertical wall, and its base (on level ground) is 5 feet from the wall.

37. A sky diver in free fall "tracks" (moves horizontally) 1 foot for every 2 feet of drop.

38. A logging chute (for bringing logs down a hill) drops $2\frac{1}{2}$ meters for every 2 meters it runs horizontally.

The slope is 65%. Find the vertical distance for each horizontal distance below.

39. 80 feet   **40.** 150 meters   **41.** 35 inches   **42.** 16 centimeters

The slope is 12%. Find the horizontal distance for each vertical distance below.

43. 24 feet   **44.** 30 meters   **45.** 3 yards   **46.** 2 kilometers

© **47.** Describe two new situations like those in Exercises **31–38** in which slope as per cent might be used.

How Steep Are Some Roads?

In Section 8.9, slopes of roads were expressed as per cents. This makes it easy to tell which of two roads is the steeper.

The steepest part of the Pennsylvania Turnpike has a slope of 3%. On the thousands of miles of the Interstate Highway System in the U.S., the steepest parts have a slope of 7%.

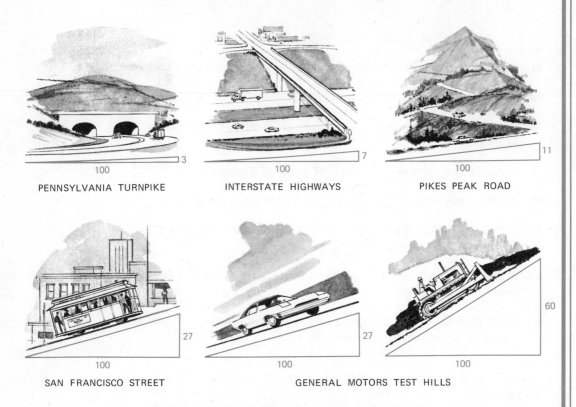

PENNSYLVANIA TURNPIKE   INTERSTATE HIGHWAYS   PIKES PEAK ROAD

SAN FRANCISCO STREET   GENERAL MOTORS TEST HILLS

For a road, any slope over 10% is considered quite steep. A drive up Pikes Peak would involve slopes of almost 11%. A road up one of San Francisco's steepest hills has a slope of 27% (this is steeper than many ski slopes).

At the General Motors Proving Ground in Milford, Michigan, there is a road with a slope of 27% for testing cars and also a grade of 60% for testing tracked vehicles, like bulldozers.

Source: General Motors Corporation, *Mathematics at Work in General Motors*, Pamphlet Number 5, 1964.

Your knowledge of graphing equations will be helpful in graphing inequalities. All points for which $y = x$, such as (4, 4), (0, 0), and $(-3, -3)$, are on the line in graph I.

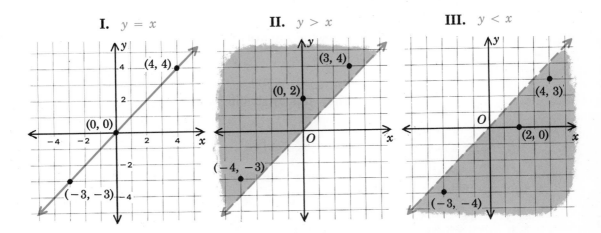

I. $y = x$ **II.** $y > x$ **III.** $y < x$

In graph II, points for which $y > x$, such as (3, 4), (0, 2), and $(-4, -3)$, are "above" the line $y = x$. In general, the graph of $y > x$ is a **half-plane** containing all the points *above* the line $y = x$.

In graph III, points for which $y < x$, such as (4, 3), (2, 0), and $(-3, -4)$, are "below" the line $y = x$. In general, the graph of $y < x$ is a half-plane containing all the points *below* the line $y = x$.

In II and III, the line $y = x$ is a **boundary line** for each half-plane. When the boundary line is drawn as a dashed line, as above, this shows that its points are *not* included in the graph.

IV. $y \leq x$

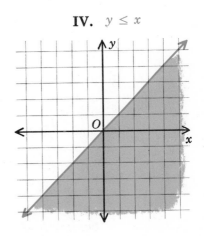

If, however, we graph $y \leq x$, then the boundary line is included in the graph. And we draw it as a solid line, as in graph IV.

The graph of $y < x$ is called an **open** half-plane, since it does not include the boundary line. The graph of $y \leq x$ is a **closed** half-plane.

Example 1: Graph $y < -4x - 2$.

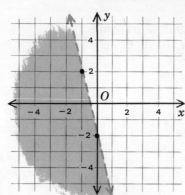

SOLUTION: Using the equation

$$y = -4x - 2,$$

graph the boundary line. Since it is not to be included in the graph, draw it as a dashed line.

Since you are graphing

$$y < -4x - 2,$$

the *open half-plane* below the line is the graph. Show this by shading as at the left.

Example 2: Graph $3x - 4y \leq 12$.

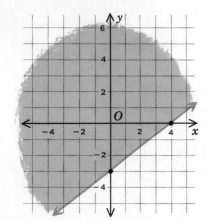

SOLUTION: Solve for y.

$$3x - 4y \leq 12$$
$$-4y \leq -3x + 12$$
$$y \geq \tfrac{3}{4}x - 3$$

Notice that multiplying both sides by $-\tfrac{1}{4}$ changes the sense of the inequality.

Next, using the equation $y = \tfrac{3}{4}x - 3$, graph the boundary line. This time draw it solid. Why?

Since $y \geq \tfrac{3}{4}x - 3$, shade above the boundary as at the left. The graph is a *closed half-plane*.

EXERCISES 8.10

Ⓐ For each exercise below,

    a. What is the equation of the boundary line?

    b. Is the graph a closed or an open half-plane?

    c. On which side of the boundary line would you shade?

1. $y < 2x$ **2.** $y > 3x$ **3.** $y > x - 1$

4. $y < x + 5$ **5.** $y \leq -\tfrac{1}{2}x$ **6.** $y \geq -\tfrac{2}{3}x$

7. $y \geq 2x - 2$ **8.** $y \leq \tfrac{1}{4}x - 2$ **9.** $y > -2$

10. $y \leq 4$ **11.** $x < 5$ **12.** $x \geq -3$

13–24. Graph the inequalities in Exercises **1–12,** using a separate pair of axes for each.

Write an equivalent inequality with only *y* on the left side. (Be careful when multiplying by a negative number.)

25. $y + x < 2$ **26.** $y - x > 3$ **27.** $y + 3 > 2x$

28. $x + y < 5$ **29.** $2x - y < 0$ **30.** $10x - 5y > 0$

31. $4x - 2y > 4$ **32.** $4x - 2y < 8$ **33.** $3y + 6 \leq 0$

34. $4y - 8 \geq 0$ **35.** $-4x - y \leq 8$ **36.** $-2x - 2y \geq 4$

37–48. Graph the inequalities in Exercises **25–36,** using a separate pair of axes for each.

Ⓒ Write an inequality for each problem.

49. A certain airplane can perform a maneuver only if the vertical distance is less than $\frac{1}{3}$ the horizontal distance.

50. A ramp for motorcycle jumping has to be built so that the horizontal distance minus twice the vertical distance is greater than or equal to 18 meters.

Graph each pair of inequalities. Use a separate pair of axes for each exercise.

51. $x > 1; y > 1$ **52.** $x < -3; y < 2$

53. $y < x; y > -x$ **54.** $y < x - 1; y > -x - 1$

55. $y \geq x + 2; y \leq x - 2$ **56.** $y \leq x + 3; y \geq x - 1$

Refer to the graphs you drew for Exercises 51–54. Then graph each compound sentence.

57. $x > 1$ and $y > 1$ **58.** $x < -3$ or $y < 2$

59. $y < x$ and $y > -x$ **60.** $y < x - 1$ or $y > -x - 1$

61. Locate in the coordinate plane 10 points in the graph of $y = x^2$. What, do you think, is the complete graph? Show what you think the graphs of $y > x^2$ and $y < x^2$ are.

CHAPTER REVIEW

8.1

1. List all the ordered pairs (x, y) that can be formed if the replacement set for x is $\{1, 0, -1\}$ and for y it is $\{0, 1\}$.

8.2

2. Graph these ordered pairs, using the same pair of axes.

(0, 0)	(5, 0)	(0, 5)	(−1, 0)	(0, −1)
(4, 3)	(−4, −3)	(4, −3)	(−4, 3)	$(1\frac{1}{2}, -\frac{1}{2})$

3. If a point is on the y-axis, what is its x-coordinate?

4. In which quadrant are all the points for which $x < 0$ and $y > 0$?

8.3

Is the equation a linear equation in two variables? If so, is it in standard form?

5. $y = -\frac{1}{2}x + 7$ **6.** $-2x + 0y = 1$ **7.** $x^2 + y = 0$

Graph the equations, using a separate pair of axes for each.

8. $y = 3x - 4$ **9.** $x + 2y = 6$

8.4

Find the slope (if any) of the line with points at:

10. $(-3, -3)$ and $(7, -3)$ **11.** $(0, 0)$ and $(4, 4)$

12. $(1, -2)$ and $(-3, 1)$ **13.** $(\frac{1}{2}, 6)$ and $(\frac{1}{2}, 3\frac{1}{2})$

8.5

Given the slopes, tell which line is steeper.

	LINE l	LINE k		LINE l	LINE k
14.	4	5	**15.**	−1	−3
16.	$\frac{7}{8}$	$-\frac{8}{9}$	**17.**	$-\frac{6}{23}$	$-\frac{7}{24}$

Given the slope and one point of a line, draw the line. Use a separate pair of axes for each exercise.

	SLOPE	POINT		SLOPE	POINT
18.	$-\frac{1}{2}$	(0, 0)	**19.**	$\frac{2}{3}$	(0, 0)
20.	4	(1, 3)	**21.**	−2	(−3, 1)
22.	0	(6, 3)	**23.**	none	(3, −7)

Change each equation to slope-intercept form. State the slope and
y-intercept of the graph, and use them to graph the equation.

24. $3x + y = 2$ **25.** $3x - 4y - 8 = 0$

Each exercise gives two facts about a line. Find the slope-intercept form
of the equation of the line.

26. slope: $-\frac{3}{2}$; y-intercept: 5

27. slope: 2; point: $(-2, -2)$

28. point one: $(2, 2)$; point two: $(5, 3)$

29. Change the answer for Exercise **28** to standard form.

30. Using the variables given, write a formula for finding the number
(c) of cents in q quarters.

31. Solve the formula found in Exercise **30** for the independent
variable. What is the new dependent variable?

32. Using the variables given, write a formula for changing temperatures from degrees Celsius (C) to degrees Kelvin (K). Two
ordered pairs of the form (C, K) are $(-273.16, 0)$ and $(0, 273.16)$.

Find the slope as a per cent.

33. A cable car rises 2 feet for every 8 feet of horizontal run.

34. A minisub descends 8 meters for every 5 meters of horizontal run.

35. The slope is 45%. Find the vertical distance if the horizontal
distance is 6 meters.

36. The slope is 150%. Find the horizontal distance if the vertical
distance is 300 feet.

Graph each inequality, using a separate pair of axes for each.

37. $y < 3x$ **38.** $y \geq -\frac{3}{4}x + 5$ **39.** $2x - y > 4$

CHAPTER SELF-TEST

Which term best completes each sentence?

a. quadrant   **b.** *x*-coordinate   **c.** slope-intercept

d. slope   **e.** *y*-coordinate   **f.** linear equation

g. coordinate   **h.** ordered pair   **i.** standard

1. The graph of a(n) _____ is a point.

2. The axes determine the _____ plane.

3. If (2, 3) are the coordinates of a point, then the _____ is 3.

4. If $x < 0$ and $y < 0$, then (x, y) is graphed in the third _____.

5. The graph of a(n) _____ is a line.

6. The equation $y = 3x + 2$ is in _____ form.

7. The _____ of a horizontal line is 0.

Graph each open sentence, using a separate pair of axes for each.

8. $y = 3x - 7$ **9.** $2x + 5y = 5$ **10.** $3x - 4y > 8$

Find the slope (if any) of the line with points at:

11. $(-2, -3)$ and $(2, 0)$ **12.** $(0, 0)$ and $(4, -8)$

13. $(-6, \frac{1}{2})$ and $(-6, 2\frac{1}{2})$

Each exercise gives two facts about a line. Find the slope-intercept form of the equation of the line.

14. slope: -2;   *y*-intercept: $\frac{1}{2}$ **15.** slope: $\frac{5}{2}$;   point: $(-2, 1)$

16. point one: $(1, -2)$;   point two: $(-2, -1)$

17. Change the answer for Exercise **16** to standard form.

18. Using the variables given, write a formula for changing temperatures from degrees Reaumur (R) to degrees Fahrenheit (F). Two ordered pairs of the form (R, F) are (80, 212) and (0, 32).

19. Find the slope as a per cent: A road goes up 45 feet for every 500 feet of horizontal run.

Chapter	Systems of
9	**Linear Sentences**

The undersea explorers are using a minisub that has a maximum speed of $4\frac{1}{2}$ mph in still water. Traveling at top speed against the current, their trip took 1 hour. Still traveling at top speed, but with the current, their return trip took 48 minutes. What was the total distance traveled?

In this chapter you will learn how to answer such a question by *solving a system of equations.*

WHAT IS A SYSTEM?

Using the ideas of *slope* and *y-intercept* from Chapter 8, we can graph equations like $x - y = -1$ and $2x + y = 4$ as follows.

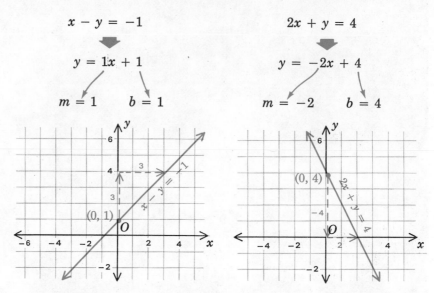

$$x - y = -1$$

$$y = 1x + 1$$

$$m = 1 \qquad b = 1$$

$$2x + y = 4$$

$$y = -2x + 4$$

$$m = -2 \qquad b = 4$$

The following "or" and "and" sentences can be formed from these two equations.

$x - y = -1$ **or** $2x + y = 4$

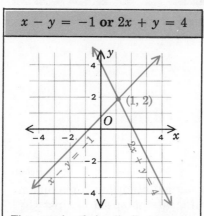

The graph of the "or" sentence is two intersecting lines. This is the set of all points whose coordinates satisfy *either* of the two equations.

$x - y = -1$ **and** $2x + y = 4$

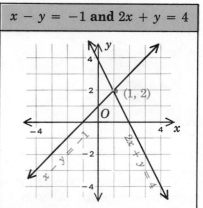

The graph of the "and" sentence is the intersection of two lines. It is the single point at (1, 2). This is the only ordered pair which satisfies *both* equations.

An "and" sentence such as

$$x - y = -1 \text{ and } 2x + y = 4$$

is often written

$$\begin{cases} x - y = -1 \\ 2x + y = 4 \end{cases}$$

 a system
of equations

and is called a *system of equations*.

REMEMBER: A system of equations is an "and" sentence.

So, the **solutions of a system of equations** are the ordered pairs which satisfy *each* equation in the system. Sometimes we find the solutions by graphing.

Example: Solve the system at the right by graphing. Then check that your solutions are correct.

$$\begin{cases} x + 2y = 2 \\ 3x - 2y = -10 \end{cases}$$

SOLUTION: We can graph a linear equation either by making a table of ordered pairs or by using the slope and y-intercept. Below, we graph one equation by each method.

For $x + 2y = 2$, we get the
table:

x	0	2	-4
y	1	0	3

For the other equation we
get: $3x - 2y = -10$

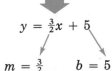

$$y = \tfrac{3}{2}x + 5$$

$$m = \tfrac{3}{2} \qquad b = 5$$

From the graph it appears that the lines intersect at $(-2, 2)$. On the next page we check this solution.

We can check that the ordered pair $(-2, 2)$ really does satisfy both equations as follows.

Check:

$$x + 2y = 2 \qquad\qquad 3x - 2y = -10$$
$$-2 + 2(2) = 2 \qquad\qquad 3(-2) - 2(2) = -10$$
$$-2 + 4 = 2 \qquad\qquad -6 - 4 = -10$$
$$2 = 2 \quad \text{T} \qquad\qquad -10 = -10 \quad \text{T}$$

EXERCISES 9.1

Ⓐ For each pair of lines named below, tell the coordinates of the point of intersection.

1. (a) and (b)

2. (a) and (c)

3. (a) and (d)

4. (b) and (c)

5. (b) and (d)

6. (c) and (d)

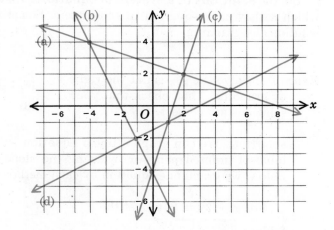

Tell whether each statement is true or false.

7. $\begin{cases} x + 3y = -6 \\ 2x - 3y = -3 \end{cases}$ means $(x + 3y = -6 \text{ or } 2x - 3y = -3)$.

8. $\begin{cases} 2x - 3y = 6 \\ x + 3y = -3 \end{cases}$ means $(2x - 3y = 6 \text{ and } x + 3y = -3)$.

9. Tell the slope and y-intercept of the graph of $6x + 2y = -2$.

10. Describe two methods you could use to graph an equation like $6x + 2y = -2$.

Ⓑ Carefully graph each system. From the graph, estimate the solutions of the system. Check your solutions. (Remember, the solutions of a system must satisfy *both* equations.)

11. $\begin{cases} 2x - y = 1 \\ x + y = 2 \end{cases}$
12. $\begin{cases} 2x - y = -5 \\ x + y = 2 \end{cases}$
13. $\begin{cases} 3x - 2y = -4 \\ x + 2y = -4 \end{cases}$

14. $\begin{cases} 2x + y = 4 \\ 2x - 3y = 12 \end{cases}$
15. $\begin{cases} x = 3 \\ y = 5 \end{cases}$
16. $\begin{cases} x = -4 \\ y = 2 \end{cases}$

17. $\begin{cases} x = -3 \\ y = -4 \end{cases}$
18. $\begin{cases} x = 7 \\ y = -1 \end{cases}$
19. $\begin{cases} 2x + y = 4 \\ y = 2 \end{cases}$

20. $\begin{cases} x = 3 \\ 2x + 3y = 0 \end{cases}$
21. $\begin{cases} y = -1 \\ 2x + 2y = 2 \end{cases}$
22. $\begin{cases} x + 4y = 8 \\ x = -4 \end{cases}$

23. $\begin{cases} x + y = 0 \\ x - y = 0 \end{cases}$
24. $\begin{cases} 2x - 3y = 0 \\ 2x + 3y = 0 \end{cases}$
25. $\begin{cases} x = \frac{1}{2} \\ y = \frac{1}{4} \end{cases}$

26. $\begin{cases} x = -\frac{1}{4} \\ y = \frac{1}{2} \end{cases}$
27. $\begin{cases} y = 3x - 2 \\ y = -2x + 3 \end{cases}$
28. $\begin{cases} y = \frac{1}{3}x - 1 \\ y = -\frac{1}{3}x - 3 \end{cases}$

Ⓒ Carefully graph each system and estimate the solutions. Use fractions where necessary.

29. $\begin{cases} x + y = 3 \\ x = y \end{cases}$
30. $\begin{cases} y = -x \\ x - y = 3 \end{cases}$
31. $\begin{cases} y = 3x \\ y = -3x + 2 \end{cases}$

32. $\begin{cases} 8x = 7 \\ 5y = 2 \end{cases}$
33. $\begin{cases} y = -2x + 2 \\ y = 2x - 4 \end{cases}$
34. $\begin{cases} x + y = 3 \\ 2x - 3y = \frac{7}{2} \end{cases}$

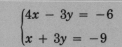

9.2 TYPES OF SYSTEMS

Each system in the preceding section had exactly one ordered pair in its solution set. But this is not always so. There are three types of systems shown in the examples below.

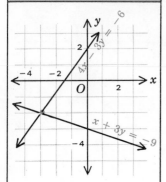

$$\begin{cases} 4x - 3y = -6 \\ x + 3y = -9 \end{cases}$$

The graphs intersect in *one point*. The solution set of the system contains **only one ordered pair**:

$$\{(-3, -2)\}.$$

Such a system is called **consistent**.

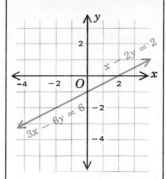

$$\begin{cases} x - 2y = 2 \\ 3x - 6y = 6 \end{cases}$$

The graphs are the *same line*. The solution set of the system contains **many (an unlimited number of) ordered pairs**:

$$\{(x, y) \mid x - 2y = 2\}.$$

Such a system is called **consistent** and **dependent**.

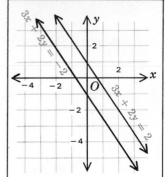

$$\begin{cases} 3x + 2y = -2 \\ 3x + 2y = 2 \end{cases}$$

The graphs are *parallel lines*. The solution set of the system is **the empty set**:

$$\{ \ \} = \varnothing.$$

Such a system is called **inconsistent**.

Example 1: For the system at the right,

   a. graph the equations.

   b. find the solution set.

$$\begin{cases} 5x - 2y = 4 \\ 10x - 4y = 8 \end{cases}$$

SOLUTION: If we multiply both sides of the first equation by 2, we get

$$2(5x - 2y) = 2(4) \quad \text{or} \quad 10x - 4y = 8,$$

which is the second equation. This tells us that the two equations are equivalent (have the same solution set). Also, the graphs *coincide* (are the same line).

We arrive at the same conclusions by changing the two equations to slope-intercept form.

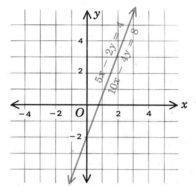

$$5x - 2y = 4 \qquad\qquad 10x - 4y = 8$$

$$-2y = -5x + 4 \qquad -4y = -10x + 8$$

$$y = \tfrac{5}{2}x - 2 \qquad\qquad y = \tfrac{5}{2}x - 2$$

Notice that for each of the equations,

$$m = \tfrac{5}{2} \quad \text{and} \quad b = -2.$$

So, we get

a. the graphs as shown.

b. the solution set is $\{(x, y) \mid 5x - 2y = 4\}$ (many solutions).

Example 2: For the system at the right,

   a. graph the equations.

   b. find the solution set.

$$\begin{cases} 3x - 2y = 4 \\ 2y = 3x - 6 \end{cases}$$

SOLUTION: First change the equations to slope-intercept form.

$$3x - 2y = 4 \qquad\qquad 2y = 3x - 6$$

$$-2y = -3x + 4 \qquad\qquad y = \tfrac{3}{2}x - 3$$

$$y = \tfrac{3}{2}x - 2$$

Now it is clear that the equations have the same slope ($m = \tfrac{3}{2}$), but different y-intercepts, -2 and -3. So the graphs are parallel lines (no points in common). Thus, we get

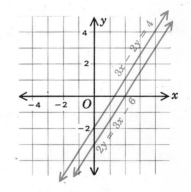

   a. the graphs as shown.

   b. the solution set is $\{\ \}$ or $\varnothing$ (no solutions).

EXERCISES 9.2

Ⓐ If a system of linear equations has an empty solution set:

1. How are the graphs of the equations related?

2. What type of system is it?

If a system of linear equations has many solutions:

3. How are the graphs of the equations related?

4. What type of system is it?

If a system of linear equations has exactly one solution:

5. How are the graphs of the equations related?

6. What type of system is it?

Look at each system and tell whether the system has exactly one solution, many solutions, or no solutions.

7. $\begin{cases} y = 3x - 5 \\ y = 3x + 2 \end{cases}$

8. $\begin{cases} y = 2x + 3 \\ y = 3x + 2 \end{cases}$

9. $\begin{cases} y = x - 5 \\ 2y = 2x - 10 \end{cases}$

10. $\begin{cases} y = \frac{1}{2}x - 4 \\ y = \frac{1}{4}x - 4 \end{cases}$

11. $\begin{cases} x - 3y = 4 \\ 3x - 9y = 12 \end{cases}$

12. $\begin{cases} y = \frac{1}{4}x - 2 \\ y = \frac{1}{2}x - 2 \end{cases}$

13. $\begin{cases} y = 5x + 3 \\ y = 5x - 3 \end{cases}$

14. $\begin{cases} x + y = 3 \\ x + y = 2 \end{cases}$

Ⓑ Change the equations of each system to slope-intercept form. Then state whether the solution set is empty, contains one ordered pair, or contains many ordered pairs.

15. $\begin{cases} 3x + 2y = -2 \\ 2x + y = -1 \end{cases}$

16. $\begin{cases} 2x - 3y = 3 \\ x - 2y = -2 \end{cases}$

17. $\begin{cases} x - 2y = 6 \\ 2x - 4y = 12 \end{cases}$

18. $\begin{cases} 2x + y = -3 \\ 2y + 6 = -4x \end{cases}$

19. $\begin{cases} 2x - 5y = 10 \\ 4x = 10y + 30 \end{cases}$

20. $\begin{cases} x - y = 6 \\ 2x = 2y + 4 \end{cases}$

21. $\begin{cases} 2x + 3y = 6 \\ 3x + 4y = 8 \end{cases}$

22. $\begin{cases} 4x - y = 5 \\ 2y = -5x - 10 \end{cases}$

23. $\begin{cases} x + y = 2 \\ x - y = 4 \end{cases}$

24. $\begin{cases} x + y = 4 \\ x - y = 2 \end{cases}$

25. $\begin{cases} y + 2 = 4x \\ 8x - 2y = -1 \end{cases}$

26. $\begin{cases} 3y - 2 = 4x \\ 12x - 9y = 1 \end{cases}$

27. $\begin{cases} 5y - 2 = 2x \\ 4x = 10y - 4 \end{cases}$

28. $\begin{cases} 3y + 5 = x \\ 3x = 9y + 15 \end{cases}$

29. $\begin{cases} x - 18 = 6y \\ 3y + 9 = \frac{1}{2}x \end{cases}$

30–44. Find the solution set of each system in Exercises 15–29. (If the solution set contains exactly one ordered pair, carefully graph the equations to find it.)

© Find the value of m which makes each system inconsistent.

45. $\begin{cases} y = mx + 3 \\ y = 4x - 2 \end{cases}$

46. $\begin{cases} y = \frac{1}{4}x - 5 \\ y = mx + 2 \end{cases}$

47. $\begin{cases} 3x - 4y = 8 \\ y = mx + 1 \end{cases}$

48. $\begin{cases} 2x - 5y = 7 \\ y = mx + 2 \end{cases}$

Find the value of b which makes each system consistent and dependent.

49. $\begin{cases} y = 4x + 2 \\ y = 4x + b \end{cases}$

50. $\begin{cases} y = 3x + b \\ 3x - y = 7 \end{cases}$

51. $\begin{cases} 5x + 10y = 6 \\ y = -\frac{1}{2}x + b \end{cases}$

52. $\begin{cases} x + y = b \\ 4x = -4y + 12 \end{cases}$

In the graphs below, the following systems are graphed in different colors—first separately, and then on the same axes.

$$\text{I. } \begin{cases} 2x - y = 5 \\ 3x + 2y = 11 \end{cases} \qquad \text{II. } \begin{cases} x = 3 \\ y = 1 \end{cases}$$

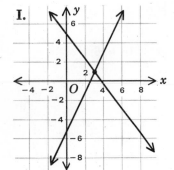 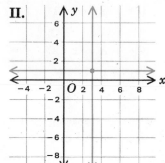 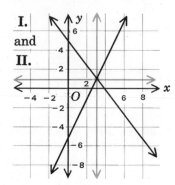

The two systems have the same solution set, $\{(3, 1)\}$. Such systems are called *equivalent systems*. You should check that $(3, 1)$ satisfies both systems.

$$\begin{cases} 2x - y = 5 \\ 3x + 2y = 11 \end{cases} \quad \text{is equivalent to} \quad \begin{cases} x = 3 \\ y = 1 \end{cases}$$

Equivalent systems are systems which have the same solution set.

Example: Solve the system at the right by drawing its graph and then finding an equivalent system of the form

$$\begin{cases} y = 3x + 10 \\ y = -\tfrac{1}{4}x - 3 \end{cases}$$

$$\begin{cases} x = a \\ y = b \end{cases} \quad \text{where } a \text{ and } b \text{ are constants.}$$

SOLUTION: Since the equations are in slope-intercept form, we can easily graph them. Their graphs are shown in black at the top of the next page.

From the graph we find that

$$\begin{cases} y = 3x + 10 \\ y = -\frac{1}{4}x - 3 \end{cases} \quad \begin{matrix} \text{is} \\ \text{equivalent} \\ \text{to} \end{matrix} \quad \begin{cases} x = -4 \\ y = -2. \end{cases}$$

For both systems,

the solution set is $\{(-4, -2)\}$.

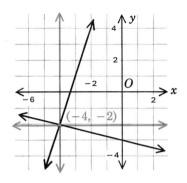

EXERCISES 9.3

Ⓐ Refer to the graphs at the right. Tell whether each system is equivalent to

$$\begin{cases} x = -1 \\ y = 3. \end{cases}$$

1. $\begin{cases} y = -x + 2 \\ y = 3x + 6 \end{cases}$ **2.** $\begin{cases} y = 3x + 6 \\ y = 3 \end{cases}$

3. $\begin{cases} y = 3x + 6 \\ x = -1 \end{cases}$ **4.** $\begin{cases} y = -x + 2 \\ y = 3 \end{cases}$

5. $\begin{cases} x = -1 \\ y = -x + 2 \end{cases}$ **6.** $\begin{cases} y = 3 \\ x = -1 \end{cases}$

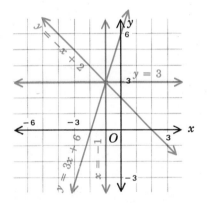

7–12. Refer to the equations graphed at the right. Name six different but equivalent systems of linear equations. Why are your systems equivalent?

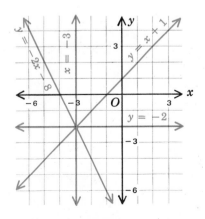

Ⓑ Graph the two systems on the same axes. Then tell whether the two systems are equivalent.

13. $\begin{cases} y = 3x - 7 \\ y = x - 3 \end{cases}$ $\begin{cases} x = 2 \\ y = -1 \end{cases}$ **14.** $\begin{cases} y = 4x - 4 \\ y = -x - 4 \end{cases}$ $\begin{cases} x = 0 \\ y = -4 \end{cases}$

15. $\begin{cases} y = -x + 4 \\ y = -x \end{cases}$ $\begin{cases} x = 2 \\ y = 2 \end{cases}$ **16.** $\begin{cases} x = -2 \\ y = x + 1 \end{cases}$ $\begin{cases} x = -2 \\ y = 3 \end{cases}$

Graph each system and find an equivalent system of the form $\begin{cases} x = a \\ y = b \end{cases}$ where a and b are constants.

17. $\begin{cases} x = 3 \\ 2y = -x + 3 \end{cases}$ **18.** $\begin{cases} y + 3 = 2x \\ y = -3 \end{cases}$ **19.** $\begin{cases} x + y = 0 \\ 2x = 3y \end{cases}$

20. $\begin{cases} x - 2y = 0 \\ x = y \end{cases}$ **21.** $\begin{cases} x + y = 2 \\ x - y = 0 \end{cases}$ **22.** $\begin{cases} x + y = 3 \\ x + 1 = 3y \end{cases}$

23. $\begin{cases} x - y = 0 \\ x + y = -2 \end{cases}$ **24.** $\begin{cases} 3y = x + 20 \\ y + 3x = -10 \end{cases}$ **25.** $\begin{cases} 5x + y = 5 \\ x + y = -3 \end{cases}$

26. $\begin{cases} y = 3x - 16 \\ 3y + x = -8 \end{cases}$ **27.** $\begin{cases} x + 4y = 8 \\ 2x - y = 7 \end{cases}$ **28.** $\begin{cases} 2x + 7y = 1 \\ 2x + 5y = 3 \end{cases}$

Ⓒ Estimate the solutions of each system by graphing. Then use your estimate to write a simpler system in the form at the right. (a and b are constants.) $\begin{cases} x = a \\ y = b \end{cases}$

29. $\begin{cases} y = 1.2x + 3.6 \\ y = -0.4x \end{cases}$ **30.** $\begin{cases} y = -2.3x + 4 \\ y = 0.6x \end{cases}$

Tell whether the two systems are equivalent.

31. $\begin{cases} y = 2x + 2 \\ y = 2x + 3 \end{cases}$ and $\begin{cases} 2x + y = -2 \\ 2x + y = 1 \end{cases}$

32. $\begin{cases} 3x - y = 6 \\ 6x - 2y = 12 \end{cases}$ and $\begin{cases} y - 3x = -6 \\ 2y - 6x = -12 \end{cases}$

9.4 SUBSTITUTION METHOD

It is often easier and faster to solve a system of equations by algebraic methods rather than by graphing. One such method is the *substitution method*.

Example 1: Use the substitution method to solve $\begin{cases} x + 2y = 9 \\ 2x - y = 8. \end{cases}$

SOLUTION:

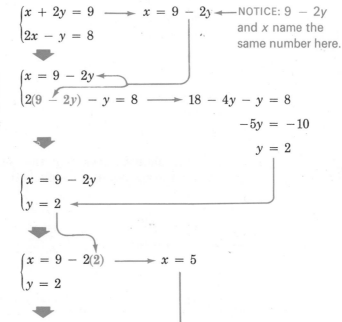

- Solve the first equation for x.

$$\begin{cases} x + 2y = 9 \\ 2x - y = 8 \end{cases} \longrightarrow x = 9 - 2y \longleftarrow \text{NOTICE: } 9 - 2y \text{ and } x \text{ name the same number here.}$$

- Substitute the result in the second equation and solve for y. (Also write the first equation in its new form.)

$$\begin{cases} x = 9 - 2y \\ 2(9 - 2y) - y = 8 \end{cases} \longrightarrow 18 - 4y - y = 8$$
$$-5y = -10$$
$$y = 2$$

- Replace the second equation with the simpler equivalent equation.

$$\begin{cases} x = 9 - 2y \\ y = 2 \end{cases}$$

- Substitute the value of y in the first equation and solve for x.

$$\begin{cases} x = 9 - 2(2) \\ y = 2 \end{cases} \longrightarrow x = 5$$

- Replace the first equation with the simpler equivalent equation.

$$\begin{cases} x = 5 \\ y = 2 \end{cases}$$

Each of the systems derived above is equivalent to the original system. It is clear that (5, 2) is the solution of the last system above. We now check that this solution satisfies both equations of the original system.

Check:
$$x + 2y = 9 \qquad\qquad 2x - y = 8$$
$$5 + 2(2) = 9 \qquad\qquad 2(5) - (2) = 8$$
$$9 = 9 \quad \text{T} \qquad\qquad 8 = 8 \quad \text{T}$$

For convenience, we often shorten the substitution method.

Example 2: Use substitution to solve $\begin{cases} 4s + t = 2 \\ 2s - 4t = -5. \end{cases}$

SOLUTION:

- Solve the first equation for t.

$$4s + t = 2$$
$$t = 2 - 4s$$

- Substitute the result for t in the second equation and solve for s.

$$2s - 4(2 - 4s) = -5$$
$$2s - 8 + 16s = -5$$
$$18s = 3$$
$$s = \tfrac{1}{6}$$

- Substitute the value of s in the first equation and solve for t.

$$t = 2 - 4(\tfrac{1}{6})$$
$$t = \tfrac{4}{3}$$

You should check that the solution is $(\tfrac{1}{6}, \tfrac{4}{3})$. (Notice that $\tfrac{1}{6}$ and $\tfrac{4}{3}$ are given in the alphabetical order of the variables.)

EXERCISES 9.4

Ⓐ Tell how you would use substitution to solve each system.

1. $\begin{cases} x = 3 \\ x + y = 8 \end{cases}$

2. $\begin{cases} x = y - 2 \\ y = 6 \end{cases}$

3. $\begin{cases} x = 2y \\ x + 3y = 10 \end{cases}$

4. $\begin{cases} x - 3y = 2 \\ y = x \end{cases}$

5. $\begin{cases} 2x - y = 6 \\ 3y = 12 \end{cases}$

6. $\begin{cases} m + n = 3 \\ m = n + 1 \end{cases}$

Ⓑ Solve each system by substitution.

7. $\begin{cases} 2m + n = 1 \\ m - n = 8 \end{cases}$

8. $\begin{cases} a + 7b = 20 \\ a - b = 4 \end{cases}$

9. $\begin{cases} 3x - 4y = 3 \\ 2x + y = 2 \end{cases}$

10. $\begin{cases} 3c - 2d = -4 \\ 3c + d = 2 \end{cases}$

11. $\begin{cases} 4m + 3n = 5 \\ 2m - n = -5 \end{cases}$

12. $\begin{cases} 4s + 3t = 1 \\ 4s + t = -5 \end{cases}$

13. $\begin{cases} 3s + 7t = 10 \\ 4s - t = 3 \end{cases}$

14. $\begin{cases} 5x - 3y = -13 \\ x + 4y = 2 \end{cases}$

15. $\begin{cases} 5p + 7q = 1 \\ 4p - 2q = 16 \end{cases}$

16. $\begin{cases} 3m + 8n = 22 \\ 10m - 2n = 16 \end{cases}$

17. $\begin{cases} \frac{1}{2}x - \frac{1}{5}y = 1 \\ 5x + 2y = 10 \end{cases}$

18. $\begin{cases} \frac{1}{2}x - \frac{1}{4}y = 2 \\ 3x + 2y = 5 \end{cases}$

19. $\begin{cases} 3x - y = 1 \\ 2x + 2y = 2 \end{cases}$

20. $\begin{cases} 2x + y = 1 \\ 3x - 6y = -1 \end{cases}$

© **21.** $\begin{cases} 3x - y = 7 \\ 2x + 2y = 5 \end{cases}$

22. $\begin{cases} \frac{1}{4}x + y = -\frac{7}{2} \\ \frac{1}{2}x - \frac{1}{4}y = 1 \end{cases}$

23. $\begin{cases} 3x + 2y = 4 \\ 2x - 4y = 5 \end{cases}$

24. $\begin{cases} \frac{1}{2}x - \frac{1}{4}y = 2 \\ 2x - y = 3 \end{cases}$

25. $\begin{cases} 5x + 3y = 4 \\ x - 4y = 3 \end{cases}$

26. $\begin{cases} 5x - 3y = 7 \\ \frac{5}{2}x - \frac{3}{2}y = \frac{7}{2} \end{cases}$

27. The length of a rectangle is 3 inches more than the width. The perimeter is 42 inches. Use a system of linear equations to find the length and width of the rectangle.

$l = \text{length}$

$\text{perimeter} = 2l + 2w$

$w = \text{width}$

9.5 MULTIPLICATION–ADDITION METHOD

Sometimes, it is easier to solve a system of equations by the *multiplication-addition method*. This method involves two useful ideas.

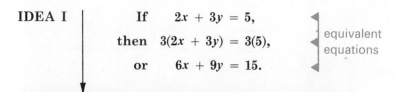

IDEA I

If $2x + 3y = 5,$

then $3(2x + 3y) = 3(5),$ equivalent equations

or $6x + 9y = 15.$

If we **multiply** both members of an equation by the same number, the result is an equivalent equation.

IDEA II

If $2x + 3y = 5,$

and $3x - 3y = 10,$

then $5x + 0 = 15$ or $x = 3.$

If we **add** the corresponding members of two equations in two variables, the result is sometimes a single equation in only one variable.

Example 1: Solve $\begin{cases} 2x + 3y = 6 \\ x + 2y = 5. \end{cases}$

SOLUTION:

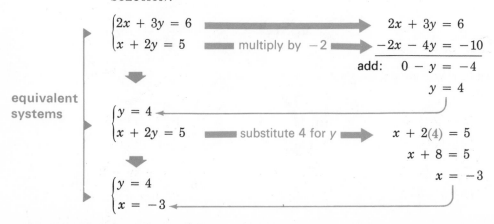

equivalent systems

$\begin{cases} 2x + 3y = 6 \\ x + 2y = 5 \end{cases}$ multiply by -2 $\begin{array}{r} 2x + 3y = 6 \\ -2x - 4y = -10 \end{array}$

add: $0 - y = -4$

$y = 4$

$\begin{cases} y = 4 \\ x + 2y = 5 \end{cases}$ substitute 4 for y $x + 2(4) = 5$

$x + 8 = 5$

$x = -3$

$\begin{cases} y = 4 \\ x = -3 \end{cases}$

Finally, we check the solution in the original equations.

Check: $2x + 3y = 6$ $x + 2y = 5$
           $2(-3) + 3(4) = 6$ $(-3) + 2(4) = 5$
           $-6 + 12 = 6$ $-3 + 8 = 5$
           $6 = 6$ T $5 = 5$ T

So, the solution is $(-3, 4)$.

Example 2: Solve $\begin{cases} 4s + 2t = -2 \\ 2s - 3t = 1. \end{cases}$

SOLUTION: The multiplication-addition method is often shortened.

$\begin{cases} 4s + 2t = -2 \\ 2s - 3t = 1 \end{cases}$ ▬▬ multiply by 3 ⟹ $12s + 6t = -6$

                                          ▬▬ multiply by 2 ⟹ $4s - 6t = 2$

add: $16s + 0 = -4$

$s = -\frac{4}{16}$ or $-\frac{1}{4}$

Substitute $-\frac{1}{4}$ $4(-\frac{1}{4}) + 2t = -2$
for s in one $-1 + 2t = -2$
of the original $2t = -1$
equations. $t = -\frac{1}{2}$

$\begin{cases} s = -\frac{1}{4} \\ t = -\frac{1}{2} \end{cases}$

So, the solution is $(-\frac{1}{4}, -\frac{1}{2})$. You should check that this solution satisfies *both* original equations.

EXERCISES 9.5

Ⓐ Tell how you would use the multiplication-addition method to solve each system.

1. $\begin{cases} x + y = 4 \\ x - y = 4 \end{cases}$ 2. $\begin{cases} 2x - y = 4 \\ x + y = 2 \end{cases}$ 3. $\begin{cases} x + 2y = 6 \\ -x + 3y = -1 \end{cases}$

4. $\begin{cases} 2x - y = 5 \\ 2x + y = 3 \end{cases}$ 5. $\begin{cases} 3x + y = 4 \\ x - 2y = -1 \end{cases}$ 6. $\begin{cases} 2x - 2y = 2 \\ x + y = 5 \end{cases}$

7. $\begin{cases} 2x + y = 12 \\ 3x + y = 17 \end{cases}$

8. $\begin{cases} x + 3y = 9 \\ x + 2y = 7 \end{cases}$

9. $\begin{cases} 2x - 3y = 12 \\ 4x + 3y = 24 \end{cases}$

10. $\begin{cases} 2x - 3y = -3 \\ 3x + 3y = 18 \end{cases}$

11. $\begin{cases} 3x + 2y = 8 \\ 3x - 2y = 4 \end{cases}$

12. $\begin{cases} 2m + 4n = 10 \\ 2m - 4n = 2 \end{cases}$

13. $\begin{cases} 2a - 5b = 12 \\ 2a - 3b = 12 \end{cases}$

14. $\begin{cases} 3s - 2t = 7 \\ 3s + 5t = 14 \end{cases}$

15. $\begin{cases} 2x + 3y = 12 \\ 4x - y = 10 \end{cases}$

16. $\begin{cases} 2x - 3y = 22 \\ 4x + y = 2 \end{cases}$

17. $\begin{cases} 3p + 2q = 2 \\ p - 4q = 3 \end{cases}$

18. $\begin{cases} 4s + 5t = 7 \\ 2s - t = 0 \end{cases}$

19. $\begin{cases} 4s + t = 4 \\ 3s - 2t = 3 \end{cases}$

20. $\begin{cases} 3m + 4n = 0 \\ 2m - 2n = 7 \end{cases}$

21. $\begin{cases} a - 5b = 0 \\ 2a - 3b = 7 \end{cases}$

22. $\begin{cases} 3x + 4y = 4 \\ x - 2y = 0 \end{cases}$

23. $\begin{cases} 3x - 3y = 6 \\ 2x + y = 1 \end{cases}$

24. $\begin{cases} 3x + 3y = 6 \\ 2x - y = 1 \end{cases}$

Ⓒ 25. $\begin{cases} \frac{1}{2}x + \frac{1}{2}y = 3 \\ \frac{1}{4}x - \frac{1}{2}y = 3 \end{cases}$

26. $\begin{cases} 2x - \frac{1}{4}y = 3 \\ 4x - \frac{1}{2}y = 6 \end{cases}$

27. $\begin{cases} 3x + 4y = 7 \\ 3x + 4y = 8 \end{cases}$

28. The sum of two numbers is 33. The difference of the same two numbers is 11. Find the numbers.

29. Show that if (m, n) is a solution of system **I** at the right, then (m, n) is also a solution of system **II**. (Assume all letters except x and y name constants.)

I. $\begin{cases} ax + by - c = 0 \\ dx + ey - f = 0 \end{cases}$

II. $\begin{cases} k(ax + by - c) + j(dx + ey - f) = 0 \\ dx + ey - f = 0 \end{cases}$

Another Way to Solve Systems

A **determinant** is a number named by an array such as $\begin{vmatrix} 2 & 3 \\ -2 & 4 \end{vmatrix}$.

Example: $\begin{vmatrix} 2 & 3 \\ -2 & 4 \end{vmatrix} = (2)(4) - (-2)(3) = 8 + 6 = 14$

The determinant $\begin{vmatrix} a & c \\ b & d \end{vmatrix}$ is equal to $ad - bc$.

Determinants can be used to solve a system of two linear equations in two variables. The numerals **I**, **II**, and **III** show how the three determinants used below are related to the coefficients and constants of the equations.

$$\begin{cases} 2x + 3y = 6 \\ 4x + (-2)y = 1 \end{cases}$$

I   **II**   **III**

 SYSTEM

I   **II**

$D = \begin{vmatrix} 2 & 3 \\ 4 & -2 \end{vmatrix} = (2)(-2) - (4)(3) = -4 - 12 = -16$

III   **II**

$D_x = \begin{vmatrix} 6 & 3 \\ 1 & -2 \end{vmatrix} = (6)(-2) - (1)(3) = -12 - 3 = -15$

I   **III**

$D_y = \begin{vmatrix} 2 & 6 \\ 4 & 1 \end{vmatrix} = (2)(1) - (4)(6) = 2 - 24 = -22$

 DETERMINANTS

$x = \dfrac{D_x}{D} = \dfrac{-15}{-16} = \dfrac{15}{16}$ The solution is $(\frac{15}{16}, \frac{11}{8})$.

$y = \dfrac{D_y}{D} = \dfrac{-22}{-16} = \dfrac{11}{8}$ (Check these results.)

 SOLVING FOR x AND y

Use determinants to solve each system.

1. $\begin{cases} 2x + y = 6 \\ x + 3y = 8 \end{cases}$ **2.** $\begin{cases} 2x - 5y = -9 \\ 3x + 7y = 1 \end{cases}$ **3.** $\begin{cases} 4x + 6y = 0 \\ 6x - 3y = 4 \end{cases}$

9.6 SOLVING PROBLEMS

Systems of two equations in two variables are very useful for solving certain kinds of problems.

Example 1: Find two numbers whose sum is 14 and whose difference is 6.

SOLUTION: Let x = the larger of the two numbers.

Let y = the smaller of the two numbers.

We can use a system of equations to show how x and y are related.

$$\begin{cases} x + y = 14 \\ x - y = 6 \end{cases}$$

The sum of the two numbers is 14.

The difference of the two numbers is 6.

By the multiplication-addition method we get,

$$\begin{array}{l} x + y = 14 \\ \underline{x - y = 6} \\ 2x + 0 = 20 \\ x = 10 \end{array}$$

$(10) + y = 14$

$y = 4.$

You should check that 4 and 10 satisfy the conditions stated in the original problem.

Example 2: Kim is 4 years older than Dean. Eight years ago, Kim was twice as old as Dean. What are their ages now?

SOLUTION: It is often helpful to organize the given information in a chart.

	Kim	Dean	Relation
Age now	k	d	$k - d = 4$
Age 8 years ago	$k - 8$	$d - 8$	$k - 8 = 2(d - 8)$

We can use this information as shown on the next page.

From the chart we get a system of two equations in k and d.

$$\begin{cases} k - d = 4 \\ k - 8 = 2(d - 8) \end{cases} \xleftarrow[\text{to}]{\overset{\text{is}}{\longleftarrow \text{equivalent} \longrightarrow}} \begin{cases} k - d = 4 \\ k - 2d = -8 \end{cases}$$

Multiplying the second equation by -1 and solving, we get

$$\begin{array}{c} k - d = 4 \\ \underline{-k + 2d = 8} \\ d = 12 \end{array} \qquad \begin{array}{c} k - (12) = 4 \\ k = 16. \end{array}$$

We conclude that Kim is 16 years old and Dean is 12 years old. (Be sure you check these results.)

EXERCISES 9.6

Ⓐ Each problem below can be translated into one of the following systems. Tell which one.

I. $\begin{cases} 2x + y = 85 \\ 3x + 2y = 140 \end{cases}$ II. $\begin{cases} x + y = 140 \\ x = 4y \end{cases}$

III. $\begin{cases} x - y = 5 \\ x + y = 27 \end{cases}$ IV. $\begin{cases} x + y = 27 \\ 2x + 3 = y \end{cases}$

1. One number is 5 more than another and their sum is 27. Find the numbers.

2. The sum of two numbers is 140. One number is 4 times the other. Find the numbers.

3. Daren is 5 years older than her sister Annette. The sum of their ages is 27. Find the age of each.

4. A 140-foot cable must be cut into two pieces with one piece four times as long as the other. How long must the pieces be?

5. Two hamburgers and a Coke cost 85¢. Three hamburgers and two Cokes cost $1.40. What is the cost of a hamburger? A Coke?

6. In an algebra class of 27 students, the number of girls is 3 more than twice the number of boys. How many are boys? Girls?

Ⓑ **7–12.** Solve each problem stated in Exercises **1–6**.

Translate each problem into a system of two equations in two variables and solve.

13. The sum of two numbers is 12 and their difference is 4. Find the numbers.

14. The sum of a number and twice a second number is 16. The first number is 4 greater than the second. Find the numbers.

15. The larger of two numbers is equal to three times the smaller. If twice the larger is added to three times the smaller, the sum is 27. Find the numbers.

16. Five times the smaller of two numbers is 4 greater than the larger. Three times the larger is 27 greater than 2 times the smaller. Find the numbers.

17. Dan is 6 years older than Dave. In 5 years, the sum of their ages will be 36. What are their ages now?

18. Paula is twice as old as Trudy. Seven years ago, the sum of their ages was 13. How old is each now?

19. Three times Nancy's age is 6 more than twice Roger's age. The sum of their ages is 32. Find their ages.

20. Jill is 3 times as old as Juli. In 10 years, Jill will be twice as old as Juli. Find their ages now.

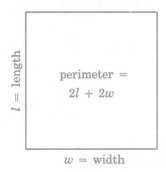

perimeter =
$2l + 2w$

l = length

w = width

21. Twice the length of a rectangle is equal to five times its width. The perimeter of the rectangle is 77 meters. Find the length and width.

22. The perimeter of a rectangle is 14 centimeters. Twice the width is equal to $\frac{1}{3}$ the length. Find the length and the width.

23. Twice the sum of two numbers is 32. Twice their difference is 4. Find the numbers.

24. Find two numbers such that the sum of 3 times the first and 2 times the second is 16, and such that 2 times the first is 2 more than 3 times the second.

© **25.** A pet shop sold 20 rabbits for $192. Some of the rabbits sold for $7 each and the rest for $11 each. How many rabbits were sold at each price?

26. Jabbar scored 23 times in a basketball game. If he scored 34 points, two for each field goal and one for each free throw, how many field goals did he make? How many free throws?

27. Gail sold 7 adult and 3 student tickets for a school play and collected $10.25. Her sister sold 3 adult and 7 student tickets and collected $7.25. What was the cost of each type of ticket?

28. In Fairbanks, Alaska, the longest period of daylight is 18 hours longer than the shortest period of darkness. Both periods occur in the same 24 hours. How long is each period?

29. For an advertising campaign, the Superauto Supply Company gave away 9,000 miniature cars and trucks. The cars cost 13¢ each and the trucks cost 15¢ each. The company spent a total of $1290 on the giveaways. How many of each kind did they buy?

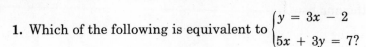

1. Which of the following is equivalent to $\begin{cases} y = 3x - 2 \\ 5x + 3y = 7? \end{cases}$

   a. $y = 3x - 2$ or $5x + 3y = 7$

   b. $y = 3x - 2$ and $5x + 3y = 7$

Find the solution set of each system by graphing.

2. $\begin{cases} x - 5y = 10 \\ 3y = -x - 6 \end{cases}$

3. $\begin{cases} 3x + 2y = 3 \\ 6x + 4y = 12 \end{cases}$

Determine whether each system has exactly one solution, many solutions, or no solutions.

4. $\begin{cases} 3x - y = 4 \\ y = 3x - 4 \end{cases}$

5. $\begin{cases} 2x - y = 5 \\ 4x - 2y = 5 \end{cases}$

6. $\begin{cases} 2x + 3y = 5 \\ -x + 4y = 3 \end{cases}$

Tell whether the two systems are equivalent.

7. $\begin{cases} y = x \\ x + 2y = 6 \end{cases}$ $\begin{cases} x = 2 \\ y = 2 \end{cases}$

8. $\begin{cases} x - 3y = 12 \\ 2x + 3y = 3 \end{cases}$ $\begin{cases} x = 6 \\ y = 2 \end{cases}$

Solve by the substitution method. (Check your solutions.)

9. $\begin{cases} x = 2y \\ 2y + x = 8 \end{cases}$

10. $\begin{cases} x + 3y = 2 \\ 2x + 3y = 13 \end{cases}$

11. $\begin{cases} 2x + y = 5 \\ 3x + 2y = 7 \end{cases}$

Solve by the multiplication-addition method. (Check your solutions.)

12. $\begin{cases} 4x - 2y = 0 \\ x + 2y = 5 \end{cases}$

13. $\begin{cases} 2x - 2y = -6 \\ x + y = 9 \end{cases}$

14. $\begin{cases} 3x + 2y = 1 \\ 2x - 3y = 5 \end{cases}$

15. Seven years ago, Mary was twice as old as Nita. Today, Mary is 4 years older than Nita. Find their present ages.

Most of the problems in this section are of two types, *digit problems* and *mixture problems*.

Example 1: The sum of the digits of a two-digit number is 12. If the digits are interchanged, they name a second number which is 36 greater than the first. Find the first number.

SOLUTION:

Let t = tens digit of first number.

Let u = units digit of first number.

Now we can represent the two numbers as follows.

$$10t + u \longleftarrow \text{first number}$$

$$10u + t \longleftarrow \text{second number}$$

From the statement of the problem, we get a system.

$\begin{cases} u + t = 12 \longleftarrow \\ 10u + t = (10t + u) + 36 \longleftarrow \end{cases}$ $\begin{array}{l} \text{The sum of the digits of the} \\ \text{first number is 12.} \\ \text{The second number is 36} \\ \text{greater than the first number.} \end{array}$

$\begin{cases} u + t = 12 \\ 9u - 9t = 36 \end{cases}$

$\begin{cases} u + t = 12 \\ u - t = 4 \end{cases}$ $\longrightarrow$ $\begin{array}{l} u + t = 12 \\ u - t = 4 \end{array}$

$$\text{add: } 2u \quad = 16$$

$$u \quad = 8$$

$$(8) + t = 12$$

$$t = 4$$

So, the first number is: $10t + u = 10(4) + 8 = 48$. You should check that 4 and 8 satisfy the conditions stated in the problem.

Example 2: A lab technician has some 40% alcohol solution and some 60% alcohol solution. She needs to make 1000 grams of solution which is 48% alcohol. How much of each available solution should she combine?

SOLUTION:

Let x = grams of 40% solution.

Let y = grams of 60% solution.

Analyzing the problem, we find two conditions must be met.

Condition 1
$$\left(\begin{array}{c}\text{weight of 40\%}\\\text{solution}\end{array}\right) + \left(\begin{array}{c}\text{weight of 60\%}\\\text{solution}\end{array}\right) = \left(\begin{array}{c}\text{weight of final}\\\text{solution}\end{array}\right)$$

$$x + y = 1000$$

Condition 2
$$\left(\begin{array}{c}\text{alcohol in}\\\text{40\% solution}\end{array}\right) + \left(\begin{array}{c}\text{alcohol in}\\\text{60\% solution}\end{array}\right) = \left(\begin{array}{c}\text{alcohol in}\\\text{final solution}\end{array}\right)$$

$$0.40x + 0.60y = 0.48(1000)$$

So, the system we must solve is:

$$\begin{cases} x + y = 1000 \\ 0.40x + 0.60y = 0.48(1000). \end{cases}$$

Mult. 1st equation by -40.

Mult. 2nd equation by 100.

$$-40x - 40y = -40000$$
$$\underline{40x + 60y = 48000}$$
$$0 + 20y = 8000$$
$$y = 400$$

$$x + (400) = 1000$$
$$x = 600$$

So, the technician should combine 600 grams of the 40% solution with 400 grams of the 60% solution. Be sure you check these results.

EXERCISES 9.7

Ⓐ Translate each problem into a system of equations. Be sure to tell what each variable represents.

1. The tens digit of a two-digit number is 4 greater than the units digit. The sum of the digits is 10. Find the number.

2. A number is 4 times the sum of its two digits. The tens digit is 2 less than the units digit. What is the number?

3. How many kilograms of 60% alcohol solution and how many kilograms of 80% alcohol solution should be mixed to get 20 kilograms of 70% alcohol solution?

4. How many pints of 15% vinegar solution should be added to 10 pints of 20% vinegar solution to get a solution that is 18% vinegar?

Ⓑ 5–8. Solve each problem stated in Exercises 1–4.

Translate each problem into a system of two equations in two variables and solve. (Tell what each variable represents.)

9. The units digit of a two-digit number is twice the tens digit. The number is 6 greater than 5 times the units digit. Find the number.

10. The tens digit of a two-digit number is 3 greater than the units digit. Eight times the sum of the digits is 1 less than the number. Find the number.

11. The sum of the digits of a two-digit number is 6. If the digits are interchanged, they name a number which is 3 times the original tens digit. Find the original number.

12. The sum of the digits of a two-digit number is 11. If the digits are interchanged, the new number named is 27 greater than the original number. What is the original number?

13. A company has some tea worth 90¢ a pound and some tea worth $1.20 a pound. They wish to make a blend of tea worth $1.00 a pound. How much of each kind of tea must be used to make 60 pounds of blended tea?

14. From a soil analysis, Mr. Beatty learned that his lawn will be healthier if he applies 60 pounds of fertilizer which is 21% nitrogen. He already has a supply of fertilizer, some 10% nitrogen and some 30% nitrogen. How much of each kind should be mixed together for the lawn?

15. A gasoline station mixes two types of gasoline to the customer's order. One type costs 36¢ a gallon and the other costs 46¢ a gallon, If a customer wants 15 gallons for $6.00, how much of each type should be included?

16. An alloy (mixture) of metals is 20% copper and another alloy is 50% copper. How much of each alloy should be used to make 100 grams of alloy which is 45% copper?

© 17. The numerator of a fraction is 7 more than twice the denominator. The reciprocal of the fraction equals 0.4. Find the fraction.

18. Find a way to represent the difference between a three-digit integer and the integer named by reversing the order of the digits. Is this difference *always* divisible by 99? Explain.

9.8 SYSTEMS OF INEQUALITIES

When we look for *common solutions* of two or more inequalities, we are concerned with a *system of inequalities*.

$$\begin{cases} y < -\tfrac{1}{2}x + 2 \\ y > 3x - 3 \end{cases}$$

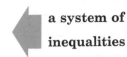 a system of inequalities

This system is another way of writing the "and" sentence

$$y < -\tfrac{1}{2}x + 2 \quad \text{and} \quad y > 3x - 3.$$

The two inequalities and the system are graphed below.

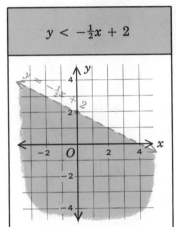

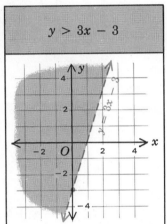

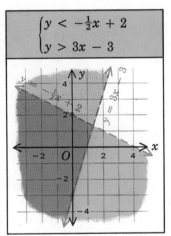

A system consisting of three or more inequalities can be graphed in a similar way.

Example: Graph $\begin{cases} y \leq -x + 3 \\ x \geq 1 \\ y \geq -1. \end{cases}$

SOLUTION: The graph is the intersection of three closed half-planes as shown at the right. Study this graph carefully.

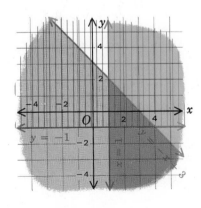

EXERCISES 9.8

Ⓐ Match each system with its graph.

1. $\begin{cases} x > 1 \\ y < 1 \end{cases}$

2. $\begin{cases} y < x \\ x > 2 \end{cases}$

3. $\begin{cases} y < x + 1 \\ x > 2 \end{cases}$

4. $\begin{cases} y \geq 2x + 1 \\ x \leq -2 \end{cases}$

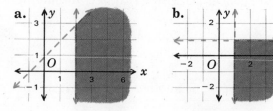

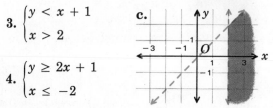

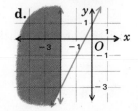

Ⓑ Graph each system.

5. $\begin{cases} x \leq 4 \\ y \geq 2 \end{cases}$

6. $\begin{cases} x \geq -2 \\ y \leq 3 \end{cases}$

7. $\begin{cases} y \geq 2x \\ y \geq -1 \end{cases}$

8. $\begin{cases} y \leq 3x \\ y \leq -2 \end{cases}$

9. $\begin{cases} y \geq 2x + 2 \\ y \leq 4 \end{cases}$

10. $\begin{cases} y \leq 3x - 2 \\ x \geq -3 \end{cases}$

11. $\begin{cases} y < x - 1 \\ y > 2x - 1 \end{cases}$

12. $\begin{cases} y > -x + 2 \\ y > x - 2 \end{cases}$

13. $\begin{cases} x + y < 2 \\ x - y > 3 \end{cases}$

14. $\begin{cases} x - y < 4 \\ x + y > 3 \end{cases}$

15. $\begin{cases} y - 3 \leq 0 \\ x + 2y \geq 4 \end{cases}$

16. $\begin{cases} x + 4 \geq 0 \\ x - 2y \geq -6 \end{cases}$

Ⓒ 17. $\begin{cases} x \geq 3 \\ y \geq 1 \\ x + y < 5 \end{cases}$

18. $\begin{cases} y > -2 \\ x + y < 5 \\ x - y > 5 \end{cases}$

19. $\begin{cases} x - y < 0 \\ x - y > -4 \\ x + y > -4 \end{cases}$

20. $\begin{cases} y - 2x \geq 0 \\ y \geq -2x \\ 4 \geq y \end{cases}$

21. $\begin{cases} y \leq -\frac{3}{4}x + 6 \\ y \leq -3x + 3 \\ y \geq 0 \\ x \geq 0 \end{cases}$

22. $\begin{cases} x \geq -1 \\ x \leq 4 \\ y < -x + 5 \\ y > -x - 1 \end{cases}$

You probably recognize the formula $r \cdot t = d$. It gives the distance (d) traveled in a certain time (t) at a constant rate (r). This formula is useful for solving motion problems.

Example 1: Bernie and Brian paddle their canoe 2 miles downstream (with the current) to a friend's campsite. By paddling at a constant rate, they arrive in $\frac{1}{2}$ hour.

Later, they paddle at the same rate upstream (against the current) for 1 hour to return to their own campsite.

How fast do they paddle (speed in still water)? How fast is the current?

SOLUTION:

Let $x =$ the boys' paddling speed (mph).

Let $y =$ the speed of the current (mph).

A chart will be helpful.

	Rate (r)	Time (t)	Distance (d)	$r \cdot t = d$
Downstream	$x + y$	$\frac{1}{2}$	2	$(x + y)\frac{1}{2} = 2$
Upstream	$x - y$	1	2	$(x - y)1 = 2$

From the chart we get a system of two equations.

$$\begin{cases} (x + y)\frac{1}{2} = 2 \\ (x - y)1 = 2 \end{cases} \quad \Rightarrow \quad \begin{cases} x + y = 4 \\ x - y = 2 \end{cases}$$

By the multiplication-addition method we have

$$2x = 6 \quad \text{or} \quad x = 3. \quad \text{Then } y = 1.$$

These values check with the given conditions. So the boys' paddling speed is 3 mph and the speed of the current is 1 mph.

The *lever* is one of the simplest machines studied in science. A familiar example of a lever is a playground seesaw.

 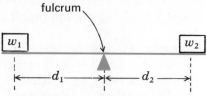

Let: w_1 = weight 1. d_1 = distance 1.

w_2 = weight 2. d_2 = distance 2.

Then, from physics we learn that we can use the formula

law of levers

$$w_1 d_1 = w_2 d_2$$

to solve lever problems.

Example 2: A 180-pound man wants to use a 10-foot lever to lift a 720-pound weight. How far from the fulcrum should the 720-pound weight be placed?

SOLUTION:

A sketch is useful.

Let x = distance from man to fulcrum (in feet).

Let y = distance from weight to fulcrum (in feet).

Since the lever is 10 feet long: ⟶ $x + y = 10$.
From the formula $w_1 d_1 = w_2 d_2$: ⟶ $180x = 720y$.
So we must solve the system,

$$\begin{cases} x + y = 10 \\ 180x = 720y \end{cases} \quad \text{or} \quad \begin{cases} x + y = 10 \\ x = 4y. \end{cases}$$

By substitution, $(4y) + y = 10$ or $y = 2$. Then $x = 4(2)$ or $x = 8$. (You should check these values.)

So we conclude that the fulcrum should be placed 2 feet from the 720-pound weight.

EXERCISES 9.9

Ⓐ Tell what system of equations you would use to solve each problem.

1. A pleasure boat makes a 24-mile trip downstream in 4 hours. It makes the return trip in 6 hours. Find the speed of the boat in still water and the speed of the current.

2. At his fastest, Bill can row downstream at 9 mph and upstream at 3 mph. Find Bill's rowing speed in still water and the speed of the current.

3. Two children sit 10 feet apart to balance a seesaw. If one child weighs 60 pounds and the other weighs 40 pounds, how far is each from the fulcrum?

4. Using a 14-foot lever, a person who weighs 120 pounds is just able to lift a 216-pound weight. How far is the fulcrum from the person? From the weight?

Ⓑ 5–8. Solve each problem in Exercises 1–4. (Make a sketch whenever it will help.)

Solve each problem.

9. Shelia rides her bicycle 18 miles with the wind in 2 hours. It takes her 3 hours to return against the wind. What is Shelia's riding speed and the speed of the wind?

10. A small airplane flies 600 miles in 5 hours against the wind. Returning with the wind requires only 4 hours. Find the speed of the airplane and the speed of the wind.

11. A meter stick balances when the fulcrum is at its center (the 50-centimeter point). A weight of 60 grams is then placed at the 10-centimeter point. What weight can be placed at the 60-centimeter point to make the stick balance again?

12. The sum of the weights of Lew and Rena is 180 pounds. A seesaw balances when Lew sits 8 feet from the fulcrum while Rena sits 10 feet from the fulcrum. How much does each weigh?

13. A speedboat raced 30 miles with the current in $\frac{1}{2}$ hour. Racing against the current, the boat took $\frac{3}{5}$ hour to make the return trip. What was the still-water speed of the boat and the speed of the current?

14. Flying against the wind, an airplane travels 2880 miles in $4\frac{1}{2}$ hours. Flying with the wind, the airplane can travel the same distance in 4 hours. Find the speed of the plane in still air and the speed of the wind.

15. Two weights balance on a lever when one is 4 feet from the fulcrum and the other is 6 feet from the fulcrum. If their positions are interchanged, 6 pounds must be added to the smaller weight for them to balance. How heavy is each weight?

16. Two weights balance on a lever when one is 6 feet from the fulcrum and the other is 8 feet from the fulcrum. If 4 pounds are added to each weight, the weights may be moved to 8 and 10 feet from the fulcrum, respectively, to balance again. How heavy is each weight?

© 17. Solve the problem given on page 303.

18. A woman leaves an airport on a plane headed due east. By mistake, her baggage leaves one hour later on a plane headed due west. The woman is traveling 60 mph faster than her baggage. Four hours after she left, the woman and her baggage are 4370 miles apart. How fast is each plane flying if they fly at constant rates and make no stops?

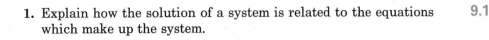

1. Explain how the solution of a system is related to the equations which make up the system.

9.1

Find the solution set of each system by graphing.

2. $\begin{cases} y = 3x - 2 \\ y = -x + 2 \end{cases}$

3. $\begin{cases} 2y = x + 4 \\ x + y = 5 \end{cases}$

4. When looking at the graph of a system of equations, how can you tell whether the system has exactly one solution, many solutions, or no solutions?

9.2

Tell whether each system has exactly one solution, many solutions, or no solutions.

5. $\begin{cases} y = 3x + 4 \\ y = 3x - 4 \end{cases}$

6. $\begin{cases} 3x - 2y = 1 \\ 9x - 6y = 3 \end{cases}$

7. $\begin{cases} y = 2x - 3 \\ y = -x + 6 \end{cases}$

8. When are two systems of equations equivalent?

9.3

9. Are the two systems at the right equivalent?

$\begin{cases} y = -1 \\ x = -2 \end{cases}$

$\begin{cases} y = \frac{3}{2}x + 2 \\ y = -2x - 5 \end{cases}$

Use the substitution method to solve each system.

9.4

10. $\begin{cases} 3x + 2y = 7 \\ y = x - 4 \end{cases}$

11. $\begin{cases} y - x = 5 \\ 4x - y = 11 \end{cases}$

Use the multiplication-addition method to solve each system.

9.5

12. $\begin{cases} x - 2y = 3 \\ 3x + 2y = 1 \end{cases}$

13. $\begin{cases} 2x - 3y = 10 \\ 3x + 2y = 2 \end{cases}$

Solve each problem.

9.6   **14.** The sum of two numbers is 30. Twice their difference is 3 greater than the smaller number. Find the numbers.

15. Naomi is 6 years older than Pedro. Four years ago, Naomi was twice as old as Pedro. How old is each now?

9.7   **16.** The sum of the digits of a two-digit number is 11. If the digits are interchanged, they name a second number which is 45 greater than the first. What is the first number?

17. How many grams of 15% alcohol solution and how many grams of 35% alcohol solution should be mixed to get 48 grams of a solution which is 30% alcohol?

9.8   Graph each system of inequalities.

18. $\begin{cases} y < x + 3 \\ y > -\frac{1}{2}x \end{cases}$ **19.** $\begin{cases} x \geq -3 \\ y \geq -\frac{5}{3}x \end{cases}$

9.9   **20.** At what point must the fulcrum be placed so that a 5-pound weight and a 7-pound weight will balance when placed at opposite ends of a 60-centimeter lever?

21. A certain passenger airplane cruises 150 mph faster than a business jet. The business jet cruises at a speed which is $\frac{3}{4}$ of the speed of the passenger airplane. Find the cruising speed of each aircraft.

Choose the lettered term which best completes each sentence.

    a. consistent   **b.** empty set   **c.** dependent

    d. equivalent   **e.** system   **f.** inconsistent

1. A(n)_____ system has exactly one solution.

2. The sentence "$y = 2x$ and $y = x - 3$" can be written as a(n)_____ of equations.

3. A(n)_____ system has an empty solution set.

4. The systems at the right are consistent and _____.
$$\begin{cases} x = 2 \\ y = 3 \end{cases} \text{and} \begin{cases} y = -\tfrac{1}{2}x + 4 \\ y = 3 \end{cases}$$

5. A consistent and _____ system has many solutions.

Tell whether each system is *consistent*, *consistent and dependent*, or *inconsistent*. Then, solve each system.

6. $\begin{cases} y = 3x + 2 \\ y = 3x + 4 \end{cases}$
    7. $\begin{cases} y = 3x + 2 \\ 2y = 6x + 4 \end{cases}$
    8. $\begin{cases} x - y = 3 \\ x + y = 7 \end{cases}$

Graph each of the following systems.

9. $\begin{cases} 3y = x + 9 \\ y = -2x - 4 \end{cases}$
    10. $\begin{cases} x \le 5 \\ y \ge 2 \end{cases}$
    11. $\begin{cases} y \ge 2x - 5 \\ 3x + 2y \le 4 \end{cases}$

Solve each problem.

12. The sum of the digits of a two-digit number is 12. The number equals 21 times the units digit. Find the number.

13. A class of 40 students must be divided into two groups so that one is 4 greater than 5 times the other. How many students should be in each group?

14. A motorboat can go 15 miles downstream in $\tfrac{1}{2}$ hour. The return trip takes $\tfrac{3}{4}$ hour. Find the speed of the boat (in still water) and the speed of the current.

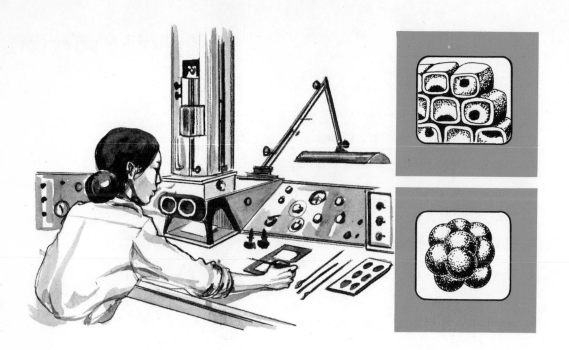

Chapter 10

Division of Polynomials

All living things are made up of *cells*. The cube is a common shape for plant cells, while the sphere is a common shape for animal cells.

Scientists who study living things might have to find the ratio of the surface area of a cell to its volume. This would involve quotients like the following.

$$\frac{\text{Surface area of cube}}{\text{Volume of cube}} = \frac{6s^2}{s^3} \qquad \frac{\text{Surface area of sphere}}{\text{Volume of sphere}} = \frac{4\pi r^2}{\frac{4}{3}\pi r^3}$$

In this chapter, you will study how such quotients can be simplified. And you will also see how division of monomials and polynomials can be involved in solving problems about ratios and rates.

340

Quotients involving powers can be simplified as shown in the following examples.

$$\frac{5^4}{5^4} = \frac{5 \cdot 5 \cdot 5 \cdot 5}{5 \cdot 5 \cdot 5 \cdot 5}$$

$$= 1$$

$$\frac{5^7}{5^4} = \frac{(5 \cdot 5 \cdot 5)(5 \cdot 5 \cdot 5 \cdot 5)}{5 \cdot 5 \cdot 5 \cdot 5} \longleftarrow \text{7 factors}$$
$$\longleftarrow \text{4 factors}$$

$$= 5 \cdot 5 \cdot 5 \qquad \longleftarrow \text{7 } - \text{ 4 factors}$$

$$= 5^{7-4}$$

$$= 5^3$$

$$\frac{5^4}{5^7} = \frac{5 \cdot 5 \cdot 5 \cdot 5}{(5 \cdot 5 \cdot 5)(5 \cdot 5 \cdot 5 \cdot 5)} \qquad \longleftarrow \text{4 factors}$$
$$\longleftarrow \text{7 factors}$$

$$= \frac{1}{5 \cdot 5 \cdot 5} \qquad \longleftarrow \text{7 } - \text{ 4 factors}$$

$$= \frac{1}{5^{7-4}}$$

$$= \frac{1}{5^3}$$

The examples above suggest the following properties for division of powers.

division
of powers

Let a be any nonzero real number, and let m and n be any positive integers.

▶ If $m = n$,

then $\dfrac{a^m}{a^n} = 1$.

▶ If $m > n$,

then $\dfrac{a^m}{a^n} = a^{m-n}$.

▶ If $m < n$,

then $\dfrac{a^m}{a^n} = \dfrac{1}{a^{n-m}}$.

Notice that a cannot be 0 in the fractions above since division by 0 is not defined.

Examples: Simplify each expression.

1. $\dfrac{4^6}{4^4}$
2. $\dfrac{(-2)^7}{(-2)^{12}}$
3. $\dfrac{4s^3t^5}{12s^3t^2}$
4. $\dfrac{24x^9y^2}{-6x^4y^5}$

SOLUTIONS:

1. $\dfrac{4^6}{4^4} = 4^{6-4}$

$\qquad = 4^2 = 16$

2. $\dfrac{(-2)^7}{(-2)^{12}} = \dfrac{1}{(-2)^{12-7}}$

$\qquad\qquad = \dfrac{1}{(-2)^5}$

$\qquad\qquad = \dfrac{1}{-32} = -\dfrac{1}{32}$

3. $\dfrac{4s^3t^5}{12s^3t^2} = \dfrac{4}{12} \cdot \dfrac{s^3}{s^3} \cdot \dfrac{t^5}{t^2}$

$\qquad\quad = \tfrac{1}{3} \cdot 1 \cdot t^{5-2}$

$\qquad\quad = \tfrac{1}{3}t^3$

4. $\dfrac{24x^9y^2}{-6x^4y^5} = \dfrac{24}{-6} \cdot \dfrac{x^9}{x^4} \cdot \dfrac{y^2}{y^5}$

$\qquad\qquad = -4 \cdot x^{9-4} \cdot \dfrac{1}{y^{5-2}}$

$\qquad\qquad = -4x^5 \cdot \dfrac{1}{y^3}$

$\qquad\qquad = -\dfrac{4x^5}{y^3}$

Division by 0 is not defined. Therefore, when a divisor (denominator) contains a variable, as in Examples 3 and 4, any value which makes the divisor 0 must be excluded from the replacement set. For the rest of this chapter, we will consider such values to be excluded automatically, so you can assume that no divisors are 0.

Another property of powers is suggested by the following example.

$$\left(\frac{2}{5}\right)^3 = \frac{2}{5} \cdot \frac{2}{5} \cdot \frac{2}{5} = \frac{2 \cdot 2 \cdot 2}{5 \cdot 5 \cdot 5} = \frac{2^3}{5^3}$$

power of a quotient

Let a and b be any real numbers where $b \neq 0$, and let n be any positive integer.

$$\left(\frac{a}{b}\right)^n = \frac{a^n}{b^n}$$

Example 5: Simplify $\left(\dfrac{-3x}{-x}\right)^4$.

SOLUTION: $\left(\dfrac{-3x}{-x}\right)^4 = \dfrac{(-3x)^4}{(-x)^4}$ Power of a quotient

$$= \dfrac{(-3x)^4}{(-1x)^4}$$ Mult. prop. of -1

$$= \dfrac{(-3)^4 x^4}{(-1)^4 x^4}$$ Power of a product

$$= \dfrac{(-3)^4}{(-1)^4}$$

$$= \dfrac{81}{1} = 81$$

ANOTHER WAY: $\left(\dfrac{-3x}{-x}\right)^4 = \left(\dfrac{-3x}{-1x}\right)^4$

$$= 3^4 = 81$$

EXERCISES 10.1

Ⓐ Which property of powers is illustrated by each equation?

1. $\dfrac{a^6}{a^4} = a^{6-4}$ **2.** $\left(\dfrac{3}{4}\right)^3 = \dfrac{3^3}{4^3}$ **3.** $\dfrac{2^8}{2^{10}} = \dfrac{1}{2^{10-8}}$

4. $\dfrac{(3x)^5}{(3x)^2} = (3x)^{5-2}$ **5.** $\left(\dfrac{1}{2}\right)^7 = \dfrac{1^7}{2^7}$ **6.** $(2t)^5 = 2^5 t^5$

7–12. Complete the solutions for simplifying Exercises 1–6.

Simplify each expression.

13. $\dfrac{r^8}{r^3}$ **14.** $\dfrac{s^7}{s^4}$ **15.** $\dfrac{t^9}{t^{12}}$ **16.** $\dfrac{u^3}{u^8}$

17. $\dfrac{10^{11}}{10^8}$ **18.** $\dfrac{(-3)^6}{(-3)^9}$ **19.** $\dfrac{(-2)^5}{(-2)^7}$ **20.** $\dfrac{10^6}{10^4}$

21. $\dfrac{(-7)^5}{(-7)^5}$ **22.** $\left(\dfrac{1}{2}\right)^3$ **23.** $\dfrac{(-5)^4}{(-5)^4}$ **24.** $\left(\dfrac{2}{5}\right)^2$

25. $\left(\dfrac{-s}{t}\right)^6$ **26.** $\left(\dfrac{r}{-w}\right)^7$ **27.** $\dfrac{x^5}{x^3}$ **28.** $\dfrac{y^7}{y^5}$

Ⓑ **29.** $\dfrac{-5^5}{-5^2}$ **30.** $\dfrac{-4^6}{-4^3}$ **31.** $\dfrac{(0.4)^3}{0.4}$ **32.** $\dfrac{(0.6)^4}{-0.6}$

33. $\dfrac{(ab)^8}{(ab)^6}$ **34.** $\dfrac{(cd)^9}{(cd)^7}$ **35.** $\dfrac{(xy)^3}{(xy)^7}$ **36.** $\dfrac{(ab)^2}{(ab)^6}$

37. $\dfrac{r^8 s^{12}}{r^4 s^5}$ **38.** $\dfrac{a^7 b^{14}}{a^4 b^9}$ **39.** $\dfrac{m^3 n^8}{m^7 n^{10}}$ **40.** $\dfrac{t^2 v^6}{t^5 v^{11}}$

41. $\dfrac{x^{17} y^5}{x^9 y^8}$ **42.** $\dfrac{z^6 w^7}{z^9 w^2}$ **43.** $\dfrac{4 \times 10^8}{2 \times 10^5}$

44. $\dfrac{9 \times 10^{11}}{3 \times 10^6}$ **45.** $\dfrac{2.4 \times 10^{12}}{6.0 \times 10^9}$ **46.** $\dfrac{4.8 \times 10^7}{8.0 \times 10^5}$

47. $\dfrac{3.6 \times 10^5}{0.9 \times 10^4}$ **48.** $\dfrac{3.5 \times 10^7}{0.7 \times 10^6}$ **49.** $(2p)^7 \cdot \dfrac{1}{(2p)^3}$

50. $(3q)^8 \cdot \dfrac{1}{(3q)^4}$ **51.** $\dfrac{(2a)^4}{a^2} \div \dfrac{(2a)^2}{a^4}$ **52.** $\dfrac{(3b)^5}{b^2} \div \dfrac{(3b)^3}{b^4}$

53. $(2w)^4 \cdot \dfrac{1}{2w}$ **54.** $(3s)^3 \cdot \dfrac{1}{3s}$ **55.** $\dfrac{(-5r)^5}{(-5r)^2}$

56. $\dfrac{(-7p)^4}{(-7p)^2}$ **57.** $\left(\dfrac{2x}{3y}\right)^3$ **58.** $\left(\dfrac{3r}{2s}\right)^4$

Ⓒ Simplify each expression. Each exponent is a positive integer.

59. $\dfrac{-24m^2(m-n)^7}{6m^3(m-n)^6}$ **60.** $\dfrac{12r^2(r-s)^6}{-4r^4(r-s)^5}$ **61.** $\dfrac{r^{5a} s^{3b} t^{2c}}{r^{2a} s^b t^c}$

62. $\dfrac{x^{3d} y^{4e} z^{2f}}{x^{2d} y^{3e} z^f}$ **63.** $\dfrac{7^{3a}}{7^{2a}} \cdot \dfrac{7^{4a}}{7^a}$ **64.** $\dfrac{5^{5b}}{5^{3b}} \div \dfrac{5^{3b}}{5^{2b}}$

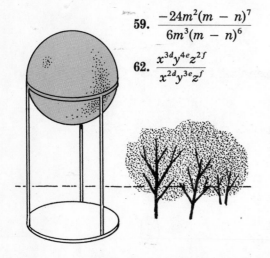

65. A spherical-shaped water tank rests on a tower whose circular base has the same radius as the tank. What is the ratio of the surface area of the tank to the area of the base? (HINT: Area of a circle = πr^2, and surface area of a sphere = $4\pi r^2$.) If 10 gallons of paint are needed to paint the circular base, how many gallons are needed to paint the tank?

You have already had some practice in dividing monomials. For example, the expression

$$\frac{x^8}{x^3}$$

means "divide the monomial x^8 by the monomial x^3." Applying the rule for division of powers, you have

$$\frac{x^8}{x^3} = x^{8-3} = x^5. \qquad (x \neq 0.\ \text{Why?})$$

In this section, you will get some more practice in *dividing monomials*, or in *simplifying quotients of monomials*

Example 1: Simplify $\dfrac{12x^7}{27x^3}$.

SHORT SOLUTION:

$$\frac{12x^7}{27x^3} = \frac{\overset{4}{\cancel{12}}x^{7-3}}{\underset{9}{\cancel{27}}}$$

$$= \frac{4x^4}{9}$$

DETAILED SOLUTION:

$$\frac{12x^7}{27x^3} = \frac{12}{27} \cdot \frac{x^7}{x^3}$$

$$= \frac{4 \cdot 3}{9 \cdot 3} \cdot x^{7-3}$$

$$= \frac{4}{9} x^4 \text{ or } \frac{4x^4}{9}$$

Example 2: Simplify $\dfrac{-54r^9s^5}{66r^4s^8}$.

SHORT SOLUTION:

$$\frac{-54r^9s^5}{66r^4s^8} = -\frac{\overset{9}{\cancel{54}}r^{9-4}}{\underset{11}{\cancel{66}}s^{8-5}}$$

$$= -\frac{9r^5}{11s^3}$$

DETAILED SOLUTION:

$$\frac{-54r^9s^5}{66r^4s^8} = \frac{-54}{66} \cdot \frac{r^9}{r^4} \cdot \frac{s^5}{s^8}$$

$$= \frac{-9 \cdot 6}{11 \cdot 6} \cdot r^{9-4} \cdot \frac{1}{s^{8-5}}$$

$$= -\frac{9}{11} \cdot r^5 \cdot \frac{1}{s^3}$$

$$= -\frac{9r^5}{11s^3}$$

A quotient of two monomials is in *simplest form* if the numerical quotient is in simplest form and no variable occurs more than once. For instance, in Example 2, the numerical quotient $-\frac{9}{11}$ is in simplest form and each of r and s occurs no more than once as a base. Thus, the quotient $-\frac{9r^5}{11s^3}$ is in simplest form.

EXERCISES 10.2

Ⓐ Simplify each expression.

1. $\dfrac{4x}{2x}$

2. $\dfrac{8y}{4}$

3. $\dfrac{10z}{5}$

4. $\dfrac{6x}{3x}$

5. $\dfrac{-7}{14w}$

6. $\dfrac{15s}{10s}$

7. $\dfrac{a^2}{2a}$

8. $\dfrac{b^2}{3b}$

9. $\dfrac{2m^3}{m}$

10. $\dfrac{-9}{18t}$

11. $\dfrac{21r}{14r}$

12. $\dfrac{7s^5}{s}$

13. $\dfrac{13x^5}{x^2}$

14. $\dfrac{-s^3}{5s^6}$

15. $\dfrac{t^2}{-3t^5}$

16. $\dfrac{11y^7}{y^4}$

17. $\dfrac{9w^4}{18w^4}$

18. $\dfrac{-8x^3}{-5x^2}$

Ⓑ 19. $\dfrac{49x^6}{-28x^4}$

20. $\dfrac{56y^8}{-14y^5}$

21. $\dfrac{24m^3}{72m^6}$

22. $-\dfrac{36n^4}{68n^7}$

23. $\dfrac{84x^9}{-7x^4}$

24. $\dfrac{96y^{10}}{-8y^6}$

25. $\dfrac{64s^6}{16s^{10}}$

26. $\dfrac{88t^5}{11t^{11}}$

27. $\dfrac{18xy^2}{6xy}$

28. $\dfrac{21m^2n}{7mn}$

29. $\dfrac{-28x^5}{7x^3}$

30. $\dfrac{32y^7}{-8y^3}$

31. $\dfrac{-44x^4}{-11x^7}$

32. $\dfrac{-36x^3}{-6x^8}$

33. $\dfrac{39x^2y^2}{13xy}$

34. $\dfrac{26m^2n^2}{13mn}$

35. $\dfrac{19y^3s^2}{-38y^2s}$

36. $\dfrac{-17x^4t^2}{34x^3t}$

Simplify each expression.

Example: $\left(\dfrac{x}{y}\right)^2 \cdot \left(\dfrac{y}{x}\right)^3 = \dfrac{x^2}{y^2} \cdot \dfrac{y^3}{x^3}$

$$= \dfrac{x^2 \cdot y^3}{y^2 \cdot x^3}$$

$$= \dfrac{y^{3-2}}{x^{3-2}}$$

$$= \dfrac{y}{x}$$

37. $\left(\dfrac{a}{b}\right)^4 \cdot \left(\dfrac{b}{a}\right)^2$

38. $\left(\dfrac{r}{s}\right)^3 \cdot \left(\dfrac{s}{r}\right)^2$

39. $\left(\dfrac{m}{n}\right)^2 \cdot \left(\dfrac{n}{m}\right)^2$

40. $\left(\dfrac{x}{y}\right)^3 \cdot \left(\dfrac{y}{x}\right)^3$

41. $\left(\dfrac{2x}{3}\right)^2 \cdot \left(\dfrac{3}{x}\right)^2$

42. $\left(\dfrac{4r}{5}\right)^2 \cdot \left(\dfrac{10}{r}\right)^2$

© **43.** $\left(\dfrac{xy}{2}\right)^3 \cdot \left(\dfrac{4}{xy}\right)^2$

44. $\left(\dfrac{3}{ab}\right)^2 \cdot \left(\dfrac{ab}{6}\right)^2$

45. $\left(\dfrac{3xy}{4}\right)^2 \cdot \left(\dfrac{2}{xy}\right)^3$

46. $\left(\dfrac{cd}{5}\right)^4 \cdot \left(\dfrac{5}{2cd}\right)^2$

47. $\left(\dfrac{4mn}{3}\right)^2 \cdot \left(\dfrac{m}{n}\right)^3$

48. $\left(\dfrac{x}{y}\right)^5 \cdot \left(\dfrac{4xy}{5}\right)^3$

Simplify each expression. Each exponent is a positive integer.

49. $\dfrac{8x^a}{2x^a}$

50. $\dfrac{3x^{2b}}{6x^b}$

51. $\dfrac{-2y^c}{3y^{2c}}$

52. $\dfrac{-3y^{4m}}{2y^{3m}}$

53. $\dfrac{12x^{2a}}{-4x^{4a}}$

54. $\dfrac{18x^{3a}}{-9x^{6a}}$

55. $\dfrac{-24x^b}{-14x^{4b}}$

56. $\dfrac{-36x^{3a}}{16x^{3a}}$

57. $\dfrac{-54y^{3a}}{-18y^{2a}}$

Simplify each expression.

58. $\dfrac{12x^5}{4x^2} + \dfrac{-8x^4}{2x^2} - \dfrac{5x}{x}$

59. $\dfrac{34x^3}{2} - \dfrac{27x^6}{9x^3} + \dfrac{15x^5}{5x^4}$

60. $\dfrac{17x^9}{x^7} + \dfrac{20x^7}{5x^6} - \dfrac{8x}{2}$

61. $\dfrac{-3x^4}{2x^2} + \dfrac{7x^5}{8x^4} - \dfrac{17x}{x}$

First, let's consider an example without any variables.

Example 1: Divide: $\dfrac{30 + 20}{5}$.

SHORT SOLUTION:

$$\frac{30 + 20}{5} = \frac{30}{5} + \frac{20}{5}$$

$$= 6 + 4$$

$$= 10$$

DETAILED SOLUTION:

$$\frac{30 + 20}{5} = (30 + 20) \div 5$$

$$= (30 + 20) \cdot \frac{1}{5}$$

$$= 30 \cdot \frac{1}{5} + 20 \cdot \frac{1}{5} \quad \text{Why?}$$

$$= \frac{30}{5} + \frac{20}{5}$$

$$= 6 + 4$$

$$= 10$$

The method used above can also be used in dividing any polynomial by a monomial.

Example 2: Divide: $\dfrac{8x^2 + 4x}{2x}$.

SHORT SOLUTION:

$$\frac{8x^2 + 4x}{2x} = \frac{8x^2}{2x} + \frac{4x}{2x}$$

$$= 4x + 2$$

DETAILED SOLUTION:

$$\frac{8x^2 + 4x}{2x} = (8x^2 + 4x) \div 2x$$

$$= (8x^2 + 4x) \cdot \frac{1}{2x}$$

$$= 8x^2 \left(\frac{1}{2x} \right) + 4x \left(\frac{1}{2x} \right)$$

$$= \frac{8x^2}{2x} + \frac{4x}{2x}$$

$$= 4x + 2$$

Notice that if we omit the steps shown in red in the preceding example, the remaining steps are identical to those in the short solution.

Extending this method, we can divide a polynomial of more than two terms by a monomial. Only a short solution is shown in each example below.

Example 3: Divide: $\dfrac{24y^4 + 16y^3 + 12y^2}{4y^2}$.

SOLUTION: $\dfrac{24y^4 + 16y^3 + 12y^2}{4y^2}$

$= \dfrac{24y^4}{4y^2} + \dfrac{16y^3}{4y^2} + \dfrac{12y^2}{4y^2}$

$= 6y^2 + 4y + 3$

Example 4: Divide: $\dfrac{28x^2 - 14x + 3}{14x}$.

SOLUTION: $\dfrac{28x^2 - 14x + 3}{14x}$

$= \dfrac{28x^2}{14x} - \dfrac{14x}{14x} + \dfrac{3}{14x}$

$= 2x - 1 + \dfrac{3}{14x}$

EXERCISES 10.3

Ⓐ Express each fraction as a sum or difference as in the example.

Example: $\dfrac{7x^2 - 14x}{7x} = \dfrac{7x^2}{7x} - \dfrac{14x}{7x}$.

1. $\dfrac{3x + 6}{3}$

2. $\dfrac{7x - 14}{7}$

3. $\dfrac{3x^2 - 6x}{3x}$

4. $\dfrac{8r^2 + 4r}{4r}$

5. $\dfrac{10x^2 - 2x}{2x}$

6. $\dfrac{13x^2 - 11x}{x}$

7. $\dfrac{19w^3 - 6w^2}{w^2}$

8. $\dfrac{8y - 16y^2}{8y}$

9. $\dfrac{22z - 11z^3}{11z}$

10. $\dfrac{24x^2 + 12x}{6x}$

11. $\dfrac{15y^2 - 30y}{5y}$

12. $\dfrac{2m^3 - m^2}{m^2}$

13–24. Simplify the answers you obtained in Exercises 1–12.

Ⓑ Divide as indicated.

25. $\dfrac{32x^3 - 16x^2}{8x^2}$

26. $\dfrac{15w^2 - 10}{5}$

27. $\dfrac{7x^2 + 14x}{7x}$

28. $\dfrac{16 - 8x}{8}$

29. $\dfrac{20 - 10w - 5w^2}{-5}$

30. $\dfrac{7 - 14s + 21s^2}{-7}$

31. $\dfrac{y^3 + y^2 + y}{y}$

32. $\dfrac{x^4 - x^3 + x^2}{x^2}$

33. $\dfrac{7n^2 - 28n - 35}{7}$

34. $\dfrac{9m^2 - 27m - 45}{9}$

35. $\dfrac{13x^3 - 39x^2}{13x}$

36. $\dfrac{11y^3 - 33y^2}{11y}$

37. $\dfrac{28w^4 + 42w^3 - 14w^2}{7w^2}$

38. $\dfrac{32z^4 - 40z^3 - 16z^2}{8z^2}$

39. $\dfrac{30 - 12x - 36x^2}{-6}$

40. $\dfrac{40 - 16x - 64x^2}{-8}$

41. $\dfrac{22x^2 - 33x - 9}{11}$

42. $\dfrac{24y^2 - 36y - 11}{12}$

43. $\dfrac{17w^3 - 34w^2}{-17w^2}$

44. $\dfrac{19z^3 - 38z^2}{-19z^2}$

45. $\dfrac{48x^5 - 32x^4}{8x^3}$

46. $\dfrac{56y^7 - 35y^5}{7y^4}$

47. $\dfrac{x^3 + 7x^2 - 3x + 2}{x}$

48. $\dfrac{y^3 - 5y^2 + 2y + 3}{y}$

49. $\dfrac{4c^2d^2 - 8cd}{4cd}$ **50.** $\dfrac{9m^2n^2 - 18mn}{9mn}$

51. $\dfrac{-10x^3 - 15x^2 + 5x}{-5x}$ **52.** $\dfrac{-12x^3 + 18x^2 - 6x}{-6x}$

© **53.** $(18ax^3 + 6ax^2 - 12ax) \div (6ax)$

54. $(16by^3 + 12by^2 - 8by) \div (-4by)$

55. $(9cx^4 - 15cx^3 + 5cx^2) \div (3cx^2)$

56. $(8dx^5 + 12dx^3 - 7dx^2) \div (4dx^2)$

57. $(6x^3y^3 - 9x^2y^2 + xy - 1) \div (3xy)$

58. $(4a^3b^2c - 8a^2bc^3 + ab^3c^4) \div (4abc)$

59. A smaller warm-blooded animal, like a rabbit, must take in more food for its size than a larger warm-blooded animal, like a lion. This is related to the ratio of each animal's surface area to its volume. In some studies, biologists represent animals with cylinders of appropriate size and compute the following ratio.

$$\dfrac{\text{Surface area of cylinder}}{\text{Volume of cylinder}} = \dfrac{2\pi r^2 + 2\pi rh}{\pi r^2 h}$$

What is this ratio in simplest form?

60. After 2 seconds of free fall, the distance that a sky diver falls in the next few seconds (t) can be estimated by the formula

$$d = 64t + 16t^2.$$

Therefore,

$$\dfrac{d}{t} = \dfrac{64t + 16t^2}{t}.$$

Since $\dfrac{d}{t}$ = speed, this formula gives the speed that a sky diver attains in the t seconds after the initial 2 seconds of the dive. What is the right side of the formula in simplest form?

10.4 DIVIDING A POLYNOMIAL BY A BINOMIAL

Dividing a polynomial by a binomial is similar to dividing one integer by another. Compare the two examples below.

Problem	$20 + 1 \overline{)600 + 70 + 5}$	$2x + 1 \overline{)6x^2 + 7x + 5}$

Divide
1st term of dividend by
1st term of divisor

$$20 + 1 \overline{)\overset{\boxed{30}}{600 + 70 + 5}} \qquad 2x + 1 \overline{)\overset{\boxed{3x}}{6x^2 + 7x + 5}}$$

Multiply
divisor by
1st term of quotient

$$20 + 1 \overline{)\overset{30}{600 + 70 + 5}} \qquad 2x + 1 \overline{)\overset{3x}{6x^2 + 7x + 5}}$$
$$\boxed{600 + 30} \qquad\qquad \boxed{6x^2 + 3x}$$

Subtract
partial product
from dividend

$$20 + 1 \overline{)\overset{30}{600 + 70 + 5}} \qquad 2x + 1 \overline{)\overset{3x}{6x^2 + 7x + 5}}$$
$$\underline{600 + 30} \qquad\qquad \underline{6x^2 + 3x}$$
$$\boxed{40 + 5} \qquad\qquad \boxed{4x + 5}$$

Divide
1st term of remainder by
1st term of divisor

$$20 + 1 \overline{)\overset{30 \boxed{+\ 2}}{600 + 70 + 5}} \qquad 2x + 1 \overline{)\overset{3x \boxed{+\ 2}}{6x^2 + 7x + 5}}$$
$$\underline{600 + 30} \qquad\qquad \underline{6x^2 + 3x}$$
$$40 + 5 \qquad\qquad 4x + 5$$

Multiply
divisor by
2nd term of quotient

$$20 + 1 \overline{)\overset{30 + 2}{600 + 70 + 5}} \qquad 2x + 1 \overline{)\overset{3x + 2}{6x^2 + 7x + 5}}$$
$$\underline{600 + 30} \qquad\qquad \underline{6x^2 + 3x}$$
$$40 + 5 \qquad\qquad 4x + 5$$
$$\boxed{40 + 2} \qquad\qquad \boxed{4x + 2}$$

Subtract
2nd partial product
from previous remainder

$$20 + 1 \overline{)\overset{30 + 2}{600 + 70 + 5}} \qquad 2x + 1 \overline{)\overset{3x + 2}{6x^2 + 7x + 5}}$$
$$\underline{600 + 30} \qquad\qquad \underline{6x^2 + 3x}$$
$$40 + 5 \qquad\qquad 4x + 5$$
$$\underline{40 + 2} \qquad\qquad \underline{4x + 2}$$
$$\boxed{3} \qquad\qquad\quad \boxed{3}$$

Stop

When the remainder is less than the divisor

When the remainder is 0 or when the degree of the remainder is less than the degree of the divisor

The check for each type of problem involves showing that the following statement is true for each.

$(30 + 2)(20 + 1) + 3$

$= (600 + 30 + 40 + 2) + 3$

$= (600 + 70 + 2) + 3$

$= 600 + 70 + 5$

$(3x + 2)(2x + 1) + 3$

$= (6x^2 + 3x + 4x + 2) + 3$

$= (6x^2 + 7x + 2) + 3$

$= 6x^2 + 7x + 5$

If the remainder is zero in any division process, then the divisor is a factor of the dividend.

Example: Find the quotient $(8x^2 - 6x - 9) \div (4x + 3)$.

SOLUTION:

$$\dfrac{8x^2}{4x}$$

$$\dfrac{-12x}{4x}$$

$$\begin{array}{r} 2x \quad - \quad 3 \\ 4x + 3\overline{\smash{)}8x^2 - 6x - 9} \\ 8x^2 + 6x \quad\quad \longleftarrow \quad 2x(4x + 3) \\ \hline -12x - 9 \\ -12x - 9 \quad \longleftarrow \quad -3(4x + 3) \\ \hline 0 \end{array}$$

Check: $(2x - 3)(4x + 3) = 8x^2 + 6x - 12x - 9$

$$= 8x^2 - 6x - 9$$

Thus, $4x + 3$ is a factor of $8x^2 - 6x - 9$.

EXERCISES 10.4

Ⓐ **1–20.** For each of Exercises **21–40,** find the first term in the quotient and the first partial product.

21. $x + 1\overline{)x^2 + 2x + 1}$ **22.** $y + 2\overline{)y^2 + 4y + 4}$

23. $z + 2\overline{)z^2 + 5z + 6}$ **24.** $m + 4\overline{)m^2 + 5m + 4}$

25. $x - 3\overline{)x^2 - x - 6}$ **26.** $y - 5\overline{)y^2 - 2y - 15}$

27. $x - 4\overline{)x^2 - 7x + 12}$ **28.** $y - 2\overline{)y^2 - 5y + 6}$

29. $z + 6\overline{)z^2 + 9z + 18}$ **30.** $x + 7\overline{)x^2 + 9x + 14}$

31. $m - 5\overline{)m^2 + 3m - 40}$ **32.** $y - 6\overline{)y^2 + 3y - 54}$

33. $\dfrac{6x^2 + 5x - 6}{2x + 3}$ **34.** $\dfrac{4y^2 - 16y + 15}{2y - 5}$

35. $\dfrac{18z^2 + 27z + 4}{3z + 4}$ **36.** $\dfrac{10x^2 + 29x + 21}{5x + 7}$

37. $\dfrac{6x^2 - 5x + 1}{2x - 1}$ **38.** $\dfrac{4x^2 - 20x + 21}{2x - 7}$

39. $\dfrac{15y^2 + 28y + 5}{3y + 5}$ **40.** $\dfrac{12y^2 + 36y + 15}{6y + 3}$

Find each quotient and remainder.

41. $(27y^2 - 24y + 8) \div (9y - 2)$

42. $(25r^2 - 20r + 11) \div (5r + 2)$

43. $(48m^2 + 8m + 7) \div (12m - 1)$

44. $(63y^2 + 3y + 10) \div (-7y + 2)$

Ⓒ The second polynomial is a factor of the first. Use division to help you factor the first polynomial completely.

45. $x^3 + 3x^2 + 3x + 1;\quad x + 1$

46. $x^3 - 3x^2 - x + 3;\quad x - 1$

47. $4x^3 + 12x^2 + 11x + 3;\quad 2x + 3$

48. $9x^3 - 12x^2 + x + 2;\quad 3x - 2$

49–60. For each of Exercises **29–40**, what value of the variable must be excluded to avoid division by 0?

10.5 MORE DIVISION OF POLYNOMIALS

Before dividing a polynomial by a binomial, it is helpful to arrange the terms in descending powers of the variable.

Example: Find the quotient: $(-7x + x^3 + 6) \div (x - 2)$.

SOLUTION: First arrange the terms of the polynomial $-7x + x^3 + 6$ in descending powers of x as follows.

$$x^3 + (-7x) + 6 \quad \text{or} \quad x^3 - 7x + 6.$$

Note that there is no x^2 term in this polynomial. To make the division process easier, insert "$0x^2$" in the polynomial as shown below.

$$x^3 + 0x^2 - 7x + 6$$

Division Process:

$$
\begin{array}{r}
x^2 + 2x - 3 \\
x - 2{\overline{\smash{\big)}\,x^3 + 0x^2 - 7x + 6}} \\
\underline{x^3 - 2x^2} \\
2x^2 - 7x + 6 \\
\underline{2x^2 - 4x} \\
-3x + 6 \\
\underline{-3x + 6} \\
0
\end{array}
$$

Check:

$$
\begin{array}{r}
x^2 + 2x - 3 \\
x - 2 \\
\hline
x^3 + 2x^2 - 3x \\
-2x^2 - 4x + 6 \\
\hline
x^3 + 0x^2 - 7x + 6
\end{array}
$$

EXERCISES 10.5

Ⓐ Arrange the terms of each polynomial in descending powers of x and fill in the necessary powers of x.

Example: $3 + x^2 = x^2 + 0x + 3$

1. $5 + 7x^2$

2. $2x + x^2 + 6$

3. $8 + x^2 - 2x$

4. $x^3 + 4 - x$

5. $-2x^3 + x^4 + 5$

6. $-8 + x^3$

SECTION 10.5   MORE DIVISION OF POLYNOMIALS   355

7. $(-55x + 28 + 25x^2) \div (5x - 4)$

8. $(-84x + 36 + 24x^2) \div (8x - 4)$

9. $(-24a^2 - 35 + 58a) \div (-6a + 7)$

10. $(-16b^2 - 55 + 98b) \div (-8b + 5)$

Find each quotient and remainder.

11. $\dfrac{4x^3 + 5x - 9}{2x - 3}$

12. $\dfrac{9x^3 + 5x - 8}{3x - 2}$

13. $\dfrac{6x^3 - 35x^2 + 4}{6x + 1}$

14. $\dfrac{4x^3 + 17x^2 + 3}{4x + 1}$

15. $\dfrac{2x^3 + 9x^2 + 5x - 9}{x + 3}$

16. $\dfrac{3x^3 + 8x^2 + x - 7}{x + 2}$

17. $\dfrac{-57 + 20t^2 - 21t}{-4t + 9}$

18. $\dfrac{-70 + 24s^2 - 38s}{-4s + 11}$

19. $\dfrac{10w^2 - 18 + 23w}{2w + 3}$

20. $\dfrac{16 + 3y - 10y^2}{5y + 1}$

Ⓒ The second polynomial is a factor of the first. Use division to help you factor the first polynomial completely.

21. $x^3 + 8;\quad x + 2$

22. $x^3 - 8;\quad x - 2$

23. $x^3 - 1;\quad x - 1$

24. $x^3 + 1;\quad x + 1$

25. $8x^3 + 1;\quad 2x + 1$

26. $27x^3 - 8;\quad 3x - 2$

27. $x^4 - 5x^2 + 6;\quad x^2 - 2$

28. $x^4 - 6x^2 + 8;\quad x^2 - 2$

29. A concrete patio is 4 feet longer than it is wide. The owner wants to double its area and increase the width by 4 feet. What must the new length be?

30. Lee Ann skates x feet per minute for $2x + 4$ minutes. Chris skates the same distance as Lee Ann but at a rate of $x + 2$ feet per minute. How many minutes does it take Chris?

31. The aquarium shown below is filled by using a jar which holds $x + 5$ cubic inches of water. How many jars of water are needed to fill the aquarium to within 5 inches of the top?

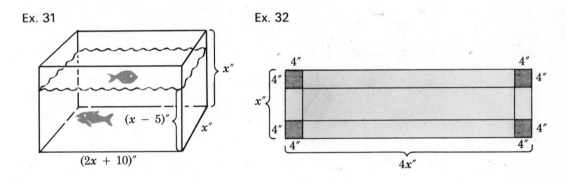

Ex. 31

x''
$(x - 5)''$
x''
$(2x + 10)''$

Ex. 32

$4''$ $4''$
$4''$ $4''$
x''
$4''$ $4''$
$4''$ $4''$
$4x''$

32. The rectangular piece of sheet metal shown above is 4 times as long as it is wide. From each corner a 4-inch square is cut, and the sheet is folded and welded to form a metal box which is open at the top. The outer surface is then covered by wood veneer strips each of which covers $4x + 16$ square inches of surface. How many of these strips are needed?

SELF-QUIZ: 10.1 to 10.5

Simplify each expression.

1. $\dfrac{5^6}{5^4}$

2. $\dfrac{(-4)^3}{(-4)^5}$

3. $\dfrac{(3r)^6}{(3r)^3}$

4. $\left(\dfrac{4}{5}\right)^3$

5. $\dfrac{42x^8}{7x^2}$

6. $\dfrac{m^5 n^7}{m^8 n^4}$

7. $\dfrac{12x^3}{16x^2}$

8. $\dfrac{-32y^2}{12y^4}$

Divide as indicated.

9. $\dfrac{3y + 9}{3}$

10. $\dfrac{4x^2 + 2x}{2x}$

11. $(10y^2 + 15y - 5) \div 5y$

12. $(16x^4 + 4x^3 - 8x^2) \div 4x^2$

13. $x + 1 \overline{)2x^2 - x - 3}$

14. $(6x^2 + 17x + 5) \div (3x + 1)$

15. $(3x^3 - 4x - 7) \div (x + 1)$

16. $(4x + 2x^3 - 7x^2 + 3) \div (2x + 1)$

When finding quotients of powers in Section 10.1, we considered three cases.

When $m = n$,
$$\frac{a^m}{a^n} = 1.$$

When $m > n$,
$$\frac{a^m}{a^n} = a^{m-n}.$$

When $m < n$,
$$\frac{a^m}{a^n} = \frac{1}{a^{n-m}}.$$

It would be simpler if we could find some way to use the second case not only when $m > n$, but also when $m = n$ and when $m < n$.

If $\frac{a^m}{a^n} = a^{m-n}$, where $a \neq 0$, is to be true	But, we already know it is true that	This suggests we should define
when $m = n$, then $\frac{a^9}{a^9} = a^{9-9} = a^0.$	$\frac{a^9}{a^9} = 1.$	a^0 as 1.
when $m < n$, then $\frac{a^3}{a^9} = a^{3-9} = a^{-6}.$	$\frac{a^3}{a^9} = \frac{1}{a^{9-3}} = \frac{1}{a^6}.$	a^{-6} as $\frac{1}{a^6}.$

Therefore, to make

$$\frac{a^m}{a^n} = a^{m-n}$$

true for *all* cases, we state the following definitions of *zero exponent* and *negative integer exponent*.

Let a be any nonzero real number, and let n be any *positive* integer.

a^0 means 1. 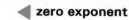 **zero exponent**

a^{-n} means $\frac{1}{a^n}$. 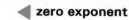 **negative integer exponent**

Notice that the preceding definitions *exclude* 0 as a base. This is necessary because division by 0 is not defined. Thus, we cannot let $0^{-n} = \frac{1}{0^n}$, and we say that

$$\boxed{0^{-n} \text{ is } \textit{not defined.}}$$

Also, we will not let $0^0 = 1$ because 0^0 can lead to division by 0 as follows.

$$0^0 = 0^{n-n}$$

$$= \frac{0^n}{0^n}$$

Thus,

$$\boxed{0^0 \text{ is } \textit{not defined.}}$$

We will continue to assume that 0 divisors are excluded, and we will also agree that values for the variables which lead to 0^0 are excluded.

Examples: For each expression, write an equivalent expression with only positive exponents. Then simplify the result.

1. $4^{-3} \cdot 5^0$ **2.** $2^{-2} \cdot 2^{-3}$ **3.** $(2 \cdot y)^{-4}$ **4.** $\dfrac{a^{-2}}{a^{-3}}$ **5.** $\left(\dfrac{3x}{y}\right)^{-2}$

SOLUTIONS:

1. $4^{-3} \cdot 5^0$

$= \dfrac{1}{4^3} \cdot 1$

$= \dfrac{1}{4^3}$

$= \dfrac{1}{64}$

2. $2^{-2} \cdot 2^{-3}$

$= \dfrac{1}{2^2} \cdot \dfrac{1}{2^3}$

$= \dfrac{1}{2^2 \cdot 2^3}$

$= \dfrac{1}{2^{2+3}}$

$= \dfrac{1}{2^5}$

$= \dfrac{1}{32}$

3. $(2 \cdot y)^{-4}$

$= \dfrac{1}{(2y)^4}$

$= \dfrac{1}{2^4 y^4}$

$= \dfrac{1}{16y^4}$

4. $\dfrac{a^{-2}}{a^{-3}} = \dfrac{\dfrac{1}{a^2}}{\dfrac{1}{a^3}}$

$\qquad = \dfrac{1}{a^2} \cdot \dfrac{a^3}{1}$

$\qquad = \dfrac{a^3}{a^2}$

$\qquad = a^{3-2} = a$

5. $\left(\dfrac{3x}{y}\right)^{-2} = \dfrac{1}{\left(\dfrac{3x}{y}\right)^2}$

$\qquad = \dfrac{1}{\dfrac{(3x)^2}{y^2}}$

$\qquad = 1 \cdot \dfrac{y^2}{(3x)^2}$

$\qquad = \dfrac{y^2}{3^2 \cdot x^2}$

$\qquad = \dfrac{y^2}{9x^2}$

EXERCISES 10.6

Ⓐ Using the definitions of zero and negative integer exponents, give the meaning of each of the following, if possible.

1. 1^0

2. 2^0

3. 16^0

4. $(1,000,000)^0$

5. 0^0

6. x^0

7. 6^{-1}

8. 6^{-2}

9. 7^{-3}

10. 8^{-4}

11. 0^{-7}

12. x^{-9}

13. $(-3)^{-2}$

14. $(-4)^{-3}$

15. $\left(\dfrac{2}{3}\right)^{-2}$

16. $\left(\dfrac{x}{y}\right)^{-3}$

Ⓑ For each given expression, write an equivalent expression which involves only positive exponents. Then simplify the result.

17. 2^{-1}

18. 3^{-1}

19. 4^{-1}

20. 5^{-1}

21. x^{-1}

22. y^{-1}

23. $\left(\dfrac{1}{2}\right)^{-1}$

24. $\left(\dfrac{1}{3}\right)^{-1}$

25. $\left(\dfrac{1}{4}\right)^{-1}$

26. $\left(\dfrac{1}{5}\right)^{-1}$

27. $\left(\dfrac{1}{x}\right)^{-1}$

28. $\left(\dfrac{1}{y}\right)^{-1}$

29. $\left(\dfrac{2}{3}\right)^{-1}$

30. $\left(\dfrac{3}{4}\right)^{-1}$

31. $\left(\dfrac{3}{2}\right)^{-1}$

32. $\left(\dfrac{4}{3}\right)^{-1}$

33. $\left(\dfrac{x}{y}\right)^{-1}$ **34.** $\left(\dfrac{y}{x}\right)^{-1}$ **35.** $(-2)^{-1}$ **36.** $(-3)^{-1}$

37. $(-4)^{-1}$ **38.** $(-5)^{-1}$ **39.** $(-x)^{-1}$ **40.** $(-y)^{-1}$

41. $\left(-\dfrac{1}{2}\right)^{-1}$ **42.** $\left(-\dfrac{1}{3}\right)^{-1}$ **43.** $\left(-\dfrac{1}{x}\right)^{-1}$ **44.** $\left(-\dfrac{1}{y}\right)^{-1}$

45. $\left(-\dfrac{2}{3}\right)^{-1}$ **46.** $\left(-\dfrac{3}{4}\right)^{-1}$ **47.** $\left(-\dfrac{x}{y}\right)^{-1}$ **48.** $\left(-\dfrac{c}{d}\right)^{-1}$

49. 2^{-2} **50.** 2^{-3} **51.** 3^{-3} **52.** 3^{-4}

53. x^{-3} **54.** r^{-6} **55.** $(-2)^{-2}$ **56.** $(-3)^{-2}$

57. $(-2)^{-3}$ **58.** $(-3)^{-3}$ **59.** $(-x)^{-2}$ **60.** $(-y)^{-4}$

61. $(-r)^{-3}$ **62.** $(-m)^{-5}$ **63.** $\left(\dfrac{1}{2}\right)^{-2}$ **64.** $\left(\dfrac{1}{3}\right)^{-2}$

65. $\dfrac{1}{a^{-5}}$ **66.** $\dfrac{1}{b^{-4}}$ **67.** $\dfrac{1}{x^{-3}}$ **68.** $\dfrac{1}{y^{-2}}$

© **69.** $2^{-2} \cdot 2^0$ **70.** $3^{-2} \cdot 3^{-3}$ **71.** $(3x)^{-2}$

72. $\dfrac{m^{-2}}{m^{-3}}$ **73.** $\left(\dfrac{2y}{3}\right)^{-2}$ **74.** $\dfrac{4^0}{4^{-2}}$

75. $3^0 \cdot 3^{-1}$ **76.** $2^{-1} \cdot 2^{-3}$ **77.** $(5y)^{-3}$

78. $\left(\dfrac{3y}{5}\right)^{-2}$ **79.** $\left(\dfrac{5^{-1}}{5^{-2}}\right)^0$ **80.** $\dfrac{m^2 m^{-3}}{m^{-2}}$

Rewrite each expression as shown in the example.

Example: $3x + 4 + \dfrac{5}{x} = 3x^1 + 4x^0 + 5x^{-1}$

81. $5x + 7 + \dfrac{3}{x}$ **82.** $4x + 3 + \dfrac{9}{x}$

83. $x - 7 + \dfrac{9}{x}$ **84.** $7 + \dfrac{2}{x} + \dfrac{3}{x^2}$

85. Are the expressions you wrote in Exercises 81–84 polynomials? Why?

In the previous section, we defined a^0 and a^{-n} so that $\dfrac{a^m}{a^n} = a^{m-n}$ holds true for all integers m and n. Also, with these definitions, the other properties of powers hold for all integer exponents (positive, negative, and zero). We will state these properties here and refer to them as the properties of integer exponents.

Let a and b be any nonzero real numbers, and let m and n be any integers.

1. $a^m \cdot a^n = a^{m+n}$ **2.** $(ab)^m = a^m b^m$

3. $\dfrac{a^m}{a^n} = a^{m-n}$ **4.** $\left(\dfrac{a}{b}\right)^n = \dfrac{a^n}{b^n}$

properties
of integer
exponents

Examples: Simplify each of the following by first using the appropriate property above. Then simplify as far as possible, using other properties.

  1. $(-4x)^0 \cdot (-4x)^{-3}$ **2.** $(wz)^{-4}$

SOLUTIONS:

  1. $(-4x)^0 \cdot (-4x)^{-3}$ **2.** $(wz)^{-4}$

$\quad = (-4x)^{0+(-3)}$ $= w^{-4}z^{-4}$

$\quad = (-4x)^{-3}$ $= \dfrac{1}{w^4} \cdot \dfrac{1}{z^4}$

$\quad = (-4)^{-3} x^{-3}$

$\quad = \dfrac{1}{(-4)^3} \cdot \dfrac{1}{x^3}$ $= \dfrac{1}{w^4 z^4}$ or $\dfrac{1}{(wz)^4}$

$\quad = \dfrac{1}{-64} \cdot \dfrac{1}{x^3}$

$\quad = -\dfrac{1}{64x^3}$

Examples: Simplify each of the following by first using the appropriate property. Then simplify as far as possible, using other properties.

3. $\dfrac{(-2r)^3}{(-2r)^{-5}}$

4. $\left(\dfrac{5m}{n}\right)^{-4}$

SOLUTIONS:

3. $\dfrac{(-2r)^3}{(-2r)^{-5}} = (-2r)^{3-(-5)}$

$\phantom{\dfrac{(-2r)^3}{(-2r)^{-5}}} = (-2r)^{3+5}$

$\phantom{\dfrac{(-2r)^3}{(-2r)^{-5}}} = (-2r)^8$

$\phantom{\dfrac{(-2r)^3}{(-2r)^{-5}}} = (-2)^8 r^8$

$\phantom{\dfrac{(-2r)^3}{(-2r)^{-5}}} = 256r^8$

4. $\left(\dfrac{5m}{n}\right)^{-4} = \dfrac{(5m)^{-4}}{n^{-4}}$

$\phantom{\left(\dfrac{5m}{n}\right)^{-4}} = \dfrac{5^{-4}m^{-4}}{n^{-4}}$

$\phantom{\left(\dfrac{5m}{n}\right)^{-4}} = \dfrac{n^4}{5^4 m^4}$

$\phantom{\left(\dfrac{5m}{n}\right)^{-4}} = \dfrac{n^4}{625m^4}$

EXERCISES 10.7

Ⓐ Simplify by using the properties of integer exponents. Your answers should contain no zero or negative exponents.

1. $2^4 \cdot 2^{-2}$

2. $(7a)^0$

3. $\left(\dfrac{1}{2}\right)^{-3}$

4. $\dfrac{3^{-5}}{3^{-5}}$

5. $\dfrac{4^{-6}}{4^{-6}}$

6. $\dfrac{5^3}{5^5}$

7. $3^{-5} \cdot 3^8$

8. $(-3)^{-2}(-3)$

9. $(-4)(-4)^{-3}$

10. $\left(\dfrac{1}{3}\right)^{-2}$

11. $\left(\dfrac{2}{3}\right)^{-3}$

12. $\left(\dfrac{3}{4}\right)^{-2}$

13. $\dfrac{4^2}{4^5}$

14. $\dfrac{5^9}{5^7}$

15. $\dfrac{3^5}{3^8}$

16. $(rs)^{-3}$

17. $(wt)^{-4}$

18. $5^{-3} \cdot 5^5$

19. $\dfrac{(-3)^4}{(-3)^7}$

20. $\dfrac{(-2)^5}{(-2)^7}$

21. $\left(\dfrac{m}{n}\right)^5$

22. $\dfrac{z^{11}}{z^{11}}$

23. $\dfrac{4^8}{4^{11}}$

24. $\left(\dfrac{s}{t}\right)^8$

Ⓑ **25.** $(2r)^{-3}(2r)^{-1}$

26. $(3s)^{-2}(3s)^{-1}$

27. $(-2w)^{-4}$

28. $(-3z)^{-3}$

29. $\dfrac{(ab)^{-8}}{(ab)^2}$

30. $\dfrac{(cd)^{-9}}{(cd)^4}$

31. $\left(\dfrac{2k}{5}\right)^{-3}$

32. $\left(\dfrac{3m}{4}\right)^{-4}$

33. $(4st)^{-4}$

34. $(5mt)^{-3}$

35. $\left(\dfrac{3xy}{4}\right)^0$

36. $\left(\dfrac{5ab}{-2}\right)^0$

37. $\dfrac{2.8 \times 10^5}{1.4 \times 10^{-2}}$

38. $\dfrac{3.4 \times 10^7}{1.7 \times 10^{-3}}$

39. $\dfrac{4.8 \times 10^{-8}}{2.4 \times 10^{-10}}$

40. $\dfrac{7.2 \times 10^{-7}}{9.0 \times 10^{-11}}$

41. $\dfrac{720x^{-3}y^{12}}{-96x^{-2}y^8}$

42. $\dfrac{560m^{-4}n^{10}}{-16m^{-11}n^3}$

43. $\dfrac{51r^2s^{-3}}{3r^{-8}s^5}$

44. $\dfrac{80a^3b^{-3}}{180a^{-3}b^3}$

45. $\dfrac{27a^3b^4c^{-2}}{810a^3b^{-1}}$

46. $\dfrac{32c^3d^{-3}}{640c^{-1}de^{-2}}$

47. $\dfrac{330x^3y^3z^2}{77(xyz)^{-2}}$

48. $\dfrac{65(rst)^{-1}}{13r^{-1}s^{-2}t^{-3}}$

Given $a < 0$, tell whether the given power is a positive or a negative number.

49. a^4 **50.** a^3 **51.** a^5 **52.** a^6

Given $a > 0$, tell whether the given power is a positive or a negative number.

53. a^{-2} **54.** a^{-3} **55.** a^{-5} **56.** a^{-4}

Ⓒ Find the solution set of each equation.

57. $\dfrac{x}{4^{-2}} = 16$

58. $\dfrac{x}{5^{-3}} = 25$

59. $\dfrac{x}{5^3} = \dfrac{1}{5^4}$

60. $\dfrac{x}{3^7} = \dfrac{1}{3^5}$

61. $\dfrac{x}{3^{-2}} = \dfrac{3^{-2}}{3^{-5}}$

62. $\dfrac{x}{4^0} = \dfrac{4^2}{4^{-2}}$

The Lost Planet Aztex

Over 16 million years ago, a planet 90 times the mass of Earth orbited the sun between Mars and Jupiter. Then it disappeared in the greatest explosion our solar system is known to have experienced. Only fragments of the lost planet Aztex still exist.

This news was announced in the summer of 1972 by the Canadian scientist Professor Michael Ovenden. He had discovered the "footprint" of the lost planet by doing mathematical calculations of the orbits of the planets. To do these gigantic calculations, Ovenden had to call on experts in England, the United States, and Mexico.

Finally, he developed a procedure which enabled him to run on a computer the entire evolution of the solar system in 10 seconds. As he ran the calculations, they only "fit together properly" if he assumed that the lost planet existed. Professor Ovenden is now using mathematics to help find out what made Aztex, the lost planet, blow up.

Scientists such as Professor Ovenden frequently use *scientific notation* in expressing very large or very small numbers. For example, the distance from the earth to the sun is often expressed as 9.3×10^7 miles. This is scientific notation for 93,000,000 miles. The diameter of a hydrogen atom is 4×10^{-9} inches in scientific notation. For other examples of numbers expressed in scientific notation (including the measures of some very interesting objects), see: Davis, Philip J., *The Lore of Large Numbers*, New York: Random House, Inc., 1961, pages 125–135.

Simplify each expression. 10.1

1. $\dfrac{4^8}{4^6}$ **2.** $\dfrac{(-3)^5}{(-3)^5}$ **3.** $\dfrac{2^3}{2^8}$ **4.** $\dfrac{(-2x)^8}{(-2x)^5}$

Simplify each quotient of monomials. 10.2

5. $\dfrac{-18r}{12r}$ **6.** $\dfrac{-32x^7}{-48x^3}$ **7.** $\dfrac{44y^4}{-11y^9}$

Simplify each quotient. 10.3

8. $\dfrac{4x + 8}{4}$ **9.** $\dfrac{3y^2 - 9y}{3y}$ **10.** $\dfrac{12s^5 + 4s^3}{4s^3}$

Find each quotient. 10.4

11. $x + 3\overline{)x^2 + 7x + 12}$ **12.** $2x - 5\overline{)6x^2 - 19x + 10}$

Find the quotient and remainder for each. 10.5

13. $(x + 6x^2 - 5) \div (3x - 4)$

14. $(1 + 6w + 28w^2) \div (-7w + 2)$

15. $(8x^3 - 1) \div (2x - 1)$

For each expression, write an equivalent expression which involves only positive exponents. Then simplify the result. 10.6

16. x^{-1} **17.** $(2)^{-3}$ **18.** $\left(\dfrac{1}{3}\right)^{-2}$ **19.** $4^{-2} \cdot 9^0$

Simplify each expression. Your answers should contain no zero or negative exponents. 10.7

20. $\dfrac{(2y)^2}{(2y)^{-3}}$ **21.** $(3x)^{-3}(3x)^{-1}$ **22.** $(-4w)^0(-4w)^{-3}$

CHAPTER SELF-TEST

Which lettered choice *best* matches each numbered item?

1. $\left(\dfrac{1}{2}\right)^3 = \dfrac{1^3}{2^3}$

2. $\dfrac{2^3}{2^2} = 2^{3-2}$

3. $5^0 = 1$

4. $3^{-2} = \dfrac{1}{3^2}$

a. division of powers

b. power of a quotient

c. multiplication of powers

d. definition of zero exponent

e. definition of negative integer exponent

Find each quotient.

5. $\dfrac{3^5}{3^3}$

6. $\dfrac{(-3)^2}{(-3)^5}$

7. $\dfrac{4^3}{4^3}$

8. $\dfrac{s^5 t^8}{s^9 t^5}$

9. $\dfrac{9x}{-3x}$

10. $\dfrac{-24r^3}{16r^2}$

11. $\dfrac{8m^8 n^3}{6m^2 n^8}$

12. $\dfrac{6x + 14}{2}$

13. $\dfrac{10s^3 - 5s^2}{5s^2}$

14. $\dfrac{9t^2 - 18t + 7}{-9}$

15. $\dfrac{12y - 9y^2 + 3y^3}{3y}$

16. $x + 3\overline{)x^2 + 8x + 15}$

17. $3x - 2\overline{)-5x + 12x^2 - 2}$

18. $3x + 1\overline{)27x^3 + 1}$

Simplify each expression.

19. 2^{-1}

20. 3^0

21. y^{-2}

22. $4^0 \cdot 6^{-2}$

23. $\left(\dfrac{1}{5}\right)^{-2}$

24. $\dfrac{w^8}{w^{-2}}$

Rational Expressions

If the train pictured above travels at a constant rate, then the distance (d) that it travels is equal to the rate (r) multiplied by the time (t).

$$d = rt$$

You have already used this idea in solving problems. Sometimes, the following variations of the formula above are used.

$$r = \frac{d}{t} \qquad\qquad t = \frac{d}{r}$$

In each case, the right side of the formula is a *rational expression*. You will work with such expressions in this chapter.

11.1 RATIONAL EXPRESSIONS DEFINED

Recall how rational numbers are related to integers.

Rational number		Integers
$\frac{2}{3}$	$=$	$2 \div 3$
$\frac{6}{12}$	$=$	$6 \div 12$
$-7 = \dfrac{-7}{1}$	$=$	$-7 \div 1$

A **rational number** is any number that can be expressed as the quotient of two *integers* (divisor not 0). In a similar way, **rational expressions** are related to *polynomials*. (A polynomial is a monomial or the sum or difference of monomials.)

Rational expression		Polynomials
$\dfrac{2x}{y}$	$=$	$2x \div y$
$\dfrac{11y}{y^2 - 4}$	$=$	$11y \div (y^2 - 4)$
$x + 7 = \dfrac{x + 7}{1}$	$=$	$(x + 7) \div 1$
$\dfrac{x^2 - 9}{x^2 + 2x - 3}$	$=$	$(x^2 - 9) \div (x^2 + 2x - 3)$

A **rational expression** is any expression that can be written as the quotient of two polynomials (divisor not 0).

By the definition above, all polynomials—even constant polynomials like -2, $\frac{3}{5}$, or 0—are also rational expressions.

Not rational expressions

$$\sqrt{y}$$

$$\frac{x}{x^2 - 2\sqrt{x}}$$

When the divisor (denominator) of a rational expression contains variables, any values that would give a 0 divisor must be excluded from the replacement sets.

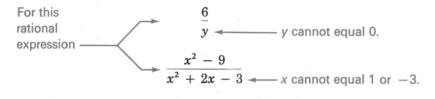

For this rational expression — $\dfrac{6}{y}$ ← y cannot equal 0.

$\dfrac{x^2 - 9}{x^2 + 2x - 3}$ ← x cannot equal 1 or -3.

You can assume that such values are automatically excluded, unless stated otherwise.

If the numerator and denominator of a rational expression are equal, then that expression is a name for 1.

$$\frac{4}{4} = 1 \qquad \frac{x + 2}{x + 2} = 1 \qquad \frac{s(s - 1)}{s^2 - s} = 1$$

Given a rational expression, you can find an equivalent rational expression by multiplying by 1 as follows.

Given rational expression		Multiply by 1		Equivalent rational expression
$\dfrac{2}{3}$	$=$	$\dfrac{2}{3} \cdot 1 = \dfrac{2}{3} \cdot \dfrac{5}{5}$	$=$	$\dfrac{10}{15}$
$\dfrac{2}{x}$	$=$	$\dfrac{2}{x} \cdot 1 = \dfrac{2}{x} \cdot \dfrac{5}{5}$	$=$	$\dfrac{10}{5x}$
$\dfrac{2}{x}$	$=$	$\dfrac{2}{x} \cdot 1 = \dfrac{2}{x} \cdot \dfrac{-3}{-3}$	$=$	$\dfrac{-6}{-3x}$
$\dfrac{y - 3}{y^2}$	$=$	$\dfrac{y - 3}{y^2} \cdot 1 = \dfrac{y - 3}{y^2} \cdot \dfrac{y}{y}$	$=$	$\dfrac{y^2 - 3y}{y^3}$

EXERCISES 11.1

Ⓐ

1. A _____ is any number that can be expressed as the quotient of two integers (divisor not 0).

2. A rational expression is any expression that can be written as _____.

Tell whether or not each expression is a rational expression.

3. $(x + 1) \div (x^2 - 4)$ **4.** $\dfrac{x + 1}{x^2 - 4}$ **5.** $(2y^2 - y + 7) \div 1$

6. $2y^2 - y + 7$ **7.** $3t^2$ **8.** $\frac{1}{2}$

9. 0.5 **10.** -3 **11.** $\sqrt{x}$

12. $\dfrac{r + 1}{0}$ **13.** $\dfrac{3\sqrt{x} + 2}{1}$ **14.** $\dfrac{y + 2}{\sqrt{y^2 - 9}}$

15. $\dfrac{x}{y}$ **16.** $\dfrac{x - 1}{y - 1}$ **17.** $\dfrac{x^2 y^3}{-2xy}$

Is the given rational expression a name for 1 ?

18. $\dfrac{-3}{-3}$ **19.** $\dfrac{-3}{3}$ **20.** $\dfrac{x - 2}{x - 2}$ **21.** $\dfrac{7x}{7 + x}$ **22.** $\dfrac{x}{y}$

Ⓑ Copy. But replace each ? so that the equation is correct for finding equivalent rational expressions.

23. $\dfrac{2}{3} = \dfrac{2}{3} \cdot \,?$ **24.** $\dfrac{2}{3} = \dfrac{2}{3} \cdot \dfrac{5}{?}$ **25.** $\dfrac{2}{3} = \dfrac{2}{3} \cdot \dfrac{?}{-3}$

26. $\dfrac{2}{3} = \dfrac{10}{?}$ **27.** $\dfrac{2}{3} = \dfrac{?}{-9}$ **28.** $\dfrac{5}{x} = \dfrac{5}{x} \cdot \,?$

29. $\dfrac{5}{x} = \dfrac{20}{?}$ **30.** $\dfrac{5}{x} = \dfrac{?}{-x}$ **31.** $\dfrac{y}{-3} = \dfrac{?}{3}$

32. $\dfrac{-2t}{-7} = \dfrac{2t}{?}$ **33.** $\dfrac{x}{y} = \dfrac{x^2}{?}$ **34.** $\dfrac{a}{b} = \dfrac{?}{ab}$

35. $\dfrac{x}{2} = \dfrac{x(\,?\,)}{2x + 6}$ **36.** $\dfrac{3}{c} = \dfrac{?}{c^2 - 2c}$

37. $\dfrac{x + 3}{x - 1} = \dfrac{?}{x^2 + x - 2}$ **38.** $\dfrac{y - 5}{y + 2} = \dfrac{y^2 - 25}{?}$

Ⓒ Which values must be excluded from the replacement set of each variable so that the denominator will not equal 0 ?

39. $\dfrac{5}{t}$ **40.** $\dfrac{3q + 2}{2q}$ **41.** $\dfrac{3m + 5}{m(m - 1)}$

42. $\dfrac{y + 2}{y^2 + y}$ **43.** $\dfrac{n}{(n - 1)(n + 3)}$ **44.** $\dfrac{8}{x^2 - 5x + 6}$

11.2 SIMPLIFYING RATIONAL EXPRESSIONS

The procedures used in simplifying rational numbers can also be used to simplify rational expressions.

Example 1: Simplify each rational expression.

a. $\dfrac{24}{36}$ **b.** $\dfrac{14r^2s^2}{21r^3s}$

SOLUTIONS:

a. $\dfrac{24}{36} = \dfrac{2^3 \cdot 3}{2^2 \cdot 3^2}$

> Completely factor both numerator and denominator.

$= \dfrac{(2^2 \cdot 3) \cdot 2}{(2^2 \cdot 3) \cdot 3}$

> Find the greatest common factor by grouping the common factors.

$= \dfrac{(2^2 \cdot 3)}{(2^2 \cdot 3)} \cdot \dfrac{2}{3}$

$= 1 \cdot \dfrac{2}{3}$

$= \dfrac{2}{3}$

b. $\dfrac{14r^2s^2}{21r^3s} = \dfrac{2 \cdot 7r^2s^2}{3 \cdot 7r^3s}$ *Another way* $\quad \dfrac{14r^2s^2}{21r^3s} = \dfrac{\overset{2}{\cancel{14}}s^{2-1}}{\underset{3}{\cancel{21}}r^{3-2}}$

$\qquad = \dfrac{(7r^2s) \cdot 2s}{(7r^2s) \cdot 3r}$

$\qquad = \dfrac{(7r^2s)}{(7r^2s)} \cdot \dfrac{2s}{3r} \qquad\qquad\qquad = \dfrac{2s}{3r}$

$\qquad = 1 \cdot \dfrac{2s}{3r}$

$\qquad = \dfrac{2s}{3r}$

A rational expression is in **simplest (or standard) form** if the greatest factor common to its numerator and denominator is 1.

Example 2: Change each rational expression to simplest form.

a. $\dfrac{2m^2 - 4m}{m^3 - 4m}$
b. $\dfrac{x^2 + 5x + 6}{x^2 - 9}$

SOLUTIONS:

a. $\dfrac{2m^2 - 4m}{m^3 - 4m} = \dfrac{2m(m - 2)}{m(m^2 - 4)}$

$\qquad\qquad = \dfrac{2m(m - 2)}{m(m + 2)(m - 2)}$

$\left.\rule{0pt}{40pt}\right\}$ Completely factor both numerator and denominator.

$\qquad\qquad = \dfrac{m(m - 2)}{m(m - 2)} \cdot \dfrac{2}{m + 2}$

Find the greatest common factor by grouping the common factors.

$\qquad\qquad = 1 \cdot \dfrac{2}{m + 2}$

$\qquad\qquad = \dfrac{2}{m + 2}$

b. $\dfrac{x^2 + 5x + 6}{x^2 - 9} = \dfrac{(x + 2)(x + 3)}{(x + 3)(x - 3)}$

$\qquad\qquad = \dfrac{x + 3}{x + 3} \cdot \dfrac{x + 2}{x - 3}$

$\qquad\qquad = 1 \cdot \dfrac{x + 2}{x - 3}$

$\qquad\qquad = \dfrac{x + 2}{x - 3}$

EXERCISES 11.2

Ⓐ Change each rational expression to simplest form.

1. $\dfrac{2 \cdot 2}{3 \cdot 2}$
2. $\dfrac{4}{6}$
3. $\dfrac{x \cdot x}{2 \cdot x}$

4. $\dfrac{x^2}{2x}$
5. $\dfrac{6t}{12st}$
6. $\dfrac{2a^2 b}{6a^2 b^2}$

7. $\dfrac{2(x + 2)}{3(x + 2)}$
8. $\dfrac{2(x + 2)}{(x + 2)^2}$
9. $\dfrac{(r - 3)^3}{3(r - 3)^2}$

10. $\dfrac{(x + 2)(x + 3)}{(x + 2)(x - 2)}$

11. $\dfrac{(m - 3)(m + 1)}{(m + 4)(m - 3)}$

12. $\dfrac{t - 1}{t^2 - 1}$

Ⓑ **13.** $\dfrac{a - 2}{a^2 - 4}$

14. $\dfrac{m + 3}{m^2 - 9}$

15. $\dfrac{4x - 4}{3x - 3}$

16. $\dfrac{5r - 10}{7r - 14}$

17. $\dfrac{x^2 - 6x + 9}{x^2 - 9}$

18. $\dfrac{y^2 + 4y + 4}{y^2 - 4}$

19. $\dfrac{3x - 6}{x^2 - 4x + 4}$

20. $\dfrac{6y + 18}{y^2 + 6y + 9}$

21. $\dfrac{m^2 - 5m}{m^2 - 6m + 5}$

22. $\dfrac{t^2 + 4t}{t^2 + 5t + 4}$

23. $\dfrac{x^2 - 3x + 2}{x^2 - 4}$

24. $\dfrac{y^2 + 5y + 6}{y^2 - 9}$

25. $\dfrac{3t^2 - 27}{6t + 12}$

26. $\dfrac{4s^2 - 64}{8s - 24}$

27. $\dfrac{m^2 - 2m + 1}{m^2 - 3m + 2}$

28. $\dfrac{n^2 + 4n + 4}{n^2 + 5n + 6}$

29. $\dfrac{x^2 + 6x + 5}{x^2 + 7x + 10}$

30. $\dfrac{y^2 + 4y + 3}{y^2 + 8y + 15}$

31. $\dfrac{s^2 - 4s - 12}{s^2 - 4}$

32. $\dfrac{t^2 - 5t - 6}{t^2 - 36}$

33. $\dfrac{x^2 + 6x + 8}{x^2 + 8x + 16}$

34. $\dfrac{y^2 - 7y + 10}{y^2 - 4y + 4}$

35. $\dfrac{m^2 - 9m + 20}{m^2 - 7m + 10}$

36. $\dfrac{n^2 - 9n + 18}{n^2 - 8n + 12}$

Ⓒ Sometimes, simplest form is defined to include listing the polynomials in the numerator and denominator in descending order and also making the leading coefficient in the denominator positive.

Example: $\dfrac{x^2 + 2x}{4 - x^2} = \dfrac{x(x + 2)}{-1(x^2 - 4)} = \dfrac{x(x + 2)}{-1(x + 2)(x - 2)}$

$$= \dfrac{x}{-1(x - 2)}$$

$$= \dfrac{-1}{-1} \cdot \dfrac{x}{-1(x - 2)} = \dfrac{-x}{x - 2}$$

Change to simplest form as in the example.

37. $\dfrac{3}{2 - x}$

38. $\dfrac{x - 2}{2 - x}$

39. $\dfrac{n^2 + n - 2}{4 - n^2}$

40. $\dfrac{2s^2 - 2}{12 + 8s - 4s^2}$

41. $\dfrac{x^3 - 7x^2 + 10x}{10 - 3x - x^2}$

42. $\dfrac{u^3 - 16u}{16 - u^2}$

11.3 MULTIPLICATION

Rational expressions are multiplied in much the same way as rational numbers. To find the product of two rational expressions, write the product of their numerators over the product of their denominators. Then express this result in simplest form.

Example 1: Find each product and express it in simplest form.

$$\text{a. } \frac{5}{6} \cdot \frac{12}{25} \qquad \text{b. } \frac{3x}{y^2} \cdot \frac{5y^3}{3x^2} \qquad \text{c. } \frac{x+1}{2x+1} \cdot \frac{2x+1}{x-1}$$

SOLUTIONS:

a. $\dfrac{5}{6} \cdot \dfrac{12}{25} = \dfrac{5 \cdot 12}{6 \cdot 25}$

Another way:

$$= \frac{5 \cdot 2^2 \cdot 3}{2 \cdot 3 \cdot 5^2} \qquad\qquad \frac{5}{6} \cdot \frac{12}{25} = \frac{5 \cdot 12}{6 \cdot 25}$$

$$= \frac{(2 \cdot 3 \cdot 5) \cdot 2}{(2 \cdot 3 \cdot 5) \cdot 5} \qquad\qquad = \frac{5 \cdot 6 \cdot 2}{6 \cdot 5 \cdot 5}$$

$$= \frac{(2 \cdot 3 \cdot 5)}{(2 \cdot 3 \cdot 5)} \cdot \frac{2}{5} \qquad\qquad = 1 \cdot \frac{2}{5}$$

$$= 1 \cdot \frac{2}{5} = \frac{2}{5} \qquad\qquad = \frac{2}{5}$$

b. $\dfrac{3x}{y^2} \cdot \dfrac{5y^3}{3x^2} = \dfrac{(3x)(5y^3)}{(y^2)(3x^2)}$

$$= \frac{(3xy^2)(5y)}{(3xy^2)(x)}$$

$$= 1 \cdot \frac{5y}{x} = \frac{5y}{x}$$

c. $\dfrac{x+1}{2x+1} \cdot \dfrac{2x+1}{x-1} = \dfrac{(x+1)(2x+1)}{(2x+1)(x-1)}$

$$= \frac{(2x+1)(x+1)}{(2x+1)(x-1)}$$

$$= 1 \cdot \frac{x+1}{x-1} = \frac{x+1}{x-1}$$

Example 2: Find the product and express it in simplest form.

$$\frac{s^2 - 2s - 3}{s^2 - 3s} \cdot \frac{s^2 + 2s}{s^2 - 4}$$

SOLUTION:

$$\frac{s^2 - 2s - 3}{s^2 - 3s} \cdot \frac{s^2 + 2s}{s^2 - 4} = \frac{(s^2 - 2s - 3)(s^2 + 2s)}{(s^2 - 3s)(s^2 - 4)}$$

$$= \frac{(s - 3)(s + 1)s(s + 2)}{s(s - 3)(s + 2)(s - 2)}$$

$$= \frac{s(s - 3)(s + 2)(s + 1)}{s(s - 3)(s + 2)(s - 2)}$$

$$= 1 \cdot \frac{s + 1}{s - 2} = \frac{s + 1}{s - 2}$$

EXERCISES 11.3

Ⓐ Find each product and express it in simplest form.

1. $\dfrac{1}{3} \cdot \dfrac{3}{5}$

2. $\dfrac{2}{3} \cdot \dfrac{5}{4}$

3. $\dfrac{5}{1} \cdot \dfrac{2}{5}$

4. $\dfrac{m}{2} \cdot \dfrac{n}{3}$

5. $\dfrac{3x}{2} \cdot \dfrac{1}{x}$

6. $\dfrac{1}{y} \cdot \dfrac{y}{x}$

7. $\dfrac{x}{y} \cdot \dfrac{x}{y}$

8. $\dfrac{x}{y} \cdot \dfrac{y}{x}$

9. $\dfrac{x}{y^2} \cdot \dfrac{y}{x^2}$

10. $\dfrac{2m}{n} \cdot \dfrac{n^2}{4m}$

11. $\dfrac{x + 2}{3} \cdot \dfrac{2}{x + 2}$

12. $\dfrac{m - 5}{5} \cdot \dfrac{m}{m - 5}$

Ⓑ **13.** $\dfrac{2m}{15n} \cdot \dfrac{5n^2}{4m}$

14. $\dfrac{5m^2}{n} \cdot \dfrac{4n}{3m}$

15. $\dfrac{3xy^2}{2x} \cdot \dfrac{8x^2}{9x^2y}$

16. $\dfrac{6s^3t}{5s^2} \cdot \dfrac{10t}{3s^2}$

17. $\dfrac{16a^2b^3}{6a} \cdot \dfrac{9ab^2}{4b^3}$

18. $\dfrac{12r^4n}{8r^2} \cdot \dfrac{5n^2}{3rn}$

19. $\dfrac{5x - 5}{3} \cdot \dfrac{9}{x - 1}$

20. $\dfrac{x - 3}{7} \cdot \dfrac{14}{x - 3}$

21. $\dfrac{a^2 - 4}{2} \cdot \dfrac{4}{a + 2}$

22. $\dfrac{12}{m - 3} \cdot \dfrac{m^2 - 9}{15}$

23. $\dfrac{t^2 - 4t}{t + 2} \cdot \dfrac{t^2 - 4}{2t - 8}$

24. $\dfrac{3s - 6}{s^2 - 9} \cdot \dfrac{s + 3}{s^2 - 2s}$

25. $\dfrac{3x + 9}{x} \cdot \dfrac{x^2}{x^2 - 9}$

26. $\dfrac{x^2}{x^2 - 16} \cdot \dfrac{4x - 16}{x}$

27. $\dfrac{4a}{3a - 12} \cdot \dfrac{5a - 20}{16a^2}$

28. $\dfrac{4b + 16}{3b^2} \cdot \dfrac{9b}{5b + 20}$

29. $\dfrac{3m - 12}{2m + 8} \cdot \dfrac{4m + 16}{6m - 24}$

30. $\dfrac{8n + 24}{2n - 6} \cdot \dfrac{3n - 9}{4n + 12}$

31. $\dfrac{m^2 - 2m + 1}{5m} \cdot \dfrac{10m^2}{m - 1}$

32. $\dfrac{y^2 + 2y + 1}{8y} \cdot \dfrac{2y}{y + 1}$

33. $\dfrac{x^2 + 4x + 4}{x - 4} \cdot \dfrac{x - 4}{3(x + 2)}$

34. $\dfrac{t + 3}{t - 3} \cdot \dfrac{t^2 - 6t + 9}{2(t + 3)}$

35. $\dfrac{m^2 - 16}{2m + 8} \cdot \dfrac{m + 4}{m^2 + 8m + 16}$

36. $\dfrac{x + 2}{x^2 - 4} \cdot \dfrac{x^2 + 4x + 4}{2x + 4}$

37. $\dfrac{(a - 2)^2}{a^2 - 4a + 4} \cdot \dfrac{a^2 - 4}{4a - 8}$

38. $\dfrac{3b - 9}{b^2 - 9} \cdot \dfrac{b^2 + 6b + 9}{(b + 3)^2}$

39. $\dfrac{x - 5}{x + 2} \cdot \dfrac{x^2 - 4}{x - 2}$

40. $\dfrac{y^2 - 16}{y + 4} \cdot \dfrac{y - 2}{y - 4}$

41. $\dfrac{a^2 + 5a + 6}{a - 1} \cdot \dfrac{a^2 - 1}{a + 3}$

42. $\dfrac{b - 2}{b^2 - 1} \cdot \dfrac{b - 1}{b^2 - 5a + 6}$

43. $\dfrac{x^2 - x - 6}{x + 3} \cdot \dfrac{x^2 + 3x}{3x - 9}$

44. $\dfrac{y^2 - 2y - 3}{y^2 - 9} \cdot \dfrac{y^2 + 4y + 3}{y^2 - 1}$

© **45.** $\dfrac{x - 3}{x + 5} \cdot \dfrac{x^2 - 25}{3 - x}$

46. $\dfrac{y^2 - 36}{7 - y} \cdot \dfrac{y - 7}{6 - y}$

47. $\dfrac{m - n}{m + n} \cdot \dfrac{m^2 + 2mn + n^2}{m^2 - 2mn + n^2} \cdot \dfrac{m^2 - n^2}{m + n}$

48. $\dfrac{a}{a - 5} \cdot \dfrac{a^2 - 6a + 5}{a^2 - 1} \cdot \dfrac{a^2 - 4a - 5}{a^2 - 5a}$

49. $\dfrac{4 - b}{b^2} \cdot \dfrac{b^2 - 16}{b^2 - 4b} \cdot \dfrac{4b^3}{16 - b^2}$

50. $\dfrac{x^2 + 7x + 12}{x^2 + 2x - 8} \cdot \dfrac{x^2 + 3x - 10}{x^2 + 8x + 15}$

As with rational numbers, the quotient of two rational expressions can be found by "inverting the divisor and multiplying."

Examples: Find each quotient and express it in simplest form.

1. $\dfrac{3}{4} \div \dfrac{15}{16}$

2. $\dfrac{m-n}{m} \div \dfrac{m+n}{m}$

3. $\dfrac{x^2-4}{x^2+2x} \div \dfrac{x^2+x-6}{2x+4}$

SOLUTIONS:

1. $\dfrac{3}{4} \div \dfrac{15}{16} = \dfrac{3}{4} \cdot \dfrac{16}{15}$

$$= \dfrac{3 \cdot 4 \cdot 4}{4 \cdot 3 \cdot 5}$$

$$= \dfrac{3 \cdot 4 \cdot 4}{3 \cdot 4 \cdot 5}$$

$$= 1 \cdot \dfrac{4}{5} = \dfrac{4}{5}$$

2. $\dfrac{m-n}{m} \div \dfrac{m+n}{m} = \dfrac{m-n}{m} \cdot \dfrac{m}{m+n}$

$$= \dfrac{m \cdot (m-n)}{m \cdot (m+n)}$$

$$= 1 \cdot \dfrac{m-n}{m+n} = \dfrac{m-n}{m+n}$$

3. $\dfrac{x^2-4}{x^2+2x} \div \dfrac{x^2+x-6}{2x+4} = \dfrac{x^2-4}{x^2+2x} \cdot \dfrac{2x+4}{x^2+x-6}$

$$= \dfrac{(x+2)(x-2)2(x+2)}{x(x+2)(x+3)(x-2)}$$

$$= \dfrac{(x+2)(x-2)2(x+2)}{(x+2)(x-2)x(x+3)}$$

$$= 1 \cdot \dfrac{2(x+2)}{x(x+3)} = \dfrac{2x+4}{x^2+3x}$$

EXERCISES 11.4

Ⓐ By what should each ? be replaced?

1. $\dfrac{3}{4} \div \dfrac{3}{5} = \dfrac{3}{4} \cdot \,?$

2. $\dfrac{x^3 y}{5x} \div \dfrac{2x}{x^2 y^2} = \dfrac{x^3 y}{5x} \cdot \,?$

3. $\dfrac{x+6}{6} \div \dfrac{x}{3} = \dfrac{x+6}{6} \cdot \,?$

4. $\dfrac{s^2-4}{s^2-3s} \div \dfrac{s^2+4s+4}{s-3} = \dfrac{s^2-4}{s^2-3s} \cdot \,?$

Find each quotient and express it in simplest form.

5. $\dfrac{2}{5} \div \dfrac{3}{5}$

6. $\dfrac{6}{a} \div \dfrac{6}{b}$

7. $\dfrac{3}{x} \div \dfrac{7}{x}$

8. $\dfrac{mn}{3} \div \dfrac{mn}{5}$

9. $\dfrac{x+3}{x} \div \dfrac{x+3}{3}$

10. $\dfrac{y}{y-1} \div \dfrac{5}{y-1}$

Ⓑ 11. $\dfrac{n-7}{n+7} \div \dfrac{n+2}{n+7}$

12. $\dfrac{x+3}{x-5} \div \dfrac{x+3}{x+6}$

13. $\dfrac{x^2-4}{x} \div \dfrac{x+2}{x}$

14. $\dfrac{x-2}{x} \div \dfrac{x^2-2x}{x}$

15. $\dfrac{m^2-4}{m^2-9} \div \dfrac{m-2}{m-3}$

16. $\dfrac{x^2-16}{x^2-25} \div \dfrac{x+4}{x+5}$

17. $\dfrac{r^2-25}{r^2+5r} \div \dfrac{r-5}{1}$

18. $\dfrac{t^2-16}{t^2-4t} \div \dfrac{t+4}{1}$

19. $\dfrac{x^2-2x+1}{x+1} \div (x-1)$

20. $\dfrac{y^2-4y+4}{y+2} \div (y-2)$

21. $\dfrac{x^2-9}{x+2} \div \dfrac{x^2+6x+9}{2x+4}$

22. $\dfrac{m^2-4}{m-2} \div \dfrac{m^2-4m+4}{3m-6}$

23. $\dfrac{x^2-x-12}{x^2-9} \div \dfrac{3x-12}{x+3}$

24. $\dfrac{y^2-2y-15}{y^2-9} \div \dfrac{2y-10}{y+3}$

25. $\dfrac{m^2+8m+16}{m+4} \div \dfrac{m^2-16}{m-4}$

26. $\dfrac{x^2-6x+9}{x-3} \div \dfrac{x^2-9}{x+3}$

27. $\dfrac{3x}{x^2 + 6x + 9} \div \dfrac{6x^2}{x^2 + 3x}$

28. $\dfrac{10y^2}{y^2 + 5y} \div \dfrac{2y}{y^2 + 10y + 25}$

29. $\dfrac{a - 5}{a^2 + 3a - 10} \div \dfrac{5a - 25}{a^2 - 2a}$

30. $\dfrac{7b - 21}{b^2 - 4b} \div \dfrac{b - 3}{b^2 - 6b + 8}$

31. $\dfrac{m^2 + 2m}{4m - 5} \div \dfrac{2m^2 + 4m}{16m - 20}$

32. $\dfrac{x^2 - 3x}{3x + 7} \div \dfrac{2x^3 - 6x^2}{9x + 21}$

© **33.** $\dfrac{x + 2}{x^2 + x - 6} \div \dfrac{x^2 - 4}{2 - x}$

34. $\dfrac{r^2 - 3r}{9 - r^2} \div \dfrac{r}{3 + r}$

35. $\dfrac{\frac{x - 2}{3}}{\frac{x^2 - 4}{5}}$

36. $\dfrac{\frac{y + 3}{5}}{\frac{y^2 - 9}{10}}$

37. $\dfrac{\frac{x^2 - y^2}{12}}{\frac{x + y}{4}}$

The speed of an object on a rotating wheel or sphere is the circumference of the circle on which it travels divided by the time required for one full rotation; that is, speed $= \dfrac{2\pi r}{t}$.

38. A merry-go-round makes a full rotation in $\frac{1}{3}$ minute. Find Tanya's speed (in feet per minute) if she is 24 feet from the center. Use $\frac{22}{7}$ for π.

39. For the merry-go-round in Exercise 38, find Cindy's speed if she is 12 feet from the center.

40. Using division, show that Tanya's speed (Exercise 38) is 2 times Cindy's speed (Exercise 39).

41. Find $\dfrac{2\pi r_1}{t} \div \dfrac{2\pi r_2}{t}$. Use the result to show that Tanya's speed is 2 times Cindy's speed.

42. Show that, due to the earth's rotation, the speed of a person at the equator ($r_1 \approx 3963$ miles) is about 1.4 times that of a person in Minneapolis ($r_2 \approx 2802$ miles).

11.5 ADDITION AND SUBTRACTION

To add or subtract rational expressions with the same denominator, add (or subtract) the numerators, writing this result over the common denominator. Then, if necessary, express in simplest form.

Examples: Find each sum or difference and express it in simplest form.

1. $\dfrac{3m + 1}{3} + \dfrac{2}{3}$

2. $\dfrac{x^2 + 3x}{x^2 - 1} - \dfrac{x - 1}{x^2 - 1}$

SOLUTIONS:

1.
$$\dfrac{3m + 1}{3} + \dfrac{2}{3} = \dfrac{(3m + 1) + 2}{3}$$

$$= \dfrac{3m + (1 + 2)}{3}$$ First, add.

$$= \dfrac{3m + 3}{3}$$

$$= \dfrac{3(m + 1)}{3 \cdot 1}$$ Then, if necessary, express in simplest form.

$$= 1 \cdot \dfrac{m + 1}{1} = m + 1$$

2.
$$\dfrac{x^2 + 3x}{x^2 - 1} - \dfrac{x - 1}{x^2 - 1} = \dfrac{x^2 + 3x - (x - 1)}{x^2 - 1}$$ Be sure you subtract the entire numerator.

$$= \dfrac{x^2 + 3x - x + 1}{x^2 - 1}$$

$$= \dfrac{x^2 + 2x + 1}{x^2 - 1}$$

$$= \dfrac{(x + 1)(x + 1)}{(x + 1)(x - 1)}$$

$$= 1 \cdot \dfrac{x + 1}{x - 1} = \dfrac{x + 1}{x - 1}$$

EXERCISES 11.5

Ⓐ Find each sum or difference and express it in simplest form.

1. $\dfrac{2}{7} + \dfrac{3}{7}$

2. $\dfrac{3}{4} - \dfrac{1}{4}$

3. $\dfrac{2}{x} + \dfrac{3}{x}$

4. $\dfrac{3a}{4} - \dfrac{a}{4}$

5. $\dfrac{2x}{4y} - \dfrac{x}{4y}$

6. $\dfrac{5}{m} - \dfrac{5}{m}$

7. $\dfrac{m+2}{m} + \dfrac{3}{m}$

8. $\dfrac{t+3}{2t} + \dfrac{t+5}{2t}$

Ⓑ **9.** $\dfrac{x}{x^2-1} - \dfrac{1}{x^2-1}$

10. $\dfrac{y}{y^2-1} + \dfrac{1}{y^2-1}$

11. $\dfrac{a^2}{a^2-4} - \dfrac{4}{a^2-4}$

12. $\dfrac{b^2-2}{b^2-1} + \dfrac{1}{b^2-1}$

13. $\dfrac{3m+2}{m+2} + \dfrac{m+6}{m+2}$

14. $\dfrac{5n+3}{2n+3} - \dfrac{n-3}{2n+3}$

15. $\dfrac{5x}{x-6} - \dfrac{3x}{x-6}$

16. $\dfrac{3y}{y+7} - \dfrac{5y}{y+7}$

17. $\dfrac{m^2+m}{m+3} - \dfrac{m^2-3}{m+3}$

18. $\dfrac{n^2+2n}{n-4} - \dfrac{n^2+8}{n-4}$

19. $\dfrac{x^2+2x}{x-2} + \dfrac{-3x-2}{x-2}$

20. $\dfrac{y^2-3y}{y+1} + \dfrac{2y-2}{y+1}$

21. $\dfrac{2m^2+2m}{m-3} - \dfrac{m^2+2m+9}{m-3}$

22. $\dfrac{5n^2-6n}{n-3} - \dfrac{4n^2-9}{n-3}$

23. $\dfrac{x^2-2x}{x-4} + \dfrac{16-6x}{x-4}$

24. $\dfrac{25-5y}{y-5} + \dfrac{y^2-5y}{y-5}$

25. $\dfrac{mn}{(m+n)^2} + \dfrac{n^2}{(m+n)^2}$

26. $\dfrac{x^2}{(x-y)^2} - \dfrac{xy}{(x-y)^2}$

27. $\dfrac{3x-2}{x^2+5x+6} - \dfrac{2x-5}{x^2+5x+6}$

28. $\dfrac{2r^2-7}{2r^2-8} + \dfrac{2r-5}{2r^2-8}$

Ⓒ **29.** $\dfrac{5m}{m^2-n^2} - \dfrac{2m+4n}{m^2-n^2} - \dfrac{2m-3n}{m^2-n^2}$

30. $\dfrac{x+7}{x^2-x-6} + \dfrac{x+3}{x^2-x-6} - \dfrac{x+13}{x^2-x-6}$

To add (or subtract) rational expressions with different denominators, we can first change them to equivalent expressions with the same denominator, preferably the least common denominator (LCD). Then we can proceed as in Section 11.5.

Examples: Find each sum and express it in simplest form.

1. $\dfrac{3}{5x^2} + \dfrac{7}{10x}$ 2. $\dfrac{3}{2n + 4} + \dfrac{3}{n^2 + 2n}$

SOLUTIONS:

1. $\dfrac{3}{5x^2} + \dfrac{7}{10x} = \dfrac{3}{5x^2} + \dfrac{7}{2 \cdot 5x}$

> Completely factor each denominator. Then choose the *greatest* power of each factor.

LCD is $2 \cdot 5 \cdot x^2$.

$= \dfrac{2 \cdot 3}{2 \cdot 5x^2} + \dfrac{7 \cdot x}{2 \cdot 5x \cdot x}$

> Multiply the numerator and the denominator of each rational expression by those factors that are in the LCD but not in the given denominator.

$= \dfrac{6}{2 \cdot 5 \cdot x^2} + \dfrac{7x}{2 \cdot 5 \cdot x^2}$

$= \dfrac{6 + 7x}{2 \cdot 5 \cdot x^2}$

$= \dfrac{7x + 6}{10x^2}$

> Since neither 2, 5, nor x is a *factor* of $7x + 6$, the result is in simplest form.

2. $\dfrac{3}{2n + 4} + \dfrac{3}{n^2 + 2n} = \dfrac{3}{2(n + 2)} + \dfrac{3}{n(n + 2)}$ LCD is $2n(n + 2)$.

$= \dfrac{3n}{2(n + 2)n} + \dfrac{2 \cdot 3}{2 \cdot n(n + 2)}$

$= \dfrac{3n}{2n(n + 2)} + \dfrac{6}{2n(n + 2)}$

$= \dfrac{3n + 6}{2n(n + 2)}$

$= \dfrac{3(n + 2)}{2n(n + 2)} = \dfrac{3}{2n}$

Example 3: Find the difference and express it in simplest form.

$$\frac{2x}{x^2 - 4} - \frac{1}{x - 2}$$

SOLUTION:

$$\frac{2x}{x^2 - 4} - \frac{1}{x - 2} = \frac{2x}{(x + 2)(x - 2)} - \frac{1}{x - 2} \quad \begin{array}{l} \text{LCD is} \\ \longrightarrow (x + 2)(x - 2). \end{array}$$

$$= \frac{2x}{(x + 2)(x - 2)} - \frac{(x + 2) \cdot 1}{(x + 2)(x - 2)}$$

$$= \frac{2x - (x + 2)}{(x + 2)(x - 2)} \longleftarrow \begin{array}{l} \text{Be sure you} \\ \text{subtract the} \\ \text{entire numerator.} \end{array}$$

$$= \frac{2x - x - 2}{(x + 2)(x - 2)} \longleftarrow$$

$$= \frac{x - 2}{(x + 2)(x - 2)}$$

$$= \frac{(x - 2) \cdot 1}{(x - 2)(x + 2)} = \frac{1}{x + 2}$$

EXERCISES 11.6

Ⓐ What is the LCD in each exercise?

1. $\dfrac{2}{3} - \dfrac{1}{6}$

2. $\dfrac{1}{4} + \dfrac{1}{6}$

3. $\dfrac{1}{x} + \dfrac{1}{2x}$

4. $\dfrac{5}{x^2} + \dfrac{2}{x}$

5. $\dfrac{2}{3y} + \dfrac{5}{6y}$

6. $\dfrac{9}{10y^2} - \dfrac{2}{5y^2}$

7. $\dfrac{3}{2b} - \dfrac{3}{ab^2}$

8. $\dfrac{2}{5t} - \dfrac{t + 1}{t^2}$

9. $\dfrac{2}{y - 2} - \dfrac{1}{y + 2}$

10. $\dfrac{5}{2(x - 1)} - \dfrac{3}{2(x + 1)}$

Ⓑ **11–20.** Find each sum or difference in Exercises 1–10 and express it in simplest form.

Find each sum or difference and express it in simplest form.

21. $\dfrac{m}{n} - \dfrac{n}{m}$

22. $\dfrac{x}{y} + \dfrac{2y}{3x}$

23. $\dfrac{m+2}{3} + \dfrac{m-1}{6}$

24. $\dfrac{x-3}{6} - \dfrac{x-1}{10}$

25. $\dfrac{3}{m^2+m} + \dfrac{3}{m+1}$

26. $\dfrac{5}{t-1} - \dfrac{5}{t^2-t}$

27. $\dfrac{3a}{(a-3)^2} - \dfrac{2}{a-3}$

28. $\dfrac{3}{a+2} + \dfrac{a}{(a+2)^2}$

29. $\dfrac{y+1}{y-5} + \dfrac{y}{2y-10}$

30. $\dfrac{5m+6}{3m+9} - \dfrac{m}{m+3}$

31. $\dfrac{4x}{x^2-16} - \dfrac{2}{x+4}$

32. $\dfrac{-18}{y^2-9} + \dfrac{3}{y-3}$

33. $\dfrac{5}{a-2} + \dfrac{3}{a^2-4a+4}$

34. $\dfrac{m}{m+1} - \dfrac{2}{m^2+2m+1}$

35. $\dfrac{2}{1} + \dfrac{3}{x-4}$

36. $\dfrac{4}{1} - \dfrac{5}{y-2}$

37. $m - \dfrac{3m}{m-2}$

38. $n - \dfrac{4n}{n-5}$

39. $\dfrac{n}{n^2-9} - \dfrac{1}{2n-6}$

40. $\dfrac{m}{m^2-16} + \dfrac{2}{3m-12}$

41. $\dfrac{x^2+3x+3}{x^2+5x+6} + \dfrac{3}{x+3}$

42. $\dfrac{y^2+4y-5}{y^2-2y-3} - \dfrac{2}{y+1}$

© 43. $\dfrac{4}{x-2} + \dfrac{3}{2-x}$

44. $\dfrac{3}{7-x} - \dfrac{4}{x-7}$

45. $\dfrac{2}{x} + \dfrac{3}{y} + \dfrac{4}{z}$

46. $\dfrac{5}{m} - \dfrac{3}{n} + \dfrac{4}{p}$

47. $\dfrac{5}{x^2-2x+1} + \dfrac{3}{x+1} - \dfrac{4}{x-1}$

The given expression is a rational expression. True or False?

1. $\dfrac{3}{7}$

2. $x^2 + x$

3. $\dfrac{1}{\sqrt{x}}$

4. $\dfrac{n}{n+1}$

Copy. But replace each ? so that the equation is correct for finding equivalent rational expressions.

5. $\dfrac{x}{y^2} = \dfrac{xy}{?}$

6. $\dfrac{a}{3} = \dfrac{?}{3a-6}$

Change each rational expression to simplest form.

7. $\dfrac{24a^2}{36ab}$

8. $\dfrac{x(x-2)}{x^2-4x+4}$

9. $\dfrac{2t^2-8}{2t+4}$

Compute as indicated. Express each result in simplest form.

10. $\dfrac{3y}{2} \cdot \dfrac{12x}{y}$

11. $\dfrac{5r+15}{2r-6} \cdot \dfrac{3r-9}{r+3}$

12. $\dfrac{x^2-x-6}{x^2-4} \div \dfrac{x-3}{x-2}$

13. $\dfrac{12a^2}{a^2+3a} \div \dfrac{2a}{a^2+6a+9}$

14. $\dfrac{4s}{s+3} + \dfrac{12}{s+3}$

15. $\dfrac{7m+3}{4m} - \dfrac{5m+3}{4m}$

16. $\dfrac{5}{3y-9} + \dfrac{3}{y-3}$

17. $\dfrac{a^2-5a+19}{a^2-3a-4} - \dfrac{3}{a-4}$

11.7 RATIONAL EXPRESSIONS IN EQUATIONS

A rational expression may occur as part of an equation. Such an equation can be solved by using the properties of equality along with the properties of rational expressions.

Example 1: Solve $2 - \dfrac{1}{x} = \dfrac{5}{x}$.

SOLUTION: $2 - \dfrac{1}{x} = \dfrac{5}{x}$ Find LCD. (In this case, it is x.)

$x\left(2 - \dfrac{1}{x}\right) = x \cdot \dfrac{5}{x}$ Mult. prop. of =, using LCD.

$2x - 1 = 5$

$2x = 6$

$x = 3$

Check: $2 - \dfrac{1}{3} = \dfrac{5}{3}$

$\dfrac{6}{3} - \dfrac{1}{3} = \dfrac{5}{3}$

$\dfrac{5}{3} = \dfrac{5}{3}$ T   Thus, $x = 3$.

In solving the equation above, we multiplied both sides by an expression containing a variable. This process might introduce apparent solutions (called *extraneous roots*), which are not really solutions. Extraneous roots can be eliminated by checking.

Example 2: Solve $\dfrac{x}{x-3} + 2 = \dfrac{3}{x-3}$.

SOLUTION: $\dfrac{x}{x-3} + 2 = \dfrac{3}{x-3}$ ⟶ LCD is $(x-3)$.

$(x-3)\left(\dfrac{x}{x-3} + 2\right) = (x-3)\dfrac{3}{x-3}$

$x + (x-3)2 = 3$

$x + 2x - 6 = 3$

$3x = 9$

$x = 3$

Check: $\dfrac{3}{3-3} + 2 = \dfrac{3}{3-3}$

$$\tfrac{3}{0} + 2 = \tfrac{3}{0}$$

Since division by 0 is not defined, 3 is an extraneous root. Thus, the solution set is { }.

You could also have excluded 3 as a possible solution by noting that, in the given equation, 3 must be excluded from the replacement set of x to avoid a 0 divisor.

Example 3: Solve $\dfrac{5}{y+3} = \dfrac{3}{y-1}$.

SOLUTION:

$$\dfrac{5}{y+3} = \dfrac{3}{y-1} \qquad\longrightarrow\qquad \begin{array}{l}\text{LCD is}\\ (y+3)(y-1).\end{array}$$

$$(y+3)(y-1)\dfrac{5}{y+3} = (y+3)(y-1)\dfrac{3}{y-1}$$

$$(y-1)5 = (y+3)3$$

$$5y - 5 = 3y + 9$$

$$2y = 14$$

$$y = 7$$

Check: $\dfrac{5}{7+3} = \dfrac{3}{7-1}$

$$\tfrac{5}{10} = \tfrac{3}{6}$$

$$\tfrac{1}{2} = \tfrac{1}{2} \quad \textsf{T} \qquad \text{Thus, } y = 7.$$

In Example **3**, each side of the given equation is a fraction. For such equations, we can use a shortcut. The second step can be omitted, and the third step can be found from the first by "cross-multiplying."

$$\dfrac{5}{y+3} \diagdown\!\!\!\!\diagup \dfrac{3}{y-1}$$

That is, we can multiply the numerator of each side by the denominator of the other.

EXERCISES 11.7

Ⓐ What is the LCD in each case?

1. $\dfrac{8}{c} = 4$

2. $\dfrac{12}{y} = 4$

3. $\dfrac{7}{3y} = \dfrac{1}{3}$

4. $\dfrac{15}{3x} = \dfrac{-1}{6}$

5. $\dfrac{2}{3x} = \dfrac{1}{9}$

6. $\dfrac{1}{m} = \dfrac{1}{12}$

7. $\dfrac{m}{3} = \dfrac{1}{2}$

8. $\dfrac{x}{4} = \dfrac{3}{2}$

9. $\dfrac{3}{x + 2} = 3$

10. $2 = \dfrac{4}{y - 3}$

11. $\dfrac{2}{x} + 4 = \dfrac{2}{x}$

12. $\dfrac{3}{y} - 2 = \dfrac{3}{y}$

13. $\dfrac{x}{2} - \dfrac{x}{3} = 8$

14. $\dfrac{n}{6} + \dfrac{n}{4} = 5$

15. $\dfrac{4}{y} + \dfrac{3}{2y} = \dfrac{11}{2}$

16. $\dfrac{3}{x} - \dfrac{2}{3x} = \dfrac{14}{3}$

17. $\dfrac{5}{x} = \dfrac{7}{x - 4}$

18. $\dfrac{3}{y} = \dfrac{2}{y - 5}$

19. $\dfrac{2x}{x + 1} + \dfrac{3}{x} = 2$

20. $\dfrac{2}{m} + \dfrac{5m}{m + 1} = 5$

Ⓑ **21–40.** Solve each equation given in Exercises 1–20. (Be sure to check each solution.)

Solve each equation.

41. $\dfrac{-x}{x - 2} + \dfrac{x}{x - 2} - 2 = 0$

42. $\dfrac{3}{y - 3} - \dfrac{y}{y - 3} - 5 = 0$

43. $\dfrac{m - 2}{m - 5} = \dfrac{m - 3}{m + 5}$

44. $\dfrac{n + 4}{n - 2} = \dfrac{n + 5}{n - 3}$

45. $\dfrac{1 - y}{1 + y} = \dfrac{2}{3}$

46. $\dfrac{1 + z}{3 - z} = \dfrac{3}{5}$

47. $\dfrac{7}{5m - 2} = \dfrac{3}{2m}$

48. $\dfrac{1}{3n + 5} = \dfrac{-2}{49}$

49. $\dfrac{5}{x + 5} = \dfrac{3}{x + 7}$

50. $\dfrac{7}{x} = \dfrac{2}{x + 5}$

51. $\dfrac{m - 2}{m + 1} = \dfrac{m + 1}{m - 2}$

52. $\dfrac{n + 3}{n + 2} = \dfrac{n + 2}{n + 3}$

53. $\dfrac{x - 2}{x + 2} = \dfrac{x - 4}{x + 4}$

54. $\dfrac{y - 2}{y - 5} = \dfrac{y + 3}{y + 5}$

55. $\dfrac{x - 4}{x + 4} - \dfrac{x + 4}{x - 4} = 0$

56. $\dfrac{1 - x}{1 + x} - 1 = \dfrac{2}{1 + x}$

57. $\dfrac{3}{y - 1} - 2 = \dfrac{5 - 2y}{y + 1}$

58. $\dfrac{8}{x - 3} - 3 = \dfrac{2 - 3x}{x + 3}$

© **59.** $\dfrac{3x^2 - 10}{2x^2 - 5x} - 1 = \dfrac{x}{2x - 5}$

60. $\dfrac{7y^2 + 8}{3y^2 - 4y} - 2 = \dfrac{y}{3y - 4}$

61. $\dfrac{4}{x - 2} - \dfrac{2x - 3}{x^2 - 4} = \dfrac{5}{x + 2}$

62. $\dfrac{5}{x + 3} - \dfrac{3}{x - 3} = \dfrac{3x - 1}{x^2 - 9}$

The following equations result in equations that can be solved by factoring as in Section 7.7. Solve, and be sure to check each solution.

63. $4m - 3 = \dfrac{m + 13}{m + 1}$

64. $5n - 4 = \dfrac{n - 8}{n - 3}$

65. $4m - \dfrac{2m - 4}{m + 2} - 2 = 0$

66. $\dfrac{x^2 - 4}{x + 3} = 2 - \dfrac{x - 2}{x + 3}$

67. $\dfrac{3x - 5}{x^2 + 4x + 3} + \dfrac{2x + 2}{x + 3} = \dfrac{x - 3}{x + 1}$

68. $\dfrac{x - 10}{5} - \dfrac{x - 10}{3x} = 0$

Using Rational Expressions

To find a defect in a telephone or telegraph line, a repair crew might use the formula below.

$$\frac{x}{2l - x} = \frac{r_1}{r_2}$$

Here's how the formula works. From the way telephone (or telegraph) service has been affected, the repair crew has a general idea of where the fault is located. They connect the faulty wire to a good wire at point B.

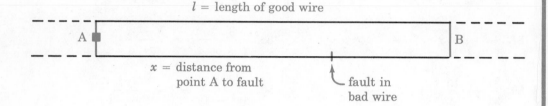

l = length of good wire

A   B

x = distance from point A to fault

fault in bad wire

At point A, they connect the two wires with testing equipment that gives two readings—the values for r_1 and r_2 in the formula. These readings are resistances to a current sent through the wires by the testing equipment, and they are given in units called *ohms*.

The length l is found by measuring the distance between points A and B.

For example, the repair crew might find that $r_1 = 500$ ohms, $r_2 = 1000$ ohms, and $l = 50$ miles. Substituting in the formula gives

$$\frac{x}{2 \cdot 50 - x} = \frac{500}{1000}.$$

1. Solve the equation above to find how far the fault is from point A.

2. Find the distance from point A to the fault if $r_1 = 250$ ohms, $r_2 = 750$ ohms, and $l = 55$ miles.

The preceding is just one example of the use of rational expressions. They occur frequently in many activities. One of these is sports.

Baseball

$$\text{Batting average} = \frac{H}{A_b} \qquad \text{where} \begin{cases} H = \text{hits} \\ A_b = \text{times at bat} \end{cases}$$

$$\text{Fielding average} = \frac{C - E}{C} \qquad \text{where} \begin{cases} C = \text{fielding chances} \\ E = \text{errors} \end{cases}$$

Basketball

$$\text{Free-throw percentage} = \frac{P}{F} \qquad \text{where} \begin{cases} P = \text{free throws made} \\ F = \text{free throws shot} \end{cases}$$

Averages or percentages like those above are computed to the nearest thousandth. Solve each problem.

3. Find the fielding average of a baseball player who made 3 errors in 50 fielding chances.

4. A baseball player can expect to have 250 times at bat. How many hits does the player need to have a batting average of 0.300?

5. A basketball player made 9 free throws and had a free-throw percentage of 0.750. How many free throws did the player shoot?

11.8 SOLVING PROBLEMS

Time is involved in all the problems in this section. These problems can, however, be grouped into two different types.

The first type involves this idea:

(rate of travel) × (time) = (distance traveled).

The second type makes use of a similar idea:

(rate of work) × (time) = (work produced).

Example 1: A nurse can do the morning rounds of a certain hospital wing in 20 minutes. It takes a student nurse 30 minutes to do the same rounds. How long will it take them if they both work at these rounds?

SOLUTION: Since the nurse can do the complete task in 20 minutes, she can do $\frac{1}{20}$ of the task in one minute. So, her rate of work is $\frac{1}{20}$ of the rounds per minute.

The rate of work of the student nurse is $\frac{1}{30}$ of the rounds per minute.

Let t = time (in minutes) required by both working together.

A table is often helpful.

	Rate of work	×	Time	=	Work produced
Nurse	$\frac{1}{20}$		t		$\frac{t}{20}$
Student nurse	$\frac{1}{30}$		t		$\frac{t}{30}$

Time is the same for each person since they are working together.

The sum of these is the work produced by both working together.

The work produced by both persons will be 1 set of rounds completed. So,

$$\frac{t}{20} + \frac{t}{30} = 1 \qquad \text{LCD is 60.}$$

$$60\left(\frac{t}{20} + \frac{t}{30}\right) = 60 \cdot 1$$

$$3t + 2t = 60$$

$$5t = 60$$

$$t = 12 \qquad \text{Check.}$$

Thus, together, they can complete the rounds in 12 minutes.

Example 2: On a fishing trip, Joan and her father rented a small boat with a battery-powered motor. The top speed of the boat in still water is 3 miles per hour. At top speed, an 8-mile trip downstream took the same amount of time as a 2-mile trip upstream. What is the rate of the current?

SOLUTION: Since (rate) × (time) = (distance),

(distance) ÷ (rate) = (time).

Let c = rate of current in miles per hour.

	Distance	÷ Rate	= Time
Downstream (with current)	8	$3 + c$	$\dfrac{8}{3 + c}$
Upstream (against current)	2	$3 - c$	$\dfrac{2}{3 - c}$

$$\frac{8}{3 + c} = \frac{2}{3 - c} \qquad \blacktriangleleft \text{ The problem says the times are equal.}$$

$$8(3 - c) = 2(3 + c)$$

$$24 - 8c = 6 + 2c$$

$$18 = 10c$$

$$c = \tfrac{18}{10} = \tfrac{9}{5} \text{ or } 1\tfrac{4}{5} \qquad \text{Check.}$$

Thus, the rate of the current is $1\tfrac{4}{5}$ miles per hour.

EXERCISES 11.8

Ⓐ Answer Exercises 1–5 by referring to the problem in Exercise 9, below.

1. What is Dori's rate of work per hour? (That is, how much of the car can she do in one hour?)

2. What is her brother's rate of work per hour?

3. Let t be the number of hours it takes them to wash and polish the car together. What expression will represent the work produced by Dori? By her brother?

4. What equation can be used to solve this problem?

5. Discuss what the following statement means: In solving "work" problems like Exercise 9, we must assume that in working together, the individuals can continue to work at their same rates.

Answer Exercises 6–8 by referring to the problem in Exercise 10, below.

6. Let w = speed of wind. Tell how to complete the table.

	Distance	÷	Rate	=	Time
With wind					
Against wind					

7. What equation can we use to solve this problem?

8. In solving a problem like Exercise 10, what do we assume about the speed of the wind?

Ⓑ Solve each problem.

9. Dori can wash and polish the family car in 2 hours, and her brother can do it in 3 hours. How long will it take them, working together?

10. The cruising speed of a certain airplane is 180 miles per hour in still air. At cruising speed, the plane flew 500 miles with the wind in the same amount of time it took to fly 400 miles back (against the wind). What is the speed of the wind?

11. At top speed, a motorboat traveled 35 miles downstream in the same amount of time it took to return 25 miles upstream. The top speed of the boat in still water is 30 miles per hour. What is the speed of the current?

12. Dr. Tolski, a chemist, can do a certain set of experiments in 4 hours. Her laboratory assistant can do it in 6 hours. How long will it take them, working together?

13. With a large tractor, a field can be plowed in 8 hours. It takes 14 hours to plow the field with a smaller tractor. How long will it take using both tractors?

14. A tugboat on the Mississippi River traveled 160 miles downstream in the same amount of time it took to return 40 miles upstream. The rate of the current is 6 miles per hour. What is the speed of the boat in still water?

15. With one pipe, a railroad tank car can be filled in 12 hours. Another pipe can fill it in 16 hours. How long will it take to fill the car using both pipes?

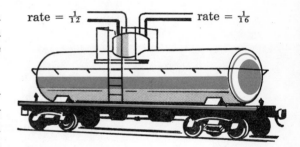

rate = $\frac{1}{12}$ rate = $\frac{1}{16}$

16. A water-storage tank can be filled by one pump in 4 hours and emptied by another pump in 8 hours. How long will it take to fill an empty tank if both pumps are operating?

17. With two printing presses, the morning edition of the *Times* can be printed in 5 hours. The faster of the two presses can print the edition in 7 hours. How long would the slower press need?

18. Two tank trucks can fuel a jet in 12 minutes. The truck that fuels slower can fuel the jet in 30 minutes. How long would the truck that fuels faster need?

19. A tank can be filled by one pump in 14 minutes and by another pump in 28 minutes. A third pump can empty the tank in 21 minutes. How long will it take to fill an empty tank if all three pumps are operating?

20. Solve Exercise 19 if the second pump is shut off after 5 minutes.

11.9 FORMULAS

Equations which involve rational expressions may contain more than one variable. This happens often in formulas. Sometimes, it is convenient to solve such an equation for one of the variables.

Example 1: Solve $\dfrac{3}{2x} - 3 = \dfrac{1}{5y}$ for y.

SOLUTION: $\dfrac{3}{2x} - 3 = \dfrac{1}{5y}$ LCD is $10xy$.

$$10xy\left(\frac{3}{2x} - 3\right) = 10xy\left(\frac{1}{5y}\right)$$

$$15y - 30xy = 2x$$

$$(15 - 30x)y = 2x$$

$$y = \frac{2x}{15 - 30x}$$

Example 2: Solve $TA = \dfrac{2R}{R - r}$ for R. (This formula is used when working with pulleys.)

SOLUTION: $\dfrac{TA}{1} = \dfrac{2R}{R - r}$

$$TA(R - r) = 1 \cdot 2R$$

$$RTA - rTA = 2R$$

$$RTA - 2R = rTA$$

$$R(TA - 2) = rTA$$

$$R = \frac{rTA}{TA - 2}$$

EXERCISES 11.9

Ⓐ 1. In Example 1, if you had to solve for x, what would be the next equation after step 3?

2. In Example **2**, if you had to solve for r, what would be the next equation after step 3?

Ⓑ Solve each equation for x.

3. $\dfrac{2}{x} + \dfrac{3}{y} = 5$

4. $\dfrac{3}{4x} - 2 = \dfrac{2}{3y}$

5. $\dfrac{1}{2x} + \dfrac{2}{3y} = 7$

6. $5x - 2 = \dfrac{3}{2y}$

7. $\dfrac{2x - 3}{x} = \dfrac{2}{y}$

8. $\dfrac{2y + 5}{y - 1} = \dfrac{3}{x}$

9–14. Solve each equation in Exercises 3–8 for y.

Solve each formula for the variable indicated.

15. $t = \dfrac{d}{r}$; for d

16. $t = \dfrac{d}{r}$; for r

17. $TA = \dfrac{m}{h}$; for T

18. $TA = \dfrac{m}{h}$; for h

19. $F = \dfrac{Mm}{d^2}$; for m

20. $F = \dfrac{Mm}{d^2}$; for d^2

21. $S = \dfrac{n}{2}(a + t)$; for n

22. $S = \dfrac{n}{2}(a + t)$; for t

23. $S = \dfrac{a}{1 - r}$; for r

24. $\dfrac{P}{D} = Q + \dfrac{R}{D}$; for Q

25. $\dfrac{P}{D} = Q + \dfrac{R}{D}$; for D

26. $\dfrac{1}{r} = \dfrac{1}{r_1} + \dfrac{1}{r_2}$; for r_1

27. $\dfrac{P}{D} = Q + \dfrac{R}{D}$; for R

28. $m = \dfrac{y_2 - y_1}{x_2 - x_1}$; for y_1

29. $y = mx + b$; for x

30. $A = P + Prt$; for P

31. $A = P + Prt$; for r

32. $A = \frac{1}{2}h(b_1 + b_2)$; for b_1

© The formula below may be used when working with lenses (for example, the lens in a camera).

$$\frac{1}{f} = \frac{1}{u} + \frac{1}{v}$$

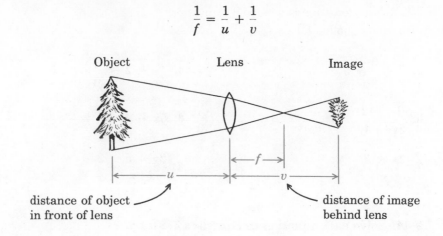

Object   Lens   Image

distance of object in front of lens

distance of image behind lens

The variable *f* stands for the *focal length* of the lens. Its value is determined by the curvature of each lens. Solve each problem.

33. The focal length of a lens is $\frac{3}{25}$ meter. The image of an object appears $\frac{1}{8}$ meter behind the lens. How far in front of the lens is the object?

34. An object is 3 *meters* in front of a lens, and its image appears 12.5 *centimeters* behind the lens. What is the focal length of the lens?

35. The focal length of a lens is 0.48 foot. Inez stands 12 feet in front of the lens. How far behind the lens will her image be?

The given expression is a rational expression. True or False?

1. $\dfrac{\sqrt{n}}{3}$ **2.** $\dfrac{x+1}{x^2}$ **3.** $\dfrac{x^2}{0}$ **4.** $r^2 - 9$

Copy. But replace each ? so that the equation is correct for finding equivalent rational expressions.

5. $\dfrac{-3a}{4a^2} = \dfrac{6a^2}{?}$ **6.** $\dfrac{x+1}{x-1} = \dfrac{?}{x^2-1}$

Change each rational expression to simplest form.

7. $\dfrac{42x^2y}{14x^3y^2}$ **8.** $\dfrac{m^3 - 9m}{m^3 + 6m^2 + 9m}$ **9.** $\dfrac{2x+6}{x^2+5x+6}$

Compute as indicated. Express each result in simplest form.

10. $\dfrac{4ab}{u} \cdot \dfrac{2au}{b}$ **11.** $\dfrac{x^2 - 16}{2x} \cdot \dfrac{12x^2}{2x - 8}$

12. $\dfrac{y^2 - 3y + 2}{y^2 - 1} \cdot \dfrac{y + 1}{y - 1}$

13. $\dfrac{6}{x^2 - 1} \div \dfrac{3}{x + 1}$ **14.** $\dfrac{a^2 - 2a + 1}{a + 1} \div (a - 1)$

15. $\dfrac{m^2 - m - 6}{m^2 - 9} \div \dfrac{m + 2}{m + 3}$

16. $\dfrac{y^2 - 3y}{y - 4} + \dfrac{y - 8}{y - 4}$ **17.** $\dfrac{m^2 + 6m}{m^2 - 4} - \dfrac{2m - 4}{m^2 - 4}$

18. $\dfrac{7}{3x^2} - \dfrac{2}{x}$ **19.** $\dfrac{9}{x^2 - 3x} + \dfrac{x + 3}{x}$

20. $\dfrac{y + 3}{y - 2} - \dfrac{4y - 13}{y^2 - 5y + 6}$

11.7   Solve each equation.

21. $\dfrac{3x - 1}{2x + 4} = \dfrac{4}{5}$

22. $\dfrac{1}{y} + \dfrac{y}{y - 3} = 1$

23. $\dfrac{2x - 3}{x} + \dfrac{3}{x} - 1 = 0$

11.8   Solve each problem.

24. Eva swam 100 meters with the current in the same amount of time that it took her to swim 80 meters back (against the current). The speed of the current is 5 meters per minute. What would be her speed if she were swimming in still water?

25. A tank can be filled by one pump in 36 minutes and emptied by another pump in 40 minutes. How long will it take to fill an empty tank if both pumps are operating?

11.9   Solve each equation for the variable indicated.

26. $5 = \dfrac{4}{3x} - \dfrac{2}{y}$;   for y

27. $t = \dfrac{v - c}{p}$;   for c

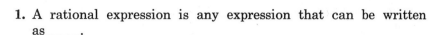

1. A rational expression is any expression that can be written as _____.

2. A rational expression is in _____ if the greatest factor common to its numerator and denominator is 1.

Compute as indicated. Express each result in simplest form.

3. $\dfrac{6xy^2}{2t} \cdot \dfrac{4t}{12xy}$

4. $\dfrac{5}{x - 3} \cdot \dfrac{x^2 - 9}{15}$

5. $\dfrac{a^2 - 6a + 9}{2a + 6} \div \dfrac{a - 3}{a + 3}$

6. $\dfrac{x^2 - 4}{x^2 - 9} \div \dfrac{x - 2}{x + 3}$

7. $\dfrac{5p}{p - 7} + \dfrac{4p}{p - 7}$

8. $\dfrac{x^2 - 3x}{x + 2} - \dfrac{2 - 4x}{x + 2}$

9. $\dfrac{4}{t - 1} - \dfrac{4}{t^2 - t}$

10. $\dfrac{x + 3}{x + 1} + \dfrac{8}{x^2 - 2x - 3}$

Solve each equation.

11. $\dfrac{x}{x - 3} - \dfrac{5}{x + 3} = 1$

12. $\dfrac{3}{x - 4} = \dfrac{2}{x - 6}$

13. $\dfrac{3y - 4}{y - 2} - \dfrac{2}{y - 2} - 2 = 0$

14. One pump can fill a tank in 30 hours, and a second pump can fill the tank in 24 hours. If both pumps are used, how long will it take to fill the tank?

15. A rowing team can row 12 miles per hour in still water. If they row 10 miles downstream in the same amount of time that they row 5 miles upstream, what is the speed of the current?

16. Solve the equation $y = \dfrac{3x - 2}{x - 1}$ for x.

17. Solve the formula $\dfrac{2S}{a + t} = n$ for t.

Ch. 8   Tell which of the ordered pairs are solutions of $4x + 2y = 4$.

1. $(0, 2)$ **2.** $(1, 3)$ **3.** $(2, -2)$ **4.** $(-4, 6)$

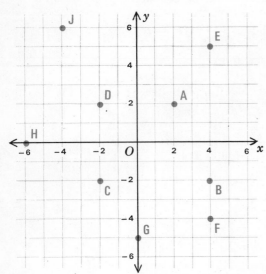

Refer to the graph.

5. What are the coordinates of point E? Of G?

6. Which point is the graph of $(-2, 2)$? Of $(-6, 0)$?

7. A line contains points F and G. Express the slope of the line as a fraction and then as a per cent.

8. Find the slope-intercept form of the equation of each line described below.

   a. slope $= -\frac{3}{2}$; contains point E

   b. contains points B and J

Tell whether the equation is in standard form. Then graph it.

9. $y = 3x + 4$ **10.** $2x + 3y = 9$

For each equation, find the slope and y-intercept of its graph.

11. $-3x + 5y = 15$ **12.** $2x - 2y + 6 = 0$

13. The cost (c) of a bus trip equals the cost of a ticket plus a charge for each transfer (t). Two ordered pairs of the form (t, c) are $(3, 60)$ and $(5, 70)$. Write a formula to show how c and t are related.

Ch. 9   Graph each system. Then tell whether the system has no solutions, exactly one solution, or many solutions.

14. $\begin{cases} 2x - y = 3 \\ 3x - y = 2 \end{cases}$ **15.** $\begin{cases} y = \frac{2}{3}x + 1 \\ y - 2 = \frac{2}{3}x \end{cases}$ **16.** $\begin{cases} y \le 3 \\ 2y < x + 2 \end{cases}$

Solve each system.

17. $\begin{cases} m = n + 6 \\ m + 3n = 14 \end{cases}$
18. $\begin{cases} s + 2t = 0 \\ s + 3t = -1 \end{cases}$
19. $\begin{cases} 2x - y = -3 \\ 4x + 5y = 15 \end{cases}$

20. Some 20% silver alloy is to be mixed with some 60% silver alloy to make 200 grams of 45% silver alloy. How much of each alloy will be needed?

Find each quotient.   Ch. 10

21. $\dfrac{s^3}{s^9}$ 22. $\dfrac{(-2)^3}{(-2)^4}$ 23. $\left(\dfrac{3}{2}\right)^3$ 24. $\dfrac{9x^2y^6}{3x^3y^2}$ 25. $\dfrac{2m^2 - 4m}{2m}$

26. $2x\overline{)2x^2 + 6x + 4}$ 27. $2y - 3\overline{)4y^3 - 6y^2 + 4y - 6}$

Simplify each expression.

28. $5^0 \cdot 2^{-1}$ 29. x^{-2} 30. $3^{-2} \cdot 3^{-1}$ 31. $(\tfrac{1}{3})^{-2}$ 32. $m^6 \div m^{-3}$

Compute as indicated. Express each result in simplest form.   Ch. 11

33. $\dfrac{(s + 1)}{(s + 2)} \cdot \dfrac{(s - 2)}{(s + 1)}$ 34. $\dfrac{m^2}{m^2 - 9} \cdot \dfrac{3m + 9}{m}$

35. $\dfrac{y^2 - 2y}{y} \div \dfrac{y - 2}{y}$ 36. $\dfrac{x - 2}{x^2} + \dfrac{2}{x^2}$ 37. $\dfrac{3m}{2m - 8} - \dfrac{m + 2}{m - 4}$

Solve each equation.

38. $\dfrac{2x - 7}{x} - \dfrac{3}{x} + 3 = 0$ 39. $\dfrac{m + 4}{m - 2} = \dfrac{m + 1}{m}$

40. Working together, two city water pumps can fill a new water tower in 16 hours. The faster of the two pumps could fill the tower in 24 hours. How long would the slower pump need?

41. Solve the formula $\quad r = \dfrac{A - P}{Pt} \quad$ for P.

12 *Radicals*

Storms are of four general types: tornadoes, hurricanes, thunderstorms, and cyclones. Weather forecasters can use the formula below to estimate how long a storm will last.

$$t = \sqrt{\frac{d^3}{216}}$$

The right side of this formula is a *radical*. In this chapter, you will learn how to simplify and use radicals. (The formula above is explained further on page 416.)

You have already found powers of numbers, for example,

$$7^2 = 7 \cdot 7 = 49$$
$$4^3 = 4 \cdot 4 \cdot 4 = 64$$
$$3^4 = 3 \cdot 3 \cdot 3 \cdot 3 = 81$$

Now let's reverse the process of finding a power. That is, we want to express a given number as some base to a given power.

Example 1: Express 25 as some base to the 2nd power.

SOLUTION: Think▶ $25 = ?^2$ Answer▶ $25 = 5^2$

Example 2: Express 8 as some base to the 3rd power.

SOLUTION: Think▶ $8 = ?^3$ Answer▶ $8 = 2^3$

Since	Can be expressed as	We say	We write
25	5^2	a 2nd *root* of 25 is 5	$\sqrt{25} = 5$
8	2^3	a 3rd *root* of 8 is 2	$\sqrt[3]{8} = 2$
81	3^4	a 4th *root* of 81 is 3	$\sqrt[4]{81} = 3$
32	2^5	a 5th *root* of 32 is 2	$\sqrt[5]{32} = 2$

The expressions $\sqrt{25}$, $\sqrt[3]{8}$, $\sqrt[4]{81}$, and $\sqrt[5]{32}$ above are called **radicals.** The word *radical* comes from a Latin word meaning "root." The sign $\sqrt{}$ is thought to be a form of the letter *r*.

radical▶

The index is always an integer greater than 1. When no index is written, it is understood to be ^{2}, that is, $\sqrt{25} = \sqrt[2]{25}$. In general, a radical indicates the operation of finding a number, called a **root**, whose power as given by the index equals the radicand.

Example 3: Find **a.** $\sqrt{9}$ **b.** $\sqrt[3]{27}$ **c.** $\sqrt[4]{16}$

SOLUTIONS: **a.**   Think ▶ $9 = ?^2$ NOTE: Recall from
            Answer ▶ $9 = 3^2$ Chapter 5 that $\sqrt{9}$
            Thus ▶ $\sqrt{9} = 3$ indicates the *positive*
            square root of 9.

b.   Think ▶ $27 = ?^3$ **c.**   Think ▶ $16 = ?^4$
       Answer ▶ $27 = 3^3$ Answer ▶ $16 = 2^4$
       Thus ▶ $\sqrt[3]{27} = 3$ Thus ▶ $\sqrt[4]{16} = 2$

EXERCISES 12.1

Ⓐ Give the *positive* number that correctly completes each equation.

1. $4 = ?^2$ 2. $16 = ?^2$ 3. $36 = ?^2$ 4. $64 = ?^2$

5. $\sqrt{4} = ?$ 6. $\sqrt{16} = ?$ 7. $\sqrt{36} = ?$ 8. $\sqrt{64} = ?$

9. $64 = ?^3$ 10. $125 = ?^3$ 11. $\frac{1}{16} = (?)^4$ 12. $\frac{16}{81} = (?)^4$

13. $\sqrt[3]{64} = ?$ 14. $\sqrt[3]{125} = ?$ 15. $\sqrt[4]{\frac{1}{16}} = ?$ 16. $\sqrt[4]{\frac{16}{81}} = ?$

Ⓑ Find roots as indicated.

17. $\sqrt{81}$ 18. $\sqrt{100}$ 19. $\sqrt[3]{216}$ 20. $\sqrt[3]{1000}$

21. $\sqrt[4]{256}$ 22. $\sqrt[4]{625}$ 23. $\sqrt[5]{243}$ 24. $\sqrt[5]{1024}$

25. $\sqrt[6]{64}$ 26. $\sqrt[6]{729}$ 27. $\sqrt{\frac{4}{9}}$ 28. $\sqrt{\frac{9}{16}}$

29. $\sqrt[3]{\frac{8}{27}}$ 30. $\sqrt[3]{\frac{27}{64}}$ 31. $\sqrt[4]{\frac{81}{16}}$ 32. $\sqrt[4]{\frac{256}{81}}$

33. $\sqrt[5]{\frac{1}{32}}$ 34. $\sqrt[5]{\frac{1}{243}}$ 35. $\sqrt[4]{1}$ 36. $\sqrt[5]{1}$

37. $\sqrt[6]{1}$ 38. $\sqrt[7]{1}$ 39. $\sqrt[8]{0}$ 40. $\sqrt[9]{0}$

41. $-\sqrt{9}$ 42. $-\sqrt{25}$ 43. $-\sqrt[4]{16}$ 44. $-\sqrt[4]{81}$

Ⓒ 45. $\sqrt[3]{-8}$ 46. $\sqrt[3]{-27}$ 47. $\sqrt[5]{-32}$ 48. $\sqrt[5]{-243}$

49. $\sqrt{-4}$ 50. $\sqrt[4]{-16}$ HINT: Be careful with
                                                Exercises **49–50.**

In the rest of this book, we will work mainly with radicals representing *second* (or *square*) *roots*. But most of the ideas can be extended to radicals representing other roots.

The equations below suggest that to multiply two radicals with the *same index*, you can multiply their radicands.

$$\sqrt{25} \cdot \sqrt{4} = \sqrt{100} \qquad\qquad \sqrt{9} \cdot \sqrt{16} = \sqrt{144}$$

$$\quad\downarrow \qquad \downarrow \qquad\quad \downarrow \qquad\qquad\qquad \downarrow \qquad \downarrow \qquad\quad \downarrow$$

$$\quad 5 \;\cdot\; 2 \;=\; 10 \qquad\qquad\qquad 3 \;\cdot\; 4 \;=\; 12$$

In general, this property is stated for square roots as follows.

Let *a* and *b* be any nonnegative real numbers. Then

$$\sqrt{a} \cdot \sqrt{b} = \sqrt{ab}.$$

---

multiplication
of square roots

This property is true even when the radicands are not perfect squares.

Examples: Find each product as a single radical.

1. $\sqrt{2} \cdot \sqrt{5}$ **2.** $\sqrt{3x} \cdot \sqrt{7y}$

SOLUTIONS:

1. $\sqrt{2} \cdot \sqrt{5} = \sqrt{2 \cdot 5}$ **2.** $\sqrt{3x} \cdot \sqrt{7y} = \sqrt{(3x)(7y)}$

$\qquad\qquad = \sqrt{10}$ $\qquad\qquad\qquad\qquad = \sqrt{21xy}$

When the radicands contain variables, as in Example 2, we will assume that the replacement set for each variable is the set of *positive* real numbers. This will avoid such problems as the square roots of negative numbers not existing (as real numbers) and division by 0 not being defined.

For division, there is a property similar to the multiplication property above. That is, to divide two radicals with the same index, you can divide their radicands. For square roots, this property is stated as follows.

**division of
square roots**

Let a and b be any nonnegative real numbers ($b \neq 0$). Then

$$\frac{\sqrt{a}}{\sqrt{b}} = \sqrt{\frac{a}{b}}.$$

Examples: Find each quotient as a single radical.

3. $\dfrac{\sqrt{15}}{\sqrt{3}}$

4. $\dfrac{\sqrt{24r^2 s}}{\sqrt{8rs}}$

SOLUTIONS:

3. $\dfrac{\sqrt{15}}{\sqrt{3}} = \sqrt{\dfrac{15}{3}}$

$= \sqrt{5}$

4. $\dfrac{\sqrt{24r^2 s}}{\sqrt{8rs}} = \sqrt{\dfrac{24r^2 s}{8rs}}$

$= \sqrt{3r}$

EXERCISES 12.2

Ⓐ Find each product in two ways:

a. First find the square roots; then multiply.

b. First multiply the radicands; then find the square root of the product.

1. $\sqrt{4} \cdot \sqrt{9}$

2. $\sqrt{4} \cdot \sqrt{16}$

3. $\sqrt{x^2} \cdot \sqrt{y^2}$

4. $\sqrt{1} \cdot \sqrt{49}$

5. $\sqrt{100} \cdot \sqrt{4}$

6. $\sqrt{\frac{1}{4}} \cdot \sqrt{16}$

Find each quotient in two ways:

a. First find the square roots; then divide.

b. First divide the radicands; then find the square root of the quotient.

7. $\dfrac{\sqrt{16}}{\sqrt{4}}$

8. $\dfrac{\sqrt{81}}{\sqrt{9}}$

9. $\dfrac{\sqrt{100}}{\sqrt{25}}$

10. $\dfrac{\sqrt{49}}{\sqrt{49}}$

11. $\dfrac{\sqrt{4}}{\sqrt{9}}$

12. $\dfrac{\sqrt{x^2}}{\sqrt{y^2}}$

Ⓑ Find each product or quotient as a single radical.

13. $\sqrt{2} \cdot \sqrt{3}$

14. $\sqrt{3} \cdot \sqrt{5}$

15. $\sqrt{3} \cdot \sqrt{10}$

16. $\sqrt{10} \cdot \sqrt{7}$

17. $\sqrt{\frac{1}{2}} \cdot \sqrt{6}$

18. $\sqrt{6} \cdot \sqrt{\frac{1}{3}}$

19. $\dfrac{\sqrt{6}}{\sqrt{2}}$

20. $\dfrac{\sqrt{6}}{\sqrt{3}}$

21. $\dfrac{\sqrt{42}}{\sqrt{7}}$

22. $\dfrac{\sqrt{30}}{\sqrt{6}}$

23. $\dfrac{\sqrt{\frac{1}{3}}}{\sqrt{\frac{1}{6}}}$

24. $\dfrac{\sqrt{\frac{10}{3}}}{\sqrt{\frac{2}{3}}}$

25. $\sqrt{2x} \cdot \sqrt{3}$

26. $\sqrt{2} \cdot \sqrt{3x}$

27. $\sqrt{5r} \cdot \sqrt{3s}$

28. $\sqrt{7k} \cdot \sqrt{5m}$

29. $\sqrt{2} \cdot \sqrt{x + 3}$

30. $\sqrt{5 - y} \cdot \sqrt{3}$

31. $\dfrac{\sqrt{15x}}{\sqrt{5}}$

32. $\dfrac{\sqrt{12y}}{\sqrt{6}}$

33. $\dfrac{\sqrt{3x}}{\sqrt{x}}$

34. $\dfrac{\sqrt{5k}}{\sqrt{k}}$

35. $\dfrac{\sqrt{12x^2}}{\sqrt{4x}}$

36. $\dfrac{\sqrt{35y^3}}{\sqrt{7y^2}}$

37. $\dfrac{\sqrt{16m^3n^2}}{\sqrt{8m^2n}}$

38. $\dfrac{\sqrt{25c^5d^7}}{\sqrt{5c^4d^6}}$

39. $\dfrac{\sqrt{x^2 + x}}{\sqrt{x}}$

40. $\dfrac{\sqrt{x^3 + x^2}}{\sqrt{x^2}}$

41. $\dfrac{\sqrt{3x^2 - 6x}}{\sqrt{3x}}$

42. $\dfrac{\sqrt{14x^3 - 7x^2}}{\sqrt{7x}}$

Ⓒ **43.** $\sqrt[3]{2} \cdot \sqrt[3]{3}$

44. $\sqrt[4]{2} \cdot \sqrt[4]{3}$

45. $\sqrt[5]{8} \cdot \sqrt[5]{10}$

46. $\dfrac{\sqrt[3]{16}}{\sqrt[3]{4}}$

47. $\dfrac{\sqrt[4]{50}}{\sqrt[4]{25}}$

48. $\dfrac{\sqrt[5]{125}}{\sqrt[5]{25}}$

49. $\sqrt[n]{a} \cdot \sqrt[n]{b}$

50. $\dfrac{\sqrt[n]{a}}{\sqrt[n]{b}}$

51. Use $a = 9$ and $b = 16$ to show that $\sqrt{a} + \sqrt{b} \neq \sqrt{a + b}$.

52. Use $a = 100$ and $b = 64$ to show that $\sqrt{a} - \sqrt{b} \neq \sqrt{a - b}$.

12.3 SIMPLIFYING RADICALS

The multiplication and division properties stated in Section 12.2 can be used in reverse to change the form of radicals.

Examples:

1. $\sqrt{8} = \sqrt{4 \cdot 2}$
$= \sqrt{4} \cdot \sqrt{2}$
$= 2\sqrt{2}$

2. $\sqrt{\dfrac{3}{2}} = \dfrac{\sqrt{3}}{\sqrt{2}}$
$= \dfrac{\sqrt{3}}{\sqrt{2}} \cdot 1$
$= \dfrac{\sqrt{3}}{\sqrt{2}} \cdot \dfrac{\sqrt{2}}{\sqrt{2}}$
$= \dfrac{\sqrt{6}}{2}$ or $\frac{1}{2}\sqrt{6}$

Such changes of form are often needed to perform other operations with radicals. However, in Examples **1** and **2**, we did not just change the form. We changed the expressions to *simplest* (or *standard*) *form*.

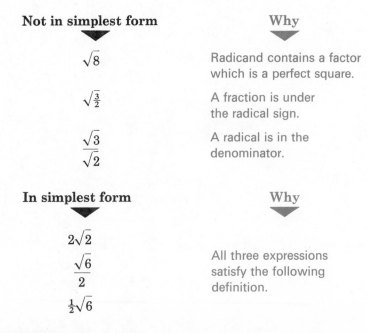

Not in simplest form	**Why**
$\sqrt{8}$	Radicand contains a factor which is a perfect square.
$\sqrt{\frac{3}{2}}$	A fraction is under the radical sign.
$\dfrac{\sqrt{3}}{\sqrt{2}}$	A radical is in the denominator.

In simplest form	**Why**
$2\sqrt{2}$	
$\dfrac{\sqrt{6}}{2}$	All three expressions satisfy the following definition.
$\frac{1}{2}\sqrt{6}$	

A radical expression representing a square root is in **simplest** (or **standard**) **form** when

1. The radicand contains no integer factor (other than 1) that is a perfect square;

2. No fraction is under a radical sign;

3. No radical is in a denominator.

Examples: Change each radical to simplest form.

3. $\sqrt{48}$ **4.** $\sqrt{4x^5}$ **5.** $\sqrt{\dfrac{a}{3}}$

SOLUTIONS:

3. $\sqrt{48} = \sqrt{16 \cdot 3}$

$\qquad = \sqrt{16} \cdot \sqrt{3}$

$\qquad = 4\sqrt{3}$

$\boxed{\textit{Another way}} \quad \sqrt{48} = \sqrt{4} \cdot \sqrt{12}$

$\qquad\qquad\qquad = 2\sqrt{12}$

$\qquad\qquad\qquad = 2 \cdot \sqrt{4} \cdot \sqrt{3}$

$\qquad\qquad\qquad = 2 \cdot 2 \cdot \sqrt{3}$

$\qquad\qquad\qquad = 4\sqrt{3}$

4. $\sqrt{4x^5} = \sqrt{4 \cdot x^2 \cdot x^2 \cdot x}$

$\qquad\quad = \sqrt{4} \cdot \sqrt{x^2} \cdot \sqrt{x^2} \cdot \sqrt{x}$

$\qquad\quad = 2 \cdot x \cdot x\sqrt{x}$

$\qquad\quad = 2x^2\sqrt{x}$

5. $\sqrt{\dfrac{a}{3}} = \dfrac{\sqrt{a}}{\sqrt{3}}$

$\qquad\quad = \dfrac{\sqrt{a}}{\sqrt{3}} \cdot \dfrac{\sqrt{3}}{\sqrt{3}}$

$\qquad\quad = \dfrac{\sqrt{3a}}{3} \quad \text{or} \quad \tfrac{1}{3}\sqrt{3a}$

In Example 5, the process of changing

$$\dfrac{\sqrt{a}}{\sqrt{3}} \qquad \text{to} \qquad \dfrac{\sqrt{3a}}{3}$$

is called *rationalizing the denominator*.

EXERCISES 12.3

Ⓐ Tell why the expression is *not* in simplest form.

1. $\sqrt{12}$ 2. $\sqrt{\frac{2}{3}}$ 3. $\sqrt{3x^2}$ 4. $\sqrt{a^2b}$

5. $\sqrt{\frac{1}{2}}$ 6. $\frac{1}{\sqrt{2}}$ 7. $\frac{\sqrt{2}}{\sqrt{3}}$ 8. $\frac{\sqrt{a}}{\sqrt{b}}$

For each number, find the *largest* integer factor which is a perfect square.

Example: For the number 20, this factor is 4.

9. 8   10. 12   11. 18   12. 50

13. 27   14. 40   15. 28   16. 75

Change each expression to simplest form.

17. $\sqrt{4 \cdot 3}$ 18. $\sqrt{12}$ 19. $\sqrt{9 \cdot 2}$ 20. $\sqrt{18}$

21. $\frac{\sqrt{2}}{\sqrt{3}}$ 22. $\sqrt{\frac{2}{3}}$ 23. $\frac{\sqrt{a}}{\sqrt{b}}$ 24. $\sqrt{\frac{a}{b}}$

Ⓑ 25. $\sqrt{20}$ 26. $\sqrt{24}$ 27. $\sqrt{27}$ 28. $\sqrt{40}$

29. $\sqrt{\frac{1}{2}}$ 30. $\sqrt{\frac{1}{3}}$ 31. $\sqrt{\frac{1}{a}}$ 32. $\sqrt{\frac{1}{xy}}$

33. $\sqrt{28}$ 34. $\sqrt{32}$ 35. $\sqrt{50}$ 36. $\sqrt{75}$

37. $\sqrt{\frac{4}{3}}$ 38. $\sqrt{\frac{9}{2}}$ 39. $\sqrt{\frac{4}{a}}$ 40. $\sqrt{\frac{9}{b}}$

41. $\sqrt{\frac{3}{4}}$ 42. $\sqrt{\frac{5}{4}}$ 43. $\sqrt{\frac{2}{9}}$ 44. $\sqrt{\frac{7}{9}}$

45. $\sqrt{3x^2}$ 46. $\sqrt{5y^4}$ 47. $\sqrt{a^2b}$ 48. $\sqrt{a^4b}$

49. $\sqrt{\frac{3}{4a^2}}$ 50. $\sqrt{\frac{5}{9a^2}}$ 51. $\sqrt{\frac{n}{4a^2}}$ 52. $\sqrt{\frac{n}{9a^2}}$

53. $\sqrt{45}$ 54. $\sqrt{54}$ 55. $\sqrt{63}$ 56. $\sqrt{80}$

57. $\sqrt{x^3}$ 58. $\sqrt{y^5}$ 59. $\sqrt{4r^5}$ 60. $\sqrt{8d^3}$

Changing to simplest form can be used to extend the square-root table on page 555. Find each square root as in the examples.

Examples:

$$\sqrt{200} = \sqrt{100 \cdot 2}$$
$$= 10\sqrt{2}$$
$$\approx 10(1.414) \quad \text{or} \quad 14.14$$

$$\sqrt{0.5} = \sqrt{\tfrac{5}{10}}$$
$$= \frac{\sqrt{5}}{\sqrt{10}} \cdot \frac{\sqrt{10}}{\sqrt{10}}$$
$$= \frac{\sqrt{50}}{10}$$
$$\approx \frac{7.071}{10} \quad \text{or} \quad 0.7071$$

61. $\sqrt{300}$ 62. $\sqrt{500}$ 63. $\sqrt{25 \cdot 7}$ 64. $\sqrt{36 \cdot 5}$

65. $\sqrt{160}$ 66. $\sqrt{250}$ 67. $\sqrt{288}$ 68. $\sqrt{363}$

69. $\sqrt{0.3}$ 70. $\sqrt{0.7}$ 71. $\sqrt{0.03}$ 72. $\sqrt{0.07}$

73. $\sqrt{1.25}$ 74. $\sqrt{1.33}$ 75. $\sqrt{1.2}$ 76. $\sqrt{1.5}$

77. $\sqrt{2.5}$ 78. $\sqrt{3.6}$ 79. $\sqrt{4.9}$ 80. $\sqrt{6.4}$

Besides radicals for square roots, other radicals can be simplified in a similar way. Simplify each radical as in the examples.

Examples:

$$\sqrt[3]{16} = \sqrt[3]{8 \cdot 2}$$
$$= \sqrt[3]{8} \cdot \sqrt[3]{2}$$
$$= 2\sqrt[3]{2}$$

$$\sqrt[4]{\tfrac{5}{3}} = \frac{\sqrt[4]{5}}{\sqrt[4]{3}}$$
$$= \frac{\sqrt[4]{5}}{\sqrt[4]{3}} \cdot \frac{\sqrt[4]{3^3}}{\sqrt[4]{3^3}}$$
$$= \frac{\sqrt[4]{5 \cdot 3^3}}{\sqrt[4]{3 \cdot 3^3}} = \frac{\sqrt[4]{135}}{3} \quad \text{or} \quad \tfrac{1}{3}\sqrt[4]{135}$$

81. $\sqrt[3]{24}$ 82. $\sqrt[4]{32}$ 83. $\sqrt[3]{54}$ 84. $\sqrt[4]{48}$

85. $\dfrac{\sqrt[3]{5}}{\sqrt[3]{3}}$ 86. $\sqrt[3]{\tfrac{1}{2}}$ 87. $\dfrac{\sqrt[4]{3}}{\sqrt[4]{5}}$ 88. $\sqrt[4]{\tfrac{2}{7}}$

On page 406, we gave the formula,

$$t = \sqrt{\frac{d^3}{216}},$$

for estimating how long a storm (tornado, hurricane, thunderstorm, or cyclone) will last.

Any of the four types of storms covers a surface that can be considered circular. Using pictures from weather satellites or reports from a network of weather stations, forecasters can find the diameter d of a storm (in miles). Then, substituting in the formula, they can compute the time t, in hours.

Let's see how this formula works. But first, let's simplify the radical.

$$t = \sqrt{\frac{d^3}{216}}$$

$$= \frac{\sqrt{d^2 \cdot d}}{\sqrt{36 \cdot 6}}$$

$$= \frac{d\sqrt{d}}{6\sqrt{6}} \cdot \frac{\sqrt{6}}{\sqrt{6}}$$

$$= \frac{d\sqrt{6d}}{36}$$

If a hurricane has a diameter of 100 miles, how long can it be expected to last?

$$t = \frac{100\sqrt{6 \cdot 100}}{36}$$

$$= \frac{100 \cdot 10\sqrt{6}}{36}$$

$$\approx \frac{1000(2.449)}{36} \quad \text{or about 68 hours}$$

Another formula involving a radical is

$$s = \sqrt{30fd}.$$

This can be used to estimate the speed s (in miles per hour) that a car was traveling from the distance d (in feet) which the car skidded.

The variable f in this formula represents a number, called the coefficient of friction, that is determined by the kind of road (concrete, asphalt, gravel, tar) and its condition (wet, dry).

For a dry, concrete road, $f = 0.8$. If the skid marks are 40 feet long, estimate how fast the car was traveling.

$$s = \sqrt{30(0.8)40}$$
$$= \sqrt{960}$$
$$= \sqrt{64 \cdot 15}$$
$$= 8\sqrt{15}$$
$$\approx 8(3.873) \quad \text{or about 31 mph}$$

Actually, the formula gives a good estimate of speed only if

  I. All four tires skid for the full braking distance;

  II. The car comes to a stop without hitting another object.

If condition I is not met, the formula gives too high a speed. If condition II is not met, the formula gives too low a speed.

See if you can use the formulas.

1. Estimate how long a thunderstorm will last if its diameter is 50 miles.

2. The coefficient of friction for a wet, concrete road is 0.4. If the skid marks are 100 feet long, estimate how fast the car was traveling.

12.4 ADDITION AND SUBTRACTION

Unlike radicals

Why

$\sqrt{2}$ and $\sqrt{3}$ have different radicands

$\sqrt[3]{5}$ and $\sqrt{5}$ have different index numbers

Like radicals

Why

$\sqrt{3}$ and $5\sqrt{3}$

$\sqrt[3]{5}$ and $2\sqrt[3]{5}$

$-2\sqrt{3y}$ and $5\sqrt{3y}$

In each pair, the index numbers are the same and the radicands are the same

You know that like terms can be added (or subtracted) by using the *distributive property* but unlike terms cannot. Similarly, like radicals can be added (or subtracted) but unlike radicals cannot.

Examples: Find each sum or difference.

   1. $3\sqrt{2} + 5\sqrt{2}$ **2.** $2\sqrt{x} - 4\sqrt{x}$

SOLUTIONS:

   1. $3\sqrt{2} + 5\sqrt{2} = (3 + 5)\sqrt{2}$ **2.** $2\sqrt{x} - 4\sqrt{x} = (2 - 4)\sqrt{x}$

                      $= 8\sqrt{2}$ $= -2\sqrt{x}$

Sometimes, unlike radicals can first be simplified and changed to like radicals. Then they can be added or subtracted.

Example 3: Simplify: $\sqrt{12} + \sqrt{27}$.

   SOLUTION: $\sqrt{12} + \sqrt{27} = 2\sqrt{3} + 3\sqrt{3}$

                            $= (2 + 3)\sqrt{3}$

                            $= 5\sqrt{3}$

Example 4: Simplify: $\sqrt{18} - \sqrt{8} + \sqrt{\frac{1}{2}}$.

SOLUTION: $\sqrt{18} - \sqrt{8} + \sqrt{\frac{1}{2}} = 3\sqrt{2} - 2\sqrt{2} + \frac{1}{2}\sqrt{2}$

$$= (3 - 2 + \tfrac{1}{2})\sqrt{2}$$

$$= (1 + \tfrac{1}{2})\sqrt{2}$$

$$= \tfrac{3}{2}\sqrt{2} \quad \text{or} \quad \frac{3\sqrt{2}}{2}$$

EXERCISES 12.4

Ⓐ Simplify each expression.

1. $4\sqrt{2} + 6\sqrt{2}$
     2. $5\sqrt{3} + 2\sqrt{3}$
     3. $7\sqrt{5} - 5\sqrt{5}$

4. $12\sqrt{7} - 8\sqrt{7}$
     5. $4\sqrt{x} - 6\sqrt{x}$
     6. $15\sqrt{y} - 17\sqrt{y}$

Ⓑ 7. $\sqrt{8} + 3\sqrt{2}$
     8. $2\sqrt{2} + \sqrt{18}$
     9. $\sqrt{12} - \sqrt{3}$

10. $\sqrt{27} - 2\sqrt{3}$
     11. $5\sqrt{a} + 3\sqrt{a}$
     12. $\frac{1}{2}\sqrt{b} + \frac{1}{2}\sqrt{b}$

13. $\sqrt{2x} + \sqrt{8x}$
     14. $\sqrt{27y} + \sqrt{3y}$
     15. $\sqrt{20} + \sqrt{45}$

16. $\sqrt{50} + \sqrt{32}$
     17. $\sqrt{8} + \sqrt{\frac{1}{2}}$
     18. $\sqrt{27} + \sqrt{\frac{1}{3}}$

19. $\sqrt{8} + \sqrt{18} - 5\sqrt{2}$
     20. $\sqrt{12} - 2\sqrt{3} + \sqrt{27}$

21. $\sqrt{24} + \sqrt{6} - \sqrt{\frac{3}{2}}$
     22. $\sqrt{40} + \sqrt{10} + \sqrt{\frac{2}{5}}$

23. $\sqrt{9x} + \sqrt{x} + \sqrt{\dfrac{x}{4}}$
     24. $\sqrt{2y} + \sqrt{8y} + \sqrt{\dfrac{y}{2}}$

25. $x\sqrt{18x} + \sqrt{8x^3}$
     26. $3y\sqrt{12y} + \sqrt{75y^3}$

27. $n^2\sqrt{50} + \sqrt{32n^4}$
     28. $\sqrt{48x^4} + x^2\sqrt{27}$

29. $\sqrt{63} + \sqrt{28} - \sqrt{\frac{1}{7}}$
     30. $\sqrt{54} - \sqrt{\frac{1}{6}} + \sqrt{24}$

Ⓒ 31. $4\sqrt[3]{3} - 2\sqrt[3]{3}$
     32. $7\sqrt[4]{5} + 3\sqrt[4]{5}$

33. $3\sqrt[3]{2x} + \sqrt[3]{16x}$
     34. $-4\sqrt[3]{3x} + \sqrt[3]{81x}$

35. $\sqrt[3]{16x^4} - \sqrt[3]{54x^4}$
     36. $\sqrt[3]{128s^5} - \sqrt[3]{16s^5}$

37. $\sqrt[4]{48} - 2\sqrt[4]{243}$
     38. $\sqrt[4]{32x} - \sqrt[4]{162x}$

39. $\sqrt[5]{64x} + \sqrt[5]{2x}$
     40. $\sqrt[6]{128} - \sqrt[6]{2}$

Find each root.

1. $\sqrt{144}$　　　　**2.** $\sqrt[3]{64}$　　　　**3.** $\sqrt[4]{81}$

4. $\sqrt{\frac{25}{16}}$　　　　**5.** $\sqrt[3]{\frac{27}{8}}$　　　　**6.** $\sqrt[4]{\frac{81}{256}}$

Find each product or quotient as a single radical.

7. $\sqrt{7} \cdot \sqrt{5}$　　　　　　　　**8.** $\sqrt{x} \cdot \sqrt{y}$

9. $\dfrac{\sqrt{18}}{\sqrt{3}}$　　　　　　　　**10.** $\dfrac{\sqrt{x}}{\sqrt{y}}$

Change each expression to simplest form.

11. $\sqrt{27}$　　　　**12.** $\sqrt{72}$　　　　**13.** $\sqrt{5x^4}$

14. $\sqrt{\dfrac{1}{n}}$　　　　**15.** $\sqrt{\dfrac{2}{3}}$　　　　**16.** $\sqrt{\dfrac{4d^3}{3}}$

Using the table on page 555, find a decimal approximation for each square root.

17. $\sqrt{600}$　　　**18.** $\sqrt{275}$　　　**19.** $\sqrt{0.6}$　　　**20.** $\sqrt{0.08}$

Simplify.

21. $\sqrt{8} + \sqrt{\frac{1}{2}}$　　　　　　　**22.** $\sqrt{12} - \sqrt{27}$

23. $\sqrt{5x^3} + x\sqrt{20x}$　　　　　　**24.** $\sqrt{24} - \sqrt{\frac{2}{3}} + \sqrt{54}$

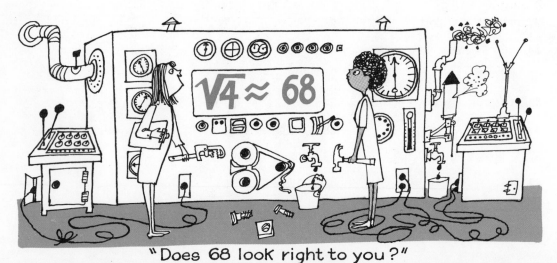

"Does 68 look right to you?"

If the replacement set for x does *not* contain *negative* numbers, then we can write

$$\sqrt{x^2} = x. \qquad \boxed{x \text{ cannot be negative.}}$$

However, if the replacement set *does contain negative* numbers, the sentence above is not correct. For example, let $x = -3$. Then the sentence above would give

$$\sqrt{x^2} = \sqrt{(-3)^2}$$
$$= -3.$$

But $\sqrt{(-3)^2}$ stands for the positive square root of $(-3)^2$. That is, if $x = -3$,

$$\sqrt{x^2} = \sqrt{(-3)^2}$$
$$= \sqrt{9}$$
$$= 3.$$

In general,

$$\sqrt{x^2} = |x|. \qquad \boxed{x \text{ may be negative.}}$$

For example,

$$\sqrt{(-7)^2} = |-7| \qquad\qquad \sqrt{7^2} = |7|$$
$$= 7 \qquad\qquad\qquad = 7$$

Examples: Change each radical to simplest form. Assume that negative replacements for the variables are permitted.

1. $\sqrt{2y^2}$ 2. $\sqrt{\dfrac{8}{r^2}}$

SOLUTIONS:

1. $\sqrt{2y^2} = \sqrt{2} \cdot \sqrt{y^2}$

        $= \sqrt{2} \cdot |y|$

        $= |y|\sqrt{2}$

2. $\sqrt{\dfrac{8}{r^2}} = \dfrac{\sqrt{8}}{\sqrt{r^2}}$

        $= \dfrac{2\sqrt{2}}{|r|}$ or $\dfrac{2}{|r|}\sqrt{2}$

EXERCISES 12.5

Ⓐ Change each radical to simplest form. Assume that negative replacements for the variables are permitted.

1. $\sqrt{(-2)^2}$ 2. $\sqrt{2^2}$ 3. $\sqrt{11^2}$ 4. $\sqrt{(-11)^2}$

5. $\sqrt{n^2}$ 6. $\sqrt{\left(\dfrac{a}{b}\right)^2}$ 7. $\sqrt{x^2y^2}$ 8. $\sqrt{\dfrac{a^2}{3}}$

Ⓑ 9. $\sqrt{8c^2}$ 10. $\sqrt{12d^2}$ 11. $\sqrt{20r^2}$

12. $\sqrt{18g^2}$ 13. $\sqrt{\dfrac{3}{4a^2}}$ 14. $\sqrt{\dfrac{5}{9b^2}}$

15. $\sqrt{32x^2}$ 16. $\sqrt{50y^2}$ 17. $\sqrt{8(mn)^2}$

18. $\sqrt{18(xy)^2}$ 19. $\sqrt{12m^2n^2}$ 20. $\sqrt{27x^2y^2}$

21. $\sqrt{\dfrac{r^2}{2}}$ 22. $\sqrt{\dfrac{s^2}{5}}$ 23. $\sqrt{\dfrac{8n^2}{3}}$

24. $\sqrt{\dfrac{12t^2}{5}}$ 25. $-2\sqrt{x^2}$ 26. $-5\sqrt{8y^2}$

27. $x\sqrt{x^2}$ 28. $y^3\sqrt{y^2}$ 29. $\sqrt{(x+2)^2}$

30. $\sqrt{(y-3)^2}$ 31. $\sqrt{18(x+y)^2}$ 32. $\sqrt{27(m-n)^2}$

Ⓒ Tell whether negative replacements can be permitted for the variable. Then change the radical to simplest form, using the absolute value symbol only if necessary.

Example: For $\sqrt{x^3}$, the radical is defined only if $x^3 \geq 0$. So, negative replacements for x cannot be permitted because if $x < 0$, then $x^3 < 0$.

$$\sqrt{x^3} = \sqrt{x^2} \cdot \sqrt{x}$$

$$= x\sqrt{x}, \quad \text{where } x \geq 0$$

33. $\sqrt{8y^3}$ 34. $\sqrt{x^4}$ 35. $\sqrt{n^5}$ 36. $\sqrt{r^6}$

An equation in which a variable occurs under a radical sign is called a *radical equation*.

Example 1: Solve $\sqrt{x-2} = 3$.

SOLUTION: $\sqrt{x-2} = 3$ Given

$(\sqrt{x-2})^2 = 3^2$ Square both sides.

$x - 2 = 9$ Solve the resulting

$x = 11$ equation.

Check: $\sqrt{11-2} = 3$

$\sqrt{9} = 3$

$3 = 3$ T   Thus, $x = 11$

The importance of *checking* is emphasized by radical equations. The process of squaring both sides often introduces apparent solutions (called *extraneous roots*) which are not really solutions of the given equation.

Example 2: Solve $x = 1 + \sqrt{3-x}$.

SOLUTION:

$x = 1 + \sqrt{3-x}$ Given

$x - 1 = \sqrt{3-x}$ Isolate radical on one side.

$(x-1)^2 = (\sqrt{3-x})^2$ Square both sides.

$x^2 - 2x + 1 = 3 - x$

$x^2 - x - 2 = 0$ Solve by factoring

$(x-2)(x+1) = 0$ as in Section 7.7.

$x - 2 = 0$ or $x + 1 = 0$

$x = 2$ $x = -1$

Check: $2 = 1 + \sqrt{3-2}$ $-1 = 1 + \sqrt{3 - (-1)}$

$2 = 1 + \sqrt{1}$ $-1 = 1 + \sqrt{4}$

$2 = 2$ T $-1 = 3$ F

So, -1 is an extraneous root. The solution set is $\{2\}$.

EXERCISES 12.6

Ⓐ 1. What equation results from squaring both sides of $\sqrt{x} = -3$?

2. Does the value found for x in Exercise 1 check in $\sqrt{x} = -3$?

3. What is the solution set of $\sqrt{x} = -3$?

4. Why should you expect this solution set by just inspecting the given equation?

Tell what equation would result from squaring both sides.

5. $\sqrt{x + 1} = 5$ 6. $\sqrt{2y} = 4$ 7. $-3 = \sqrt{3r}$

8. $7 = \sqrt{26 - n}$ 9. $\sqrt{\frac{1}{3}x} = 2$ 10. $-y = \sqrt{y}$

11. $\sqrt{5m - 2} = \sqrt{3}$ 12. $\sqrt{n + 3} = 2\sqrt{3}$

13. $\sqrt{3x^2 - 3} = 3$ 14. $\sqrt{5y^2 + 5} = 5$

Ⓑ 15–24. Solve each equation given in Exercises 5–14.

Solve each equation.

25. $1 + \sqrt{y - 1} = y$ 26. $x = 2 + \sqrt{x - 2}$

27. $n - \sqrt{n + 3} = -1$ 28. $x = 2 + \sqrt{7 - 2x}$

29. $3 + \sqrt{10 - 6k} = k$ 30. $r - 2\sqrt{5 - 2r} = 4$

Ⓒ 31. $\sqrt{2 - t} = \sqrt{t - 2}$ 32. $\sqrt{s - 5} = -\sqrt{5 - s}$

Solve the problems, using these formulas from page 416:

$$s = \sqrt{30fd} \qquad\qquad t = \frac{d\sqrt{6d}}{36}$$

33. Suppose you drive at 30 miles per hour, apply the brakes, and measure the skid marks to be 50 feet long. What is the coefficient of friction f?

34. For a wet, tar road, $f = 0.5$. At 45 mph, what would be the braking distance d? (NOTE: Due to reaction time, the *total* stopping distance would be about 50 feet longer.)

35. If a storm lasted for 1 hour, estimate what its diameter was.

On a number line, the distance between two points can be found as follows. Subtract the coordinate of either point from that of the other. Then take the absolute value of this difference.

Example 1: Find the distance PQ.

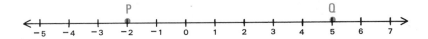

SOLUTION: $PQ = |5 - (-2)|$ or $PQ = |-2 - 5|$

$\qquad\qquad = |7|$ $\qquad\qquad\qquad = |-7|$

$\qquad\qquad = 7$ $\qquad\qquad\qquad = 7$

Using this idea and the Pythagorean theorem, we can now find the distance between two points in the coordinate plane.

Example 2: P is at $(-1, 2)$ and Q at $(3, 5)$. Find the distance PQ.

SOLUTION: As in the graph below, horizontal and vertical lines through P and Q intersect at R, forming right triangle PRQ.

All points on a horizontal line have the same y-coordinate, so R has the same y-coordinate as P. Similarly, all points on a vertical line have the same x-coordinate, so R has the same x-coordinate as Q. Thus, R is at $(3, 2)$.

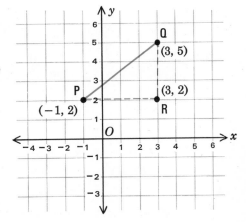

$PR = |-1 - 3|$ $\qquad$ $QR = |2 - 5|$

$\quad = 4$ $\qquad\qquad\qquad = 3$

Using the Pythagorean theorem,

$(PQ)^2 = (PR)^2 + (QR)^2$

$\qquad = 4^2 + 3^2$

$\qquad = 16 + 9$

$\qquad = 25$

So, $\sqrt{(PQ)^2} = \sqrt{25}$

$\qquad PQ = 5$

Example 2 can be generalized to find a formula for the distance between any two points in the coordinate plane.

Let P be at (x_1, y_1) and Q at (x_2, y_2). Drawing the horizontal and vertical lines, we can locate R at (x_2, y_1).

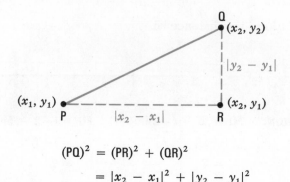

$$(PQ)^2 = (PR)^2 + (QR)^2$$
$$= |x_2 - x_1|^2 + |y_2 - y_1|^2$$

We can replace the absolute value signs with ( ) because $|n|^2 = (n)^2$, regardless of whether n is positive, negative, or zero.

$$(PQ)^2 = (x_2 - x_1)^2 + (y_2 - y_1)^2$$

Taking the square root of each side, we conclude the following.

distance formula

Let P be a point at (x_1, y_1) and Q a point at (x_2, y_2). Then, the distance from P to Q is

$$PQ = \sqrt{(x_2 - x_1)^2 + (y_2 - y_1)^2}.$$

Example 3: P is at $(5, 1)$ and Q at $(-1, -2)$. Use the distance formula to find PQ.

SOLUTION:
$$PQ = \sqrt{(x_2 - x_1)^2 + (y_2 - y_1)^2}$$
$$= \sqrt{(-1 - 5)^2 + (-2 - 1)^2}$$
$$= \sqrt{(-6)^2 + (-3)^2}$$
$$= \sqrt{36 + 9}$$
$$= \sqrt{45}$$
$$= \sqrt{9 \cdot 5} = 3\sqrt{5}$$

EXERCISES 12.7

Ⓐ Find the distance between the two points on a number line whose coordinates are given.

1. 3 and 7   **2.** 0 and 5   **3.** 0 and -5

4. -2 and 3   **5.** 2 and -3 **6.** -2 and -3

Find the coordinates of point R.

7. 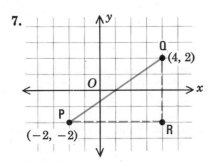   **8.**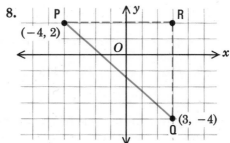

Ⓑ **9.** Refer to the graph in Exercise 7. Find:

   a. PR   **b.** QR   **c.** PQ

10. Refer to the graph in Exercise 8. Find:

   a. PR   **b.** QR   **c.** PQ

Using the distance formula, find the distance between the two points whose coordinates are given. Express radicals in simplest form.

11. $(3, 4)$ and $(0, 0)$ **12.** $(0, 0)$ and $(6, 8)$

13. $(4, 3)$ and $(1, 3)$ **14.** $(-2, 5)$ and $(-2, 8)$

15. $(-1, 4)$ and $(4, -8)$ **16.** $(6, -7)$ and $(-2, 8)$

17. $(1, 5)$ and $(3, 1)$ **18.** $(4, 3)$ and $(1, 6)$

19. $(3, -1)$ and $(-3, 2)$ **20.** $(5, 1)$ and $(-1, -1)$

21. $(-2, -8)$ and $(-7, -3)$ **22.** $(-7, -9)$ and $(-1, -3)$

Ⓒ **23.** Can the point at $(3, 4)$ be the center of the circle which passes through points at $(-1, 1)$, $(7, 7)$, and $(0, 0)$?

24. The distance between points at $(2, -1)$ and $(x, 3)$ is 5. Find all possible values of x.

CHAPTER REVIEW

12.1 Find each root.

    1. $\sqrt{121}$ **2.** $\sqrt[3]{343}$ **3.** $\sqrt[4]{10,000}$ **4.** $\sqrt{\frac{100}{121}}$

12.2 Find each product or quotient as a single radical.

    5. $\sqrt{\frac{2}{3}} \cdot \sqrt{15}$ **6.** $\sqrt{3a} \cdot \sqrt{2b}$ **7.** $\dfrac{\sqrt{54}}{\sqrt{9}}$ **8.** $\dfrac{\sqrt{34x^2}}{\sqrt{2x}}$

12.3 Change each expression to simplest form.

    9. $\sqrt{28}$ **10.** $\sqrt{125}$ **11.** $\sqrt{4x^3}$ **12.** $\sqrt{\dfrac{1}{mn}}$

Using the table on page 555, find a decimal approximation for each square root.

    13. $\sqrt{800}$ **14.** $\sqrt{0.08}$ **15.** $\sqrt{0.8}$ **16.** $\sqrt{176}$

12.4 Simplify.

    17. $7\sqrt{3} - 4\sqrt{3}$ **18.** $\sqrt{12} + \sqrt{\frac{3}{4}}$

    19. $\sqrt{8s} + \sqrt{18s}$ **20.** $\sqrt{\frac{8}{5}} + \sqrt{40} - \sqrt{\frac{2}{5}}$

12.5 Change each expression to simplest form. Assume that negative replacements for each variable are permitted.

    21. $\sqrt{x^2}$ **22.** $\sqrt{24r^2}$ **23.** $\sqrt{\dfrac{a^2}{2}}$

12.6 Solve.

    24. $\sqrt{y - 2} = 3$ **25.** $3\sqrt{2} = \sqrt{\frac{1}{2}n}$

    26. $\sqrt{t^2 + 2} = \sqrt{6}$ **27.** $x = 2 + \sqrt{10 - 3x}$

12.7 Using the distance formula, find the distance between the two points whose coordinates are given. Express radicals in simplest form.

    28. $(4, 8)$ and $(1, 5)$ **29.** $(0, -3)$ and $(2, 3)$

Which lettered term best completes each sentence?

   a. radical   **b.** index   **c.** root   **d.** distance

   e. radicand   **f.** unlike   **g.** like   **h.** simplest

1. A fourth _____ of 16 is 2.

2. $\sqrt{8}$ is not in _____ form.

3. In $\sqrt[3]{5}$, the _____ is 3.

4. In $\sqrt[3]{5}$, the _____ is 5.

5. $\sqrt{12}$ and $\sqrt[3]{12}$ are _____ radicals.

6. $\sqrt{x + 1} = 2$ is a(n) _____ equation.

7. For $\sqrt{x} = -2$, the number 4 is an extraneous _____.

8. The radical $\sqrt{(x_2 - x_1)^2 + (y_2 - y_1)^2}$ is in the _____ formula.

9. Find: **(a)** $\sqrt{49}$;   **(b)** $\sqrt[3]{8}$;   **(c)** $\sqrt[4]{81}$;   **(d)** $\sqrt{x^2}$.

10. Find as a single radical: **(a)** $\sqrt{m} \cdot \sqrt{n}$;   **(b)** $\dfrac{\sqrt{r}}{\sqrt{s}}$.

Change each expression to a radical in simplest form.

11. $\sqrt{12}$ **12.** $\sqrt{\frac{2}{3}}$ **13.** $8\sqrt{5} + \sqrt{5}$

14. $\sqrt{4y} - \sqrt{y}$ **15.** $\sqrt{27} + \sqrt{\frac{1}{3}}$ **16.** $\sqrt{200} - (\sqrt{18} + \sqrt{8})$

Using the table on page 555, find a decimal approximation for:

17. $\sqrt{700}$ **18.** $\sqrt{0.7}$

Solve.

19. $\sqrt{n + 1} = 2$ **20.** $x = 1 + \sqrt{7 - x}$

Find the distance between the two points whose coordinates are given. Express radicals in simplest form.

21. $(2, 3)$ and $(0, 1)$ **22.** $(-2, 7)$ and $(-4, 3)$

13 *Quadratics*

A paving machine like the one shown can be set to lay and finish different widths of concrete. Due to working conditions, it may be necessary to set the machine to pave 450 square feet while laying a strip that is 7 feet longer than it is wide. At what width should the machine be set?

This problem can be solved by using the equation

$$w(w + 7) = 450,$$

which is equivalent to

$$w^2 + 7w - 450 = 0.$$

In this chapter, you will consider several methods of solving equations of this type.

An open sentence stating that two polynomials are equal is called a *polynomial equation.* A polynomial equation in one variable is named according to the highest degree of its variable.

In each of these equations

$x + 2 = -4$	$x^2 = 8 - 2x$	$x^3 + 2x^2 = 3x$
$2n + 3 = 7$	$3s^2 = -75$	$y^3 = 2y + 1$
$y = 5$	$t^2 = 5$	$m^3 = 5$
$2m - 4 = 0$	$s^2 + 7s + 2 = 0$	$x^3 + 4x^2 = 1$

the highest degree of the variable is

⟩ 1   2   3

The equations are called

⟩ linear   quadratic   cubic

A quadratic equation in the form $ax^2 + bx + c = 0$, where x is any variable, a, b, and c are real numbers, and $a \neq 0$, is in **standard form**. If the polynomial $ax^2 + bx + c$ can be factored, the following property can be used to solve the equation.

If a product of real numbers is 0, then one or more of the numbers is 0.

zero product property

Example 1: Solve $x^2 + 5x + 6 = 0$.

SOLUTION: $x^2 + 5x + 6 = 0$

$(x + 2)(x + 3) = 0$ Factoring

$x + 2 = 0$ or $x + 3 = 0$ By the zero product property

$x = -2$ $x = -3$

Check:

$(-2)^2 + 5(-2) + 6 = 0$ or $(-3)^2 + 5(-3) + 6 = 0$

$4 - 10 + 6 = 0$ $9 - 15 + 6 = 0$

$0 = 0$ T $0 = 0$ T

Thus, the solution set of $x^2 + 5x + 6 = 0$ is $\{-2, -3\}$. The numbers -2 and -3 are **roots** of the equation $x^2 + 5x + 6 = 0$.

Example 2: Solve $2y^2 + 5y = 12$.

SOLUTION: $2y^2 + 5y = 12$ Expressing in standard form

$2y^2 + 5y - 12 = 0$ ← $ax^2 + bx + c = 0$

$(2y - 3)(y + 4) = 0$ Factoring

$2y - 3 = 0$ or $y + 4 = 0$ By the zero product property

$y = \frac{3}{2}$ $y = -4$

Thus, the solution set of $2y^2 + 5y = 12$ is $\{\frac{3}{2}, -4\}$. Check.

Example 3: Solve: **a.** $3n^2 + n = 0$ **b.** $4x^2 = 9$

            c. $4y^2 + 12y + 9 = 0$

SOLUTIONS:

a. $3n^2 + n = 0$ **b.** $4x^2 = 9$

      $n(3n + 1) = 0$ $4x^2 - 9 = 0$

$n = 0$ or $3n + 1 = 0$ $(2x + 3)(2x - 3) = 0$

$n = 0$ $n = -\frac{1}{3}$ $2x + 3 = 0$ or $2x - 3 = 0$

                                    $x = -\frac{3}{2}$ $x = \frac{3}{2}$

c. $4y^2 + 12y + 9 = 0$

        $(2y + 3)^2 = 0$

$2y + 3 = 0$ or $2y + 3 = 0$

$2y = -3$ $2y = -3$

$y = -\frac{3}{2}$ $y = -\frac{3}{2}$ ◀ Two equal roots

                                             Solution set: $\{-\frac{3}{2}\}$

Check these solutions.

EXERCISES 13.1

Ⓐ Find an equivalent quadratic equation in standard form.

1. $x^2 + 3x = -2$ **2.** $x^2 + 4x = -3$ **3.** $y^2 + 6 = -7y$

4. $y^2 + 8 = -6y$ **5.** $w^2 = w + 12$ **6.** $r^2 = r + 20$

7. $30 = m^2 + m$ **8.** $42 = n^2 + n$ **9.** $-x - 72 = -x^2$

10. $-x - 56 = -x^2$ **11.** $x^2 = x + 6$ **12.** $x^2 = 3x + 10$

Solve each equation by using the zero product property.

13. $5x = 0$ **14.** $x(x + 2) = 0$ **15.** $4y(y + 3) = 0$

16. $0 = 9y$ **17.** $x(x - 5) = 0$ **18.** $(x - 2)(x - 1) = 0$

19. $0 = (x + 8)(x + 12)$ **20.** $(5 - n)(7 + n) = 0$

Ⓑ **21–32.** Solve each equation in Exercises **1–12** by the factoring method.

Solve each equation by the factoring method.

33. $x^2 - 49 = 0$ **34.** $x^2 - 4 = 0$ **35.** $p^2 + 7p = 0$

36. $q^2 + 11q = 0$ **37.** $x^2 = 15x - 50$ **38.** $y^2 = 14y - 48$

39. $-x^2 = 6x + 9$ **40.** $-y^2 = 8y + 16$ **41.** $2n^2 + n = 3$

42. $3p^2 + 5p = 2$ **43.** $6x^2 - 12x = 0$ **44.** $5x^2 - 10x = 0$

45. $s^2 = 4s - 4$ **46.** $a^2 = 6a - 9$ **47.** $3r^2 = 12r$

48. $15t = 3t^2$ **49.** $9n^2 = 49$ **50.** $4m^2 = 25$

51. $s^2 + 2s - 35 = 0$ **52.** $t^2 + 2t - 15 = 0$

53. $9x^2 - 24x + 16 = 0$ **54.** $16n^2 - 24n + 9 = 0$

Find a quadratic equation that has the given roots.

Example: If $x = 1$ or $x = -2$, then $x - 1 = 0$ or $x + 2 = 0$.
So $(x - 1)(x + 2) = 0$, and $x^2 + x - 2 = 0$.

55. $\{2, 5\}$ **56.** $\{-3, 0\}$ **57.** $\{-4, -5\}$

58. $\{7, -1\}$ **59.** $\{0, -4\}$ **60.** $\{-7, 3\}$

Solve by using the zero product property.

Example: $n(2n + 1)(n - 2) = 0$
$n = 0$ or $2n + 1 = 0$ or $n - 2 = 0$
$n = 0$ $n = -\frac{1}{2}$ $n = 2$

61. $x(x - 6)(x + 4) = 0$ **62.** $(r - 1)(r - 2)(r - 3) = 0$

Ⓒ **63.** $12x^3 - 25x^2 - 7x = 0$ **64.** $9m^3 - 42m^2 = -49m$

65. $18x^3 - 45x^2 = 0$ **66.** $36t^3 = 12t$

13.2 THE SQUARE ROOT PROPERTY

In Example **3b** on page 432, the equation $4x^2 = 9$ is solved by factoring. The equation $x^2 = n^2$, where n is any real number, can be solved in the same way.

$x^2 = n^2$	Given
$x^2 - n^2 = 0$	Expressing in standard form
$(x + n)(x - n) = 0$	Factoring
$x + n = 0$ or $x - n = 0$	By the zero product property
$x = -n \qquad x = n$	

square root property for equations

> Let n be any real number.
>
> If $x^2 = n^2$, then $x = n$ or $x = -n$.

$x = n$ or $x = -n$ may also be written $x = \pm n$.

This property is useful in solving equations of the type $(x + a)^2 = c$, where a is any real number, c is a nonnegative real number, and the replacement set for x is the set of real numbers.

Example 1: Solve $(x + 3)^2 = 16$.

SOLUTION:
$$(x + 3)^2 = 16$$
$$(x + 3)^2 = (\pm 4)^2$$
$$x + 3 = \pm 4$$
$$x + 3 = 4 \quad \text{or} \quad x + 3 = -4$$
$$x = 1 \qquad\qquad x = -7$$

Check: $(1 + 3)^2 = 16$ or $(-7 + 3)^2 = 16$

$\qquad\quad 4^2 = 16 \qquad\qquad\qquad (-4)^2 = 16$

$\qquad\quad 16 = 16$ T $\qquad\qquad 16 = 16$ T

This method may also be used to find irrational roots as in the next example. Any radicals involved should be simplified.

Example 2: Solve $(x - 5)^2 = 8$.

SOLUTION:

$$(x - 5)^2 = 8$$
$$(x - 5)^2 = (\pm\sqrt{8})^2$$
$$x - 5 = \pm\sqrt{8}$$
$$x = 5 \pm \sqrt{8} \longrightarrow \quad \text{That is, } x = 5 + \sqrt{8} \text{ or } x = 5 - \sqrt{8}.$$
$$x = 5 \pm 2\sqrt{2}$$

Check: $[(5 \pm 2\sqrt{2}) - 5]^2 = 8$
$$(\pm 2\sqrt{2})^2 = 8$$
$$8 = 8 \quad \textsf{T}$$

Example 3: Solve $x^2 + 6x + 9 = 49$.

SOLUTION: perfect-square trinomial

$$\overbrace{x^2 + 6x + 9} = 49$$
$$(x + 3)^2 = (\pm 7)^2$$
$$x + 3 = \pm 7$$
$$x = -3 \pm 7$$
$$x = 4 \quad \text{or} \quad x = -10 \qquad \text{Check these roots.}$$

EXERCISES 13.2

Ⓐ In using the square root property for equations to solve a quadratic equation of the form $(x + a)^2 = c$,

1. must c be nonnegative?

2. must c be a perfect square?

Express each equation in the form $(x + a)^2 = c$.

3. $x^2 + 2x + 1 = 4$ **4.** $y^2 + 4y + 4 = 9$

5. $y^2 - 3 = 6$ HINT: $y^2 = (y + 0)^2$ **6.** $3 + x^2 = 7$

7. $(s - 2)^2 - 9 = 0$ **8.** $0 = 16 - (t - 5)^2$

9. $r^2 - 81 = 0$ **10.** $64 - n^2 = 0$

Use the square root property for equations to solve each equation.

11. $x^2 = 25$ **12.** $w^2 - 1 = 0$ **13.** $4s^2 = 16$

14. $4 = 9y^2$ **15.** $m^2 = 3$ **16.** $n^2 - 49 = 0$

17. $x^2 - 7 = 2$ **18.** $s^2 = 18$ **19.** $x^2 - 40 = 9$

20. $t^2 = 50$ **21.** $32 = 2y^2$ **22.** $72 = w^2$

Ⓑ **23–30.** Solve each equation in Exercises 3–10.

Solve each equation.

31. $(x + 1)^2 = 81$ **32.** $(x + 2)^2 = 64$

33. $(m - 4)^2 = 1$ **34.** $(n - 3)^2 = 1$

35. $(y + 7)^2 = 16$ **36.** $(y + 5)^2 = 25$

37. $36 = (r - 8)^2$ **38.** $49 = (s - 6)^2$

39. $x^2 + 8x + 16 = 9$ **40.** $x^2 + 6x + 9 = 25$

41. $m^2 - 21 = 4$ **42.** $n^2 - 19 = 17$

43. $(s + 3)^2 - 3 = 13$ **44.** $(t + 6)^2 - 3 = 33$

45. $(m - 4)^2 = 8$ **46.** $(n - 3)^2 = 18$

47. $x^2 - 54 = 0$ **48.** $y^2 - 48 = 0$

49. $(s - 10)^2 = 64$ **50.** $(t - 9)^2 = 25$

51. $8 = x^2 - 18x + 81$ **52.** $12 = y^2 - 16y + 64$

53. $m^2 - 121 = 0$ **54.** $n^2 - 144 = 0$

55. $81 - x^2 = 5$ **56.** $79 - y^2 = 7$

57. $(x - 20)^2 = 100$ **58.** $(y - 30)^2 = 100$

Ⓒ **59.** $(x + \frac{1}{3})^2 = \frac{16}{9}$ **60.** $(y + \frac{1}{2})^2 = \frac{9}{4}$

61. $(x - \sqrt{6})^2 = 24$ **62.** $(y - \sqrt{7})^2 = 28$

63. $(4x - 5)^2 = 32$ **64.** $(7x - 6)^2 = 28$

65. $(7y - 14)^2 = 49$ **66.** $(8m - 16)^2 = 64$

In Chapter 7, on page 233, we "completed the square" to form perfect-square trinomials. For example, given $x^2 - 10x$, we complete the square as follows.

$$x^2 - 2 \cdot x \cdot 5 + ?^2$$
$$x^2 - 2 \cdot x \cdot 5 + 5^2$$

In a perfect-square trinomial, the middle term is $+2$ or -2 times the square roots of the first and last terms.

$$x^2 - 10x + 25 \quad \longleftarrow \quad \text{The perfect-square trinomial}$$

$$(x - 5)^2 \quad \longleftarrow \quad \text{The trinomial factored}$$

This method can be used to solve quadratic equations that cannot be solved easily by factoring.

Example 1: Solve $x^2 - 10x - 2 = 0$.

SOLUTION:

$$x^2 - 10x - 2 = 0$$
$$x^2 - 10x = 2$$

Rewrite the given equation in the form $x^2 - bx = c$. Then decide how to complete the square as shown above.

$$x^2 - 10x + 5^2 = 2 + 25$$

Add the necessary number to **both** sides of the equation.

$$(x - 5)^2 = 27$$

Factor.

$$x - 5 = \pm\sqrt{27}$$

Sq. root prop. for $=$

$$x = 5 \pm 3\sqrt{3}$$

Check: First check the root $5 + 3\sqrt{3}$.

$$(5 + 3\sqrt{3})^2 \quad -10(5 + 3\sqrt{3}) - 2 \quad = 0$$

$$25 + 2 \cdot 15\sqrt{3} + (3\sqrt{3})^2$$
$$25 + 30\sqrt{3} + 27$$
$$52 + 30\sqrt{3}$$

$$(-10 \cdot 5 - 10 \cdot 3\sqrt{3}) - 2$$
$$(-50 - 30\sqrt{3}) - 2$$
$$-52 - 30\sqrt{3}$$

$$52 + 30\sqrt{3} \quad -52 - 30\sqrt{3} = 0$$
$$0 = 0 \quad \top$$

Now check the root $5 - 3\sqrt{3}$.

Example 2: Solve $5x^2 + 30x = 2$.

SOLUTION:

$$5x^2 + 30x = 2$$

$$x^2 + 6x = \tfrac{2}{5}$$

$$\left.\begin{array}{l} x^2 + 2 \cdot x \cdot 3 + ?^2 = \tfrac{2}{5} + ?^2 \\[4pt] x^2 + 2 \cdot x \cdot 3 + 3^2 = \tfrac{2}{5} + 9 \end{array}\right\}$$

$$(x + 3)^2 = \tfrac{47}{5}$$

$$x = -3 \pm \tfrac{1}{5}\sqrt{235}$$

{ Rewrite the equation in the form $x^2 + bx = c$ by using the mult. prop. of $=$.

◀ Complete the square.

⟵ Use the square root property for equations to solve this equation.

Notice that in $x^2 + bx = c$, the square is always completed by adding $\left(\tfrac{b}{2}\right)^2$ to both sides.

EXERCISES 13.3

Ⓐ What number must be added to both sides of each equation to complete the square?

1. $x^2 + 2 \cdot x \cdot 2 = 12$ **2.** $x^2 - 2 \cdot x \cdot 3 = 7$

3. $x^2 - 2x = 24$ **4.** $x^2 + 6x = 16$

5. $x^2 - 6x = -8$ **6.** $x^2 + 8x = -12$

7. $x^2 + 3x = -\tfrac{1}{4}$ **8.** $x^2 + 7x = \tfrac{3}{4}$

9. $x^2 - \tfrac{3}{2}x = \tfrac{7}{16}$ **10.** $x^2 + \tfrac{6}{5}x = \tfrac{7}{25}$

Ⓑ **11–20.** Solve each equation in Exercises **1–10** by completing the square.

Solve by completing the square.

21. $x^2 + 2x - 8 = 0$ **22.** $x^2 + 2x - 3 = 0$

23. $y^2 + 6y + 8 = 0$ **24.** $y^2 + 8y + 7 = 0$

25. $x^2 + \tfrac{4}{3}x = \tfrac{4}{3}$ **26.** $x^2 + \tfrac{8}{3}x = 1$

27. $x^2 = x + 6$ **28.** $x^2 = x + 12$

29. $0 = r^2 - 9r + \tfrac{1}{4}$ **30.** $0 = s^2 - 7s + \tfrac{9}{4}$

31. $x^2 + 6 = 5x$

32. $x^2 - 6 = 5x$

33. $m^2 + 10m + 7 = 0$

34. $n^2 + 12n + 12 = 0$

35. $x^2 + 12x = 0$

36. $x^2 + 14x = 0$

37. $2x^2 - x - 6 = 0$

38. $3x^2 - 7x - 6 = 0$

39. $5x^2 - 6x = 11$

40. $8x^2 - 32x = -5$

41. $4x^2 - 6x = \frac{27}{4}$

42. $5x^2 - 32x = -8$

43. $7x^2 + 28x + 3 = 0$

44. $2x^2 + 12x = 7$

45. $3x^2 - 8 = 2x$

46. $8x^2 - 2x = 3$

Ⓒ Solve by completing the square as in the example below.

Example: $9x^2 - 30x = 2$

$(3x)^2 - 2 \cdot 3x \cdot 5 + ?^2 = 2 + ?^2$

$(3x)^2 - 2 \cdot 3x \cdot 5 + 5^2 = 2 + 25$

$(3x - 5)^2 = 27$ ⟵ Use the square root property for equations to solve this equation.

$x = \frac{5}{3} \pm \sqrt{3}$

47. $9r^2 + 12r = 32$

48. $4s^2 + 12s = 27$

49. $16m^2 = 8m + 3$

50. $25n^2 = 30n + 16$

51. $4x^2 + 28x = 95$

52. $9y^2 + 60y = 44$

Write each equation in the form $x^2 + mx = n$, and then solve by completing the square.

53. $(2x - 3)^2 - x(x + 3) = 0$

54. $(3x - 4)(2x + 3) + (6x + 10) = 0$

55. $(x + 2)^2 + 4(x + 2) = 12$

56. $x^2 + 2x + c = 0$

57. $x^2 + bx + c = 0$

58. $ax^2 + bx + c = 0$

13.4 THE QUADRATIC FORMULA

The method of completing the square can be used to solve any quadratic equation. Recall that, in the standard form of the quadratic equation, a, b, and c are any real numbers and $a \neq 0$. We will now complete the square for a general quadratic equation.

(1) $\quad ax^2 + bx + c = 0$ Standard form of quadratic equation

(2) $\quad\quad ax^2 + bx = -c$ Add $-c$ to both sides of eq. (1).

(3) $\quad\quad x^2 + \dfrac{b}{a}x = -\dfrac{c}{a}$ Multiply both sides of eq. (2) by $\dfrac{1}{a}$.

Now complete the square for the left side of equation (3) and factor the resulting polynomial.

(4) $\quad x^2 + 2 \cdot x \cdot \dfrac{b}{2a} + ?^2 = -\dfrac{c}{a} + ?^2$

(5) $\quad x^2 + 2 \cdot x \cdot \dfrac{b}{2a} + \left(\dfrac{b}{2a}\right)^2 = -\dfrac{c}{a} + \left(\dfrac{b}{2a}\right)^2$

(6) $\quad\quad\quad\quad \left(x + \dfrac{b}{2a}\right)^2 = -\dfrac{c}{a} + \left(\dfrac{b}{2a}\right)^2$

Before using the square root property for equations on equation (6), we can write the right side of the equation in a form that will be more convenient.

$$-\frac{c}{a} + \left(\frac{b}{2a}\right)^2 = -\frac{c}{a} + \frac{b^2}{(2a)^2}$$

$$= \frac{b^2}{(2a)^2} - \frac{c}{a}$$

$$= \frac{b^2}{(2a)^2} - \frac{c}{a} \cdot \frac{2^2 a}{2^2 a}$$

$$= \frac{b^2 - 4ac}{(2a)^2}$$

$$= \left(\frac{\sqrt{b^2 - 4ac}}{2a}\right)^2$$

Equation (6) can now be expressed as follows.

(7) $\left(x + \dfrac{b}{2a}\right)^2 = \left(\dfrac{\sqrt{b^2 - 4ac}}{2a}\right)^2$ If $b^2 - 4ac \geq 0$, we can use the square root property for equations on eq. (7).

(8) $x + \dfrac{b}{2a} = \pm \dfrac{\sqrt{b^2 - 4ac}}{2a}$

(9) $x = -\dfrac{b}{2a} \pm \dfrac{\sqrt{b^2 - 4ac}}{2a}$ Add $-\dfrac{b}{2a}$ to both sides of eq. (8).

(10) $x = \dfrac{-b \pm \sqrt{b^2 - 4ac}}{2a}$ Add as indicated on the right side of eq. (9).

Checking these roots in the original equation, we find we can conclude the following.

Let a, b, and c be any real numbers, and let $ax^2 + bx + c = 0$.

Then $$x = \dfrac{-b \pm \sqrt{b^2 - 4ac}}{2a}$$

providing that $a \neq 0$ and $b^2 - 4ac \geq 0$.

quadratic formula

We can use this formula to solve any quadratic equation.

Example 1: Solve $3x^2 - x - 2 = 0$.

SOLUTION:
$$\overset{a}{\underset{\downarrow}{3x^2}} \ \overset{b}{\underset{\downarrow}{- 1x}} \ \overset{c}{\underset{\downarrow}{- 2}} = 0 \quad \text{and} \quad x = \dfrac{-b \pm \sqrt{b^2 - 4ac}}{2a}$$

Substituting, $x = \dfrac{-(-1) \pm \sqrt{(-1)^2 - 4 \cdot 3 \cdot (-2)}}{2 \cdot 3}$

$= \dfrac{1 \pm \sqrt{25}}{6}$

$= \dfrac{1 \pm 5}{6}$

Thus, $x = 1$ or $x = -\frac{2}{3}$. Check these roots.

Example 2: Solve $3x^2 + 5x + 1 = 0$.

SOLUTION:

$$\overset{a}{\underset{\downarrow}{3x^2}} + \overset{b}{\underset{\downarrow}{5x}} + \overset{c}{\underset{\downarrow}{1}} = 0 \quad \text{and} \quad x = \frac{-b \pm \sqrt{b^2 - 4ac}}{2a}$$

Substituting, $x = \dfrac{-5 \pm \sqrt{5^2 - 4 \cdot 3 \cdot 1}}{2 \cdot 3}$

$$= \frac{-5 \pm \sqrt{13}}{6}$$

Thus, $x = -\frac{5}{6} + \frac{1}{6}\sqrt{13}$ or $x = -\frac{5}{6} - \frac{1}{6}\sqrt{13}$. Check these roots.

These roots can be expressed as decimal approximations by using the square-root table on page 555.

$$x = \frac{-5 \pm \sqrt{13}}{6}$$

$$x \approx \frac{-5 \pm 3.606}{6}$$

$$x \approx \frac{-1.394}{6} \quad \text{or} \quad x \approx \frac{-8.606}{6}$$

$$x \approx -0.232 \qquad x \approx -1.434$$

EXERCISES 13.4

(A) What are the values of a, b, and c for each equation?

1. $x^2 + 3x + 2 = 0$

2. $x^2 - 5x + 6 = 0$

3. $n^2 + n - 2 = 0$

4. $m^2 - 2m = 3$

5. $2r^2 + 11r + 12 = 0$

6. $2s^2 + 5 = 11s$

7. $5 = -3x^2 + 8x$

8. $4x^2 = 8x - 3$

9. $5x^2 - 6x = 8$

10. $3x^2 - 6x = 0$

(B) 11–20. Use the quadratic formula to solve each equation in Exercises 1–10.

Solve by using the quadratic formula. Express irrational roots in simplest radical form.

21. $x^2 + 8x + 8 = 0$ **22.** $x^2 + 6x + 6 = 0$

23. $x^2 - 4x + 1 = 0$ **24.** $x^2 - 6x + 2 = 0$

25. $s^2 = 5s - 1$ **26.** $t^2 = 7t - 2$

27. $y^2 + 2y = 1$ **28.** $y^2 + 4y = 1$

29. $-x^2 + 5x + 4 = 0$ **30.** $-x^2 + 7x + 2 = 0$

31. $5x^2 = 7x$ **32.** $3x^2 = 5x$

33. $x^2 - 3x - 2 = 0$ **34.** $x^2 - x - 3 = 0$

35. $m^2 + 9m + 6 = 0$ **36.** $n^2 + 11n + 8 = 0$

37. $x^2 = 11x - 30$ **38.** $x^2 = 9x - 20$

39. $8x^2 + 3x = 0$ **40.** $6x^2 + 4x = 0$

41. $3x^2 + 6x + 1 = 0$ **42.** $2x^2 + 4x + 1 = 0$

43. $2x^2 + 4x = 3$ **44.** $2x^2 + 6x = 3$

45. $5x^2 + 8x + 2 = 0$ **46.** $5x^2 + 10x + 1 = 0$

47. $2r^2 = 5r + 7$ **48.** $2s^2 = s + 10$

49. $9x^2 = 6x$ **50.** $8x^2 = 10x$

51–56. Express each irrational root for Exercises **41–46** as a decimal approximation to the nearest tenth.

© Solve each equation.

57. $x^2 + \frac{7}{3}x = \frac{2}{3}$ **58.** $mx^2 + nx + p = 0$

59. $w^2 + 2\sqrt{3}w + 3 = 0$ **60.** $\sqrt{2}x^2 + 2x - 2\sqrt{2} = 0$

HINT: For Exercises 61–64, first multiply both sides by the LCD. Then solve the resulting quadratic equation.

61. $-\dfrac{1}{x + 1} = \dfrac{3}{x} + 2$ **62.** $\dfrac{1}{x - 2} = \dfrac{2}{x} + 1$

63. $\dfrac{2}{x} + 3x = 8$ **64.** $\dfrac{2}{x} + \dfrac{5}{2} = x$

Stop!

On page 416, a formula is shown that is used to estimate the speed of a car from its skid marks. But the skid marks show only the distance traveled during braking. *Stopping distance* is the sum of *braking distance* and *reaction distance* (the distance traveled from the time the driver sees danger to the time he brakes).

braking distance + reaction distance = stopping distance

$$d_B = \frac{s^2}{30f} \qquad d_R = 1.1s \qquad d = \frac{s^2}{30f} + 1.1s$$

Distances are in feet.
s = speed in mph
f = coefficient of friction

in standard form: $\quad s^2 + 3.3fs - 30fd = 0$

If a car required a stopping distance of 74 feet on a dry, concrete road ($f = 0.8$), estimate how fast the car was traveling.

$s^2 + 3.3(0.8)s - 30(0.8)(74) = 0$ ⟶ Substituting .

$s^2 + 2.64s - 1776 = 0$

$$s = \frac{-2.64 + \sqrt{(2.64)^2 - 4 \cdot 1 \cdot (-1776)}}{2 \cdot 1}$$

Using the quadratic formula (The negative radical is not useful here.)

$$\approx \frac{-2.64 + \sqrt{7110.97}}{2}$$

$\approx -1.32 + 42.16 \quad \text{or} \quad 40.84 \longrightarrow$ So s is about 41 mph.

Estimate how fast a car was traveling if

1. It stops in 100 feet on a dry, oiled-gravel road ($f = 0.5$).

2. It stops in 300 feet on a wet, concrete road ($f = 0.4$).

Solve each equation by the factoring method.

1. $x^2 - 9 = 0$ **2.** $x^2 + 3x = 0$

3. $x^2 + 4x + 4 = 0$ **4.** $x^2 + 7x + 10 = 0$

5. $m^2 + m = 30$ **6.** $3x^2 + 2x - 8 = 0$

Solve by using the square root property for equations.

7. $r^2 = 20$ **8.** $5s^2 = 20$

9. $(y + 7)^2 = 9$ **10.** $\dfrac{(x - 4)^2}{2} = 8$

11. $(y + \frac{1}{2})^2 = \frac{1}{4}$ **12.** $t^2 - 10t + 25 = 3$

Solve each equation by completing the square. Express each irrational root in simplest radical form.

13. $x^2 + 4x = 12$ **14.** $y^2 + 5y = 0$

15. $m^2 + 6m - 3 = 0$ **16.** $x^2 = 3x + 54$

17. $0 = 5s^2 - 8s + 3$ **18.** $2t^2 - 3t = 4$

Solve each equation by using the quadratic formula. Express each irrational root in simplest radical form.

19. $x^2 + 7x + 12 = 0$ **20.** $2x^2 + 5x - 3 = 0$

21. $6x^2 = 10x$ **22.** $3x^2 + x = 4$

23. $x^2 - 4x + 2 = 0$ **24.** $2x^2 = -2x + 3$

In Section 13.4, you learned that $ax^2 + bx + c = 0$ has real roots (as given by the quadratic formula) if $b^2 - 4ac \geq 0$. The expression $b^2 - 4ac$ is called the **discriminant** of the equation, and its value also tells us if the real roots are equal.

Examples:

1. $x^2 + 3x - 1 = 0$ $\longrightarrow$ $a = 1, b = 3, c = -1$

$$x = \frac{-3 \pm \sqrt{3^2 - 4 \cdot 1 \cdot (-1)}}{2 \cdot 1}$$

$$= \frac{-3 \pm \sqrt{13}}{2}$$

$\boxed{b^2 - 4ac > 0}$

$$x = \frac{-3 + \sqrt{13}}{2} \quad \text{or} \quad x = \frac{-3 - \sqrt{13}}{2}$$

$\boxed{\text{The roots are unequal.}}$

2. $x^2 + 4x + 4 = 0$ $\longrightarrow$ $a = 1, b = 4, c = 4$

$$x = \frac{-4 \pm \sqrt{4^2 - 4 \cdot 1 \cdot 4}}{2 \cdot 1}$$

$$= \frac{-4 \pm \sqrt{0}}{2}$$

$\boxed{b^2 - 4ac = 0}$

$$x = -2 \quad \text{or} \quad x = -2$$

$\boxed{\text{The roots are equal.}}$

3. $2x^2 + x + 1 = 0$ $\longrightarrow$ $a = 2, b = 1, c = 1$

$$x = \frac{-1 \pm \sqrt{1^2 - 4 \cdot 2 \cdot 1}}{2 \cdot 2}$$

$$= \frac{-1 \pm \sqrt{-7}}{4}$$

$\boxed{\begin{array}{l} b^2 - 4ac < 0 \\ \text{There are no real roots.} \end{array}}$

EXERCISES 13.5

Ⓐ If the discriminant of a quadratic equation has the value given, does the equation have real roots?

1. 4	**2.** -3	**3.** 0	**4.** 8	**5.** $-(-9)$
6. $-\frac{1}{2}$	**7.** 29	**8.** 49	**9.** -49	**10.** 24

Find the value of the discriminant of each equation and then describe the roots. (Are they real? If so, are they equal?)

11. $p^2 + 4p + 2 = 0$ **12.** $q^2 + 3q + 1 = 0$

13. $x^2 + 2 = 0$ **14.** $y^2 + 3 = 0$

15. $4x^2 + 9 = 12x$ **16.** $4x^2 + 25 = 20x$

17. $3m^2 + 6m + 4 = 0$ **18.** $2n^2 + 5n + 4 = 0$

19. $4 = 3x^2 + 11x$ **20.** $2 = 5x^2 + 9x$

21. $-5s^2 + s + 1 = 0$ **22.** $-7t^2 + t + 1 = 0$

23. $\frac{1}{2}x^2 + \sqrt{6}x + 2 = 0$ **24.** $\frac{1}{4}y^2 + \sqrt{11}y + 8 = 0$

25. $\frac{3}{4}m^2 + \frac{1}{4} = 0$ **26.** $\frac{2}{3}n^2 + \frac{1}{3} = 0$

27–50. Find the value of the discriminant of each equation in Exercises **27–50** on page 443 and describe the roots.

Ⓒ If a, b, and c are rational numbers and the discriminant is a perfect square, the roots of $ax^2 + bx + c = 0$ are also rational. However, if the discriminant is positive but not a perfect square, the roots are irrational.

Find the value of the discriminant of each equation and describe the roots. (Are they real? Equal? Rational?)

51. $x^2 - 2x - 3 = 0$ **52.** $3x^2 + 4x - 12 = 0$

53. $9y^2 + 12y + 4 = 0$ **54.** $2w^2 + 4w + 8 = 0$

55. $3t^2 - 3t = -5$ **56.** $5s^2 = 20$

If a, b, and c are real numbers, describe the roots of $ax^2 + bx + c = 0$ in each case.

57. $a = 0$, $b \neq 0$, $c \neq 0$ **58.** $a \neq 0$, $b \neq 0$, $c = 0$

59. $b = 0$, a and c have the same sign   **60.** $b^2 = 4ac$

61. $b = 0$, a and c have opposite signs

13.6 SOLVING PROBLEMS

Quadratic equations are often useful in solving everyday problems. The steps for solving problems, which were shown in a flow chart in Chapter 3, are repeated in the example below.

Example 1: The strip of paving described on page 430 is 7 feet longer than it is wide. Its area is 450 square feet. What are its length and width?

SOLUTION: The strip is 7 feet longer than it is wide; its area is 450 square feet.

▷ Read the problem carefully.

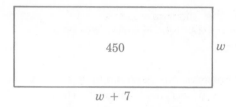

w

▷ Draw a diagram if possible.

$w + 7$

Let w = the width of the strip in feet. Then $w + 7$ = the length of the strip in feet.

▷ Choose a variable.

The area, which is 450 square feet, can also be represented as $w(w + 7)$.

So $$w(w + 7) = 450$$

▷ Write and solve an open sentence.

$$w^2 + 7w = 450$$

$$w^2 + 7w - 450 = 0$$

$$(w - 18)(w + 25) = 0$$

$$w - 18 = 0 \quad \text{or} \quad w + 25 = 0$$

$$w = 18 \qquad\qquad w = -25$$

Since the width cannot be negative, $w = 18$ and $w + 7 = 25$. That is, the strip is 18 feet across and 25 feet long. Check to see that these dimensions fit the problem.

▷ Interpret the result. There are two solutions for the equation, but one of them cannot be used in answering the problem.

Example 2: The sum of two numbers is 11 and their product is 28. Find the numbers.

SOLUTION: Let n = one number.

Then $11 - n$ = the other number.

$$n(11 - n) = 28$$

$$11n - n^2 = 28$$

$$n^2 - 11n + 28 = 0 \qquad \longleftarrow \text{ Solve this equation.}$$

$$\left. \begin{array}{ll} n = 4 \quad \text{or} & n = 7 \\ 11 - n = 7 & 11 - n = 4 \end{array} \right\} \quad \begin{array}{l} \text{Both solutions for the} \\ \text{equation give the same} \\ \text{answer to the problem.} \end{array}$$

Check to see that 4 and 7 are the required numbers.

Example 3: The sum of the squares of two consecutive odd integers is 74. Find the integers.

SOLUTION: Let x = the smaller integer.

Then $x + 2$ = the other integer.

$$x^2 + (x + 2)^2 = 74$$

$$2x^2 + 4x + 4 = 74$$

$$x^2 + 2x + 2 = 37$$

$$x^2 + 2x - 35 = 0 \qquad \longleftarrow \text{ Solve this equation.}$$

$$\left. \begin{array}{ll} x = -7 \quad \text{or} & x = 5 \\ x + 2 = -5 & x + 2 = 7 \end{array} \right\} \quad \begin{array}{l} \text{Each solution for the} \\ \text{equation gives a different} \\ \text{answer to the problem.} \end{array}$$

There are two possible answers to the problem, the integers -7 and -5, and the integers 5 and 7. Check these results.

EXERCISES 13.6

Ⓐ 1. In Example **1**, why is there only one answer to the problem, though the equation used to solve it has two solutions?

2. In Example **2**, why is there only one answer to the problem, though the equation used to solve it has two solutions?

Match each problem with the quadratic equation that could be used to solve it.

a. $\frac{1}{3}x^2 = 12$ **b.** $x(21 - x) = 80$ **c.** $x(x + 10) = 56$

d. $4x^2 = 16$ **e.** $x(x + 2) = 80$ **f.** $x^2 + x = 56$

g. $x \cdot 3x = 48$ **h.** $x(14 - x) = 48$ **i.** $x(x + 1) = 56$

j. $4x^2 = 64$ **k.** $x(x + 12) = 64$ **l.** $x(x - 7) = 0$

3. The product of two numbers is 48. One of the numbers is three times the other. Find the numbers.

4. One number is $\frac{1}{4}$ of another and their product is 16. Find the numbers.

5. Find two numbers whose product is 64 and whose difference is 12.

6. Find two numbers whose product is 56 and whose difference is 10.

7. Find two consecutive integers whose product is 56.

8. Find two consecutive even integers whose product is 80.

9. Find two numbers whose sum is 14 and whose product is 48.

10. Find two numbers whose sum is 21 and whose product is 80.

11. The sum of a number and its square is 56. Find the number.

12. The product of some number and the number that is 7 less is 0. Find the numbers.

13. Four times the area of a square is 64 square feet. Find the length of each side.

14. One-third the area of a square is 12 square meters. Find the length of each side.

Ⓑ 15–26. Solve each problem in Exercises 3–14.

Solve.

27. A rectangle is 5 centimeters longer than it is wide. Its area is 66 square centimeters. Find its length and width.

28. The width of a rectangle is 7 meters less than its length. Its area is 44 square meters. Find its length and width.

A home-building contractor gives purchasers a choice of outdoor concrete work. The basic plan calls for a 3 by 24 foot concrete sidewalk. Other choices, requiring the same amount of concrete as the sidewalk, are described below.

29. The purchaser may have a patio that is twice as long as it is wide. What are its length and width?

30. The purchaser may have a patio that is just a foot longer than it is wide. What are its length and width?

31. Two cars leave the same intersection at the same time and move at right angles to each other. One car travels 30 miles per hour and the other car travels 40 miles per hour. What is the distance between the cars after 2 hours? (HINT: Use the Pythagorean theorem.)

32. What is the distance between the cars in Exercise **31** after 3 hours?

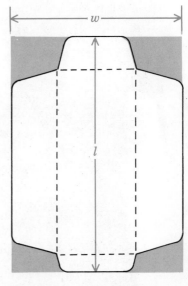

© Paper for all-purpose envelopes is available in sheets 5 feet long by 3 feet wide (so each sheet has an area of 2,160 square inches). A sheet can be cut without waste into rectangles, each of which makes one envelope "blank" as shown in the diagram. Make a manufacturer's size-chart by finding width and length in each exercise.

	Number of envelopes cut from each sheet	Size of each blank width	length
33.	6	w	$w + 2$
34.	10	$\frac{1}{3}(2l)$	l
35.	18	$l - 2$	l
36.	24	w	$2w + 3$
37.	36	w	$2w + 2$
38.	48	$\frac{1}{2}(l + 1)$	l
39.	60	w	$2w + 1$
40.	108	$l - 1$	l

Many times, the application of a formula results in a quadratic equation.

Example 1: $A = \frac{1}{2}bh$, where A is the area of a triangle, b is the length of its base and h is its height. The base of a given triangle is 2 centimeters longer than three times the height, and the area is 28 square centimeters. Find the height of the triangle.

SOLUTION: Since $b = 3h + 2$ and $A = 28$,

$$28 = \tfrac{1}{2}(3h + 2)h.$$

Then $3h^2 + 2h - 56 = 0$.

$$h = -\tfrac{14}{3} \quad \text{or} \quad h = 4$$

Thus, the height is 4 centimeters. Check this result.

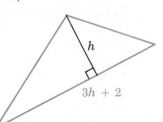

Example 2: An object falls d feet in t seconds, where $d = 16t^2$. How long will it take each drop of water to reach the bottom of a 100-foot waterfall?

SOLUTION:

$$d = 16t^2 \quad \blacktriangleleft \text{ Substitute 100 for } d \text{ in this formula.}$$

$$100 = 16t^2$$

$$\tfrac{100}{16} = t^2$$

$$\pm\sqrt{\tfrac{100}{16}} = t$$

$$\pm\tfrac{10}{4} = t$$

So $t = -2\frac{1}{2}$ or $t = 2\frac{1}{2}$.

Each drop of water takes $2\frac{1}{2}$ seconds to reach the bottom. (Check this result.)

EXERCISES 13.7

Ⓐ In each case, what substitution has been made in the formula to obtain the quadratic equation?

FORMULA	QUADRATIC EQUATION
1. $A = \pi r^2$	$9\pi = \pi r^2$
2. $d = 16t^2$	$16t^2 = 64$
3. $S = 4\pi r^2$	$36\pi = 4\pi r^2$
4. $S = \pi r^2 + \pi rl$	$\pi r^2 + 4\pi r = 77\pi$
5. $V = 2\pi r(r + h)$	$32\pi = 2\pi r^2 + 12\pi r$
6. $h = vt - 16t^2$	$120t - 16t^2 = 200$

7. A linear equation would result if a number were substituted for _____ in the formula of Exercise **5**.

8. To understand the result when a formula is used to solve a problem, it (is, is not) necessary to know the units in which any measurements were made.

Ⓑ **9–14.** Solve each quadratic equation in Exercises **1–6**.

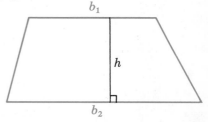

The formula for the area (A) of a trapezoid is
$$A = \tfrac{1}{2}h(b_1 + b_2),$$
where h, b_1, and b_2 are the measures of the altitude and the two bases.

15. If the area of a trapezoid is 40 square meters, and if $b_1 = h$ and $b_2 = h + 6$, find the altitude.

16. If the area of a trapezoid is 26 square meters, and if $b_1 = 2h$ and $b_2 = h + 1$, find the altitude.

17. If the area of a trapezoid is 60 square inches, and if $h = 2b_1$ and $b_2 = b_1 + 2$, find the altitude.

18. If the area of a trapezoid is 90 square feet, and if $h = 6b_2$ and $b_1 = b_2 + 4$, find the altitude.

19. The spillway shown has a cross-sectional area of 100 square feet. The width of the spillway at the bottom is one-third its width at the top. To carry enough water, the spillway must be twice as deep as it is wide at the bottom. How deep must it be?

20. A spillway similar to the one described in Exercise 19 has a cross-sectional area of 90 square feet. It is four times as wide at the top as at the bottom and the depth must be equal to the width at the bottom. How deep is this spillway?

$$d = \tfrac{1}{2}gt^2$$

distance an object falls

time of fall

acceleration due to gravity

Air resistance is ignored. If t is in seconds, use 9.8 for g to find d in meters.

21. If a stone is dropped 78.4 meters to the ground, how many seconds does the stone fall?

22. If a flowerpot falls from a window and lands 122.5 meters below, how many seconds does it fall?

23. If a diver "falls" from a diving board 8 meters above the water, how much later does he strike the water?

24. If supplies are dropped from an airplane 200 meters above the ground, how much later do they hit the ground?

Gravity on the moon is about one-sixth the gravity on earth. Use the formula $d = \tfrac{1}{2}gt^2$, with $g = \tfrac{1}{6}(9.8)$, in the exercises below.

25. About how many seconds does it take for a tool to fall $3\tfrac{3}{4}$ meters from a landing module to the surface of the moon?

26. An astronaut in a landing module on the moon drops a package 2.4 meters to a companion. How much time does the drop require?

$$h = vt - 16t^2$$

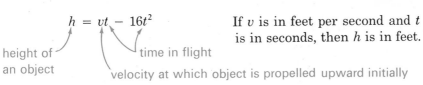

height of an object — time in flight — velocity at which object is propelled upward initially

If v is in feet per second and t is in seconds, then h is in feet.

27. If a ball is thrown upward at 80 feet per second, in how many seconds does it reach 100 feet?

28. In how many seconds does the ball in Exercise **27** reach 96 feet? (HINT: The ball reaches 96 feet on its way up and again on its way down.)

29. If a ball is thrown upward at 72 feet per second, in how many seconds does it reach 81 feet?

30. In how many seconds does the ball in Exercise **29** reach 56 feet? (See the HINT for Exercise **28**.)

© 31. Solve the formula $d = \frac{1}{2}gt^2$ for t.

32. Solve the formula $h = vt - 16t^2$ for t. (HINT: Use the quadratic formula.)

33. The formula $S = \frac{1}{2}n(n + 1)$ gives the sum (S) of the first n positive integers. Solve the formula for n.

34. If the sum of the integers from 1 to n is 276, what is n?

35. The sum (S) of the first n positive even integers is given by the formula $S = n(n + 1)$. Solve this formula for n.

36. If the sum of the first n even integers is 156, what is n?

*

13.8 QUADRATIC INEQUALITIES

$$x^2 + 2x - 3 < 0 \qquad x^2 + 2x - 3 \leq 0$$
$$x^2 + 2x - 3 > 0 \qquad x^2 + 2x - 3 \geq 0$$

The sentences above are **quadratic inequalities**. To solve them, we first graph the solution set of $x^2 + 2x - 3 = 0$, which is $\{-3, 1\}$. Notice that the graph of these roots separates the real number line into three intervals.

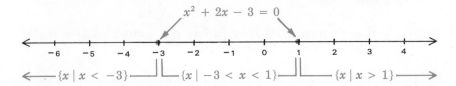

• By evaluating $x^2 + 2x - 3$ for at least one number between -3 and 1, we can show that, in this interval, $x^2 + 2x - 3 < 0$.

| Let $x =$ | -2 | Then $x^2 + 2x - 3 =$ | $(-2)^2 + 2(-2) - 3 = -3$ |

Thus, the solution set of $x^2 + 2x - 3 < 0$ is $\{x \mid -3 < x < 1\}$. In the graph of this set, hollow dots at -3 and 1 show that these **boundary points** are *not* in the graph.

$x^2 + 2x - 3 < 0$

• The solution set of $x^2 + 2x - 3 \leq 0$ is the *union* of the solution sets of $x^2 + 2x - 3 = 0$ and $x^2 + 2x - 3 < 0$, or $\{x \mid -3 \leq x \leq 1\}$.

$x^2 + 2x - 3 \leq 0$

• By evaluating $x^2 + 2x - 3$ for numbers less than -3 and also for numbers greater than 1, we can show that, in both these intervals, $x^2 + 2x - 3 > 0$.

| Let $x =$ | -4 | Then $x^2 + 2x - 3 =$ | $(-4)^2 + 2(-4) - 3 = 5$ |
| | 4 | | $4^2 + 2 \cdot 4 - 3 = 21$ |

So the solution set for $x^2 + 2x - 3 > 0$ is $\{x \mid x < -3 \quad \text{or} \quad x > 1\}$.

• The solution set for $x^2 + 2x - 3 \geq 0$ is $\{x \mid x \leq -3 \quad \text{or} \quad x \geq 1\}$.

Example 1: Find and graph the solution set of $2x^2 - 3x < 5$.

 SOLUTION: First, rewrite the inequality so the right side is 0.

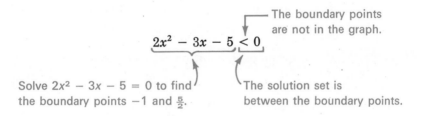

The boundary points are not in the graph.

Solve $2x^2 - 3x - 5 = 0$ to find the boundary points -1 and $\frac{5}{2}$.

The solution set is between the boundary points.

So, for $2x^2 - 3x < 5$, the solution set is $\{x \mid -1 < x < \frac{5}{2}\}$.

Example 2: Find and graph the solution set of $x^2 - 4 \geq 0$.

 SOLUTION:

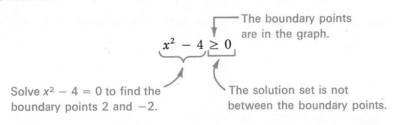

The boundary points are in the graph.

Solve $x^2 - 4 = 0$ to find the boundary points 2 and -2.

The solution set is not between the boundary points.

So, for $x^2 - 4 \geq 0$, the solution set is $\{x \mid x \leq -2 \text{ or } x \geq 2\}$.

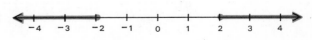

EXERCISES 13.8

Ⓐ Describe each set graphed.

1.

2.

3.

4.

5.

6.

What three intervals would you consider in graphing each sentence?

7. $(x + 1)(x + 2) < 0$ 8. $(x + 1)(x + 3) < 0$

9. $(x - 2)(x + 3) > 0$ 10. $(x - 3)(x + 2) > 0$

11. $(x - 4)(x - 2) < 0$ 12. $(x - 5)(x - 3) < 0$

13. $(x + 6)(x - 5) > 0$ 14. $(x + 5)(x - 4) > 0$

15. $(3x - 5)(x - 4) > 0$ 16. $(2x - 3)(x - 5) > 0$

Ⓑ **17–26. Find and graph each solution set in Exercises 7–16.**

Find and graph the solution set of each inequality.

27. $x^2 + 5x + 6 < 0$ 28. $x^2 + 7x + 12 < 0$

29. $y^2 + y - 2 \geq 0$ 30. $y^2 + 2y - 3 \geq 0$

31. $x^2 - 8x + 15 \leq 0$ 32. $x^2 - 9x + 14 \leq 0$

33. $y^2 + 2y > 8$ 34. $y^2 - y > 6$ 35. $x^2 + 9x < 0$

36. $x^2 + 7x < 0$ 37. $x^2 \geq 25$ 38. $x^2 \geq 16$

39. $2x^2 \leq 3x + 9$ 40. $2x^2 \leq -x + 10$

41. $0 > 9r^2 - 15r + 4$ 42. $0 > 4s^2 - 8s + 3$

43. $4p^2 - 5p - 6 > 0$ 44. $4q^2 - 9q - 9 > 0$

Ⓒ Graph each set.

45. $\{x \mid 1 < x < 3\} \cup \{x \mid x \geq 1\}$ 46. $\{x \mid x \geq 1\} \cap \{x \mid x \leq 2\}$

47. $[\{y \mid y > -1\} \cup \{y \mid y < 1\}] \cap \{y \mid -1 < y < 1\}$

48. $\{x \mid x < -2 \text{ or } x > 1\} \cap \{x \mid x > -3 \text{ and } x < 2\}$

Some Uses of Quadratic Equations

In Section 13.7, you worked with several formulas for vertical motion. There are many other formulas whose use may lead to quadratic equations. Several of these are illustrated below.

$$d^2 = kht^2$$

t is time required to travel distance d.

k is determined by gravity and friction.

$$E = mc^2$$

m is the mass of a material.

E is its potential energy.

c is the velocity of light.

$$x^2 = ah$$

a is determined by the spread of the arch.

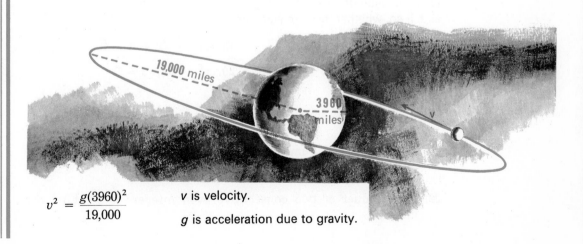

$$v^2 = \frac{g(3960)^2}{19{,}000}$$

v is velocity.

g is acceleration due to gravity.

CHAPTER REVIEW ◆

13.1 Solve each equation by the factoring method.

    1. $2x^2 + 6x = 0$ **2.** $x^2 - 8x + 16 = 0$

    3. $s^2 + 2s - 15 = 0$ **4.** $2t^2 - 7t + 3 = 0$

13.2 Use the square root property for equations in solving each equation.

    5. $4m^2 = 12$ **6.** $(x + 6)^2 = 16$

    7. $(y - 3)^2 = 18$ **8.** $r^2 + 14r + 49 = 5$

13.3 Solve each equation, using the method of completing the square. Express each irrational root in simplest radical form.

    9. $w^2 + 6w = -5$ **10.** $m^2 + 4m - 14 = 0$

    11. $9x^2 = 12x + 5$ **12.** $3s^2 - 6s = -2$

13.4 Solve each equation by using the quadratic formula. Express each irrational root in simplest radical form.

    13. $y^2 + 5y = 14$ **14.** $3r^2 + 7r = 0$

    15. $2x^2 - 8x + 3 = 0$ **16.** $5m^2 - 2m = 1$

13.5 Find the value of the discriminant and then tell whether the roots are real and, if so, whether they are equal or unequal.

    17. $x^2 + 6x + 9 = 0$ **18.** $2x^2 - 7x + 3 = 0$

    19. $-3x^2 = -6x + 1$ **20.** $x^2 + x + 2 = 0$

13.6 Solve each problem by using a quadratic equation.

    21. The sum of two numbers is 13 and their product is 40. Find the numbers.

    22. The product of two consecutive even integers is 48. Find the integers.

23. The area of a rectangle is 45 square centimeters. Its length is one centimeter less than twice its width. Find its dimensions.

24. One leg of a right triangle is 3 units longer than the other leg. The hypotenuse is 15 units long. How long is each leg?

Evaluate each formula for the indicated variable. 13.7

25. $d = 16t^2$; $d = 36$; $t =$ _____.

26. $S = \pi r^2 + \pi r l$; $r = 3$; $l = 3r$; $S =$ _____. (Use 3.14 for π.)

27. The formula for the sum S of the first n positive integers is $S = \frac{1}{2}n(n + 1)$. How many consecutive positive integers, beginning with 1, must be added to give a sum of 78?

28. An object falls d feet in t seconds, where $d = 16t^2$. How many seconds will it take an object to fall 64 feet?

Find and graph the solution set of each inequality. 13.8

29. $x^2 + 5x < 0$ **30.** $y^2 + 9y + 20 > 0$

31. $w^2 - 3w \leq 40$ **32.** $3w^2 - 8w - 16 \geq 0$

CHAPTER SELF-TEST

Which lettered term best describes each numbered item?

1. If $mn = 0$, then $m = 0$ or $n = 0$.
2. $ax^2 + bx + c = 0$
3. If $m^2 = n^2$, then $m = \pm n$.
4. $b^2 - 4ac$
5. $x = \dfrac{-b \pm \sqrt{b^2 - 4ac}}{2a}$
6. $ax^2 + bx + c \leq 0$

   a. discriminant
   b. quadratic inequality
   c. zero product property
   d. square root property for equations
   e. quadratic formula
   f. quadratic equation

Use the following equations in Exercises 7–12.

   a. $x^2 = 10x - 25$ b. $(y + 5)^2 = 3$
   c. $w^2 - 8w = 2$ d. $6s + 2 = -3s^2$

7. Write each equation in standard form.

8. Find the value of the discriminant for each equation and describe the roots.

9. Solve equation **a** by factoring.

10. Use the square root property of equations to solve equation **b**.

11. Solve equation **c** by completing the square.

12. Use the quadratic formula to solve equation **d**.

13. A rectangle has an area of 65 square inches. It is 8 inches longer than it is wide. Find its length and width.

14. Maria is 3 years older than Martin and the product of their ages is 180. Find their ages.

Ex. 15

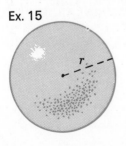

15. The formula for the surface area of a sphere is $S = 4\pi r^2$, where r is the measure of the radius. Find the radius of a sphere whose surface area is 16π square meters.

Find and graph the solution set of each inequality.

16. $x^2 + 4x < 0$ 17. $y^2 - 7y + 12 \geq 0$

Relations
and Functions

The word *relation* is used often in everyday language. For the scene pictured above, we might say that there is a *relation* between the speed of a tennis ball and the force with which it is hit by a racket.

The algebraic use of the word relation is similar to its everyday use. But in algebra, we define *exactly* what is meant by *relation*. We will do so in this chapter. Then you will study relations, mainly a special type of relation called a *function*.

463

Some parts of the country have a sales tax. The table below lists four sales amounts and what each tax would be for a tax rate of 5%.

Amount of sale	Amount of tax at 5%
$0.60	$0.03
2.00	0.10
4.99	0.25
5.00	0.25

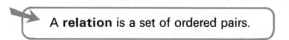

The matching diagram to the right of the table shows how the table *pairs* each member in one set with a member in another set. Thus, the information above could also be listed as a set of ordered pairs.

$$\{(0.60, 0.03), \ (2.00, 0.10), \ (4.99, 0.25), \ (5.00, 0.25)\}$$

The amount of tax is *related* to the amount of sale. And this is an example of how *relation* is defined in algebra.

> A **relation** is a set of ordered pairs.

Sets of ordered pairs are used often in algebra. For example, you have used them in solving and graphing open sentences in two variables. So, you have already been working with relations. The following definition is helpful in exploring relations.

The **domain** of a relation is the set containing the first members of its ordered pairs. The **range** of a relation is the set containing the second members of its ordered pairs.

Example 1: State the domain and range of the relation

$$\{(0, 0), \ (1, 1), \ (1, -1), \ (4, 2), \ (4, -2)\}.$$

SOLUTION: Domain = $\{0, 1, 4\}$; Range = $\{-2, -1, 0, 1, 2\}$.

In Example 1, notice that even though 1 occurs as the first member of two ordered pairs, it is listed only once in giving the domain. Similarly, members in the range would not be repeated.

Often, an open sentence in two variables can be used to describe a relation. For example, we can use

$$y = 2x$$

and specify that x can have any value in the domain $\{1, 2, 3, 4, \cdots, 300\}$. See the diagram at the right.

Thus, the relation we have described is

$\{(1, 2), (2, 4), (3, 6), (4, 8), \cdots, (300, 600)\}$

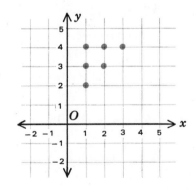

It is also possible to show a relation as a graph.

Example 2: Graph the relation

$$\{(1, 2), (1, 3), (1, 4), (2, 3), (2, 4), (3, 4)\}.$$

SOLUTION: Since a relation is a set of ordered pairs, we graph relations in the coordinate plane. Simply use the usual graphing methods to show the points that correspond to the ordered pairs in the relation.

The *domain* corresponds to the *horizontal* axis (*x*-axis) and the *range*, to the *vertical* axis (*y*-axis).

EXERCISES 14.1

Ⓐ 1. What are the ordered pairs of the relation shown at the right?

2. Name the 5 ways that relations have been described or shown in this section.

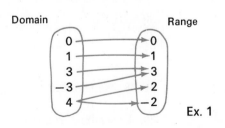

Ex. 1

State the domain and range of each relation below.

3. $\{(2, -2), (1, -1), (0, 0), (-1, 1), (-2, 2)\}$

4. $\{(0, 0), (1, 1), (-1, 1), (2, 2), (-2, 2)\}$

5. $\{(0, 0), (1, 1), (1, -1), (4, 2), (4, -2)\}$

6. $\{(1, 0), (2, 0), (2, 1), (3, 0), (3, 1), (3, 2)\}$

Ⓑ **7–10.** For each relation in Exercises **3–6**, draw a matching diagram as shown in Exercise **1**.

Copy and complete each table so that it shows one of the relations in Exercises 3–6.

11.

Given number	Its absolute value
2	
1	
0	
−1	
−2	

12.

Given number	One of its square roots
	−2
	−1
	0
	1
	2

13.

Given number					
A smaller number	0	0	1	0	1	2

14.

Given number	2	1	0	−1	−2
Its opposite					

Which of the relations in Exercises 3–6 can be described by using the given open sentence?

15. $y = -x$ **16.** $y < x$ **17.** $y = \pm\sqrt{x}$ **18.** $y = |x|$

19–22. Graph each relation in Exercises 3–6.

Let x have any value in the domain $\{0, 1, 4, 9\}$. List the ordered pairs in each relation.

23. $y = 2x$ **24.** $y = x + 2$ **25.** $y = 2x + 2$ **26.** $y = 2x - 2$

27. $y = x$ **28.** $y = x^2$ **29.** $y = x^2 - x$ **30.** $y = \pm\sqrt{x}$

31–38. Repeat Exercises **23–30**, but let the domain be $\{0, \frac{1}{4}, \frac{4}{9}, 1\}$.

Ⓒ **39.** Describe a relation from everyday life that can be thought of as a set of ordered pairs.

When an open sentence is used to describe a relation, it is important to know which variable stands for any member in the domain. The variable used for the domain (often x) is called the *independent* variable. The variable used for the range (often y) is called the *dependent* variable.

Domain: $\{1, 2, 3, 4, 5\}$

Relation described by: $y > x$ $y = x + 2$

Some ordered pairs:

x	y
1	2
1	3
2	3
2	4

x	y
1	3
2	4
3	5
4	6

Each value of the independent variable in the relation described by $y = x + 2$ determines exactly one value for the dependent variable. A relation of this type is called a **function.**

A **function** is a relation in which each member of the domain is paired with only one member in the range. That is, no two ordered pairs of a function have the same first member.

Example 1: Is the relation described by $y > x$ above a function?

SOLUTION: Since 1 is paired with both 2 and 3, this relation is *not* a function. Each value for the independent variable *does not* determine exactly one value for the dependent variable.

In a function,

this cannot occur

$$1 \begin{cases} 2 & (1, 2) \\ 3 & (1, 3) \end{cases}$$

but this can occur

Two ordered pairs in a function can, however, have the same second member. For example, if the domain is $\{-2, 0, 2\}$, the relation described by $y = x^2$ is

$$\{(-2, 4), (0, 0), (2, 4)\}.$$

$$\begin{matrix} -2 \searrow & & (-2, 4) \\ & 4 & \\ 2 \nearrow & & (2, 4) \end{matrix}$$

Each value for the independent variable determines only one value for the dependent variable, so this relation is a function.

There is a simple method called the **vertical line test** which is used to tell from the graph of a relation if it is a function.

Example 2: For each relation graphed below, tell if it is a function. Then state its domain and range.

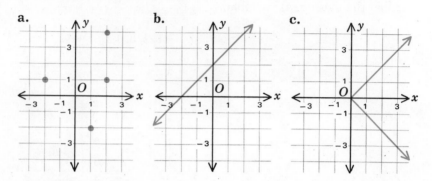

a.   b.   c.

SOLUTION: Notice that for relations **a** and **c**, you could draw a vertical line which crosses each graph at more than one point. This means that more than one ordered pair has the same first member. Consequently, **a** and **c** are not functions.

Relation	Function	Domain	Range
a.	No	$\{-2, 1, 2\}$	$\{-2, 1, 4\}$
b.	Yes	{real numbers}	{real numbers}
c.	No	{nonnegative real numbers}	{real numbers}

EXERCISES 14.2

Ⓐ Tell which of the following relations are functions.

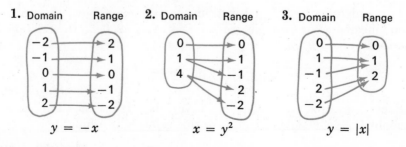

1. Domain   Range   **2.** Domain   Range   **3.** Domain   Range

$$y = -x$$ $$x = y^2$$ $$y = |x|$$

4. {(3, 8), (3, 5), (2, 4)}

5. {(6, 1), (5, 1), (4, 1)}

6. {(1, 1), (2, 2), (3, 3), (4, 4)}

7. The variable that stands for any member in the domain of a relation is called the ____ .

8. Each value of the ____ variable for a function determines exactly one value for the ____ variable.

Which graphs are graphs of functions? If the relation is not a function, give two ordered pairs with the same first member.

9.

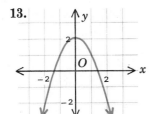

10.

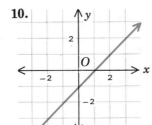

11.

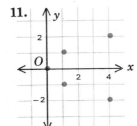

12.

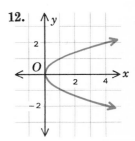

13.

14.

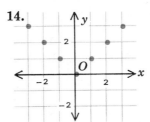

15.

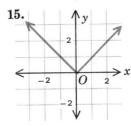

16.

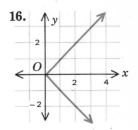

Ⓑ **17–24.** State the domain and range of each relation in Exercises 9–16.

Graph each relation using the domain given. Then determine if the relation is a function.

25. $y = 3x$,   {2, 1, 0, -1, -2}

26. $y = 2x + 1$,   {2, 1, 0, -1, -2}

27. $y = |x|$,   {-4, -2, 0, 2, 4}

28. $x = |y|$,   {0, 2, 4, 6, 8}

29. $y = x^2$,   {2, 1, 0, -1, -2}

30. $y = -x^2$,   {2, 1, 0, -1, -2}

31. $x = -y^2$,   {-16, -9, -4, 0}

32. $x = y^2$,   {0, 4, 9, 16}

Ⓒ **33.** $y > x$,   {real numbers}

34. $y < x$,   {real numbers}

35. $y = 3$,   {real numbers}

36. $x = 3$,   {3}

14.3 FUNCTION NOTATION

Functions are often named by using letters such as f, g, and h.

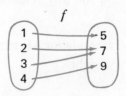

If we call the function above f, then we can write

$$f = \{(1, 5), (2, 7), (3, 7), (4, 9)\}.$$

We say $\begin{cases} f \text{ matches 1 to 5.} \\ f \text{ matches 2 to 7.} \\ f \text{ matches 3 to 7.} \\ f \text{ matches 4 to 9.} \end{cases}$ We write $\begin{cases} f: 1 \to 5. \\ f: 2 \to 7. \\ f: 3 \to 7. \\ f: 4 \to 9. \end{cases}$

Example 1: Function g is described as $g: x \to x^2 - 4x + 2$. Find the range values to which g matches 1, 0, and -2.

SOLUTION:

$g: 1 \to 1^2 - 4(1) + 2 = -1$. So g matches 1 to -1.

$g: 0 \to 0^2 - 4(0) + 2 = 2$. So g matches 0 to 2.

$g: -2 \to (-2)^2 - 4(-2) + 2 = 14$. So g matches -2 to 14.

Another notation commonly used with functions follows.

The symbol $f(x)$ stands for the value in the range of f to which any value x in the domain is matched.

$f(x)$ is read "f of x" or "f at x" and *does not* stand for "f times x."

Example 2: Function f is defined as $f(x) = x^2 + 2x - 1$. Find $f(2)$ and $f(-1)$.

SOLUTION: $f(2) \quad = (2)^2 \quad + 2(2) \quad - 1 = \quad 7$
$$f(-1) = (-1)^2 + 2(-1) - 1 = -2$$

EXERCISES 14.3

Ⓐ Match each description with a diagram.

1. $f: x \rightarrow 2x$ **2.** $g: x \rightarrow -x$ **3.** $h: x \rightarrow |x|$

a.

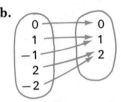

b.

c.

For each relation below, tell whether each value of x determines exactly one value $f(x)$. Then tell if the relation is a function.

4.

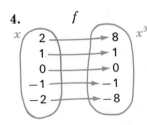

5.

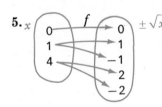

6.

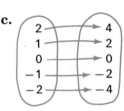

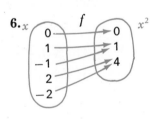

Use the diagram in Exercise 6 to complete Exercises 7–14.

7. f matches 1 to _____.

8. $f(-1) =$ _____

9. $f(2) =$ _____

10. $f(-2) =$ _____

11. $f(0) =$ _____

12. $f(x) =$ _____

13. $f: x \rightarrow$ _____

14. $y =$ _____

For Exercises 15–18, use $f: x \rightarrow 2x$.

15. f matches 3 to _____.

16. f matches _____ to 2.

17. f matches 0 to _____.

18. $f(-1) =$ _____

For Exercises 19–22, use $f(x) = x + 1$.

19. $f(0) =$ _____ **20.** $f(5) =$ _____ **21.** $f(\_) = 3$ **22.** $f(\_) = 0$

Ⓑ For Exercises 23–28, use $f: x \rightarrow 7x - 4$.

23. f matches 8 to _____. **24.** f matches _____ to -4.

25. $f(-4) =$ _____ **26.** $f(3) =$ _____

27. $f(\_\_\_) = 24$ **28.** $f(\_\_\_) = 38$

Use functions f and g below to find the values listed.

$$f: x \rightarrow 4x - 3$$
$$g: x \rightarrow x^2 - 5x + 8$$

29. $f(2)$ **30.** $f(3)$ **31.** $f(-4)$ **32.** $f(-3)$ **33.** $f(4.3)$

34. $g(5)$ **35.** $g(4)$ **36.** $g(-3)$ **37.** $g(-2)$ **38.** $g(\frac{1}{2})$

Give the set of ordered pairs for each function.

DESCRIPTION	DOMAIN
39. $f(x) = 4x - 5$	$\{1, 2, 3\}$
40. $f(x) = 2x - 7$	$\{1, 3, 5\}$
41. $f(x) = x^2 - 3x + 4$	$\{-1, 0, 1\}$
42. $f(x) = x^2 + 5x - 4$	$\{-2, 0, 2\}$

Graph each relation and use the vertical line test to determine if it is a function. The domain for each is the set of real numbers.

43. $y = x - 2$ **44.** $y = 2x + 4$ **45.** $y = -3$

46. $y = 2$ **47.** $x = -2$ **48.** $x = 4$

49. $2x + 3y = 6$ **50.** $4x - 3y = 12$ **51.** $f(x) = x + 2$

52. $f(x) = 2x - 4$ **53.** $f: x \rightarrow -3$ **54.** $f: x \rightarrow 2$

Ⓒ Function f is defined as $f: x \rightarrow 3x - 10$. Find the given expressions.

Example: $f(a - 3) = 3(a - 3) - 10 = 3a - 19$

55. $f(b + 4)$ **56.** $f(x + 10)$ **57.** $f(2c - 3)$ **58.** $f(x^2 + 2)$

Linear equations were graphed in Chapter 8. From the equation $y = 2x - 3$, we can tell the following about its graph.

$$\text{slope} = 2$$

$$y\text{-intercept} = -3$$

Using these two facts, the graph can be drawn as below.

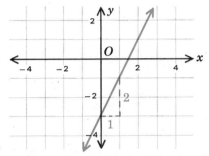

No vertical line in the plane would intersect this graph at more than one point. Therefore, $y = 2x - 3$ describes a function. If we call this function f, then we can write

$$f(x) = 2x - 3$$

or

$$f\colon x \to 2x - 3.$$

We say f is a *linear function*. Both the domain and range are the set of real numbers.

A **linear function** is any set of ordered pairs (x, y) that is the solution set of an equation of the form

$$y = mx + b,$$

where m and b are constants $(m \neq 0)$.

Notice that for a linear function, y or $f(x)$ is equal to a *first-degree* polynomial in x.

Example 1: Does the equation $4x + 3y = 12$ describe a linear function?

SOLUTION: The equation $4x + 3y = 12$ can be changed to slope-intercept form.

$$4x + 3y = 12$$
$$3y = -4x + 12$$
$$y = -\tfrac{4}{3}x + 4$$

Since y is equal to a first-degree polynomial in x, the equation $y = -\tfrac{4}{3}x + 4$ describes a linear function. Since $4x + 3y = 12$ is equivalent to $y = -\tfrac{4}{3}x + 4$, it follows that $4x + 3y = 12$ describes a linear function.

Example 2: Graph the linear function described by $y = -\tfrac{4}{3}x + 4$.

SOLUTION: We can graph three ordered pairs of the function (two to determine the line and a third to serve as a check).

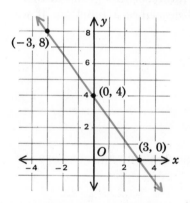

$$y = -\tfrac{4}{3}(0) + 4 = 4$$
$$y = -\tfrac{4}{3}(3) + 4 = 0$$
$$y = -\tfrac{4}{3}(-3) + 4 = 8$$

x	y
0	4
3	0
-3	8

If we call this function g, then

$$g: x \rightarrow -\tfrac{4}{3}x + 4$$

or

$$g(x) = -\tfrac{4}{3}x + 4.$$

The graph of $y = 3$ is shown below. The equation $y = 3$ can be written as $y = 0 \cdot x + 3$. Since $m = 0$, this equation does not determine a linear function. However, $y = 3$ does determine a *constant function.* Every element of the domain is matched to 3.

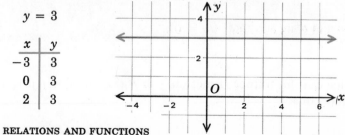

$y = 3$

x	y
-3	3
0	3
2	3

> A function that can be described by an equation of the type $y = k$, where k is a real number, is a **constant function.**

Notice that for a constant function, y or $f(x)$ is equal to a constant.

EXERCISES 14.4

Ⓐ Tell whether each equation describes a linear function, a constant function, or neither.

1. $y = x - 5$ **2.** $y = 0 \cdot x + 2$ **3.** $y = x^2$

4. $y = \frac{3}{4}x$ **5.** $y = \frac{1}{2}x$ **6.** $y = 7$

7. $y = -4$ **8.** $2x + 3y = 6$ **9.** $-3x + y = 5$

10. $y = \dfrac{x - 1}{2}$ **11.** $4x = 9y - 18$ **12.** $-2y = 10x$

13. $3y - 6x = 9$ **14.** $x = 6$

Ⓑ **15–28.** Determine the slope of the graph of each equation in Exercises 1–14, if possible. If not possible, write *no slope.*

Graph the ordered pairs in each table and determine whether the ordered pairs belong to a linear function, a constant function, or neither.

29.

x	-4	-2	0
y	-2	-1	0

30.

x	-3	0	3
y	-1	0	1

31.

x	-2	0	2
y	1	3	5

32.

x	0	3	6
y	4	7	10

33.

x	-4	0	2
y	-4	0	2

34.

x	-6	0	3
y	-2	-2	-2

35.

x	-1	0	1
y	-7	-4	-1

36.

x	-1	0	1
y	-2	-5	-2

Graph each linear function. Each domain is the set of real numbers.

37. $y = -\frac{1}{2}x + 3$ **38.** $y = -\frac{1}{3}x + 2$

39. $2x - 3y = 6$ **40.** $3x - 4y = 12$

41. $5x = y - 10$ **42.** $4x = y - 8$

43. $3x + 5y = 10$ **44.** $7x + 3y = 9$

45. $m(x) = 4x - 5$ **46.** $n(x) = 5x - 4$

47. $h(x) = -2x + 3$ **48.** $k(x) = -3x + 5$

49. $f: x \to \frac{1}{4}x - 2$ **50.** $g: x \to \frac{1}{3}x - 4$

Use the functions in Exercises 45–50 to find the following.

51. $m(2)$ **52.** $n(3)$ **53.** $h(0)$ **54.** $k(0)$

55. $m(-3)$ **56.** $n(-2)$ **57.** $h(\frac{1}{2})$ **58.** $k(\frac{1}{3})$

59. $f(12)$ **60.** $g(9)$ **61.** $f(-8)$ **62.** $g(-6)$

© Graph each function.

Example: Graph $f(x) = \begin{cases} 2 \text{ if } x \geq 0 \\ 2x \text{ if } x < 0 \end{cases}$

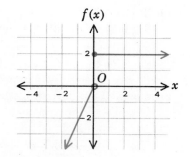

SOLUTION: For $x \geq 0$, the graph is determined by $f(x) = 2$. For $x < 0$, the graph is determined by $f(x) = 2x$. The graph is shown at the right.

63. $f(x) = \begin{cases} 3 \text{ if } x < 0 \\ x \text{ if } x \geq 0 \end{cases}$ **64.** $g(x) = \begin{cases} x \text{ if } x \geq 0 \\ -x \text{ if } x < 0 \end{cases}$

65. $h(x) = \begin{cases} 2x + 1 \text{ if } x > 0 \\ 0 \text{ if } x = 0 \\ -2 \text{ if } x < 0 \end{cases}$ **66.** $k(x) = \begin{cases} x + 2 \text{ if } x > 0 \\ 0 \text{ if } x = 0 \\ -2 \text{ if } x < 0 \end{cases}$

The approximate relation between the pressure p in pounds per square inch and the depth d, in feet, of water in a swimming pool is given in the table below.

Depth in feet (d)	Pressure in lbs. per sq. in. (p)
1	0.43
2	0.86
3	1.29
4	1.72
5	2.15

The relation between p and d can be graphed as follows.

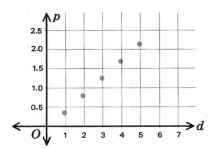

Notice that for convenience we can use a different-sized unit on each axis.

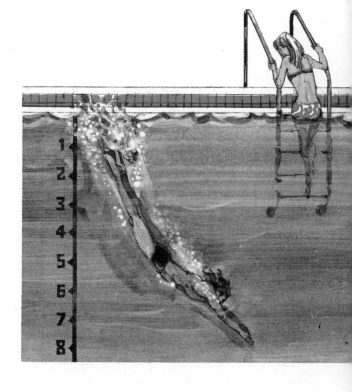

This relation can be described by the equation $p = 0.43d$. Since every value of d is matched to exactly one value for p, the relation is a function.

You have seen that a linear function is described by an equation of the form $y = mx + b$ where $m \neq 0$. When $b = 0$, the function is called a *direct variation*. So $p = 0.43d$ describes a direct variation.

A **direct variation** is a linear function that can be described by an equation of the form,

$$y = kx, \quad \text{where } k \neq 0.$$

Notice that for a direct variation, y or $f(x)$ is equal to a first-degree *monomial* in x.

In the direct variation $p = 0.43d$,

> p is said to *vary directly* as d, or
> p is said to be *directly proportional* to d.

0.43 is called   the *constant of variation* or
the *constant of proportionality*.

Example 1: The weight m of an object on the moon varies directly as its weight e on the earth. If an astronaut weighs 150 pounds on earth and 25 pounds on the moon, what would Tina weigh on the moon if she weighs 114 pounds on earth?

SOLUTION:

Write a direct-variation equation:	$m = ke$
Substitute 25 for m and 150 for e:	$25 = k \cdot 150$
Solve for k:	$k = \frac{25}{150} = \frac{1}{6}$
Substitute $\frac{1}{6}$ for k in $m = ke$:	$m = \frac{1}{6}e$
Substitute 114 for e:	$m = \frac{1}{6} \cdot 114$
Solve for m:	$m = 19$

Thus, Tina would weigh 19 pounds on the moon.

Example 2: Peggy earns \$7.20 in working 4 hours. If the amount m of money earned is directly proportional to the number h of hours worked, how many hours must she work to earn \$21.60?

SOLUTION:

Write a direct-variation equation:	$m = kh$
Substitute 7.20 for m and 4 for h:	$7.20 = k \cdot 4$
Solve for k:	$k = 1.80$
Substitute 1.80 for k in $m = kh$:	$m = 1.80h$
Substitute 21.60 for m:	$21.60 = 1.80h$
Solve for h:	$h = 12$

Thus, Peggy must work 12 hours.

EXERCISES 14.5

(A) Which equations describe direct variations?

1. $y = 3x$

2. $y = 7x$

3. $y = 4$

4. $y - 2x = 0$

5. $2x - y = 0$

6. $\dfrac{y}{x} = 2$

7. $xy = 12$

8. $x = 7y$

9. $2x - 3y = 6$

10. $\dfrac{x}{2y} = 4$

11. $y = x + 3$

12. $x = y + 3$

Complete each exercise by using the graph of the direct variation below.

13. When $x = 2$, $y = $ _____.

14. When $x = 6$, $y = $ _____.

15. When $y = 2$, $x = $ _____.

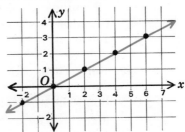

16. The slope of the line is _____.

17. The constant of variation is _____.

18. The equation for this direct variation is _____.

(B) Write an equation of the type $y = kx$ to show the relationship between the variables given. (Use k as the constant of variation.)

19. Distance d in miles varies directly as the time t in hours.

20. Cost c of beef in dollars varies directly as the number of pounds p.

21. Circumference C of a circle varies directly as the diameter d.

22. Weight w of a pipe in pounds is directly proportional to its length l in feet.

Write new equations for Exercises 19–22 if the constants of variation are respectively:

23. $k = 60$

24. $k = 1.39$

25. $k = \pi$

26. $k = 1.2$

Use the direct-variation equations found in Exercises 23–26 to find:

27. d if $t = 6$ hours

28. c if $p = 4$ pounds

29. C if $d = 5$ inches (Use 3.14 for π.)

30. w if $l = 15$ feet

31. The number m of meters in a linear measurement varies directly as the number c of centimeters in the measurement. Nick measured the length of a table and found it was 150 centimeters or 1.5 meters. How wide is the table in meters if its width in centimeters is 91?

32. A trip of 90 miles required 6 gallons of gasoline. If the number g of gallons of gasoline used varies directly as the number m of miles traveled, how many gallons are required for a trip of 135 miles?

33. Kelly earns $13.50 for working 6 hours. If the amount m of money she earns is directly proportional to the number h of hours she works, how much does she earn for working 10 hours?

34. Karen received $12.25 interest on the $245 in her savings account. If the interest i is directly proportional to the amount a of money in her account, how much interest will Karen receive for the same period of time if she has $360 in her account?

© **35.** The surface area A of a sphere varies directly as the square of the radius r. If a sphere with radius 2 inches has an area of 16 square inches, what area will a sphere have if its radius is 8 inches?

36. The area A of a square varies directly as the square of the length s of its side. If s is doubled, how does A change? If the area of a square is 81 square meters, what is the area of a square with sides twice as long?

You know that $y = 3x$ describes a direct variation. If (x_1, y_1) and (x_2, y_2) are solutions of $y = 3x$, then

$$y_1 = 3x_1 \quad \text{and} \quad y_2 = 3x_2.$$

If $x_1 \neq 0$ and $x_2 \neq 0$, then we can find the **ratios** (quotients) $\dfrac{y_1}{x_1}$ and $\dfrac{y_2}{x_2}$.

$$\frac{y_1}{x_1} = 3 \quad \text{and} \quad \frac{y_2}{x_2} = 3. \quad \text{So, } \frac{y_1}{x_1} = \frac{y_2}{x_2}.$$

An equation such as $\dfrac{y_1}{x_1} = \dfrac{y_2}{x_2}$ which states that two ratios are equal is called a **proportion**. The numbers x_1 and y_2 are called **means**, and y_1 and x_2 are called **extremes**.

Example 1: (2, 6) and (5, 15) are solutions of $y = 3x$. Write a proportion for the numbers in these ordered pairs. Identify the means and extremes.

SOLUTION: Let $(x_1, y_1) = (2, 6)$ and $(x_2, y_2) = (5, 15)$. So,

$$\frac{y_1}{x_1} = \frac{y_2}{x_2} \quad \text{becomes} \quad \frac{6}{2} = \frac{15}{5}.$$

The extremes are 6 and 5. The means are 2 and 15. Notice that the product of the extremes in $\frac{6}{2} = \frac{15}{5}$ is equal to the product of the means. That is, $6 \cdot 5 = 2 \cdot 15$.

In general, if a, b, c, and d are real numbers ($b \neq 0$ and $d \neq 0$), the form of the proportion $\frac{a}{b} = \frac{c}{d}$ can be changed as follows.

$$\frac{a}{b}(bd) = \frac{c}{d}(bd)$$

$$ad = cb \quad \text{or} \quad ad = bc.$$

In a proportion the product of the extremes is equal to the product of the means.

Proportions are useful in solving direct-variation problems.

Example 2: Solve Example 2 in Section 14.5 by using a proportion. (If Peggy earns $7.20 in working 4 hours, how many hours must she work to earn $21.60?)

SOLUTION: In words, you can write the proportion:

$$\frac{\text{amount Peggy earns in 4 hr.}}{4 \text{ hr.}} = \frac{\text{amount Peggy will earn in } x \text{ hr.}}{x \text{ hr.}}$$

Since $21.60 is the amount Peggy will earn in x hours, you can rewrite the proportion as

$$\frac{7.20}{4} = \frac{21.60}{x}$$

$$7.20(x) = 4(21.60)$$

$$x = \frac{4(21.60)}{7.20}$$

$$x = 12$$

So Peggy must work 12 hours to earn $21.60.

Example 3: Solve the proportion $\dfrac{5}{x + 3} = \dfrac{3}{2x - 1}$.

SOLUTION: $\dfrac{5}{x + 3} = \dfrac{3}{2x - 1}$

$$5(2x - 1) = (x + 3)3$$

$$10x - 5 = 3x + 9$$

$$7x = 14$$

$$x = 2$$

Check: $\dfrac{5}{2 + 3} = \dfrac{3}{2 \cdot 2 - 1}$ Solution set is $\{2\}$.

$$\frac{5}{5} = \frac{3}{3}$$

$$1 = 1 \quad \text{T}$$

EXERCISES 14.6

Ⓐ In each exercise, the two ordered pairs belong to a direct variation. Give a proportion for each.

Example: $(4, 16)$; $(5, 20)$

SOLUTION: $\frac{16}{4} = \frac{20}{5}$

1. $(2, 3)$; $(4, 6)$ **2.** $(1, 5)$; $(4, 20)$ **3.** $(6, 2)$; $(3, 1)$

4. $(8, 2)$; $(4, 1)$ **5.** $(-2, 3)$; $(-10, 15)$ **6.** $(9, -6)$; $(3, -2)$

Give the means and extremes for each proportion.

7. $\dfrac{8}{2} = \dfrac{12}{3}$ **8.** $\dfrac{r}{s} = \dfrac{x}{y}$

Ⓑ In each table, y varies directly as x. Write a proportion and solve it for the given letter.

9.

x	1	2	3
y	4	a	12

10.

x	3	2	1
y	9	6	b

11.

x	-2	-4	-6
y	c	2	3

12.

x	-2	-6	-10
y	3	d	15

13.

x	$\frac{1}{6}$	c	7
y	$\frac{1}{3}$	$\frac{2}{3}$	14

14.

x	$\frac{1}{4}$	f	3
y	$\frac{1}{2}$	$\frac{2}{3}$	6

Solve each proportion.

15. $\dfrac{4}{5} = \dfrac{x}{30}$ **16.** $\dfrac{5}{6} = \dfrac{y}{36}$ **17.** $\dfrac{1}{7} = \dfrac{-2}{a}$

18. $\dfrac{1}{11} = \dfrac{-3}{b}$ **19.** $\dfrac{3}{2} = \dfrac{5}{m}$ **20.** $\dfrac{4}{3} = \dfrac{5}{n}$

21. $\dfrac{12}{3x} = \dfrac{10}{3}$ **22.** $\dfrac{8}{3x} = \dfrac{16}{3}$ **23.** $\dfrac{4}{x+1} = \dfrac{2}{1}$

24. $\dfrac{6}{x+1} = \dfrac{3}{1}$ **25.** $\dfrac{s+2}{3} = \dfrac{2s}{4}$ **26.** $\dfrac{t+3}{5} = \dfrac{2t}{7}$

27. $\dfrac{-3}{m-5} = \dfrac{4}{m+2}$ **28.** $\dfrac{2}{n-6} = \dfrac{-4}{n+3}$

29. $\dfrac{-5}{2x-7} = \dfrac{-2}{3x+5}$

30. $\dfrac{-6}{2y+11} = \dfrac{-2}{3y-4}$

31–34. Solve Exercises 31–34 in Section 14.5 by using proportions.

Solve each problem by using a proportion.

35. On a certain map, 1 inch represents 48 miles. What distance on the map represents 216 miles?

36. A photographer has a $5'' \times 7''$ snapshot. How long will an enlargement be if its width is $17\frac{1}{2}''$?

37. The commission that a saleswoman receives is directly proportional to her sales. If sales of \$300 bring her a commission of \$36, how much commission will she get on sales of \$800?

38. A farmer mixes feed for cattle in the ratio of 1 bushel of soybean meal to 9 bushels of ground corn. How many bushels of soybean meal must be mixed with 54 bushels of ground corn?

39. A recipe for brownies requires $\frac{1}{2}$ teaspoon of baking powder for $\frac{3}{4}$ cup of flour. If the recipe is changed to include 3 cups of flour, how many teaspoons of baking powder are required?

40. A board 24 inches long is to be cut into two pieces whose lengths are in the ratio of 3 to 5. What will the length of each part be? (HINT: Let x and $24 - x$ equal the lengths of the two pieces.)

41. A baseball player got 10 hits in the first 30 times at bat. To keep the same batting average, how many hits should he have after 66 at bats?

42. On a 15-question quiz, you answer 12 questions correctly. All questions are of equal value. How many points did you score if the score for all correct answers is 100 points?

© Show that if $\dfrac{a}{b} = \dfrac{c}{d}$, then

43. $\dfrac{a}{c} = \dfrac{b}{d}$

44. $\dfrac{d}{b} = \dfrac{c}{a}$

45. $\dfrac{b}{a} = \dfrac{d}{c}$

46. $\dfrac{a+b}{b} = \dfrac{c+d}{d}$

Give the domain and range of each relation.

1. $\{(1, 2), (7, 3), (1, 4), (3, 4)\}$ **2.** $\{(2, 6), (8, 1), (5, 2), (2, 3)\}$

3. $\{(-4, 6), (3, 2), (5, 5)\}$ **4.** $\{(1, 1), (2, 2), (3, 3), (0, 0)\}$

5–8. For each of Exercises 1–4, tell if the relation is a function.

For Exercises 9–12 refer to the function below.

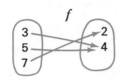

9. f matches 5 to _____.   **10.** f matches _____ to 2.

11. $f(3) =$ _____   **12.** $f(\_\_\_) = 2$

For the function $g: x \rightarrow 3x - 5$,

13. g matches -2 to _____.   **14.** $g(4) =$ _____

Tell whether each equation describes a linear function, a constant function, or neither.

15. $y = \sqrt{x}$ **16.** $y = 7$ **17.** $2x - y = 4$

18–19. Graph each equation in Exercises **16–17**.

20. If $y = 5x$, then y varies directly as _____, and the constant of variation is _____.

21. The amount a of money that Barbara earns is directly proportional to the number h of hours she works. If she earns \$9.00 in working 6 hours, how much will she earn in working 8 hours? Solve by using an equation of the type $y = kx$.

22. Solve Exercise **21** by using a proportion.

23. Solve: $\dfrac{2}{2x - 1} = \dfrac{-2}{3x + 2}$

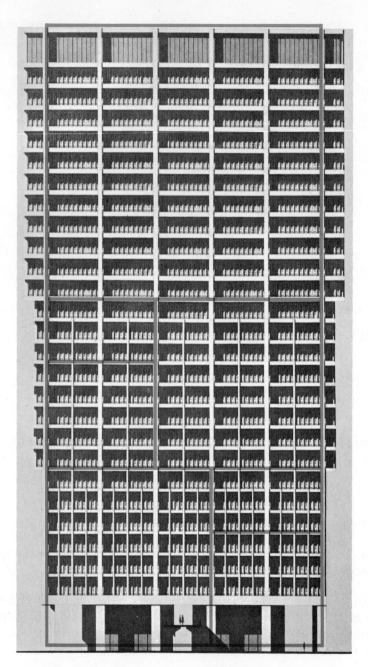

In the building shown above, you can see a variety of rectangles. Many of them are **Golden Rectangles**. Supposedly, Golden Rectangles have the most visually-pleasing shape of all rectangles, and since ancient times, examples occur frequently in art and architecture.

A Golden Rectangle is any rectangle which when placed next to a square will give another rectangle whose length and width are proportional to its own length and width.

That is, $\dfrac{l}{w} = \dfrac{w+l}{l}$.

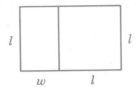

How many Golden Rectangles can you find outlined in red in the picture of the building?

The proportion above is called the **Divine Proportion**, and the ratio $\dfrac{l}{w}$ is called the **Golden Ratio**. We can find the value of the Golden Ratio by using the quadratic formula to solve the Divine Proportion for $\dfrac{l}{w}$. But first, the proportion must be changed to a quadratic equation in standard form.

$$\frac{l}{w} \cdot \frac{l}{w} = \frac{w+l}{l} \cdot \frac{l}{w}$$ First multiply both sides by $\dfrac{l}{w}$.

$$\left(\frac{l}{w}\right)^2 = \frac{w+l}{w}$$

$$\left(\frac{l}{w}\right)^2 = 1 + \frac{l}{w}$$

$$\left(\frac{l}{w}\right)^2 - \frac{l}{w} - 1 = 0$$ Let $\dfrac{l}{w} = x$ and solve by using the quadratic formula.

$$x = \frac{l}{w} = \frac{-(-1) \pm \sqrt{(-1)^2 - 4 \cdot 1 \cdot (-1)}}{2 \cdot 1} = \frac{1 \pm \sqrt{5}}{2} \quad \text{or} \quad \tfrac{1}{2}(1 \pm \sqrt{5})$$

In this case $\tfrac{1}{2}(1 - \sqrt{5})$ gives a negative value, but we are interested only in the positive value of $\dfrac{l}{w}$. So, $\dfrac{l}{w} = \tfrac{1}{2}(1 + \sqrt{5}) \approx \tfrac{1}{2}(1 + 2.24)$ or 1.62.

For some interesting applications of the Golden Ratio, see:

Bergamini, David, *Mathematics* (Life Science Library Series), New York: Time-Life Books, 1963, pages 94–97.

Huntley, H. E., *The Divine Proportion: A Study in Mathematical Beauty*, New York: Dover Publications, Inc., 1970.

14.7 QUADRATIC FUNCTIONS

None of the equations below describe linear or constant functions.

$$y = x^2$$
$$y = -x^2 + 5$$
$$y = x^2 - 3x + 2$$

Each equation does describe a *quadratic function*. For any value we assign to x, there is exactly one corresponding value for y.

A **quadratic function** is any set of ordered pairs (x, y) that is the solution set of an equation of the form $y = ax^2 + bx + c$, where a, b, and c are constants and $a \neq 0$.

Notice that for a quadratic function, y or $f(x)$ is equal to a second-degree polynomial in x. The graphs of quadratic functions are not straight lines.

Example 1: Graph the quadratic function described by

$$y = x^2.$$

SOLUTION: Make a table of several ordered pairs. Then plot each point. Since the points do not lie on a straight line, it is necessary to graph several points.

x	y
-3	9
-2	4
-1	1
0	0
1	1
2	4
3	9

Enough points are plotted to tell the general curve of the graph. So we draw a smooth curve through these points.

The graph of a quadratic function such as $y = x^2$ is called a **parabola.** Note that the point $(0, 0)$ is the *minimum point* of the curve above. That is, it is the lowest point on the graph. Some parabolas have a *maximum point* instead of a minimum point. The maximum or minimum point is also called the **vertex** of the parabola.

Example 2: Graph the function described by

$$y = -2x^2.$$

SOLUTION: Make a table of ordered pairs, plot the points, and draw a smooth curve through the points.

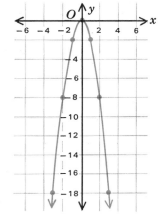

x	y
-3	-18
-2	-8
-1	-2
0	0
1	-2
2	-8
3	-18

Notice that $(0, 0)$ is the vertex of the parabola for $y = -2x^2$, just as it was for $y = x^2$. In this case, however, $(0, 0)$ is a maximum, rather than a minimum, point.

The graph of any equation of the form $y = ax^2$, where $a \neq 0$, is a parabola with its vertex at the origin. If $a > 0$, the parabola opens upward. If $a < 0$, the parabola opens downward.

Many quadratic functions, however, have graphs whose vertex is not the origin. Consider the following.

Example 3: Graph the function described by

$$y = x^2 + 4x + 3.$$

SOLUTION: Make a table of ordered pairs. In this case, the vertex is $(-2, -1)$. Usually it is wise to graph several points on each "side" of the vertex.

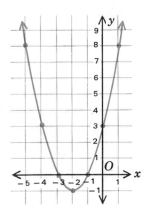

x	y
-5	8
-4	3
-3	0
-2	-1
-1	0
0	3
1	8

For any quadratic function, the vertical line through the vertex of its graph is an *axis of symmetry*. That is, if the coordinate plane were "folded" along this line, the two "halves" of the parabola would coincide. This fact is helpful in graphing.

EXERCISES 14.7

Ⓐ Tell which equations describe quadratic functions.

1. $y = 2x^2$ **2.** $y = 4x - 9$ **3.** $y = \frac{1}{2}x^2 - 8x$

4. $y = 5 - 2x - x^2$ **5.** $y = x^3 - 4$ **6.** $y = 2x^2 + x - 3$

For each quadratic function described below, tell whether the vertex of the graph is at the origin.

7. $y = 4x^2$ **8.** $y = x^2 + 1$ **9.** $y = \frac{1}{2}x^2$

10. $y = -\frac{1}{3}x^2$ **11.** $y = 2x^2 - 3$ **12.** $y = 3x^2 + x$

13. Will the graph of $y = 5x^2$ open upward or downward?

14. Will the graph of $y = -4x^2$ open upward or downward?

Ⓑ Find the value of y for each value of x given in the table. Then graph each function, using {real numbers} as the domain.

15. $y = 3x^2$

x	-2	-1	0	1	2
y					

16. $y = -\frac{1}{3}x^2$

x	-2	-1	0	1	2
y					

17. $y = 2x^2 - 5$

x	-2	-1	0	1	2
y					

18. $y = x^2 - 4x$

x	0	1	2	3	4
y					

19. $y = x^2 - 2x + 1$

x	-1	0	1	2	3
y					

20. $y = x^2 + 2x - 3$

x	-3	-2	-1	0	1
y					

Graph each function. Let the domain be {real numbers}. Plot at least the points whose x-values are -3, -2, -1, 0, 1, 2, and 3.

21. $y = \frac{1}{4}x^2$ **22.** $y = \frac{1}{5}x^2$ **23.** $y = -4x^2$

24. $y = -3x^2$ **25.** $y = x^2 - 2x + 2$ **26.** $y = x^2 - 2x + 3$

27. $y = x^2 - 4$ **28.** $y = x^2 - 9$ **29.** $y = x^2 + 3x$

30. $y = x^2 + x$ **31.** $y = x^2 - 4x$ **32.** $y = x^2 - 4x + 3$

Ⓒ In each exercise, graph the functions on the same set of axes.

33. $y = x^2$ **34.** $y = \frac{1}{2}x^2$ **35.** $y = x^2$

       $y = x^2 + 3$ $y = \frac{1}{2}(x - 2)^2$ $y = (x - 1)^2 + 2$

       $y = x^2 - 3$ $y = \frac{1}{2}(x + 2)^2$ $y = (x - 1)^2 - 2$

If the graph of a function contains the point at $(a, 0)$, then a is called an *x-intercept* of the graph, and a is also called a **zero** of the function.

The graph of a linear function is a line that is not horizontal. Thus, its graph intersects the x-axis at exactly one point, and a linear function has *exactly one* zero.

Example 1: Find the zero of the linear function described by

$$y = 2x + 4.$$

SOLUTION: The zero can be found by two methods.

I. Graph the function and determine where it intersects the x-axis. The point of intersection is at $(-2, 0)$. So, -2 is the zero in this case.

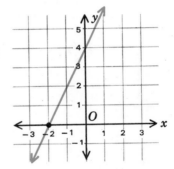

II. Find the value of x for which $y = 0$. That is, let $y = 0$ in $y = 2x + 4$ and solve the resulting equation:

$$0 = 2x + 4$$

$$-4 = 2x$$

$$x = -2$$

Thus, -2 is the zero of this function.

The graph of a quadratic function can intersect the x-axis in 2, 1, or 0 points. See the graphs on the following page. Thus, a quadratic function may have 2, 1, or no zeros.

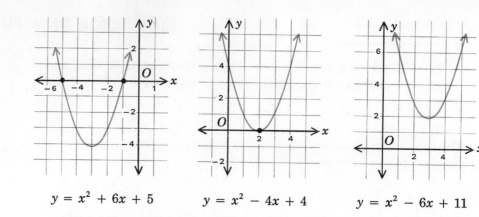

$$y = x^2 + 6x + 5 \qquad y = x^2 - 4x + 4 \qquad y = x^2 - 6x + 11$$

Example 2: Find the zeros of the quadratic function described by

$$y = 4x^2 - 8x - 5.$$

SOLUTION: Again, the zeros can be found by two methods.

I. Graph the equation $y = 4x^2 - 8x - 5$.

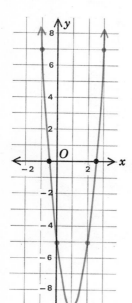

x	y
3	7
2	-5
1	-9
0	-5
-1	7

From the graph at the left we can estimate that $-\frac{1}{2}$ and $\frac{5}{2}$ (or $2\frac{1}{2}$) are zeros of the function.

II. Find the values of x for which $y = 0$ by letting $y = 0$ in the equation $y = 4x^2 - 8x - 5$ and solving.

$$4x^2 - 8x - 5 = 0$$
$$(2x + 1)(2x - 5) = 0$$
$$x = -\tfrac{1}{2} \quad \text{or} \quad x = \tfrac{5}{2}$$

Thus $-\frac{1}{2}$ and $\frac{5}{2}$ are the zeros of the function.

Since the graphing method for finding the zeros of a function gives estimates only, the second method is often preferred.

EXERCISES 14.8

Ⓐ 1. How many zeros does a linear function have? How many zeros
   may a quadratic function have?

From the graphs, give the zeros of each function if they exist.

2.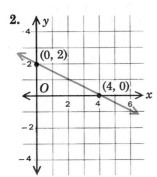

3.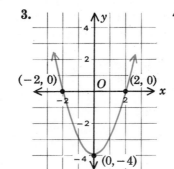

4.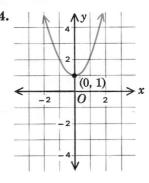

Ⓑ Find the zeros (if any) of each function without graphing.

   5. $y = x + 3$ **6.** $y = x - 2$ **7.** $y = 3x - 9$

   8. $y = 4x - 12$ **9.** $y = x^2 + 1$ **10.** $y = (x - 3)(x - 1)$

   11. $y = x^2 - 4$ **12.** $y = x^2 - 9$ **13.** $y = (x - 1)(x - 2)$

   14. $y = x^2 + 4$ **15.** $y = -x^2 + 9$ **16.** $y = -x^2 + 16$

Find the zeros (if any) of each function by the graphing method.

   17. $y = 2x + 5$ **18.** $y = 2x + 7$ **19.** $y = x(x - 6)$

   20. $y = x(x - 9)$ **21.** $y = x^2 - 3x + 2$ **22.** $y = x^2 - 4x + 3$

   23. $y = x^2 + 3$ **24.** $y = x^2 + x - 6$ **25.** $y = x^2 - x - 6$

   26. $y = x^2 + 2$ **27.** $y = x^2 - 6x + 9$ **28.** $y = x^2 + 4x + 4$

Find the zeros of each function, using the quadratic formula.

   29. $y = x^2 + 3x - 10$ **30.** $y = 2x^2 - 3x - 1$

   31. $y = 3x^2 - x - 1$ **32.** $y = x^2 + 4x + 5$

Ⓒ Find the zeros of each *cubic* function.

   33. $y = x(x - 4)(x + 3)$ **34.** $y = x^3 - 3x^2 - 4x$

14.9 SOLVING PROBLEMS

Quadratic functions are useful in solving problems for which a maximum or a minimum value is desired.

Example: Part of a parking lot is going to be fenced off as a bin to collect materials for recycling. The bottom of the bin will be rectangular. Using 24 yards of fence, what dimensions for the rectangle will give the *maximum* area?

SOLUTION: The perimeter of the base is 24. So

$$2l + 2w = 24$$

$$l + w = 12$$

$$l = 12 - w.$$

See the diagram.

Let A = the area of the base. Then

$$A = w(12 - w) \quad \text{or} \quad A = -w^2 + 12w.$$

Since A is equal to a second-degree polynomial in w, this equation describes a quadratic function. We can say that the area A is a function of the width w.

Graphing this function, we get the partial parabola below.

w	A
0	0
1	11
2	20
3	27
4	32
5	35
6	36
7	35
8	32
9	27
10	20
11	11
12	0

For this problem the domain of the function does not contain values where $w < 0$ or $w > 12$. Such values of w would determine negative values for A, and the area cannot be negative.

The highest point of the graph is at (6, 36). So, the maximum area possible is 36. Since $A = 36$ when $w = 6$, the width is 6 yards and the length is $12 - w$ or 6 also. The rectangle must be 6 by 6 yards square.

EXERCISES 14.9

Ⓐ If a ball is thrown upward vertically at a starting speed of 96 feet per second, the height h (in feet above the starting point) that it will reach at the end of t seconds is given by the quadratic equation

$$h = 96t - 16t^2.$$

This equation describes the quadratic function graphed below.

t	h
0	0
1	80
2	128
3	144
4	128
5	80
6	0

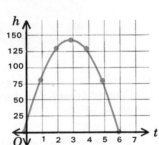

1. What is the maximum point of the graph?

2. What is the maximum height reached by the ball?

3. After 1 second, how high is the ball?

4. After 5 seconds, how high is the ball?

5. Where is the ball at 0 seconds?

6. Where is the ball after 6 seconds?

Ⓑ 7. If a ball is thrown upward vertically at a starting speed of 64 feet per second, the height h reached by the ball after t seconds is given by the equation $h = 64t - 16t^2$. Graph this function using the values 0, 1, 2, 3, 4, for t.

In Exercises 8–10, refer to the graph drawn for Exercise 7.

8. Find the maximum height reached by the ball.

9. After how many seconds is the height of the ball 48 feet? (There are two answers.)

10. After how many seconds does the ball return to its starting height?

11. A piece of sheet metal 28 inches wide is to be bent upward at each end to form a chute which has a rectangular cross section. Find the dimensions of the chute that will give the maximum cross-sectional area. HINT: Graph the function described by $A = x(28 - 2x)$.

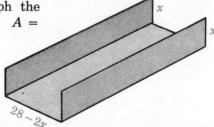

12. Find two numbers whose sum is 12 if the sum of their squares is to be a minimum. HINT: Graph the function described by the equation $s = x^2 + (12 - x)^2$.

13. Toni has 32 feet of fencing to use in making a rectangular pen for her pet rabbit. What dimensions for the pen will give the maximum area? HINT: See the example on pages 494–495.

14. What dimensions of a rectangular sheet of copper with a perimeter of 40 centimeters will give the maximum area?

© 15. The sum of the measures of the base and altitude of a triangle is 16 inches. Find the measure of the base that will give the maximum area.

16. Find the number which when added to the square of the same number will give a minimum sum. What is that sum?

Suppose the area of a rectangle remains constant at 24, while the length b of the base and the length h of the altitude vary. This relation is expressed by the equation

$$bh = 24.$$

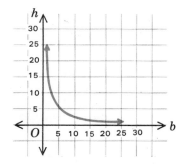

Let $b =$	1	2	3	4	6	8	12	24
Then $h =$	24	12	8	6	4	3	2	1

Notice that when

> b is 3, h is 8
> b is 6, h is 4

when b is doubled, h is halved.

> b is 4, h is 6
> b is 12, h is 2.

when b is tripled, h is divided by 3.

This is an example of an *inverse variation*.

An **inverse variation** is a function that can be described by an equation of the form

$$y = \frac{k}{x}, \quad \text{or} \quad xy = k,$$

where $x \neq 0$ and k is a nonzero constant.

The equation $y = \frac{k}{x}$ can be written as $y = k \cdot \frac{1}{x}$. Thus, y is directly proportional to $\frac{1}{x}$, the multiplicative *inverse* of x. This gives us reason to say that

> y is *inversely proportional* to x, or
> y *varies inversely* as x.

> k is the *constant of variation* or
> the *constant of proportionality*.

In the example above, $bh = 24$ can be written as $h = \frac{24}{b}$. So h varies inversely as b, and 24 is the constant of variation.

Example: The rate r of travel over a given distance varies inversely as the time t of travel. At 45 miles per hour, it takes 3 hours to travel a certain distance. How long will it take to travel this distance at 30 miles per hour?

SOLUTION:

Write an inverse-variation equation:	$r = \dfrac{k}{t}$
Substitute 45 for r and 3 for t:	$45 = \dfrac{k}{3}$
Solve for k:	$k = 135$
Substitute 135 for k in $r = \dfrac{k}{t}$:	$r = \dfrac{135}{t}$
Substitute 30 for r:	$30 = \dfrac{135}{t}$
Solve for t:	$t = \dfrac{135}{30} = \dfrac{9}{2}$

Thus, it will take $4\frac{1}{2}$ hours to travel the distance at 30 miles per hour.

EXERCISES 14.10

(A) For each equation, tell whether it describes a direct or an inverse variation.

1. $y = 5x$

2. $y = 7x$

3. $\dfrac{y}{x} = 3$

4. $\dfrac{y}{x} = 7$

5. $\dfrac{6}{x} = y$

6. $\dfrac{4}{x} = y$

7. $xy = 12$

8. $xy = 10$

9. $6 = \dfrac{y}{2x}$

10. $8 = \dfrac{y}{3x}$

11. $y = \dfrac{14}{3x}$

12. $y = \dfrac{1}{2} \cdot \dfrac{1}{x}$

Complete each exercise for the graph of
the inverse variation shown.

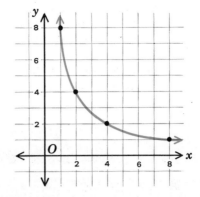

13. When $x = 2$, $y =$ _____ .

14. When $x = 8$, $y =$ _____ .

15. The constant of variation is _____ .

16. The equation of this inverse variation is _____ .

Ⓑ Write an equation of the form $y = \dfrac{k}{x}$ to show the relationship between the
variables given. Use k as the constant of variation.

17. The volume V of a gas kept at a constant temperature varies
inversely as the pressure p.

18. The current I in an electrical circuit is inversely proportional
to the resistance R when the voltage remains constant.

19. The time t required to travel a fixed distance is inversely proportional to the rate r of travel.

20. The interest rate r required to give a certain income varies
inversely as the amount A of money invested.

Find the constant of variation k if y varies inversely as x.

21. $y = 8$ when $x = 2$ **22.** $y = 7$ when $x = 5$

23. $y = 1.5$ when $x = 4$ **24.** $y = \frac{8}{3}$ when $x = \frac{3}{4}$

25. $y = 3.2$ when $x = 0.5$ **26.** $y = 1\frac{2}{3}$ when $x = \frac{3}{5}$

Solve each problem. (HINT: Refer to the Example and to Exercises 17–20.)

27. Suppose the area of a triangle remains constant, while the length
a of the altitude and the length b of the base vary. If the altitude
is 6 centimeters when the base is 10 centimeters, find the altitude
when the base is 20 centimeters.

28. In Exercise **27**, find the altitude when the base is 30 centimeters.

29. It takes 6 hours for the train below to travel a certain distance at the rate of 50 miles per hour. How long would it take the train to travel this distance at 75 miles per hour?

30. In Exercise **29**, find how long it would take to travel the distance at the rate of 60 miles per hour.

31. If a gas is kept at a constant temperature and the pressure is 15 pounds per square inch, the volume is 24 cubic feet. What will the volume be when the pressure is 30 pounds per square inch?

32. In Exercise **31**, find the volume of the gas when the pressure is 45 pounds per square inch.

33. If $10,000 invested at 6% gives a certain income, how much money must be invested at 5% to give the same income?

34. In Exercise **33**, how much money must be invested at 6.4% to give the same income?

© **35.** For a light source of a given intensity, the illumination I on a flat surface varies inversely as the square of its distance from the light source. If a lamp bulb 2 feet from a flat surface gives 20 lumens of illumination per square foot on the surface, how many lumens does each square foot of the surface receive when it is held 4 feet from the bulb?

14.11 INVERSE VARIATION AND PROPORTIONS

We have used proportions to solve problems involving direct variation. Proportions can also be used to solve problems about inverse variation.

If (x_1, y_1) and (x_2, y_2) are solutions of $y = \frac{4}{x}$, then

$$y_1 = \frac{4}{x_1} \quad \text{and} \quad y_2 = \frac{4}{x_2}.$$

So, $x_1 y_1 = 4 \quad$ and $\quad x_2 y_2 = 4.$

Then $x_1 y_1 = x_2 y_2.$

Multiplying both sides of this equation by $\frac{1}{x_2 y_1}$, we get

$$x_1 y_1 \left(\frac{1}{x_2 y_1}\right) = x_2 y_2 \left(\frac{1}{x_2 y_1}\right)$$

or

$$\boxed{\frac{x_1}{x_2} = \frac{y_2}{y_1}.}$$

In this proportion, x_1 and y_1 are the extremes, and x_2 and y_2 are the means.

Example 1: $(3, 8)$ and $(6, 4)$ are solutions of $y = \frac{24}{x}$. Write a proportion for the numbers in these ordered pairs.

SOLUTION: Let $(x_1, y_1) = (3, 8)$ and $(x_2, y_2) = (6, 4)$.

By substitution, $\frac{x_1}{x_2} = \frac{y_2}{y_1}$

becomes $\frac{3}{6} = \frac{4}{8}.$

You should check that $\frac{3}{6} = \frac{4}{8}$ is correct. The product of the extremes should equal the product of the means.

Example 2: Solve the problem in the example in Section 14.10 by using a proportion. (At 45 miles per hour, a given distance can be traveled in 3 hours. How long will it take to travel the same distance at 30 miles per hour?)

SOLUTION: Let r_1 and t_1 be the rate and time for the first trip, and let r_2 and t_2 be the rate and time for the second trip. Then

$$r_1 = 45, \quad t_1 = 3, \quad r_2 = 30, \quad \text{and} \quad t_2 = ?$$

Since this is an inverse variation, you can write

$$\frac{r_1}{r_2} = \frac{t_2}{t_1} \quad \text{or} \quad \frac{45}{30} = \frac{t_2}{3}.$$

Solving this equation, you have

$$30t_2 = 3 \cdot 45$$

$$30t_2 = 135$$

$$t_2 = \frac{135}{30} = \frac{9}{2}$$

Thus, it will take $4\frac{1}{2}$ hours to travel the same distance at 30 miles per hour.

EXERCISES 14.11

(A) In each exercise, the two ordered pairs belong to an inverse variation. Give a proportion for each.

1. $(1, 6)$; $(3, 2)$ **2.** $(5, 4)$; $(2, 10)$ **3.** $(8, 3)$; $(4, 6)$

4. $(\frac{1}{2}, 12)$; $(2, 3)$ **5.** $(1, 3)$; $(9, \frac{1}{3})$ **6.** $(12, 3)$; $(6, 6)$

7. $(28, 2)$; $(7, 8)$ **8.** $(7, 6)$; $(21, 2)$ **9.** $(5, 10)$; $(25, 2)$

10. $(3, 8)$; $(12, 2)$ **11.** $(5, 8)$; $(4, 10)$ **12.** $(\frac{1}{4}, 4)$; $(\frac{1}{5}, 5)$

(B) In each table, y varies inversely as x. Write a proportion and solve it for the given letter.

13.

x	1	2	3
y	12	a	4

14.

x	2	3	6
y	9	6	b

15.

x	5	10	35
y	c	7	2

16.

x	8	f	12
y	3	6	2

17.

x	5	4	g
y	8	10	20

18.

x	h	33	22
y	6	2	3

19–26. Solve Exercises **27–34** in Section 14.10 by using proportions.

Solve each problem by using a proportion.

27. The number of equal steps required to walk a given distance varies inversely as the length of each step. If it takes 120 steps of length 3 feet each to walk this distance, how many steps of length 2 feet are needed to walk this distance?

28. The time required to complete a certain project is inversely proportional to the number of people employed. If 2 people can complete the work in 3 days, how many days will 4 people require?

29. The number of revolutions made by a wheel rolling over a given distance varies inversely as the wheel's circumference C. A wheel of circumference 20 inches makes 100 turns in going a certain distance. How many turns will be required of a wheel of circumference 25 inches?

30. If two toothed gears mesh so that one can turn the other, the speeds of the gears vary inversely as the number of teeth in the gears. One of the gears has 16 teeth and a speed of 150 revolutions per minute. If the other gear has 50 teeth, what is its speed?

© 31. Solve Exercise **35** in Section 14.10 by using a proportion.

CHAPTER REVIEW ◆

14.1   Graph each relation. Then state the domain and range of the relation.

1. $\{(2, 1),\ (2, -2),\ (3, 4)\}$ **2.** $\{(3, 4),\ (4, 4),\ (5, 1),\ (2, 6)\}$

14.2   Tell which of the following relations are functions.

3. $\{(7, 8),\ (5, 2),\ (7, 1),\ (9, 3)\}$ **4.** $\{(4, 6),\ (3, 6),\ (5, 6),\ (2, 6)\}$

5.

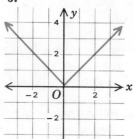

6.

7.

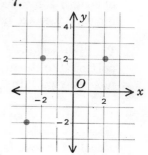

14.3   Refer to function f shown at the right.

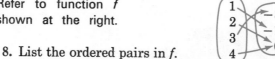

8. List the ordered pairs in f.

9. f matches 2 to _____.   **10.** $f(3) =$ _____

Given the function $f\colon x \to 4x + 3$,

11. $f(-3) =$ _____   **12.** _____ is matched to 3.

14.4   Tell whether each equation determines a linear function, a constant function, or neither.

13. $3x - 2y = 12$ **14.** $y = -2$ **15.** $x = 3$

16–18. Graph each equation in Exercises **13–15.**

14.5   **19.** y varies directly as x, and $y = 18$ when $x = 3$. Find the constant of variation and write a direct-variation equation of the form $y = kx$.

Does the given equation describe a direct variation?

20. $x = 7y$ **21.** $\dfrac{y}{x} = 3$ **22.** $y = \dfrac{4}{x}$ **23.** $3x - y = 3$

24. Within limits, the length l that a spring stretches varies directly as the weight w attached. If a weight of 24 grams stretches the spring 3 centimeters, how far will a weight of 36 grams stretch the spring? Solve this problem by an equation of the form $y = kx$.

25. Solve the problem in Exercise **24** by using a proportion.   **14.6**

26. Solve: $\dfrac{-3}{2x + 1} = \dfrac{1}{x - 4}$.

Graph each quadratic function.   **14.7**

27. $y = 2x^2$ **28.** $y = x^2 - 2$ **29.** $y = x^2 - 3x - 4$

Find the zeros (if any) of each function.   **14.8**

30. $y = 2x - 9$ **31.** $y = x^2 + x - 30$ **32.** $y = 3x^2 - 2x + 1$

33. A sheet of copper 32 inches wide is to be bent upward at each end to form a chute with a rectangular cross section. Find the dimensions of the chute that will give the maximum cross-sectional area.   **14.9**

34. If y varies inversely as x and $y = 8$ when $x = 3$, find y when $x = 4$.   **14.10**

35. What is the constant of variation in Exercise **34**?

36. The time t needed to travel a certain distance varies inversely as the rate r of travel. If it takes 8 hours to travel a certain distance at the rate of 36 miles per hour, how long would it take to travel this distance at the rate of 48 miles per hour?

37. Solve the problem in Exercise **34** by using a proportion.   **14.11**

38. Solve the problem in Exercise **36** by using a proportion.

CHAPTER SELF-TEST

Which lettered item *best* matches each numbered item?

1. A function described by $y = mx + b$, where m and b are constants, $m \neq 0$

2. A function described by $y = k$

3. A function described by $y = \dfrac{k}{x}$, $x \neq 0$, and k is a nonzero constant

4. A function described by $y = ax^2 + bx + c$, where a, b, c are real numbers, $a \neq 0$

5. The set $\{2, 3, 7\}$ for the function $\{(1, 2), (4, 3), (5, 7)\}$.

a. direct variation
b. domain
c. range
d. inverse variation
e. quadratic function
f. linear function
g. constant function

Tell if each relation is a function.

6. $\{(3, -1), (1, 2), (3, 5)\}$

7. $\{(6, 2), (5, -1), (7, 2)\}$

Using the function $f: x \rightarrow 3x - 8$, complete each exercise.

8. $f(2) = $ _____

9. f matches -1 to _____.

Does the given equation describe a direct variation or an inverse variation?

10. $y = \dfrac{10}{x}$

11. $y = 5x$

12. $xy = 6$

13. $4 = \dfrac{y}{x}$

Find the zeros of each function.

14. $y = -2x + 6$

15. $y = x^2 + 2x - 15$

16–17. Graph the functions in Exercises 14–15.

18. The amount A of money Sue earns by baby-sitting varies directly as the number n of hours she works. If she earned $9.00 for sitting 6 hours last week, how much will she earn for sitting 8 hours this week?

Tell which of the ordered pairs are solutions of $3x - 4y = 8$. **Ch. 8**

1. $(1, -2)$ **2.** $(0, -2)$ **3.** $(2, \frac{1}{2})$ **4.** $(4, 1)$

Refer to the graph.

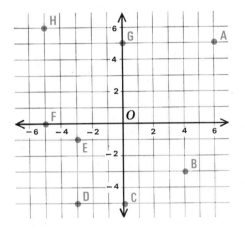

5. What are the coordinates of point H? D?

6. Which point is the graph of $(4, -3)$?

7. A line contains points E and A. Express the slope of the line as a fraction, and then as a per cent.

8. Find the slope-intercept form of the equation of each line described below.

   a. slope $= \frac{3}{2}$; contains point G

   b. contains points F and C

Tell whether the equation is in standard form. Then graph it.

9. $y = 2x + 6$ **10.** $3x + 5y = 10$

11. When a car is rented for one day, the fee (f) equals a charge for each mile (m) driven plus a minimum charge. Two ordered pairs of the form (m, f) are $(60, 24.20)$ and $(200, 41.00)$. Write a formula to show how f and m are related.

Graph each system. Then tell whether the system has no solutions, exactly one solution, or many solutions. **Ch. 9**

12. $\begin{cases} y = \frac{1}{4}x + 2 \\ y - 1 = \frac{1}{4}x \end{cases}$ **13.** $\begin{cases} 3x - y = 5 \\ x - y = 1 \end{cases}$ **14.** $\begin{cases} y \leq 2 \\ 2y > 4x - 2 \end{cases}$

Solve each system.

15. $\begin{cases} 4p - 2q = -4 \\ 3p + 5q = 10 \end{cases}$ **16.** $\begin{cases} x = 3y + 1 \\ 6x + 2y = -14 \end{cases}$ **17.** $\begin{cases} 4m - 5n = -13 \\ 2m + n = 9 \end{cases}$

18. Some 30% antifreeze solution is to be mixed with some 60% antifreeze solution to make 30 kilograms of 50% antifreeze solution. How much of each solution will be needed?

Ch. 10   Find each quotient.

19. $\dfrac{(-3)^2}{(-3)^3}$ **20.** $\left(\dfrac{2}{5}\right)^2$ **21.** $\dfrac{m^4}{m^7}$ **22.** $\dfrac{10s^3t^5}{2s^2t^3}$

23. $3m\overline{\smash{)}9m^2 + 18m}$ **24.** $2x - 1\overline{\smash{)}6x^2 + 9x - 6}$

Simplify each expression.

25. $3^{-2} \cdot 2^0$ **26.** s^{-3} **27.** $2^{-3} \cdot 2^{-2}$ **28.** $\left(\dfrac{1}{2}\right)^{-1}$ **29.** $\dfrac{x^7}{x^{-2}}$

Ch. 11   Compute as indicated. Express each result in simplest form.

30. $\dfrac{2y - 4}{y^2} \cdot \dfrac{y}{y^2 - 4}$ **31.** $\dfrac{m + 3}{m} \div \dfrac{m^2 + 3m}{m}$

32. $\dfrac{3}{t^3} + \dfrac{t - 3}{t^3}$ **33.** $\dfrac{x^2 - 3}{x + 3} - \dfrac{2x^2}{3x + 9}$

Solve each equation.

34. $\dfrac{4m - 8}{m} - \dfrac{10}{m} + 2 = 0$ **35.** $\dfrac{s + 2}{s + 3} = \dfrac{s - 2}{s}$

36. Julie can mow a lawn in 45 minutes, and Mary can mow the same lawn in 30 minutes. If they use identical mowers, how long will it take them, working together?

37. Solve the formula $F = \dfrac{Mm}{d^2}$ for m.

Ch. 12   Find the roots indicated.

38. $\sqrt{9}$ **39.** $\sqrt[3]{8}$ **40.** $\sqrt{10000}$ **41.** $\sqrt[4]{\frac{1}{81}}$

Find each product or quotient.

42. $\sqrt{2} \cdot \sqrt{5}$ **43.** $\sqrt{8} \cdot \sqrt{\frac{1}{2}}$ **44.** $\dfrac{\sqrt{15}}{\sqrt{5}}$ **45.** $\dfrac{\sqrt{\frac{9}{2}}}{\sqrt{\frac{3}{2}}}$

Simplify each expression.

46. $\sqrt{24}$ **47.** $\sqrt{75x}$ **48.** $\sqrt{\frac{2}{5}}$

49. $2\sqrt{3} + \sqrt{3}$ **50.** $\sqrt{27} - 2\sqrt{3}$ **51.** $3\sqrt{x} + \sqrt{4x}$

Change each radical to simplest form.

52. $\sqrt{(-3)^2}$ **53.** $\sqrt{20y^2}$ **54.** $\sqrt{\dfrac{x^2}{3}}$

Solve each equation.

55. $\sqrt{m - 3} = 5$ **56.** $2 + \sqrt{x - 2} = x$

Find the distance between the two points whose coordinates are given.

57. $(6, 0)$ and $(4, 2)$ **58.** $(1, -6)$ and $(7, -2)$

Solve by using the *zero product property* or the *square root property*. **Ch. 13**
Factor first if necessary.

59. $x(x - 1) = 0$ **60.** $y^2 - y - 2 = 0$

61. $s^2 = 4s + 12$ **62.** $(x - 6)^2 = 25$

Solve by *completing the square*.

63. $x^2 + 14x + 40 = 0$ **64.** $y^2 = 6y - 4$

Solve by using the quadratic formula.

65. $2m^2 - 3m - 2 = 0$ **66.** $x^2 = 4x - 1$

Find the value of the discriminant for each equation and describe the roots.

67. $3m^2 + 3 = -6m$ **68.** $y^2 + 6 = 0$

69. Helen is 11 years older than Elsa and the product of their ages is 126. Find their ages.

70. The formula for the volume of a right circular cylinder is $V = \pi r^2 h$. (Refer to the figure.) If $V = 36\pi$ cubic meters and $h = 4$ meters, find r.

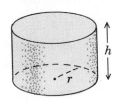

Find and graph the solution set of each inequality.

71. $x^2 + 4x + 3 < 0$ **72.** $x^2 + x - 6 \geq 0$

For Exercises 73–78, refer to the relations below.

a. {(1, 1), (3, 2), (4, 3), (6, 3)}   **b.** {(3, 4), (5, 4), (3, 3)}

73–74. Graph each relation.

75–76. State the domain and range of each relation.

77–78. Tell whether each relation is a function.

Tell whether each relation graphed is a function.

79. 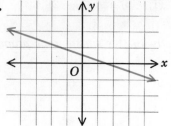   **80.**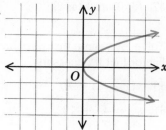

81. Graph the relation described by $y = x^2 - 2$ if the domain is {$-3, 0, 2, 5$}. Is this relation a function?

Given the function $f: x \rightarrow -2x + 1$,

82. $f(-2) =$ _____.   **83.** _____ is matched to 9.

Does the given equation describe a direct variation, an inverse variation, or is it a proportion?

84. $xy = 9$ **85.** $\dfrac{x}{2} = \dfrac{5}{8}$ **86.** $y = 4x$

Graph each quadratic function.

87. $y = x^2$ **88.** $y = 2x^2 - 3$

Find the zeros of each function.

89. $y = -\frac{1}{3}x + 3$ **90.** $y = x^2 - 2x - 3$

91. The amount (A) of gasoline used in a car varies directly as the number (m) of miles driven. If 15 gallons of gas were used to drive 210 miles, how much gas will be used to drive 882 miles?

Trigonometry

Trigonometry began as a branch of mathematics dealing with the measurement of parts (sides and angles) of triangles. In this chapter we will explore some of the uses of trigonometry.

First, it is necessary to know a little about *similar triangles*. Notice the right triangle shown in the photograph above. It is similar to the actual right triangle formed by the building that was photographed. We might say that by taking the photograph the larger triangle was shrunk to a smaller one which has the *same shape* but a different size.

15.1 WHAT ARE SIMILAR TRIANGLES?

Similar triangles have the same shape, but may differ in size. The three triangles below are similar.

Each of these triangles could be transformed into any one of the others if the following were possible. First, uniformly "shrink" or "expand" one of the triangles until it is the desired size. Then move it into the exact position of the other triangle.

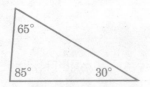 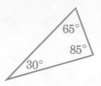

For any two of these triangles, each angle of one can be paired with an angle of the other that has the same measure. Another way to say this is "in similar triangles, corresponding angles are *congruent*." *Corresponding sides* are opposite congruent angles.

You may suspect that corresponding sides of similar triangles are related in some way. Consider the following ratios involving the similar right triangles below. (In the equations, a symbol such as AC stands for the length of the line segment.)

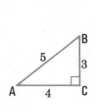 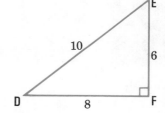

$$\frac{AC}{DF} = \frac{4}{8} = \frac{1}{2} \qquad \frac{BC}{EF} = \frac{3}{6} = \frac{1}{2} \qquad \frac{AB}{DE} = \frac{5}{10} = \frac{1}{2}$$

This suggests that the ratios of the measures of corresponding sides are equal for similar triangles. Equations like those above, which state that ratios are equal, are called **proportions**, so we can say:

> In similar triangles, corresponding sides are **proportional**.

Example: For the similar triangles shown, complete the given proportions.

$$\frac{15}{10} = \frac{12}{?} \qquad \frac{12}{8} = \frac{?}{6} \qquad \frac{9}{?} = \frac{15}{10}$$

SOLUTION: Since corresponding sides are proportional,

$$\frac{15}{10} = \frac{12}{8} \qquad \frac{12}{8} = \frac{9}{6} \qquad \frac{9}{6} = \frac{15}{10}$$

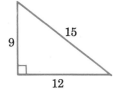

EXERCISES 15.1

Ⓐ Match each triangle in 1–4 with that triangle in a–d to which it is similar.

1.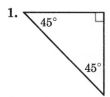

2.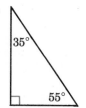

a.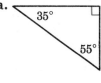

b.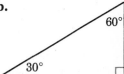

3.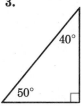

4.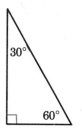

c.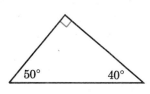

d.

Ⓑ For each pair of triangles, complete the given proportions.

5. $\dfrac{4.9}{?} = \dfrac{5}{2.5}$

$\dfrac{7}{3.5} = \dfrac{?}{2.45}$

$\dfrac{?}{2.5} = \dfrac{7}{3.5}$

Ex. 5

6. $\dfrac{4.5}{3} = \dfrac{7.5}{?}$

$\dfrac{7.5}{5} = \dfrac{?}{4}$

$\dfrac{6}{?} = \dfrac{4.5}{3}$

Ex. 6

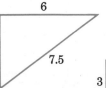

Ex. 7

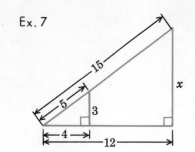

7. $\dfrac{3}{?} = \dfrac{5}{15}$

$\dfrac{4}{12} = \dfrac{?}{x}$

$\dfrac{5}{15} = \dfrac{4}{?}$

Ex. 8

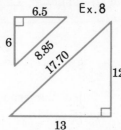

8. $\dfrac{8.85}{17.70} = \dfrac{6}{?}$

$\dfrac{6.5}{?} = \dfrac{8.85}{17.70}$

$\dfrac{?}{12} = \dfrac{6.5}{13}$

Ex. 9

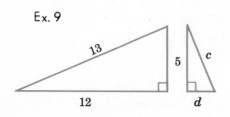

9. $\dfrac{12}{5} = \dfrac{5}{?}$

$\dfrac{?}{d} = \dfrac{13}{c}$

$\dfrac{13}{?} = \dfrac{12}{5}$

Ex. 10

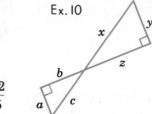

10. $\dfrac{?}{y} = \dfrac{c}{x}$

$\dfrac{c}{x} = \dfrac{b}{?}$

$\dfrac{b}{z} = \dfrac{?}{y}$

© Similar triangles can be used to find unknown distances by using distances which are known. Use the fact that corresponding sides of similar triangles are proportional to solve each problem.

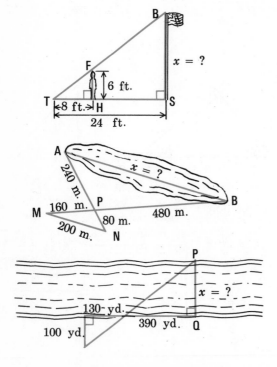

11. When the shadow of a 6-foot-tall person is 8 feet long, the shadow of a flagpole is 24 feet long. If the tips of the shadows are at the same point on the ground, how tall is the pole? (HINT:Triangles TFH and TBS are similar. What ratios must be equal?)

12. To find the distance across a lake, measurements were made as shown in the figure. Find the distance from A to B. (HINT: Triangles ABP and MNP are similar.)

13. Use similar triangles to find the width (PQ) of the river.

How to Measure a Pyramid and Lose a Girl Friend

About 600 B.C. there was an unusually successful Greek merchant named Thales (thā-lēz), who became very wealthy. He then turned his talents to the study of many subjects, including mathematics.

A story is told that one evening, while walking with a girl, Thales became so interested in studying the stars that he stumbled and fell into a ditch. The girl, angry about the lack of attention, asked sharply, "How can you expect to learn anything about the stars if you don't know what's going on at your feet?"

Another story about Thales says that he was much admired for a method by which he computed the height of the Great Pyramid in Egypt. He is said to have placed a stick in the ground and then waited until the length of its shadow was equal to the length of the stick. It had occurred to him that, at such a time, he could determine the height of the pyramid by measuring its shadow. (He also allowed for the distance from the center of the pyramid to an outside edge.)

Thales' method involved similar triangles. Can you explain why?

15.2 SINE, COSINE, AND TANGENT RATIOS

A right triangle has one right angle and two *acute angles* (angles measuring less than 90 degrees). In a right triangle, the side opposite the right angle is called the **hypotenuse** and the other two sides are called **legs**.

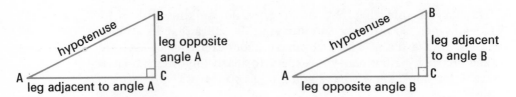

Once an acute angle has been chosen, the legs may be identified as shown above. For each acute angle, there are three ratios which are most commonly used. They are called *trigonometric ratios*. The definitions below are stated for angle A, but can also be applied to angle B.

Name	Abbreviation		Ratio
sine of angle A	sin A	=	$\dfrac{\text{leg opposite angle A}}{\text{hypotenuse}}$
cosine of angle A	cos A	=	$\dfrac{\text{leg adjacent to angle A}}{\text{hypotenuse}}$
tangent of angle A	tan A	=	$\dfrac{\text{leg opposite angle A}}{\text{leg adjacent to angle A}}$

Example 1: For right triangle MPN, find sin M, cos M, and tan M.

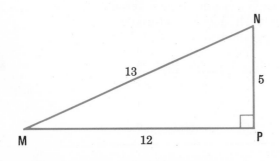

SOLUTION:

$$\sin M = \frac{\text{leg opp. M}}{\text{hypotenuse}} = \frac{5}{13} \approx 0.385$$

$$\cos M = \frac{\text{leg adj. to M}}{\text{hypotenuse}} = \frac{12}{13} \approx 0.923$$

$$\tan M = \frac{\text{leg opp. M}}{\text{leg adj. to M}} = \frac{5}{12} \approx 0.417$$

Example 2: For right triangle MPN, find sin N, cos N, and tan N.

SOLUTION:

$$\sin N = \frac{\text{leg opp. N}}{\text{hypotenuse}} = \frac{12}{13} \approx 0.923$$

$$\cos N = \frac{\text{leg adj. to N}}{\text{hypotenuse}} = \frac{5}{13} \approx 0.385$$

$$\tan N = \frac{\text{leg opp. N}}{\text{leg adj. to N}} = \frac{12}{5} = 2.4$$

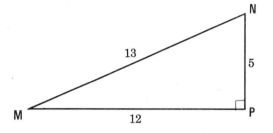

EXERCISES 15.2

Ⓐ Use triangle HJK to find the given ratios in fraction form.

1. $\sin H = \frac{?}{?}$ **2.** $\sin K = \frac{?}{?}$

3. $\cos H = \frac{?}{?}$ **4.** $\cos K = \frac{?}{?}$

5. $\tan H = \frac{?}{?}$ **6.** $\tan K = \frac{?}{?}$

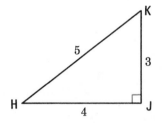

Use triangle PRQ to find the given ratios in fraction form.

7. $\sin P = \frac{?}{?}$ **8.** $\sin Q = \frac{?}{?}$

9. $\cos P = \frac{?}{?}$ **10.** $\cos Q = \frac{?}{?}$

11. $\tan P = \frac{?}{?}$ **12.** $\tan Q = \frac{?}{?}$

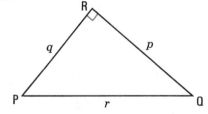

Ⓑ Compute, to the nearest thousandth, the sine, cosine, and tangent for both acute angles of each triangle.

13.

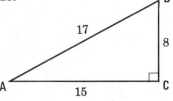

14.

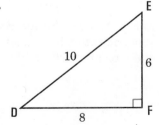

15.

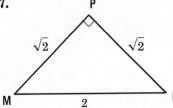

16.

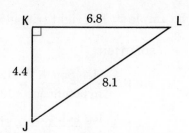

17.

18.

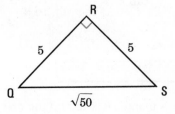

© In Exercises 19–30, refer to triangles ABC and DEF where angles A and D have the same measure and angles B and E have the same measure.

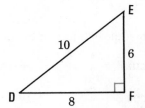

Find each ratio below in fraction form.

19. sin A	**20.** cos A	**21.** tan A
22. sin D	**23.** cos D	**24.** tan D
25. sin B	**26.** cos B	**27.** tan B
28. sin E	**29.** cos E	**30.** tan E

31. What do the results for Exercises **19–30** suggest about the trigonometric ratios for angles having the same measure (like angles A and D or angles B and E)?

One reason that the sine, cosine, and tangent ratios are useful is that they do not depend on the size of the triangle.

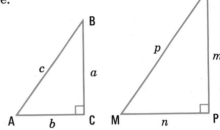

For example, in the diagram, angle A and angle M have the same measure and the two triangles are similar. Thus the corresponding sides are proportional.

$$\frac{a}{c} = \frac{m}{p} \qquad \frac{b}{c} = \frac{n}{p} \qquad \frac{a}{b} = \frac{m}{n}$$

This shows that the sine, cosine, and tangent ratios *do not* depend on the size of the right triangle. Once the measurement of an acute angle is determined, these trigonometric ratios are determined. It is handy to have a table of these ratios. Part of such a table follows. A more complete table appears on page 556.

angle A	sin A	cos A	tan A
26°	0.438	0.899	0.488
27	.454	.891	.510
28	.469	.883	.532
29	.485	.875	.554
30	.500	.866	.577
31	.515	.857	.601
32	.530	.848	.625
33	.545	.839	.649
34	.559	.829	.675
35	.574	.819	.700

Example 1: Find sin 29°, cos 29°, and tan 29°.

SOLUTION: In the column headed **angle** A, find 29°. Directly opposite 29° in the column headed **sin** A, read 0.485.

$$\sin 29° \approx 0.485$$

(Nearly all values in the table are approximations.) Similarly you should find the following.

$$\cos 29° \approx 0.875 \qquad \tan 29° \approx 0.554$$

Example 2: What is the degree measure of the angle whose

      a. cosine is 0.839?

      b. tangent is 0.700?

SOLUTION:

a. In the column headed **cos** A, find 0.839. Directly opposite 0.839 in the column headed **angle** A, read 33°.

$$\cos 33° \approx 0.839$$

So the measure of the angle whose cosine is 0.839 is approximately 33°.

b. Similarly, tan 35° ≈ 0.700. So, the measure of the angle whose tangent is 0.700 is approximately 35°.

Trigonometric ratios can often be used to find unknown parts of right triangles as shown in the following example.

Example 3: Use the figure. Find x if

      a. sin A ≈ 0.827.

      b. tan A ≈ 1.470.

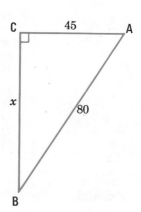

SOLUTION:

a. $\sin A = \dfrac{x}{80}$ and sin A ≈ 0.827

$$\therefore \frac{x}{80} \approx 0.827 \qquad x \approx 80(0.827)$$

$$x \approx 66.2$$

b. $\tan A = \dfrac{x}{45}$ and tan A ≈ 1.470

$$\therefore \frac{x}{45} \approx 1.470 \qquad x \approx 45(1.470)$$

$$x \approx 66.2$$

EXERCISES 15.3

Ⓐ Use the table on page 556 to find sine ratios for the following.

1. 30°   2. 60°   3. 88°   4. 45°

5. 27°   6. 48°   7. 72°   8. 5°

Find the cosine ratios for the following.

9. 55°   10. 30°   11. 60°   12. 20°

13. 5°   14. 72°   15. 85°   16. 45°

Find the tangent ratios for the following.

17. 27°   18. 48°   19. 45°   20. 60°

21. 85°   22. 5°   23. 78°   24. 30°

Find angle A to the nearest 1°.

25. $\sin A \approx 0.122$ 26. $\tan A = 1$ 27. $\sin A \approx 0.999$

28. $\cos A = 0.5$ 29. $\cos A \approx 0.940$ 30. $\tan A \approx 0.700$

Ⓑ Find each of the following.

31. $\sin 20°$ 32. $\cos 42°$ 33. $\tan 66°$

34. $\sin 3°$ 35. $\cos 3°$ 36. $\tan 3°$

37. $\sin 35°$ 38. $\cos 15°$ 39. $\tan 70°$

40. $\sin 65°$ 41. $\cos 55°$ 42. $\tan 89°$

43. As the size of the angle increases, does the

   a.   sine ratio for that angle increase or decrease?

   b.   cosine ratio for that angle increase or decrease?

   c.   tangent ratio for that angle increase or decrease?

44. If sin A = cos A, what is the degree measure of angle A?

45. Which is larger, cos 76° or tan 15°?

46. Which is larger, sin 20° or cos 70°?

Use the figure. Give your results to the nearest tenth.

47. Find *m* if sin M = 0.107.

48. Find *m* if sin M = 0.5.

49. Find *n* if cos M = 0.891.

50. Find *n* if cos M = 0.015.

51. Find *m* if *n* = 10 and tan M = 9.949.

52. Find *m* if *n* = 50 and tan M = 1.732.

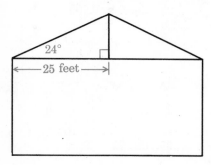

© **53.** Compute (sin A)² + (cos A)² ≈ ? for angle A with a measure of

    a. 20°   **b.** 42°   **c.** 66°   **d.** 87°

Now round each of your results to the nearest integer. What do you conclude? Test your conclusion on angles having other measures.

54. An architect is designing a roof to have a pitch of 24 degrees. If the distance from the center of the house to a wall is 25 feet, how high above the outside walls will the peak of the roof be? (See figure.)

There are many practical problems that you can solve by using trigonometric ratios. The terms *angle of elevation* and *angle of depression* are often useful in such problems.

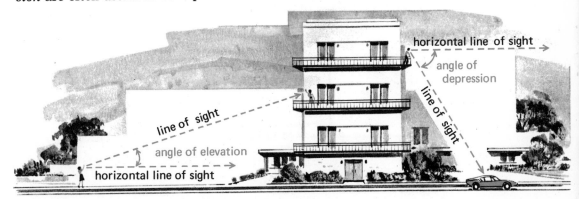

Example 1: A tree casts a shadow 25 meters long when the angle of elevation of the sun is 36°. How tall is the tree?

SOLUTION: It is helpful to make a sketch as at the right.

$$\tan 36° = \frac{x}{25} \qquad x = 25(\tan 36°)$$

$$x \approx 25(0.727)$$

$$x \approx 18.175$$

So, the tree is approximately 18.175 meters tall.

Example 2: A minisub is 50 meters higher than an undersea research base and the angle of the depression to the base is 10°. What is the distance from the sub to the base?

SOLUTION: $\sin 10° = \dfrac{50}{x} \qquad x = \dfrac{50}{\sin 10°}$

$$x \approx \frac{50}{0.174}$$

$$x \approx 287.4$$

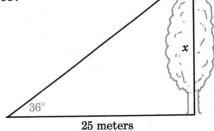

So, the sub is approximately 287.4 meters from the base.

EXERCISES 15.4

Ⓐ Make a sketch whenever necessary. Give your answers to the nearest tenth.

1. How tall is the building?

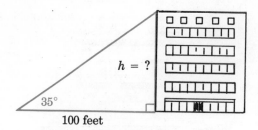

$h = ?$

35°

100 feet

2. How long is the ladder?

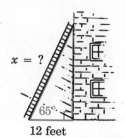

$x = ?$

65°

12 feet

3. How wide is the river?

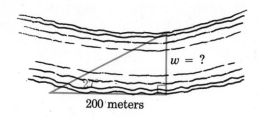

$w = ?$

27°

200 meters

4. How high is the balloon?

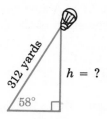

312 yards

$h = ?$

58°

5. How high is the kite?

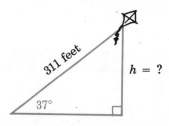

311 feet

$h = ?$

37°

6. How wide is the lake?

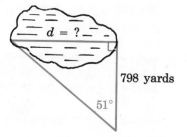

$d = ?$

798 yards

51°

Ⓑ **7.** A telephone pole casts a shadow 21 feet long when the angle of elevation of the sun is 52°. How tall is the pole?

8. A woman casts a shadow 10 feet long when the angle of elevation of the sun is 28°. How tall is the woman?

9. How long must a brace to a TV tower be if it is attached to the tower 37 feet above the ground and forms an angle of 52° with the tower?

10. From a point 107 meters above the ground in a control tower, the angle of depression to a taxiing airplane is 31°. How far is the airplane from the observer in the tower?

11. How long a ladder does the fire department need to reach the top of a building 60 feet tall? The angle of elevation of the ladder should be about 70°.

12. How long a ladder is needed to reach a window 10 meters above the ground if the angle of elevation of the ladder is 75°?

13. Use the figure at the right. Find how high the bridge is above point P.

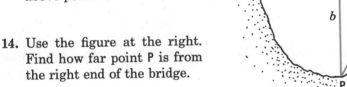

14. Use the figure at the right. Find how far point P is from the right end of the bridge.

Make a sketch for each problem. Give your answers for Exercises 15–18 to the nearest degree.

15. An escalator 72 feet long raises passengers 21 feet from the first to the second floor. What angle does the escalator make with the first floor?

16. A mountain train rises 10 feet for every 175 feet it moves along the track. Find the angle of elevation of the track.

17. A pilot flying at an altitude of 38,000 feet wants to land at an airport 100 miles (528,000 feet) ahead. If she now descends to the airport by maintaining a constant angle with the horizontal, what should that angle be?

18. A thundercloud is sighted 12,500 feet above a point on the ground that is 28,100 feet from a weather observation post. What is the angle of elevation of the thundercloud from the observation post?

In Exercises 19–20, give your answers to the nearest foot.

19. A surveyor stands 125 feet from the foot of a building and with the aid of a transit finds the angle of elevation of the top of the building to be 27°. How tall is the building?

20. A moon capsule is resting on the surface of the moon directly below a spaceship in its orbit 10 miles above the moon. Two astronauts find the angle of elevation from their position to the spaceship to be 78°. How far are they from the moon capsule?

© Make a sketch whenever necessary. Give angle measures to the nearest degree and other measures to the nearest tenth.

21. A boat sails southwesterly in a direction 60° from due south. After holding this course for 80 miles, how far south has it traveled? How far west?

22. From the top of a building 100 feet high, the angles of elevation and depression of the top and bottom of an industrial smokestack are 30° and 20°. How tall is the smokestack?

23. A mountaintop is 1 kilometer above the cities seen at points A and B. The angles of depression of the two cities are 25° and 40°. How far apart are the two cities?

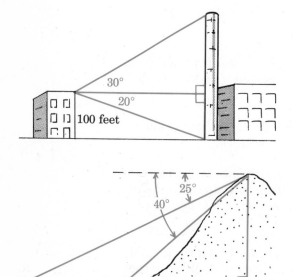

1. Write the word that best completes each sentence.

    a. Similar triangles have the same _____.

    b. Corresponding angles of similar triangles are _____.

    c. Corresponding sides of similar triangles are _____.

2. Explain the meaning of the sine, the cosine, and the tangent of an angle.

15.1

15.2

Find *x* to the nearest foot for each triangle below.

15.3

3.
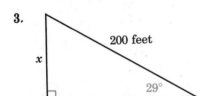
200 feet
x
29°

4.
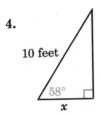
10 feet
58°
x

5.
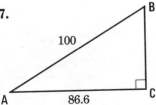
18°
40 feet
x

6.
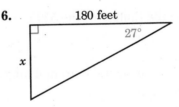
180 feet
27°
x

In each triangle below, find angle A to the nearest 1°.

7.
B
100
A
86.6
C

8.
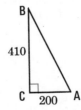
B
410
C
200
A

9. Make drawings to illustrate the meaning of

    a. angle of elevation.   **b.** angle of depression.

15.4

10. The tallest building in the city casts a shadow 593 feet long when the angle of elevation of the sun is 64°. How tall is the building, to the nearest foot?

CHAPTER SELF-TEST

1. Which of the following are true of similar triangles?

   a. Corresponding sides are congruent.

   b. Corresponding angles are congruent.

   c. The triangles are the same shape.

   d. Corresponding sides are proportional.

2. Use the diagram. Replace each ? to make a true sentence.

   a. $\sin P = \frac{?}{?}$

   b. $\cos P = \frac{?}{?}$

   c. $\tan P = \frac{?}{?}$

   d. $\cos Q = \frac{?}{?}$

   e. $\tan Q = \frac{?}{?}$

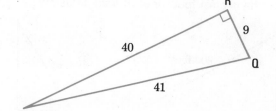

3. Use the table on page 556 to estimate the following ratios.

   a. $\sin 65°$ **b.** $\cos 60°$ **c.** $\tan 89°$

4. Use the same table to find angle A to the nearest 1°.

   a. $\tan A \approx 0.213$ **b.** $\cos A \approx 0.070$ **c.** $\sin A \approx 0.358$

5. Use the diagram. If $\sin 41° \approx 0.656$ and $\cos 41° \approx 0.755$, find the following to the nearest tenth.

   a. AB

   b. BC

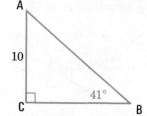

6. To the nearest foot, how high is a flying kite if the kite string is 100 feet long and forms an angle of 44° with the ground? (Assume the string is straight. Make a sketch.)

7. To the nearest degree, what is the angle of elevation of the sun when a 6-foot person casts an 8-foot shadow? (Make a sketch.)

Heads, I'll go fishing. Tails, I'll shoot baskets. If the coin stands on end, I'll cut the grass.

* Chapter

16 *Probability*

Are the boy's chances of going fishing or shooting baskets better than his chances of cutting the grass? A whole branch of mathematics, called **probability**, deals with chance. In fact, probability started when mathematicians became interested in games of chance.

Now, the uses of probability are growing very rapidly in many fields such as insurance, medicine, industry, and politics.

Most people have at some time flipped a coin or rolled dice. You may think these things have nothing to do with mathematics. However, both of these activities involve ideas of probability.

Ⓑ EXERCISES 16.1

Experiment 1

When an ordinary coin is tossed, we expect two equally likely outcomes, heads or tails. If a coin is tossed for many **trials**, it seems that heads would occur about half the time and tails about half the time. To test this, toss a coin for 50 trials and record the results in a table like the following.

Heads	
Tails	
Total trials	50

1. What is the ratio of the number of heads to the total number of trials?

2. What is the ratio of the number of tails to the total number of trials?

3. If a coin were tossed 1000 times, about how many times would you expect heads to occur?

4. Is it possible that heads would occur 700 times out of 1000 tosses of a coin?

Experiment 2

If an ordinary die (singular of dice) is rolled, we expect six equally likely outcomes: *1, 2, 3, 4, 5,* or *6* dots. Roll a die 60 times and record your results in a table.

Outcome	Number of times
1	
2	
3	
4	
5	
6	
Total trials	60

5. Since there are 6 possible outcomes, does it seem likely that each outcome would occur $\frac{1}{6}$ of the time? Did this happen in your experiment?

6. If you roll a die 600 times, about how many times would you expect to get a *3*? How many times would you expect to get a *7*?

When two coins are tossed, there are four equally likely outcomes. Represent heads by *H* and tails by *T*. Now toss a penny and a dime for 40 trials. Record the results in a table.

Experiment 3

Outcome		Number of times
(*penny*)	(*dime*)	
H	H	
H	T	
T	H	
T	T	
Total trials		40

7. Are two heads as likely to occur as one head and one tail? Why?

8. Is it possible for two heads to occur in all 40 trials? Is it likely?

Put 7 marbles of one color (say red) and 3 marbles of another color (say black) in a sack. Mix them up. Select one marble without looking, record the color, then replace the marble and mix again. Do this for 50 trials. All the marbles should be the same size. Why?

Experiment 4

Red	Black	Total trials
		50

9. Which color is most likely to be selected in any one trial? Why?

10. In what per cent of the trials would you expect black to be selected? Red?

11. In 100 trials, about how many times would you expect black to be selected?

12. Are "selecting red" and "selecting black" equally likely outcomes?

A thumbtack was tossed 100 times. There were two outcomes, *A* and *B*, as shown below.

Out of the 100 tosses, outcome *A* occurred 71 times and outcome *B* occurred 29 times. From only this information, how likely does it seem that outcome *A* will occur in any future toss?

> In an experiment with chance, if an outcome occurs *s* times out of *n* trials, the **experimental probability** of that outcome is $\frac{s}{n}$.

Suppose you tossed a die for 60 trials and the results were as follows.

Outcome	1	2	3	4	5	6
Number of times	11	9	10	12	8	10

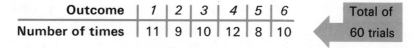

Total of 60 trials

Then, experimental probability of *1* $= \frac{11}{60}$,

experimental probability of *2* $= \frac{9}{60} = \frac{3}{20}$,

$\vdots$

and so forth.

Since *7* resulted 0 times out of the 60 trials,

an impossible outcome → experimental probability of *7* $= \frac{0}{60} = 0$.

Also, since a result *less than 7* occurred in every trial,

a certain outcome → experimental probability of a result less than *7* $= \frac{60}{60} = 1$.

> The experimental probability of an outcome is never less than 0 and never greater than 1.

EXERCISES 16.2

Ⓐ A student tossed a die 50 times to obtain this table.

Outcome	1	2	3	4	5	6
Number of times	8	7	9	10	8	8

Find the experimental probability of obtaining a(n):

1. *2*   2. *5*   3. *3*   4. *6*

5. *1*   6. *4*   7. *8*   8. *0*

9. even number   10. odd number

11. *2* or *3*   12. *3* or *6*

13. prime number   14. number less than *10*

15. If a particular outcome occurs every time an experiment is performed, what is its experimental probability?

16. If a particular outcome never occurs, what is its experimental probability?

Ⓑ Use your results from Experiments 1–4 in Section 16.1.

17. For Experiment 1, find the experimental probability:
   a. of heads.   b. of tails.

18. For Experiment 2, find the experimental probability:
   a. of a *1*.   b. of a *5*.

19. For Experiment 3, find the experimental probability:
   a. of 2 heads.   b. of 2 tails.

20. For Experiment 4, find the experimental probability:
   a. of red.   b. of black.

Perform the following experiments.

21. Write the letters *A*, *C*, and *T* on three identical slips of paper. Fold the slips so that the letters are not visible. Put them in a box and have someone draw the letters out one at a time, recording the letters in the order they are selected. Repeat this for 30 trials. Find the experimental probability of spelling "cat" by this *random selection* of letters.

22. Throw two dice for a total of 60 trials. For each trial, record the sum of the dots on the two faces. Then find the experimental probability of each possible sum. Use a table as follows.

Sum	2	3	4	5	6	7	8	9	10	11	12
Number of times											
Experimental probability											

© **23.** A consumer survey was made to determine automobile buying habits of the public. Out of 75 persons who reported that they planned to buy a car within the next six months, only 33 had actually done so six months later.

Question: *If we choose at random one of the persons who reported that they planned to buy a car in the next six months, what is the experimental probability that the person actually bought one?*

United Foods Corporation conducted a test to determine the tastiness of a new food product. Fifty people were asked to taste the product and rate it from +3 (excellent) to −3 (terrible). Here are the results for the product (called *product H*) and for a competing product (called *product C*).

Rating	Frequency C	Frequency H
+3	1	5
+2	5	11
+1	15	19
0	17	13
−1	8	1
−2	3	1
−3	1	0
Total tasters	50	50

Questions: *If we choose one of the tasters at random, what is the experimental probability that the taster rated:*

24. *product H with +2 or higher?*

25. *product C with −2 or less?*

What Are Odds?

Probabilities are often expressed in terms of "odds." Suppose an outcome A occurs s times out of n equally likely outcomes in an experiment. Then n does *not* occur in $n - s$ cases.

Odds *in favor of A* $= \dfrac{\text{number of times } A \text{ occurs}}{\text{number of times } A \text{ does not occur}} = \dfrac{s}{n - s}$

Odds *against A* $= \dfrac{\text{number of times } A \text{ does not occur}}{\text{number of times } A \text{ occurs}} = \dfrac{n - s}{s}$

So the odds in favor of A are s to $n - s$. The odds against A are $n - s$ to s.

Sometimes odds are rather amazing. The following article appeared in the *Chicago Tribune*.

The winning hand

REDDITCH, England, Nov. 24 (UPI)—Whist Player Jack Spenser shouted, "Abundance declared," and laid down his hand of 13 spades. His companions followed with 13 hearts, 13 diamonds, and 13 clubs, defying odds of 2,223,520,000,000,000,000,000,-000,000 to 1, give or take a few thousand.

For Spenser to get a perfect hand would have overcome odds of 158,753,389,899 to 1, but for all four men to get perfect hands defied odds that are, in the words of a university mathematics expert, "so vast it is incomprehensible for most people."

Spenser, a factory serving manager, has been playing whist—a parent game of bridge—once a week for three years with Ewart Clark, a store clerk; Sidney Mayneor, a factory worker; and Ernest French, a retired farmer.

Who won the game? Mayneor, who held diamonds as trumps—which, in whist, are determined by the suit of the last card dealt.

(Courtesy United Press International)

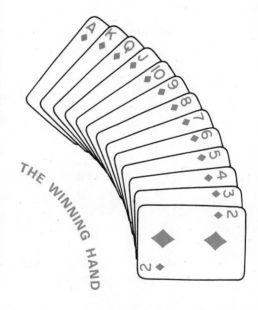

THE WINNING HAND

16.3 SAMPLE SPACES

When a coin is tossed, the possible outcomes are heads or tails. When a die is tossed, the possible outcomes are *1, 2, 3, 4, 5,* or *6* dots.

> The set of all possible outcomes in an experiment with chance is called a **sample space**. Each member of the sample space is called a **sample point**.

Example 1: In an experiment, each person is asked to name a prime number less than 20. What is the sample space?

SOLUTION: The prime numbers less than 20 are 2, 3, 5, 7, 11, 13, 17, and 19. So,

$$\text{sample space} = \{2, 3, 5, 7, 11, 13, 17, 19\}.$$

Example 2: A penny and a die are tossed at the same time. List the sample space.

SOLUTION: Let H stand for heads and T stand for tails. H and T each can occur with any of the six possible outcomes for the die. So there are 12 sample points. One way to list the sample space is by using ordered pairs.

$$\left\{ \begin{array}{llllll} (H,1), & (H,2), & (H,3), & (H,4), & (H,5), & (H,6) \\ (T,1), & (T,2), & (T,3), & (T,4), & (T,5), & (T,6) \end{array} \right\}$$

Example 3: List the sample space for an experiment in which three coins are tossed.

SOLUTION: Sometimes a *tree diagram* is helpful in listing the members of a sample space.

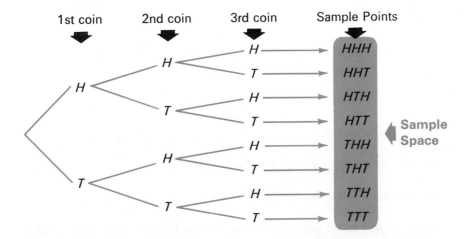

Example 4: List the sample space for an experiment in which one red die and one white die are thrown at the same time.

SOLUTION: In this case a table is helpful. Notice that each sample point is listed as an ordered pair, with the outcome of the red die always listed first.

		Red				
	1	**2**	**3**	**4**	**5**	**6**
1	*(1,1)*	*(2,1)*	*(3,1)*	*(4,1)*	*(5,1)*	*(6,1)*
2	*(1,2)*	*(2,2)*	*(3,2)*	*(4,2)*	*(5,2)*	*(6,2)*
3	*(1,3)*	*(2,3)*	*(3,3)*	*(4,3)*	*(5,3)*	*(6,3)*
4	*(1,4)*	*(2,4)*	*(3,4)*	*(4,4)*	*(5,4)*	*(6,4)*
5	*(1,5)*	*(2,5)*	*(3,5)*	*(4,5)*	*(5,5)*	*(6,5)*
6	*(1,6)*	*(2,6)*	*(3,6)*	*(4,6)*	*(5,6)*	*(6,6)*

(White is labeled vertically along the left side.)

EXERCISES 16.3

Ⓐ Refer to Examples 3 and 4 to answer Exercises 1–6.

How many sample points:

1. are in the sample space for tossing 3 coins?

2. consist of 3 tails?

3. consist of 2 heads and 1 tail (in any order)?

4. are in the sample space for tossing 2 dice?

5. In how many cases do the results of both dice total 7?

6. In how many cases do the results of both dice total 2?

Find the sample space for:

7. tossing a quarter.

8. dialing a 1-digit phone number.

9. picking 1 letter from the alphabet.

10. picking 1 letter from the set of vowels. (*Assume y is not a vowel.*)

11. selecting an even number from {0, 3, 4, 6, 9, 12}.

12. selecting two different symbols from {○, △, ∗}.

Ⓑ Draw a tree diagram to find the sample space in Exercises 13–16.

13. tossing two coins at the same time

14. selecting two marbles from a jar that contains only 1 red, 1 white, and 1 green marble

15. selecting two letters from the set {*A, B, T*}

16. selecting two numbers from the set {1, 2, 3, 4}

NOTE: The first selection is *not* replaced before making the second selection.

17. A girl has 1 white, 1 red, and 1 blue sweater. She has 1 plaid, 1 striped, and 1 paisley skirt. List a sample space for the possible sweater-skirt combinations.

18. The Model 625 5-speed bike comes with 3 types of handlebars (Racer, Butterfly, or Highrisers) and 2 types of saddles (regular or banana). List a sample space for the possible matching of handlebars to saddles.

Ⓒ **19.** Three books are chosen at random from a five-volume set. If the books are labeled *A, B, C, D,* and *E*, list the sample space for the possible selections (disregarding order). That is *ABC* and *CBA* are considered to be the same sample point.

20. A dodecahedron die has its 12 faces numbered 1 to 12. List the sample space in table form for tossing two dodecahedron dice. How many sample points are in the sample space?

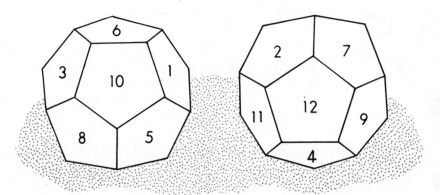

21. A bag contains 6 Ping-Pong balls numbered from 1 through 6. Three balls are chosen at random, without regard to the order of selection. List the sample space. (HINT: The sample space consists of 20 sample points.)

22. Find the number of sample points for tossing 4 coins. Use your results from this and the cases for 1, 2, and 3 coins to determine the number of sample points for tossing n coins.

16.4 THEORETICAL PROBABILITY

We may wish to predict how likely a particular outcome is *before* we have any experimental results. We use a sample space to do this.

For example, if we think of a fair coin being tossed many times, we expect that heads would occur in about half of the tosses. This seems reasonable since the sample space for tossing a coin consists of only two possible outcomes, both equally likely.

So, without ever flipping a coin, we predict that H and T would each have probability $\frac{1}{2}$. A probability determined in this way is called a *theoretical probability*.

> If a sample space consists of n equally likely sample points, the **theoretical probability** of any particular sample point is $\frac{1}{n}$.

You might think of a *theoretical probability* as the result of an imaginary experiment, while an *experimental probability* is the result of an actual experiment. When an experiment is repeated many times, the experimental probability of each outcome can be expected to be close to the theoretical probability.

> IMPORTANT: Hereafter, when we speak of a probability, we will mean a theoretical probability unless stated otherwise. The theoretical probability of an outcome A will be denoted by $P(A)$.

Example 1: In a toss of a single die, what is the probability of throwing a 5? That is, find $P(5)$.

SOLUTION: The sample space for throwing a die has 6 sample points, each equally likely. Thus, $P(5) = \frac{1}{6}$.

Example 2: If two pennies are tossed, what is the probability of throwing 2 heads?

SOLUTION: Sample space = $\{HH, HT, TH, TT\}$

So, $P(HH) = \frac{1}{4}$.

In a sample space an outcome is usually called an **event**. For Examples **1** and **2**, each *event* consists of a single sample point. But, an event may consist of more than one sample point.

For example, we might want to find the probability of rolling an even number when one die is tossed. Since 3 of the 6 sample points are even numbers,

$$P(even) = \frac{3}{6} = \frac{1}{2}. \text{ (See diagram.)}$$

sample space

event "*even number is rolled*"

> An *event* is a subset of a sample space. Suppose an event consists of *s* sample points out of a total of *n* equally likely sample points. The probability of that event is $\frac{s}{n}$.

Example 3: An ordinary deck of playing cards consists of 13 hearts and 13 diamonds (all red), as well as 13 spades and 13 clubs (all black). What is the probability of drawing a club from a well-shuffled deck?

SOLUTION: Since the sample space consists of 52 sample points and 13 of them are clubs,

$$P(clubs) = \frac{13}{52} = \frac{1}{4}.$$

EXERCISES 16.4

(A) Find the probability of each of the following.

1. rolling a *6* with a single fair die

2. rolling an odd number with a single fair die

3. picking a red marble at random from a sack containing only 3 red and 4 blue marbles of the same weight and size

Find the probability of selecting at random:

4. a vowel from the set $\{A, B, C, D, E\}$.

5. a prime number from the set $\{2, 3, 4, 5\}$.

6. an ace from an ordinary deck of 52 playing cards.

7. a red card from an ordinary deck of 52 playing cards.

8. the ace of spades from an ordinary deck of 52 playing cards.

Use the sample space for Example 3 on pages 536–537. Find:

9. *P(3 heads)*.

10. *P(1 head and 2 tails)*.

11. *P(3 tails)*.

12. *P(2 heads and 1 tail)*.

13. *P(at least 1 head)*.

14. *P(at most 1 head)*.

Ⓑ Use the sample space for Example 4 on page 537. Find:

15. *P(sum is 2)*.

16. *P(sum is 12)*.

17. *P(sum is 3)*.

18. *P(sum is 7)*.

19. *P(white die shows a 1)*.

20. *P(red die shows a 3)*.

21. *P(sum is less than 4)*.

22. *P(sum is greater than 12)*.

23. A certain sports car is available in 4 body colors: red, white, black, and aqua. The top is available in white, black, or gray. Assuming that any combination of colors is equally likely to be picked by a customer, what is the probability that someone will buy a red car with a white top?

When a dodecahedron die is tossed, what is the probability of:

24. an even number?

25. a prime number?

26. a number less than 10?

27. a number divisible by 4?

28. If a single fair coin is tossed 5 times in a row, what is the probability of getting heads in all 5 tosses?

29. The letters *E, L, O,* and *V* are written on identical cards, placed in a hat, and then drawn out one at a time. What is the probability of drawing the letters in the order *LOVE?*

30. You and 999,999 other people enter a nationwide contest in which winners are selected by random drawing. Each person is allowed to enter only once and is eligible to win only once. The first prize is a trailbike. There are two second prizes of a 10-speed bicycle, and 200 third prizes of a Hot Wheels toy car. What is the probability you will win **(a)** the trailbike? **(b)** a bicycle? **(c)** a Hot Wheels toy car? **(d)** nothing?

Probability and the Law

A policeman had noted the position of the valves on the front and rear tires on one side of a parked car. He used a technique like that used by pilots in noting directions: one valve was pointing to, say, one o'clock and the other valve to, say, six o'clock. The "nearest hour" is used in both cases.

ONE
O'CLOCK

SIX
O'CLOCK

After the allowed time had run out, the policeman found the car in the same place with the two valves still pointing toward one o'clock and six o'clock. The driver, however, denied that she had overparked. She claimed that she had driven away, come back, and parked with the wheels in the very same position as before!

The court had an expert compute the probability of such an event occurring, and the judge acquitted the driver.

Question: *Assuming twelve such positions for the valve on each of the two wheels, in how many different ways could the valves be positioned?*

POSTSCRIPT: In acquitting the driver, the judge remarked that if all *four* wheels had been checked and found to point in the same direction as before, the driver's claim would have been rejected as too improbable. In such a case, the four wheels, each with 12 positions, could combine in a total of $12 \times 12 \times 12 \times 12 = 20,736$ ways. So the probability of a chance repetition would be only $\frac{1}{20,736}$. (*Adapted from:* Tanur, Judith M., ed., *Statistics: A Guide to the Unknown*. Holden-Day, Inc., San Francisco, 1972, pages 102–103.)

The spinner shown below is constructed so that the arrow never stops on a line.

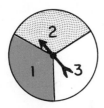

Think of tossing a die and spinning the arrow. What is the probability that the *sum* of the results will be 4 *and* 7?

Common sense tells us that the *sum* could never be both 4 *and* 7. (However, it could be either 4 or 7.) Let's look at this more closely. Let $A = \{$sum is 4$\}$ and $B = \{$sum is 7$\}$.

Die

		1	2	3	4	5	6
Spinner	1	(1,1)	(2,1)	(3,1)	(4,1)	(5,1)	(6,1)
	2	(1,2)	(2,2)	(3,2)	(4,2)	(5,2)	(6,2)
	3	(1,3)	(2,3)	(3,3)	(4,3)	(5,3)	(6,3)

$A = \{(1,3), (2,2), (3,1)\}$ $\qquad$ $B = \{(4,3), (5,2), (6,1)\}$

We want the probability of the event **A *and* B**. Thus we must find all the sample points that are in both set A and set B. In the language of sets, we must find the *intersection* of A and B. So, let $P(A \cap B)$ stand for *probability of **A *and* B***. From the sample space it is clear that the intersection of A and B is empty.

$$A \cap B = \varnothing$$
$$\text{So, } P(A \cap B) = \tfrac{0}{18} = 0.$$

> The probability of an impossible event is zero.
>
> That is, $P(\varnothing) = 0$.

Events which have no sample points in common are called **mutually exclusive events**. Two mutually exclusive events cannot both occur at the same time.

Again think of tossing a die and spinning the arrow. What is the probability that the die will come up *4* and the arrow will stop on *3*?

Let C = {arrow stops on *3*}   and D = {die comes up *4*}.

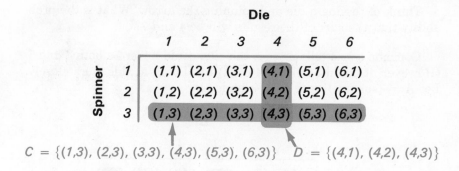

C = {(1,3), (2,3), (3,3), (4,3), (5,3), (6,3)} D = {(4,1), (4,2), (4,3)}

We want the probability of the event **C and D**. This event is the *intersection* of C and D in the sample space. Notice that this intersection is not empty. (This means C and D are *not mutually exclusive events*—they could occur at the same time.) Let $P(C \cap D)$ stand for *probability of C and D*.

$$C \cap D = \{(4,3)\}$$

So, $P(C \cap D) = \frac{1}{18}$.

EXERCISES 16.5

(A) Are the events mutually exclusive?

1. throwing heads and throwing tails when a single coin is tossed

2. getting a king and getting a spade when drawing a card from an ordinary deck of 52 playing cards

3. throwing an odd number and throwing a multiple of 3 when a die is tossed

4. winning and losing a bet

Refer to the following events and a two-dice sample space. Tell whether the events in each pair below are mutually exclusive.

      A: The sum is 4.   *B*: The second die shows a *5*.

      C: The sum is 9.   *D*: The first die shows a *2*.

           E: The same number shows on both dice.

5. *A, B*   **6.** *A, D*   **7.** *A, C*   **8.** *B, C*

9. *C, D*   **10.** *B, E*   **11.** *C, E*   **12.** *D, E*

Ⓑ Find the probabilities. Refer to the events described above.

13. $P(A)$ **14.** $P(D)$ **15.** $P(B)$ **16.** $P(E)$

17. $P(C)$ **18.** $P(A \cap D)$ **19.** $P(A \cap B)$ **20.** $P(D \cap E)$

21. $P(A \cap C)$ **22.** $P(B \cap C)$ **23.** $P(A \cap E)$ **24.** $P(B \cap D)$

Refer to a two-dice sample space.

25. What is the probability of a sum less than 2?

26. What is the probability of a sum less than 13?

27. What is the probability of an event which is impossible?

28. What is the probability of an event which is certain?

Ⓒ **29.** One card is drawn at random from an ordinary deck of 52 playing cards. What is the probability that the card is a king and from a red suit?

30. The numbers 10, 11, 12, ···, 34 are written on identical cards and placed in a bowl. If one card is drawn at random, what is the probability that the number on the card is even and its digits have a sum of 5?

16.6 PROBABILITY OF "A or B"

Suppose you want to find the probability of throwing a sum of 7 *or* 11 with two dice.

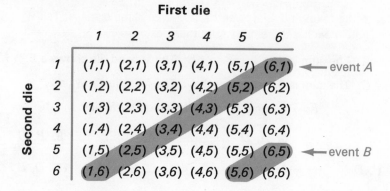

First die

Let A = {sum is 7} and B = {sum is 11}. From the sample space,

$$A = \{(1,6), (2,5), (3,4), (4,3), (5,2), (6,1)\}, \qquad B = \{(5,6), (6,5)\}.$$

Since A has 6 members and B has 2 members, you know that

$$P(A) = \tfrac{6}{36} \qquad \text{and} \qquad P(B) = \tfrac{2}{36}.$$

We want to find the probability of the event **A or B**. Thus we must find all the sample points that are in set A or set B or both. In the language of sets, we must find the *union* of A and B. So, let $P(A \cup B)$ stand for *probability of A or B*.

Since $A \cup B = \{(1,6), (2,5), (3,4), (4,3), (5,2), (6,1), (5,6), (6,5)\}$,

we conclude $\qquad P(A \cup B) = \tfrac{8}{36} \qquad$ or $\qquad \tfrac{2}{9}$.

Notice the following.

$$\tfrac{8}{36} \quad = \quad \tfrac{6}{36} \quad + \quad \tfrac{2}{36}$$

A and *B* are mutually exclusive events $\longrightarrow$ $\quad P(A \cup B) = P(A) + P(B)$

Example 1: What is the probability of throwing a sum of 2 or 12 with two dice?

SOLUTION: Let $E = \{\text{sum of 2}\} = \{(1,1)\}$ and $F = \{\text{sum of 12}\} = \{(6,6)\}$. Then, since E and F are mutually exclusive events,

$$P(E \cup F) = P(E) + P(F) = \tfrac{1}{36} + \tfrac{1}{36} = \tfrac{2}{36} = \tfrac{1}{18}.$$

For *not mutually exclusive events*, the formula used above is not correct. Consider $A = \{\text{sum is 7}\}$ and $C = \{\text{first die shows a } 3\}$ for tossing two dice.

First die

From the sample space, $P(A) = \tfrac{6}{36}$ and $P(C) = \tfrac{6}{36}$. Notice that A and C are not mutually exclusive events since $A \cap C = \{(3,4)\}$. To find $P(A)$ and $P(C)$, we counted $(3,4)$ each time. So in the sum $P(A) + P(C)$ the point $(3,4)$ is, in effect, counted twice. To adjust for this, we must subtract $P(A \cap C)$ from $P(A) + P(C)$ when computing $P(A \cup C)$.

$$P(A \cup C) = P(A) + P(C) - P(A \cap C) \qquad \longleftarrow \quad \text{A and C are not mutually exclusive events}$$
$$= \tfrac{6}{36} + \tfrac{6}{36} - \tfrac{1}{36}$$
$$= \tfrac{11}{36}$$

Actually, this formula works for any two events whether they are mutually exclusive or not. If the events are mutually exclusive, then $P(A \cap C) = 0$, and the formula becomes $P(A \cup C) = P(A) + P(C)$.

> For any two events A and B,
> $$P(A \cup B) = P(A) + P(B) - P(A \cap B).$$

Example 2: What is the probability of drawing an ace or a club from an ordinary deck of 52 playing cards?

SOLUTION: Since there are 4 aces in the deck, $P(\text{ace}) = \frac{4}{52}$. There are 13 clubs, so $P(\text{club}) = \frac{13}{52}$. These two events are not mutually exclusive because one card is both an ace and a club. So $P(\text{ace of clubs}) = \frac{1}{52}$. Now applying our formula, we have

$$P(\text{ace or club}) = P(\text{ace}) + P(\text{club}) - P(\text{ace of clubs})$$
$$= \frac{4}{52} + \frac{13}{52} - \frac{1}{52} = \frac{16}{52} \text{ or } \frac{4}{13}.$$

EXERCISES 16.6

Ⓐ Think of tossing two coins. The sample space is {*HH, HT, TH, TT*}.

A = {first coin shows heads} B = {second coin shows heads}

1. What is $P(A)$?

2. What is $P(B)$?

3. What is $P(A \cap B)$?

4. What is $P(A \cup B)$?

Ⓑ For tossing two dice, consider the following events.

A: The sum is 2. B: The first die shows a *1*.

C: The sum is 10. D: The second die shows a *4*.

E: The same number shows on both dice.

Now find the following.

5. $P(A \cup E)$ **6.** $P(A \cup B)$ **7.** $P(B \cup C)$ **8.** $P(A \cup C)$

9. $P(D \cup E)$ **10.** $P(C \cup D)$ **11.** $P(C \cup E)$ **12.** $P(A \cup D)$

Ⓒ **13.** A card is drawn at random from an ordinary deck of 52 playing cards. Find the probability that it is a queen or a diamond.

14. It is known that out of every 100 cars produced by a certain company, we can expect 6 to be defective. Of the 6, 3 will have defective headlights, 2 will have faulty wheel alignment, and 1 will have both defects. If a buyer purchases a car from this company, what is the probability that the car will have one or both of these defects?

1. In an experiment a coin is tossed for 500 trials. In how many trials would you expect "heads" to occur?

16.1

2. In an experiment, a die is rolled 600 times. In how many trials would you expect an outcome of 5?

3. The numbers 1–10 are written on separate slips of paper and put in a box. One slip is drawn, and then replaced. This is repeated for 100 trials. If "3" is drawn a total of 11 times, what is the experimental probability of "3"?

16.2

4. Two dice are rolled 50 times. A sum of 2 occurs three times. Find the experimental probability of a "sum of 2."

List a sample space for:

16.3

5. selecting a color from the American flag.

6. rolling a die and tossing a quarter.

7. matching a letter from the name *Max* with a number from the set {0, 1, 2}.

Give the theoretical probability for:

16.4

8. throwing a *4* when a die is rolled.

9. throwing 2 heads when 2 coins are tossed.

10. drawing the jack of clubs from an ordinary deck of 52 cards.

11. If two dice are rolled, let C = {sum is 6} and let D = {first die shows a *3*}. Are C and D mutually exclusive events? What is $P(C)$? $P(D)$? $P(C \cap D)$?

16.5

12. Think of rolling two dice. Let A = {sum is 5} and let B = {the second die shows a *4*}. What is $P(A)$? $P(B)$? $P(A \cap B)$? $P(A \cup B)$?

16.6

CHAPTER SELF-TEST

An experiment consists of picking a marble from a sack containing 3 red, 10 blue, and 7 white marbles. In 100 trials, the following results were obtained: red, 19 times; blue, 47 times; white, 34 times. Find the experimental probability of the following.

1. red

2. blue

3. red and blue

4. white

5. yellow

6. red, white, or blue

List a sample space for:

7. rolling a single die.

8. tossing a penny and a nickel.

9. matching a letter from the word "cat" with a letter from the word "dog."

Find the theoretical probability of:

10. getting a prime number by selecting one number at random from $\{2, 4, 7, 10\}$.

11. drawing an ace from an ordinary deck of 52 cards.

12. tossing all "heads" in a toss of 3 coins.

Consider the following events for tossing two dice.

A: The sum is 2.

B: The sum is 5.

C: The first die shows a 1.

Find the following.

13. $P(A)$

14. $P(B)$

15. $P(C)$

16. $P(A \cap B)$

17. $P(A \cap C)$

18. $P(A \cup B)$

19. Are C and B mutually exclusive events?

Complete the following proportions by referring to similar triangles ABC and DEF.

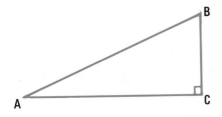

1. $\dfrac{AC}{?} = \dfrac{BC}{EF}$

2. $\dfrac{?}{DE} = \dfrac{AC}{DF}$

3. $\dfrac{BC}{EF} = \dfrac{?}{DF}$

Find each ratio in fraction form. Refer to triangle MRS.

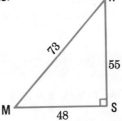

4. $\sin M = \dfrac{?}{?}$

5. $\sin R = \dfrac{?}{?}$

6. $\cos M = \dfrac{?}{?}$

7. $\cos R = \dfrac{?}{?}$

8. $\tan M = \dfrac{?}{?}$

9. $\tan R = \dfrac{?}{?}$

10. Refer to the diagram. If $\sin 17° \approx 0.292$ and $\cos 17° \approx 0.956$, find the following to the nearest tenth.

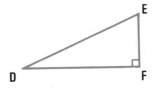

    a. DE   **b.** EF

Solve the following. Refer to the table on page 556.

11. How long is the support wire?

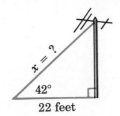

12. How wide is the stream?

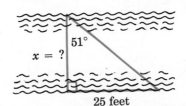

13. In an experiment, a die is tossed 100 times with the following results.

Outcome	1	2	3	4	5	6
Number of times	18	15	16	18	14	19

What is the experimental probability of each of the following?

a. *5*   **b.** *1*   **c.** *6*   **d.** an even number

List a sample space for each of the following.

14. tossing a coin   **15.** tossing a die

16. matching a number from {3, 5, 7} with a letter from {a, b}

17. selecting two names at random from the set {Roberta, Ed, Reb, Dan}, where the order of selection is important

Find the probability for each of the following.

18. rolling a *5* with a single die

19. rolling a sum of 2 when 2 dice are tossed

20. tossing 2 heads when 2 coins are tossed

21. drawing a king *or* a queen from an ordinary deck of playing cards

22. throwing a *5* on the first toss of a die *and* a *2* on the second toss

SQUARES AND SQUARE ROOTS

n	n^2	$\sqrt{n}$	n	n^2	$\sqrt{n}$	n	n^2	$\sqrt{n}$
1	1	1.000	51	2,601	7.141	101	10,201	10.050
2	4	1.414	52	2,704	7.211	102	10,404	10.100
3	9	1.732	53	2,809	7.280	103	10,609	10.149
4	16	2.000	54	2,916	7.348	104	10,816	10.198
5	25	2.236	55	3,025	7.416	105	11,025	10.247
6	36	2.449	56	3,136	7.483	106	11,236	10.296
7	49	2.646	57	3,249	7.550	107	11,449	10.344
8	64	2.828	58	3,364	7.616	108	11,664	10.392
9	81	3.000	59	3,481	7.681	109	11,881	10.440
10	100	3.162	60	3,600	7.746	110	12,100	10.488
11	121	3.317	61	3,721	7.810	111	12,321	10.536
12	144	3.464	62	3,844	7.874	112	12,544	10.583
13	169	3.606	63	3,969	7.937	113	12,769	10.630
14	196	3.742	64	4,096	8.000	114	12,996	10.677
15	225	3.873	65	4,225	8.062	115	13,225	10.724
16	256	4.000	66	4,356	8.124	116	13,456	10.770
17	289	4.123	67	4,489	8.185	117	13,689	10.817
18	324	4.243	68	4,624	8.246	118	13,924	10.863
19	361	4.359	69	4,761	8.307	119	14,161	10.909
20	400	4.472	70	4,900	8.367	120	14,400	10.954
21	441	4.583	71	5,041	8.426	121	14,641	11.000
22	484	4.690	72	5,184	8.485	122	14,884	11.045
23	529	4.796	73	5,329	8.544	123	15,129	11.091
24	576	4.899	74	5,476	8.602	124	15,376	11.136
25	625	5.000	75	5,625	8.660	125	15,625	11.180
26	676	5.099	76	5,776	8.718	126	15,876	11.225
27	729	5.196	77	5,929	8.775	127	16,129	11.269
28	784	5.292	78	6,084	8.832	128	16,384	11.314
29	841	5.385	79	6,241	8.888	129	16,641	11.358
30	900	5.477	80	6,400	8.944	130	16,900	11.402
31	961	5.568	81	6,561	9.000	131	17,161	11.446
32	1,024	5.657	82	6,724	9.055	132	17,424	11.489
33	1,089	5.745	83	6,889	9.110	133	17,689	11.533
34	1,156	5.831	84	7,056	9.165	134	17,956	11.576
35	1,225	5.916	85	7,225	9.220	135	18,225	11.619
36	1,296	6.000	86	7,396	9.274	136	18,496	11.662
37	1,369	6.083	87	7,569	9.327	137	18,769	11.705
38	1,444	6.164	88	7,744	9.381	138	19,044	11.747
39	1,521	6.245	89	7,921	9.434	139	19,321	11.790
40	1,600	6.325	90	8,100	9.487	140	19,600	11.832
41	1,681	6.403	91	8,281	9.539	141	19,881	11.874
42	1,764	6.481	92	8,464	9.592	142	20,164	11.916
43	1,849	6.557	93	8,649	9.644	143	20,449	11.958
44	1,936	6.633	94	8,836	9.695	144	20,736	12.000
45	2,025	6.708	95	9,025	9.747	145	21,025	12.042
46	2,116	6.782	96	9,216	9.798	146	21,316	12.083
47	2,209	6.856	97	9,409	9.849	147	21,609	12.124
48	2,304	6.928	98	9,604	9.899	148	21,904	12.166
49	2,401	7.000	99	9,801	9.950	149	22,201	12.207
50	2,500	7.071	100	10,000	10.000	150	22,500	12.247

SINES, COSINES, AND TANGENTS

angle A	sin A	cos A	tan A	angle A	sin A	cos A	tan A
1°	0.017	1.000	0.017	46°	0.719	0.695	1.036
2	.035	0.999	.035	47	.731	.682	1.072
3	.052	.999	.052	48	.743	.669	1.111
4	.070	.998	.070	49	.755	.656	1.150
5	.087	.996	.087	50	.766	.643	1.192
6	.105	.995	.105	51	.777	.629	1.235
7	.122	.993	.123	52	.788	.616	1.280
8	.139	.990	.141	53	.799	.602	1.327
9	.156	.988	.158	54	.809	.588	1.376
10	.174	.985	.176	55	.819	.574	1.428
11	.191	.982	.194	56	.829	.559	1.483
12	.208	.978	.213	57	.839	.545	1.540
13	.225	.974	.231	58	.848	.530	1.600
14	.242	.970	.249	59	.857	.515	1.664
15	.259	.966	.268	60	.866	.500	1.732
16	.276	.961	.287	61	.875	.485	1.804
17	.292	.956	.306	62	.883	.469	1.881
18	.309	.951	.325	63	.891	.454	1.963
19	.326	.946	.344	64	.899	.438	2.050
20	.342	.940	.364	65	.906	.423	2.145
21	.358	.934	.384	66	.914	.407	2.246
22	.375	.927	.404	67	.921	.391	2.356
23	.391	.921	.424	68	.927	.375	2.475
24	.407	.914	.445	69	.934	.358	2.605
25	.423	.906	.466	70	.940	.342	2.747
26	.438	.899	.488	71	.946	.326	2.904
27	.454	.891	.510	72	.951	.309	3.078
28	.469	.883	.532	73	.956	.292	3.271
29	.485	.875	.554	74	.961	.276	3.487
30	.500	.866	.577	75	.966	.259	3.732
31	.515	.857	.601	76	.970	.242	4.011
32	.530	.848	.625	77	.974	.225	4.331
33	.545	.839	.649	78	.978	.208	4.705
34	.559	.829	.675	79	.982	.191	5.145
35	.574	.819	.700	80	.985	.174	5.671
36	.588	.809	.727	81	.988	.156	6.314
37	.602	.799	.754	82	.990	.139	7.115
38	.616	.788	.781	83	.993	.122	8.144
39	.629	.777	.810	84	.995	.105	9.514
40	.643	.766	.839	85	.996	.087	11.430
41	.656	.755	.869	86	.998	.070	14.301
42	.669	.743	.900	87	.999	.052	19.081
43	.682	.731	.933	88	.999	.035	28.636
44	.695	.719	.966	89	1.000	.017	57.290
45	.707	.707	1.000				

LIST OF SYMBOLS

Photograph and Cartoon Credits

COVER: Freelance Photographers Guild, Inc.

Index

Coordinate(s)
of a point on a line, 8
of a point in a plane, 265
Coordinate plane, 264–267
Corresponding sides, 512
Cosine, 516–522

D

Decimals
nonrepeating, 16, 174–178
repeating, 16, 167–170
terminating, 167
Definitions in proof, 188–191
Degree
of a monomial, 197
of a polynomial, 200, 203
of a polynomial equation, 431
Denominator
least common, 162–165, 384–386
rationalizing, 413
Determinant, 321
Difference of two squares, 229–232
Direct variation, 477–484
Directed line segment, 31
Discriminant, 446–447
Disjoint sets, 130
Distance formula, 425–427
Distributive property, 64–66, 184
extended, 78
Division, 188
with fractions, 54–55, 62, 159–161
of polynomials, 345–357
of powers, 341–344
of radicals, 409–411
of rational expressions, 379–381
of real numbers, 50–55, 188
of square roots, 410–411
by zero, not defined, 51
Domain, 464–469

E

Empty set, 2, 5
as solution set, 96, 308
Equal sets, 6
Equality
addition property of, 82
multiplication property of, 85
reflexive, symmetric, transitive properties of, 115
Equation(s), 24
cubic, 431
equivalent, 82, 308–309
graphing, 269–272
as identity, 96
linear, 269–271, 282–284, 431
of lines, 285–287
polynomial, 431
quadratic, 250–253, 430–462
radical, 423–424
rational expressions in, 388–391
roots of, 431, 446–447
solving, 82–87, 93–97
square root property for, 434–436
systems of, 303–339
Equivalence
of expressions, 75, 185
of rational expressions, 371
of sentences, 82, 308–309
of sets, 6
of systems of equations, 312–314
Evaluating expressions, 20, 72–74, 203–205
Exponent(s)
in division of powers, 341
in multiplication of powers, 76, 152
negative integers as, 359–362
one as, 72
positive integers as, 72–77
in power of a product, 152
in power of a quotient, 342
properties of, 363–365
zero as, 359–362

Expression(s), 20–24
 in BASIC, 77
 closed, 20–23
 equivalent, 75, 185
 evaluating, 20, 72–74, 203–205
 multiplying, 75–77
 open, 20–23
 rational, 369–403
 simplifying, 75–80
 terms of, 78, 198, 200
Extraneous roots, 388–389, 423
Extremes, 481

F

Factor(s), 155
 greatest common, 159
 prime, 155–157
Factoring
 completely, 156, 226–227
 difference of two squares, 229–231
 over the integers, 226–227
 perfect-square trinomials, 233–235, 437
 polynomials, 226–249
 prime, of integers, 155–157
 to remove a monomial factor, 226–228
 with scissors and paper, 225, 228, 241
 to solve quadratic equations, 250–253, 431–433
 trinomials, 237–249
Finite sets, 2
Flow charts
 for factoring, 239, 244
 and inequalities, 148
 for problem solving, 88
FOIL method of multiplication, 219–220
Formula(s), 103–105, 199, 202
 distance, 425–427
 linear, 289–292

 quadratic, 440–443, 452–455, 459
 using radicals, 416–417
 using rational expressions, 392–393, 398–400
Fractions, 53–55, 61–63
 addition and subtraction with, 162–165
 division with, 159–161
 multiplication with, 159–161, 189
 reducing, 61, 159
 standard form for, 54, 61, 159–161
Function(s), 467–477, 488–497
 constant, 474–475
 graphing, 473–476, 488–490
 linear, 473–476
 notation for, 470–472
 quadratic, 488–490
 vertical line test for, 468
 zeros of, 491–493

G

Goldbach's conjecture, 192
Golden ratio, 486–487
Graphing
 compound sentences, 134–140
 equations, 269–272
 functions, 473–476, 488–490
 inequalities, 110–111, 119–120, 297–299
 integers, 8–9
 irrational numbers, 179
 ordered pairs, 264–268
 quadratic inequalities, 456–458
 rational numbers, 13, 16
 real numbers, 16
 relations, 465
 systems of equations, 304–307
 whole numbers, 8
Greatest common factor, 159
Grouping symbols, 20, 24

H

Half-plane, 297
Hypotenuse, 178, 516

I

Identity
additive, 34
equation as, 96
multiplicative, 56
Identity property
of addition, 34, 184
of multiplication, 56, 184
Inconsistent equations, 308
Index of a radical, 407
Inductive reasoning, 184
Inequalities, 24, 110
comparing numbers using, 112–114
graphing, 110–111, 119–120, 297–299
and order properties, 115–117
quadratic, 456–458
solving, 118–124
systems of, 331–332
Inequality
addition properties of, 118
multiplication properties of, 122
transitive properties of, 115–116
Infinite sets, 2
Integers, 8–11
as exponents, 72–77, 359–362
factoring over, 226–227
graphing, 8–9
negative, 8–9
positive, 8–9
prime factors of, 155–157
subsets of, 9
Intersection of sets, 130–133, 135
Inverse
additive, 34, 42–43, 209
multiplicative, 56

Inverse property
of addition, 34, 184
of multiplication, 56, 184
Inverse variation, 497–503
Irrational numbers, 16, 178–181
decimal approximations for, 174–178
graphing, 179

L

Least common denominator, 162–165
of rational expressions, 384–386
Legs of a right triangle, 178, 516
Like radicals, 418–419
Like terms, 78, 198
Line(s)
boundary, 297
equations of, 269, 285–287
intersecting, 279–308
parallel, 279, 308
perpendicular, 281
slope of, 274–281
Linear equation, 269–271, 431
slope-intercept form of, 282–284
standard form of, 270
Linear function, 473–476
Linear polynomial, 203

M

Means, 481
Member of a set, 2
Mixed numeral, 61
Monomial, 197–200
degree of, 197
division by, 345–351
as a factor, 226–228
Multiplication
with fractions, 54–55, 62, 159–161, 189
inverse operation of, 188
of polynomials, 215–222

of powers, 76, 152
properties of, 56–59, 184
of radicals, 409–411
of rational expressions, 376–378
of real numbers, 46–49, 189
of square roots, 409–411
Multiplication properties
of < and >, 122
of opposites, 57
Multiplication property
of equality, 85
of negative one, 57, 185–186
of zero, 46, 185–186
Multiplicative identity, 56
Multiplicative inverse, 56

N

Natural numbers, 8
Number line
for integers, 8–9
order on, 14, 110
for rational numbers, 13, 16
for real numbers, 16
for whole numbers, 8

O

One
as a coefficient, 197
as an exponent, 72
as the multiplicative identity, 56, 371
Open expressions, 20–23
Open half-plane, 297
Open sentences, 24, 82, 260–263
Operations
inverse, 42, 188
order of, 20
Opposite(s), 8, 34
addition property of, 186
multiplication properties of, 57
of a polynomial, 209
"Or" sentences, 134–140, 304

Order
on a number line, 14, 110
of operations, 20
properties of, 115–117
Ordered pairs, 261–263, 464
graphing, 264–267
Ordinate, 265

P

Parabola, 488–490
Per cent, 293
Perfect square, 174
Perfect-square trinomials, 233–235
Point, coordinate(s) of
on a line, 8
in a plane, 265
Polynomial(s), 200–202
addition of, 208–211
degree of, 200, 203
division of, 345–357
evaluating, 203–205
factoring, 226–249
multiplication of, 215–222
opposite (additive inverse) of, 209
subtraction of, 212–214
terms of, 198, 200
zeros of, 204, 207
Polynomial equation, 431
Power(s), 72, 407
division of, 341–344
multiplication of, 76, 152
of a product, 152
of a quotient, 342
Prime factors, 155–157
Prime numbers, 155, 158, 192
Principal square root, 171
Probability, 529–552
of "A and B," 545–547
of "A or B," 548–550
experimental, 532–534
and odds, 535
theoretical, 540–544

Answers to Selected Exercises

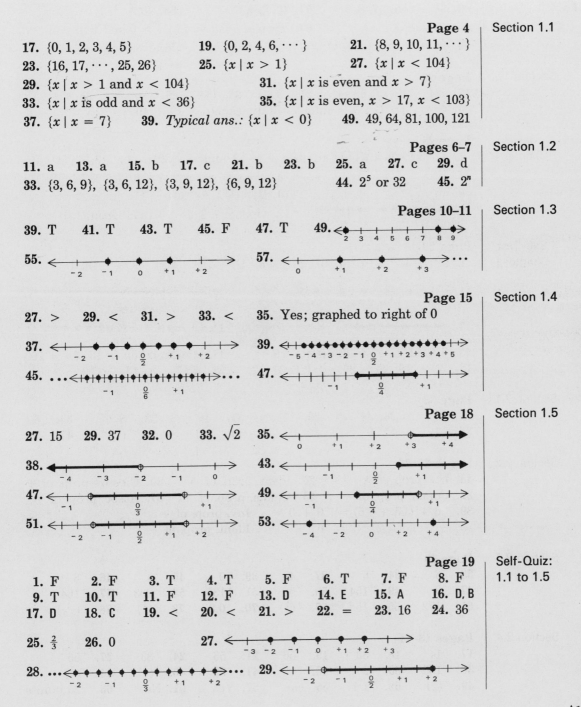

Page 4 | Section 1.1

17. $\{0, 1, 2, 3, 4, 5\}$ **19.** $\{0, 2, 4, 6, \cdots\}$ **21.** $\{8, 9, 10, 11, \cdots\}$

23. $\{16, 17, \cdots, 25, 26\}$ **25.** $\{x \mid x > 1\}$ **27.** $\{x \mid x < 104\}$

29. $\{x \mid x > 1$ and $x < 104\}$ **31.** $\{x \mid x$ is even and $x > 7\}$

33. $\{x \mid x$ is odd and $x < 36\}$ **35.** $\{x \mid x$ is even, $x > 17, x < 103\}$

37. $\{x \mid x = 7\}$ **39.** *Typical ans.:* $\{x \mid x < 0\}$ **49.** 49, 64, 81, 100, 121

Pages 6–7 | Section 1.2

11. a **13.** a **15.** b **17.** c **21.** b **23.** b **25.** a **27.** c **29.** d

33. $\{3, 6, 9\}$, $\{3, 6, 12\}$, $\{3, 9, 12\}$, $\{6, 9, 12\}$ **44.** 2^5 or 32 **45.** 2^n

Pages 10–11 | Section 1.3

39. T **41.** T **43.** T **45.** F **47.** T **49.**

55. **57.**

Page 15 | Section 1.4

27. > **29.** < **31.** > **33.** < **35.** Yes; graphed to right of 0

37. **39.**

45. **47.**

Page 18 | Section 1.5

27. 15 **29.** 37 **32.** 0 **33.** $\sqrt{2}$ **35.**

38. **43.**

47. **49.**

51. **53.**

Page 19 | Self-Quiz: 1.1 to 1.5

1. F **2.** F **3.** T **4.** T **5.** F **6.** T **7.** F **8.** F

9. T **10.** T **11.** F **12.** F **13.** D **14.** E **15.** A **16.** D, B

17. D **18.** C **19.** < **20.** < **21.** > **22.** = **23.** 16 **24.** 36

25. $\frac{2}{3}$ **26.** 0 **27.**

28. **29.**

A1

Section 1.6

Pages 22–23
21. 6 **23.** 14 **25.** 12 **27.** 5 **29.** $n + 3$ **33.** $y - 12$
35. $4r$ **39.** $15 - 4t$ **41.** $a - 7$ **43.** $9 + 3y$ **45.** $p + 1$
49. $3k$ **55.** $\{7, 8, 9\}$ **57.** $\{0, 2, 4, 6, \cdots\}$ **63.** $\{0, 1, \frac{3}{2}, 4\}$
65. $\{0, 1, 2, 3, \cdots\}$ **67.** *Typical answer:* $\{x \mid x \geq 0 \text{ and } x \text{ is even}\}$
75. $2x + 2y$ or $2(x + y)$; xy **76.** $t - \frac{1}{2}; t - 1\frac{1}{4}; t - 3\frac{1}{2}$

Section 1.7

Page 26
17. $\{2\}$ **19.** $\{0, 1\}$ **21.** $\{3, 4\}$ **23.** $\{\frac{1}{2}\}$ **29.** $\{^-4\}$ **33.** ^+I
35. $\varnothing$ **37.** Let d = number of dimes; $5(d + 6) + 10d = 255$

Review, Chapter 1

Page 28
1. a. $\{x \mid x \text{ is a whole number}, x > 12, \text{ and } x < 20\}$; **c.** $\{13, 14, \cdots, 19\}$
2. F **3.** T **6.** $\{\cdots, ^-3, ^-2, ^-1\}$
8.
10. M: $^-(\frac{10}{7})$; P: $^+(\frac{4}{7})$ **11.** $\{x \mid x < {}^+2\}$

13. Open; $\{7, 6, 4\}$ **17.** Open; $\{3\}$

Self-Test, Chapter 1

Page 29
1. a **2.** k **3.** g **4.** b **5.** j **6.** d **7.** h **8.** l **9.** e **10.** i

11. **12.**

13. **14.**

15. 7, 9, 11, 13 **16.** $100m - 9$ **17.** n nickels; $5n + 10 \cdot 2n = 200$
18. $\{2\}$ **19.** $\varnothing$ **20.** $\{0, 1, 2, 3\}$ **21. a.** 7 **b.** 13 **c.** 0

Section 2.1

Page 33
27. $^+1$ **28.** $^+6$ **29.** $^+1$ **31.** $^-4$ **32.** $^-3$ **35.** $^-6$
38. $^+1$ **41.** 0 **42.** 0 **44.** $^-(\frac{1}{2})$ **45.** $^+(\frac{2}{3})$ **47.** $^+(\frac{1}{6})$

Section 2.2

Pages 35–36
23. Inv. prop. of + **25.** Ident. prop. of + **30.** Closure prop. of +
32. Comm. prop. of + **35.** Comm. prop. of + **37.** Assoc. prop. of +
39. $^-6 + (^+5 + ^-5) = {}^-6 + 0$ Inv. prop. of +
               $= {}^-6$ Ident. prop. of +

Section 2.3

Page 40
33. $^-6$ **34.** $^+5$ **37.** $^-4$ **39.** $^+9$ **45.** $^+4$ **46.** $^-6$
47. $^-9$ **49.** $^-154$ **50.** $^-56$ **51.** $^+135$ **53.** $^-233$ **57.** $^-164$
61. $^-172$ **65.** $^-153$ **67.** $^+(\frac{5}{7})$ **70.** $^+0.8$ **73.** $^+(\frac{1}{4})$ **78.** $^-(\frac{1}{12})$

Section 2.4

Pages 43–44
17. $^-14$ **18.** $^-33$ **19.** $^+56$ **21.** $^-56$ **24.** $^+33$ **27.** $^+56$
30. $^-185$ **35.** $^-2$ **40.** $^+19$ **41.** $^-39$ **43.** $^+(\frac{3}{7})$ **44.** $^-(\frac{2}{7})$
49. $^+(\frac{1}{6})$ **52.** $^+1.4$ **55.** No **57.** Yes **61.** No **63.** $^-25$ points

1. $^+5$ 2. $^+9$ 3. $^-9$ 4. $^-5$ 5. $^-11$ 6. $^-21$ 7. $^+11$ 8. $^+21$
9. $^-1$ 10. $^-10$ 11. $^-10$ 12. $^-11$ 13. $^-11$ 14. Comm. prop.
15. Inv. prop.   16. Ident. prop.   17. Closure prop.   18. Inv. prop.
19. Assoc. prop.   20. $^+11$ 21. $^+19$ 22. $^-11$ 23. $^-19$
24. $^-10$ 25. $^+30$ 26. $^+10$ 27. $^-30$ 28. $^-44$

27. $^+1$ 30. $^+1$ 31. $^-126$ 33. $^+192$ 35. $^+60$ 38. $^+48$
41. $^-192$ 43. 0   46. $^-180$ 47. $^-4620$ 49. $^-288$ 53. $^+9176$
57. $^-\left(\frac{6}{35}\right)$ 58. $^-\left(\frac{12}{55}\right)$ 59. $^-\left(\frac{8}{49}\right)$ 61. $^-0.56$ 65. $^+\left(\frac{8}{3}\right)$ 67. $^-\left(\frac{9}{8}\right)$

27. $^-6$ 28. $^+6$ 31. $^+6$ 33. $^-6$ 36. $^+9$ 39. $^-5$
41. $^+9$ 45. $^+40$ 46. $^-1.8$ 47. $^-0.9$ 51. $^-1°$ 53. $^-32$

13. $\frac{7}{40}$ 17. $\frac{8}{21}$ 19. $-\frac{49}{100}$ 20. $-\frac{5}{42}$ 23. $-\frac{8}{75}$ 27. $\frac{63}{200}$
30. $-\frac{24}{143}$ 31. $\frac{6}{25}$ 33. $-\frac{24}{125}$ 37. $-\frac{8}{9}$ 40. $\frac{70}{9}$ 43. $-\frac{81}{32}$

25. Comm. prop. of ·   27. Assoc. prop. of ·   30. Ident. prop. of ·
33. Mult. prop. of -1 37. Inv. prop. of ·   41. Mult. props. of opp.
43. $-5 \cdot (4 \cdot \frac{1}{4}) = -5 \cdot 1$ Inv. prop. of ·
$\qquad\qquad\qquad = -5$ Ident. prop. of ·

1. -10 2. 10   3. 10   4. -10 5. -48 6. 48
7. 48   8. -48 9. -48 10. 70   11. -175 12. -375
13. Clos. prop.   14. Mult. prop. of 0   15. Comm. prop.
16. Ident. prop.   17. Inv. prop.   18. Assoc. prop.
19. -4 20. 4   21. -4 22. 4   23. -4 24. 4   25. 4
26. -4 27. -25 28. -19 29. 18   30. -50 31. $-\frac{12}{35}$ 32. $-\frac{4}{9}$
33. $\frac{18}{77}$ 34. $-\frac{2}{45}$ 35. $-\frac{7}{48}$ 36. $\frac{27}{35}$ 37. $-\frac{15}{112}$ 38. $\frac{54}{65}$ 39. $-\frac{16}{225}$

13. $\frac{2}{5}$ 15. $\frac{3}{4}$ 18. $\frac{1}{8}$ 21. $-\frac{1}{20}$ 24. $\frac{11}{5}$ 27. $-\frac{2}{3}$
29. $-\frac{7}{8}$ 35. $-\frac{1}{9}$ 37. $\frac{1}{15}$ 40. $\frac{9}{1000}$ 45. $-\frac{2}{5}$ 51. 0
55. $-\frac{4}{21}$ 60. $\frac{16}{25}$ 61. $\frac{1}{8}$ 65. $\frac{1}{15}$ 67. $\frac{1}{18}$ 74. $-\frac{5}{12}$
77. $\frac{1}{4}$ 83. $-\frac{13}{12}$ 84. $-\frac{2}{9}$ 89. $\frac{41}{18}$ 93. $-\frac{33}{8}$ 99. $-\frac{1}{4}$

9. -6 10. -6 11. -40 15. -133 18. -120 21. 14
25. -5 29. x 33. $4x$ 36. $a+b$ 39. $-3x$ 41. $3x^2$

1. $3 + 2 = 5$ 3. $3 + (-2) = 1$ 5. Comm.   7. Assoc.

A3

9. Clos.   10. -1 11. 1   12. -7 13. 7   19. -10
22. 12   23. -12 24. -2 25. 2   32. -32 34. -12
35. 12   36. 12   37. -12 41. 63   46. -8 47. 8
48. -8 55. 9   56. 0.8   57. -8 58. $-\frac{2}{5}$ 59. $-\frac{3}{7}$
60. $\frac{2}{3}$ 62. $\frac{12}{35}$ 63. $-\frac{10}{63}$ 64. $-\frac{7}{30}$ 66. $\frac{4}{45}$ 70. Inv.
71. Ident.   75. $-\frac{3}{5}$ 77. $-\frac{1}{3}$ 78. $\frac{1}{2}$ 82. $-\frac{7}{16}$ 83. -12 86. 6

Self-Test, Chapter 2

Page 70

1. e   2. l   3. c   4. g   5. b   6. f   7. a
8. j   9. k   10. i   11. n   12. m   13. h   14. d
15. 12   16. -58 17. 35   18. -111 19. 8   20. 96   21. -42
22. 121   23. -6 24. 219   25. -4 26. -150 27. 8   28. 10
29. 2   30. -120 31. -11 32. -77 33. $-\frac{2}{9}$ 34. $\frac{12}{5}$ 35. $-\frac{2}{3}$
36. $-\frac{27}{245}$ 37. $\frac{3}{2}$ 38. $\frac{4}{5}$ 39. $-\frac{1}{12}$ 40. $\frac{6}{5}$ 41. $-\frac{7}{9}$

Section 3.1

Page 74

11. -128 13. 343   19. 625   21. 0.00032   23. $\frac{1}{64}$ 33. 500
35. 3   41. 32   43. a^4 45. 25^2 49. $(xy)^3$ 51. $(2x)^3$

Section 3.2

Page 77

13. $-21n$ 15. $4ab$ 17. $15cd$ 19. $36m^2$ 21. $21t^4$ 25. $77s^6t^5$
27. $-28m^7$ 29. $12n^5s^3$ 31. $-15r^2s^3$ 33. $30d^3e^3f$ 35. $-3cd^5$

Section 3.3

Pages 79–80

17. $4x - 8$ 19. $8s + t$ 21. Cannot be simplified   27. e, g
29. c, e, h   31. $42x - 35$ 33. $17t - 63$ 35. 0   41. $12x - 13$
45. $-13a - 3b$ 51. $8x - 4y$ 55. $30x^2 + 28x + 6$

Self-Quiz: 3.1 to 3.3

Page 81

1. -243 2. 72   3. 225   4. 0.16   5. 11   6. 9
7. 81   8. 37   9. 15^2 10. $(ab)^3$ 11. $-16r$ 12. $6a^2$
13. $15pq$ 14. $-6s$ 15. $-21mn^3$ 16. $30xy^2$ 17. $13d - 2c$
18. $4p^2q$ 19. $x^2y + 2xy$ 20. $10a$ 21. $6x + 4$ 22. $17m - 8n$
23. $11pm$ 24. $24m + 24n$ 25. $10a - 20p$

Section 3.4

Pages 83–84

31. a, b, d, h   33. a, e, g   35. $\{-20\}$, or $x = -20$, or -20 37. 26
41. -21 43. -1 47. 1   53. $\frac{1}{4}$ 61. $a - b$

Section 3.5

Pages 86–87

31. a, g, h, k, m   33. b, e, o, p   35. -14 39. -14 41. 10
47. -8 51. 4   59. 3   63. $-\frac{52}{3}$ 67. $\frac{d}{a-c}$

Section 3.6

Pages 90–91

13. 15 yrs.   15. 6   17. \$1.75   19. 5780 ft.   21. 4 sec.
23. 12 hrs.   25. Cindy: 30 mi.; Kathy: 15 mi.   27. \$540
28. 6.4 ft.   29. 41 grams   31. 11 birds   34. 10:30 A.M.

1. Yes   **2.** Yes   **3.** No   **4.** Yes   **5.** No   **6.** Yes
7. -15 **8.** -3 **9.** -8 **10.** 40   **11.** 10   **12.** $\frac{1}{6}$
13. 14 yrs. old   **14.** Ron: $0.75; Wayne: $3   **15.** 42 yards

17. Yes   **19.** Yes   **21.** No   **23.** Yes   **25.** 6
27. 1   **29.** -2 **31.** $\frac{3}{4}$ **35.** 18   **39.** -4
47. $\frac{2}{3}$ **51.** 2   **57.** $-\frac{2}{5}$ **59.** 2   **69.** $ax + (-c) = 0; x = \dfrac{c}{a}$

11. $\{-5\}$ **13.** {rational numbers}   **15.** $\{4\}$ **19.** $\varnothing$ **21.** $\{\frac{1}{2}\}$
27. $\{16\}$ **29.** $\{16\}$ **33.** $\varnothing$ **39. a.** Any set not containing 1
b. $\{1\}$ **c.** Any set containing 1 and at least one other member

7. 5, 31   **9.** 200 by 280 meters   **11.** 16 yrs. old   **13.** 17, 18, 19
15. 14, 16, 18   **17.** 73   **19.** 160 by 360 feet   **21.** 6 lbs.
23. $70   **25.** 18 nickels, 11 dimes   **27.** 22, 23, 24   **29.** 26 mph

7. 15,700 sq. m.   **9.** 1538.6 cu. in.   **15.** 56 volts   **17.** 113°
19. $427.80   **23.** 560 km.   **25.** 43 mph   **27.** 7 hours   **29.** $t = \dfrac{d}{r}$

1. b. $3 \cdot 3 \cdot 3 \cdot 3$;   **c.** 4;   **d.** 3;   **e.** 81   **3. b.** $(-2)(-2)(-2)(-2)$;   **e.** 16
4. $-48s$ **7.** No   **9.** $-17y^2$ **12.** $9 - 15x$ **13.** $45wz$ **15.** Yes
17. 6   **20.** 1   **21.** -3 **24.** 17 yrs.   **26.** 4   **30.** {rational numbers}
31. $\varnothing$ **33.** 9   **35.** 5 quart., 9 dimes   **38.** 50.24 sq. m.; 100.48 cu. m.

1. g   **2.** a   **3.** d   **4.** i   **5.** h   **6.** e   **7.** f
8. $-x - 4y$ **9.** $9st$ **10.** $5r + 8$ **11.** 9   **12.** $\frac{1}{2}$ **13.** -2
14. {rational nos.}   **15.** Dee is 12; Dick is 36.
16. $V = 1130.4$ cu. in.   **17.** $h = \dfrac{2A}{b}$

15.   **17.**

19.   **23.**

13. $<$ **17.** $<$ **21.** $=$ **23.** $>$ **25.** $\frac{2}{4} > \frac{1}{4}$
29. $\frac{-1}{4} > \frac{-2}{4}$ **30.** $\frac{-12}{15} < \frac{-10}{15}$ **35.** $\frac{-18}{63} > \frac{-28}{63}$

49. $3 + 1 = 4$ **53.** $-3 + 8 = 5$ **55.** $-3 < 1$

Section 4.3

Page 117
15. $6 < 21$ **17.** $5x < 7x$ **20.** $12 = 8 + 4$
21. $5 - 7a > 36$ **25.** Less than 12 seconds   **27.** More than $150

Section 4.4

Pages 120–121

17. 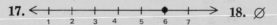   **18.** $\varnothing$

21. $m < -4$    **27.** $q > -20$

29. $x < -8$ **31.** $a < 2$ **34.** $s < 12$ **37.** $x < -6$ **39.** $x < 2.8$

Section 4.5

Page 124
19. $x < 5$ **21.** $m > \frac{7}{4}$ **22.** $q < \frac{6}{5}$ **27.** $r > 27$ **28.** $s > \frac{3}{4}$
29. $m < -12$ **31.** $t > -2$ **37.** $y > \frac{1}{5}$ **41.** $x < 0$ **45.** $x < -6.8$

Section 4.6

Pages 127–128
13. Any number less than 6   **15.** 14 nickels   **16.** Any integer less than 11
17. Any integer greater than 17   **18.** $x > 16\frac{2}{3}$; in full hours, 17
19. $x < \frac{17}{5}$; 3 hamburgers   **21.** More than 2600   **23.** 3 hamburgers

Self-Quiz:
4.1 to 4.6

Page 129
1. $>$ **2.** $>$ **3.** $<$ **4.** $>$ **5.** $=$ **6.** $>$ **7.** $<$ **8.** $<$ **9.** $<$
10. Comparison property   **11.** Add. prop. of $>$ **12.** Trans. prop. of $>$

13.   **14.**   **15.**

16. $m < p$ **17.** $x < 5$ **18.** $x > 26$ **19.** $x > 5$ **20.** $x < \frac{9}{2}$
21. $x > \frac{7}{9}$ **22.** $x < \frac{13}{11}$ **23.** $t > 6\frac{2}{3}$; in full hours, 7

Section 4.7

Page 132
21. $\{-8, -4\}$ **23.** $\{6\}$ **25.** A **26.** C **30.** $\{-8, -6, -4, 6\}$
33. $\varnothing$ **35.** G **38.** $\{-7, -5\}$ **39.** G **41.** I **44.** G

Section 4.8

Page 137
9. a. $x < -3$ or $x = -3$ **11. a.** $x > 6$ or $x = 6$
   b. $\{x \mid x < -3\} \cup \{-3\}$ **b.** $\{x \mid x > 6\} \cup \{6\}$
   c. 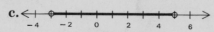   **c.**

13. a. $x > -3$ and $x < 5$ **17. a.** $x > -5$ or $x < -5$
   b. $\{x \mid x > -3\} \cap \{x \mid x < 5\}$ **b.** $\{x \mid x > -5\} \cup \{x \mid x < -5\}$
   c.   **c.**

31. $x \leq \frac{1}{3}$ **32.** $y \leq -2$ **33.** $x \geq 3$ **35.** $x < 3$

17. $7, -7$ **19.** $\frac{1}{4}, -\frac{1}{4}$ **23.** $-5 < x < 5$ **27.** $x > 7$ or $x < -7$

28. $-9 \le y \le 9$ **31.** $s > 4.3$ or $s < -4.3$ **33.** $-9, 15$

35. $-4, -10$ **37.** $-3.4, 3.4$ **39.** $3 < x < 7$ **43.** $-1 < t < \frac{4}{3}$

44. $-\frac{3}{2} < s < 3$ **45.** $-\frac{3}{2} < r < \frac{5}{2}$ **47.** $c < -8$ or $c > 2$

49. $c \le 4$ or $c \ge 8$ **53.** $\varnothing$ **55.** Any real number

13. $x \le 7$ **17.** $0.25 < x < 0.75$ **21.** $x \ge 3$ **23.** $-\frac{2}{9} < x < \frac{5}{9}$

25. Any number greater than or equal to 7 **27.** Any number between 2 and 4

28. $-2 < x < 2$ **31.** $x < 0$ or $x > 2$ **32.** $8\frac{4}{7}$ or more hours

1. **3.**

5. $>$ **7.** $<$ **9.** $=$ **11.** $>$ **14.** $m > 7$

15. $13 > x + 5$ **18.** $3 < 9$ **20.** $2x = 3m$ **22.** $x < 4$ **23.** $y > 4$

25. $x > -\frac{1}{9}$ **29.** $t > -2$ **30.** $x < 0$

32. Less than 35 nickels **33.** More than $9\frac{3}{5}$ hours

35. $\{3\}$ **36.** $\varnothing$ **38.** $\{-2, -1, 1, 3, 5\}$

41. **42.**

45. $-4, 4$ **48.** $-2 \le t \le 6$ **49.** Any number between 10 and 12

1. e **2.** h **3.** d **4.** f **5.** b **6.** $<$ **7.** $>$ **8.** $<$ **9.** $<$

10. **11.**

12. $x \le 10$ **13.** $n > 2$ **14.** $m > -\frac{22}{3}$ **15.** $t \le -5$ or $t \ge 5$

16. $\{-1, 1\}$ **17.** $\{-2, -1, 0, 1, 2\}$ **18.** $\{1\}$

19. $\frac{2}{15}$ or greater **20.** Between $1.50 and $1.875 per hour

17. -3^5 or $(-3)^5$ or -243 **19.** $(-1)^8$ or 1 **22.** $3^2 x^2$ or $9x^2$

23. $-2^3 s^3, (-2)^3 s^3$, or $-8s^3$ **29.** x^{22} **32.** $6^2 x^2$ or $36x^2$

35. $-3^5, (-3)^5$, or -243 **39.** $(-3)^6$ or 729 **41.** $-6^3, (-6)^3$, or -216

43. $x^6 y^2$ **47.** $x^5 y^5$ **55.** $r^6 s^6$ **57.** $3^5 z^5$ or $243z^5$

66. $20x^8 y^5$ **69.** $-3^5 r^5, (-3)^5 r^5$, or $-243r^5$ **71.** s^{12} **83.** 3^{3x+4}

25. $-1 \cdot 2^3 \cdot 3$ **28.** 2^5 **29.** $2^2 \cdot 5^2$ **31.** $-1 \cdot 5^3$ **33.** $3^3 \cdot 5$

42. $2^2 \cdot 3 \cdot 5^2$ **45.** $-1 \cdot 2^3 \cdot 3^3$ **47.** $2^3 \cdot 3 \cdot 5^2$ **49.** $2^5 \cdot 7$ **51.** $-1 \cdot 11^2$

54. $-1 \cdot 2 \cdot 13^2$ **55.** 5^4 **57.** $13 \cdot 17$ **61.** 2 **62.** 2; is not

Pages 160–161

21. $\frac{2}{3}$ **24.** $-\frac{4}{7}$ **27.** $-\frac{9}{7}$ **35.** $-\frac{5}{6}$ **37.** $\frac{1}{6}$ **39.** $-\frac{2}{9}$ **41.** $\frac{5}{16}$

43. $\frac{9}{1}$ or 9   **46.** $-\frac{1}{6}$ **53.** $\frac{45}{104}$ **55.** $\frac{3}{4}$ **57.** $-\frac{1}{4}$ **61.** $-\frac{8}{27}$

65. $\frac{1}{1}$ or 1   **69.** $-\frac{29}{93}$ **72.** $\frac{21}{8}$ **73.** $\frac{2}{b}$ **77.** $\frac{-s^2}{7r}$ **81.** $\frac{1}{xyz}$

Pages 163–165

13. $\frac{13}{15}$ **16.** $\frac{13}{18}$ **19.** $\frac{31}{96}$ **21.** $-\frac{157}{210}$ **25.** $\frac{1}{36}$ **26.** $-\frac{4}{75}$ **30.** $\frac{103}{504}$

31. $-\frac{41}{144}$ **33.** $\frac{107}{78}$ **37.** $\frac{7}{8}$ in.   **40.** $2\frac{1}{2} \div \frac{1}{3} = 7\frac{1}{2}$ tsp.   **41.** $\frac{113}{144}$

43. $\frac{7}{12}$ **45.** $-\frac{7}{30}$ **47.** $-\frac{79}{180}$ **51.** $\frac{139}{210}$ **53.** $\frac{217}{240}$ inch   **55.** No

Page 166

1. $2^3 a^3$ or $8a^3$ **2.** r^6 **3.** $x^5 y^3$ **4.** $c^5 d^5$ **5.** $-12n^5$

6. $-32x^5$ **7.** $r^7 s^7$ **8.** $15s^5 t^5$ **9.** $-42x^5 y^8$ **10.** $2 \cdot 5^2$

11. $-1 \cdot 2^3 \cdot 7$ **12.** $-1 \cdot 2^2 \cdot 3^2 \cdot 5$ **13.** $2^5 \cdot 3^2$ **14.** $-\frac{1}{4}$ **15.** $\frac{9}{16}$

16. $-\frac{7}{4}$ **17.** $\frac{3}{4}$ **18.** $\frac{3}{4}$ **19.** $-\frac{49}{30}$ **20.** $-\frac{4}{21}$

21. $\frac{7}{16}$ **22.** $\frac{29}{36}$ **23.** $\frac{7}{144}$ **24.** $-\frac{29}{120}$ **25.** $-\frac{7}{72}$ **26.** $\frac{29}{48}$ in.

Pages 169–170

21. $0.\overline{1}$ **24.** $0.28\overline{0}$ **25.** $6.\overline{3}$ **29.** $0.\overline{09}$ **30.** $0.\overline{18}$

33. $-0.\overline{45}$ **35.** $-14.\overline{72}$ **37.** $0.156250\overline{}$ **39.** $1.\overline{148}$ **44.** $-1.4\overline{3}$

45. $0.\overline{142857}$ **49.** $\frac{5}{9}$ **52.** $\frac{29}{9}$ **53.** $\frac{6}{11}$ **55.** $\frac{7}{6}$ **57.** $\frac{52}{111}$

60. $\frac{19}{2}$ **63.** $-\frac{182}{99}$ **70.** $\frac{1}{4} = \frac{1}{2 \cdot 2} = \frac{1 \cdot 5 \cdot 5}{2 \cdot 2 \cdot 5 \cdot 5} = \frac{25}{100} = 0.250\overline{}$

Pages 172–173

15. 4   **19.** -9 **22.** 11   **23.** -11 **25.** 12   **29.** $\frac{3}{4}$ **32.** $\frac{4}{5}$

33. $\frac{5}{2}$ **35.** $-\frac{6}{7}$ **39.** $\frac{10}{11}$ **44.** 0.3   **48.** -0.8 **49.** -1.1 **51.** $\sqrt[3]{-27} = -3$

Pages 176–177

33. 3.16   **34.** 3.46   **37.** 4.47   **42.** 6.40   **47.** 10.44   **53.** 12.124

73. Divide the radicand by the average found in the preceding step.

74. Are the divisor and quotient the same for the decimal places required?

75. Find the average of the quotient and divisor from the preceding step.

Pages 180–181

19. 529   **21.** 4.796   **24.** 9216   **25.** 9.055   **28.** 12.207

29. 3.606   **31.** 2.236   **33.** 7.071   **35.** 11.7 ft.   **37.** 8.5 km.

Page 183

1. $0.2\overline{0}$ **2.** $0.8\overline{3}$ **3.** $1.8\overline{63}$ **4.** $-0.\overline{216}$ **5.** $\frac{2}{5}$ **6.** $\frac{40}{99}$

7. $-\frac{22}{15}$ **8.** 7   **9.** 9   **10.** -11 **11.** $\frac{5}{8}$ **12.** 8.06

13. 9.11   **14.** 2116   **15.** 6.782   **16.** 15,876   **17.** 10.817   **18.** 6.708

19. 6.928   **20.** 11.6 feet

Page 187

9. Dist. prop.   **13.** Comm. prop. of $\cdot$ **14.** Comm. prop. of $+$

15. Ident. prop. of $\cdot$ **17.** Assoc. prop. of $+$ **19.** Inv. prop. of $\cdot$

20. Mult. prop. of 0   **22.** Add. props. of opposites

For Ex. 25 and 26, reasons for steps of proof are given.

25. Mult. prop. of -1;   Assoc. prop. of $\cdot$;   Mult. prop. of -1

26. Comm. prop. of $\cdot$;   Proved in Ex. **25**;   Comm. prop. of $\cdot$

Pages 190–191 | Section 5.10

Reasons for given steps and final statement are shown.

13. Subt. prop.;   Assoc. prop. of $+$;   Subt. prop.;
  $\therefore a + (b - c) = (a + b) - c$

15. Def. of fractions;   Proved on p. 188;   Inv. prop. of $\cdot$; $\therefore \dfrac{a}{a} = 1$

18. Subt. prop.;   Add. prop. of opposites;   Assoc. prop. of $+$;   Subt. prop.;
  $\therefore a - (b + c) = (a - b) - c$

19. Subt. prop.;   Proved in Ex. **18**;   Subt. prop.;   Proved in Ex. 28, p. 187;
  $\therefore a - (b - c) = (a - b) + c$

Pages 193–194 | Review, Chapter 5

1. x^9 **2.** $4^2 m^2$ or $16m^2$ **3.** $a^5 b^3$ **7.** $2^2 \cdot 7$ **8.** $-1 \cdot 2 \cdot 3^3$ **11.** $-\frac{1}{3}$

12. $\frac{5}{12}$ **13.** $-\frac{20}{9}$ **15.** $-\frac{2}{3}$ **17.** $-\frac{4}{15}$ **19.** $-\frac{2}{45}$ **21.** $\frac{83}{150}$ **24.** $1.25\overline{0}$

26. $0.\overline{481}$ **28.** $\frac{6}{5}$ **30.** $\frac{25}{18}$ **31.** 8   **34.** $-\frac{9}{11}$ **35.** 4.69   **37.** 7.211

40. Add. prop. of opposites   **42.** Dist. prop.   **44.** Ident. prop. of $+$

For Ex. 46 and 47, reasons for steps of proof and final statement are shown.

46. Def. of fractions;   Proved on p. 188, $\therefore \dfrac{a}{b} = a \cdot \dfrac{1}{b}$

47. Proved in Ex. **46**,   p. 194;   Mult. prop. of -1;   Assoc. prop. of $\cdot$;
  Proved in Ex. **46**,   p. 194;   Mult. prop. of -1; $\therefore \dfrac{-a}{b} = -\dfrac{a}{b}$

Page 195 | Self-Test, Chapter 5

1. f   **2.** a   **3.** d   **4.** b   **5.** e   **6.** g   **7.** r^6

8. $2^5 y^5$ or $32y^5$ **9.** $(-2)^4 a^4$ or $16a^4$ **10.** $-12m^4 n^3$ **11.** $-\frac{9}{16}$

12. $\frac{49}{120}$ **13.** $-\frac{19}{36}$ **14.** $-\frac{61}{189}$ **15.** $-1 \cdot 2 \cdot 3^2 \cdot 5^2$ **16.** $1.\overline{45}$

17. $\frac{7}{33}$ **18.** -13 **19.** $\frac{11}{7}$ **20.** 5.29   **21.** 8.5 ft.

22. *Reasons:* Subt. prop.;   Inv. prop. of $+$;   *Final step:* $\therefore a - a = 0$

Pages 198–199 | Section 6.1

33. Yes   **35.** No   **37.** Yes   **39.** No   **43.** Yes
46. No   **47.** Yes   **50.** Yes   **51.** $-21m^4 n^2$ **53.** $-96m^3 n^3$

Page 201 | Section 6.2

19. Monomial   **22.** Binomial   **23.** Trinomial   **29.** Binomial
33. Polynomial with 4 terms   **39.** 1   **43.** 4
49. 2   **53.** 4   **57.** 3   **59.** $\sqrt{11}\, x^2 + \sqrt{2}\, x$
63. $x^4 - 7x^3 - 3x^2 + x$ **67.** $-5y^3 + 7y^2 + 6y - 2$

Page 205 | Section 6.3

27. -20 **28.** 34   **31.** 34   **35.** 240   **39.** 2664   **43.** 22.5
49. 389   **51.** 4   **53.** 1, -1 **55.** -4 **59.** 3   **65.** 0, 2

Self-Quiz:
6.1 to 6.3

Page 206

1. Coefficient: 5; $\sqrt{3}$; $-\frac{1}{2}$; -11.   Degree: 0; 1; 3; 4
2. $\{4, \sqrt{5}\}$; $\{-6x^2, \sqrt{2}\,x^2, \frac{1}{2}x^2\}$; $\{3mn, -15mn\}$ **3.** a, h, i
4. b, c, e, f   **5.** d, g   **6.** h   **7.** b
8. a, d, f, g   **9.** c, e, i   **10.** $-7x^3 + 4x^2 + 3x - 5$ **11.** -10
12. 18   **13.** 12   **14.** 4   **15.** $-2, 2$ **16.** $2, 4$

Section 6.4

Pages 210–211

19. $12y + 2$ **23.** $\frac{1}{2}x - 18$ **25.** $7p + 7$ **29.** $12x^2 + 4$
33. $5t^2 - 6t - 7$ **37.** 0   **41.** 0   **43.** $8xy^2$
45. $1.1r + 0.8s - 2t$ **47.** $8x + 6$ **49.** $11x^3y - 12x^2y + 10xy$

Section 6.5

Pages 213–214

19. $-2x + 5y$ **23.** $-10x + 14$ **27.** $-4x^2 - 16x + 9$
29. $-7st - 5s$ **33.** $-\frac{3}{4}x$ **35.** $4y^2 + 2y + 10$
37. $-4m^2n^2 - 3mn - 6$ **41.** $4x^2y^2 + 11xy$ **43.** $8x^2 - 11x + 14$
45. $18p^2 - 6$ **47.** $3x - 6$ **49.** -4

Section 6.6

Pages 216–218

15. $6a^3b + 14a^2b^2 - 12ab^3$ **16.** $30m^4n - 10m^3n + 15m^2n$
21. $x^2 + 5x + 6$ **23.** $m^2 - 25$ **27.** $49 - y^2$
31. $\frac{1}{4}x^2 - \frac{1}{4}$ **35.** $35x^2 - 74x + 35$ **39.** $x^3 + x^2 - x + 2$
43. $x^2 - 15x + 56$ **49.** $x^3 + y^3$ **51.** $10a^3 - 4a^2b - 8ab^2 + 2b^3$
53. $30x^2 - 6x$ **55.** $36k^2 - 36k + 9$ **57.** $49 + 112b + 64b^2$

Section 6.7

Pages 221–222

19. $19 \cdot 21 = (20 - 1)(20 + 1) = 400 - 1 = 399$
25. $24 \cdot 26 = (25 - 1)(25 + 1) = 625 - 1 = 624$ **27.** $15x^2 + 16x - 15$
35. $\frac{1}{4}x^2y^2 - 4$ **43.** $t^2 + 6t + 9$ **49.** $2x^2 + 6x - 6$
51. $7pq - q^2$ **55.** $43p^2 + 9p - 6$ **61.** $x^2y - y^3$

Review,
Chapter 6

Page 223

1. Yes, 3, 0   **2.** Yes, 4, 1   **3.** No   **7.** Yes, $\sqrt{2}$, 3
9. Yes   **11.** No   **13.** $5p$, monomial   **14.** $m^4 - 4$, binomial
18. $x^4 + 2x^3 + 7x^2 - 3x$, none of these   **19.** 35, 252, 3, 144, -16, 54
21. $8x + 5$ **23.** $4m^2 + 5m - 5$ **25.** -5
28. $4x^2 - 17x + 3$ **29.** $4t^2 - 12t$ **31.** $36x^2 - 4$
32. $p^3 - p^2 + 2$ **33.** $4m^2 + 12mn + 9n^2$ **34.** $40p^2 - 19pq - 14q^2$

Self-Test,
Chapter 6

Page 224

Answers for 1–13 may vary.   **1.** $3y$ **2.** $2x^2 - 3$ **3.** $3x + 2y - 7$
4. $5x^2 - 5y + 16$ **5.** 3 is coefficient in $3m^2n$
6. $7ab$ and $-5ab$ **7.** -11 **8.** $-19a + 2$ **9.** $3x^2 + 7x - 5$
10. $y^3 - 2y^2 + 7y - 11$ **11.** $-19a$ and 2 are terms of $-19a + 2$
12. 2 is zero of $-5x + 10$ **13.** $19a - 2$ is opposite of $-19a + 2$
14. $3x + 18$ **15.** $2x^2 + 4x$ **16.** $12x^2 - 28x$ **17.** $-2x^2 - 7x + 9$

18. $9x^2 - 12x + 11$ **19.** $2x^2 - 12x + 14$ **20.** $5x^2 + 40x + 10$
21. $-6x^3 + 15x^2 - 36x$ **22.** $x^2 - 5x - 14$ **23.** $18x^2 - 3x - 15$
24. $9a^2b^2 - 30ab + 25$ **25.** $x^3 + 14x^2y + 21xy^2 - 36y^3$
26. $25m^2 - 30m + 9$ **27.** $3m^3n^3 - 12m^2n^2 + 33mn$
28. $x^2 + 8xy + 16y^2$ **29.** $4m^3 + 25m^2n + 3mn^2 - 18n^3$
30. -2 **31.** 1 **32.** -3 **33.** $16x^2 + 60x$ **34.** $4x^3 + 20x^2$

Pages 227–228 | Section 7.1

21. $9(2y - 1)$ **27.** $-3(r + 5t)$ **29.** $x(3x + 2)$ **33.** $b^2(a + 1)$
35. $x(xy + 1)$ **37.** $y^2(7y - 5)$ **39.** $6x^2(4x^2 - 3x + 2)$
41. $3b(b^2 + 2b - 4)$ **43.** $7ab(4a^2 - 3a + 1)$ **45.** $(a + b)(c + d)$
47. $(x - y)(r + s)$ **51.** $(5x + 1)(r^2 - 2)$ **53.** $(x + y)(m + n)$

Page 231 | Section 7.2

27. $(8 + y)(8 - y)$ **29.** $(x + 5y)(x - 5y)$ **35.** $(7m + 3n)(7m - 3n)$
37. $2(1 + y)(1 - y)$ **41.** $3(t + 3s)(t - 3s)$ **43.** $7(mn + 1)(mn - 1)$
45. $8(1 + 2st)(1 - 2st)$ **49.** $x^2(1 + y)(1 - y)$ **51.** $13(st + 2w)(st - 2w)$
57. 200 **59.** $14,200$ **67.** -25 **73.** $(m^2 + n^2 + 4)(m^2 - n^2 - 2)$

Pages 234–235 | Section 7.3

13. $(2x + s)^2$ **15.** Not perf. sq. **17.** $(4x - 3y)^2$
19. $25; (x + 5)^2$ **21.** $16; (m - 4)^2$ **23.** $2pq; (p + q)^2$
25. $4ef; (2e + f)^2$ **27.** $16b^2; (3a - 4b)^2$ **33.** $25; (8x - 5)^2$
35. $(4s - t)^2$ **37.** $(x + 10)^2$ **39.** $(p - q)^2$ **41.** $(mn - 2)^2$
43. $(9 - t)^2$ **47.** $(7m + 1)^2$ **49.** $(1 - 7p)^2$ **51.** $(4x - 5y)^2$
53. $(4xy + 1)^2$ **55.** $(x + 2)(x - 2)$ **57.** $2(x^2 + 2x + 6)$
65. $(x^2 + 8)^2$ **67.** $(a^2 - 2b^2)^2$ **71.** $(m - n - 1)^2$

Page 240 | Section 7.4

11. $(x + 3)(x + 1)$ **13.** $(x - 7)(x - 1)$ **17.** $(m - 3)(m + 2)$
33. $5(x + 3)(x + 1)$ **35.** $(3x - 1)^2$ **41.** $(6x + 5y)(6x - 5y)$
45. $12t(t - 2)$ **50.** $(x + 3)(x - 3)(x^2 - 2)$

Page 245 | Section 7.5

11. $(2y + 7)(y + 2)$ **13.** $(2n - 5)(n - 1)$ **16.** $(2x - 3)(2x - 1)$
21. $(6b + 1)(b - 5)$ **23.** $(3y + 4)(3y - 2)$ **25.** $(5m - 1)(2m + 5)$
29. $(8b - 5)(b + 3)$ **37.** $(4q - 3)(2q - 3)$ **41.** $(6s - 11t)(2s + t)$
43. $x^2(x + 2)(x - 2)$ **52.** $5, 7$ **53.** $1, -1, 5, -5$

Page 246 | Self-Quiz: 7.1 to 7.5

1. 2 **2.** $7p$ **3.** $3x$ **4.** x^2 **5.** $9(x + 2)$ **6.** $y(11y - 6)$
7. $5mn(1 + n)^2$ **8.** $4z(3z + 4)$ **9.** $(w + u)(w - u)$
10. $(x + 5y)(x - 5y)$ **11.** $(7m + 4n)(7m - 4n)$ **12.** $(3mn + 8p)(3mn - 8p)$
13. $(u - 5)^2$ **14.** $(t + 7)^2$ **15.** $(3s - 4t)^2$
16. $(2x + 9y)^2$ **17.** $(a + 8)(a + 2)$ **18.** $(c - 12)(c - 1)$
19. $(x - 6)(x + 2)$ **20.** $(y + 16)(y - 1)$ **21.** $(3x - 4)(x + 1)$
22. $(5p + 3)(p + 2)$ **23.** $3(2y + 3)(y - 1)$ **24.** $(4z + 3)(z - 3)$

Pages 248–249

13. $5(x + 3)(x - 3)$ **15.** $-1(x + 3)^2$ **16.** $(a^2 + 4)(a + 2)(a - 2)$
18. $(m + 1)^2(m - 1)$ **22.** $a(x + 1)(x - 1)$ **25.** $3(x + 2)(x + 3)$
29. $(p^2 + q^2)(p + q)(p - q)$ **31.** $(x + 1)(x - 1)(x + 3)(x - 3)$
33. $3x(2x - 1)(x + 1)$ **35.** $2m(3n + 5p)(3n - 5p)$
43. $-m(m + 8)$ **45.** $4(p + 2)^2(p - 2)^2$ **47.** $9x^2(y + 2z)(y - 2z)$
49. $\frac{1}{2}(x + 10)$ **51.** $\frac{1}{9}(p + 3)(p - 3)$ **53.** $\frac{1}{16}(4t + 1)(4t - 1)$
55. $\frac{1}{36}(3x + 2y)(3x - 2y)$ **65.** $(x - y + 2)(x - y - 1)$

Pages 252–253

15. $3, -3$ **17.** $-1, -3$ **19.** 3 **21.** $0, 8$
25. $2, 3$ **27.** $-\frac{7}{5}, -1$ **29.** $\frac{3}{5}, \frac{1}{2}$ **31.** $-4, -3$
35. 4 **41.** $-5, 5$ **47.** $0, 6$ **55.** $20, 8$ meters
57. $6, 8$ in. **60.** $0, -2, 3$ **64.** $3, 7$ sec. **66.** 400 ft., 5 sec.

Page 254

1. $5(m - n)$ **3.** $6q(2p + r)$ **5.** $x - 3$
7. $(m + n)(m - n)$ **9.** $(x - 7)^2$ **13.** $(r - 13)(r - 1)$
15. $(x + 8)(x - 4)$ **17.** $(2c + 1)(c - 2)$ **19.** $(3y - 2)(y - 2)$
21. $(t + 6)(t - 5)$ **23.** $6(s - 1)^2$ **25.** $p(p^2 - 8p - 1)$
27. $(x^2 + y^2)(x + y)(x - y)$ **29.** $\frac{1}{4}(m + 6)(m - 6)$ **32.** $0, 6$ **33.** -6

Page 255

1. e **2.** d **3.** a **4.** c **5.** $5x(y - 4z)$ **6.** $(5a - 1)^2$
7. $9(s + 2t)(s - 2t)$ **8.** $(x - 6)(x - 1)$ **9.** $(2p + 3q)^2$
10. $(c + 3)(c + 5)$ **11.** $(y - 4)(y + 3)$ **12.** $(2x + 3)(x + 7)$
13. $(5x + 2)(x - 6)$ **14.** $(3x - 7)(x - 2)$ **15.** $5a(m + 2)(m - 2)$
16. $2(x - 2)^2$ **17.** $(r^2 - 2)(r + 1)(r - 1)$
18. $(4xy + 9)(4xy - 9)$ **19.** $\frac{1}{4}(hk + m)(hk - m)$ **20.** $\frac{1}{5}(x - 5)^2$
21. $3x - 7y$ **22.** $0, 4$ **23.** $2, 9$ **24.** $\frac{5}{4}, -\frac{3}{2}$
25. $-2, 2$ **26.** $0, \frac{1}{2}, -\frac{2}{3}$ **27.** $\frac{5}{3}$ **28.** $4, 16$ cm.

Pages 262–263

15. $(1, 1), (1, 2)$ **16.** $(2, 0), (2, 1)$ **18.** $(0, 1), (0, 2), (1, 1), (1, 2)$
23. $x - 2y = 0$; sentences using $(0, 0), (2, 1)$ are true; sentences using $(0, 1), (0, 2), (2, 0), (2, 2)$ are false.
25. $3x + 1 < y$; sentences using $x = 0$ are false; all others are true.

Page 267

43. 0 **44.** 0 **45.** Vertical **46.** Horizontal **47.** Right
49. First **50.** Third **51.** Fourth **52.** Second **53.** y-axis

Pages 271–272

25. a. $y = \frac{1}{2}$ **b.** $y = 0$ **c.** $y = -5\frac{1}{2}$ **26. a.** $y = 1$ **b.** $y = 0$ **c.** $y = 2$
For Ex. 31–49, two points on each graph are given.
31. $(0, 3), (-3, 0)$ **34.** $(0, -5), (5, 0)$ **35.** $(0, 0), (1, 2)$
42. $(0, 0), (4, -1)$ **43.** $(0, 3), (1, 5)$ **49.** $(0, 3), (6, 0)$

1. F 2. T 3. F 4. T 5. T
6. $(0, -\frac{1}{2})$, $(0, 0)$, $(0, 1)$, $(1, -\frac{1}{2})$, $(1, 0)$, $(1, 1)$ 8. 0 9. Third
10. Yes; yes 11. No 12. Yes; no
For Ex. 13–15, two points on each graph are given.
13. $(0, -5)$, $(1, -3)$ 14. $(0, 4)$, $(2, 3)$ 15. $(0, 8)$, $(12, 0)$

15. 1 18. -1 19. 2 21. $-\frac{1}{3}$ 24. $\frac{4}{3}$ 25. -2 27. $\frac{4}{3}$ 29. 4
31. 1 33. $\frac{3}{2}$ 36. $-\frac{2}{3}$ 37. $\frac{8}{35}$ 39. 3 40. 11 43. Line k

13. l 14. l 17. l 20. k 21. k 23. l
For Ex. 25–42, one more point on each graph is given.
25. $(0, 2)$ 27. $(0, 7)$ 30. $(2, 5)$ 35. $(2, -2)$ 39. $(1, -6)$ 42. $(4, 0)$

21. $y = \frac{2}{3}x + 5; \frac{2}{3}; 5$ 22. $y = \frac{3}{5}x + 7; \frac{3}{5}; 7$
33. $y = -\frac{3}{2}x - 3; -\frac{3}{2}; -3$ 35. $y = x + \frac{3}{2}; 1; \frac{3}{2}$
37. $y = x + 0; 1; 0$ 39. $y = 0 \cdot x + 2; 0; 2$
For Ex. 43–50, two points on each graph are given. 43. $(0, -3)$, $(2, -6)$
46. $(0, \frac{5}{4})$, $(1, \frac{9}{4})$ 47. $(0, 0)$, $(1, 1)$ 50. $(0, -4)$, $(1, -4)$
51. The x-coordinate of the point where the line intersects the x-axis

13. $2x - y = -3$ 15. $x - 3y = 6$ 17. $7x - y = 0$ 18. $y = 3$
19. $y = \frac{2}{3}x + 1; 2x - 3y = -3$ 21. $y = 2x - 8; 2x - y = 8$
23. $y = -\frac{2}{3}x + 2; 2x + 3y = 6$ 25. $y = x + 2; x - y = -2$
29. $y = 2; y = 2$ 35. $y = x + 1$ 41. $y = -2x - 11$ 45. $x = -2$

1. 1 2. -2 3. 0 4. None 5. k 6. k 7. l 8. Neither
For Ex. 9–14, one more point on each graph is given.
9. $(5, 5)$ 10. $(5, -1)$ 11. $(-1, -6)$ 12. $(1, -4)$ 13. $(5, 1)$ 14. $(2, 0)$
15. $y = \frac{3}{2}x + 5; \frac{3}{2}; 5$ 16. $y = -\frac{1}{3}x - 4; -\frac{1}{3}; -4$
   $(0, 5)$, $(2, 8)$ are on the line. $(0, -4)$, $(3, -5)$ are on the line.
17. $y = 4x - 2$ 18. $y = -\frac{2}{5}x + \frac{12}{5}$ 19. $y = \frac{4}{3}x - \frac{17}{3}$ 20. $4x - 3y = 17$

11. $c = 10d$ 14. $d = \frac{1}{100}c$ 15. $i = 12f$ 17. $p = 4s$ 19. $c = 38.9g$
21. {whole nos.} 26. {nonnegative reals} 29. {nonnegative rationals}
31. $f = \frac{1}{12}i; f$ 33. $s = \frac{1}{4}p; s$ 37. $f = 0.15c + 2$ 41. $w = 5.5h - 220$

15. $\frac{3}{4}$ 17. $\frac{21}{20}$ 20. $\frac{1}{6}$ 23. 6 ft. 28. 50 meters 31. 5%
33. 50% 35. 150% 36. 385% 38. -125% 39. 52 ft. 43. 200 ft.

Page 299 (*Graphs are described.*)

13. Open half-plane below line through $(0, 0)$ and $(1, 2)$

14. Open half-plane above line through $(0, 0)$ and $(1, 3)$

17. Closed half-plane below line through $(0, 0)$ and $(2, -1)$

24. Closed half-plane to right of line through $(-3, 0)$, $(-3, 1)$

25. $y < -x + 2$ **26.** $y > x + 3$ **29.** $y > 2x$ **35.** $y \geq -4x - 8$

39. Open half-plane above line through $(0, -3)$ and $(2, 1)$

45. Closed half-plane below line through $(0, -2)$ and $(1, -2)$

Pages 300–301

1. $(1, 0)$, $(1, 1)$, $(0, 0)$, $(0, 1)$, $(-1, 0)$, $(-1, 1)$ **3.** 0   **4.** Second

5. Yes; no   **8.** $(0, -4)$, $(1, -1)$ are on the line.   **10.** 0   **12.** $-\frac{3}{4}$

13. None   **14.** k **16.** k **18.** $(2, -1)$ is also on the line.

20. $(0, -1)$ is also on the line.   **22.** $(0, 3)$ is also on the line.

24. $y = -3x + 2$; -3; 2   **26.** $y = -\frac{3}{2}x + 5$ **28.** $y = \frac{1}{3}x + \frac{4}{3}$

30. $c = 25q$ **32.** $K = C + 273.16$ **33.** 25%   **35.** 2.7 meters

37. The graph is the open half-plane below the line through $(0, 0)$, $(1, 3)$.

38. The graph is the closed half-plane above the line through $(0, 5)$, $(4, 2)$.

Page 302

1. h   **2.** g   **3.** e   **4.** a   **5.** f   **6.** c   **7.** d

8. $(0, -7)$, $(1, -4)$ are on the line.   **9.** $(0, 1)$, $(5, -1)$ are on the line.

10. The graph is the open half-plane below the line through $(0, -2)$, $(4, 1)$.

11. $\frac{3}{4}$ **12.** -2 **13.** None   **14.** $y = -2x + \frac{1}{2}$ **15.** $y = \frac{5}{2}x + 6$

16. $y = -\frac{1}{3}x - \frac{5}{3}$ **17.** $x + 3y = -5$ **18.** $F = \frac{9}{4}R + 32$ **19.** 9%

Page 307

11. $(1, 1)$ **13.** $(-2, -1)$ **15.** $(3, 5)$ **18.** $(7, -1)$

19. $(1, 2)$ **21.** $(2, -1)$ **23.** $(0, 0)$ **29.** $(\frac{3}{2}, \frac{3}{2})$

Pages 310–311

15. $\begin{cases} y = -\frac{3}{2}x - 1 \\ y = -2x - 1 \end{cases}$ **17.** $\begin{cases} y = \frac{1}{2}x - 3 \\ y = \frac{1}{2}x - 3 \end{cases}$ **19.** $\begin{cases} y = \frac{2}{5}x - 2 \\ y = \frac{2}{5}x - 3 \end{cases}$

One ordered pair   Many ordered pairs   Empty solution set

30. $(0, -1)$ **31.** $(12, 7)$ **33.** $\{(x, y) \mid y = -2x - 3\}$ **35.** $\varnothing$

Page 314

13. Equivalent   **15.** Not equivalent   **17.** $\begin{cases} x = 3 \\ y = 0 \end{cases}$ **19.** $\begin{cases} x = 0 \\ y = 0 \end{cases}$

21. $\begin{cases} x = 1 \\ y = 1 \end{cases}$ **23.** $\begin{cases} x = -1 \\ y = -1 \end{cases}$ **25.** $\begin{cases} x = 2 \\ y = -5 \end{cases}$ **27.** $\begin{cases} x = 4 \\ y = 1 \end{cases}$

Pages 316–317

7. $(3, -5)$ **9.** $(1, 0)$ **11.** $(-1, 3)$ **15.** $(3, -2)$ **19.** $(\frac{1}{2}, \frac{1}{2})$

Page 320

7. $(5, 2)$ **9.** $(6, 0)$ **13.** $(6, 0)$ **17.** $(1, -\frac{1}{2})$ **21.** $(5, 1)$

7. 11 and 16   **9.** Annette: 11; Daren: 16   **11.** Hamburger: 30¢; Coke: 25¢

13. $\begin{cases} x + y = 12 \\ x - y = 4 \end{cases}$ 8 and 4

15. $\begin{cases} x = 3y \\ 2x + 3y = 27 \end{cases}$ Larger: 9 / Smaller: 3

19. $\begin{cases} 3n = 2r + 6 \\ n + r = 32 \end{cases}$ Nancy: 14 / Roger: 18

21. $\begin{cases} 2l = 5w \\ 2l + 2w = 77 \end{cases}$ Length: $27\frac{1}{2}$ m. / Width: 11 m.

1. b   **2.** $(0, -2)$ **3.** $\varnothing$ **4.** Many solutions   **5.** No solutions

6. One solution   **7.** Equivalent   **8.** Not equivalent

9. $(4, 2)$ **10.** $(11, -3)$ **11.** $(3, -1)$ **12.** $(1, 2)$

13. $(3, 6)$ **14.** $(1, -1)$ **15.** Mary: 15; Nita: 11

5. 73   **6.** 24   **7.** 10 kg. 60%, 10 kg. 80%   **8.** $6\frac{2}{3}$ pt.

9. t = tens digit
u = units digit
$\begin{cases} u = 2t \\ 10t + u = 5u + 6 \end{cases}$
The number is 36.

13. x = number of lbs. of 90¢ tea
y = number of lbs. of \$1.20 tea
$\begin{cases} 0.90x + 1.20y = 1.00(60) \\ x + y = 60 \end{cases}$
40 lb. of 90¢ tea
20 lb. of \$1.20 tea

15. x = number of gal. at 36¢
y = number of gal. at 46¢
$\begin{cases} 0.36x + 0.46y = 6.00 \\ x + y = 15 \end{cases}$
9 gal. of 36¢ gasoline
6 gal. of 46¢ gasoline

5.

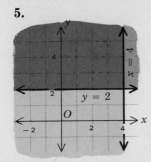

11.

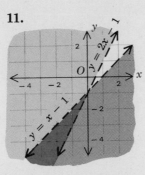

15.

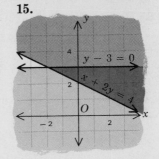

5. Boat: 5 mph; Current: 1 mph   **11.** 240 grams

13. Boat: 55 mph; Current: 5 mph   **15.** 4.8 lb., 7.2 lb.

1. The solution of a system consists of all ordered pairs which satisfy each equation in the system.

2. $(1, 1)$ **4.** See graphs on page 308.

5. No solutions   **8.** When they have the same solution set

9. Yes   **11.** $(5\frac{1}{3}, 10\frac{1}{3})$ **13.** $(2, -2)$ **14.** $11\frac{2}{5}, 18\frac{3}{5}$ **16.** 38

20. 35 cm. from 5 lb. weight, or 25 cm. from 7 lb. weight.

21. Passenger airplane: 600 mph; Business jet: 450 mph

Page 339

1. a   **2.** e   **3.** f   **4.** d   **5.** c   **6.** Incon.; $\varnothing$

7. Con. and dep.; $\{(x, y) \mid y = 3x + 2\}$ **8.** Con.; $(5, 2)$

9. 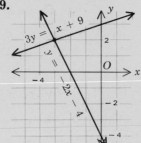   **10.** 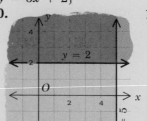   **11.**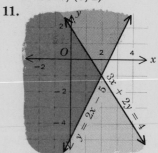

12. 84   **13.** 6, 34   **14.** Boat: 25 mph; Current: 5 mph

---

Section 10.1

Page 344

29. -125 **30.** -64 **31.** 0.16   **32.** -0.216 **34.** $c^2 d^2$

35. $\dfrac{1}{x^4 y^4}$ **37.** $r^4 s^7$ **41.** $\dfrac{x^8}{y^3}$ **43.** 2000   **45.** 400

50. $81q^4$ **51.** $4a^4$ **53.** $8w^3$ **57.** $\dfrac{8x^3}{27y^3}$ **59.** $-\dfrac{4(m - n)}{m}$

Section 10.2

Pages 346–347

19. $-\dfrac{7x^2}{4}$ **20.** $-4y^3$ **21.** $\dfrac{1}{3m^3}$ **25.** $\dfrac{4}{s^4}$ **27.** $3y$ **30.** $-4y^4$ **31.** $\dfrac{4}{x^3}$

35. $-\dfrac{ys}{2}$ **37.** $\dfrac{a^2}{b^2}$ **41.** 4   **43.** $2xy$ **49.** 4   **57.** $3y^a$ **60.** $17x^2$

Section 10.3

Pages 350–351

25. $4x - 2$ **30.** $-1 + 2s - 3s^2$ **35.** $x^2 - 3x$ **41.** $2x^2 - 3x - \dfrac{9}{11}$

46. $8y^3 - 5y$ **49.** $cd - 2$ **51.** $2x^2 + 3x - 1$ **60.** $64 + 16t$

Section 10.4

Page 354

21. $x + 1$ **22.** $y + 2$ **25.** $x + 2$ **27.** $x - 3$ **32.** $y + 9$

35. $6z + 1$ **37.** $3x - 1$ **39.** $5y + 1$ **41.** $3y - 2$; rem. 4

45. $(x + 1)^3$ **47.** $(2x + 3)(2x + 1)(x + 1)$ **49.** $z \neq -6$ **54.** $y \neq \dfrac{5}{2}$

Section 10.5

Pages 356–357

7. $5x - 7$ **8.** $3x - 9$ **9.** $4a - 5$ **11.** $2x^2 + 3x + 7$; rem. 12

13. $x^2 - 6x + 1$; rem. 3   **17.** $-5t - 6$; rem. -3 **20.** $-2y + 1$; rem. 15

21. $(x + 2)(x^2 - 2x + 4)$ **27.** $(x^2 - 2)(x^2 - 3)$ **30.** $2x$ minutes

---

Self-Quiz:
10.1 to 10.5

Page 358

1. 25   **2.** $\dfrac{1}{16}$ **3.** $27r^3$ **4.** $\dfrac{64}{125}$ **5.** $6x^6$

6. $\dfrac{n^3}{m^3}$ **7.** $\dfrac{3x}{4}$ **8.** $-\dfrac{8}{3y^2}$ **9.** $y + 3$ **10.** $2x + 1$

11. $2y + 3 - \dfrac{1}{y}$ **12.** $4x^2 + x - 2$ **13.** $2x - 3$ **14.** $2x + 5$

15. $3x^2 - 3x - 1$; rem. -6 **16.** $x^2 - 4x + 4$; rem. -1

17. $\dfrac{1}{2^1} = \dfrac{1}{2}$ **23.** $\dfrac{1}{\left(\frac{1}{2}\right)^1} = 2$ **29.** $\dfrac{1}{\left(\frac{2}{3}\right)^1} = \dfrac{3}{2}$ **38.** $\dfrac{1}{(-5)^1} = -\dfrac{1}{5}$

43. $\dfrac{1}{\left(-\frac{1}{x}\right)^1} = -x$ **47.** $\dfrac{1}{\left(-\frac{x}{y}\right)^1} = -\dfrac{y}{x}$ **54.** $\dfrac{1}{r^6}$ **63.** $\dfrac{1}{\left(\frac{1}{2}\right)^2} = 4$

65. $\dfrac{1}{\frac{1}{a^5}} = a^5$ **71.** $\dfrac{1}{(3x)^2} = \dfrac{1}{9x^2}$ **76.** $\dfrac{1}{2^1} \cdot \dfrac{1}{2^3} = \dfrac{1}{16}$ **80.** $\dfrac{m^2 m^2}{m^3} = m$

25. $\dfrac{1}{16r^4}$ **26.** $\dfrac{1}{27s^3}$ **29.** $\dfrac{1}{a^{10}b^{10}}$ **31.** $\dfrac{125}{8k^3}$ **33.** $\dfrac{1}{256s^4 t^4}$

35. 1 **37.** 2×10^7 or $20{,}000{,}000$ **41.** $-\dfrac{15y^4}{2x}$ **48.** $5st^2$

49. Positive **53.** Positive **56.** Positive

1. 16 **2.** 1 **3.** $\dfrac{1}{3^2}$ **5.** $-\dfrac{3}{2}$ **7.** $-\dfrac{4}{y^5}$ **8.** $x + 2$ **10.** $3s^2 + 1$

11. $x + 4$ **13.** $2x + 3$; rem. 7 **15.** $4x^2 + 2x + 1$; rem. 0

16. $\dfrac{1}{x^1} = \dfrac{1}{x}$ **18.** $\dfrac{1}{\left(\frac{1}{3}\right)^2} = 9$ **20.** $32y^5$ **22.** $-\dfrac{1}{64w^3}$

1. b **2.** a **3.** d **4.** e **5.** 9 **6.** $-\dfrac{1}{27}$

7. 1 **8.** $\dfrac{t^3}{s^4}$ **9.** -3 **10.** $-\dfrac{3r}{2}$ **11.** $\dfrac{4m^6}{3n^5}$ **12.** $3x + 7$

13. $2s - 1$ **14.** $-t^2 + 2t - \dfrac{7}{9}$ **15.** $4 - 3y + y^2$ **16.** $x + 5$

17. $4x + 1$ **18.** $9x^2 - 3x + 1$ **19.** $\dfrac{1}{2}$ **20.** 1

21. $\dfrac{1}{y^2}$ **22.** $\dfrac{1}{3^6}$ **23.** 25 **24.** w^{10}

23. $\dfrac{2}{3} = \dfrac{2}{3} \cdot 1$ (Or ? may be replaced by any other name for 1.)

24. $\dfrac{2}{3} = \dfrac{2}{3} \cdot \dfrac{5}{5}$ **25.** $\dfrac{2}{3} = \dfrac{2}{3} \cdot \dfrac{-3}{-3}$ **26.** $\dfrac{2}{3} = \dfrac{10}{15}$

29. $\dfrac{5}{x} = \dfrac{20}{4x}$ **31.** $\dfrac{y}{-3} = \dfrac{-y}{3}$ **33.** $\dfrac{x}{y} = \dfrac{x^2}{xy}$

35. $\dfrac{x}{2} = \dfrac{x(x+3)}{2x+6}$ **36.** $\dfrac{3}{c} = \dfrac{3c-6}{c^2-2c}$ **37.** $\dfrac{x+3}{x-1} = \dfrac{x^2+5x+6}{x^2+x-2}$

13. $\dfrac{1}{a+2}$ **15.** $\dfrac{4}{3}$ **17.** $\dfrac{x-3}{x+3}$ **18.** $\dfrac{y+2}{y-2}$ **19.** $\dfrac{3}{x-2}$

21. $\dfrac{m}{m-1}$ **25.** $\dfrac{t^2-9}{2t+4}$ **29.** $\dfrac{x+1}{x+2}$ **37.** $\dfrac{-3}{x-2}$ **38.** -1

13. $\dfrac{n}{6}$ **14.** $\dfrac{20m}{3}$ **15.** $\dfrac{4y}{3}$ **17.** $6a^2 b^2$ **19.** 15

21. $2a - 4$ **23.** $\dfrac{t^2-2t}{2}$ **26.** $\dfrac{4x}{x+4}$ **27.** $\dfrac{5}{12a}$ **29.** 1

31. $2m^2 - 2m$ **32.** $\dfrac{y+1}{4}$ **36.** $\dfrac{x+2}{2x-4}$ **39.** $x-5$ **41.** $a^2 + 3a + 2$

Section 11.4   Pages 380–381

11. $\dfrac{n-7}{n+2}$ **13.** $x-2$ **14.** $\dfrac{1}{x}$ **15.** $\dfrac{m+2}{m+3}$ **17.** $\dfrac{1}{r}$

19. $\dfrac{x-1}{x+1}$ **21.** $\dfrac{2x-6}{x+3}$ **23.** $\dfrac{x+3}{3x-9}$ **25.** 1 **31.** 2

Section 11.5   Page 383

9. $\dfrac{1}{x+1}$ **11.** 1 **13.** 4 **15.** $\dfrac{2x}{x-6}$ **16.** $\dfrac{-2y}{y+7}$

17. 1 **19.** $x+1$ **21.** $m+3$ **23.** $x-4$ **24.** $y-5$

Section 11.6   Pages 385–386

11. $\dfrac{1}{2}$ **13.** $\dfrac{3}{2x}$ **17.** $\dfrac{3ab-6}{2ab^2}$ **19.** $\dfrac{y+6}{y^2-4}$

21. $\dfrac{m^2-n^2}{mn}$ **23.** $\dfrac{m+1}{2}$ **25.** $\dfrac{3}{m}$ **27.** $\dfrac{a+6}{a^2-6a+9}$

31. $\dfrac{2}{x-4}$ **33.** $\dfrac{5a-7}{a^2-4a+4}$ **37.** $\dfrac{m^2-5m}{m-2}$ **41.** $\dfrac{x+3}{x+2}$

Self-Quiz: 11.1 to 11.6   Page 387

1. T   **2.** T   **3.** F   **4.** T

5. $\dfrac{x}{y^2} = \dfrac{xy}{y^3}$ **6.** $\dfrac{a}{3} = \dfrac{a^2-2a}{3a-6}$ **7.** $\dfrac{2a}{3b}$ **8.** $\dfrac{x}{x-2}$

9. $t-2$ **10.** $18x$ **11.** $\dfrac{1.5}{2}$ **12.** 1 **13.** $6a+18$

14. 4 **15.** $\dfrac{1}{2}$ **16.** $\dfrac{14}{3y-9}$ **17.** $\dfrac{a-4}{a+1}$

Section 11.7   Pages 390–391

21. 2 **22.** 3 **24.** -30 **27.** $\dfrac{3}{2}$ **29.** -1 **31.** $\varnothing$

33. 48 **36.** $\dfrac{1}{2}$ **39.** -3 **40.** $\dfrac{2}{3}$ **41.** $\varnothing$ **44.** -1

46. $\dfrac{1}{2}$ **49.** -10 **51.** $\dfrac{1}{2}$ **53.** 0 **55.** 0 **57.** $\dfrac{5}{2}$

Section 11.8   Pages 396–397

9. $1\frac{1}{5}$ hr.   **10.** 20 mph   **12.** $2\frac{2}{5}$ hr.   **13.** $5\frac{1}{11}$ hr.   **15.** $6\frac{6}{7}$ hr.

Section 11.9   Page 399

3. $x = \dfrac{2y}{5y-3}$ **4.** $x = \dfrac{9y}{8+24y}$ **7.** $x = \dfrac{3y}{2y-2}$

9. $y = \dfrac{3x}{5x-2}$ **10.** $y = \dfrac{8x}{9-24x}$ **13.** $y = \dfrac{2x}{2x-3}$

15. $d = rt$ **17.** $T = \dfrac{m}{hA}$ **20.** $d^2 = \dfrac{Mm}{F}$ **21.** $n = \dfrac{2S}{a+t}$

22. $t = \dfrac{2S-na}{n}$ **24.** $Q = \dfrac{P-R}{D}$ **29.** $x = \dfrac{y-b}{m}$ **32.** $b_1 = \dfrac{2A-hb_2}{h}$

Review, Chapter 11   Pages 401–402

1. F   **4.** T   **5.** $\dfrac{-3a}{4a^2} = \dfrac{6a^2}{-8a^3}$ **7.** $\dfrac{3}{xy}$

8. $\dfrac{m-3}{m+3}$ **10.** $8a^2$ **12.** $\dfrac{y-2}{y-1}$ **13.** $\dfrac{2}{x-1}$ **14.** $\dfrac{a-1}{a+1}$

16. $y + 2$ **18.** $\dfrac{7 - 6x}{3x^2}$ **20.** $\dfrac{y - 2}{y - 3}$ **21.** 3   **23.** $\varnothing$

24. 45 meters per minute   **26.** $y = \dfrac{6x}{4 - 15x}$ or $y = \dfrac{-6x}{15x - 4}$

Page 403 | Self-Test, Chapter 11

1. The quotient of two polynomials (divisor not 0)   **2.** Simplest (or standard) form   **3.** y **4.** $\dfrac{x + 3}{3}$

5. $\dfrac{a - 3}{2}$ **6.** $\dfrac{x + 2}{x - 3}$ **7.** $\dfrac{9p}{p - 7}$ **8.** $x - 1$ **9.** $\dfrac{4}{t}$

10. $\dfrac{x - 1}{x - 3}$ **11.** 12   **12.** 10   **13.** $\varnothing$ **14.** $13\frac{1}{3}$ hr.

15. 4 mph   **16.** $x = \dfrac{y - 2}{y - 3}$ **17.** $t = \dfrac{2S - an}{n}$

Page 408 | Section 12.1

17. 9   **19.** 6   **22.** 5   **23.** 3   **26.** 3   **27.** $\frac{2}{3}$ **29.** $\frac{2}{3}$ **32.** $\frac{4}{3}$

33. $\frac{1}{2}$ **36.** 1   **37.** 1   **39.** 0   **42.** -5 **43.** -2 **45.** -2 **47.** -2

Page 411 | Section 12.2

13. $\sqrt{6}$ **18.** $\sqrt{2}$ **19.** $\sqrt{3}$ **23.** $\sqrt{2}$ **26.** $\sqrt{6x}$ **29.** $\sqrt{2x + 6}$

31. $\sqrt{3x}$ **34.** $\sqrt{5}$ **37.** $\sqrt{2mn}$ **39.** $\sqrt{x + 1}$ **42.** $\sqrt{2x^2 - x}$ **43.** $\sqrt[3]{6}$

Pages 414–415 | Section 12.3

25. $2\sqrt{5}$ **30.** $\frac{1}{3}\sqrt{3}$ **37.** $\frac{2}{3}\sqrt{3}$ **42.** $\frac{1}{2}\sqrt{5}$ **45.** $x\sqrt{3}$ **57.** $x\sqrt{x}$

61. $10\sqrt{3} \approx 17.32$ **65.** $4\sqrt{10} \approx 12.648$ **67.** $12\sqrt{2} \approx 16.968$

71. $\frac{1}{10}\sqrt{3} \approx 0.1732$ **73.** $\frac{1}{2}\sqrt{5} \approx 1.118$ **75.** $\frac{1}{5}\sqrt{30} \approx 1.0954$

Page 419 | Section 12.4

7. $5\sqrt{2}$ **10.** $\sqrt{3}$ **11.** $8\sqrt{a}$ **13.** $3\sqrt{2x}$ **18.** $\frac{10}{3}\sqrt{3}$ **19.** 0

23. $\frac{9}{2}\sqrt{x}$ **25.** $5x\sqrt{2x}$ **28.** $7x^2\sqrt{3}$ **29.** $\frac{34}{7}\sqrt{7}$ **31.** $2\sqrt[3]{3}$ **34.** $-\sqrt[3]{3x}$

Page 420 | Self-Quiz: 12.1 to 12.4

1. 12   **2.** 4   **3.** 3   **4.** $\frac{5}{4}$ **5.** $\frac{3}{2}$

6. $\frac{3}{4}$ **7.** $\sqrt{35}$ **8.** $\sqrt{xy}$ **9.** $\sqrt{6}$ **10.** $\sqrt{\dfrac{x}{y}}$ or $\frac{1}{y}\sqrt{xy}$

11. $3\sqrt{3}$ **12.** $6\sqrt{2}$ **13.** $x^2\sqrt{5}$ **14.** $\frac{1}{n}\sqrt{n}$ **15.** $\frac{1}{3}\sqrt{6}$

16. $\frac{2}{3}d\sqrt{3d}$ **17.** 24.49   **18.** 16.585   **19.** 0.7746   **20.** 0.2828

21. $\frac{5}{2}\sqrt{2}$ **22.** $-\sqrt{3}$ **23.** $3x\sqrt{5x}$ **24.** $\frac{14}{3}\sqrt{6}$

Page 422 | Section 12.5

9. $2|c|\sqrt{2}$ **12.** $3|g|\sqrt{2}$ **13.** $\dfrac{1}{2|a|}\sqrt{3}$ **17.** $2|mn|\sqrt{2}$ **21.** $\frac{1}{2}|r|\sqrt{2}$

24. $\frac{2}{5}|t|\sqrt{15}$ **27.** $x|x|$ **29.** $|x + 2|$ **32.** $3|m - n|\sqrt{3}$ **34.** Yes; x^2

Page 424 | Section 12.6

15. 24   **17.** $\varnothing$ **18.** -23 **20.** 0   **21.** 1   **23.** $-2, 2$

25. 1, 2   **27.** 1   **29.** $\varnothing$ **31.** 2   **33.** $\frac{3}{5}$ or 0.6   **35.** 6 mi.

Page 427

9. **a.** 6   **b.** 4   **c.** $2\sqrt{13}$ **11.** 5   **14.** 3   **15.** 13

17. $2\sqrt{5}$ **19.** $3\sqrt{5}$ **22.** $6\sqrt{2}$ **23.** Yes   **24.** 5, -1

Page 428

1. 11   **2.** 7   **5.** $\sqrt{10}$ **7.** $\sqrt{6}$ **8.** $\sqrt{17x}$ **9.** $2\sqrt{7}$

11. $2x\sqrt{x}$ **12.** $\frac{1}{mn}\sqrt{mn}$ **13.** 28.28   **15.** 0.8944   **17.** $3\sqrt{3}$ **19.** $5\sqrt{2s}$

21. $|x|$ **24.** 11   **26.** 2, -2 **28.** $3\sqrt{2}$

Page 429

1. c   **2.** h   **3.** b   **4.** e   **5.** f   **6.** a   **7.** c

8. d   **9. a.** 7   **b.** 2   **c.** 3   **d.** $|x|$, or x if $x \geq 0$

10. a. $\sqrt{mn}$ **b.** $\sqrt{\frac{r}{s}}$ or $\frac{1}{s}\sqrt{rs}$ **11.** $2\sqrt{3}$ **12.** $\frac{1}{3}\sqrt{6}$ **13.** $9\sqrt{5}$

14. $\sqrt{y}$ **15.** $\frac{10}{3}\sqrt{3}$ **16.** $5\sqrt{2}$ **17.** 26.46   **18.** 0.8367

19. 3   **20.** 3   **21.** $2\sqrt{2}$ **22.** $2\sqrt{5}$

Page 433

21. $-1, -2$ **23.** $-6, -1$ **25.** 4, -3 **29.** 9, -8 **33.** 7, -7

35. 0, -7 **37.** 5, 10   **39.** -3 **41.** 1, $-\frac{3}{2}$ **47.** 0, 4

49. $\frac{7}{3}, -\frac{7}{3}$ **53.** $\frac{4}{3}$ **55.** $x^2 - 7x + 10 = 0$ **61.** 0, 6, -4

Page 436

23. 1, -3 **25.** 3, -3 **27.** 5, -1 **29.** 9, -9 **37.** 2, 14

39. $-1, -7$ **41.** 5, -5 **45.** $4 + 2\sqrt{2}, 4 - 2\sqrt{2}$ **47.** $3\sqrt{6}, -3\sqrt{6}$

55. $2\sqrt{19}, -2\sqrt{19}$ **59.** 1, $-\frac{5}{3}$ **61.** $3\sqrt{6}, -\sqrt{6}$

Pages 438–439

11. 2, -6 **13.** 6, -4 **17.** $-\frac{3}{2} + \sqrt{2}, -\frac{3}{2} - \sqrt{2}$ **19.** $\frac{7}{4}, -\frac{1}{4}$

21. $-4, 2$ **25.** $-2, \frac{2}{3}$ **29.** $\frac{9}{2} + 2\sqrt{5}, \frac{9}{2} - 2\sqrt{5}$ **35.** 0, -12

41. $\frac{9}{4}, -\frac{3}{4}$ **47.** $\frac{4}{3}, -\frac{8}{3}$ **53.** $x^2 - 5x = -3; \frac{5}{2} + \frac{1}{2}\sqrt{13}, \frac{5}{2} - \frac{1}{2}\sqrt{13}$

Pages 442–443

11. $-1, -2$ **13.** 1, -2 **17.** 1, $\frac{5}{3}$ **21.** $-4 + 2\sqrt{2}, -4 - 2\sqrt{2}$

25. $\frac{5}{2} + \frac{1}{2}\sqrt{21}, \frac{5}{2} - \frac{1}{2}\sqrt{21}$ **29.** $\frac{5}{2} + \frac{1}{2}\sqrt{41}, \frac{5}{2} - \frac{1}{2}\sqrt{41}$ **31.** 0, $\frac{7}{5}$

41. $-1 + \frac{1}{3}\sqrt{6}, -1 - \frac{1}{3}\sqrt{6}$ **51.** $-0.2, -1.8$ **53.** $-2.6, 0.6$

57. $-\frac{7}{6} + \frac{1}{6}\sqrt{73}, -\frac{7}{6} - \frac{1}{6}\sqrt{73}$ **61.** $-\frac{3}{2} + \frac{1}{2}\sqrt{3}, -\frac{3}{2} - \frac{1}{2}\sqrt{3}$

Page 445

1. 3, -3 **2.** 0, -3 **3.** -2 **4.** $-5, -2$ **5.** 5, -6

6. $\frac{4}{3}, -2$ **7.** $2\sqrt{5}, -2\sqrt{5}$ **8.** 2, -2 **9.** $-10, -4$ **10.** 0, 8

11. 0, -1 **12.** $5 + \sqrt{3}, 5 - \sqrt{3}$ **13.** 2, -6 **14.** 0, -5

15. $-3 + 2\sqrt{3}, -3 - 2\sqrt{3}$ **16.** 9, -6 **17.** 1, $\frac{3}{5}$

18. $\frac{3}{4} + \frac{1}{4}\sqrt{41}, \frac{3}{4} - \frac{1}{4}\sqrt{41}$ **19.** $-3, -4$ **20.** $\frac{1}{2}, -3$ **21.** 0, $\frac{5}{3}$

22. 1, $-\frac{4}{3}$ **23.** $2 + \sqrt{2}, 2 - \sqrt{2}$ **24.** $-\frac{1}{2} + \frac{1}{2}\sqrt{7}, -\frac{1}{2} - \frac{1}{2}\sqrt{7}$

Page 447

11. 8, real, unequal **13.** −8, not real **15.** 0, real, equal
27–50. Roots real, unequal **27.** 8 **29.** 41 **31.** 49 **33.** 17
52. 160; real, uneq., irr. **57.** One real, not 0 **61.** Real, unequal

Pages 450–451

15. 4, 12 or −4, −12 **19.** 7, 8 or −7, −8 **23.** 7 or −8 **25.** 4 feet
27. 11 cm., 6 cm. **29.** 12 feet, 6 feet **31.** 100 mi. **33.** 18 by 20 in.

Pages 453–455

9. 3, −3 **13.** 2, −8 **15.** 5 meters **19.** 10 feet **21.** 4 sec.
25. $2\frac{1}{7}$ sec. **27.** $2\frac{1}{2}$ sec. **28.** 2, 3 sec. **33.** $n = -\frac{1}{2} \pm \frac{1}{2}\sqrt{1 + 8S}$

Page 458

17. $-2 < x < -1$ **19.** $x < -3$ or $x > 2$ **21.** $2 < x < 4$
23. $x < -6$ or $x > 5$ **25.** $x < \frac{5}{3}$ or $x > 4$ **27.** $-3 < x < -2$

Pages 460–461

1. 0, −3 **2.** 4 **5.** $\sqrt{3}, -\sqrt{3}$ **6.** −2, −10
7. $3 + 3\sqrt{2}, 3 - 3\sqrt{2}$ **9.** −1, −5 **12.** $1 + \frac{1}{3}\sqrt{3}, 1 - \frac{1}{3}\sqrt{3}$
13. 2, −7 **15.** $2 + \frac{1}{2}\sqrt{10}, 2 - \frac{1}{2}\sqrt{10}$ **17.** 0; real, eq.
19. 24; real, uneq. **21.** 8, 5 **23.** 5 cm. by 9 cm.
25. $t = \pm\frac{3}{2}$ **27.** 12 **29.** $-5 < x < 0$ **30.** $y < -5$ or $y > -4$

Page 462

1. c **2.** f **3.** d **4.** a **5.** e **6.** b
7. a. $x^2 - 10x + 25 = 0$ **b.** $y^2 + 10y + 22 = 0$ **c.** $w^2 - 8w - 2 = 0$
d. $3s^2 + 6s + 2 = 0$ **8. a.** 0; real, eq. **b.** 12; real, uneq.
c. 72 ; real, uneq. **d.** 12; real, uneq.
9. $(x - 5)^2 = 0; x = 5$ **10.** $y + 5 = \pm\sqrt{3}; y = -5 \pm \sqrt{3}$
11. $(w - 4)^2 = 18; w = 4 \pm 3\sqrt{2}$ **12.** $s = \frac{-6 \pm \sqrt{36 - 24}}{6}; s = -1 \pm \frac{1}{3}\sqrt{3}$
13. 13 inches, 5 inches **14.** Martin: 12; Maria: 15 **15.** 2 meters
16. $-4 < x < 0$ **17.** $y \leq 3$ or $y \geq 4$

Page 466

7.

Domain Range

11. See Ex. 4. **13.** See Ex. 6.
15. Ex. 3 **18.** Ex. 4
23. {(0, 0), (1, 2), (4, 8), (9, 18)}
28. {(0, 0), (1, 1), (4, 16), (9, 81)}
31. {(0, 0), $(\frac{1}{4}, \frac{1}{2})$, $(\frac{4}{9}, \frac{8}{9})$, (1, 2)}

Page 469

17. Domain: {−2, −1, 0, 1, 2, 3} **20.** Domain: {nonneg. real numbers}
Range: {−3, −2, −1, 0, 1, 2} Range: {real numbers}

Section 14.3 | **Page 472**
23. 52   **25.** -32 **28.** 6   **31.** -19 **33.** 14.2   **38.** $\frac{2}{4}3$
39. $\{(1, -1), (2, 3), (3, 7)\}$ **41.** $\{(-1, 8), (0, 4), (1, 2)\}$
43. The graph is a line containing $(0, -2)$ and $(2, 0)$; yes.
48. The graph is a line containing $(4, 0)$ and $(4, 2)$; no.
53. The graph is a line containing $(0, -3)$ and $(2, -3)$; yes.

Section 14.4 | **Pages 475–476**
15. 1   **17.** No slope   **19.** $\frac{1}{2}$ **20.** 0
25. $\frac{4}{9}$ **29.** Linear   **32.** Linear   **34.** Constant
For Exercises 37–43, two points on the line are given.
37. $(0, 3), (6, 0)$ **41.** $(0, 10), (-2, 0)$ **43.** $(0, 2), (-5, 5)$
51. 3   **54.** 5   **57.** 2   **59.** 1   **61.** -4

Section 14.5 | **Pages 479–480**
19. $d = kt$ **22.** $w = kl$ **23.** $d = 60t$ **27.** 360
31. 0.91 meters   **34.** $18   **35.** 256 square inches

Section 14.6 | **Pages 483–484**
9. $\frac{1}{4} = \frac{2}{a}$ or $\frac{2}{a} = \frac{3}{12}$, $a = 8$ **12.** $\frac{-2}{3} = \frac{-6}{d}$ or $\frac{-6}{d} = \frac{-10}{15}$, $d = 9$
15. 24   **17.** -14 **20.** $\frac{1}{4}5$ **23.** 1   **28.** 3   **35.** $4\frac{1}{2}$ in.

Self-Quiz:
14.1 to 14.6 | **Page 485**
Domain: **1.** $\{1, 3, 7\}$ **2.** $\{2, 5, 8\}$ **3.** $\{-4, 3, 5\}$ **4.** $\{0, 1, 2, 3\}$
Range: $\{2, 3, 4\}$ $\{1, 2, 3, 6\}$ $\{2, 5, 6\}$ $\{0, 1, 2, 3\}$
5. No   **6.** No   **7.** Yes   **8.** Yes   **9.** 4   **10.** 7   **11.** 4
12. 7   **13.** -11 **14.** 7   **15.** Neither   **16.** Constant   **17.** Linear
18. The line contains $(0, 7), (3, 7)$.   **19.** The line contains $(0, -4), (2, 0)$.
20. $x, 5$ **21.** $12.00   **22.** $12.00   **23.** $-\frac{1}{5}$

Section 14.7 | **Page 490**

15.

x	-2	-1	0	1	2
y	12	3	0	3	12

16.

x	-2	-1	0	1	2
y	$-\frac{4}{3}$	$-\frac{1}{3}$	0	$-\frac{1}{3}$	$-\frac{4}{3}$

17.

x	-2	-1	0	1	2
y	3	-3	-5	-3	3

18.

x	0	1	2	3	4
y	0	-3	-4	-3	0

20.

x	-3	-2	-1	0	1
y	0	-3	-4	-3	0

21.

x	-3	-2	-1	0	1	2	3
y	$\frac{9}{4}$	1	$\frac{1}{4}$	0	$\frac{1}{4}$	1	$\frac{9}{4}$

24.

x	-3	-2	-1	0	1	2	3
y	-27	-12	-3	0	-3	-12	-27

29.

x	-3	-2	$-\frac{3}{2}$	-1	0	1	2	3
y	0	-2	$-\frac{9}{4}$	-2	0	4	10	18

Section 14.8 | **Page 493**
5. -3 **6.** 2   **9.** None   **12.** $-3, 3$ **13.** 1, 2   **15.** $-3, 3$
Graphs not shown for Ex. 17–27.   **17.** $-\frac{5}{2}$ **19.** 0, 6   **22.** 1, 3
23. None   **24.** 2, -3 **27.** 3   **30.** $\frac{3}{4} + \frac{1}{4}\sqrt{17}, \frac{3}{4} - \frac{1}{4}\sqrt{17}$ **32.** None

8. 64 ft.   **9.** 1, 3 sec.   **11.** $x = 7, 28 - 2x = 14$ **13.** 8 by 8 ft.

17. $V = \dfrac{k}{p}$ **18.** $I = \dfrac{k}{R}$ **21.** 16   **23.** 6   **25.** 1.6

27. 3 cm.   **32.** 8 cu. ft.   **33.** $12,000   **35.** 5 lumens

13. $\dfrac{1}{2} = \dfrac{a}{12}$ or $\dfrac{2}{3} = \dfrac{4}{a}$; $a = 6$ **15.** $\dfrac{5}{10} = \dfrac{7}{c}$ or $\dfrac{5}{35} = \dfrac{2}{c}$; $c = 14$

17. $\dfrac{5}{g} = \dfrac{20}{8}$ or $\dfrac{4}{g} = \dfrac{20}{10}$; $g = 2$ **19.** $\dfrac{6}{x} = \dfrac{20}{10}$; 3 cm.

22. $\dfrac{6}{x} = \dfrac{60}{50}$; 5 hr.   **23.** $\dfrac{15}{30} = \dfrac{x}{24}$; 12 cu. ft.

26. $\dfrac{10{,}000}{x} = \dfrac{6.4}{6}$; $9,375   **27.** $\dfrac{120}{x} = \dfrac{2}{3}$; 180 steps

1.

Domain: {2,3}
Range: {−2,1,4}

4. Yes   **6.** No   **8.** (1, −1), (2, 0), (3, −3), (4, 0)

10. −3   **11.** −9   **13.** Linear   **15.** Neither

16. The graph is a line through (4, 0) and (0, −6).

19. $y = 6x$ **20.** Yes   **22.** No   **25.** $\dfrac{3}{24} = \dfrac{y}{36}$; $4\frac{1}{2}$ cm.

27. The graph is a parabola with vertex at (0, 0) and points at (−2, 8) and (2, 8).   **30.** $\dfrac{9}{2}$ or $4\frac{1}{2}$

32. No zeros   **33.** 8 in. deep by 16 in. across

34. 6   **38.** $\dfrac{36}{48} = \dfrac{t}{8}$; $t = 6$ hr.

1. f   **2.** g   **3.** d   **4.** e   **5.** c   **6.** No   **7.** Yes   **8.** −2   **9.** −11

10. Inv.   **11.** Dir.   **12.** Inv.   **13.** Dir.   **14.** 3   **15.** 3 and −5

16. The graph is a line through (0, 6), (3, 0).   **17.** The graph is a parabola through (−5, 0), (3, 0); vertex (−1, −16).   **18.** $12

5. 2.45; 4.9; 5   **6.** 5; 6; 4   **7.** x; 3; 12   **9.** d; 5; c

10. a; z; a **11.** 18 feet   **12.** 600 meters   **13.** 300 yards

13. $\sin A \approx 0.471$ $\cos A \approx 0.882$ $\tan A \approx 0.533$
$\sin B \approx 0.882$ $\cos B \approx 0.471$ $\tan B = 1.875$

15. $\sin G = \frac{1}{2}\sqrt{3} \approx \frac{1}{2}(1.732) \approx 0.866$ $\sin K = 0.500$
$\cos G = 0.500$ $\cos K \approx 0.866$
$\tan G \approx 1.732$ $\tan K = \dfrac{1}{\sqrt{3}} = \dfrac{\sqrt{3}}{3} \approx 0.577$

31. 0.342   **32.** 0.743   **35.** 0.999   **37.** 0.574   **39.** 2.747

43. a. Increases   **44.** 45°   **47.** 10.7   **49.** 89.1   **51.** 99.5

Section 15.4	**Pages 524–526**

7. 26.9 ft.   **8.** 5.3 ft.   **9.** 60.1 ft.   **11.** 63.8 ft.   **13.** 190.5 ft.
15. 17°   **16.** About 3°   **19.** 63.8 ft.   **20.** 11,222 ft.

Review,
Chapter 15   **Page 527**

1. a. Shape   **b.** Congruent   **2.** See definitions, page 516.   **3.** 97 ft.
4. 5 ft.   **7.** 30°   **9.** See drawing at top of page 523.   **10.** 1216 ft.

Self-Test,
Chapter 15   **Page 528**

1. b, c, d **2. a.** $\frac{9}{41}$ **b.** $\frac{40}{41}$ **c.** $\frac{9}{40}$ **d.** $\frac{9}{41}$ **e.** $\frac{40}{9}$
3. a. 0.906   **b.** 0.500   **c.** 57.290   **4. a.** 12°   **b.** 86°   **c.** 21°
5. a. 15.2   **b.** 11.5   **6.** 70 ft.   **7.** 37°

Section 16.1   **Pages 530–531**

3. 500   **4.** Yes   **6.** 100; 0   **7.** No; two heads can occur in only *one way*
(HH), but a head and a tail can occur in two ways (HT and TH).   **11.** 30

Section 16.2   **Page 534**

23. $\frac{11}{25}$ **25.** $\frac{2}{25}$

Section 16.3   **Page 538**

13. Coin 1   Coin 2   **15.** Selection 1   Selection 2

```
        H — HH                              B ——— AB
H <                               A <
        T — HT                              T ——— AT

        H — TH                              A ——— BA
T <                               B <
        T — TT                              T ——— BT

                                            A ——— TA
                                  T <
                                            B ——— TB
```

Section 16.4   **Page 542**

15. $\frac{1}{36}$ **17.** $\frac{1}{18}$ **18.** $\frac{1}{6}$ **19.** $\frac{1}{6}$ **23.** $\frac{1}{12}$ **24.** $\frac{1}{2}$ **27.** $\frac{1}{4}$

Section 16.5   **Page 547**

13. $\frac{1}{12}$ **14.** $\frac{1}{6}$ **17.** $\frac{1}{9}$ **18.** $\frac{1}{36}$ **19.** 0   **23.** $\frac{1}{36}$ **25.** 0   **27.** 0

Section 16.6   **Page 550**

5. $\frac{1}{6}$ **6.** $\frac{1}{6}$ **8.** $\frac{1}{9}$ **9.** $\frac{11}{36}$ **13.** $\frac{4}{13}$

Review,
Chapter 16   **Page 551**

1. 250   **3.** $\frac{11}{100}$ **5.** $\{R, W, B\}$
6. $\{1H, 1T, 2H, 2T, 3H, 3T, 4H, 4T, 5H, 5T, 6H, 6T\}$
8. $\frac{1}{6}$ **9.** $\frac{1}{4}$ **11.** No; $\frac{5}{36}$; $\frac{1}{6}$; $\frac{1}{36}$

Self-Test,
Chapter 16   **Page 552**

1. $\frac{19}{100}$ **2.** $\frac{47}{100}$ **3.** 0   **4.** $\frac{17}{50}$ **5.** 0   **6.** 1
7. $\{1, 2, 3, 4, 5, 6\}$ **8.** $\{HH, HT, TH, TT\}$
9. $\{$cd, co, cg, ad, ao, ag, td, to, tg$\}$ **10.** $\frac{1}{2}$ **11.** $\frac{1}{13}$
12. $\frac{1}{8}$ **13.** $\frac{1}{36}$ **14.** $\frac{1}{9}$ **15.** $\frac{1}{6}$ **16.** 0   **17.** $\frac{1}{36}$
18. $\frac{5}{36}$ **19.** No